The Official® Price Guide to
Military Collectibles

The Official® Price Guide to
Military Collectibles

Richard Austin

Sixth Edition

House of Collectibles

The Ballantine Publishing Group · New York

Copyright ©1998 by Richard Austin

All rights reserved under International and Pan-American Copyright Conventions

Published by: House of Collectibles
The Ballantine Publishing Group
201 East 50th Street
New York, NY 10022

Distributed by The Ballantine Publishing Group, a division of Random House, Inc., New York, and simultaneously in Canada by Random House of Canada Limited, Toronto.

http://www.randomhouse.com

Manufactured in the United States of America

ISSN: 0747-5691

ISBN: 0-676-60052-2

Cover design by Dreu Pennington-McNeil

Cover photo © George Kerrigan

Sixth Edition: April 1998

10 9 8 7 6 5 4 3 2 1

Contents

Acknowledgments

Many people contributed to this volume. So many have been involved along the way that I am sure I will leave someone out. For this I apologize.

First I want to thank everyone at Ballantine Books/ House of Collectibles, my publisher, for their patience and assistance. I would especially like to thank my editor, Randy Ladenheim-Gil, for all her efforts.

Harry L. Rinker and his staff at Rinker Enterprises deserve a special thanks for the assistance and input on this project. The research assistance and availability of images were extremely helpful. Kathy Williamson and Barbara Davison deserve special thanks for their many hours of data entry work.

Steven Flood, Heather Paulhamus, and the rest of the staff at AAG International deserve thanks for their assistance and for the use of several fine images used in this book.

Special thanks also to D. Levy Morgan, Director of Public Realtions and Katharine Knight, Marketing Director at Butterfield & Butterfield for their assistance and images provided. Also thanks to their staff members who assisted.

David W. Uhrig deserves a special thanks for the military vehicle images and information and insight he provided into that market.

The staff at Roger S. Steffen Historical Militaria and Christie's in New York and London also deserve special thanks for providing catalogs and other information for use in this book. Special photographic assistance was also provided by Sarah Austin and Alison Dancho.

Thanks to the many collectors and dealers whose assistance, pricing information, and other input were indispensible in the preparation of this book. Also a thanks to those who contributed images and allowed objects to be photographed for inclusion in the book.

Finally a special thanks to my wife, Diane, and my children, Sarah and Angela. Without their love, support and assistance I would have never completed this project.

To the readers of this book, a thanks in advance. I welcome any suggestions for improving the book or any corrections. Please send them to me care of:

House of Collectibles
201 East 50th Street
New York, NY 10022

Introduction

Welcome to the sixth edition of *The Official Price Guide to Military Collectibles*. The field of militaria collecting has changed drastically since the last edition of this book was published in 1985. In those twelve years, few comprehensive and reliable price guides about militaria were written.

The trend in militaria publishing during this period has been toward extreme specialization. Hundreds of specialty books on militaria, ranging from the 48-page monographs that sell for $10 to $15 to the 200+-page hardcover books that retail for $30 to $70, were produced. Multiple titles can now be found on subjects such as the M1 Garand rifle, German military helmets (Imperial and/or Third Reich eras), military awards and medals (by specific country), military uniforms (by country and branch of service), and edged weapons (by type, country, or manufacturer). The photographic content and detailed text make many of these specialty volumes very useful for identification purposes. Unfortunately, if a collector or dealer is interested in more than one specific category of militaria, he would have to purchase multiple books at a cost that could easily exceed a hundred dollars. Another shortcoming of these specialty books is that few include any pricing information. The new edition of *The Official Price Guide to Military Collectibles* seeks to remedy this situation.

The main purpose of *The Official Price Guide to Military Collectibles* is to provide in one volume and at an attractive price a comprehensive reference, identification, and price guide to militaria, for use by collectors, dealers, re-enactors, and historians. This new edition is also unique in the broad scope of its coverage. Some of the topics covered in the book that are often missing from other publications include firearms, field pieces, military vehicles, and homefront collectibles. Some high-value, extremely rare objects have been included but the focus is on more reasonably priced, commonly available objects of general interest to the groups listed above. For many objects there are also multiple listings illustrating a variety of prices, conditions, and sources.

The market for militaria is worldwide. The United States and England are the most active countries in terms of dealer and collector activity. Although the guide concentrates on the American militaria market, listings have also been included from European sources. Civilian organizations and their objects have not been included. All prices, however, are stated in terms of U.S. dollars.

Organization of the Book

The format of this guide is very different from the previous editions. The 8⅜ x 10⅞ inch size allows larger print size and larger, more detailed images to be used. This makes the book easier to read and increases the overall usefulness of the book.

The book is divided into sixteen chapters, each of which covers a broad militaria category (e.g., edged weapons, firearms). Each chapter opens with a brief one-page introduction. Within this introduction are included such details as collectors' clubs, periodicals, and museums that are relevant to the category. These types of resources can be invaluable to the collector and dealer.

The chapters are then divided into subchapters which highlight more detailed topics within the broad category (e.g., bayonets and swords within the edged-weapons chapter). The object listings are then sorted into the correct subcategory.

The object listings are the heart of the book. To be useful, the listings have been kept as detailed as possible. Within the subcategory, the objects are arranged by origin—with American objects displayed first, then German, then all other countries'—then by description. For some objects, additional descriptive data such as details of construction, use in service, period of service, etc., has been added.

In addition to the main text, the guide includes several helpful sections. Following this introduction is a listing of the abbreviations used throughout the text.

After the listings themselves is a glossary of military terms used in the guide and a large bibliography. The books listed are only a sample of recent titles that collectors and others should find helpful. Most of the books listed are still available from regular sources such as publishers, bookstores, book dealers, and specialty catalogs. Many more specialized titles that are out of print may also be of interest to collectors. These can often be found at flea markets, antique shows, gun shows, and in used book stores.

The final section is the index, which provides a detailed listing of the items and their location within the text.

Condition and Pricing

Militaria, like all other collectibles, whether common or rare, are profoundly affected by their condition at the time they are sold. If an object is damaged, shows repairs, has been altered, or is incomplete, the final price realized at sale may be severely affected. Items that are in the condition closest to that at time of issuance, of course, have the greatest value.

Most militaria items by the very nature of the way they

were used will show some normal wear and tear. It would be unusual to find field equipment or combat uniforms in mint condition. Repairs made to objects while in the field at the time of its original use will of course have less effect on the overall condition and value of a piece than one that was made years later.

The completeness of an object also has a significant impact on its condition and ultimate value. Uniforms that are lacking their original insignia, badges, pins, and ribbons, or that have had these items replaced, are typically less valuable than an intact example. Original packaging has become an extremely desirable feature in many categories of collectibles. This also applies to militaria. Many of the mass-produced World War II and later militaria items from many countries can still be found in their original packaging. If you have two identical objects and one is intact in its original packaging and the other is not, the packaged example would be expected to be of higher value.

Evaluating the condition of an object is a very subjective procedure which can vary widely from one auction house or dealer to another. One difficulty in compiling a book like this is that different rating systems are used by different sources. For the purposes of this book we have simply reported the condition as it was listed by the auction house or dealer. A simple condition rating system is used:

Mint	Above Average
Excellent	Average
Very Good	Below Average
Good	Poor

For the reasons stated above there will be few items that would be rated as being in mint condition. At the lower end of the rating scale, few items have been included that are in below-average or poor condition.

Militaria prices are ultimately determined by an object's rarity, condition, and desirability. One of the most important intended uses of this book is to provide collectors and dealers with accurate and recent pricing information so comparisons can be made to other similar objects found in the field. An effort has been made to show a range of prices and conditions for multiple examples of the same basic object. A broad variety of object listings from scarce to common are included in the guide, but the majority of the listings are common objects readily available on the market.

The listings and prices used for this guide were gathered between 1995 and 1997 from a wide variety of sources, including auction house prices, realized lists and catalogs, gun shows, advertisements in collectors' periodicals, newsletters, lists from dealers, and purchases and sales reported by both collectors and dealers. No changes or alterations have been made to the prices included in this guide except for simple rounding.

This book is designed to be used as a buyer's guide for militaria. The prices represent an approximation of the amount that a collector would have to pay on the open market to purchase an object. Do not expect, however, to be able to necessarily get these prices for objects that you may want to sell. There are many variables that affect the ability of sellers to get the top price for an object they are interested in selling. Beyond the basic condition, rarity, and desirability of an object, other factors such as knowing whom to sell it to and where to advertise the object also have a large effect on the final selling price.

Fakes, Fantasies, and Reproductions

The militaria collectibles market, as with many other categories of collectibles, is filled with vast quantities of fakes, fantasies, and reproductions. Fakes are objects that are made with the express purpose of deceiving dealers and collectors into thinking that the object is original. Fantasies are objects that are similar to original militaria items but never really existed. Reproductions (or repros) are exact copies of original objects.

These items are of great concern to all who are interested in collecting and studying militaria. By definition, none of the objects that fall into the three categories have any real value. Only by careful study and communication within the trade can these objects be detected and removed from the market.

Fakes can take the form of new objects made and distressed to be passed off as originals. Fakes that are harder to spot are original objects that have been altered in some way to enhance their desirability and value. Third Reich-era fakes have become a real problem since World War II. They are becoming even more difficult to detect, as many of these fakes are now thirty to forty years old.

Fantasy items are another area of concern. An example would be a pistol assembled from original but nonmatching parts. The assembled pistol never existed as an original object and was not used during the time period it would have been in service. Another example would be an object manufactured and used for civilian purposes being identified as a piece of militaria.

Reproductions are another great problem in the militaria field. Under many situations, reproductions are actually legitimately needed. Re-enactors often use reproduction uniforms, equipment, and insignia because originals are too expensive or not available. If reproductions were properly identified, there would be no problem. Unfortunately the vast majority of reproductions are unmarked. Some unscrupulous dealers try to pass these items off as legitimate objects.

Another problem with reproductions is that many of them have been in existence for a long time. In the 1800s, reproductions of early armor and edged weapons were made and sold throughout England and Europe. Many of these objects are now a hundred to two hundred years old and are difficult to authenticate. For many decades after the American Civil War, reproduction uniforms and equipment from both sides were produced. Today, these objects are often knowingly or unknowingly put on the market as originals.

How do you detect fakes, fantasies, and reproductions? The key to authenticating militaria, as with other collectibles, is to *know the objects*. Read about, study, examine, and handle as many objects as possible. If an object doesn't look right or feel right, don't buy it. If an object has no visible wear, is not worn in the correct areas, lacks detail, or is missing the proper markings or identification numbers, be suspicious. If a dealer has several of what should be a rare item, ask questions before taking the plunge and buying one of them. If the explanation is lacking, walk away.

Sources of Information

The listings, prices, and the other information in this guide are obtained from a wide variety of sources. Militaria collectors and dealers deserve much credit for the development and evolution of this collecting category into a strong and established market. Without a well-established market mechanism, no category can long survive.

The first source of information about militaria is from the hundreds of books that have been published over the years by collectors and scholars on various topics. The breadth and depth of militaria topics covered is astounding. No collecting category can long survive unless there is a backbone of research and study available to dealers, collectors, and potential collectors.

The next source are the magazines, newspapers, and newsletters published by various groups to further the knowledge of their members on topics of interest to them. One of the most valuable sources of information about the militaria market deserves special mention:

Military Trader, Antique Trader Publications, 100 Bryan Street, Dubuque, IA 52003.

Occasional articles on militaria appear in the following trade newspapers, but the most important information for collectors and dealers are the show and auction listings.

Antique Week, PO Box 90, Knightstown, IN 46148
Maine Antique Digest, PO Box 358, Waldoboro, ME 04572.

Dealers are another key source of information about the militaria market. Without their input and insight about the market, this guide would have been difficult to produce. Dealers recognize the need for detailed and accurate reporting of the prices and objects being bought and sold.

Individual collectors have also provided valuable information about the current pricing trends, insights into the market activity in their areas of specialization, and access to their collections.

Working out in the field gathering information from collectors and dealers on a first-hand basis is also important. Informational interviews via the phone are another method of gathering information. Computer technology, such as E-mail and browsing the World Wide Web, open up the world to researchers looking for militaria information. There are even a few online militaria auction sites.

Finally, the following auction houses frequently handle militaria, firearms, or other military-related objects. Their cooperation by providing auction catalogs and prices-realized lists is most appreciated.

AAG International
1266-B Sans Souci Parkway
Wilkes-Barre, PA 18702
(717) 822-5300

Butterfield and Butterfield
220 San Bruno Avenue
San Francisco, CA 94103
(415) 861-7500

Christie's
8 King Street
St. James, London SW1Y 6QT
0171-839 9060

Garth's Auction
2690 Stratford Road
PO Box 369
Delaware, OH 43015
(614) 362-4771

Hake's Americana and Collectibles
PO Box 1444
York, PA 17405
(717) 848-1333

Historical Collectible Auctions
PO Box 975
Burlington, NC 27215
(910) 570-2803

James D. Julia
PO Box 830
Fairfield, ME 04937
(207) 453-7904

Manion's International Auction House, Inc
PO Box 12214
Kansas City, Kansas 66112
(913) 299-6692

Robert W. Skinner, Inc.
Bolton Gallery
357 Main Street
Bolton, MA 01740
(508) 779-6241

Sotheby's
1334 York Avenue
New York, NY 10021
(212) 606-7000

Roger S. Steffen Historical Militaria
14 Murnan Road
Cold Spring, KY 41076
(606) 431-4499

Swann Galleries, Inc.
104 E. 25th Street
New York, NY 10010
(212) 254-4710

State of the Militaria Market

In 1997 it appears that the pricing for militaria has stabilized for the majority of items on the market and the pace of activity is sluggish. An analysis of a variety of auction sales results reveals that 25 to 40 percent of lots typically do not sell. The amount of high-quality militaria that is not sold through dealers and auctions continues to decline.

In fact there has been little change in the U.S. market in the past ten years in terms of activity by country. The most active continue to be:

Nazi German
American
Imperial German

Activity by category in the U.S. market is a little more difficult to gauge. In general, the most active categories continue to be:

Headgear
Edged Weapons
Firearms
Uniforms
Metallic Insignia

The expected increase in interest in militaria, due to the fifty-year anniversaries of World War II, does not seem to have occurred. Also the expected influx of higher-quality World War II militaria into the market from veterans and the families of veterans has also not noticeably taken place.

The occasional auction of high-end esoteric militaria from the early 1800s and before still manages to stir up excitement and a frenzy of interest from upscale collectors. Much of this activity takes place in the European market, with the English offices of Christie's and Sotheby's leading the way. The U.S. auction house of Butterfield and Butterfield has also become a major player in this market.

The question about the future of militaria that needs to be examined now is where is the next generation of collectors of militaria going to come from? Typical high school students know and care little about World War I and World War II. Their future as militaria collectors is doubtful.

As generations die out, frequently the demand for objects that interested them also disappears. How many collectors of World War I militaria are still active? As the World War II generation passes on, collectors and dealers need to nurture and pass on the interest and love of militaria collecting to the next generation or one day there will be no collectors with which to deal.

Abbreviations

AAC: Army Air Corps
AAF: Army Air Forces
Abn: Airborne
Adv: Advanced
AF: Air Force
AFB: Air Force Base
AG: Army Green
Alum: Aluminum
AN: Army–Navy (Standardization Program)
ANC: Army Nurses Corps
ANG: Air National Guard
Arty: Artillery
ARVN: Army of the Republic of Vietnam
B & W: Black and White
BAR: Browning Automatic Rifle
Bde: Brigade
Bds: Boards
BDU: Battle Dress Uniform
Bevo: Bandfabrik Ewald Vorsteher—Major manufacturer of cloth badges in Nazi Germany
BMR: Bomber
BN: Battalion
c: Circa
CAC: Coastal Artillery Corps
Cal: Caliber
Camo: Camouflage
Cav: Cavalry
Cb: Clasp Back
CBI: China-Burma-India
CBR: Chemical, Biological, Radiological
CIB: Combat Infantry Badge
cm: Centimeter
CMD: Command
col: Colonel
cond: Condition
CPO: Chief Petty Officer
CW: Civil War
DAF: Deutsche Arbeitsfront—German Labor Front
DAK: Deutsches Afrikakorps—German Africa Corps
dbl: Double
DDR: East Germany
DE: Double Edged
DI: Distinctive Insignia
diam: Diameter
Div: Division
DJ: Deutsches Jungvolk—German Young People
DK: Deutsches Kreuz—German Cross
DOD: Department of Defense

DRGM: Deutsches Reichsgebrauchsmuster—Nationally used pattern
DRK: Deutsches Rotes Kreuz—German Red Cross
DUC: Distinguished Unit Citation
EG&A: Eagle, Globe, and Anchor (U.S. Marine Corps Emblem)
EK: Eisernes Kreuz—Iron Cross
EL: Eichenlaub—Oak Leaves
EM: Enlisted Man
Embr: Embroidered
Engr: Engineer
ERDL: Engineer Research and Development Laboratory
ETO: European Theater of Operations
Exc: Excellent
FA: Field Artillery
FIG: Fighter Interceptor Group
FTR: Fighter
GAR: Grand Army of the Republic
GDR: West Germany
Ges. Gesch: Gesetzlich Geschutzt—Legally Protected
GRP: Group
hb: Hardbound
HBT: Herringbone Twill
HJ: Hitlerjugend—Hitler Youth
hmkd: Hallmarked
HQ: Headquarters
IC: Iron Cross (See **EK**)
Illus: Illustrations
Inf: Infantry
INTCP: Interceptor
JG: Jagdgeschwader—Luftwaffe Fighter Wing
JM: Jungmaedel—Young Girls
KC: Knights Cross (See **RK**)
KM: Kriegsmarine
KVK: Kriegsverdienstkreuz—War Merit Cross
KVM: Kriegsverdienstmedaille—War Merit Medal
LDO: Leistungsgemeinschaft der Deutschen Ordenhersteller—Administration of German Manufacturers
Lieut: Lieutenant
Lt: Light
LW: Luftwaffe
M: Model
MG: Machine Gun
MK: Mark
mm: Millimeters
MP: Military Police
Msgt: Master Sergeant
mtd: Mounted

NATO: North Atlantic Treaty Organization
NCO: Noncommisioned Officer
NS: Studentenbund—National Socialist Student League
NSBO: Nationalsozialistische Betriebsorganisation—National Socialist Factory Organization
NSDAP: Nationalsozialistische Deutsche Arbeiterpartei—National Socialist German Worker's Party
NSFK: Nationalsozialistisches Fliegerkorps—National Socialist Flying Corps
NSKK: Nationalsozialistisches Kraftfahrkorps—National Socialist Motor Corps
NSRK: Nationalsozialistisches Reiterkorps—National Socialist Riding Corps
NVA: North Vietnamese Army
OD: Olive Drab
OG: Olive Green
OKH: Oberkommando des Heeres—High Command of the Army
OKL: Oberkommando der Luftwaffe—High Command of the Air Force
OKM: Oberkommando der Kriegsmarine—High Command of the Navy
OKW: Oberkommando der Wehrmacht—High Command of the Armed Forces
ORD: Ordnance
O/S: Overseas
OSS: Office of Strategic Studies
OT: Organisation Todt
OWI: Office of War Information
Pb: Pin Back
Pfc: Private First Class
PO: Petty Officer
Qm: Quartermaster
QR: Quick Release
RAD: Reichsarbeitsdienst—National Labor Service
RAF: Royal Air Force
rb: Ribbon
RB-NR: Reichsbetriebsnummer—National Factory Code Number
RCT: Regimental Combat Team
rect: Rectangular
Regt: Regiment
RIA: Rock Island Arsenal
RK: Ritterkreuz—Knight's Cross
RL: Reichsleiter—NSDAP official
RLB: Reichsluftschutzbund—National Air Raid Protection Force
RN: Royal Navy

Rt: Right
RZM: Reichszeugmeisterie—National Material Control Board
SA: Sturmabteilung—Assault Detachment
SAC: Strategic Air Command
SAW: Spanish American War
Sb: Screw Back
sb: Soft Bound
sgt: Sergeant
shd: Shoulder
SMG: Sub Machine Gun
Spec: Specification
SQDN: Squadron
S/S: Stainless Steel
SS: Schutzstaffel—Protection Squad
SS-BW: SS Bekleidungswerk—SS Clothing Factory
SS-SD: SS Sicherheitsdienst—SS Security Service
SS-TV: SS Totenkopfverbande—SS Death's Head Units
SS-VT: SS Verfugungstruppe—SS Special Purpose Troops
Svc: Service
T-: Technical
TAC: Tactical Air Command
TENO: Technische Nothilfe—Technical Emergency Service
UCV: Union of Confederate Veterans
USA: United States Army
USAF: United States Air Force
USCG: United States Coast Guard
USMA: United States Military Academy
USMC: United States Marine Corps
USN: United States Navy
USNA: United States Naval Academy
UN: United Nations
USSR: Union of Soviet Socialist Republics
WAAC: Women's Army Auxiliary Corps
WAC: Women's Army Corps
WAF: Women in Air Force
WASP: Women's Air Force Service Pilots
WAVES: Women Accepted for Volunteer Emergency Service
WBA: Wehrmachtbekleidungsamt—Armed Forces Clothing Office
WO: Warrant Officer
WWI: World War One
WWII: World War Two

CHAPTER ONE

Early Militaria (Pre-1800)

The objects in this chapter are for the most part high end and one of a kind. Mass production of products on a wide scale was still decades away, and craftsmen were responsible for creating these objects.

Most of the desirable objects from this period reside in museums and private collections. When collections are sold or disposed of, the sales are most often handled by a Christie's or Butterfield and Butterfield. The occasional object from this period will turn up on the market with other firms, but this is usually only a few pieces at best.

When being sold by Christie's or Butterfield and Butterfield, detailed examinations are made of the objects and extensive descriptions are prepared. The condition of the objects are described in great detail and the history or provenance of the object is researched.

The sale catalogs for these objects are lavishly illustrated and extremely interesting reading on their own. The catalogs are usually available several months before a sale takes place. The buyers for these collections include high-end individual collectors as well as institutional buyers making purchases for their collections and organizations.

Three-quarter Suit of Armor

Collecting Tips

The major categories of early militaria include armor, edged weapons, and early firearms. I have included a small section on early clothing or uniforms but such items are unusual. Due to their expense, you would be well advised to narrow your collecting category of interest (e.g., English military flintlock pistols 1770–1800). The more specialized you are, the more you can know about a category and the less likely you are to make costly mistakes. Over time you can modify your area of interest.

Fakes and Frauds

With objects of this age, fakes and frauds can present problems. Many fakes are themselves more than a hundred years old. Medieval armor was all the rage in 19th Century Europe. Many reproduction suits from that period exist and will pass as original if you do not know what details to examine.

Care and Display

Preservation to prevent further deterioration is the first priority with these objects. Consult with experts before any work is attempted. Restoration or repairs should should not be undertaken at all unless absolutely necessary.

Armor

Backplate, Italy, Late 16th Century. Ten rounded upward lapping lames each with shaped edge bordered by horizontal double line, plain shoulderplate bordered by rivets. Avg. cond. $1224

Breastplate, German, Early 16th Century. Of globular form with prominent inward turn at the neck, flange at the bottom for the missing skirt, and semi-circular arm openings bordered by rivet holes. Movable gussets missing, some patching, rust patinated overall. 13¼" high. Good cond. $1159

Breastplate, France, Early 1800s. Russed iron, medial ridge ending in blunt point at bottom, bordered by large brass-headed lining rivets, front engraved with three narrow bands and conventional foliage flanked by large trophies of arms with borders. Above avg. cond. . . . $6468

Breastplate, Italy, Late 16th Century. "Pisan" type. Of peasecod form with characteristic etched decoration arranged in bands with, at the top, a tower (armorer's mark?) above embossed volutes framing male and female profile heads. Single narrow skirtplate (gussets missing and skirtplate defective). Item is 18½ inches high. Good cond. $1546

Buckler, Italy, 16th Century. Wood covered with parchment, mounted with wrought-iron strips. Avg. cond. $1311

Cabasset, Spain, 17th Century. One-piece construction. Downcurving brim with roped rim. Five rivets retain their brass rosettes. Dark patina and some pitting present. A number of holes at the peak. Avg. cond. $748

Spanish Cabasset

Close Helmet, Italy, 1570–80. One-piece skull with high roped comb, blunt visor with single vision slit. Good cond. $6817

Close Helmet, Italy, Late 16th Century. Blackened iron, one-piece skull and high roped comb, the latter engraved on each side with trophy of arms, large shaped riveted patch carrying small plume holder in rear, stamped at back of neck "GP" (Galleria Prima). Avg. cond. $1485

Close Helmet, France, c1580s. One-piece skull and high roped comb, pointed visor with single vision slit, etched with bands with sprigged edges containing running scrolling foliage, bird scenes on comb, child figure and animals. Good cond. $6992

Close Helmet, France, c1570. Two-piece skull with high roped comb, riveted plume holder formed as shaped shield embossed with a lion mask at rear. Good cond. $13,984

Close Helmet, Todenkopf or Savoyard Type, Italy, c1630. Two-piece skull with tubular plume holder at rear. Solid mask visor with small ventilation slit over mouth and upper edge scooped out for vision on either side. Neckstrap with brass buckle. Decorated with hatched medial band between fillets from base of skull to visor, remaining engraved against a stippled ground with design of running foliage bearing flowers and fruit and framing cartouches, classical female figures. Avg. cond. . . $1050

Gauntlet, Mitten, Germany, 17th Century. For right hand. Made of russet steel, pointed cuff with recessed border encircled by row of lining rivets, original leather straps, iron buckle wrist strap, buff leather lining with figure 9 or 6 painted on palm, 15" long. Good cond. $2798

Lobster-tailed Pot, European, 1625–1650. With ribbed hemispherical one-piece skull with separate ring-shaped finial. Pointed fixed fall with turned edge pierced for the adjustable nasal bar. Bluntly pointed neck guard of four plates. Pierced single-plate ear pieces (retaining leathers broken). Hammered surface rough throughout. Pot is 11" high. Good cond. $1345

Mail Shirt, 16th Century. Riveted links, hip length, open in front with short sleeves, lower edge finished with two rows of riveted brass rings. Good cond. $3321

Mail Sleeve, Germany, 16th Century. Small rings riveted throughout. Avg. cond. $786

Morion, Spain, Late 16th Century. One-piece , with tall skull rising to a pronounced stalk. The base is encircled by a row of dome-headed rivets. Downturned brim rising to a point fore and aft with a turned and roped border. 11" high. Above avg. cond. $1932

Morion, Comb, Spain, 17th Century. One-piece construction. Peaked brim with rolled and roped rim and etched with decorative banding. Rivet backed with steel rosettes. Struck with the Nuremburg city mark. Comb etched with jousting knights on a field of vines. Skull etched with scene of St. George and the dragon on one side and St. Martin on the other. Dark patina overall and some pitting.

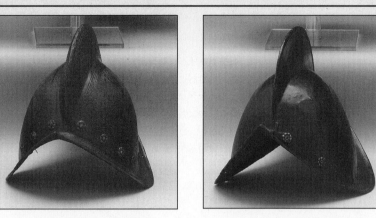
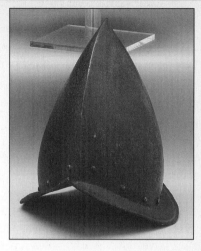

Left, **Spanish Comb Morion with St. George and St. Martin scene;** *center,* **Spanish Comb Morion;** *right,* **Spanish Peaked Morion**

A few dents and one hole at the crest. Two rivets missing. Above avg. cond. $2588

Morion, Comb, France, 1580. Iron with high roped comb, narrow downturned brim with turned and roped edges, etched overall with interlaced strapwork forming quatrefoil panels framing trophies of arms, armor and musical instruments. Good cond. $2447

Morion, Comb, Spain, 17th Century. Two-piece construction with high crest or comb. Brim peaked front and back. Rolled edges. Brass blossom form rivets. Mounted with plume holder. Dark patina and some pitting overall. A few dents. Three rivets missing and two others broken. Above avg. cond. $1265

Morion, Peaked, Spain, 17th Century. Elongated one-piece skull having stalk at apex. Brim peaked front and back. Rim rolled and slightly roped. Dark patina and some pitting. Also one rivet is missing and there is a small tear present on left side of brim. Above avg. cond. . . . $2300

Pauldron, For Right Shoulder, Italy, c1510. Steel covering outside and back, mainplate with three downward lapping lames below and two upward above. Avg. cond. $1227

Suit of Armor, Full, Articulated Miniature, Late 19th Century. Blued steel, comprised of close helmet with one-piece skull and ribbed tail-like plume holder at rear. Full arm defenses, breastplate and backplate, full leg defenses with sabatons, decorated with line engraving, gilt brass rivets, hinges and buckles. Shield of blued steel. Good cond. $1748

Targe, Circular, Scotland. Wood covered with leather. Punched interlace design, central brass boss engraved, interior lined in rough deerskin and two iron staples for arm straps. Good cond. $3146

Three-quarter Suit of Armor, Germany, c1540. Suit consists of a close helmet, one-piece skull with a low roped comb; sharply pointed visor with two horizontal sights and rows of circular and slotted breaths; two-lame neck defense with lower roped edge.

Gorget with spirally roped collar joined to the main plates by single intermediary lames, outer lames with sprocket pins for the pauldrons. Breastplate with sharply pointed central ridge, strongly roped rims and traces of four lames.

Backplate of simple form with roped bands. Long tassets of ten lames, the knee caps with seven roped ridges. Pauldrons with five plates, the upper with sunken cross banding and the upper and lower with spiral roped rims.

Upper and lower arm defense of simple form. Gauntlets with sunken cross banding on the cuffs, six metacarpal plates and roped knuckle plates.

Areas of light pitting and some helmet repairs present. Minor restoration has been performed. Owned by William Randolph Hearst from 1947–52. Above avg. cond. $37,375

Vambraces, Pair, Germany, 16th Century. Upper and lower cannons linked by articulated plates to bracelet cowters with heart-shaped tandon protectors with embossed heart. Avg. cond. $1050

Firearms

Cannon Tube, France, 1794. Two-stage 40" barrel with 2" bore and keyhole moulding at touchhole. Has faint inscription in French and dated "L'An 2" (1794). Tube has fine patina. Good cond. $5175

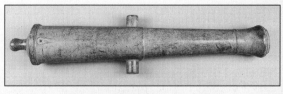

Cannon Tube, French, 1794

Cannon, Naval (Pair), Unknown, Late 18th Century. Each 40" bronze tube has a 2¼ inch bore. Simple mouldings at muzzle breech and trunnions. Gray painted naval-style carriages appear to be contemporary to the tubes. Tubes have light patina. Carriages have scattered blemishes but sound. Above avg. cond. $6900

Carbine, Flintlock, Cavalry, German, c1780. The 22" barrel of .75 cal. is formed with flared cannon-type muzzle. Has five engraved brass bands and decorative sighting tube at breech. Lockplate with relief scrolls. Varnished walnut stock with carved mouldings along front end. Ramrod missing. Barrel has brown staining and wear to engraving. Lockplate shows brown patina and has light pitting on lower jaw. Stock shows repaired crack at butt. Good cond. $4313

Flintlock Cavalry Carbine, c1780

Howitzer, India, c1750. Bronze. Multi-staged with raised mouldings and compressed cascable. Inscribed "Lt. Colonel Claude Martin, Lucknow, 1786," and engraved "Taken By Lord Clyde At Lucknow, March 1758," on stepped four-wheeled mahogany carriage. Good cond. $6642

Musket, Flintlock, Model 1777, France, c1800. 43" barrel of .71 cal. Unmarked lockplate. Varnished walnut stock. Bands marked "DT." Barrel has light brown patina, pitting at breech, lock has dark brown stain. Stock has crack at counterplate and numerous marks. Forward sling swivel broken. Lacks ramrod. Avg. cond. $805

Musket, Wheelock, Germany, c1600. Military type. A 37" barrel of .53 cal., with octagonal breech section, fore and rear sights. Large flat lockplate, with decorated springs and safety catch. Varnished figured walnut stock. Barrel has light brown patina. Lock shows old cleaned surface. Some light marks on the stock. Missing one swivel and the ramrod. Good cond. $6325

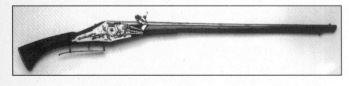

Wheelock Musket, Germany, c1600

Musketoon, Flintlock, Model 1786, France, c1800. 26½ inch barrel of .62 cal. Lockplate marked "D No.26." Walnut stock. Light gray-brown patina on metal throughout.

Stock has extensive worm holes especially at butt. Replacement comb. Below avg. cond. $748

Pistol, Flintlock, Cavalry, England, c1800, Barnett. The 7" .62 cal. barrel is marked "D-C8147" on top. Lockplate marked "BARNETT." Varnished walnut stock marked "J.B." in ramrod channel. Brass furniture with wooden ramrod. Barrel has minor pitting. Minor stains on lock. Even wear and some minor marks on wood stock. Above avg. cond. $920

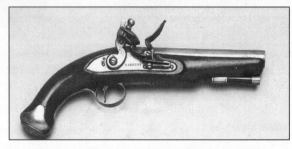

Flintlock Cavalry Pistol by Barnett, c1800

Pistol, Flintlock, Grenade Launching, Germany, 1750. Brass barrel, flat beveled lock engraved with scrollwork against punched ground. Walnut stock and iron mounts. Good cond. $1486

Pistol, Flintlock, Model 1777, France, 1781, St. Etienne. The 7½ inch barrel, of .68 cal., has proof marks on left side and tang inscribed "No. 88." Brass action marked "St. Etienne." Varnished walnut grip with markings on right side "7.B 1781" and a fleur-de-lys over the "B." Barrel has pitting. Some marks on brass and wood grip. Ramrod missing. Good cond. $1265

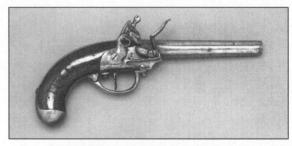

Flintlock Pistol, Model 1777

Flintlock Pistol, Model AN IX (1801)

Pistol, Flintlock, Model An IX (1801), France, c1805. The 8" barrel of .68 cal. is marked "1 B" at breech. Lock marked "B" near cock, is otherwise unmarked. Walnut stock. Ramrod present. Light brown patina to old cleaned surfaces. Lockplate has light pitting. Bronze pan shows a solder repair. Some wear and age marks on brass and wood grip. Above avg. cond. $2588

Pistol, Flintlock, Officer, France, c1800. Has 5½ inch octagonal brass barrel. Rounded brass lockplate, with floral decorations at tail, fine beaded border at pan. Engraved trigger guard with classical motifs. Brass pommel cap engraved with crescent moon within starburst. Walnut stock with checkered wrist. Barrel and lockplate show minor marks. Fore-end of stock extensively repaired. Ramrod missing. Good cond. $978

Officer's Flintlock Pistol, French, c1800

Edged Weapons

Backsword, Basket-hilted, England, 1750. Double-edged blade, brass hilt with slender circular guard bars, bun-shaped pommel, shagreen (leather) covered wooden grip. Good cond. $1224

Backsword, Officer, England, 1750–80. Tapered hollow ground single-edged blade, stamped on each face of the forte with orb and cross marks and "Andrea Ferara." Iron hilt, lion's head pommel and iron-mounted leather covered wooden scabbard. Good cond. $1136

Briquet, Infantry, France, c1790s. Unmarked 23½ inch blade. Brass hilt comprising pierced oval guard with shell finial and integral knucklebow; two outboard branches with a panel of a rampant lion holding a phrygian cap with national cockade aloft on a pole with a dragon and cannon below. One-piece ribbed grip. No scabbard. Blade of light

Infantry Briquet, French, c1790s, 23½-inch blade

gray metal shows light spotting. Hilt shows dark patina. Good cond. $748

Briquet, Infantry, France, c1790. Unmarked 28" blade with back edge fuller. Simple brass stirrup hilt. No scabbard. Blade with mottled gray metal shows some pitting. Hilt cleaned. Good cond. $518

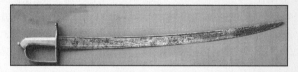

Infantry Briquet, French, c1790s, 28-inch blade

Briquet, Model 1770 Infantry Grenadier, France, Late 18th Century. Unmarked 23" blade. Brass hilt of standard pattern. No scabbard. Blade with mottled gray metal, some pitting and small nicks to edge. Hilt with dark patina. Avg. cond. $460

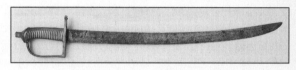

Briquet, Model 1770, Infantry Grenadier

Broadsword, Italy, Early 16th Century. Tapered 31" blade with strong full-length diamond section rib. Bronze crossguard; quillion block with stepped ridge conforming to the blade rib; quillions of flattened section widening at the tips and of recurved "S" configuration. Black letter and twine (?) wrapped wooden grip. Bronze fishtail pommel. Blade shows overall light pitting; edges and tip worn and showing small notches. Grip cracked and showing some damage to the leather. Good cond. $4888

Broadsword, Cavalry, Spain, n/a, 1781, Royal Toledo Manufactory. Double-edged blade stamped on one face with a crowned "R" mark and a "Co. III" and on the other with "C" and "To 1781," the iron hilt has asymmetrical double upturned shells, slender arms, vertically recurved quillions and knuckle-guard with moulded button terminals, globular pommel, and wire-bound wooden grip reinforced with longitudinal iron strips, in original iron-mounted leather scabbard with trumpet-shaped mouth reinforce, the locket with suspension ring. 35¼ inch blade. The inscriptions refer to King Carlo III of Spain (1759–88) and the manufacturer. Above avg. cond. ....
....$1345

Fauchard, Chinese, China, c1750. 32" long. Made of iron with intricate scrollwork motifs of birds, back with ornamental spike and dark finish overall. Good cond. ..
....$600

Glaive, France, c1790. For L'Ecole de Mars (School of

Mars). Straight 19" blade of diamond section. Brass and steel hilt of standard pattern. Brass scabbard with red wool inserts. Blade has dark patina and pitting. Scabbard shows repairs and is missing the decorative panel above the chape. Avg. cond. $863

Plug Bayonet, England, c1690. Slightly curved 11½ inch blade with 4" false edge and worn armorer's mark. Brass crossguard and capstan pommel with finials in the form of a putti. Simple wood grip of typical form. Blade has scattered minor pitting and grip has minor blemishes. Avg. cond. $2185

Plug Bayonet, English, c1690, 11½-inch blade

Plug Bayonet, England, c1690. Straight 11¼ inch blade with impressed armorer's mark on either side. Bronze quillions and pommel, all with head finials. Baluster-form turned wood grip. Blade has dark patina and areas of minor pitting. Small bruises on grip. Good cond. $2588

Plug Bayonet, English, c1690, 11¼-inch blade

Rapier, Swept Hilt, Italy, c Early 17th Century. Narrow 42" blade of diamond section. Steel hilt comprising large fluted shells enclosed by multiple branches of flattened ovoid section, the quillions and knucklebow with scrolled ends. Large tapered ovoid pommel. Wood grip lacking the wire wrapping. Mottled gray metal showing areas of light pitting overall. Several branches of the hilt repaired. Avg. cond. $2070

Saber, Model 1792 Mounted Artillery, France, c1790. Unmarked 23½ inch blade with 6" false edge. Brass stirrup hilt of standard pattern with animal-form grip. Black leather scabbard with brass mounts, the throat mount with buff leather frog tab. Blade has small patches of light pitting. Scabbard scuffed. Avg. cond. $1035

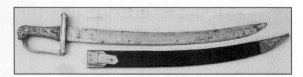

Saber with Scabbard, Model 1792, Mounted Artillery

Saber, Model 1792 Mounted Chasseur, France, c1790. Slightly curved 31" blade engraved with conventional motifs. Brass stirrup hilt with double languets, straight quillion and copper-wire-wrapped grip. Blade shows light pitting. Grip possibly rewrapped. Avg. cond. $431

Saber, Officer, England, c1800. Curved hollow-ground blade, etched and gilt, "GR" monogram and horizontal ribbed ivory grip. Avg. cond. $315

Short Saber, Infantry Officer, France, c1790s. Slightly curved 28½ inch blade engraved with the motto "Vaincre/ ou/Mourir" on one side and an allegorical figure of France on the obverse. Bronze hilt comprising a solid guard/knucklebow; two branches incorporating an allegorical figure of France as a warrior a la antique with a lion, cannon and stand of flags; helmet-form pommel. Fluted ebony grip. No scabbard. Blade has light pitting overall. Hilt with traces of gilt finish and two repaired fractures to the branches. Grip with one chip. Good cond. ... $1610

Infantry Officer's Short Saber

Short Sword, France, c1790s. Unmarked 27" blade. One-piece brass hilt comprising straight quillion; single, broad branch; and ribbed grip. Leather scabbard with brass mounts. Blade cleaned and showing light spotting and patches of pitting toward point. Scabbard scuffed with break above chape. Avg. cond. $863

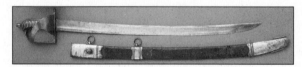

Short Sword with Scabbard, France, c1790s

Short Sword, Model 1790 Artillery, France, c1790. Straight 23" double fullered blade. Brass hilt with straight quillions and eagle head grip. Brass-mounted black leather scabbard. Blade showing light mottling and minor pitting. Hilt cleaned. Scabbard scuffed and missing the tip mount. Avg. cond. $1380

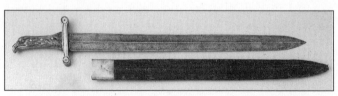

Short Sword with Scabbard, Model 1790, Artillery

Spadroon, Infantry Officer, England, c1800. Blade of hollow diamond section etched and gilt, blued ground with scrollwork, trophies, the royal arms and "For My Country & King." Gilt copper hilt with original leather scabbard. Good cond. $1136

Spear Point, Persia, c500 B.C. Bronze 7" blade with flat median ridge and open 6" socket. Has dark green patina and minor chips. Avg. cond. $575

Sword, Hand and a Half, German, c1541. Narrow 41" blade engraved on either side of the forte with a crown, intwined initials and the date 1541. Long down-curved quillions. Quillion block with two side rings. Leather-covered grip. Elongated ovoid pommel with fluted sides. Blade shows some pitting. Above avg. cond. $3738

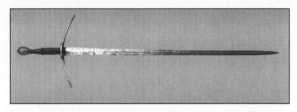

Hand-and-a-half Sword, German, c1541

Sword, Heavy Cavalry Trooper, France, c1790. Straight, unmarked 36" blade. Brass hilt comprising a broad "D"-form guard pierced with a series of circles. Grip/pommel with fluted bands. Leather and wire wrapped grip. Leather-covered scabbard with brass mounts. Blade with dark patina and scattered areas of pitting. Grip scuffed. Scabbard leather scuffed. Mounts with scattered dents, soldered repairs and split at drag. Avg. cond. $805

Sword, Light Cavalry Officer, England, c1800. Etched and gilt blade against blued ground, on one face the royal arms, laurel wreath, trophy of arms and a demi winged horse, on other side a floral spray, a crowned "GR" monogram, a cavalryman, and a crowned Irish harp. Good cond. $1573

War Axe Head, Germany, c13th Century. Excavated item. Hand forged with mounting ring for handle intact. Several runes cut into side of blade. Avg. cond. $264

War Hammer, Poland or Turkey, 17th Century. The iron head comprising a hammerhead of rectangular section balanced by a long, fluted, down-curved, beak-shaped fluke, decorated overall with narrow engraved bands of wriggle-

work and circles of radiating lines, with silver ferrules above and below the head chased with repeated flower-heads within shaped frames, on leather-covered wooden shaft with deep silver ferrule at the bottom decorated en suite. Approx. 27½" long. Good cond. $4250

Clothing

Coatee, Guarde Nationale, Colonel, France, Army, c1795. Of coarse navy blue wool with scarlet wool collar and cuffs piped in white. Buff wool turnbacks piped in red. Brass buttons reading "Republique Francaise" with laurel branches around a fasces. Correct gold bullion fringed epaulettes. Bullion flaming bombs adorn the tail turnbacks. Lined in buff cotton. Overall condition is a result of some moth damage, heavy wear and age. Fair cond. $3163

Coatee, Infantry, Officer, France, Army, c1780. Of scarlet red melton wool with black silk velvet collar and cuffs and with black silk turnbacks. Tails with buff wool turnbacks and black piping. Silver-faced infantry buttons with "I" in relief. Letter "M" monogrammed on lining. Heavy moth damage and age contribute to the overall poor condition of the garment. Poor cond. $1265

French Officer's Coatee, c1780

CHAPTER TWO
Uniforms and Footwear

This chapter encompasses a broad range of military clothing. By no means is this a comprehensive listing of all of the various examples of military clothing that have ever existed, but instead a snapshot of the examples seen on the market over the past two years. Except for the Uniforms subchapter, most of the listings here are for individual pieces or pairs of clothing.

Since clothing tends to be fragile, very little has survived from the period prior to WWI unless it was carefully stored or preserved. Rodent and insect damage is frequently seen.

Military clothing tends to fall into three broad categories: dress uniforms, combat (field) uniforms, and fatigue (utility or work) uniforms. Combat clothing, due to the conditions under which it was worn, is least likely to have survived. Also, combat uniforms tended to be left behind when soldiers left the combat area. In actual service, the distinction between combat and fatigue uniforms was often blurred.

European military uniforms frequently are more elaborate or formal looking than their American counterparts. American officers' clothing is often very similar to the enlisted man's version.

Third Reich military clothing tends to be the most highly sought after. Clothing from SS or Waffen SS units, camouflaged combat clothing, and clothing from specialty units such as Panzers and Paratroopers command the highest prices.

Imperial German Uhlan Officer's Tunic

Collecting Tips
Several approaches to uniform collecting are widely followed. First is to concentrate on the uniforms of a particular country or organization in that country (e.g., Waffen SS combat uniforms). Use period photos to assemble realistic combinations of clothing. A second approach would be to collect one type of item such as belt buckles.

Fakes and Frauds
Third Reich uniforms and accessories are often targets for this type of activity. Reproduction belt buckles usually lack the detail of the originals. Former West German uniforms and movie props are modified to give them the appearance of Third Reich-era examples.

Collectors Clubs
Company of Military Historians, Westbrook, CT, (203) 399-9460, Newsletter
Association of American Military Uniform Collectors, Elyria, OH (216) 365-5321, Newsletter
Imperial German Military Collectors Association, Keyport, NJ, (908) 739-1799, Newsletter

Museums
West Point Museum, USMA, West Point, NY, (914) 938-2203
National Infantry Museum, Ft. Benning, GA, (405) 544-4762

Belts and Buckles—U.S.

Belt, Dress, USA, USMC, WWI. For dress blue uniform. White buff leather. No fittings or buckle. Approx. 40" long. Below avg. cond. $20

Belt, Dress, EM, USA, USMC, WWII. For dress blue uniform. White web belt with rectangular gilt brass buckle with design of 1937 pattern EG&A device in center. Above avg. cond. $50

Belt, Sam Browne, Officer, USA, Army, 1922. Stitched brown leather belt with brass fittings. No cross-strap. Includes brown leather pistol clip ammo pouch and equipment. All pieces are QMC marked and 1922 dated. Good cond. $23

Belt, Sam Browne, Officer, USA, Army, 1930s. Russet brown shell leather belt with gilt brass fittings and matching cross-strap. Size 33. Well marked. Above avg. cond. $40

Belt, Sam Browne, Officer, USA, Army, WWI. Stitched brown leather belt with brass fittings and matching shoulder strap. Above avg. cond. $30

Belt, Sam Browne, Officer, USA, Army, WWI. 2.25" wide stitched brown leather belt with cross-strap and brass fittings. Avg. cond. $20

Belt, Sam Browne, Officer, USA, Army, WWII. Dark brown with brass fittings. Avg. cond. $23

Belt, Sam Browne, Officer, USA, Army, WWI. Stitched brown leather belt with brass fittings, matching cross-strap and leather sword hanger with brass snap hooks. Belt and cross-strap are named to a 1st Lieut. in 305th Inf, Co. L. About size 30. Avg. cond. $41

Belt, Sam Browne, Officer, USA, Army, WWI. Stitched brown leather belt with brass fittings and matching cross-strap. Good cond. $22

Belt, Sam Browne, Officer, USA, Army, 1930s. 2.25"-wide stitched dark tan leather belt with matching cross-strap and gilt brass fittings. Size 32. Above avg. cond. $22

Belt, Sam Browne, Officer, USA, Army, 1930s. Handsome brown leather belt with brass fittings and cross belt plus sword hanger with nickel silver chain. Near mint cond. $97

Belt, Trouser, USA, Army, WWI. Dark tan web with brass end. USQMD/1917 marked. Has brass friction-style buckle. About 32" length. Above avg. cond. $84

Belt, Trouser, USA, Army, WWI, Russell. Dark tan web with brass end. Russell/USQMD marked. Has brass fric-

tion-style buckle. About 37" length. Good cond. . . .$14

Belt, Web Trouser, Officer, USA, Army, WWII, Gemsco. 36" long lt OD web belt with gilt tip. In Gemsco maker's box marked "U.S. Officers Web Belt" on lift-off lid. Above avg. cond. $38

Belts and Buckles—Germany

Belt, Cavalry EM, Imperial Germany, Army, WWI. With sword hanger. Open face brass buckle, blue felt-lined white leather dress belt. Good cond. $101

Belt, Cavalry, Prussian, Imperial Germany, Army, WWI. Gray buckle with bronks. Brown leather belt stamped size 116. Back inked "J.R.49." Avg. cond. $35

Belt, Combat, Germany, Army, WWII. Black leather. Leather tongue and steel hook. Size 100. Avg. cond. $26

Belt, Combat, Germany, Army, 1937. Black leather. Leather tongue, alum hook, size 95 and 1937 date and maker. Avg. cond. $25

Belt, DAK, Germany, Army, WWII. Olive-green web body with leather tongue, green steel hook, inked size 88 and maker. Dated 1941. Exc. cond. $72

Belt, EM, Germany, Army, 1940. Stamped pebbled alum body. By "F.K.O." and same maker to black leather tab. Black leather combat belt, leather tongue, steel hook, 1940 date and maker. Size 115 and inked "R.L.M." Avg. cond. $72

Belt, EM, Germany, Army, WWII. Pebbled alum body and four tab roundel. Black leather belt. Avg. cond. $40

Belt, EM, Germany, Army, WWII. Stamped pebbled alum body with paint. By "R.S.&S." Leather tab with maker and "6./J.R.110." Black combat belt, leather tongue and alum hook. About size 100. Below avg. cond. $80

Belt, EM, Germany, Army, WWII. Stamped pebbled alum body by "F.K.O." Late war brown leather belt, bent steel hook and holes to body. Size 105. Brown belt loop with nickel D-ring and extra clip. Avg. cond. $35

Belt, EM, Germany, Army, WWII. Stamped pebbled alum body and four tab roundel. Marked "olc." Black leather belt, tongue and riveted hook. Size 105. Above avg. cond. $42

Belt, EM, Germany, Army, 1936/1938. Stamped pebbled alum body with gray paint. Brown leather tab marked with 1938 date and maker. Black leather belt with tongue, alum hook, 1936 date, maker and unit stamp. Size 92. Avg. cond. $61

Belt, EM, Germany, Army, WWII. Stamped steel by

"ESL43" with gray paint. Black leather dress belt, tongue stamped "Croupon358" and riveted nickel hook. About size 90. Avg. cond. $39

Belt, EM, Germany, Army, WWII. Stamped steel with gray paint. By "JFS." Black leather belt with tongue, steel hook, 1942 dated and maker. Size 85. Avg. cond. . . . $87

Belt, EM, Germany, Army, WWII. Pebbled gray body with four tab roundel having silver painted finish. Black patent leather belt, gray felt backing, riveted hooks and leather tongue. About size 85. Avg. cond. $50

Belt, EM, Germany, Army, 1942. Stamped steel with gray paint. Brown leather tab, 1942 dated and maker. Black belt, moved leather tongue, alum hook, 1942 date and maker. About size 90. Good cond. $73

Belt, EM, Bavarian, Imperial Germany, Army, WWI. Stamped steel with gray paint. Black leather belt with steel hook, leather tongue, stamped "5 Fd.A.R.1916" and size 95. Avg. cond. $118

Belt, EM, Prussian, Imperial Germany, Army, WWI. Stamped steel with gray paint. Black leather belt with steel hook and leather tongue. Size 108. Leipzig maker, 1916 dated and Army issue. Marked "BAXIX 16." Avg. cond. .
. . . . $50

Belt, EM, Prussian, Imperial Germany, Army, WWI. Brass body with nickel crown. Black leather belt with leather tongue and brass hook. Approx. 90 cm. Avg. cond.
. . . . $45

Belt, EM, Prussian, Imperial Germany, Army, WWI. 50mm. Brass buckle with nickel roundel. 45mm belt with tongue. Size 100. Below avg. cond. $35

Belt, EM, Prussian, Imperial Germany, Army, WWI. 45mm. Brass body with nickel roundel. Brown leather belt. Below avg. cond. $20

Belt, EM, Prussian, Imperial Germany, Army, WWI. Stamped steel with gray paint. Black leather belt with tongue and steel hook. About size 90. Avg. cond. . . $45

Belt, EM, Prussian, Imperial Germany, Army, WWI. 45mm brass body with nickel roundel. Brown leather belt with brass hook and leather tongue. Good cond. . . . $71

Belt, EM, Prussian, Imperial Germany, Army, WWI. Stamped steel with gray paint. Black belt, tongue and steel hook. Size 105. Avg. cond. $28

Belt, EM, Prussian, Imperial Germany, Army, WWI. Stamped steel with gray paint. Brown leather tab by "Lieferungs-Gen. Itzehoe 1918." Black leather belt with leather tongue, steel hook and faint 1916 maker. Size 105. Above avg. cond. $82

Belt, Luftwaffe, EM, Germany, Luftwaffe, 1941. Stamped steel with blue-gray paint. 1941 date/maker marked on brown leather tab. Black leather belt marked with maker and size 95. Avg. cond. $75

Belt, Luftwaffe, EM, Germany, Luftwaffe, 1942. Stamped steel with gray paint. Tab marked "41" and maker. Black belt, steel hook, leather tongue and stamped "1942 R.Z.f.H.7." Size 95. Good cond. $40

Belt, Luftwaffe, EM, Germany, Luftwaffe, 1941, H. Aurich, Dresden. Stamped steel with blue-gray paint. Brown tab marked "H.Aurich Dresden 1941." Black combat belt with steel hook, cut-down tongue and added gull device from collar tab. Size 85. Avg. cond. $37

Belt, Luftwaffe, EM, Germany, Luftwaffe, WWII. Stamped pebbled alum body and four tab roundel with early down-tailed eagle design. Brown leather belt, leather tongue, riveted nickel hook and blue felt backing. About size 105. Above avg. cond. $75

Belt, Luftwaffe, EM, Germany, Luftwaffe, WWII. Pebbled gray body and four tab roundel. Black leather belt with moved tongue, riveted hook and stamped "10JR1888." Below avg. cond. $48

Belt, Luftwaffe, EM, Germany, Luftwaffe, WWII. Stamped alum buckle with 2nd eagle design. Brown leather dress belt, tongue and riveted hook. About size 80. Below avg. cond. $30

Belt, Luftwaffe, Officer, Germany, Luftwaffe, WWII. Alum. brocade facing with two gray and one red stripe. Two brocade loops, blue-gray wool backing with grommets for size adjustments. Frosted silver finish to stamped buckle with two rivets holding gold down-tailed eagle. Good cond. $325

Belt, Luftwaffe, Officer, Germany, Luftwaffe, WWII. Alum. brocade facing with stripes. Blue-gray twill wool backing has grommet size adjustment and some moth holes. Two brocade loops. Stamped buckle with silver frosted finish and gold down-tail eagle attached with two rivets. Larger size. Good cond. $257

Belt, Medical Officer, Bavarian, Imperial Germany, Army, WWI Era. Round buckle with wreath, Bavarian crown belt is of silver brocade with two wide blue stripes and blue cloth backed. Good cond. $155

Belt, Naval, EM, Germany, Navy, WWII. Dark blue-gray paint to stamped steel buckle by "JFS." Black leather belt has rare Eagle-M. Size 96, leather tongue and steel hook. Exc. cond. $97

Belt, Naval, Officer, Imperial Germany, Navy, WWI. Large circular gilt buckle with anchor, W and crown. Silver brocade belt with backing black and gold stripes. Above avg. cond. $177

Belt, Naval, Officer, Imperial Germany, Navy, WWI. Gold crowned anchor buckle. Silver brocade facing with two black stripes and center red strip. Blue wool backing and grommet size adjustment for about 90. One hidden hinged brass hanger loop. Two brocade loops. Above avg. cond. $139

Belt, Naval, Officer, Imperial Germany, Navy, WWI. Solid brass casting to crowned-W-anchor in wreath with gold finish. Silver brocade facing with one red & two black stripes. Grommet size adjustment about 100. Blue wool backing. Good cond. $144

Belt, Naval, Officer, Germany, Navy, WWII. Silver brocade facing with two black stripes. Brocade loops. Blue wool backing with grommet adjustment for size 90. Hidden loops for dagger. Stamped brass buckle with gold details. Above avg. cond. $157

Belt, Naval, Officer, Imperial Germany, Navy, WWI. 1.5" wide. Dark brown russet leather with circular gilt buckle with wreath, W and anchor complete with two lion head slides and hook for dagger hanger. Brass keepers present. Above avg. cond. $85

Belt, NSDAP, Official, Germany, NSDAP, WWII. 60mm brown leather belt with two leather loops, leather tongue, inked size "95" and stamped "RZM Kernstuck L2/682/42." Gold finished alum buckle hmkd "RZM M4/46" and loop by "RZM M4/77." Above avg. cond. $177

Belt, Officer, Germany, Army, WWII. Field gray wool backed with silver wire base and two centered green stripes. Alum belt buckle with pressed-in catch, all fittings and slide straps. Avg. cond. $150

Belt, Officer, Germany, Army, WWII. Bright alum facing with green stripes, brocade loops, wool backing, grommet size adjustment and stamped alum buckle. About size 95. Above avg. cond. $155

Belt, Officer, Germany, Army, WWII. Alum. brocade facing with green stripes. Gray wool backing. Leather tongue. Stamped alum buckle with prongs to loop. Below avg. cond. $66

Belt, Officer, Germany, Army, WWII. Bright alum brocade facing with two green stripes. Gray wool backing, 2 brocade loops, leather tongue and size 110. Gray finished alum buckle with prongs to loop. 6" diam. brown leather case with buckle-strap closure. Above avg. cond. $200

Belt, Officer, Germany, Army, WWII. Silver bullion tape with two green stripes and green wool backing. About size

34. Stamped alum buckle. Above avg. cond. $145

Belt, Officer, Prussian, Imperial Germany, Army, WWI. Brocade facing with two gray stripes. Two brocade loops and all have green twill wool backing. Leather tongue with pronged loop. Gold finish to brass buckle with affixed "WII" center by three-prongs. Exc. cond. $111

Belt, Open Face, NSDAP Official, Germany, NSDAP, WWII. 55mm brown leather body and stamped "Croupon Herst.-NR.610." Brown belt loop, nickel D-ring belt loop and brass pebbled buckle with claws. Avg. cond. $75

Belt, Open Face, NSDAP Official, Germany, NSDAP, WWII (1938). Gold finished pebbled body with open claws. 60mm black leather cut-down body is about size 90. Stamped "Croupon 1249 1938." Avg. cond. $37

Belt, Open Face, SS, Officer, Germany, SS, WWII. 45mm-wide black leather belt with leather loop intact. Gray pebbled buckle with claws. About size 110. Stamped SS runes in hexagon at loop. Below avg. cond. $108

Belt, RAD, EM, Germany, RAD, WWII. Stamped pebbled alum body and maker trademark. Leather tab with 36 maker. Black leather belt, tongue, alum hook and size 95. Stamped "B.A.Br. 9 38." Avg. cond. $60

Belt, RAD, Officer, Germany, RAD, WWII. Stamped alum disc maker marked "A DRGM 37" for Assmann. Alum brocade facing has three brown stripes and both brocade loops. Leather tongue stamped size 93 and alum loop with prongs. Brown wool backing. Below avg. cond. $225

Belt, RAD, Officer, Germany, RAD, WWII. Alum brocade facing with three brown stripes and brown twill wool backing. Two brocade loops and leather tongue for size around 90. Above avg. cond. $75

Belt, Red Cross, Officer, Germany, Red Cross, WWII. Alum disc with eagle and laurel leaf wreath. Marked "Ges.Gesch 2." Black leather belt with tongue and two sets of factory-added holes to body behind tongue. Leather loop and alum loop. Tongue stamped "H" & about size 90. Above avg. cond. $282

Belt, SA, Member, Germany, SA, WWII. Brass body with two solder holes on common brass roundel. Black leather is pliable, leather tongue, steel hook and size 100. Above avg. cond. $45

Belt, SA, Member, Germany, SA, WWII. Brass body with two solder holes to brass roundel and common swastika. Dark brown leather belt, tongue and riveted hook. About size 95. Above avg. cond. $73

Belt, SA, Member, Germany, SA, WWII. Stamped brass body with common eagle/swastika and bright nickel finish overall. Black leather dress belt, tongue and riveted hook. About size 95. Above avg. cond. $99

Belt, Sash, Officer, Prussian, Imperial Germany, Army, c1896. Darkening to brocade with white cloth backing, large tassels and large loop with grommets to adjust size. Avg. cond. $33

Belt, Sash, Officer, Prussian, Imperial Germany, Army, Pre-1896. Darkening to brocade with white cloth backing, large tassels and hinged silver metal hook/loop fittings. Avg. cond. $25

Belt, SS, EM, Germany, SS, WWII. Stamped nickel body by "O&C ges.gesch." Black leather belt with leather tongue and riveted nickel hook. About size 95. Has stamped "RZM/SS" in circles. Avg. cond. $293

Belt, SS, EM, Germany, SS, WWII. Stamped alum marked "RZM 36/39 SS." Black leather belt, tongue, steel hook and size 90. Above avg. cond. $250

Belt, SS, EM, Germany, SS, 1943. Stamped with silver paint. Unmarked. Black leather body, steel hook, tongue, stamped size 95 and 43 dated RB-NR. Above avg. cond. $282

Belt, SS, EM, Germany, SS, 1937, A. Fischer, Berlin. Stamped nickel body by "O&C Ges. Gesch." White fiber belt by "A. Fischer Berlin C.2 1937," alum hook and leather tongue stamped "RZM 4/38 SS." Attached white fiber covered leather bayonet frog by "A. Fischer Berlin C.2 1937." Exc. cond. $1200

Belt, SS, Officer, Germany, SS, WWII. Stamped alum disc has been attached to incorrect alum hook stamped "A DRGM 37." Hook should have "RZM/SS" marks instead of "37" (Assmann). Black leather belt, tongue, gray felt backing and pronged loop has leather tab. Below avg. cond. $500

Belt, Stahlhelm, Member, Germany, Stahlhelm, WWII. Bright brass body with frosted silver helmet roundel with title and half-wreath. Two solder holes. Belt about size 80 with tongue and riveted hook. Above avg. cond $75

Belt, Stahlhelm, Member, Germany, Stahlhelm, WWII. Last pattern. Stamped steel with gray paint, crowned eagle holding shield and title on helmet. Black leather belt with riveted alum hook and moved tongue. About size 80. Avg. cond. $55

Belt, Tropical, EM, Germany, Army, WWII (1941). Olive web belt with leather tongue, steel hook and inked size "90." Stamped steel buckle with green paint. Marked "GB 41" and web tab inked "Leppe." Above avg. cond. . .$155

Belt, Tropical, EM, Germany, Army, WWII (1940). Stamped steel body with gray paint and maker marked

"ESL 40." Tan leather tab with same maker and date. Olive web belt, leather tongue, rust to steel hook, inked RB-NR and size 85. Exc. cond. $95

Belt, Tropical, EM, Germany, Army, 1942. Olive-tan web body with web tongue, steel hook, inked size 100, 1942 date, and maker. Stamped steel buckle with olive paint and web tab. Near mint cond. $212

Belt, Tropical, EM, Germany, Army, WWII. Tan web belt, steel hook, olive tongue and inked "95." Stamped steel buckle with gray paint and olive tab. Near mint cond. . . . $125

Belt, Web, DAK, Germany, Army, 1941, G.Reinhardt, Berlin. Green web belt, leather tongue, olive painted loop, inked size "98" and stamped "G.Reinhardt Berlin 1941." Near mint cond. $143

Belt, Web, DAK, Germany, Army, 1941, G.Reinhardt, Berlin. Olive-green web belt, olive painted hook, leather tongue inked size "115" and stamped "G.Reinhardt Berlin 1941." Near mint cond. $177

Belt, White Parade Dress, EM, Prussian, Imperial Germany, Army, WWI. 40mm. This is a smaller size buckle than the standard. Brass body with nickel roundel. White patent leather belt with leather tongue, gray hook and white felt backing. Size 104. Avg. cond. $49

Belt, With Cross-Strap, Hitler Youth Member, Germany, Hitler Youth, WWII. Gray injected buckle with details and "RZM M4/72." Black paper ersatz belt, riveted hook and leather tongue stamped "RZM DJ etc." Two imitation pigskin/paper belt loops and cross-strap with nickel fittings. Both clips stamped "DRGM M5/8c RZM A." Avg. cond. $120

Belt, With Cross-Strap, SS, Officer, Germany, SS, WWII. Stamped alum. disc with details. Back stamped "RZM SS 36/38 OLC." Prongs on fixed loop. Black leather belt, leather tongue, leather loop, alum. end loop. Black leather cross-strap, nickel fittings and one clip stamped "A" for Assmann. Two black leather belt loops with nickel D-rings. Near mint cond. $906

Buckle, Butcher, Imperial Germany, Army, WWI. 45mm. Dark-brass body with two rivets to nickel silver cowhead and cleavers at center. Cast-brass prong bar and soldered hook. Styled after M1850. Avg. cond. $95

Buckle, Butcher, Imperial Germany, Army, WWI. 45mm brass body is 85mm long. Two rivets to cast-brass full-body cow standing on ground. Cast-brass prong bar and soldered hook at back. Avg. cond. $124

Buckle, Coastal Arty, EM, Germany, Navy, 1937. Stamped steel body by "Rodo" with dark blue/black paint. Tab marked 1937/maker. Above avg. cond. $28

Buckle, Coastal Arty, EM, Germany, Navy, WWII. Stamped steel with blue/black paint. Good cond. . . . $50

Buckle, DAF Member, Germany, DAF, WWII. Stamped alum. by "RZM M4/24" with silver paint. With paper tag and same inked RZM-maker. Exc. cond. $79

Buckle, DAF Member, Germany, DAF, WWII. Stamped alum with cogged wheel swastika. By "RZM M4/27." Good cond. $66

Buckle, EM, Germany, Army, WWII. Stamped gray pebble body with four tab roundel. Silver painted finish. Exc. cond. $35

Buckle, EM, Germany, Army, 1937. Stamped pebbled alum body by "Dr.F.&Co." Brown tab dated 1937 and maker marked. Below avg. cond. $40

Buckle, EM, Germany, Army, 1937. Stamped pebbled alum body with gray paint. Brown leather tab, dated 1937 and maker marked. Below avg. cond. $27

Buckle, EM, Germany, Army, 1940. Stamped pebbled alum. Brown tab dated 1940 and maker marked. Avg. cond. $27

Buckle, EM, Germany, Army, WWII. Stamped pebbled alum. Marked "JMO 39." Avg. cond. $40

Buckle, EM, Germany, Army, 1936. Stamped pebbled alum body. Brown leather tab marked with 1936 date, maker and unit. Good cond. $70

Buckle, EM, Germany, Army, 1941. Stamped steel with gray paint, excellent details and marked "N&H 1941." Brown tab marked with date and maker. Near mint cond. $93

Buckle, EM, Austrian, Germany, Army, WWI. 50mm. Stamped brass. Stamped crowned-shield proof to top corner. Above avg. cond. $45

Buckle, EM, Bavarian, Imperial Germany, Army, WWI. Stamped steel with crown details and "In Treue Fest" with wreath. Below avg. cond. $31

Buckle, EM, Bavarian, Imperial Germany, Army, WWI. 45mm variation. Brass body with nickel roundel. Avg. cond. $46

Buckle, EM, Hannoverian, Imperial Germany, Army, WWI. 65mm. Brass body with brass roundel. Above avg. cond. $68

Buckle, EM, Prussian, Imperial Germany, Army, WWI. 50mm. Brass body with nickel roundel. Three solder holes. Above avg. cond. $68

Buckle, EM, Prussian, Imperial Germany, Army, WWI. 45mm copper/tombac body with nickel roundel. Marked

"J.R.Gebrauchs=Musterschutz No2748." Avg. cond. $25

Buckle, EM, Saxon, Imperial Germany, Army, WWI. 45mm. Stamped steel. Avg. cond. $48

Buckle, EM, Saxon, Imperial Germany, Army, WWI. 45mm. Tombak body with nickel roundel with crowned "JG" monogram. Below avg. cond. $270

Buckle, EM, Tropical, Germany, Army, 1941. Stamped steel body with "41" behind bar. Olive web tab. Avg. cond. $90

Buckle, EM, Wurttemberg, Imperial Germany, Army, WWI. Stamped steel with gray finish. Good cond.   . $47

Buckle, EM, Wurttemberg, Imperial Germany, Army, WWI. Stamped steel with gray finish. Above avg. cond. $40

Buckle, EM, Wurttemberg, Imperial Germany, Army, WWI. 45mm brass body with two solder holes to nickel roundel. Brown leather tab. Above avg. cond. $50

Buckle, Fire Defense, EM, Germany, WWII. 45mm stamped steel body with silver paint. Title to roundel with oak leaf half-wreath and shield center with diagonal bar. Avg. cond. $50

Buckle, Fire Defense, Officer, Rheinland, Germany, WWII. Stamped brass disc with dark silver finish. Shield center and laurel leaf wreath border. Loop with prongs. Avg. cond. $32

Buckle, Hitler Youth (HJ), Germany, Hitler Youth (HJ), WWII. Stamped alum by "RZM M4/42." Avg. cond. $21

Buckle, Luftwaffe, EM, Germany, Luftwaffe, 1940. Stamped steel with blue-gray paint. Brown leather tab with 1940 date and maker. Avg. cond. $31

Buckle, Luftwaffe, EM, Germany, Luftwaffe, WWII. Stamped steel with blue-gray paint. Avg. cond. $34

Buckle, Luftwaffe, EM, Germany, Luftwaffe, WWII. Stamped pebbled alum with wear to 2nd eagle design. Avg. cond. $28

Buckle, Luftwaffe, EM, Germany, Luftwaffe, 1939. Stamped pebbled alum body. Brown leather tab marked 1939 and maker. Avg. cond. $45

Buckle, Luftwaffe, EM, Germany, Luftwaffe, WWII (1936). Stamped pebbled alum body with down-tailed eagle. Maker trademarked. Brown tab marked "36" and maker name. Avg. cond. $50

Buckle, Naval Administration Official, Germany, Navy, WWII. Alum body. Marked "EJL." Avg. cond. $20

Buckle, Naval Administration Official, Germany, Navy,

WWII. 60mm solid alum disc with no loop to back. "EJL" hallmark. Avg. cond. $35

Buckle, Naval EM, Imperial Germany, Navy, WWI (1914), Wimmer & Lewy, Leipzig. 45mm. Brass body has domed back stamped "Wimmer & Lewy Leipzig 1914." Affixed nickel roundel with flat-sided crown. Below avg. cond. $40

Buckle, Naval Officer, Imperial Germany, Navy, WWI. 40mm brass disc with gold finish to laurel leaf wreath and crowned-W anchor in center. Loop to back side. Good cond. $80

Buckle, Naval, EM, Germany, Navy, 1938. Stamped alum with gold wash. Hmkd "R.S.&S." Brown tab with 1938 date, maker and Eagle-M stamp. Avg. cond. $124

Buckle, Naval, EM, Germany, Navy, 1938. Stamped alum with gold finish. Brown leather tab with 1938 date, maker and Eagle-M. Good cond. $100

Buckle, Naval, Officer, Germany, Navy, WWII. 60mm. Solid heavy gray metal by "FLL" with gold finish. Loop to back side. Avg. cond. $50

Buckle, Naval, Officer, Germany, Navy, WWII. Brass. 60mm heavy cast body with gold finish to anchor and laurel leaf wreath. Avg. cond. $50

Buckle, Naval, Officer, Germany, Navy, WWII. Heavy stamped 60mm brass body with gold finish. Loop to back side and extra loop. Above avg. cond. $70

Buckle, Naval, Officer, Germany, Navy, WWII. Solid gray metal 60mm disc with gold finish. Hmkd "FLL." No loop. Above avg. cond. $35

Buckle, Naval, Officer, Germany, Navy, WWII. Solid alum body with gold finish at highlights of anchor and laurel leaf wreath. Hmkd "EJL." Avg. cond. $23

Buckle, NSBO, Germany, NSBO, WWII. Brass body, attached roundel with logo center and oak leaf wreath border. Two solder holes. Good cond. $50

Buckle, NSBO, EM, Germany, NSBO, WWII. 45mm brass body with two solder holes to stamped brass roundel having full oak leaf wreath logo center. Above avg. cond. $56

Buckle, NSDAP Official, Germany, NSDAP, WWII. 60mm. Solid alum body with gold finished eagle and wreath hmkd "RZM M4/24." Oak leaves on prong loop and extra loop. Above avg. cond. $90

Buckle, NSDAP Official, Germany, NSDAP, WWII. Gold finish to solid body, marked "RZM M4/87." Oak leaves to loop with prongs. Exc. cond. $59

Buckle, Officer, Germany, Army, WWII. Stamped gray alum disc with same alums loop to both sides. Above avg. cond. $40

Buckle, Officer, Germany, Army, WWII. Stamped alum disc with loop. Prongs to alum loop. Exc. cond. . . . $76

Buckle, Officer, Brunswick, Imperial Germany, Army, WWI. Stamped buckle has frosted silver finish to laurel leaf wreath. 92nd tradition skull with crossbones below is nickel cap style with 2 prongs through buckle holes. Belt loop to back-side. Above avg. cond. $164

Buckle, Officer, Prussian, Imperial Germany, Army, WWI. Stamped steel disc, laurel leaf wreath border, Crowned "WII" center and traces of brown paint. Loop to back side. Avg. cond. $35

Buckle, Officer, Prussian, Imperial Germany, Army, WWI. Matte silver finish with keeper. Circular oak leaf pattern with "W" and crown device in center. Near mint cond. $85

Buckle, Officer, Prussian, Imperial Germany, Army, WWI. 48mm dia. Gilt buckle with crowned "W II" cipher. Has hinged left rectangular anchor for belt and broad hook on reverse. Above avg. cond. $55

Buckle, RAD, EM, Germany, RAD, WWII. Stamped pebbled alum body. Hmkd "R.S.&S." with gray wash. Above avg. cond. $33

Buckle, RAD, EM, Germany, RAD, WWII. Stamped pebbled alum body. Brown leather tab marked with maker name and date. Near mint cond. $67

Buckle, RAD, EM, Germany, RAD, WWII. Stamped pebbled alum body with gray finish. By "A 38" for Assmann. Avg. cond. $50

Buckle, Red Cross, EM, Germany, Red Cross, WWII. Gray finished stamped pebbled alum body with eagle/wreath. By "olc ges.gesch." Avg. cond. $73

Buckle, Red Cross, EM, Germany, Red Cross, WWII. Stamped pebbled gray alum body with eagle and wreath. "Ges.Gesch.1." Avg. cond. $135

Buckle, Red Cross, Officer, Germany, Red Cross, WWII. Stamped brass laurel leaf wreath body has silver cross attached to center with two prongs. Three extra holes for prongs. Loop to back side. Below avg. cond. $80

Buckle, RLB, EM, Germany, RLB, WWII. 3rd Type. Stamped steel with dark blue-gray paint. Brown tab marked with 1941 date and maker. Above avg. cond. $244

Buckle, RLB, EM, Germany, RLB, WWII. 2nd Type. Stamped alum with Luftschutz winged swastika/wreath. Avg. cond. $30

Buckle, SA, Member, Germany, SA, WWII. 45mm dark brass body, two solder holes and common swastika on brass roundel. Avg. cond. $40

Buckle, SA, Member, Germany, SA, WWII. Brass body with common nickel roundel having two solder holes. Avg. cond. $50

Buckle, SA, Member, Germany, SA, WWII. Brass body with common brass roundel attached with two solder holes. Avg. cond. $40

Buckle, SA, Member, Germany, SA, WWII. 35mm. Brass body. Dark nickel roundel with two solder holes. Avg. cond. $45

Buckle, SA, Member, Germany, SA, WWII. Brass body with dark brass roundel and slanted swastika. Two solder holes. Avg. cond. $36

Buckle, SA, Member, Germany, SA, WWII. Brass body, two solder holes, and common swastika to brass roundel. Avg. cond. $28

Buckle, SA, Member, Germany, SA, WWII. Common roundel with wear to silver finish. Brass body and two solder holes. Avg. cond. $45

Buckle, SA, Member, Germany, SA, WWII. Dark brass body and common roundel with two solder holes. Avg. cond. $27

Buckle, SA, Member, Germany, SA, WWII. Stamped brass body with common swastika. Below avg. cond. $25

Buckle, SA, Member, Germany, SA, WWII. Bright plated finish to smooth body and two solder holes on roundel with common swastika. Above avg. cond. $90

Buckle, SS, EM, Germany, SS, WWII. Stamped steel with silver painted front and back. Above avg. cond. . . . $135

Buckle, SS, EM, Germany, SS, WWII. Stamped alum body. Marked "RZM 822/38 SS." Avg. cond. $187

Buckle, SS, EM, Germany, SS, WWII. Stamped alum with silver paint. By "RZM 155/39 SS." Above avg. cond. $387

Buckle, SS, EM, Germany, SS, WWII. Stamped steel with silver paint. Marked "RZM 155/43 SS." Above avg. cond. $171

Buckle, SS, EM, Germany, SS, WWII. Stamped alum with silver paint. Marked "RZM 822/37 SS." Near mint cond. $349

Buckle, SS, EM, Germany, SS, WWII. Stamped steel with silver painted finish. Exc. cond. $130

Buckle, SS, EM, Germany, SS, WWII. Stamped steel with

gray paint. Marked "Rodo." Combat style. Above avg. cond. $244

Buckle, SS, Officer, Germany, SS, WWII. Stamped non-magnetic metal disc with silver paint and excellent details. Back stamped "RZM SS 36/43 OLC." With extra loop and black printed paper tag. Near mint cond. $900

Buckle, SS, Officer, Germany, SS, WWII. Alum stamped with pressed-in keeper bar. Hmkd "OLC SS 36/39 RZM" on bar. Alum two-pronged keeper attached and unattached keeper bar with two prongs. Avg. cond. $339

Buckle, Stahlhelm, Member, Germany, Stahlhelm, WWII. Brass body with nickel roundel having three solder holes. Above avg. cond. $56

Buckle, Telegrapher, Prussian, Imperial Germany, Army, WWI. Stamped steel. Good cond. $225

Buckle, Tropical, EM, Germany, Army, WWII. Stamped steel. Marked "Dr.F&C.42" with OG paint. Exc. cond. $48

Buckle, Tropical, EM, Germany, Army, 1941. Stamped steel by "CTD 1941" with olive paint. Above avg. cond. $42

Hate Belt, With 10 Devices, Imperial Germany, Army, WWI. Prussian EM belt buckle. Brass with nickel roundel and unmarked leather tab. Maker to brown belt with brass hook and tongue. Nine different buttons and silver badge with profiles of Wilhelm II/Franz Josef. Avg. cond. . $40

Hate Belt, With 18 Devices, Imperial Germany, Army, WWI. Brown body with steel hook and moved leather tongue. Was size 100. Most buttons and devices affixed with catches or loops intact. Unique silver disc with early race car, enamel 1914 EK with oak leaves on Arty ring, etc. Above avg. cond. $95

Belts and Buckles——Other

Belt, Parade, Army Officer, Soviet Union, Army, 1980s. Gilded buckle with hammer and sickle on star in wreath motif, on elongated oval planchet. Yellow cloth belt with multi-colored flecking. Exc. cond. $20

Boots——U.S.

Boots, Arctic, Felt, USA, Army, Korean War. Ex-large size with white felt bodies, thick composition soles, two-buckle canvas and leather uppers and lace insteps. Above avg. cond. $20

Boots, Arctic, Felt, USA, Army, Korean War. Thick white felt bodies with thick composition soles, lace insteps, white canvas/leather two-buckle uppers. Size large. With thick white wool felt liners. Avg. cond. $21

Boots, Cavalry, USA, Army, Pre-WWII. Smooth russet brown leather with cap toes, laced fronts, leather soles and rubber heels. Faint ink stamp markings inside. Size 8½E. Good cond. $133

Boots, Cavalry, USA, Army, 1930s. 17"-tall brown leather bodies with two leg strap closures, lace insteps and cap toes. Top of each have had 2.75"-tall section of russet brown leather added with top strap restitched in place. About size 8/9. Avg. cond. $75

Boots, Combat, USA, USMC, Korean War. Size 10W dark brown leather with cap toes, neoprene soles and lace fronts. Tongue has faint USMC inspector markings. Below avg. cond. $12

Boots, Combat, Leather, USA, Army, 1988. Size 11½R in black leather with molded rubber soles and speed lace fronts. 1988 dated. Near mint cond. $35

Boots, Combat, Leather, USA, Army, 1989. Size 8½R in black leather with molded rubber soles and speed lace fronts. 1989 dated. Near mint cond. $35

Boots, Combat, Leather, USA, Army, 1986. Size 9½R in black leather with cleated soles and speed laces. 1986 dated. Exc. cond. $35

Boots, Combat, Leather, USA, Army, 1986. Size 9½R black leather, cleated soles and speed laces. 1986 dated. Near mint cond. $35

Boots, Combat, Leather, USA, Army, 1988. Size 9R in black leather with speed lace fronts and molded rubber soles. 1988 dated. Near mint cond. $35

Boots, Combat, Leather, Female, USA, Army, 1977. Size 4N black leather bodies with lace fronts and "tire tread" soles. 1977 dated. Near mint cond. $20

Boots, Combat, Leather, Female, USA, Army, 1980. Size 3XW black leather bodies with lace fronts and "tire tread" soles. 1980 dated. Near mint cond. $20

Boots, Combat, Tropical, USA, Army, 1969. Size 10W. Black leather bodies with OD canvas uppers, lace fronts, and cleated soles. 1969 dated. Spike protective marked. Above avg. cond. $66

Boots, Combat, Tropical, USA, Army, 1966. Size 12XN. Black leather bodies with cleated soles, OD canvas uppers and lace fronts. 1966 dated. Spike protective marked. Near mint cond. $100

Boots, Combat, Tropical, USA, Army, 1965. Size 11N. Black leather bodies with OD canvas uppers, lace fronts and cleated soles. 1965 dated. Above avg. cond. . . . $50

Boots, Combat, Tropical, USA, Army, 1988. "Jungle" boots. Size 10½W. Dark OD canvas uppers, black leather bodies and cleated soles. Spike protective marked. 1988 dated. Near mint cond. $40

Boots, Combat, Tropical, USA, Army, Vietnam War . Black leather bodies with cleated soles, dark OD canvas uppers, and lace fronts. Size 13N. Exc. cond. $20

Boots, Combat, Tropical, USA, Army, 1968. Size 10XN. Black leather bodies with OD canvas uppers, cleated soles and lace fronts. Spike protective marked. 1968 dated. Avg. cond. $25

Boots, Combat, Tropical, USA, Army, 1966. Size 8W with black leather bodies, OD canvas uppers, lace fronts and cleated soles. 1966 dated. Above avg. cond. . . . $49

Boots, Combat, Tropical, USA, Army, 1970s. Patterned after Vietnam issue but with black nylon canvas uppers, black leather bodies, "speed lace fronts," cleated soles and drain vents. Size 8W. Instructional card still attached. Last of the "jungle" boots. Exc. cond. $35

Boots, Combat, Tropical, USA, Army, 1964. Jungle boots. Size 11W with black leather bodies, OD canvas uppers, lace fronts and 1964-dated spec tags. Above avg. cond. $39

Boots, Field, USA, Army, WWII. 17" tall in smooth brown leather with cap toes, lace insteps and three leg-strap tops. 1941 dated Qm markings. Size 9D. Included pair US-marked nickel spurs. Above avg. cond. . . . $145

Boots, Field, USA, Army, 1931. Approx. 17" tall in russet brown leather with full lace fronts and rubber soles and heels. Avg. cond. $90

Boots, Field, M1917, USA, Army, WWI. Ankle high in brown leather with lace fronts, leather soles and heels with hobnails. Large size. Avg. cond. $591

Boots, Field, Officer, USA, Army, WWI. Approx. 14" tall. Medium shade of brown leather with rawhide lace fronts, cap toes, leather and rubber soles. Above avg. cond. . $76

US Army Officer's Field Boots (WWI)

Boots, Jump, Airborne, USA, Army, WWII. Dark brown leather with cap toes and lace fronts. About size 8. Avg. cond. $125

Boots, Jump, Airborne, USA, Army, WWII. Issue in brown leather with cap toes, lace fronts and beveled heels. Size 9½B. Some use. Have been cleaned up and have good appearance. Above avg. cond. $200

US Army Parachute Jump Boots (Corcoran, WWII)

Boots, Jump, Parachute, USA, Army, Airborne, WWII, Corcoran. Dark brown leather with rawhide lace fronts, woven Corcoran label, cap toes and beveled heels. Size 9C. Avg. cond. $177

Boots, Jump, Parachute, USA, Army, Airborne, Korean War Era. Size 10½R in dark brown leather with cap toes, replacement laces and neoprene soles. Avg. cond. $12

Boots, Jump, Parachute, USA, Army, Airborne, WWII, Corcoran. Russet brown leather with cap toes, beveled heels and rawhide lace fronts. Lacks most of woven maker's label but embossed Corcoran markings remain. Size 9D. Avg. cond. $210

Boots, Jump, Parachute, USA, Army, Airborne, WWII, Corcoran. Smooth dark brown leather with cap toes, beveled heels and rawhide lace fronts. Embossed Corcoran markings inside top of each. Size 8½D. Avg. cond. $365

Boots, Riding, Officer, USA, Army, 1930s. Approx 17"-tall brown leather bodies with lace insteps, leather soles and web pull loops inside each. About size 9. Avg. cond. $61

Boots, Riding, Officer, USA, Army, WWII. 18" tall in russet brown leather with leather heels and black web pulls inside each. About size 10. Above avg. cond. $91

Boots, Service, Combat, USA, Army, 1956. Size 10 R in black leather with cap toes, lace fronts and neoprene soles. 1956 dated Qm markings. Above avg. cond. $52

Boots, Service, Combat, Russet, USA, Army, Korean War. Size 10½ in smooth russet brown leather with cap toes, neoprene soles and lace fronts. Exc. cond. . . . $44

Boots, Service, Combat, Russet, USA, Army, Korean War. Smooth russet brown leather with cap toes, neoprene soles and lace fronts. Size 9. In original carton. Exc. cond. $46

Boots, Service, Combat, Russet, USA, Army, 1950s. Russet brown leather with cap toes, lace fronts and neoprene soles. In original issue box. Size 8½. Exc. cond. $49

Boots, Service, Combat, Russet, USA, Army, 1950s. Russet brown leather with cap toes, lace fronts and neoprene soles. Markings faint. About size 10. Exc. cond. $35

Boots, Service, Combat, Russet, USA, Army, 1950s. Size 8½ in smooth russet brown leather with cap toes, neoprene soles and lace fronts. Avg. cond. $29

Boots, Service, Combat, Two-buckle, USA, Army, 1944. Dubbed brown roughout leather bodies with laced insteps and smooth leather two-buckle uppers. 1944 dated. Avg. cond. $65

Boots, Service, Combat, Two-buckle, USA, Army, WWII. Roughout brown leather bodies with laced insteps and smooth leather two-buckle uppers. Size 6AA. 1944 dated Qm markings. Exc. cond. $82

Boots, Service, Combat, Two-buckle, USA, Army, WWII. Roughout brown leather bodies with laced insteps and two-buckle smooth leather uppers. Size 9D. Avg. cond. $143

Boots, Service, Combat, Two-buckle, USA, Army, WWII. Dubbed dark brown roughout leather bodies with lace insteps and two-buckle smooth leather uppers. Size 7½D. Avg. cond. $66

Boots, Service, Combat, Two-buckle, USA, Army, WWII. Size 12A. Roughout brown leather bodies with rawhide lace insteps and smooth leather two-buckle uppers. Faint Qm markings. Show little use. Exc. cond. $171

Boots, Service, Combat, Two-buckle, USA, Army, WWII. Dark leather bodies. Laced insteps and two-buckle leather uppers. Size 11½E. Have metal tap nailed to each heel. Avg. cond. $91

Boots, Service, Combat, Two-buckle, USA, Army, WWII. Size 7D in dark brown roughout leather with lace insteps and smooth two-buckle leather uppers. Avg. cond. $44

Boots, Shoepac,12-Inch, M1944, USA, Army, WWII. Dark brown impregnated leather uppers with molded soles and rawhide laces. 1944 dated Qm markings. Size 8. Includes pair heavy white knit socks. Above avg. cond. $59

Boots, Shoepac,12-Inch, M1944, USA, Army, WWII. Size 10N. Dark impregnated leather bodies with molded black rubber soles. No laces. 1945 dated Qm markings. Approx. 12" tall. Above avg. cond. $20

Boots, Ski, USA, Army, WWII. Brown leather bodies with "square" toes, white lace fronts and leather soles and heels. Size 8. Faint Qm markings appear 1942 dated. Avg. cond. $47

Boots, Ski, Mountain, USA, Army, WWII. Brown leather with square toes, lace fronts and heavy cleated soles. Size 9D. Faint Qm markings. Avg. cond. $20

Boots, Ski, Mountain, USA, Army, WWII. Size 8½E in dark brown leather with heavily cleated soles and lace insteps. Faint Qm markings. Show little use. Above avg. cond. $135

Boots, Ski, Mountain, USA, Army, WWII. Dark brown leather ankle-high bodies with square toes, rawhide lace insteps and heavily cleated soles. Size 7EE. Above avg. cond. $50

Boots, Ski, Mountain, USA, Army, WWII. Dark brown leather with square toes, lace fronts and heavily cleated soles. 1943 dated issue markings. Exc. cond. $65

Boots—Germany

Boots, Cavalry, Officer, Germany, Army, WWII. Black leather. 18½" tall, scalloped tops, two broken cloth loops, leather soles and heels with heavy duty horseshoes. Spur tabs above heels. Avg. cond. $66

Boots, Combat, Low-quarter, Germany, Army, WWII. 6"-tall black leather bodies, eight grommets and six hook fronts. Leather soles and heels with hobnails, large toe plates, horseshoes and stamped "1010 40." Exc. cond. $447

Boots, Combat, Officer, Germany, Luftwaffe, WWII. Black leather. 17½"-tall leather-lined uppers with loops. Luftwaffe-style stitched leather soles and heels. Hobnails added to edges of soles with toe plates and horseshoes. Avg. cond. $95

Boots, Combat, Officer, Germany, Army, WWII. Black leather. 16" tall with leather-lined uppers having cloth straps and back buckle strap. Two broken cloth straps. Leather soles and heels with hobnails, toe plates and horseshoes. Good cond. $94

Boots, Combat, Officer, Germany, Army, WWII. Black leather. 16½"-tall leather-lined uppers with loops. Leather soles and heels with added hobnails to edge, toe plates and horseshoes. Avg. cond. $135

Boots, Combat, Officer, Germany, Army, WWII. 16½"-tall black leather bodies, leather-lined uppers and cloth loops. Leather soles and heels with hobnails and four toe plates to each. Avg. cond. $135

German WWII Officer's Combat Boots

Boots, Jack, Germany, Army, WWII. Black leather. 16" tall. Side stamped "31.5.39." About size 11 with leather soles showing remains of hobnails. Leather heels with horseshoes and rubber centers. Avg. cond. $205

Boots, Jack, Germany, Army, WWII. Black leather. 16"-tall bodies. Leather soles and heels. Hobnails, toe plates and horseshoes. Avg. cond. $126

Boots, Jack, Germany, Army, WWII. Black leather. 17½"-tall bodies with replacement cloth loops. Leather soles and heels with hobnails, toe plates and horseshoes. Avg. cond. $107

Boots, Jack, Germany, Army, WWII. Custom made. Black leather. Combat style but leather lining to 16½"-tall bodies with repaired loops. Leather soles and heels with hobnails, toe plates and horseshoes. Trademark man-logo inside. Avg. cond. $85

Boots, Jump, Germany, Luftwaffe, Paratrooper, WWII. Early pattern side laced. Black leather. 10" tall, six grommet and twelve hooks on sides with laces. Luftwaffe-style sewn leather soles and heels with toe/heel plates. Avg. cond. $800

Boots, Lace-up, SA, Germany, Army, WWII. Brown leather. 16"-tall bodies with 18 grommets and 22 hooks. Brown cloth laces. Leather soles and heels and removed/missing toe plates/horseshoes. Avg. cond. $244

Boots, Low-quarter, Tropical, Germany, Army, WWII. About 7"-tall white web uppers, black leather lowers and wooden soles. Two buckle strap closure on front slash. Soles inked "#41" with some hobnails, toe plates and horseshoe heels. Exc. cond. $118

Boots, Mountain, Germany, Army, WWII. Heavy black leather style with original laces. Cleats, hobnails all intact. Size 8–9. Above avg. cond. $150

Boots, Mountain, Germany, Army, WWII. Black leather. 6" tall with gray wool trim to opening, 14 grommets and cloth laces. Leather soles and heels filled with steel cleats. Stamped "28 5." Avg. cond. $229

Boots, Mountain , Germany, Army, WWII. 5½"-tall dark brown leather bodies with gray wool trim to openings, 12 grommets. Leather soles and heels with hobnails and border cleats. Avg. cond. $115

Boots, Officer, Germany, Luftwaffe, WWII. Black leather. 15" tall, leather-lined upper and buckle strap sides. Luftwaffe-style sewn leather soles and heels with horseshoes. Above avg. cond. $114

Boots, Officer, East Germany, Army, 1980s. Pair, black grained leatherette, jet boot style with pull-on tabs, black thread soles and heels. Unissued. Good cond. $31

Boots, Officer, Germany, Army, WWII. Black leather. 15½"-tall, leather-lined uppers with cloth/leather loops, leather soles, heels and horseshoes. Avg. cond. $65

Boots, Officer, Germany, Army, WWII. Black leather. 16"-tall leather-lined uppers with broken cloth loops. Leather soles and heels both covered with black rubber and toe plates. Below avg. cond. $72

Boots, Officer, Germany, Army, 1941. Black leather. 16" tall with leather-lined uppers, cloth loops and looks to be 1941 dated. Polished bodies. Leather soles and heels with toe plates and horseshoes. Avg. cond. $110

Boots, Officer, Germany, Luftwaffe, WWII. Black leather. 17" tall with buckle closure. Cloth loops and partial leather-lined. Luftwaffe-style sewn leather soles. Avg. cond. $72

Boots, Officer, Germany, Army, WWII. Black leather. 16½" tall with leather lining and cloth loops. Leather soles with metal toe plates and black rubber heels by "Berson." Above avg. cond. $82

Boots, Officer, Germany, Army, WWII. Black leather. 17"-tall leather-lined bodies with cloth pull-on straps. Leather soles and heels. Above avg. cond. $118

Boots, Officer, Germany, Army, WWII. Black leather. 16"-tall leather-lined bodies with cloth loops. Leather soles and heels. Avg. cond. $50

Boots, Sentry, Germany, Army, WWII. 12"-tall gray felt

bodies with black leather fittings and wooden soles. Two roller buckle closure straps. Inked cloth maker tags with date. Soles also inked size "32." Exc. cond. $82

Boots, Sentry, Germany, Army, 1939. 11"-tall gray wool bodies with black leather lowers, fittings and soles. Two roller buckle closure front and inside leather tab dated 1939. Above avg. cond. $90

Boots, Ski, Germany, Army, WWII. 10" tall with green canvas uppers, brown leather lowers and wooden soles. Four leather roller buckle closure straps. Steel horseshoe and toe fitting on each. Wood stamped "28 Rata 42 623." Includes French fleece/leather liners with zipper sides. Above avg. cond. $135

Boots, Winter, Germany, Army, 1944. 17½" tall with gray felt uppers having buckle strap closure, cloth loops and leather maker tag "1944 28½ E.Pretzsch etc." Scuffed brown leather lowers. Leather soles and heels with leather fittings. Avg. cond. $160

Boots, Winter, Officer , Germany, Luftwaffe, WWII. 17"-tall smooth black leather and suede bodies. Adjustment strap around top and across ankle. Metal zipper to side. White felt lined. Unused double-stitched leather soles and heels. Near mint cond. $350

Boots—Other

Boots, Combat, Cuban, Cuba, Army, 1980. Cuban Army Issue. Ankle length, black leather uppers, rubber soles, and one shoelace. Above avg. cond. $21

Breeches—U.S.

Breeches, EM, USA, Army, WWI. Brown wool with zinc US Army button fly and lace calves. Medium size. Avg. cond. $26

Breeches, Officer, USA, Army, WWI. OD wool with button fly and lace calves. About size 30" waist. Avg. cond. $23

Breeches, Officer, USA, Army, 1930s. Lt OD gabardine with button front, lace calves and reinforced thigh areas. Faint 1930s date. Above avg. cond. $24

Breeches, Officer, USA, Army, WWI. Dark tan cotton twill with button calves and zinc US Army button fly. Approx. 42" waist. Avg. cond. $20

Breeches, Officer, USA, Army, WWI. Dark tan cotton twill with zinc US Army button fly and lace calves. Avg. cond. $16

Breeches, Officer, USA, Army, WWI. Lt OD whipcord with button calves and fly. Includes dark tan cotton belt. Approx. 30" waist. Avg. cond. $16

Breeches, Officer, "Pink," USA, Army, 1930s. Gabardine with button fly, lace calves and large white suede patches. Faint maker's label. About size 30" waist. Avg. cond. $25

Breeches, Officer, "Pink," USA, Army, 1930s. Private purchase in "pink" gabardine with button fly, lace calves and stitched thigh panels. About size 28" waist. Above avg. cond. $20

Breeches, Officer, "Pink," USA, Army, WWII. Gabardine with button fly, suede patches and button tan cotton calves. Medium size. Avg. cond. $16

Breeches, Officer, "Pink," USA, Army, 1930s. Private purchase in gabardine with zip fly, button calves and off-white suede thigh panels. Faintly named and 1930s era dated. About size 30/32" waist. Avg. cond. $27

Breeches, Officer, Summer, USA, Army, 1937. 35" x 23" in dark tan cotton with lace calves, zinc US Army buttons and 1937 dated Qm label. Paper Qm inspector tags still stapled to body. Exc. cond. $40

Breeches—Germany

Breeches, Riding, Germany, Army, WWII. Gray wool body, three slash pockets and watch slash. Five-button fly, suspender buttons, belt loops and side adjustment belts. Slash cuffs with five buttons. Below avg. cond. . . . $135

Breeches, Riding, Germany, Army, WWII. Gray wool. Four pockets with buttons and watch slash. Six-button front with closure strap and side belt adjustments. Metal "Zipp" zippers on cuffs. Avg. cond. $109

Breeches, Riding, Germany, Army, WWII. Stone-gray twill wool body. Twenty-two grommets on cuff slashes with laces. Four slash pockets and watch slash. Bevo maker tag "Gunter Viohl etc." Avg. cond. $85

Breeches, Riding, Germany, Luftwaffe, WWII. Blue-gray body, three pockets with button flaps, watch slash, belt loops, and side adjustment belts. Avg. cond. $225

Breeches, Riding, Germany, SS, 1934. Black wool with inked "V.A.-SS.1934." Four slash pockets and watch slash. Four-button fly with hook, suspender buttons, belt loops and back adjustment belts. Slash cuffs with four buttons and tie strings. Below avg. cond. $390

Breeches, Riding, Germany, DAF, WWII. Blue wool. Three slash pockets and watch slash with button flaps. Six-button fly, suspender buttons, side adjustment belts and slash cuffs with tie strings. Reinforced wool seat. Black plastic buttons have cogwheel design. Above avg. cond. $82

Breeches, Riding, Germany, Army, 1942, Rudolf Wentz, Nurnberg. Gray salt and pepper twill cotton body with

reinforced seat. Three slash pockets, three-button fly with hook, belt loops, suspender buttons and back adjustment belts. Metal zipper on each tapered leg. Inked "Rudolf Wentz Nurnberg 1942." Exc. cond. $162

Breeches, Riding, Germany, Army, 1942. Gray salt and pepper twill cotton body with reinforced seat. Three slash pockets, three-button fly with hook, belt loops, suspender buttons and back adjustment belts. Metal zipper to each tapered leg. Inked "Rudolf Wentz Nurnberg 1942." Near mint cond. $162

Breeches, Riding, Pioneer, Germany, Army, WWII. Gray twill wool body, three slash pockets, watch slash, six-button fly with hook, suspender buttons, belt loops and back adjustment belt. Black wool sides and slash cuffs. Avg. cond. $118

Breeches—Other

Breeches, Officer, Air Force, Soviet Union, Air Force, c1950. Khaki wool twill, seam piping, pockets, belt loops and button calves. Above avg. cond. $20

Coats—U.S.

Coat, Foul Weather, Officer, USA, Navy, WWII. Dark OD impregnated body with black trim, double breasted front, large fold-over collar and shearling lining. Printed naval contract label in neck. Size 42. Above avg. cond. $223

Coat, Leather, Aviation Officer, USA, Navy, WWII. ¾ length in dark brown leather. Large real fur collar, double breasted front, satin and alpaca lining, matching belt and slash pockets. Woven BuAero marked spec label in neck. Size 40. Exc. cond. $237

Coat, Sack, USA, Army, 1895. Navy blue melton wool body with black mohair trimmed standing collar and front. Lined in black cotton. Each cuff is covered in black melton wool with ornate black woven trim. Woven clothier's label. Named. Avg. cond. $59

Coat, Sack, USA, Army, 1889. Navy blue melton wool body with fold-over collar and five-button front with brass 1855 pattern buttons. Inside edge of button front has ornate red felt trim. Black lining with fancy red stitching and owner's name. Ornate black stitching on each cuff. Has 1902 felt 1st Class gunner chevron on rt sleeve. Avg. cond. $75

Coat, Sack, Bandsman, USA, Army, 1895. Navy blue melton wool with standing collar, black woven trim, braid on cuffs and concealed button front. Lined in black cotton. Collar has gilt brass lyre device sewn on each side. Above avg. cond. $40

Coat, Sack, Dress, EM, USA, Army, 1902. Navy blue melton wool blouse with standing collar, lt blue piping and belt hooks at waist. Fully lined in black cotton. Has 1921 gilt brass eagle button front, gilt brass type I "US/3" and "Inf/A" collar discs. Above avg. cond. $145

Coat, Sack, EM, USA, Army, 1902. Navy blue melton wool body with six-button front, red piped standing collar, cuffs, epaulettes, rimless gilt brass eagle buttons and black cotton lining. Each sleeve has red on blue Sgt 1st Class chevron. Woven clothier's label in neck. Exc. cond. $58

Coat, Sack, EM, USA, Army, 1890s. Navy blue melton wool body with two rows of stitching on each cuff, full wool lining and fold-over collar. Has single-breasted six-button front with 1855 pattern buttons. Converted from double breasted front. Inside lining has "U.S./24 INF./ 107/B" stenciled in white. Avg. cond. $90

Coat, Sack, Officer, USA, Army, 1895. Navy blue melton wool body with black woven mohair trim on standing collar. Concealed button front and cuffs. Lined in black cotton. Woven clothier's label. Has pair open-catch pb Signal Corps insignia. Each shoulder has black cloth-covered metal button. Above avg. cond. $49

Coat, Service, Nurse, USA, Army, 1942. Size 16R in navy blue wool with maroon trim on epaulettes and woven cuff braid. 1942 dated Qm tag. Matching belt, gilt brass eagle buttons, pair pb 2nd Lieut bars and "US" and "Med/N" collar devices. Above avg. cond. $76

Overcoat, USA, WAC, WWII. Lt OD poplin body with double-breasted front, button adj tab on each cuff and slash pockets. Button-in liner and button-on hood. Named with serial number. Med. size. Average $34

Overcoat, EM, USA, Army, WWI. Heavy OD wool with dark bronze eagle buttons on double-breasted front and button tab on each cuff. Avg. cond. $20

Overcoat, EM, USA, Army, WWI. Heavy OD wool with large bronze eagle buttons on double-breasted front, straight cuffs and single bullion o/s stripe. Above avg. cond. $28

Overcoat, EM, USA, Army, 1945. Size 34R in heavy OD wool with large OD eagle buttons on double-breasted front and 1945 dated Qm label. Above avg. cond. . . $20

Overcoat, EM, USA, Army, 1941. 38R in OD wool. Has horn buttons on double-breasted front. 1941 dated Qm label. Above avg. cond. $45

Overcoat, EM, USA, Army, Airborne, 1941. Size 42R in heavy OD wool with large gilt eagle buttons on double-breasted front and 1941 dated Qm label. Theater-made 1st

Airborne Div patch on left shoulder is silk machine embr on lt blue felt and discharge patch. Above avg. cond. . . .
. . . . $41

Overcoat, EM, USA, Army, 1942. Size 38R on heavy OD wool with large OD plastic buttons on double-breasted front. 1942 dated Qm label. Above avg. cond. $21

US Army NCO's Overcoat

Overcoat, EM, USA, USMC, 1942. Size 1S in forest green wool with large bronze plastic buttons on double-breasted front. No belt. 1942–43 dated USMC Qm markings. Named. Above avg. cond. $45

Overcoat, EM, USA, USMC, 1943. Size 4S in forest green gabardine with large dark bronze plastic USMC buttons. 1942–43 dated USMC Qm markings. Above avg. cond. $20

Overcoat, EM, USA, USMC, 1942. Size 2L in forest green wool with large bronze USMC buttons on double-breasted front. 1942–43 dated USMC Qm markings. Above avg. cond. $40

Overcoat, EM, USA, Army, 1943. Size 34S in OD wool with large OD eagle buttons and 1943 dated Qm label. Above avg. cond. $40

Overcoat, EM, USA, Army, Aero Service, WWI. Heavy OD wool body with large eagle buttons on double-breasted front (one missing). Button tab at each cuff and slash pocket. Has discharge stripe, two bullion o/s stripes and silk embr on dark blue felt circular four-bladed propeller design patch. Above avg. cond. $27

Overcoat, EM, USA, Army, 1942. Size 34R in OD wool with large gilt eagle buttons on double-breasted front and nice felt on felt T-Cpl chevrons. 1942 dated Qm label. Above avg. cond. $30

Overcoat, EM, USA, Army, Air Force, 1942. Size 36R in OD wool with large OD plastic eagle buttons on double-breasted front, AAF patch on left shoulder, felt-on-felt Sgt chevrons and AAF armature specialty patch on rt cuff. 1942 dated Qm label. Above avg. cond. $24

Overcoat, EM, USA, Army, WWI. Lt OD wool coat with large bronze eagle buttons on double-breasted front, adjustable tab on each cuff and dark tan cotton lining. Has oversize multi-piece 76th Div patch on left shoulder, Cpl chevron on rt sleeve, and two bullion o/s stripes. Avg. cond. $49

Overcoat, EM, WAC, USA, Army, WWII. Lt OD poplin with large OD plastic buttons on double-breasted front. Matching belt with name label stitched to backside. Includes matching button on hood and button in OD wool liner. Medium size. Above avg. cond. $60

Overcoat, Field, USA, Army, 1953. Dark OD cotton with double-breasted front, matching belt, matching button-in liner. 1953 dated. Exc. cond. $51

Overcoat, Liner, WAC, USA, WAC, 1943. Size 12S in OD wool. Button-in style. 1943 dated Qm label. Avg. cond. $12

Overcoat, M1952, Female, USA, USMC, 1952. Wool. Size 12R in forest green. 1952 dated spec label with name tag above. Above avg. cond. $21

Overcoat, Officer, USA, Army, 1943. Lt OD melton wool with woven tailor's label. Named and 1943 dated. Converted to single-breasted front. Avg. cond. $23

Overcoat, Officer, USA, Army, WWI. Private purchase in lt OD melton wool with double-breasted front and woven clothier's label. Fully lined in cotton. Has two rows of black woven quatrefoil rank on each cuff. Above avg. cond. $45

Overcoat, Officer, USA, Army, WWI. Coarse lt shade blanket wool body. Three-quarter length. Double breasted with simulated horn buttons and patch pockets. Cotton lined with shawl collar. Avg. cond. $38

Overcoat, Officer, USA, Army, 1942, Australia. Australian made. Size 38R in heavy OD wool with large gilt brass buttons (maker hmkd) on double-breasted front. Slash pockets, belt, epaulettes, partial tan cotton lining, and spec label marked "Greatcoat US/Made in Australia/1942." Above avg. cond. $100

Overcoat, Officer, USA, USMC, 1944. Private purchase in forest green melton wool with bronze USMC buttons on double-breasted front. Woven Quantico, Va. post exchange

label. 1944 dated. Medium size. Named. Above avg. cond. $35

Overcoat, Officer, USA, Army, 1943. Size 37R in lt OD poplin with double-breasted front, matching belt and 1943 dated Qm label. Includes correct button-in liner and matching hood. Above avg. cond. $70

Overcoat, Officer, Naval, USA, Navy, 1974. Full length in navy blue melton wool with gilt buttons on double-breasted front, 1974 dated spec label, and provisions for removable shoulder boards. Size 36R. Above avg. cond. $34

Overcoat, Officer, WAC, USA, WAC, WWII. Lt OD poplin with double-breasted front. No belt. Medium size. Named. Above avg. cond. $28

Overcoat, Short Length, Officer, USA, Army, WWII. Tailor-made in OD melton wool with OD plastic double-breasted front, matching belt, ribbed satin lining and woven tailor's label in neck. 5th Army patch on left shoulder and FEAF patch on rt shoulder. Large size. Avg. cond. $75

Overcoat, Short Length, Officer, USA, Army, 1944. Lt OD melton wool with 1944 dated Qm label, salmon colored satin lining and double-breasted front. Size 38R. Avg. cond. $25

Overcoat, Short Length, Officer, USA, Army, 1942. Size 42R in OD melton wool with horn buttons on double-breasted front. 1942 dated Qm label. Avg. cond. . . . $34

Parka, Cold Weather (N-2B), USA, USAF, 1966. Sage green nylon with real fur-trimmed built-in hood, 1966 dated printed spec label, zipper/button front, several pockets, knit cuffs and waistband. Medium size. Near mint cond. $334

Parka, Cold Weather (N-2B), USA, USAF, 1974. Sage green nylon with 1974 dated spec label, simulated fur-ruff-trimmed built-in hood, zipper/button front, several pockets, knit cuffs and waistband. Medium size. Above avg. cond. $63

Parka, Cold Weather (N-2B), USA, USAF, 1971. Sage green nylon body with real fur-trimmed built-in hood, zipper/button front, several pockets, knit cuffs and waistband. 1971 dated spec label. Above avg. cond. $177

Parka, Cold Weather (N-3B), USA, USAF, 1950s. Sage green nylon with woven spec label, real fur trimmed built-in collar, zipper/button closure front, early color USAF patch design on left shoulder and several pockets. Medium size. Exc. cond. $445

Parka, Cold Weather (N-3B), USA, USAF, 1960s. Sage green nylon with sage green nylon lining, built-in hood trimmed in real wolf fur, woven spec label, zipper/button front, color printed patch design decal on left shoulder and several pockets. Large size. Exc. cond. $450

Parka, Cold Weather (N-3B), USA, USAF, 1977. Sage green cotton with built-in hood trimmed in simulated fur ruff, zipper/button front and several pockets. Reflective strip on back. 1977 dated spec label. Medium size. Avg. cond. $21

Parka, Cold Weather (N-3B), USA, USAF, 1981. Sage green cotton with simulated fur ruff trimmed built-in hood, zipper/button front and several pockets. 1981 dated spec label. Avg. cond. $32

Parka, Cold Weather (N-3B), USA, USAF, 1950s. Sage green nylon with real fur-trimmed built-in hood, several pockets and zipper/button front. Faint early USAF patch design on left shoulder. Reflective strips on sleeves and back. Size medium. Avg. cond. $93

Parka, Cold Weather (N-3B), USA, USAF, 1950s. Sage green nylon with woven spec label, zipper/button front, several pockets, real fur-trimmed built-in hood and sage green satin lining. Faint color early USAF patch design printed on left shoulder. Above Average $145

Parka, Ski, USA, Army, WWII. Reversible from lt OD to white poplin. Button/zipper closure front, built-in hood, two lower patch pockets, two upper slash pockets and web waistbelt. Size 38. Faint Qm label. Avg. cond. $37

Parka, Ski, USA, Army, WWII. Reversible. White to lt OD poplin with built-in hood, zippered neck, slash pockets with zippered openings and drawstring at waist. Named. Exc. cond. $79

Parka, Ski, USA, Army, WWII. Reversible. Darker shade of OD to white cotton with built-in real fur-trimmed hood, button neck with two three-button rows and slash pockets. Small size. Light yellowing to white side. Avg. cond. $55

Parka, Ski, USA, Army, 1942. Reversible. Lt OD to white poplin with fur-trimmed built-in hood, button neck, button tabs on cuffs and slash chest pockets. 1942 dated Qm tag. Medium size. Above avg. cond. $87

Parka, Ski, USA, Army, 1942. Reversible. Lt OD to white poplin with built-in hood, three-button neck, slash pockets and button tab on each cuff. 1942 dated Qm tag. Medium size. Hood has had fur trim removed. Named. Below avg. cond. $35

Parka, Ski, USA, Army, 1942. Size 42. Reversible from lt OD to white with 1942 dated Qm label. Zipper/button front, built-in hood, several pockets, button tab at each cuff and built-in web waistbelt. Includes correct dark brown pile liner. Above avg. cond. $240

Parka-shell, M1948, USA, USAF, 1951. Dark OD cotton with zipper/button front, built-in hood, intact web waistbelt and matching pile liner. 1951 dated USAF/Qm marked spec label (1948 pattern dated). Large size. Exc. cond. $74

Parka-shell, M1951, USA, Army, 1951. Dark OD M1951 parka-shell with 1951 dated Qm markings, built-in hood, zipper/snap closure front, correct button-in liner also with 1951 dated Qm markings. Large size. Above avg. cond. $20

Peacoat, USA, Navy, WWI. Heavy navy blue serge wool with double-breasted front. Medium size. Named. Avg. cond. $43

Peacoat, USA, Navy, WWII. Navy blue melton wool with double-breasted front. About size 38. Above avg. cond. $21

Tailcoat, Dress, Officer, USA, Navy, 1930s. Navy blue melton wool with double-breasted front, gold wire Lieut cuff braid and line stars. Has provisions for shoulder boards. Avg. cond. $27

Coats—Germany

Frock Coat, Infantry, Officer, Prussian, Imperial Germany, Army, Infantry, WWI. Royal blue melton wool with red wool collar and piping. double-breasted style with twelve copper buttons, one missing. Some light mothing. Above avg. cond. $205

Greatcoat, EM, Saxon, Imperial Germany, Army, WWI. EM from Jager number 12. Lt gray almost lilac wool body, black wool collar tabs and large black shoulder straps with red wool piping, and horn and nickel buttons. Full satin lining with slash pocket. Exc. cond. $200

Greatcoat, Admiral, Germany, Navy, WWII. Smooth black wool body instead of dark blue. Cornflower blue wool lapels, 12-button front, two slash pockets and fake French cuffs. Full black satin lining with two slash pockets. Above avg. cond. $850

Greatcoat, EM, Germany, Army, 1942. Gray wool body and collar. Partial gray satin lining with inked size and "M42/II." Avg. cond. $153

Greatcoat, EM, Germany, Army, WWII. Gray wool body and large collar. Partial gray lining with pocket, inked size and RB-NR. Avg. cond. $126

Greatcoat, EM, Germany, Army, WWII. Gray wool body and collar. Partial gray lining with inked size and date. Exc. cond. $184

Greatcoat, EM, Female, Luftwaffe, Germany, Luftwaffe, 1940. Variation. For female use. With short/small blue-gray wool body, pleated patch upper pockets, two slash lower and six-button front. French cuffs, loops and buttons for strap use. Partial gray lining with slash pocket, inked size, maker and "LBA(S)40." Avg. cond. $161

Greatcoat, EM, Prussian, Imperial Germany, Army, WWI. M1910. Stone-gray doeskin body, six nickel buttons, two slash pockets, French cuffs, white wool collar tabs and shoulder boards with red cord "WR II" and red wool crown. Full lining with pocket. Avg. cond. . . $275

Greatcoat, Flight EM, Luftwaffe, Germany, Luftwaffe, 1939. Early blue-gray wool body, wide collar, four slash pockets, 12 buttons and French cuffs. Hand-sewn yellow wool tabs with single gull each. Sewn-in wool straps with yellow wool piping. Full black wool lining, slash pocket and inked size/maker/"LBA39" tag. Exc. cond. $250

Greatcoat, NCO, Germany, Army, 1939. Gray wool body, green color and slip-on straps with pip to each. Inked maker, size and "M39." Avg. cond. $185

Greatcoat, Officer, Germany, Army, WWII. Gray wool body and green collar. Full gray satin lining with slash pocket. Above avg. cond. $150

Greatcoat, Officer, Luftwaffe, Germany, Luftwaffe, WWII. For Flak unit Lieut. Rubberized. Blue-gray stiff cloth body is impregnated for rain use. Twelve cast resin button front, slash pockets and sewn French cuffs. Slip-on shoulderboards. Exc. cond. $120

Greatcoat, Officer, Luftwaffe, Germany, Luftwaffe, WWII. Dark blue-gray wool body, full satin lining with pocket and bevo neck label "Minovsky Stuttgart." Above avg. cond. $200

Greatcoat, Officer, Prussian, Imperial Germany, Army, WWI. For Prussian reservist Lt. M1910 pattern. Stone gray body with 12 crown buttons, two slash pockets, fake French cuffs and blue wool collar. Slip-on gray boards with green piping and white bases. Seven-crown button back with strap. Full gray satin lining. Above avg. cond. $232

Greatcoat, Officer-oberst, Germany, Army, WWII. Gray doeskin body. Buttons and fittings intact. Full gray satin lining with bevo maker label at neck and oil cloth label to pocket with owner name. Sewn-in shoulderboards. Exc. cond. $200

Greatcoat, Rubberized, EM, Germany, Army, WWII. Pliable body is cut just like greatcoat. Bevo size tag "48" at neck. Gray color. Above avg. cond. $145

Greatcoat, Winter, EM, Coastal Arty, Germany, Navy, WWII. Wool body, large collar and attached hood. Twelve-

anchor button front, two slash pockets and fake French cuffs. Full blue wool lining with inked maker tag on sleeve "Gunter Schwarz etc." Avg. cond. $144

Greatcoat, Winter, Officer, Germany, Army, WWII, A.Pilain, Paris. French made. Long suede body with three wood toggle front closure and two slash pockets. Fleece lining. Inked "A. Pilain etc., Paris" and size. Above avg. cond. $350

Coats——Other

Cape, Cossack's, Soviet Union, Army, c1930. Full-length cloak, black fur, maroon lining and scarlet satin collar trim. Above avg. cond. $250

Cape, Rain, Officer, Soviet Union, Army, c1980. Khaki waterproof fabric. Button front and hood. Exc. cond. $95

Greatcoat, Artillery Officer, Hungary, Army, WWII. Khaki brown wool twill coat with double-breasted front, gilded crown buttons, brown velvet collar, and turn-back cuffs. Scalloped pocket flaps with red piping trim, lapel, rear half-belt and rear skirt piped in red. Collar mounted by red wool scalloped insignia, fields and cuffs present three horizontal gold bullion lace stripes indicating captain's rank, brown quilted satin lining mounted by oversized embroidered monogrammed shield inscribed with "SZV." Exc. cond. $380

Greatcoat, EM, Soviet Union, Army, c1980. Brown blanket wool, star buttons, and gray cotton lining. Exc. cond. $75

Greatcoat, Major General, Soviet Union, Army, c1950. Quality gray wool, double-breasted, red wool collar, and gray satin lining. Exc. cond. $195

Overcoat, EM, Soviet Union, Army. Wool overcoat, cotton lining to upper half, unusual hook and eye closure to the front and plain OD felt collar tabs. Large size. Unissued. Mint cond. $30

Gloves——U.S.

Gloves, USA, Army, Airborne, WWII. Off-white smooth and roughout horsehide five-finger bodies with adjustable web strap across each wrist. Marked "26" inside each. Above avg. cond. $145

Gloves, Dress, USA, Army, WWII. Five pairs. Five-finger design in gray knitted nylon. In issue packages. I...$20. Mint cond. $20

Gloves, Dress, WAC, USA, WAC, WWII. White doeskin. Exc. cond. $55

Gloves, Foul Weather, USA, Navy, WWII. Navy blue knit

wool bodies with gauntlets that cover much of forearm. Exc. cond. $40

Gloves, Leather, USA, USMC, WWII. Roughout tan leather five-finger bodies and gauntlets with machine-stitched smooth dark tan leather palms. Well marked. Above avg. cond. $25

Gloves, Wool, EM, USA, Army, WWII. Dark OD woolen knit bodies with dark brown leather-faced palms and woven Qm tags. Size 9. Some light soiling to palms. Above avg. cond. $53

Gloves, Wool, EM, USA, Army, WWII. Dark OD wool five-finger bodies with dark brown leather-faced palms. Size 8. Woven Qm tag in each. Exc. cond. $50

Mittens, USA, Navy, WWII. Dark tan leather with adjustable strap across wrist. USN marked. Includes OD knit liners. Above avg. cond. $20

Mittens, Arctic, USA, Army, Korean War. Dark OD cotton with lt brown leather palms with alpaca facing, adjustable straps on wrists and gauntlets. Medium size. Avg. cond. $20

Gloves—Germany

Gauntlets, Tropical, Three Finger, Germany, Army, WWII. 16" long olive-green canvas body with green leather palms/fingers. Two leather snap straps. Inked maker and size 10. Exc. cond. $48

Gloves, Germany, Army, WWII. Gray wool. Two white size rings. Above avg. cond. $40

Gloves, Germany, Army, WWII. Gray wool. Single white size band to each. Above avg. cond. $53

Gloves, Officer, Germany, Army, WWII. Gray suede leather. 10½" long with opening having two buttons. Inked maker and size 8½. Avg. cond. $145

Gloves, Officer, Germany, Army, WWII. White leather. 9½" long with slash to opening and two snaps each. Inked size 8. Above avg. cond. $82

Gloves, Officer, Germany, Army, WWII. Gray suede leather. 10" long. Slash openings with stag snaps having title to each. Below avg. cond. $20

Gloves, Officer, Germany, Army, WWII. White leather. 9" long suede bodies with slash to opening of each. Above avg. cond. $129

Gloves, Officer, Germany, Army, WWII. White leather. Wrist slash and snap. Inked "7½." Avg. cond. $35

Mittens, Germany, Army, WWII. 11½" tan canvas bodies. Have wrist buckle straps. White felt lined and bevo maker

tag "Engelhardt Erzeugnis 11." Avg. cond. $25

Mittens, Germany, Army, WWII. Gray canvas. 15½" long canvas with gray leather at thumb area. Elastic band at wrist. Buckle/strap at cuffs with wooden toggle and loop on other side. Exc. cond. $45

Mittens, Three Finger, Germany, Army, 1940, A. Brilling. 14" green canvas bodies with gray leather palms/fingers. Two gray leather snap straps to gauntlets. Inked "A.Brilling 1940 7½." Above avg. cond. $72

Mittens, Three Finger, Germany, Army, 1941. 14" long green canvas bodies with gray leather palm/finger area and two snap straps each. Inked 1941/maker and size 8. Avg. cond. $90

Mittens, Three Finger, Germany, Army, WWII. 12½" long bodies with leather-covered three-finger area. Buckle strap at wrist and elastic at opening. Inked size "7½" and other numbers. Storage age only. Above avg. cond. . $23

Mittens, Three Finger, Germany, Army, WWII. 12½" long bodies with leather-covered three-finger area. Adjustment buckle belt at wrist and elastic opening. Inked numbers. Avg. cond. $23

Mittens, Three Finger, Camo, Germany, Army, WWII. Late war. Reversible. Water pattern camo to winter white. Style used with four-part outfit. 16" long bodies with different maker camo print to each. Trigger finger, long cloth connector strap and reversible to white. Exc. cond.
.... $160

Mittens, Winter, Germany, Army, WWII. Gray canvas. 12" long with elastic around cuffs. Fleece-lined hand areas with right side having trigger finger. Inked size "3." Above avg. cond. $45

Mittens, Winter, Germany, Army, WWII. 11½" long natural suede bodies with fleece insides. Size 9. Avg. cond.
.... $20

Mittens, Winter, Luftwaffe, Germany, Luftwaffe, WWII. Off-white canvas exterior with padded interior and tie cuffs. Above avg. cond. $135

Mittens, Winter, Reversible, Germany, Army, WWII. 15½" green-gray wool side and white cotton side. Connecting strap also is gauntlet closure. Above avg. cond. $66

Blouses, Jackets, and Tunics—U.S.

Blouse, Cadet, USA, Army, 1955. From cadet at US Military Academy (West Point). Blue gray wool with black woven trim, standing collar, zip front, purple satin lining, large Sgt chevrons and cuff trim. Named and dated 1955. Avg. cond. $12

Blouse, Class "A," EM, USA, Army, Airborne, 1957. AG wool serge class "A" blouse with 1957 dated spec label. Has machine embr on black velvet 101st Airborne Div patch with attached Airborne tab on left shoulder, spec 4 chevrons, US and Inf collar discs on lt blue plastic backings, lt blue twill paratrooper oval with wide blue embr border, DUC ribbon with cluster device on rt chest, braided dress Inf aiguilette around rt shoulder and one pair of 502nd Airborne Inf Regt DI's. Avg. cond. $35

Blouse, Class "A," EM, USA, Army, Airborne, 1981. Size 36R in AG worsted. With 1981 dated spec label, white on blue Airborne tab over 6th Div patch on left shoulder, Sgt chevrons, two hashmarks, padded Canadian para wing on rt chest. Exc. cond. $28

Blouse, Class "A," EM, USA, Army, 1964. Size 37R in AG wool serge. 1964 dated with 4th Div patch on left shoulder and Pfc chevrons. Above avg. cond. $24

Blouse, CPO, USA, Navy, WWII. Dark tan cotton twill blouse with removable gilt NAVY buttons and rate on left sleeve. With athletic instructor rate. Size 38. Avg. cond. $35

US Navy WWII EM Blouse (Navy Blue)

Blouse, Dress Blue, EM, USA, USMC, Korean War Era. Navy blue melton wool with standing collar, red piping and embr on felt dress Cpl chevrons (without cross rifles). Size 36. Above avg. cond $20

Blouse, Dress Blue, EM, USA, USMC, 1930s. Pocketless body in navy blue melton wool with standing collar stitch grommeted for devices (none included), red piping and 1933–34 dated USMC Qm markings. Size 4L. Avg. cond. $35

Blouse, Dress Blue, EM, USA, USMC, Korean War Era. Navy blue melton wool with pair 1937 pattern EG&A devices on standing collar, red piping, removable buttons (lacks one small button), 1949–50 USMC Qm markings and five-place ribbon group for Korean Service. Size 34R. Above avg. cond. $18

Blouse, Dress Blue, EM, USA, USMC, 1900s. Navy blue wool serge with scarlet red epaulettes, faced standing collar and trim, 1909–10 USMC Qm markings, white and black cotton lining and gilt brass USMC buttons. Leather tab still intact in collar. Size 1L. Exc. cond. $229

Blouse, Dress White, Officer, Naval, USA, Navy, WWII. White cotton with standing collar and gilt buttons. Has WWII wool-covered shoulder boards with gold tape ensign rank and line stars. Medium size. Above avg. cond. $22

Blouse, EM, USA, Army, 1918. Lt OD wool serge four pocket blouse with standing collar and full dark tan cotton lining. 1918 dated Qm label. Bullion o/s stripe on left cuff. Avg. cond. $65

Blouse, EM, USA, USMC, WWII. Forest green wool with 1942–43 dated USMC Qm markings, 1937 pattern EG&A collar devices, 2nd Marine Div patch on left shoulder and Cpl chevrons. Missing belt. Size 1L. Avg. cond. $39

Blouse, EM, USA, USMC, WWII. Size 2L in forest green wool. With 1941–42 dated USMC Qm markings. Has 1st Marine Div patch on left shoulder, woven Pfc chevrons and Gemsco hmkd officer 1937 pattern EG&A collar devices. No belt. Above avg. cond. $66

USMC EM Blouse (No Devices)

Blouse, EM, USA, USMC, WWII. Size 5S in forest green wool. With 1944 dated USMC Qm markings, 1st Marine

Div patch on left shoulder, 1937 pattern EG&A devices and wide plastic-coated three-place ribbon bar. Trace of removed chevrons. Above avg. cond. $34

Blouse, EM, USA, USMC, WWII. Forest green wool with 1941–42 dated USMC Qm markings. Has fully embr 6th Marine Div patch on left shoulder, woven Pfc chevrons and wide plastic-coated Purple Heart ribbon bar. No belt. Size 6S. Above avg. cond. $45

Blouse, EM, USA, USMC, 1968. Forest green wool. 1968 dated. With belt. Has Lance Cpl chevrons, three-place bar for Nam service, shooting badge and 1962 pattern collar devices. Above avg. cond. $16

Blouse, EM, USA, Army, WWI. Lt OD wool serge body with dark tan cotton lining, French embr 26th Div patch on left shoulder, Cpl Musician chevron on rt sleeve and US and musician (lyre design) collar discs. About size 38. Avg. cond. $59

Blouse, EM, M1912, USA, Army, WWI. Dark tan cotton twill blouse with removable dark bronze eagle buttons and stitch grommet hole in each side of collar for discs. About size 36. Exc. cond. $25

Blouse, EM, M1912, USA, Army, WWI. Dark tan cotton 1912 pattern blouse with removable buttons, felt 6th Div patch on left shoulder, discharge stripe, US and Inf collar discs. Has wool base for two o/s stripes but bullion stripes have been removed. Avg. cond. $49

Blouse, EM, M1912, USA, Army, Aero Service, WWI. Yellow tan wool blouse with OD cotton lining, three bullion o/s stripes and patch on rt shoulder. Patch is silk embr "69" on dark blue felt above three-bladed prop. Above avg. cond. $175

Blouse, EM, M1912, USA, Army, WWI. OD wool. Fully lined in tan cotton with two bullion o/s stripes, Sgt chevron on rt sleeve and USNA and 302/Inf collar discs. Above avg. cond. $40

Blouse, EM, M1917, USA, Army, WWI. 1917 pattern in dark OD wool with full dark tan cotton lining, multi-piece felt 3rd Div patch on left shoulder, discharge stripe, three bullion o/s stripes and Pfc/Engr chevron on rt sleeve. US and B/Engr collar discs, two pb ribbon bars and pb marksman badge. Above avg. cond. $128

Blouse, EM, M1917, USA, Army, WWI. OD wool body fully lined in black cotton. With large bullion on felt 80th Div patch on left shoulder, discharge stripe, two bullion o/s stripes, US and "313/Arty/C" collar discs and Cpl chevron on rt sleeve. Avg. cond. $50

Blouse, EM, M1917, USA, Army, WWI. OD wool serge blouse with full dark tan cotton lining, gold bullion tape

on felt 33rd Div patch on left shoulder, discharge stripe, two bullion o/s stripes and corporal chevron. US and "Arty/C" collar discs. Above avg. cond. $65

Blouse, EM, M1917, USA, Army, WWI. Unlined 1917 pattern blouse in OD wool with discharge stripe, US and Arty collar discs and solid red celluloid button pinned to rt chest pocket flap. Some moth damage. Includes WWI Victory medal on wrap brooch mtd long drape ribbon with "France" clasp. Avg. cond. $66

Blouse, EM, M1917, USA, Army, WWI. OD wool with dark tan cotton lining, French cord stitched on felt 3rd Army Div patch on left shoulder, discharge and bullion o/s stripes, Cpl chevron on rt sleeve and US and A collar discs. Above avg. cond. $61

Blouse, EM, M1918, USA, Army, WWI. OD wool with full lt OD cotton lining and worn silk embr on felt 78th Div patch on left shoulder. Discharge stripe, bullion o/s stripe, Cpl chevron on rt sleeve and US and "H" collar discs. Above avg. cond. $65

Blouse, Officer, Naval, USA, Navy, Aviator, WWII. Green gabardine with gold bullion on aviator green background on left chest, black woven Lieut JG braid and line officer star on each cuff. Size 41R. Named. Avg. cond. $47

Blouse, Officer, Naval, USA, Navy, Aviator, WWII. Green gabardine with black woven ensign rank and line officer star on each cuff. Heavy bullion on black felt naval aviation wing on left chest. Size 38. Above avg. cond. $37

US Navy Officer's WWII Blouse (Navy Blue)

Blouse, Officer, Naval, USA, Navy, Aviator, WWII. Tailor made in green gabardine. Size 44XL with bronze

NAVY buttons, black woven Lieut rank and line officer star on each cuff. Above avg. cond. $37

Blouse, Service, EM, USA, AAF, WWII. OD wool serge with embr on felt AAF patch on left shoulder, Sgt chevrons, Sb US and AAF collar discs, matched pair sterling pb Air Service DI's, a four-place wide ribbon group and discharge patch. Trace of removed spec patch on rt cuff. Size 37R. Avg. cond. $40

Blouse, Service, EM, USA, AAF, WWII. OD wool serge with 20th AF patch on left shoulder, AAF patch on rt shoulder, woven S/Sgt chevrons, two o/s bars, one hashmark, US and AAF collar discs, a 3" cb sterling aerial gunner wing, four-place ribbon group and discharge patch. Size 39L. Exc. cond. $100

USAAF Enlisted Man's Service Blouse

Blouse, Service, EM, USA, Army, WWII. OD wool serge with 1942 dated Qm label and 4th Service CMD patch on left shoulder. Size 44L. Above avg. cond. $66

US Army Enlisted Man's Service Blouse

Blouse, Service, EM, USA, Army, WWII. OD wool serge with belt hooks at waist, embr on felt T-Sgt chevrons, five

o/s bars, two hashmarks and MUC wreath. Size 39L. Above avg. cond. $25

Blouse, Service, EM, USA, Army, WWII. Early WWII-style four-pocket OD wool serge blouse with removable rimless gilt brass eagle buttons, Army Service Forces patch on left shoulder, theater-made hand embr on twill CBI patch on rt shoulder, 1st Sgt chevrons, two o/s bars and one hashmark. Avg. cond. $25

Blouse, Service, EM, USA, Army, Airborne, WWII. OD wool serge four-pocket blouse with 1941 dated Qm label, OD border 17th Airborne Div patch with tab above on left shoulder, 18th Corps patch with Airborne tab on rt shoulder, woven T-Sgt chevrons, six o/s bars, sb WWII US collar device, type I medical collar disc, six ribbons and discharge patch. Left chest has pb sterling glider troop badge with officer medical collar device applied on thick maroon felt oval. Size 38XL. Exc. cond. $301

Blouse, Service, EM, USA, Army, WWII. OD wool serge with belt hooks at waist, embr on felt 8th Corps patch on left shoulder, Sgt chevrons, hashmark, US collar disc and two-place pb ribbon bar. Size 37R. Avg. cond. $20

Blouse, Service, EM, M1926, USA, Army, 1930s. Nice quality private purchase lt OD wool serge with brass eagle buttons, dark tan cotton lining, woven clothier's label, stitch grommet holes in collar for insignia (none included), belt hooks at waist, silk machine embr on lt OD felt 27th Div patch on left shoulder, felt Cpl chevrons and four hashmarks. Named. Size 36½. Above avg. cond. . . . $40

Blouse, Service, Officer, USA, Army, 1918. Lt OD wool serge with full cotton lining, woven NY tailor's label in neck and lt OD woven cuff braid. Named and 1918 dated. Has pair pb 2nd Lieut bars, US and Arty collar devices and two bullion o/s stripes. Above avg. cond. $50

Blouse, Service, Officer, USA, Army, WWI. Tailor made in lt OD wool serge. Lined in lt green cotton. Tailor's label inside. Has single Signal Corps and "U.S.R." collar devices. Above avg. cond. $45

Blouse, Service, Officer, USA, AAF, WWII. Private purchase in dark OD gabardine with matching belt. Woven clothier's label, silk embr on felt 9th AF patch on left shoulder, heavy bullion on trimmed OD wool MUC wreath on rt cuff, US collar devices, pair AAF collar devices with twin Sb posts, EAME ribbon bar and pair pb sterling 1st Lieut bars. Medium size. Above avg. cond. $34

Blouse, Service, Officer, USA, AAF, 1942. Dark OD gabardine with mismatched belt. 1942 dated Qm label and heavy bullion on felt AAF patch on left shoulder. Size 36R. Avg. cond. $20

Blouse, Service, Officer, USA, Army, WWI. Private purchase in lt OD wool serge with clothier's label in neck, woven dark tan cuff braid and full cotton lining. Has pair "coffin" lid pb 2nd Lieut bars, pair pb field clerk adjutant and USNG collar devices and two-place ribbon bar including Cuban Occupation. Above avg. cond. $68

Blouse, Service, Officer, USA, AAF, 1942. Dark OD gabardine with matching belt and 1942 dated Qm label. Has silk on felt 8th AF patch on left shoulder, pair US and AAF collar devices and 3"-wide bullion on padded blue felt backing AAF navigator wing stitched to left chest. About size 38. Avg. cond. $82

Blouse, Service, Officer, USA, AAF, WWII. OD gabardine, four pocket with matching belt. Has US and AAF collar devices, 1st Lieut bars, 8th Air Force patch and bullion pilot wing on trimmed blue wool base. Above avg. cond. $155

Blouse, Service, Officer, USA, AAF, WWII. Private purchase in dark OD gabardine with matching belt. Woven maker's label. Named and dated 1944. Has silk embr on felt 8th AF patch on left shoulder. About size 37. Above avg. cond. $37

Blouse, Service, Officer, USA, Army, WWII. Dark OD gabardine with woven clothier's label in neck and attached matching belt. Has heavy bullion on blue wool base AAF patch on left shoulder, four o/s bars, heavy bullion on wool CBI patch on rt shoulder. Size 43. Avg. cond. $69

Blouse, Service, Officer, Naval, USA, Navy, WWII. Tan cotton blouse with removable gilt NAVY buttons. Has removable Lieut line officer shoulderboards. Size 38. Exc. cond. $20

Blouse, Winter Service, EM, USA, USMC, Korean War Era. Forest green wool with bronze plastic buttons and grommet holes in collar for devices (not included). No belt. Size 38. One button missing. Has pair of Cpl (with crossed rifles) chevrons. Above avg. cond. $15

Coat, Parachute Jumper, M1942, USA, Army, Airborne, WWII. "Jump jacket." Lt OD cotton twill body with original zipper front, matching belt, zippered pocket in neck, gray metal snaps on angled pleated chest pockets and straight lower pockets and epaulettes. Has embr 101st Airborne Div patch with tab on left shoulder. Size 38. Avg. cond. . $405

Coat, Parachute Jumper, M1942, USA, Army, Airborne, WWII. "Jump jacket." Lt OD cotton body with original zipper front, zippered pocket in neck, gray metal snaps on angled chest pocket flaps and lower pocket flaps, matching belt and epaulettes. Size 38. Above avg. cond. . $400

Coat, Parachute Jumper, M1942, USA, Army, Airborne, WWII. "Jump jacket." Lt OD cotton with good original

zipper front, zippered pocket at neck, epaulettes, angled chest and straight lower pleated pockets with gray metal snaps and matching belt. Has 82nd Airborne patch and tab on left shoulder. About size 38. Avg. cond. $350

Coat, Parachute Jumper, M1942, USA, Army, Airborne, WWII. "Jump jacket." Lt OD cotton body with original zipper front, zippered pocket in neck, matching belt, good brass snaps on pocket flaps and early WWII era summer 1st Sgt chevron on each sleeve. Size 36. Collar has frayed spot at fold. Zipper missing couple teeth. Avg. cond. $370

Coat, Parachute Jumper, M1942, USA, Army, Airborne, WWII. "Jump jacket." Lt OD cotton body with replacement "Talon" zipper front, zippered pocket in neck, brass snap closures, four pleated front pockets with angled chest pockets and matching belt. Canvas reinforcement added to each elbow and lower pocket edges. Size 38. Avg. cond. . $185

Coat, Parachute Jumper, M1942, USA, Army, Airborne, WWII. "Jump jacket." Lt OD cotton with original zipper front, zippered pocket in neck, gray metal snap closures on angled chest pocket flaps and lower pockets and epaulettes. No belt. About size 38. Above avg. cond. $300

Coat, Tropical, 1st Pattern, USA, USMC, Vietnam War. "Jungle jacket." OD poplin. All tags present. Has name inked above each chest pocket as was typical of Marine Corps usage. Size small/short. Avg. cond. $118

Coat, Tropical, 1st Pattern, USA, Army, Vietnam War. "Jungle jacket." OD poplin with color US-made insignia, early color Special Forces patch and tab on left shoulder, captain and Inf collar patches, CIB, senior para wing, yellow woven on black US Army tape, bevo ARVN para wing, printed on white web name tape and bevo ARVN Special Forces patch on left chest pocket. Size medium/regular. Avg. cond. $221

Coat, Tropical, 1st Pattern, USA, Army, Vietnam War. "Jungle jacket." Medium size in OD poplin with color US-made insignia, early color Special Forces patch, tab on left shoulder, S/Sgt chevrons, combat medic badge, para wing, yellow woven on black US Army tape, bevo ARVN para wing, printed on white web name tape and bevo ARVN Special Forces patch on rt chest pocket. Avg. cond. $138

Coat, Tropical, 2nd Pattern, USA, Army, Vietnam War. "Jungle jacket." OD poplin. Size small/short. Has black and yellow "U.S. Army" and black on white name tape, color spec 4 chevrons on twill and color hand embr. "528 Medical Det. Mobile Lab" pocket patch on rt chest. Avg. cond. $105

Coat, Tropical, 2nd Pattern, USA, Army, Vietnam War. "Jungle jacket." Size small/regular in OD poplin. Avg. cond. $59

Coat, Tropical, 3rd Pattern, USA, Army, 1967. "Jungle jacket." OD poplin. 1967 dated. Has subdued insignia including tropical pattern embr on twill 1st Cav Div patch on left shoulder, 25th Div patch on rt shoulder and S/Sgt chevrons. Also includes expert infantryman badge, aircrew wing and ARVN para wing badges. Nam-made US Army and name pocket tapes. Size medium/regular. Avg. cond. $74

Coat, Tropical, 3rd Pattern, USA, Army, 1967. OD poplin. 1967 dated. Size medium/regular. Name inked. Never had any insignia. Near mint cond. $32

Coat, Tropical, 3rd Pattern, Camo, USA, Army, Vietnam War. Class 2 in ERDL pattern camo poplin. Lacks labels but color good. Never had any insignia. Small size. Above avg. cond. $76

Coat, Tropical, 3rd Pattern, Camo, USA, USMC, Vietnam War. Class 2 in ERDL pattern camo poplin with iron-on USMC stencil on left chest pocket. Size medium/long. Dated 1968. All tags. Avg. cond. $100

Coat, Tropical, 3rd Pattern, Camo, USA, Army, Vietnam War. Size large/short. In ERDL pattern camo ripstop. 1968 dated. Near mint cond. $50

Coat, Tropical, 3rd Pattern, EM, USA, Army, Vietnam War. "Jungle jacket" in OD ripstop material. Has Vietnam-made subdued twill 25th Div patch on left shoulder, Vietnam-made subdued cloth combat Inf badge and "US Army" tape on left chest. Avg. cond. $60

Jacket, Cold Weather, USA, Navy, 1983. Size medium. In OD cotton with zipper, button front and several pockets. 1983 dated. Name stenciled on left chest. "LSD 38/065" stenciled on back. Above avg. cond. $20

Jacket, Cold Weather, A-1, USA, Navy, 1963. Dark green nylon with synthetic lining, zipper/snap front, large 1963 dated spec label and slash pockets. NAVY marked. Size small. Above avg. cond. $49

Jacket, Cold Weather, CWU-7/P, USA, USAF, 1973. Sage green cotton lining, 1973 dated spec label, knit collar, zipper front, four front pockets and snap tabs at cuffs. Reflective strip stitched to front, back and each cuff. Size large. Avg. cond. $156

Jacket, Cold Weather, N-1, USA, Navy, WWII. Lt OD ribbed cotton. With alpaca collar and lining, zipper/button front and slash pockets. NAVY marked. Size 40. Spec label intact. Some fading. Avg. cond. $55

Jacket, Dress, Officer, 1937 Pattern, USA, Army, 1939. Waist length in navy blue melton wool with scarlet felt-faced lapels, ribbed black satin lining, button front, single row gold wire quatrefoil and gold wire braid with ribbed red insert on each cuff. Provisions for removable shoulderboards. Woven Panama tailor's label. Named and dated 1939. Above avg. cond. $55

Jacket, Field, BDU, Camo, USA, Army, Desert Storm. Size large/long in six-color desert camo. Has color 22nd Field Arty Support CMD patch on left shoulder and US flag patch on rt shoulder. Left chest pocket has color novelty Operation Desert Storm 1991 patch and embr on tan twill Operation Desert Storm patch on rt chest. Has brown embr on tan US Army pocket tape and name tape in Arabic letters. Exc. cond. $38

Jacket, Field, M1941, USA, Navy, WWII. Light OD cotton/wool lined with zipper/button front. Medium size, "USN" stenciled on left chest and a 4½" diam black wool squadron patch on right chest. Jacket has had a later era patch on left chest removed. Above avg. cond. $181

Jacket, Field, M1941, USA, Army, 1942. Lt OD poplin body lined in OD wool with good original zipper/button front, 1942 dated Qm tag, button tabs at cuffs and waist, slash pockets and epaulettes. Above avg. cond. $65

Jacket, Field, M1941, USA, Army, WWII. Lt OD poplin body with OD wool lining, epaulettes, zipper/button front and button tabs at cuffs and waist. Size 38R. Above avg. cond. $269

Jacket, Field, M1941, USA, Navy, WWII. Dark OD poplin with dark OD wool lining, printed size label in neck with naval contract markings, zipper/button front, slash pockets. "NAVY" marked on left chest. Left chest has trace of removed pocket tape. Size 38. Exc. cond. $93

Jacket, Field, M1941, USA, Army, WWII. Lt OD poplin with OD wool lining, size label intact in neck, good zipper/button front, slash pockets, button adjustable tab at waist and cuffs and epaulettes. Size 36R. Above avg. cond. $168

M1941 Field Jacket (Parsons)

Jacket, Field, M1941, USA, Army, WWII. Lt OD poplin with OD wool lining, zipper/button front, epaulettes, slash pockets and button tabs at cuffs and waist. Small size. Avg. cond. $28

Jacket, Field, M1941, USA, Army, WWII. Lt OD poplin with OD wool lining, size label intact in neck, zipper/button front, slash pockets, epaulettes and adjustable tabs at cuffs and waist. Left shoulder has OD border Army Service Forces patch. Each cuff stitch reinforced. Size 36R. Above avg. cond. $112

Jacket, Field, M1941, USA, Army, WWII. Lt OD poplin body with OD wool lining, zipper/button front, epaulettes, slash pockets and button tabs at cuffs and waistband. Size 42. Above avg. cond. $210

Jacket, Field, M1941, USA, Army, WWII. Lt OD poplin with OD wool lining, replacement zipper front, button tabs at cuffs and waist, slash pockets with button closure flaps and sewn on captain's bar on each epaulette. About size 36. Avg. cond. $59

Jacket, Field, M1941, Female, USA, USMC, WWII. Lt OD poplin with OD wool lining, epaulettes, zipper/button front, slash pockets and button tabs at cuffs and waist. Medium size. Above avg. cond. $84

Jacket, Field, M1943, USA, Army, WWII. Dark OD cotton with button front and label intact in neck. Faint Qm label. Size 36R. Avg. cond. $61

Jacket, Field, M1943, USA, AAF, 1945. Dark OD cotton with button front, 1945 dated Qm label, 8th Air Force patch on left shoulder and pair pb 2nd Lieut bars. Lieut's name in small ink-stamped letters above left chest pocket. Size 36L. Above avg. cond. $120

Jacket, Field, M1943, USA, Army, WWII. Dark OD cotton with button front and printed markings in neck. Faint Qm label. Has 103rd Div patch on left shoulder. Size 40R. Above avg. cond. $105

Jacket, Field, M1943, USA, Army, WWII. Dark OD cotton with button front and faint Qm label. Label in neck intact. Size 38. Avg. cond. $34

Jacket, Field, M1943, USA, Army, WWII. Dark OD cotton with button front. Size 34R. Avg. cond. $55

Jacket, Field, M1943, USA, Army, WWII. Dark OD cotton with faint Qm label. Includes M1943 field jacket hood. Size 38R. Avg. cond. $60

Jacket, Field, M1943, USA, Army, WWII. Dark OD cotton with button front. Faint Qm label. Includes M1943 field jacket hood. Avg. cond. $40

Jacket, Field, M1943, USA, Army, 1943. Dark OD cotton

with button front and 1943 dated Qm label. Size 36R. Exc. cond. $135

Jacket, Field, M1943, USA, Army, WWII. Dark OD cotton with button front and label intact in neck. Faint Qm label. About size 36. Avg. cond. $55

Jacket, Field, M1943, USA, Army, 1945. Dark OD wool with button front and 1945 dated Qm label. Dark printed markings in neck. Size 36L. Above avg. cond. $66

Jacket, Field, M1943, USA, AAF, 1945. Dark OD cotton with button front and 1945 dated Qm label. Has 15th Air Force patch on left shoulder. Size 38L. Exc. cond. . $129

Jacket, Field, M1943, USA, Army, WWII. Dark OD cotton with button front, 1944 dated Qm label and instructional label in neck. Size 36R. Exc. cond. $150

Jacket, Field, M1943, USA, Army, WWII. Dark OD cotton with button front and faint Qm label. Fully embr Army Service Forces patch on left shoulder. Size 34L. Above avg. cond. $34

Jacket, Field, M1943, Female, USA, WAC, 1944. Dark OD cotton with button front and 1944 dated Qm label. Size 18L. Avg. cond. $57

Jacket, Field, M1943, Female, USA, WAC, WWII. Dark OD cotton with button front and 1944 dated Qm label. Size 10R. Above avg. cond. $45

Jacket, Field, M1943, Female, USA, WAC, WWII. Dark OD cotton with button front. Faint Qm label. Some wash fading. Some frayed spots on collar fold. Size 10R. Avg. cond. $20

Jacket, Field, M1951, USA, Army, 1950s. Dark OD cotton with zipper and snap closure front. Has black OD web tape on rt chest and merrowed edge AG border 1st Armored Div patch on left shoulder. Exc. cond. ... $46

Jacket, Field, M1951, USA, Army, Korean War. Dark OD cotton body with zipper and snap closure front and faint Qm markings. Size medium/regular. Has OD border 7th Div patch on left shoulder, OD embr on blue twill Master Sgt chevrons, yellow-on-black woven US Army pocket tape, theater-made fully mach-embr name tape with attached unit crest design along top edge. Avg. cond. $50

Jacket, Field, M1951, USA, Army, 1960. Dark OD cotton with all labels intact and zipper/snap closure front. Dated 1960. Has subdued name tapes. Size small/reg. Above avg. cond. $24

Jacket, Field, M1951, USA, Army, 1952. Dark OD cotton with zipper front and 1952 dated Qm markings. Size small/regular. Above avg. cond. $37

Jacket, Field, M1951, USA, Army, 1952. Dark OD cotton

with 1952 dated Qm markings. Has color Berlin CMD patch on left shoulder and Pfc chevrons. Size small/reg. Avg. cond. $20

Jacket, Field, M1965, USA, Army, 1970s. Dark OD cotton with zipper and snap closure front. Has color US-made 173rd Airborne Div patch and tab on left shoulder with theater-made subdued "Ammo" tab above, early color US-made Special Forces patch and tab on rt shoulder, US embr on twill subdued Sgt chevrons, theater-made para wing, yellow-on-black US Army tape and theater-made subdued name tape. Small size. Above avg. cond. . . $38

Jacket, Field, M1965, USA, Army, 1971. OD cotton. Dated 1971. Size small/regular. Above avg. cond. . . $37

Jacket, Field, M1965, USA, Army, 1970s. In dark OD cotton with 4th Missile CMD patch on left shoulder, theater-made Korean 1st Div patch on spec 4 chevrons, yellow-on-black US Army tape and white web name tape. Size medium/regular. Avg. cond. $16

Jacket, Field, M1965, USA, Army, 1967. Dark OD cotton with zipper and snap closure front. Dated 1967. Button-in pile liner. Size medium/long. Avg. cond. $21

Jacket, Field, Wool, OD, USA, Army, WWII, England. Original "Ike jacket." ETO contract. Size 34 in OD wool serge with satin lining and Frankfurt marked Qm label. Avg. cond. $20

Jacket, Field, Wool, OD, EM, USA, Army, WWII. Original "Ike jacket." OD wool serge with 63rd Div patch on left shoulder, OD border 36th Div patch on rt shoulder, five o/s bars and discharge patch. Size 36R. Above avg. cond. $25

US Army Enlisted Man's wool Field Jacket (Ike Jacket)

Jacket, Field, Wool, OD, EM, USA, Army, Airborne, WWII. Original "Ike jacket." OD wool serge with 11th Abn Div patch with separate tab on left shoulder, 27th Div patch on rt shoulder and three o/s bars. Size 38R. Above avg. cond. $40

Jacket, Field, Wool, OD, EM, USA, AAF, WWII. Original "Ike jacket." OD wool serge with 9th Air Force patch on left shoulder, 12th Air Force patch on rt shoulder, Cpl chevrons, six o/s bars, one hashmark, AF Engr Specialty patch on rt cuff and discharge patch. Size 36L. Includes tan cotton necktie and AAF piped OD wool o/s cap. Above avg. cond. $175

Jacket, Field, Wool, OD, EM, USA, Army, WWII. "Ike jacket." Size 40R in OD wool. With theater-made CBI patch on left shoulder, T-Sgt chevrons, four o/s bars, US Army Pacific patch on rt, US and Transportation collar discs and four-place ribbon group. Avg. cond. $22

Jacket, Field, Wool, OD, Officer, USA, Army, WWII. "Ike jacket." Private purchase in OD wool serge with colorful woven maker's label and OD satin lining. 2nd Army patch on left shoulder and six o/s bars. About size 40. Avg. cond. $45

Jacket, Field, Wool, OD, Officer, USA, Army, 1945. "Ike jacket." OD wool serge with satin lining and 1945 dated Qm label. Has six o/s bars on left cuff. Size 42R. Above avg. cond. $93

Jacket, Field, Wool, OD, Officer, USA, AAF, 1944. Original "Ike jacket." OD wool serge with cotton lining. 1944 dated Qm label, 9th AF patch on left shoulder, four o/s bars, pair pb major leaves, US and AAF collar devices, 3" wide sterling hmkd cb AAF pilot wing on left chest over plastic-coated three-place ribbon bar and DUC ribbon. Size 42L. Above avg. cond. $160

Jacket, Field, Wool, OD, Officer, USA, AAF, WWII. Original "Ike jacket." British made. Dark OD whipcord tailor made lined with bright red silk. Has OG mohair cuff braid. Has 15th AF patch sewn to left shoulder. Size 38-40. Above avg. cond. $160

Jacket, Reefer, CPO, USA, Coast Guard, WWII. Size 36R. With woven US Navy label, gilt brass USCG buttons on double-breasted front, bullion CPO boatswain's mate rate, three hashmarks on left sleeve and bullion USCG shield on rt cuff. Avg. cond. $25

Jacket, Reefer, Dress White, CPO, USA, Navy, WWII. White cotton jacket with correct removable gilt buttons, CPO carpenter's mate rate, six hashmarks on left sleeve, five-place wide ribbon group. Avg. cond. $35

Jacket, Reefer, Warrant Officer, Naval, USA, Navy, WWII. Private purchase in navy blue whipcord with woven Pettibone clothier's label. Gold wire CWO rank and bullion carpenter device on each cuff. Named. About size 38. Good cond. $20

Jacket, Shell, USA, Army, Cavalry, Civil War. Dark blue wool serge body with 1855 pattern buttons, single-breasted button front, yellow piped cuffs and standing collar. Above avg. cond. $840

Jacket, Tropical, Officer, USA, AAF, WWII. "Bush jacket." Theater-made dark tan cotton jacket with button front, matching adjustable belt with brass buckle, pleated chest pockets with scalloped flaps, lower billow pockets and button cuffs. Has fully embr OD border CBI patch on left shoulder and 10th Air Force patch on rt shoulder. Embr on tan cotton 1st Lieut rank bar on each epaulette and cloth AAF pilot wing on left chest. Hash and embr CBI-made US and AAF collar patches. About size 36/38. Above avg. cond. $147

Jacket, Tropical, Officer, USA, AAF, WWII. "Bush jacket." CBI made. Dark tan cotton body with woven Calcutta maker's label in neck. Horn button front, pleated chest pockets, lower billow pockets and button cuffs. Has nice CBI-made insignia, CBI patch on left shoulder, hand embr on cotton AAF patch on rt shoulder and US and AAF collar patches. Has detachable epaulettes, each with hand embr 1st Lieut bar. About size 38. Above avg. cond. $166

Jacket, Utility, Camo, USA, Navy, Desert Storm. Size medium/long in three-color desert camo ripstop. Has brown embr on tan poplin US Navy tape in English and Arabic on left. Exc. cond. $27

Jacket, Winter Combat, USA, Army, Armored, WWII. Private purchase. Dark OD cotton body with zipper front, OD knit collar, cuffs and waistband, quilted green satin lining and slash pockets. Has OD border Armored Forces patch on left shoulder, embossed brown leather name tag stitched to left chest. Size 40. Avg. cond. $65

Jacket, Wool, OD, EM, M1950, USA, Army, Early 1950s. Last pattern "Ike jacket." OD wool serge with 40th Div patch on left shoulder, China HQ patch on rt shoulder, woven S/Sgt chevrons, multi-piece cb US and Qm collar discs. Size 38R. Above avg. cond. $35

Jacket, Wool, OD, EM, M1950, USA, Army, Korean War. Last model of "Ike jacket." In OD wool serge. Size 38R. With Korean-made bullion 8th Army patch on left and "Korea" arc on rt shoulder, "Korea" leadership loops, woven S/Sgt chevrons, two bullion o/s bars, US and Arty collar discs, three-place ribbon bar with Korean DUC ribbon on left chest pocket flap. Avg. cond. $55

Jacket, Wool, OD, EM, M1950, USA, Army, Early 1950s. Last pattern "Ike jacket." OD wool serge with large Qm

tag, 1st Army patch on left shoulder, US Army Forces Western Pacific patch on rt shoulder, OD embr on felt Master Sgt chevrons, eight hashmarks, two o/s bars, ten-place cord-stitched ribbon group on OD wool serge lt backing on left chest. Size 40R. Avg. cond. $17

Jacket, Wool, OD, EM, M1950, USA, Army, 1951. Last pattern "Ike jacket." OD wool serge with 1951 dated Qm tag. Has been converted to zipper front. Has bevo-style weave 1st Div patch on left shoulder, Cpl chevrons and single Sb Inf collar device. Size 38R. Above avg. cond. $20

Jacket, Wool, OD, MQ1, EM, USA, Army, 1948. "Ike jacket" M1946 pattern. OD wool serge with 1948 dated Qm label, bevo Supreme HQ Allied Powers, Europe patch on left shoulder. Corp chevrons. Size 36R. Avg. cond. $20

Jacket, Wool, OD, MQ1, EM, USA, Army, Late 1940s. "Ike jacket" M1946 pattern. OD wool serge with 2nd Army patch on left shoulder, US Army Forces Western Pacific patch on rt shoulder, small yellow-on-blue corp chevrons, five embr on dark OD gabardine o/s bars and two hashmarks. Size 38R. Avg. cond. $18

Jacket, Wool, OD, MQ1, EM, USA, Army, Late 1940s. "Ike jacket" M1946 pattern. OD wool serge with German-made bullion on felt 7th Army patch on and bevo "Seven Steps to Hell" tab on left shoulder, OD embr on black felt Pfc chevrons, pair pb DI's with motto "The Fifth Foremost," domed US and "5/Arty/D" collar discs, German-made plastic Army of Occupation ribbon bar and DUC ribbon. Size 34S. Above avg. cond. $40

Jacket, Wool, OD, Officer, M1950, USA, Army, Korean War. "Ike jacket." Dark OD gabardine with matching belt and ribbed buckle. With woven clothier's label, Meyer hmkd pb captain's bars, US and Arty collar devices, 8th Army patch on left shoulder and 5th Army on rt. Above avg. cond. $35

Jacket, Zouave and Vest, USA, Army, Civil War. Dark blue rough wool body with red trim and fancy red scrollwork on body. Matching dark blue vest with red tape piping. Exc. cond. $195

Jacket, Zouave and Vest, USA, Army, Civil War. Short style cut-away jacket with russet wool body having black tape-style scrollwork. Matching vest. Full lining. Exc. cond. $195

Blouses, Jackets, and Tunics—Germany

Atilla, Hussar, Imperial Germany, Army, Hussar, c1890s. Sage green wool with twisted black and white cord frogging and sleeve trim. Brass pinwheel buttons and toggles.

With silver bullion shoulderboards and cotton lining. Above avg. cond. $374

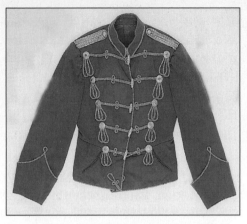

Imperial German Hussar's Attila

Attila, Hussar, Officer, Prussian, Imperial Germany, Army, Hussar, c1880s. Navy blue wool gabardine with yellow wool collar facings. Front of tunic frogged and piped in black cordage with brass pinwheel buttons, floraled bands and simulated twisted cord toggle buttons. Sleeves with three rows of bullion tape. Black cotton lining. Above avg. cond. $460

Prussian Hussar Officer's Attila

Attila, NCO, Prussian, Imperial Germany, Army, Hussar, WWI. Blue wool with white cloth frogging and silvered metal buttons. White cord shoulder straps. No unit ciphers. Exc. cond. $250

Attila, Officer, Prussian, Imperial Germany, Army, Hussar, WWI. Sherwood green with silver frogging and round frosted silver buttons. Stand-up collar with matching piping. Black flecking in cording. Lieut shoulder-boards. Full liner. Avg. cond. $300

Cape, Dress, Officer, Germany, Army, WWII. Gray doe-skin wool body with green collar. Five-button front and button strap at collar with hook. Near mint cond. . $328

Cape, Dress, Officer, Germany, Luftwaffe, WWII, W. Bentrup & Sohn, Panderborn. Blue-gray wool body and collar. Five-button front. Dark alum eagle-head clasp with chain. Bevo maker tag at neck "W. Bentrup & Sohn Panderborn etc." Above avg. cond. $350

Jacket, Dress, EM, Naval, Imperial Germany, Navy, 1915. Blue wool body with 18 nickel button front and six buttons on each cuff. Black lining, slash pocket and faint inked "BAW 6.3.15 3." Above avg. cond. $145

Jacket, Dress, EM, Naval, Imperial Germany, Navy, 1906. Dress "monkey" jacket style. Dark blue wool. Gilt crown and anchor buttons. "BAK 18.5.06" issue dates marked inside body. Above avg. cond. $158

Jacket, Dress, PO, Germany, Navy, WWI. With PO's engineer silver crowned anchor sleeve rating. Deluxe blue wool body with high-relief crown buttons, silver chain and buttons on front. Silver PO tressing to cuffs. Exc. cond. $300

Jacket, Dress, PO, Naval, Germany, Navy, WWII. Dark blue wool. Gilt brass KM buttons, gilt braid on cuffs, and embr breast eagle. PO rate in gilt metal with anchor over chevron. Red flaming bomb and chevron below. With breast chain. Named inside. Exc. cond. $315

Jacket, EM, Naval, Imperial Germany, Navy, WWI. Blue wool body with hmkd naval buttons, tunic has all buttons and also white wool chevron on left arm. Inside has Wilhelmshaven Qm issue marks, is dated Sept. 4, 1895, and has owner's name tag sewn inside with unit marks below. Two small eyelet hooks for bib retention on back. Above avg. cond. $180

Jacket, EM, Naval, Imperial Germany, Navy, 1910. High quality double-breasted jacket. With silver crown and anchor buttons. Includes yellow embr Mine Specialist patch on left sleeve with red-white-black inverted chevron above. Jacket marked "II.T.1. 42/11" WILHELMS-HAVEN 1910". Above avg. cond. $265

Jacket, Field, Camo, Germany, Army, WWII. Gray reversible to white. Gray twill cotton body and bleached white side. Hood, two pockets and waistbelt. Exc. cond. $670

Jacket, Field, Camo, Germany, Waffen-SS, WWII. Reversible. Green oak leaf side has four pleated patch pockets and five black resin button front. Large hood lacks drawstring. Slash cuffs with resin buttons. Drawstring at waist. Of the period and field made from shelter quarter. Exc. cond. $495

Jacket, Field, Camo, Germany, Army, WWII. Splinter pattern camo reversible to winter white. Hood with drawstring, waistbelt, two slash pockets and all buttons in place on front. Inked RB-NR and size III. Above avg. cond.   . $685

Jacket, Field, Camo, Germany, Army. Reversible water pattern camo to winter white. Camo print on light brown. Hood, two pockets and waistbelt. Exc. cond. $706

Jacket, Foul-weather, Naval, Germany, Navy, WWII. Black leather jacket. Below waist style with five gold fouled anchor button front and three slash pockets with flaps. Short stand-up collar. Button strap to cuffs. Black wool lined with patch and pocket. Also includes gray leather pants. Five-button front. Gray cloth lined with bevo maker "Hela Kleiderfabrik Kiel 46." Avg. cond. . . . $300

Jacket, Foul-weather, Naval, Germany, Navy, WWII. Below waist length, three slash pockets, five black resin buttons instead of anchor style and short standing collar. Black wool lined. Below avg. cond. $90

Jacket, Foul-weather, Naval, Germany, Navy, WWII. Black leather. Black wool lining to five anchor button body with stand-up collar and three slash pockets. With straight-leg leather trousers. Avg. cond. $298

Jacket, Foul-weather, Naval, Germany, Navy, 1941, Hilbert Chemnitz. Black leather. Above knee length body. Four black plastic button front, two slash chest pockets and two lower slash/flap pockets. Stamped Eagle-M on front between buttons. Full black wool lining with pocket and bevo neck label marked "Hilbert Chemnitz etc. 1941" and size 52. Jacket type associated with U-boat service. Avg. cond. $196

Jacket, Mess Dress, Officer, Germany, Navy, 1937. Blue doeskin jacket and vest. Bullion hand embr eagle. Gold tape stripe to each cuff with bullion stars. Lieut rank. Oilcloth maker label marked "Frdr. ???? Kiel" with inked owner's name and 1937 date. Pre-war quality. Exc. cond. . . . $468

Jacket, Mess Dress, Officer, Germany, Luftwaffe, WWII. Short blue-gray wool body with eight pebbled button front, flat-silver bevo eagle is zigzag sewn to wool backing and hand sewn on. Twisted alum piping to collar and sewn-in boards with one gold pip each. Gray satin lining with two slash pockets. Loops for one badge. For flight oberleutnant. Above avg. cond. $280

Jacket, Mess Dress, Officer, Naval, Germany, Navy, WWII. Blue doeskin wool body. Eight golden anchor buttons and chain with two buttons. Dark gold sleeve stripe with dark bullion star above. Gold bullion breast eagle on wool. Full black satin lining with two pockets and bevo maker tag "Offizierkleiderkasse Whaven," typed "Brodda" and inked "2.MRZ.37." Above avg. cond. $220

Jacket, Mess Dress, Official, Naval, Germany, Navy, WWII. Dark blue wool body. Ten-button front with 18mm diam silver frosted anchor buttons. Loops for one badge. Cuffs have 2"-wide silver band with ⅝"-wide band above. Silver wire embr eagle with three chevrons below. Loops present for ribbon bar. Black satin lining. Two inner pockets. Exc. cond. $475

Jacket, Motorcycle, Tropical, Germany, Army, WWII. Olive twill cotton body, belt and buttons. Inked "Lago-Mu M43/N" and size. Cloth loops for shoulder straps. Exc. cond. $285

Jacket, Pea, EM, Naval, Germany, Navy, WWII. Dark blue wool construction. Twelve anchor buttons, two slash pockets with flaps, yellow embr eagle, one blue wool collar tab and yellow embr lightning bolt to sleeve disc. Wool lined with two slash pockets and owner name to neck. Includes one pair straight-leg dark blue wool trousers. Above avg. cond. $200

Jacket, Pea, Naval, Germany, Navy, WWII. Thick navy blue heavy wool jacket. Two slash pockets. Wool lined with two pockets. Above avg. cond. $145

Jacket, Reefer, Chaplain, Naval, Germany, Navy, WWII. Dark blue twill wool body, eight-button front, three slash pockets and rt side pocket has small patch pocket inside. Dark gold bullion and sewn-on hand-embr eagle and M1942 purple velvet tabs, gold twisted piping, gold bullion wreath with cross center. Both hand sewn to collar. Full black satin lining with pocket. Exc. cond. $695

Jacket, Reefer, Official, Naval, Germany, Navy, WWII. Dark blue with double-breasted front. Ten silver fouled anchor buttons, silver bullion breast eagle on dark blue and rt silver bevo cuff stripe with silver Nazi eagle over sleeve patch. Above avg. cond. $540

Jacket, Reefer, Tech Official, Naval, Germany, Navy, WWII. Dark blue doeskin body, three alum brocade sleeve stripes, alum bullion eagle and sleeve oval eagles with two triangles. Black satin lining with two pockets. Loops for one badge. Avg. cond. $250

Jacket, Work, Germany, Luftwaffe, WWII. Reed-green HBT body. Silver-gray machine-embr breast eagle on blue-gray wool. Blue-gray wool sleeve chevron with single silver braid "V." Motor Vehicle Driver Spec Patch. Two lower patch-style pockets. Pebble finish buttons. The work jacket was worn without shoulderboards or collar tabs. Avg. cond. $250

Litewka, Officer, Bavarian, Imperial Germany, Army, WWI. For 2nd Lieut. Polished copper double row of buttons, slate gray body with red piping and light green wool turn-down collar, red tabs with matching buttons. Silver wire shoulderboards with red piping and Bavarian blue flecking. Two lower slash-style pockets. Exc. cond. $276

Rabatte, Officer, Imperial Germany, Army, Uhlan, WWI. With many loops for decorations. Lemon-yellow exterior. Light yellow silk lining. Above avg. cond. $81

Smock, Camo, Germany, Army, WWII. For Army sniper. Reversible, water pattern camo to winter white. Hood still has camo gauze for face cover with hole near seam. Tie string to slash neck, drawstring waist, two slash openings for tunic pocket use. Inked RB-NR and size II. Above avg. cond. $1000

Smock, Paratrooper, Camo, Germany, Luftwaffe, 1945. Printed water pattern camo on heavy twill cotton body. Four white plastic "RiRi" zippers on pockets and four glass buttons remain on front. Variation gray embr eagle is on gray cloth and zigzag sewn on. Tan/brown flight suit material is used for rank backing with four white felt gulls sewn to each. Inked RB-NR, size "IIa," and "45" date to inside. Above avg. cond. $1785

Tunic, Bandsman, NCO, Prussian, Imperial Germany, Army, Garde, WWI. Dark blue body with red piping. NCO lace on sleeves and collar. Yellow shoulderboards with matching yellow and blue "swallows" nests. Yellow Garde matching litzen on sleeves. Domed copper buttons. Exc. cond. $325

Tunic, Dress, Garde Officer, Prussian, Imperial Germany, Army, 1912. Dark blue wool body with domed silver buttons, silver Garde litzen on full stand-up collar and matching litzen to sleeves. Service shoulderboards of a captain with rank insignia, silver field and black flecking. Black velour collar and cuffs with matching litzen and buttons. Full liner. 1912 period. Above avg. cond. . $375

Tunic, Dress, Garde Officer, Prussian, Imperial Germany, Army, WWI. Erfurt maker label inside. Dark blue wool. Stand-up collar with heavy silver bullion Garde litzen. Matching litzen on cuff. Red piped. Copper buttons. Large silver and black loops for the shoulder epaulettes. Shoulder buttons also present. About size 40. Above avg. cond. $350

Tunic, Dress, NCO, Germany, Army, WWII. Gray twill wool body with green piping. Flat-silver bevo insignia and tarnished silver tape stripes. Loops for long ribbon bar. Red wool on back of front opening. Avg. cond. . . . $300

Tunic, Dress, NCO, Germany, Army, Arty, WWII. Twill gray wool body, green collar and cuffs with red wool piped collar, front, cuffs and back. Alum tape stripe and bullion tabs to both cuffs and collar. Red hand embr signal sleeve oval, black wound badge and 1914 EK. White embr eagle, sewn-in straps with #22 devices, pip and eleven buttons.

Green satin lining with belt, slash pocket and inked "A.R.22." Avg. cond. $420

Tunic, Dress, NCO, Germany, Army, Arty, WWII. Shoulder straps have full silver braid and two silver stars, officer quality silver embr breast eagle, Iron Cross 2nd Class ribbon in button hole and long service ribbon bar. High quality hand embr gold and silver with silver cord border radioman's specialist insignia. About size 38. Above avg. cond. $290

Tunic, Dress, Officer, Prussian, Imperial Germany, Army, Arty, WWI. Dark blue Prussian wool body with red piping on cuffs, collar, closure and tails. Deluxe copper-style domed buttons. Slip on 4th Artillery Major shoulderboards with gilt unit cipher. Black velour stand-up collar. Full lining. Matching velour cuffs. Avg. cond. $350

Tunic, Drill, EM, Germany, Army, Arty, 1942. Reed-green HBT body, four patch pockets, six removable button front, machine-sewn-on gray bevo eagle and collar tape tabs. Slip-on Arty straps. Partial gray satin lining. Inked size and 1942 date. Two alum belt ramps. Above avg. cond. $425

Tunic, Drill, EM, Germany, Luftwaffe, WWII. Reed-green HBT body with two pleated patch upper pockets, six blue-gray pebbled removable button front, loops and buttons for strap. Cloth eagle removed from breast but outline remains. Issue purple satin lining with bandage pocket. Has correct inked RB-NR, size and M1943 markings. Exc. cond. $189

Tunic, Drill, NCO, Germany, Army, WWII. Reed-green HBT body with four patch pockets and removable six-button front. Sewn-on gray embr eagle on green felt. Dark green wool collar with alum NCO edge and gray-green tape tabs machine sewn to green wool backings. Slip-on straps in dark green with white piping and worn alum NCO insignia. Inked size inside. Avg. cond. $370

Tunic, EM, Germany, Army, c1970s. Four-pocket-style tunic of wool and polyester in field gray. With alum buttons, engineer's collar insignia and white piping on cuffs and collar. Above avg. cond. $20

Tunic, EM, Germany, Army, 1978. Field gray wool and polyester tunic with four pockets and alum buttons. Technical Troops collar tabs, tab and shoulderboard and shoulder insignia of the 5th Armored Div. Above avg. cond. $25

Tunic, EM, M1944, Germany, Army, Late WWII. Waist-length gray wool body. Two unpleated front pockets with button flaps and six-button front. Below avg. cond. $165

Tunic, Field, EM, M1907/1910, Bavarian, Imperial Germany, Army, Inf, WWI. Gray wool body with turn-down collar, red piping and tails. Belt ramp buttons present. Brandenburg cuffs with subdued lion-style buttons same on front and rear. Partial lining for summer issue. Owner's name hand embr on inside. Red embr #1 on shoulder straps with 8th Company buttons. Two lower slash pockets. Exc. cond. $480

Tunic, Flight, EM, Germany, Luftwaffe, 1943. Blue-gray wool body with insignia. Purple satin partial lining with two pockets and inked RB-NR, size and "LBA(S)43." Exc. cond. $744

Tunic, Flight, EM, Germany, Luftwaffe, WWII. Blue-gray wool body. Embr gray eagle, embr two-tone radio/gunner badge, yellow collar tabs with single gull and slip-on shoulder straps. Partial gray lining with two pockets. Avg. cond. $385

Tunic, General, Bavarian, Imperial Germany, Army, 1915. Field gray feldgrau wool with stand-up gray collar with subdued gold wire general collar tabs. Red piped collar, closure and cuffs. Two lower slash pockets and subdued bronze-colored Bavarian lion buttons. Red wool slip-on general shoulderboards in subdued gold and silver with blue-white flecking. Large deluxe parade furled ribbon bar with six ribbons. Full liner. Exc. cond. . . . .
. . . . $2565

Tunic, NCO, Prussian, Imperial Germany, Army, Arty, WWI. Dark blue wool with black stand-up collar and cuffs. NCO gold braid trim. Tombak domed buttons. Fine quality blue wool shoulder straps with red embr flaming bomb and "#23" of the 23rd Field Art. Black silk lined. Red piped. Loops on breast for decorations. Avg. cond. .
. . . . $275

Tunic, Officer, Prussian, Imperial Germany, Army, Hussar, WWII. Black wool with silver frogging and buttons. Black flecking. Quatrefoil-style shoulderboards in silver wire. Full liner and inner belt. Loops for medals present. Stand-up collar. Special sewn hole for a breast house order. Above avg. cond. $340

Tunic, Parade Dress, EM, Germany, Army, Pioneer, WWII. Smooth gray wool body, green collar, cuffs and black piping. Flat-silver bevo insignia and sewn-in green straps with chain stitched b&w "#19." Inked maker name, size and "H38." Above avg. cond. $324

Tunic, Parade Dress, EM, Germany, Army, Inf, WWII. Gray wool body, green cuffs and collar with white piping overall. White wool collar and cuff tabs with alum tape litzen. Sewn-in green straps with white wool piping, white chain stitched "19" and alum #6 buttons. Flat-silver bevo eagle. Full gray lining with pocket and inked size/date. Avg. cond. $181

Tunic, Parade Dress, Officer, Germany, Army, Supply, WWII, Wilhelm Welhausen, Hannover Kassel. Tailored gray twill wool body with green cuffs and collar. Light blue wool piping overall and eight-button front. Alum bullion eagle, sewn-in oberleutnant shoulderboards, thick collar and cuff tabs. Full satin lining with pocket and neck bevo maker label "Wilhelm Welhausen Hannover Kassel." Avg. cond. $385

Tunic, Service, Germany, NSKK, WWII. Olive brown wool body, brown collar, black collar tabs, flat silver bevo sleeve eagle and black sleeve diamond with silver eagle on six-spoked wheel. Partial brown lining, inked "52" and large RZM mark on wool material. Oilcloth RZM tag "Feldbluse NSKK etc." on belt ramp strap. Large size. Exc. cond. $230

Tunic, Service, EM, Germany, Army, Inf, WWII. Gray wool body, green collar with bevo tabs and embr eagle. 1939 EK ribbon in buttonhole. Partial gray lining with inked maker and size. Exc. cond. $650

Tunic, Service, EM, Germany, Navy, Coastal Arty, WWII. Gray wool body with five gray anchor buttons. Two pleated patch upper pockets with two slash-style lower pockets and matching slash pattern cuffs. Yellow bevo breast eagle and single rank chevron. Loops and buttons for shoulder straps. No collar tabs. Full gray lining with ink size marks. Avg. cond. $252

Tunic, Service, EM, Flak, Germany, Luftwaffe, WWII. Blue-gray wool. Four alum button front, four pleated patch pockets and French cuffs. Loops for one badge. Embr eagle, machine-sewn-on red wool tabs with single gull. Slip-on wool straps with red cord piping. Gray cloth lining with pocket having bevo tag "Materla," unit "I./E./R.7 11.Batt." Above avg. cond. $397

Tunic, Service, EM, M1943, Germany, Army, WWII. Rough texture gray wool body, collar and four patch pockets. Bevo eagle is zigzag stitched and bevo tabs are machine sewn on. Loops and buttons for shoulder straps. Partial gray satin lining with inked size, RB-NR and "E44." Exc. cond. $710

Tunic, Service, EM, M1943, Germany, Army, WWII. Reed-green HBT body, four patch pockets, six-button front, machine-sewn-on gray bevo eagle and collar tape tabs. Slip-on wool straps with white cord piping. Partial satin lining. Avg. cond. $285

Tunic, Service, EM, M1943, Germany, Army, WWII. Gray wool body, four pleated patch pockets and five-button front. Same gray wool to collar instead of green and lacks tabs. Loops and buttons for strap use. No eagle but does have Russian front ribbon to buttonhole. Partial gray lining with inked maker, size and "H41." Below avg. cond. $270

Tunic, Service, Flight NCO, Germany, Luftwaffe, WWII. Blue-gray twill wool body, gray embr eagle, yellow cord collar piping, alum tape, yellow tabs and alum gull on each. Full gray satin lining shows use. 1939 EK ribbon in button hole, loops for two patches and small ribbon bar. Below avg. cond. $200

Tunic, Service, NCO, Germany, Luftwaffe, Flak, WWII. Blue-gray wool body with four-button front and four pleated patch pockets. Loops for one badge. "F" specialist patch. Eagle on wool is machine zigzag sewn on. 1939 EK ribbon at buttonhole. Alum NCO tape to collar with red wool tabs having three gray gulls each. Sewn-in straps of wool with alum tape, red wool piping and one pip each. Full black lining with one slash pocket. Exc. cond. $381

Tunic, Service, NCO, Germany, Army, Arty, WWII. Gray wool body and green collar with tape stripe. Bevo eagle, tabs and slip-on straps with two pips each. Loops for three badges and one badge on rt pocket. Partial gray lining with inked size. Exc. cond. $850

Tunic, Service, Officer, Germany, Army, Smoke Troops, 1942. Field gray wool body with dark green wool collar. Field gray pebble finish buttons. Two lower hidden pockets with flaps and two upper pleated patch style. French cuffs. Loops on chest for awards. Silver bullion hand embr breast eagle on dark green wool. Sewn-on leutnant boards with silver-gray cords on Bordeaux red. Dark green wool tabs with silver-gray bullion hand embr bars with Bordeaux red litzen. Field gray silk lining with inner waistbelt and hanger. Label in pocket dated 1942. Above avg. cond. $670

Tunic, Service, Officer, Germany, Army, Mt. Troop, WWII. Gray twill wool body, six buttons, four pleated patch pockets, French cuffs and green collar. Loops for one badge. Flat-silver bevo eagle is zigzag sewn on through lining. Bevo sleeve shield is sewn on to rt sleeve. Sewn-in gray straps on green wool with one pip each. Green wool tabs with alum bars having green plaited centers. Gray HBT satin lining with pocket and dagger clip. Above avg. cond. $495

Tunic, Service, Officer, Germany, Army, WWII, L. Kielleuthner, Muenchen. Late war light gray wool body with green collar. Insignia and three loops for ribbon bar. Full brown satin lining, two slash pockets, dagger clip and bevo neck label "L.Kielleuthner etc. Muenchen." Near mint cond. $903

Tunic, Service, Officer, Germany, Army, Cav, WWII. Gray twill wool tailored body with chest pads and shoulder pads. Green collar, six pebbled nickel button front

with 1939 EK ribbon, French cuffs, two pleated patch upper pockets and two slash lower. Loops for four badges. Alum hand-embr eagle, alum litzen on green tabs with yellow twisted centers and sewn-on gray leutnant shoulderboards on yellow. Full satin lining with pocket and printed owner's tag at neck "Reiter Ludemann 1./K.R.Hannover." Above avg. cond. $600

Tunic, Service, Officer, Germany, Army, Inf, WWII. Smooth gray doeskin wool body with French cuffs. Green wool collar, five-button front and four pleated patch pockets. Loops for ribbon bar and three badges. Beautiful bullion breast eagle and sewn-on shoulder-boards for an oberleutnant. Full satin lining with slash pocket, dagger clip and bevo neck label "Bulag Muenchen." 1939 EK ribbon at buttonhole. Avg. cond. $426

Tunic, Service, Officer, Germany, Waffen SS, Inf, WWII. Gray wool body and green collar. Four pleated patch pockets, six-button front and French cuffs. 1939 EK ribbon at buttonhole. Loops for two badges and clasp. Gray embr sleeve eagle on black. Old fighter chevron and SS embr runes collar tab with twisted alum piping. Rank tab is machine sewn on. For Obersturmfuhrer. Sewn-on boards with worn silver finished pip and #5 on each. Full satin lining with pocket and dagger clip. Above avg. cond. $2100

Tunic, Service, Officer, Germany, Army, Inf, WWII. Tailor made with padded shoulders on thick gray EM-style wool body. Green collar, four pleated patch pockets, six-button front and French cuffs. Variation bullion eagle, thick tabs and slip-on leutnant shoulderboards. Loops for badge and ribbon bar. Full satin lining with pocket. Avg. cond. $320

German Infantry Officer's Tunic

Tunic, Service, Officer, Bavarian, Imperial Germany, Army, Arty, WWI. Gray body has repaired red cord/wool piping on front opening. Eight brass lion buttons. Black piped cuffs and red on back. Loops for ribbon bar. Narrow slip-on Lieut shoulderboards. Lining inked with size "B.A.?1910" and "6.fd.A.R.etc.1913." Avg. cond. $912

Tunic, Service, Officer, M1943, Germany, Army, Inf, WWII. Heavy wool tunic. Green collar, six-button front, four pleated patch pockets and French cuffs. Flat-silver bevo officer's eagle is machine sewn. Full gray satin lining with pocket. Loops for two badges. Above avg. cond. $575

Tunic, Service, Officer, M1943, Germany, Army, Arty, WWII. Gray twill wool body, green collar, six-button front, four pleated patch pockets and French cuffs. Bullion eagle, thick tabs and sewn-in hauptmann shoulderboards. Full gray satin lining with pocket and dagger clip. Above avg. cond. $450

Tunic, Service, Officer, M1943, Germany, Army, Mt. Troop, WWII. Light gray twill wool body with green collar. Six-button front, four pleated patch pockets and French cuffs. Loops for three badges. Hand embr alum sleeve edelweiss with gold celleon flower center, black highlights and dark green felt oval. Alum bullion eagle. Alum tabs and gray sewn-in boards on light green wool. Gold pip and #3 to each. Gray satin lining with slash pocket. Exc. cond. $632

Tunic, Service, Tropical, Germany, Army, DAK, WWII. Olive twill body, five removable blue-gray pebbled button front, four patch pockets and slash cuffs. Sewn-on blue

bevo eagle and blue bevo tape tabs. Loops and buttons for straps. Partial lining and bandage pocket. Inked RB-NR, "45 98 76 68" and "M44." Exc. cond. $685

Tunic, Uhlan, Officer, Prussian, Imperial Germany, Army, Uhlan, c1890s. double-breasted tunic of navy blue wool with scarlet collar, cuffs and piping. Silver bullion collar boards, epaulette retainers and sleeve rating. Nickel-plated buttons. Black cotton lining. Above avg. cond. $316

Ulanka, Dress, NCO, Imperial Germany, Army, Uhlan, WWI. Dark blue wool with dark yellow piping, stand-up collar and lapels. Silver domed button. NCO litzen and silver rank pip of a feldwebel. Double lance chevrons on rt sleeve. Avg. cond. $475

Ulanka, EM, Imperial Germany, Army, Uhlan, WWI. Dark blue wool body, pink piping, black velvet cuffs and collar. Darkened silver tape sleeve rank. Twelve nickel buttons and blue wool shoulder straps. Full black lining. Above avg. cond. $265

Ulanka, Officer, Imperial Germany, Army, Uhlan, WWI. Dark blue wool body, yellow wool piping overall, yellow cuffs, standing collar and sewn-on plastron front, 14 nickel buttons. Full lining with pocket. Exc. cond. $271

Blouses, Jackets, and Tunics——Other

Attila, NCO, Austria-Hungary, Army, Hussar, WWI. Blue twill wool body, white piping, 16 gold buttons, white cuffs with dark brocade tape, gold front cord and dark gold shoulder cord. Black fleece collar and full black satin lining with pocket and marked "Alexander Sohr Wien etc." Exc. cond. $282

Blouse, EM, Poland, Army, WWII. British battledress blouse (jacket) of khaki wool with seven-award medal bar of Polish and British medals. Above avg. cond.   . . . $750

Blouse, EM, Poland, Army, WWII. British-made battledress khaki wool blouse (jacket) with 12 awards mounted in two medal bars. Above avg. cond. $1500

Blouse, NCO, Poland, Army, WWII. British-pattern battledress blouse (jacket) of khaki wool. Above avg. cond. $500

Blouse, Service, Dress, Canada, Army, Airborne, 1970s. Dark blue twill blouse with four flapped pockets, gilded lion buttons, embroidered gold and silver bullion Canadian parachutist winged badge, gilded metal Canadian Para Rescue badge, nine-award ribbon bar, "Canada" shoulder insignia with yellow maple leaf and white wreath on red field, American parachutist badge, original owner's name tag and black satin lining. Above avg. cond. $145

Luftwaffe Tropical Issue Tunic

Blouse, Service, Officer, England, Royal Air Force, WWII. American-made blouse (jacket) having "American Union Garment Makers" label. Blue-gray wool with four flapped pockets, blue-gray wool twill with brass crown and eagle buttons, padded and embr navigator wing, blue satin lining, and officer cuff stripes. Above avg. cond.   . . $225

British Blouse (Jacket), Army Medical Corps, WWII

Blouse, Service, Officer, England, Royal Air Force, c1955. Wing commander. Blue wool blouse (jacket) with four patch pockets with button flaps, fabric belt with nickel buckle, open lapel, silvered buttons. Cloth embroidered RAF winged badge, two-medal ribbon bar, cuff rank and gray silk lining with tailor's label. Above avg. cond. $67

Blouse, Service, Officer, Australia, Royal Australian Air Force, 1944. Khaki wool blouse (jacket) with two flapped breast pockets, concealed button front, shoulder straps with Flying Officer rank and button cuffs. Embroidered RAAF pilot winged badge with blue wreath and dark blue wool ground, 1939–45 Star ribbon and Africa Star ribbon on tunic. Above avg. cond. $225

Blouse, Service, Officer, Australia, Royal Australian Air Force, WWII. Tan cotton twill blouse (jacket) with DFM,

English Army Officer's WWII Service Blouse

strap and button epaulettes with bronze officer eagle and crown devices. Tunic breast has embroidered single wing with blue wreath and "E" destination. Three-award ribbon bar, waistbelt with bronze rail buckle and cuff with four service stripes. Named. Above avg. cond. $350

Blouse, Service, Officer, England, Army, Arty, WWII. Khaki cotton twill blouse (jacket) with brass Arty buttons and bronze collar insignias. Second Lieut shoulder strap insignias and three-award ribbon bar. Above avg. cond.   .
. . . . $150

Coatee, Royal Army, Officers, England, Army, c1830. Scarlet wool with navy blue wool collar, turnbacks, and cuffs with white piping. Gilt brass buttons with Royal crown. White wool lining and tail turnbacks. Provision for single rt shoulder epaulette. Light moth damage present and some previous repairs present. Avg. cond. $920

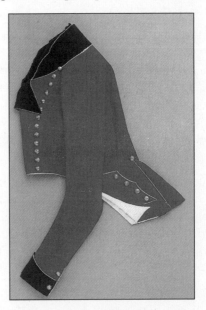

Royal Army Officer's Coatee

Jacket, Battledress, Italy, Army, Tank Corps, WWII. Second Lieut rank, khaki wool jacket with two pleated patch pockets and flaps, open lapel collar, wool Armor Corps collar tabs with silvered star, shoulder strap with hand embr gold bullion rank device and material unit sleeve shield on khaki wool. Above avg. cond. $22

Jacket, Combat, Camo, South Korea, Marines, 1980s. Camo cotton twill with pockets. Above avg. cond.   . . $30

Jacket, Field, Camo, South Vietnam, Army, c1967. Cotton twill jacket with tiger stripe camo pattern. Exc. cond.
. . . . $150

Jacket, Field, Officer, Russia, Army, c1980. Warrant Officer rank, khaki wool, pockets and khaki satin lining. Exc. cond. $26

Jacket, Officer, Soviet Union, Air Force, 1970s. For Air

Force Col. With two pockets, button at waist, shoulderboards and Guards badge. Above avg. cond. $45

Tunic, Soviet Union, Army. Heavy OD wool, lined with drab cotton twill, four pockets. Above avg. cond. .. $45

Tunic, EM, Naval, Russia, Navy, c1980. Enlisted white cotton "jumper" tunic. With issue blue-white striped undershirt. Exc. cond. $40

Tunic, Officer, Austria-Hungary, Army, WWI. Light blue double-breasted doeskin body, red piping, red cuffs and standing collar with gold brocade tape. 16 gold buttons with design. Full lining with bevo label "Kriegsministerium Wien etc." Above avg. cond. $370

Tunic, Officer, Italy, Air Force, c1950. Blue wool twill tunic with open lapel collar, four patch pockets with flaps, fabric belt, and gilded brass buttons, blue satin lining and black insignia. Above avg. cond. $20

Tunic, Officer, Greece, Air Force, WWII. Blue-gray wool tunic with brass Air Force crowned buttons, hand-embr gold bullion pilot badge with eagle and crown motif on gray wool triangular field, hand-embr gold bullion oak leaf ornamentation and gold bullion border lace, cuffs with diamond ornament, gold bullion shoulderboards with hand-embr silk bullion star rank insignia with gilded metal eagle devices and gray cotton twill lining. Fair cond. $400

Tunic, Officer, Marine, France, Marines, c1950. Khaki wool tunic with two flapped breast pockets, gold washed anchor buttons, shoulder straps with Lieut rank, gold bullion embr anchor shoulder insignia with dark blue diamond field, and seven "celo type" award ribbons. Above avg. cond. $150

Tunic, Summer, Officer, Greece, Army, WWII. For army Inf general. White cotton twill tunic with four pockets, gilded Greek shield and crown buttons, slip-on shoulderboards with gold lace mounted by two silver bullion rank pips, gilded metal crown and gilded metal crossed sword and baton insignia on shoulder-boards. Tunic complete with seven-award ribbon bar. Above avg. cond. ... $425

Vest, Officer, France, Army, WWI. Horizon blue wool vest with sky blue composition buttons, gray twill back, four slash pockets, and striped cotton ticking lining. Above avg. cond. $100

Shirts—U.S.

Fatigue Shirt, USA, USAF, 1950s. Size 14 ½ x 31. OD durapress shirt with subdued insignia and S/Sgt chevrons, pocket tapes, TAC pocket patch, and color-printed 4450th TAC Grp pocket patch. Above avg. cond. $20

Shirt, EM, USA, Army, WWII. Size 15 x 32. Lt OD wool

serge with gas flap. Has theater-made embr 36th Div patch on left shoulder and 84th Div patch on rt. Above avg. cond. $28

Shirt, EM, USA, Army, WWII. Size 16 x 34. Lt OD wool with gas flap, embr on felt 6th Cav Grp patch on left shoulder, woven T-Sgt chevrons and single hashmark. Above avg. cond. $35

Shirt, EM, USA, Army, WWII. Lt OD wool with 84th Div patch on left shoulder, 13th Corps patch on rt, sgt chevrons, US and Armor Force collar discs and sterling CIB. Size 15 x 32. Avg. cond. $20

Shirt, EM, USA, Army, WWII. Size 34R in dark OD HBT with metal star buttons and deep pleated chest pockets. Avg. cond. $20

Shirt, EM, USA, Army, WWII. Size 36R. Lt OD HBT with lt OD plastic button front, 1942 dated Qm tag, pleated chest pockets, button waistband and cuffs and adjustable tabs at waist. Above avg. cond. $32

Shirt, EM, USA, Army, WWII. Dark OD HBT with metallic star buttons and deep billow chest pockets. Medium size. Above avg. cond. $25

US Army WWII Wool Shirt (Dark Olive Drab)

Shirt, EM, USA, Army, WWII. Size 15½ x 33. Lt OD wool serge with gas flap, 1st Armored Div patch on left shoulder and Cpl chevrons. Above avg. cond. $21

Shirt, EM, USA, Army, WWII. Size 34R in dark OD HBT. With metal star buttons, gas flap, deep billow chest pockets and faint 1943 dated Qm tag. Avg. cond. .. $24

Shirt, EM, Female, USA, WAC, WWII. Dark OD HBT with size "S" tag, 1943 dated Qm tag, patch chest pockets, gas flap and OD plastic buttons. Name and service number stamped. Pleats on lower front have been unstitched. Above avg. cond. $25

Shirt, Fatigue, Camo, USA, Army, Vietnam Era. Dark pattern tiger stripe camo on ripstop. With US-style OD buttons and small patch-type chest pockets with button flaps. Sleeves neatly finished, traces of neatly removed lower pockets. Size "S" tag. Avg. cond. $20

Shirt, Fatigue, Camo, USA, Army, WWII. Reversible from green to tan spot pattern HBT with concealed button front, button cuffs, and chest pockets. About size 40. Above avg. cond. $216

Shirt, Fatigue, Camo, USA, Army, Vietnam Era. Medium weight cotton with spot pattern "duck hunter" camo on dark tan background. Black finish metal star buttons, lower patch pockets with single exposed button closure flaps, button front and straight cuffs. Medium size. Above avg. cond. $34

Shirt, Fatigue, Denim, USA, Navy, 1930s. Dark blue denim body with fold-over collar, lower patch pockets, straight cuffs, and removable metal NAVY 13 line buttons. Name label stitched into neck. About size 36. Avg. cond.
. . . . $50

Shirt, Fatigue, Denim, USA, Army, 1930s. Dark blue denim with US Army marked zinc buttons front, lower patch pockets with button closure flaps and straight cuffs. About size 36-38. Above avg. cond. $217

Shirt, Fatigue, Denim, USA, Army, 1930s. Dark blue denim body with US Army marked zinc metal buttons, lower patch pockets with button closure flaps and straight cuffs. About size 38. Avg. cond. $165

Shirt, Fatigue, EM, USA, Army, Korean War. OD HBT with metal star buttons and patch-type chest pockets. Size 38. Name inked above left chest pocket. Good cond. . . .
. . . . $20

Shirt, Fatigue, M1941, USA, USMC, WWII. Size 36 in lt OD HBT with three pockets, metal USMC buttons, USMC EG&A stencil on chest pocket and button cuffs. 1944 dated USMC Qm markings in neck. Above avg. cond. $100

Shirt, Fatigue, M1941, USA, USMC, WWII. Lt OD HBT with three pockets, metal USMC buttons and EG&A stencil on chest pocket. Size 36/38. Above avg. cond. . . $34

Shirt, Fatigue, M1941, USA, USMC, WWII. Lt OD HBT with three pockets and EG&A stencil on chest pocket. Has OD plastic button front. Size 38. Avg. cond. $32

Shirt, Fatigue, M1941, USA, USMC, WWII. OD HBT with brass USMC buttons and faint EG&A stencil on

chest pocket. Size 38. Collar has stitched repair to underside. Avg. cond. $13

Shirt, Fatigue, M1941, USA, USMC, WWII. Lt OD HBT with three pockets, metal USMC buttons and EG&A stencil on chest pocket. Name and service number inked in white on left chest. Size 36. Avg. cond. $24

Shirt, Fatigue, M1941, USA, USMC, WWII. Lt OD HBT with three pockets, metal USMC buttons and USMC EG&A stencil on chest pocket. Cpl chevron inked on each sleeve. Name direct embr in black thread on left chest pocket. Has EG&A device & USMC neatly stenciled on back. About size 38. Avg. cond. $85

Shirt, Fatigue, M1945, USA, USMC, WWII. Lt OD HBT with large internal pocket on each side of chest, gas flap and black finish metal buttons. Has Platoon Sgt chevron stenciled on each sleeve and EG&A stencil on chest pocket. Name on left chest has been inked out. Size 38. Avg. cond. $50

Shirt, Fatigue, M1945, USA, USMC, WWII. Medium size in lt OD HBT with metal USMC buttons, EG&A stencil on chest pocket and large internal pocket on each side of chest. Avg. cond. $20

Shirt, Fatigue, M1945, USA, USMC, WWII. Lt OD HBT with metal USMC buttons, dark EG&A stencil on chest pocket, large internal pocket on each side of chest and gas flap. Size "L." Lieut's name and service number stenciled on back. Above avg. cond. $51

Shirt, Fatigue, M1945, USA, USMC, WWII. Lt OD HBT with black finish buttons with brass USMC buttons, EG&A stencil on chest pocket, large internal pocket on each side of chest and gas flap. About size 42. Exc. cond.
. . . . $66

Shirt, Service, EM, USA, USMC, WWII. Distinctive mustard tan wool shirt with button front and 1942 dated spec tag. Size 3. Still has paper Qm inspection tag attached. Above avg. cond. $30

Shirt, Service, EM, USA, USMC, WWII. Distinctive "mustard" yellow wool with button front, patch chest pockets with scalloped flaps and button cuffs. Above avg. cond. $49

Shirt, Service, EM, USA, USMC, WWII. Dark tan worsted wool with scalloped pocket flaps, fully embr 3rd Amphibious Corps patch on left shoulder, forest green wool on tan twill Pfc chevrons, discharge patch and one pair 1937 pattern EG&A collar devices. Medium size. Above avg. cond. $40

Shirt, Utility, USA, Army, Vietnam Era. Lightweight OD poplin body with straight cuffs, button front, patch chest pockets with single exposed button flaps. Name inked on chest. Size 14½ x 33. Above avg. cond. $30

Shirt, Utility, USA, Army, Vietnam Era. Lightweight OD cotton shirt with A-L ink stamp. Button front with patch-type chest pockets and single exposed button flaps. Has woven nylon US Army subdued pocket tape and subdued Nam machine embr on OD nylon name tape. Above avg. cond. $28

Shirt, Utility, USA, USAF, Vietnam Era. 15½ x 33 in OG sateen with "Tech Rep" direct hand embr in white into each side of collar, hand embr in white on USAF shade blue twill "UNIVAC" and name pocket tapes. Sleeves neatly finished short. Avg. cond. $20

Shirt, Utility, USA, Army, Vietnam Era. Dark OG sateen with lt olive stitching, button front, patch chest pockets with single exposed button flaps and straight cuffs. Brown plastic buttons. Size 38. Avg. cond. $20

Shirt, Utility, Camo, USA, USMC, WWII. Reversible green to tan spot pattern HBT. Metal USMC buttons and large internal chest pockets. Back stenciled with soldier's name and unit designation (311 in half-circle). Size 38/40. Above avg. cond. $265

Shirt, Utility, Female, USA, USMC, WWII. Lt OD HBT with three pockets, metal USMC buttons and EG&A stencil on chest pocket. Size 36/38. Avg. cond. $25

Shirts—Germany

Shirt, Drill, EM, Naval, Germany, Navy, WWII. White HBT shirt. With slash pocket front and tie-string. Issue stamp to flap. Avg. cond. $55

Shirt, Drill, EM, Naval, Germany, Navy, WWII. Reed-green HBT shirt. Pullover with patch pocket front. Short collar. Slash cuffs. Lacks tie-strings at front slash. Avg. cond. $120

Shirt, EM, Naval, Germany, Navy, 1935. Heavy white body with slash pocket front and tie-strings at neck slash. 1935 dated. Above avg. cond. $50

Shirt, EM, Naval, Germany, Navy, WWII. White. One slash-style pocket. Tie-string front. Inked underside of flap "BAK 18.4.28 2" and red stitched numbers. Owner's tag removed. Avg. cond. $40

Shirt, EM, Naval, Germany, Navy, WWII, Schaffer & Vogel. White pullover body with blue cuffs and collar. Bevo blue eagle is zigzag sewn on. Inked maker "Schaffer & Vogel etc." Exc. cond. $250

Shirt, EM, Naval, Germany, Navy, 1943. White HBT body with slash pocket, tie-string and inked "BAW 1.1.43 etc." Exc. cond. $55

Shirt, Fatigue, EM, Naval, Imperial Germany, Navy, WWI. Heavy white cotton body, slash patch pocket, slash cuffs and flap on collar. Pullover style with slash having tie-string. Flap underside inked "BAW 4.11.03 3" and owner tag. Avg. cond. $45

Shirt, Naval, Germany, Navy, 1938. White. 1938 inked issue date and bevo owner tag. Blue embr eagle on white and gold metal star attached to sleeve. Above avg. cond. $221

Shirt, NSDAP, Germany, NSDAP, 1930s. "Brown " shirt of a Ortsgruppe Block Leader. Tan twill cotton body, blue cord piping on collar showing tan wool tabs with swastika tape stripes and blue cord piping. Two pleated patch pockets, six pebbled brass belt ramps with "RZM," three gold eagle buttons and oilcloth tag "RZM PO Diensthemd etc." Avg. cond. $239

Shirt, NSDAP, Germany, NSDAP, 1930s. "Brown" shirt of a Ortsgruppe Mitarbeiter. Tan twill cotton body with three removable nickel/eagle button front. Two pleated patch pockets. Four gold pebbled belt ramps. Bevo size tag "52." Blue cord piping to collar. Tan wool tabs with blue cord piping and dark silver-gold tape stripe. Machine-sewn-on tabs. Above avg. cond. $225

Shirt, NSDAP, With Breeches, Germany, NSDAP, 1930s. "Brown" shirt with breeches. Lt brown gabardine body, three gold eagle buttons and two eagle button lower closure. Partial satin lining with oilcloth RZM tag. Brown cotton collar liner. Inked inside "48 38 62" and maker/party marks to material. Twill wool breeches with oilcloth RZM tag "Stiefelhose W etc." and inked "48." Exc. cond. $795

Shirt, SA, Germany, SA, WWII. "Brown Shirt." Two pleated patch pockets. Three pebbled nickel button front and six gray pebbled belt ramps with "RZM M5/276." Composite cotton armband. Pink wool tabs have white cord piping. Inked neck "50 40." Above avg. cond. $405

Shirt, Sport, Germany, Army, WWII. White tank top with two faded black stripes around neck. Black bevo eagle on front, bevo with owner name at neck. Avg. cond. . . . $25

Shirt, Sport, Germany, SS, WWII. White tank top body with 4" diam b&w runes disc on front. Inked maker marks on lower edge. Exc. cond. $244

Shirt, Sport, Germany, Luftwaffe, WWII. White cotton tank top with large black bevo eagle machine sewn on. Avg. cond. $69

Shirt, Sport, Germany, Luftwaffe, WWII. White cotton tank top with large black bevo eagle machine sewn-on. Smaller size shirt. Avg. cond. $55

Shirt, Sport, Germany, Luftwaffe, WWII. White cotton tank top with small bevo eagle. Inked maker and size II. Above avg. cond. $75

Shirt, Tropical, Germany, Luftwaffe, WWII. Pullover style with tan cotton body, four-button slash and two pleated patch pockets. Gray embr eagle on tan triangle. Loops and buttons for shoulder straps. Avg. cond. $386

Shirt, Tropical, EM, Naval, Imperial Germany, Navy, 1906. White pullover style with blue cuffs and attached dickie. Issue marked "BAK 30.11.06.3." Tie-string front. Above avg. cond. $75

Shirts—Other

Shirt, Athletic, Fascist, Italy, WWII. White cotton sleeveless with fascist insignias. Above avg. cond. $175

Shirt, Medical Officer, Greece, Army, WWII. Tan cotton twill shirt with two flapped pockets. Collar insignia of hand-embr red cross on white wool field, Lieut rank slides and maroon velvet trim shoulder straps, and cloth-embr Caduceus sleeve insignia. Above avg. cond. $100

Shirt, Service, North Vietnam, Army, 1960s. Khaki cotton, small left chest pocket and long right unflapped pocket. Above avg. cond. $104

Shirt, Tropical, Woman's, England, Army, Post-WWII. Desert tan cotton twill shirt with two flapped pockets, khaki composition buttons and Greek/English interior ink stamp. Above avg. cond. $60

Shirt, Tropical, Woman's, England, Army, WWII. Tan cotton twill shirt with two flapped pockets and khaki finished metal buttons. Above avg. cond. $60

Shoes—U.S.

Shoes, Athletic, USA, Army, WWII. Lt OD canvas high-ankle-top canvas bodies with molded rubber soles and lace insteps. Converse brand. Size 8. Avg. cond. $20

Shoes, Athletic, USA, Army, WWII. OD canvas ankle-high with molded black rubber soles and lace insteps. Size 12. Above avg. cond. $45

Shoes, Jungle, USA, Army, WWII. Ankle-high style. Dark OD canvas with lace insteps and molded black rubber soles. Size 9½. Faint Qm markings. Above avg. cond. $80

Shoes, Service, USA, Army, WWII. Ankle-high in dark brown smooth leather with lace insteps and cap toes. About size 9. Above avg. cond. $50

Shoes, Service, USA, USMC, WWII. Dark tan roughout

leather with corded rubber soles and lace fronts. 1944 dated contract markings. Size 7D. Above avg. cond.　$98

Shoes, Service, USA, Army, WWII. Ankle-high dark brown leather with cap toes, lace fronts, composite soles. Size 9D. Avg. cond. $62

Shoes, Service, USA, Army, WWII. Smooth russet brown leather with cap toes, lace fronts, faint 1942 dated Qm markings and composite leather and rubber soles. Size 8C. Exc. cond. $187

Shoes, Service, USA, USMC, WWII. Roughout brown leather with lace insteps and corded rubber soles. Dated 1945 and USMC inspector marked. Size 14E. Exc. cond. . . . $85

Shoes, Service, USA, USMC, WWII. Roughout dark tan leather ankle-high bodies with corded rubber soles and lace fronts (no laces). USMC marked. Size 12½D. Well marked. Above avg. cond. $59

Shoes, Service, USA, Army, WWII. Ankle-high in dark brown leather with cap toes and lace fronts. Heels have steel taps. About size 9. Avg. cond. $100

Shoes, Service, Low-quarter, Officer, USA, Army, WWII. Size 7½D in smooth russet brown leather with lace insteps, leather soles and rubber heels. Well marked. Exc. cond. $103

Shoes, Service, Low-quarter, Officer, USA, Army, WWII. Size 6A in russet brown leather with lace insteps, 1945 dated Qm markings, leather soles and rubber heels. Above avg. cond. $35

Shoes, Service, Low-quarter, Officer, USA, Army, WWII. Smooth brown leather bodies with lace insteps, leather soles and rubber heels. Qm inspector marked. About size 9½. Above avg. cond. $53

Shoes, Service, Low-quarter, Officer, USA, Army, WWII. Size 8½B in russet brown leather with lace insteps, leather and neoprene soles. Well marked. Above avg. cond. $48

Shoes, Service, M1904, USA, Army, Early 1900s. Smooth brown leather ankle-high bodies with lace insteps, cap toes and leather soles. Size 7E. Contract markings. Avg. cond. $318

Shoes—Germany

Leggings, Germany, Army, 1937. Black leather. 12½" tall formed bodies with hook and buckle strap closure. Issue stamped "B.A.Fu.737." and inked "H33 W43 rechts 1937 etc." Exc. cond. $133

Puttees, Imperial Germany, Army, WWI. 3"-wide gray woven bodies are rolled and have closure strap with metal fitting. Inked tag "Gerfreiter Mockel 16.Kp.8.(Pr.)Inf.-Rgt." Exc. cond. $160

Shoes, Dress, Officer, Germany, Army, WWII. 5½" tall slip-on shoes with black elastic sides. Leather soles and heels. Mismatched spring steel stiffener and wooden style. Avg. cond. $129

Trousers—U.S.

Trousers, Cold Weather, USA, Navy, WWII. Bib front. Dark blue ribbed cotton with dark blue wool lining, built-in suspenders and woven contract label. Medium size. Above avg. cond. $11

Trousers, Cold Weather, USA, Navy, WWII. Dark blue ribbed cotton body with metal latch closure "bib" front, suspenders, navy blue wool lining and printed naval contract label. US Navy marked across front. Above avg. cond. $65

Trousers, Dress, Officer, 1937 Pattern, USA, Army, 1937. Tailor made in navy blue melton wool with button fly. Gold wire stripe down each leg with ribbed red insert. Named and dated 1937. Exc. cond. $49

Trousers, EM, USA, USMC, WWII. Size 6S in forest green wool. Well marked. Named. Above avg. cond. $45

Trousers, Fatigue, Camo, USA, Army, WWII. Reversible from green to tan spot pattern HBT. With OD plastic button fly and large cargo pocket on each thigh. Washed out Qm label. Medium waist size. Exc. cond. $250

Trousers, Fatigue, Camo, USA, Army, Vietnam War Era. Medium weight cotton with spot "duck hunter" pattern camo on lt olive background. Conventional cut with zip fly and metal star buttons. Size 30/32. Avg. cond. $23

Trousers, Fatigue, Camo, USA, Army, Vietnam War Era. Dark pattern tiger stripe camo on loose-weave medium-weight cotton with zipper fly and conventional cut pockets. Size 42 waist. Avg. cond. $59

Trousers, Fatigue, Camo, USA, Army, 1969. Size regular/medium. ERDL pattern camo ripstop. 1969 dated. More brown shades in camo. Avg. cond. $42

Trousers, Fatigue, Camo, USA, Army, Vietnam War Era. Heavyweight tiger stripe cotton camo with zipper fly, button waistband, slash-concealed front pockets, billow rear pockets and lower billow pocket on each thigh with twin exposed button-closure flaps, small pocket below on left leg. Size "S." Near mint cond. $237

Trousers, Fatigue, Camo, USA, Army, Vietnam War. ERDL pattern camo on poplin. Size large/regular. Above avg. cond. $101

Trousers, Fatigue, Camo, USA, Army, 1943. Reversible from green to tan spot pattern camo HBT. 1943 dated Qm label, OD plastic button fly and large cargo pocket on each thigh. Size 32 x 33. Still has paper inspector tags attached. Exc. cond. $160

Trousers, Fatigue, HBT, USA, Army, WWII. Size 34x32 in dark OD HBT with OD plastic button fly and 1944 dated Qm label. Exc. cond. $66

Trousers, Fatigue, HBT, USA, Army, WWII. Lt OD HBT with metal star button fly and conventional cut pockets with concealed rear pockets. Size 40x31. Above avg. cond. $45

Trousers, Fatigue, HBT, USA, Army, WWII. Dark OD HBT with metal star buttons and large billow cargo pocket on each thigh. About size 30 waist. Above avg. cond. $51

Trousers, Fatigue, HBT, Female, USA, WAC, 1943. Size XL. Dark OD HBT with button fly and two button flap hip pockets. 1943 dated Qm label. Near mint cond. $51

Trousers, Field, USA, USMC, WWII. 1944 pattern. Lt OD HBT with metal USMC buttons, large billow cargo pocket on each hip and a large pocket across rear. Size 30. Name marked on inside waist. Above avg. cond. . . $282

Trousers, Field, Camo, USA, USMC, WWII. 1943 pattern. Reversible from green to tan spot pattern camo HBT with USMC button fly and snap closure side-entry pockets. Medium waist size. Above avg. cond. $229

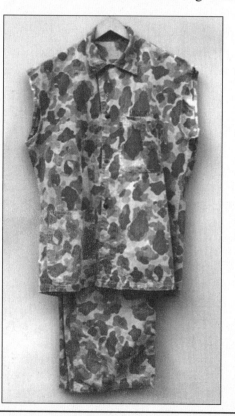

**USMC Camo
Field Trousers
with Shirt**

Trousers, Field, Female, M1943, USA, WAC, 1943. Clean OD cotton body with 1943 dated Qm label and web insteps. Size 18R. Above avg. cond. $76

Trousers, Field, Female, M1943, USA, WAC, 1944. Size 18R. Dark OD cotton with button fly, elastic insteps and 1944 dated Qm label. Name inked on waistband. Avg. cond. $21

Trousers, Field, M1941, USA, USMC, WWII. Lt OD HBT with conventional cut pockets and metal USMC buttons. Lieut's name stenciled on inside waistband. Size 30 waist. Above avg. cond. $145

Trousers, Field, M1941, USA, USMC, WWII. Lt OD HBT with metal USMC buttons and conventional cut pockets. Size 34 waist. Above avg. cond. $145

Trousers, Field, M1941, USA, USMC, WWII. Lt OD HBT with metal USMC button fly. Conventional cut. Size 34. Faint contract markings. Above avg. cond. $135

Trousers, Field, M1943, USA, Army, 1944. Size 34x32 in dark OD cotton with button fly and 1944 dated Qm label. Above avg. cond. $61

Trousers, Field, M1943, USA, Army, WWII. 42x32 in dark OD cotton with faint Qm label. Avg. cond. . . . $34

Trousers, Field, M1943, USA, Army, WWII. Size 46x32 in dark OD cotton with button fly and 1945 dated Qm label. Above avg. cond. $55

Trousers, Field, M1943, USA, Army, WWII. Size 46x32 in dark OD cotton with 1945 dated Qm label, printed markings and two paper Qm inspector tags still attached. Above avg. cond. $41

Trousers, Field, M1943, USA, Army, WWII. Size 34x32 in dark OD cotton with undated Qm label and paper Qm inspector tags still attached. Exc. cond. $66

Trousers, Field, M1943, USA, Army, 1944. Size 34x30 in dark OD cotton with button fly and 1944 dated Qm label. Above avg. cond. $59

Trousers, Field, M1951, USA, Army, 1952. Regular/large in dark OD cotton with 1952 dated Qm markings. Avg. cond. $20

Trousers, Field, Wool, USA, Army, 1945. Size 32x31 in OD wool serge with button fly and 1945 dated Qm label. Avg. cond. $19

Trousers, Field, Wool, USA, Army, 1941. Size 32x33. Lt OD wool serge. 1941 dated Qm label. Avg. cond. . . $27

Trousers, Field, Wool, USA, Army, WWII. Size 32x31 in OD wool serge with 1944 dated Qm label. Avg. cond. $19

Trousers, Field, Wool, USA, Army, 1943. Size 38x33 in lt OD wool serge. 1943 dated Qm label. Above avg. cond. $32

Trousers, Field, Wool, USA, Army, 1944. Light OD wool serge. Size 31x33. 1944 dated QM tag. Above avg. cond. $30

Trousers, Parachute Jumper, M1942, USA, Army, Airborne, WWII. Lt OD cotton twill with large pleated cargo pocket on each thigh, gray metal snap closure flaps and button fly. Washed out Qm label. About size 32. Above avg. cond. $594

Trousers, Parachute Jumper, M1942, USA, Army, Airborne, WWII. Light OD cotton. Size 30x30. Owner's name and laundry number stenciled in waistband. Original heavy OD canvas reinforced panels on knees and in the sides of pockets. Avg. cond. $1075

Trousers, Service, Officer, USA, Army, WWII. Private purchase in "pink" gabardine. About size 44. Avg. cond. . . $30

Trousers, Service, Officer, USA, Army, 1944. Dark OD gabardine with 1944 dated Qm label. Size 30. Avg. cond. $36

Trousers, Service, Officer, USA, Army, WWII. Private purchase in "pink" gabardine. Zip fly and button waistband. About size 30. Above avg. cond. $40

Trousers, Service, Tanker, USA, Army, Armored, WWII. Lt OD cotton twill with "bib" front, OD wool lining and built-in suspenders. Avg. cond. $22

Trousers, Tropical Combat, 1st Pattern, USA, Army, Vietnam Era. Size x-small/regular. In OG poplin. All tags intact. Near mint cond. $177

Trousers, Tropical Combat, 2nd Pattern, USA, Army, Vietnam Era. In OG poplin. Drawstrings in cuffs intact. Size L. Avg. cond. $48

Trousers, Tropical Combat, 2nd Pattern, USA, Army, Vietnam Era. Size large/long. OG poplin. All labels intact. Drawstrings at cuffs. Above avg. cond. $64

Trousers, Winter Service, EM, USA, Navy, WWII. In dark blue ribbon cotton with navy blue wool lining, attached suspenders, and metal latch closure "bib" front. USN marked. Woven contract label. Size medium. Above avg. cond. $40

Trousers—Germany

Coveralls, Germany, Army, 1940. Gray cloth body. Dated 1940. Exc. cond. $235

Coveralls, Winter, Germany, Luftwaffe, 1943. Black leather. Pliable body with bevo maker tag "Leder-Kuhne

Dresden etc." and owner's name. Inked 1943 date and size 3. "Zipp" alum zipper front. Avg. cond. $300

Shorts, Tropical, Imperial Germany, Army, WWI. 1915 unit marked. Gray canvas. Patch-style small front and two slash side pockets. Five gray metal button fly and suspender buttons. Adjustment belt across back. Inked "1915 F.A.14." Summer and tropical use. Above avg. cond. $95

Trousers, Camo, Germany, Waffen SS, WWII. Reinforced seat, three slash pockets, watch patch pocket, six-button fly, side adjustment belts and belt loops. Tan pocket lining and style of HBT with "peas-44" camo design on off-white side. Avg. cond. $850

Trousers, Dress, Imperial Germany, Army, WWI. Black wool with yellow piping. 14th Inf Regt unit marked. Front slash pockets. Avg. cond. $116

Trousers, Drill, Germany, Army, WWII. Reed-green HBT. Straight-leg style, three slash pockets and watch slash with paper button. Six buttons on fly, suspender buttons and side adjustment belts. Avg. cond. $355

Trousers, Drill, EM, Germany, Navy, WWII. White HBT. Flap front, gray buttons and tie-string back. Avg. cond. $80

Trousers, Fatigue, EM, Imperial Germany, Army, WWI. White. Still has paper maker/size label sewn to front. Four gray metal buttons on fly and for suspenders. Inked size, date and "5.G.B." Avg. cond. $48

Trousers, Fatigue, EM, Imperial Germany, Army, 1915. White. Four gray metal button fly. Patch-style watch pocket. Unit marked "BAX 1915. 73." Avg. cond. $145

Trousers, Fatigue, EM, Imperial Germany, Army, WWI. White body with four gray metal button fly. Patch watch pocket. High tapered back. Faint inked "Arbeits Zentrale Darmstadt." Avg. cond. $65

Trousers, Foul-weather, Germany, Navy, WWII. Black leather. Cloth lining. Three metal button fly with hook. Suspender buttons marked "Solide Neuheit." Tall back with leather adjustment straps. Exc. cond. $203

Trousers, Foul-weather, Germany, Navy, WWII. Black leather. Large stamped Eagle M on front. Two slash pockets, four-button fly and full gray cloth lining. Above avg. cond. $100

Trousers, Service, EM, Germany, Navy, WWII. White. Bell-bottom style. Flap front, stamped metal buttons and tie-string back. Owner's name marked. Above avg. cond. $66

Trousers, Straight Leg, Germany, Army, Cav, WWII. Gray twill wool bodies with golden yellow wool piping.

Slash pockets with one rear pocket. Side adjustment belts and suspender buttons. Exc. cond. $200

Trousers, Straight Leg, Germany, Navy, WWII. Dark blue wool. Straight leg with flap front. Side adjustment belts and inked marks inside. Avg. cond. $150

Trousers, Straight Leg, Germany, Luftwaffe, WWII. Blue gray twill straight-leg style. Avg. cond. $205

Trousers, Straight Leg, Germany, Army, Panzer, 1942. Black wool. Three slash pockets and watch slash. Five-button fly, suspender buttons, back adjustment belt, and straight-leg style. Dated 1942 and maker marked inside. Exc. cond. $276

Trousers, Straight Leg, Germany, Luftwaffe, WWII. Yellow wool piping on twill wool straight-leg body. Three slash pockets, watch slash, back adjustment belt and four-button fly with hook. Above avg. cond. $185

Trousers, Straight Leg, Germany, Army, Arty, WWII. Dark gray twill wool straight-leg body with wool piped sides. Standard fittings to rest. Above avg. cond. . . $187

Trousers, Straight Leg, Germany, Army, WWII. Dark gray twill wool straight-leg body with carmine wool piped sides. Standard fittings to rest. Exc. cond. $128

Trousers, Straight Leg, Germany, Army, WWII. Straight-legged twill wool bodies, dark green cord piping, four slash pockets and watch slash. Back adjustment belt and suspender buttons. Avg. cond. $135

Trousers, Straight Leg, Germany, SS, WWII. Black twill wool design with light brown wool piping on straight leg. Three-button fly with hook. Three slash pockets and watch pocket. Adjustment belts at sides, belt loops and suspender fittings. Black leather stirrup buttoned to each cuff. Exc. cond. $198

Trousers, Straight Leg, Camo, Germany, Army, WWII. Gray reversible to white. Heavy cotton quilted body. Two slash pockets, four-button fly, suspender straps and inked RB-NR. Avg. cond. $180

Trousers, Straight Leg, Camo, Germany, Army, WWII. Field-made splinter-pattern camo. Made from shelter quarter with light and dark sides. Dark side out with belt loops and three-button fly. Stamped steel buttons from quarter for fly and suspender use. Two slash pockets and right hip patch pocket is 2½" x 7½" size. Exc. cond. $325

Trousers, Straight Leg, Drill, Germany, Army, WWII. Reed-green HBT straight-leg style. Three slash pockets and watch slash with paper buttons. Six stamped steel buttons to fly, suspender buttons and side adjustment belts. Avg. cond. $285

Trousers, Straight Leg, EM, Germany, Army, WWII. Gray wool straight leg body. Three slash pockets with black resin buttons, watch slash, back adjustment belt, five-button fly and stamped metal suspender buttons. Marked "Hannover H41 76 86 109 100." Exc. cond. $643

Trousers, Straight Leg, EM, Germany, Navy, WWII. White body with flap front, gray metal buttons and adjustment side belts. Exc. cond. $65

Trousers, Straight Leg, General, Germany, Army, WWII. Gray twill wool straight leg bodies with red doeskin sides. Three slash pockets and watch pocket. Six-button fly, side adjustment belts and suspender fittings. Above avg. cond. $650

Trousers, Straight Leg, General Staff, Germany, Army, WWII. Gray twill wool straight leg bodies. Carmine wool piped seam and 1⅜" wide stripes on both sides. Three slash pockets with button flap back. Adjustment side belts, four-button fly with hook and gray satin waist trim. Watch slash pocket. Unmarked. Exc. cond. $563

Trousers, Straight Leg, Tropical, Germany, Luftwaffe, WWII. Tan twill body with built-in waistbelt, cuff belts, six-button fly, patch left leg pocket and four pockets. Inked size. Above avg. cond. $299

Trousers—Other

Sniper Suit, Camo, Soviet Union, Army, 1980s. Two-piece mesh camo, green and tan pattern, elastic to waist and cuffs of pants and button closure to top with hood. Spec tag sewn inside top. Near mint cond. $40

Trousers, Combat, Japan, Army, WWII. OG, side pockets, lined with thick light green cotton. For cold weather wear. Unissued. Near mint cond. $125

Trousers, Flight, Japan, Air Force, WWII. Brown twill, side zipper pockets, webbed belt and leg zippers. Exc. cond. $165

Trousers, Service, Soviet Union, Army, 1985. Khaki wool with side pockets. Exc. cond. $22

Trousers, Service, Camo, South Vietnam, Army, c1967. Cotton twill tiger stripe pattern camo trousers with cargo and front slash pockets. Exc. cond. $175

Trousers, Service, Officer, Soviet Union, Army, 1986. Khaki wool, red side piping and pockets. Exc. cond. $26

Trousers, Tropical, Female, England, Army, WWII. Trousers with leg pocket, cuff straps, and internal webbed waistband belt. Above avg. cond. $100

Trousers, Underwear, England, Army, WWII. Army-issue white cotton twill undertrousers complete with com-position buttons and rear adjustment ties. Above avg. cond. $70

Uniforms—U.S.

Uniform, Aero Service, EM, USA, Army, Aero Service, WWI. 1917 pattern OD wool blouse with dark tan cotton lining, multi-piece felt Advance Sector patch on left shoulder, silk machine embr on dark blue felt (faded to almost purple) 482 Aero Sqdn patch on rt shoulder, Cpl/Air Service chevron on rt sleeve, discharge stripe and two bullion o/s stripes. Includes pair lt OD wool serge breeches with zinc US Army button fly and lace calves. Above avg. cond. $105

Uniforms—Germany

Uniform, Border Guard, NCO, West Germany, Army, c1960s. Tunic and greatcoat. Tunic of green wool with four flapped pockets, dark green wool collar with silver litzen, NCO rank shoulderboards, West German sleeve eagle with gray embroidery on field gray wool field and gray satin interior lining. Greatcoat of field gray wool with double-breasted front, matching NCO buttons, dark green wool collar and gray cotton lining. Above avg. cond. . . . $100

Uniform, Dress, NCO, Germany, Army, Grenadier, WWII. Parade dress tunic with gray twill wool body, green collar and cuffs, eight-button front, lt green wool piping, alum tape stripes and tape tabs on green wool. Alum bullion eagle 2nd pattern shooting lanyard with three acorns, 1939 black wound badge of stamped brass, sewn-in straps with two pips each, and EK and KVK ribbons at buttonhole. Wool straight-leg trousers with piping. Brocade belt with alum buckle having prongs to loop. Avg. cond. $1755

Uniform, Parade Dress, NCO, Germany, Army, Arty, WWII. Gray twill wool body tunic with green collar, red wool piped collar, front, cuffs and back. Eight-button front. Alum tape tabs on red wool cuff and collar tabs. Alum NCO tape on cuffs and collar. Officer bullion eagle. Sewn-in straps with gray "XVII" and pip on each. Full lining with slash pocket and removed labels. Different shade gray twill wool straight-leg trousers with red wool piping. Early marksmanship lanyard with alum eagle shield. Avg. cond. $440

Uniform, SA, Germany, SA, 1930s. Includes wool pants, cotton shirt and brown leather cross-strap. Brown twill tunic with two pleated patch upper pockets, two patch lower, French cuffs and four pebbled alum button front. Wool composite armband. Loops for one badge. Machine-sewn-on orange wool tabs with black chain stitched "I/122" and other with silver pip with black-orange tape stripe. Black and orange twisted piping. Orange wool base to sewn-in strap with black and orange cord body. Gold satin lining with pocket. Pullover brown cotton shirt with cuff links and button on collar. Inked "SA 50/2 37." Matching wool breeches. Dark brown leather cross-strap nickel RZM clips. Exc. cond. $1063

Uniform, Service, Germany, Army, WWII. For OKW hauptmann. Gray twill body tunic with two pleated patch upper pockets, two slash lower, eight-button front and green collar. "Krim 1941/1942" sleeve shield, alum eagle, gold celleon sawtooth litzen on green collar tabs and sewn-on bright alum boards on crimson bases with two pips. Full satin lining with bevo maker label at neck and oilcloth "Wilh.Hoffmann, Glogau etc." tag on pocket with inked "Herrn Seidel 16.12.36." Different shade gray twill wool breeches with crimson piping and fittings intact. Avg. cond. $1450

Uniform, Service, EM, Naval, Imperial Germany, Navy, WWI. Each article of clothing has cloth tag with owner's name. Dark blue cap has Kiel issue stamp with Nov. 5, 1914 date and silver bevo tally, "SMS Bremen." Tunic has silver buttons, yellow rank chevron and May 10, 1907 date with Kiel issue marks. Wool pants named to sailor with June 1, 1910 date and Wilhelmshaven issue marks. Chain closure still present. Above avg. cond. $555

Uniform, Service, Officer, Germany, Waffen SS, WWII. Service tunic with gray wool body, green collar, four pleated patch pockets and six-button front. Loops for three badges, ribbon bar and 1939 EK/Russian Front ribbons at button hole. Machine-embr alum "Deutschland" cuff title, hand-embr bullion eagle, sewn-in boards and machine-sewn-on SS runes and rank tabs. Full green satin lining, dagger clip, white collar liner "Uniform 4-39" and early alum plaited adjutant aiguillette with tips. Matching wool breeches with slash cuffs having four buttons, 19"-tall black leather boots with wood forms. Above avg. cond. . $2855

Uniform, Tropical Service, Imperial Germany, Army, WWI. Blue piped for southwest Africa colonial service. Tan corduroy cloth tunic with two upper scalloped pockets and two lower pockets. Frosted silver crown colonial buttons with hallmarks. Red-white-black cord shoulder straps of Lieut Aide-de-camp Fouraguerre in white cord with red-black flecking. Full liner. Loops on both breasts for medals and badges. Matching straight-legged breeches with proper blue cord piping. Rt sleeve has cloth colonial shield in white with black bars, red canton and white stars. Above avg. cond. $700

Uniforms—Other

Uniform, Combat, Soviet Union, Army, 1980s. Jacket and trouser of olive color canvas, plastic buttons and no insignia. Small size. Above avg. cond. $40

Uniform, Combat, Camo, Russia, Army, 1980s. Camo pants and shirt OG with gray computer camo pattern. Hooded top with matching pants. Complete with drawstring. Above avg. cond. $32

Uniform, Dress, Hussar, England, Army, Hussar, WWI. Five pieces. First a busby with wicker frame and black fur exterior, white wool bag with yellow piping, yellow worsted wool front cockade, yellow worsted wool cap lines and white horsehair plume with gilded base. Busby complete with chinstrap, liner, and interior trade card to "Peter Tait & Co," of "Limerick." Dark blue wool tunic with yellow worsted wool breast frogging, domed matching yellow worsted wool buttons, narrow yellow shoulder straps, white collar with yellow worsted wool collar trim, lapel, and rear piping, cuffs in yellow worsted wool frogging, with brass ball buttons, and buff twill lining. Dark blue wool breeches with white wool side stripes, leather undershoe straps, and watch pocket. Black leather boots with soles and heels with horseshoe plates and 1911 maker's stamp. Ensemble completed with pair of white chamois leather gauntlets with white lacquered cuffs. From 13th Hussars. Above avg. cond. $1305

Uniform, Dress, Officer, Naval, Spain, Navy, Spanish American War. Blue wool coatee with double-breasted front, Lieut rank insignia on cuffs and red silk lining. Matching blue wool trousers with leg stripes. Above avg. cond. $400

Uniform, Field, Camo, Soviet Union, Army, 1981. "Computer" camo pattern. Includes cotton hooded shirt and trousers. Shirt has foliage camo loops. Exc. cond. ... $62

Uniform, Field, EM, Greece, Army, c1912–13. Includes tunic, breeches, and folding side cap. Tan cotton twill tunic with four flapped pockets, brass buttons, red buttons, red cotton twill collar tabs mounted by brass flaming grenade insignias, shoulder straps, and tan cotton twill interior lining. Breast mounted by two award ribbons. Tan cotton twill breeches with side pockets, rear pocket, and tan composition buttons. Complete with folding side cap of khaki cotton twill with brass Greek crown front insignia and national cockade in blue lacquered finish. Also includes cotton suspenders with brown leather fittings and rail buckles. Above avg. cond. $400

Uniform, Field, Officer, Soviet Union, Army, 1980s. Khaki cotton twill tunic with Lieut shoulderboards and khaki satin lining. Matching trousers. Cap with hammer and sickle insignia on visor. Above avg. cond. $93

Uniform, Field, Officer, Soviet Union, Army, 1980s. Khaki cotton twill visor cap, tunic and trousers. Tunic with major rank shoulder straps. Afghan War era. Exc. cond. $89

Uniform, Parade Dress, EM, Soviet Union, Army, 1985. For a signal troops private. Khaki wool tunic and trousers with green satin lining. Includes khaki cotton necktie. Above avg. cond. $51

Uniform, Service, EM, Italy, Army, Antiaircraft, WWII. Field gray wool felt hat with insignia of gilded crossed winged cannons. Tunic of field gray wool with pockets and lined in field gray twill. Above avg. cond. $500

Uniform, Service, EM, Naval, Soviet Union, Navy, c1980. Pullover jumper, trousers and neck havelock. Dark blue twill. Exc. cond. $45

Uniform, Service, Officer, Soviet Union, Army, Armored, 1974. Black cotton jacket with 2nd lieut rank. Black cotton trousers with waistbelt with brass rail buckle and cargo pockets. Above avg. cond. $71

Uniform, Service, Officer, Soviet Union, Army, c1985. Khaki wool tunic with seven-medal ribbon bar and khaki silk lining. Matching trousers with red side piping. Khaki cotton shirt and necktie. For Army major. Exc. cond. $136

Uniform, Service, Officer, Greece, Air Force, WWII. Blue-gray wool twill visor cap with black mohair band, hand embr gold bullion wreath and crown with blue wool cockade surmounted by brass eagle motif, crown embr gold bullion oak leaves and leather sweatband. Tunic of blue-gray wool with four flapped pockets, brass eagle and crown buttons, Greek captain rank cuff insignia, hand embr 13th Bomb Group sleeve insignia, breast with white embr eagle and crown winged badge, and seven-award ribbon bar. Tunic complete with brass rail buckle waistbelt, black interior lining and cotton twill tailor's label. Above avg. cond. $495

Uniform, Service, Officer, Hungary, Army, Arty, WWII. Brown khaki wool tunic with four flapped and scalloped pockets, gilded crown buttons, red collar tabs with gold bullion boarder piping, hand-embr gold bullion silver star showing captain rank, gold bullion shoulderboards with three small gilded crowns on cuffs, and khaki quilted cotton interior lining with Budapest tailor's label. Khaki brown twill wool riding breeches with side pockets, watch pocket, rear pocket, and interior calf leg saddling. Above avg. cond. $552

Uniform, Tropical, General Officer, Greece, Army, Inf, WWII. Desert tan cotton twill visor hat with red wool band. Tan cotton tunic with pockets and quilted khaki cotton padded lining. Cotton twill necktie included. Above avg. cond. $170

Uniform, Tropical, General Officer, Greece, Army, Inf, WWII. Tan cotton twill tunic with four flapped pockets, brass crown and shield buttons, red wool collar insignia with hand-embr gold bullion oak leaves, shoulder straps with two hand-embr silver bullion stars, gilded crossed baton and sword devices, gilded crown devices, breast with nine-award ribbons, sleeve has three hand-embr gold bullion service chevrons, and khaki satin interior lining. Tan cotton visor hat with red wool band, hand-embr gold bullion crown, silver bullion and blue wool cockade, brown leather chinstrap, blue satin interior lining, and leather sweatband. Above avg. cond. $250

CHAPTER THREE

Helmets and Headgear

Helmets and headgear have long been an extremely popular collecting category. Perhaps it is the large number of surviving examples on the market and their relatively reasonable pricing. Many militaria collectors started with a war surplus US M1 helmet that they purchased for a few dollars.

For centuries, military headgear was dominated by strange sounding types such as Kepis, Shakos, Busbies, Tschapskas, and Chapeaus. These types served many purposes such as unit decoration or distinction and unit identification. In general, however, they provided little protection to the wearer.

Around 1900, the aforementioned dress headgear was falling out of use and being replaced by more utilitarian service caps, bush hats, or campaign hats. Spiked steel or leather dress helmets that were popular in the 1880s and 1890s in several countries, including the U.S. and England, also fell out of favor, except in Germany.

It was World War One that brought the revolutionary change in military headgear. The meatgrinder of the first year of war and the massive quantities of headwounds from shrapnel and bullets resulted in the first requirements for steel combat helmets. The French were the first with their M1915 Adrian pattern helmets. More than three million were distributed to frontline troops between September 1915 and January 1916. The English Mark I or Brodie helmet followed in November 1915. The Germans re-

Prussian Model 1889 Other Ranks Guard Du Corps Cuirassier's Helmet

placed the spiked Pickelhaube with their M1916 steel helmet early in 1916.

World War Two saw a massive explosion in the quantities and types of headgear produced for the combatant countries. As with many of the categories in this book, it is generally the Third Reich examples that bring in the highest prices.

Collecting Tips

Generally try to focus on a type of headgear to collect, such as Combat Helmets or German Combat Helmets. Another approach is to collect examples from one country only, such as American helmets and headgear. Make sure that examples you consider purchasing are complete and have the correct chinstraps, liners, and insignia.

Fakes and Frauds

Frequently helmets will be made complete by the addition of random parts from other helmets. Combat helmets are frequently repainted into more desirable and expensive camo versions. Often decals or other national insignia will be added to plain examples. This is very common for German helmets. The similarity between Third Reich peaked caps and more modern German and Eastern European military and police examples has resulted in some fakes being introduced into the market. Always check for labels and removed insignia.

Berets—U.S.

Beret, USA, USMC, 1960s. English made green wool body with spec label on black cotton lining and black leather sweatband. Size 6½. Has dark bronze 1962 pattern EM visor cap device on front. Avg. cond. $20

Beret, USA, Army/Navy, Vietnam War. American advisor to South Vietnamese Junk Force. Dark blue wool with metal Junk Force emblem attached, black leather band and light blue lining. Hmkd inside with size 53. Above avg. cond. $108

Beret, Camo, USA, Navy Seals, 1970s. In woodland camo ripstop. Lined in black satin. With black vinyl sweatband and adjustable tie. Has full-size gilt Navy Seal badge on front. Above avg. cond. $20

Beret, Cavalry, USA, Army, Air Cavalry, Vietnam Era. Maroon wool body with fully embr flash on front (red-white). Below avg. cond. $20

Beret, Flash, USA, Army, Special Forces, Vietnam War. Vietnamese made. Red and yellow stripes on black field for 5th Spec Forces Grp. Exc. cond. $40

Beret, Flash, USA, Army, Rangers, Vietnam War. For 75th Ranger BN. Vietnam made. 2" x 2¼" size. Applied cotton panel and hand-embr color design on OD ripstop base. Above avg. cond. $55

Beret, Flash, USA, Army, Airborne, WWII. For member 507th Airborne Inf Regt. British-made embr flash with orange rim and black field. Unused. Mint cond. $61

Beret, Green, USA, Army, Special Forces, Vietnam War. Metal track on yellow flash with black trim. Size 7. Above avg. cond. $20

Beret, Green, USA, Army, Special Forces, 1971. Rifle green wool body with black leather sweatband and tie in rear. Black cotton lining with 1971 dated printed markings. Canadian made. Size 7. Exc. cond. $93

Beret, Green, USA, Army, Special Forces, Vietnam War. Rifle green wool. Size 6½. Hmkd Canadian Commercial Corp. Beret flash has black background with diagonal red and yellow stripes. Attached to flash is DI for 46th Special Forces Detachment. Near mint cond. $60

Beret, Green, USA, Army, Special Forces, Vietnam War. Red beret flash on front with enamel and metal special forces badge. Below avg. cond. $75

Beret, Green, USA, Army, Special Forces, 1979. Issue rifle green wool beret with 1979 dated issue markings, black cotton lining and sweatband with adjustable tie in rear. Size 6¾. Front has Special Forces crest over 7th Spe-

cial Forces Grp recognition bar. Some fading. Avg. cond. $20

Beret, Special Forces, USA, Army, c1970s. Issue rifle green wool felt beret with black sweatband with tie in rear, fully embr solid red flash on front with 1st Lieut bar. Lining removed. Size large. Above avg. cond. $35

Berets—Germany

Beret Eagle, SS, Germany, Waffen SS, WWII. For panzer beret. About 4"-wide gray machine-embr eagle on black felt. Avg. cond. $640

Beret Wreath, Army, Panzer, Germany, Army, WWII. Uncut black cloth with bevo wreath and national color cockade center. Near mint cond. $21

Beret Wreath, Army, Panzer, Germany, Army, WWII. Gray bevo wreath and tri-color pip on black. Uncut. Near mint cond. $27

Berets—Other

Beret, Spain, Army, 1960. Khaki wool, cloth eagle insignia and khaki leather trim. Lining of khaki silk with manufacturer's label. Above avg. cond. $20

Beret, Soviet Union, Army, Paratrooper, 1970s. Soviet Army paratrooper beret, blue wool with side vents, metal wreath and red star emblem. Above avg. cond. $20

Beret, EM, Soviet Union, Army, 1985. For enlisted man. Wine red wool, enameled and gilded insignia, oilcloth binding and black cotton lining. Exc. cond. $22

Beret, EM, England, Army, 1945. Khaki cotton twill lining. Exc. cond. $40

Beret, Naval Infantry, EM, Soviet Union, Navy, 1980. Black wool with insignia. Exc. cond. $20

Busbies, Kepis, Shakos and Tschapskas—U.S.

Busby, Militia, USA, Army, Militia, 1880s. Soft sided bearskin helmet. Red bag sewn to top and side with silk piping and 30mm brass button at bottom with Philadelphia hmkd. Red corded/domed cockade on front. Used by state or private militia. No inner liner on bearskin and no marks evident. Below avg. cond. $158

Kepi, 1872 Pattern, USA, Army, 1870s. Navy blue wool body with 5" diam top and long sloping back. Oilcloth trimmed leather bill with leather chinstrap, brass buckle and 1855-style eagle buttons. Hmkd Horstmann inside black cotton bag liner. Has a bronze 1874 pattern 17/Inf/F device pinned on the front. Below avg. cond. $400

Busbies, Kepis, Shakos and Tschapskas—Germany

Busby, EM, Prussian, Imperial Germany, Army, Hussar, WWI. Sealskin busby with complete liner and faint maker marks. Red kolpak with original cord retainers. Silvered frontplate with old b/w field badge. Original chinstraps (tongue broken but present). Male and female lugs gone. Reichs kokarde present. Cap lines replaced and it has had three holes punched in front to make it into a Death Head Hussar busby. Skull and crossbones replaced post-war. Avg. cond. $683

Busby, EM, Prussian, Imperial Germany, Army, Hussar, WWI. Replacement body is composed of a black coarse cloth stretched over reed and sailcloth-style inner liner, flat silver metal banner with convex scaled chinstraps. Helmet has b/w field badge with large brass number 8 on center field. Remains of old paper label inside top. Avg. cond. $500

Busby, EM, Prussian, Imperial Germany, Army, Hussar, 1916. Field gray pattern. Busby is of black sealskin with gray bandeau. Prussian b/w field badge, chinstrap and proper Reichs kokarde on the right side. Maker marked inside and 1916 dated. The busby has the white cord loops for the "schnuren" or cap cords. Exc. cond. $850

Busby, Officer, Prussian, Imperial Germany, Army, Hussar, 1911. Brown opossum fur body with red kolpak and large silver wire cap lines with black Prussian flecking. Gilt chinscales with officer silver wire field badge having black velvet center. Officer kokarde present. Deluxe calfskin liner with top inscribed "56 20/1/ 1911" indicating size and date. Frosted silver officer cross. Black leather form-fitted case with padded liner. Above avg. cond. . . .
. . . . $2100

Cover, Tschapska, Camo, Imperial Germany, Army, 1914. Gray cloth multi-piece construction with two slots, two steel rim hooks and six hooks/loops at back closure-slash. Black inked "B.A.VI 1914." Above avg. cond. $200

Shako, EM, Prussian, Imperial Germany, Army, Jaeger, WWI. Black leather body and visors. Seven-hole metal vents and gray side posts. Variation black leather chinstrap with roller buckle and gray metal end loops. Gray Jaeger eagle frontplate. Nine-finger leather liner. Avg. cond. $231

Shako, EM, Wurttemberg, Imperial Germany, Army, WWI. Black leather body and visor. Seven-hole metal vents and gray side posts. Brass frontplate. Below avg. cond. $156

Shako, Officer, Prussian, Imperial Germany, Army, Garde Jaeger, WWI. Black leather top and visor with black wool-covered body. Brass chinscales with buckle and strap. Reichs kokarde and silver bullion field badge. Dark silver Garde star with black enamel eagle and other enamel details. Leather sweatband with silk liner having inked owner's name. Exc. cond. $2296

Tschapska, NCO, M1915, Prussian, Imperial Germany, Army, Guard Uhlan, WWI. Standard helmet with leather pedestal and mortarboard. Filed badge missing. White metal eagle badge with one-piece star and center Wappen. Brass chinscales and nine-finger lining. Avg. cond. $1035

Prussian NCO Tschapska, M1915

Tschapska, NCO, M1915, Prussian, Imperial Germany, Army, Uhlan, WWI. Lancer cap with black enameled circular spike base. Two-hole vented rabatte with standard black enameled NCO mortarboard. Silver bullion field badge with correct blue center and black velvet backing. Gray metal beak edging and frosted silver helmetplate. Gray enameled chinscales and silk lining. Avg. cond. $1265

Tschapska, Officer, Prussian, Imperial Germany, Army, Uhlan, WWI. Black leather body. Silver front visor trim and line eagle plate with pierced crown. Brass chinscales with buckle strap and Reichs kokarde. Silver bullion top field badge. Leather sweatband and satin lining with faint gold maker trademark. Above avg. cond. $1500

Busbies, Kepis, Shakos and Tschapskas—Other

Bearskin, Bavaria, Army, Grenadier, c1820. Small size with silver frontplate with the Bavarian coat of arms. Crown has blue wool insert with white tape cross. Some wear and dents to frontplate. Avg. cond. $1380

Busby, Bearskin, England, Army, Grenadier, Late 1800s. Hand sewn leather body, 12" high, black bearskin fur, brass chain chinstrap and leather liner. Original paper label marked to London manufacturer having Queen Victoria royal cipher. Above avg. cond. $1155

Kepi, EM, France, Foreign Legion, 1970s. Desert tan twill, leather visor, patent leather chinstrap, brown leather sweatband and gilded Legion buttons. Exc. cond. . . $20

Kepi, EM, France, Foreign Legion, 1970s. Blue and red wool enlisted pattern, black leather visor, black patent leather chinstrap, gilded Legion buttons and black leather sweatband. Above avg. cond. $20

Kepi, Infantry, Officer, France, Army, WWI. Top of red and gray melton wool adorned with silver bullion braid. Top with quatrefoil of bullion wire. Patent leather finished pressboard visor. Bullion tape chinstrap with brass button retainers. Paper sweatband, cotton lining and label inside reading "The Russel Uniform Co./123 West 36th St./New York." Avg. cond. $161

French Infantry Officer's Kepi, c1900

Shako, EM, France, Army, Infantry, 1830s. Enlisted style. Tall black beaver body with card canvas crown, red worsted wool crown lace, brass frontplate depicting rooster with pierced and scrolled trim, flag panoply and pierced unit number "8." No chinstrap or cockades. Above avg. cond. $300

Shako, EM, M1810, France, Army, Infantry, c1812. Standard pattern with painted leather cockade and chinscales with brass chinscales and star rosettes. Leather sweatband with cloth lining. Reproduction brass frontplate of 1812 pattern. Some wear and chipped paint. Avg. cond. $1265

Shako, Grenadier, Holland, Army, Grenadier, 1870s. Black wool body with black lacquered leather crown and trim. With brass sunray frontplate surmounted by contrasting silver flaming grenade insignia, orange cockade with brass trim and silver domed button, brass lion-head chinstrap fittings and white feather plume having laurel insignia. Interior with leather sweatband. Above avg. cond. $372

Shako, Officer, England, Army, Infantry, c1815. Standard style of black felt construction with gilt brass plate bearing the Royal crown and cipher. Red and silver laced cords and black silk rosette. Lining intact and retains London maker's label. Some repairs visible. Avg. cond. . . $2875

Shako, Officer, Bavaria, Army, Grenadier, c1830s. Black leather body with silver bullion pompom and silvered plate bearing a brass grenade. Silvered chinscales with-lion mask mounts. Black leather sweatband with green cloth lining. Avg. cond. $1093

Shako, Officer, M1837, France, Army, Infantry, c1840s. Standard pattern with silver lace tape and black velvet top. Lower edge bound with black velvet. Silvered copper plate and chinscales. Grenade rosettes. Shows some wear and blemishes. Avg. cond. $690

Tschapska, General Officer, Poland, Army, WWII. Khaki twill crown, silver bullion cross lace and silver Polish eagle frontplate. Tan khaki herringbone band with hand-embr silver bullion General rank zigzag trim, two hand-embr silver bullion front stars, black leather chinstrap, black composition eagle buttons, black lacquered visor with nickel trim, leather sweatband and khaki satin lining. Exc. cond. $1000

Caps—U.S.

Cap, EM, USA, Navy, WWI. Private purchase. Navy blue melton wool with stiffener in wide flat crown. Lined in green cotton with bag liner and woven Charleston/Newport clothier's label. Has silk woven U.S.S. Florida ribbon. Above avg. cond. $68

Cap, EM, USA, Navy, WWII. "Donald Duck" style. Navy blue melton wool with gold leaf "U.S. Navy" ribbon. Size 7⅜. Little wear. Avg. cond. $14

Cap, EM, USA, Navy, WWII. "Donald Duck" style. Navy blue melton wool body with silk woven USS San Francisco (CA-38) ribbon. Small size. Above avg. cond. $40

Cap, EM, USA, Navy, WWI. Private purchase in navy

British Infantry Officer's Shako, c1815

blue melton wool lined in dark blue cotton. "Floppy" form. Has wire-woven U.S.S. Mount Vernon ribbon. Above avg. cond. $33

Cap, Fatigue, USA, Army, Korean War. Dark OD HBT with stitched bill, pleated body, and 1951 dated Qm markings. Size 7. Exc. cond. $35

Cap, Fatigue, HBT, USA, Army, 1944. Dark OD HBT with stitched semi-stiff bill, pleated body, and 1944 dated Qm tag. Size 7¼. Exc. cond. $90

Cap, Fatigue, HBT, USA, Army, WWII. Size 6¾ in dark OD HBT with pleated body and stitched bill. Above avg. cond. $12

Cap, Field, USA, Army, WWII. Dark green canvas with dark green lining, short stitched brim and fold-down earflaps with chinstrap. 1940 dated Qm tag. Still has several paper inspector tags stapled to body. Avg. cond. $25

Cap, Field, USA, Army, WWII. Dark green canvas with dark green wool lining, fold-down earflaps and stitched bill. Size 7⅛. 1941 dated Qm tag. Exc. cond. $21

Cap, Field, Pile, Model Quartermaster 1 (MQ1), USA, Army, Korean War. Dark OD cotton with alpaca-lined fold-down earflaps and 1950 dated Qm tag. Has subdued metal S/Sgt chevron on front of stitched bill. All labels intact. Size 7. Above avg. cond. $19

Cap, Garrison, Female, USA, WAC, 1944. Size 21 in tan cotton twill with WAC piping and 1944 dated Qm tag. Exc. cond. $20

Cap, Garrison, Officer, USA, Army, WWI. Also called an overseas cap. English made, British pattern in OD gabardine with two-button front with dark bronze eagle button, dark tan cotton lining. Has officer of Inf collar device pinned to left front. Avg. cond. $28

Cap, Garrison, Officer, USA, Army, WWI. Overseas cap. French made in lt OD gabardine with tall crown, red cotton lining and leather sweatband. Gilt brass AEF pin on front with "AEF" over design of two o/s stripes. Avg. cond. $20

Cap, Garrison, Officer, Female, USA, WAC, WWII. Also called an overseas cap. OD wool serge with clean dark tan cotton lining, US Army Inspector ink stamp markings and pb curve form 1st Lieut bar. Size 21. Above avg. cond. $42

Cap, Overseas, Air Cadet, USA, Army, AAF, 1941. Dark shade OD gabardine body with AAF piping, OD satin lining and 1941 dated Qm label. Size 7⅛. Above avg. cond. $34

Cap, Overseas, EM, USA, Army, 1918. English made.

US Army Overseas Cap

OD wool body with white cotton sweatband. Very well marked with broad arrow proof, 7⅛ size, maker name and 1918 date. Above avg. cond. $35

Cap, Overseas, EM, USA, Army, AAF, WWII. Tan cotton with AAF piping and small cloth-winged prop on left front. Small size. Avg. cond. $20

Cap, Overseas, EM, USA, Army, Airborne, WWII. Dark OD gabardine with Engr piping, "sharkskin" lining, "82/307 Eng" handwritten on, and maker's name on leather sweatband. Has embr on blue cotton glider patch with red border on left front. Above avg. cond. $40

Cap, Overseas, Female, USA, Navy, WAVES, WWII. Gray seersucker with woven WAVES label. Named. Avg. cond. $14

Cap, Service, Dress, Officer, Female, USA, WAVES, WWII. Visorless cap with soft white cotton top, sterling device on black woven band and black satin lining. Woven US Navy Nurse's Uniform label on ribbed sweatband. Named. Size 22. Avg. cond. $95

Cap, Service, EM, Female, USA, USMC, WWII. Soft-sided kepi-style cap with EM brass device on front. Red twist cord with knots for chinstrap. Visor in matching marine green twill with crown. Lined interior. Size 22½. Exc. cond. $20

USMC Female Service Cap

Cap, Service, EM, Female, USA, USMC, WWII. Forest green wool serge with semi-stiff visor, scarlet chincord, bronze 1937 pattern EG&A device and side buttons. Satin lined. Size 21½. Above avg. cond. $55

Cap, Service, EM, Female, USA, WAAC, WWII. OD barathea cylindrical body with matching chinstrap, OD plastic WAAC buttons, semi-stiff visor, satin lining with sweatshield, ribbed satin sweatband and WAAC marked 1943 dated Qm tag. Size 23. Fitted with gilt brass Army EM device. Above avg. cond. $72

Cap, Service, Nurse, USA, Army, ANC, WWII. Light creme-colored worsted wool with matching chinstrap, gilt brass device, stitched bill, satin lining and ribbed sweatband. Hmkd "Knox." Size 21. Above avg. cond. . . . $48

Cap, Service, Officer, Female, USA, USMC, WWII. Distinctive green cotton body with semi-stiff bill, white chincord, gilt 1937 pattern device and side buttons. Hmkd "Knox" on satin lining. Size 21½. Above avg. cond. $47

Cap, Summer Service, EM, Female, USA, WAC, WWII. Tan gabardine-covered circular top, bill and chinstrap with gilt brass device and side buttons, satin lining with foil maker's label under sweatshield and dark OD ribbed satin sweatband. Size 22½. Above avg. cond. $60

Cap, Summer Service, Nurse, USA, ANC, WWII. Tan linen kepi style with brass device centered above bill. Simulated chinstrap of same material separates bill from body. Reinforced bill with same material covering and multiple rows of stitching. Lined interior with rayon sweatband and hmkd Knox of NY. Size 22. Exc. cond. .
. . . . $70

Cap, Utility, USA, USMC, WWII. Lt OD HBT with stitched bill, pleated body and stenciled 1937 pattern EG&A device on front of crown. Named. Size 7⅜. Above avg. cond. $53

Cap, Utility, USA, USMC, 1944. Lt OD HBT with stitched bill, pleated body and 1944 dated spec tag. 1937 pattern EG&A stencil on front of crown. Owner's name inked in white marking pen on sweatband. Size small. Exc. cond. $140

Cap, Visor, 1895 Pattern, USA, Army, 1895. "Pillbox" style. Navy blue melton-wool-covered circular top with black woven band, gold wire chinstrap with 1872 pattern domed side buttons, black visor, maker markings on black cotton lining and leather sweatband. Size 7¼. Avg. cond. $60

Cap, Visor, 1895 Pattern, USA, Army, 1890s. Navy blue melton-wool-covered circular crown with two rows gold wire trim, stamped gilt wreath on front of crown with nickel "VSE" inside, thin gold wire chinstrap with 1872-

style side buttons and black oilcloth visor. Silver embossed New York maker's markings on black cotton lining. Size 6¾. With oilcloth storm cover. Avg. cond. . $72

Cap, Visor, Admiral, USA, Navy, 1950s. White cotton top with stiffener in crown, black woven band with bullion Navy officer device direct embr into front, gold wire chinstrap, gilt Navy side buttons and heavy gold bullion flag officer "scrambled eggs" on visor. "Berkshire – Flex" brand. Size 7½. Above avg. cond. $187

Cap, Visor, CPO, USA, Navy, WWII. White cotton top with CPO device on black woven band, black visor and chinstrap and gilt side buttons. Size 7¼. "Bancroft Zephyr" brand. Above avg. cond. $15

Cap, Visor, EM, USA, Army, WWII. Lt OD wool serge top with brown visor, chinstrap and dark bronze eagle side buttons. US markings on dark tan cotton lining. Has Sb Inf device on front of crown in worn dark bronze finish. Small size. Avg. cond. $55

US Army Enlisted Man's Visor Cap

Cap, Visor, EM, USA, Army, WWII. Quality cap with dark tan gabardine top with "floppy" form, gilt brass device and side buttons, dark brown semi-soft visor and mismatched front and rear chinstraps. Marked "The Crusher" model. Size 7. Above avg. cond. $160

Cap, Visor, EM, USA, USMC, Vietnam Era. Tan worsted wool top with cordovan visor and chinstrap, 1962-pattern device and side buttons. Size 6⅞. Above avg. cond. $30

Cap, Visor, EM, USA, Army, WWII. Dark OD wool body. Private purchase quality. Size 7¼. Avg. cond. $20

Cap, Visor, EM, USA, Army, WWII. Dark OD gabardine top with crown stiffener, brown visor and chinstrap and gilt brass side buttons. Satin lining hmkd "The Gordonia Caps." Size 7⅛. Above avg. cond. $37

Cap, Visor, EM, USA, Army, WWII. OD wool serge top with stiffener, gilt brass device and side buttons, brown visor and chinstrap, pressed paper sweatband and lt OD cotton lining. Size 7. Above avg. cond. $40

Cap, Visor, EM, USA, Army, WWII. OD wool serge top with crown stiffener, dark brown visor and chinstrap and gilt brass device and side buttons. Lined in lt green cotton. Patent label underneath sweat diamond. Avg. cond. . $25

Cap, Visor, EM, USA, Army, WWI. Lt OD wool serge top with brown visor and chinstrap, dark bronze side buttons. Leather sweatband with silver embossed London/Chicago maker's markings. Lined in dark tan cotton. Front of crown has dark bronze Medical officer device with open-catch Pb. Size 7. Near mint cond. $75

Cap, Visor, EM, USA, Army, AAF, WWII. Dark olive fur felt top with stiffener, brown leather visor, front and rear chinstraps, gilt brass device and side buttons and full sweatshield. Size 7½. Above avg. cond. $56

Cap, Visor, EM, USA, USMC, Korean War. Dark tan worsted wool top with cordovan visor, chinstrap and side buttons. Size 7. No device. WWII era USMC visor cap tops with stiffeners in wide crowns. Avg. cond. $21

Cap, Visor, EM, USA, Army, WWII. Dark OD gabardine top with stiffener in crown, semi-soft brown leather visor, front and rear chinstraps and gilt brass device and side buttons. Avg. cond. $20

Cap, Visor, Officer, USA, USAF, 1960s. AF blue cloth crown with blue elastic band. Gray alloy cap device 2½" high. Black patent leather chinstrap above visor anchored by two USAF buttons on side. Black leather strap with buckle around back of band also anchored at buttons. Wool-lined visor with bullion lightning and arrows emitting from clouds. Slight damage to one arrow and lightning bolt. Lined interior with leather sweatband. Hmkd Berkshire Deluxe. Above avg. cond. $72

Cap, Visor, Officer, USA, Navy, WWII. Aviation green gabardine top with stiffener, sterling device on black woven band, gold wire chinstrap with gilt side buttons, and black visor. Size 7⅛. Above avg. cond. $88

Cap, Visor, Officer, USA, USMC, WWII. Forest green wool gabardine top on wick frame, with quatrefoil, woven band, cordovan visor and chinstrap, dark bronze Meyer hmkd 1937 pattern EG&A device, side buttons and Quantico, VA maker markings. Size 7⅛. Includes storm cover. Avg. cond. $23

Cap, Visor, Officer, USA, AAF, WWII. "Crush" style. Dark OD gabardine top with floppy form, semi-soft brown leather visor and chinstrap, woven band, oversize device and side buttons. Satin lined. No sweatband. Size 7¼. Avg. cond. $59

Cap, Visor, Officer, USA, Army, WWI. Olive gabardine

top with lt OD woven band, dark bronze eagle device, dark tan visor and chinstrap, side buttons, dark tan cotton lining and leather sweatband. Size 7. Exc. cond. $175

Cap, Visor, Officer, USA, Army, WWII. OD fur felt top with "floppy" appearance, woven band, gilt brass device and side buttons, russet brown leather visor and chinstrap and maker markings on satin lining with full sweatshield. Size 7. Above avg. cond. $82

Cap, Visor, Officer, USA, Navy, 1950s. White cotton top with device on black woven band, gold wire chinstrap, NAVY side buttons and black visor. Bancroft brand. Size 7½. Avg. cond. $25

Cap, Visor, Officer, USA, USAF, 1950s. "Flight Ace" brand cap with black worsted top, soft roll crown stiffener, black woven band, silver wire chinstrap with frosted silver side buttons and heavy silver bullion "lightning bolts and clouds" on wool covered visor. Size 7⅛. Has Luxembourg maker hmkd device. For a brigadier general. Above avg. cond. $86

Cap, Visor, Officer, USA, Navy, WWII. Navy blue melton wool top with sterling device on black woven band, gold wire chinstrap and side buttons. Size 7⅛. Avg. cond. $25

Cap, Visor, Officer, USA, Navy, WWII. Navy blue melton wool top with stiffener, sterling device on black woven band, gold wire chinstrap, side buttons and black visor. Size 7¼. Above avg. cond. $40

Cap, Visor, Officer, USA, USAF, 1950s. Field grade dress cap. Black worsted wool top with woven band, frosted silver device and side buttons, silver wire chinstrap and heavy silver bullion "lightning bolts and clouds" on visor. Luxembourg brand. Size 6⅞. Avg. cond. $22

Cap, Visor, Officer, USA, Army, Korean War. Tan worsted wool top with soft roll crown stiffener, russet brown leather visor, front and rear chinstraps, oversize gilt brass device, side buttons and satin lining. "Bancroft" brand. Size 7½. Avg. cond. $30

Cap, Visor, Officer, USA, Navy, 1950s. For flag grade officer. White cotton top with sterling device on black woven band, gold wire chinstrap, side buttons and gold bullion "scrambled eggs" on visor. Hmkd Bancroft. Size 7. Avg. cond. $40

Cap, Visor, Officer, USA, Army, Korean War. Or service cap. Dark OD gabardine top with crown stiffener, woven band, brown leather visor and chinstrap, gilt brass device and side buttons. Green liner with sweatshield. Large size. Avg. cond. $42

Cap, Visor, Officer, USA, Navy, WWI. Navy melton

wool "bell crown" top with black woven mohair band with embr bullion device, gold wire chinstrap, gilt brass side buttons and black visor. Clothier's markings on black cotton lining. Size 6⅞. Above avg. cond. $90

Cap, Visor, Officer, USA, Army, WWII. Dark tan worsted wool body with "crush" form, dark tan woven band, soft brown leather visor, front and rear chinstraps, oversize gilt brass device and side buttons. "Flighter" model. Size 7⅛. Avg. cond. $90

Cap, Visor, Officer, 1902 Pattern, USA, Army, Pre-WWI. Navy blue melton wool covered "bell" crown with black woven mohair band, direct embr heavy gold bullion device on front of crown, gold wire chinstrap with 1872 pattern side buttons, black visor and maker markings on black cotton lining. Sweatband missing. Bullion still bright. Avg. cond. $68

Cap, Visor, Officer, M1926, USA, Army, 1930s. OD whipcord top with stiffener in wide crown, dark tan woven band, gilt brass device and side buttons and dark brown leather visor and chinstrap. Maker marked on lining. Capt's name inked on sweatband. Size 7. Avg. cond. $20

Cap, Visor, Officer, M1926, USA, Army, 1930s. Lt OD whipcord top with woven band, stiffener in wide crown, dark brown visor and chinstrap, gilt brass device and side buttons. Named. Faint maker markings on cotton lining. Size 7¼. Avg. cond. $26

Cap, Visor, Officer, M1938, USA, Army, WWII. Field grade. Navy blue melton wool top with gilt brass device, gold wire chinstrap with ribbed Cav piped insert, gold wire chinstrap with gilt side buttons, bullion "scrambled eggs" on wool-covered visor. Satin lined with Kansas City/St. Louis maker markings. Full sweatshield. Size 7. Above avg. cond. $53

Cap, Visor, Officer, M1938, USA, Army, WWII. Dress white version. White cotton top with stiffener, woven cap band, Gaunt/London hmkd device and gold wire chinstrap with side buttons. Size 7⅛. Norfolk, VA maker marked. With extra white cotton top and hat box. Above avg. cond. $55

Cap, Wool Knit, M1941, USA, Army, WWII. Or "Jeep" cap. Lt OD knit wool with fold-down earflaps and cardboard stiffened short bill. Size "M" tag intact. Above avg. cond. $40

Cap, Wool Knit, M1941, USA, Army, WWII. "Jeep" cap. Lt OD knit with fold-down earflaps, cardboard stiffener in short bill and size "M" tag. Above avg. cond. $33

Caps—Germany

Cap, "Coffee Can," Germany, NSFK, 1930s. Blue-gray wool-covered body has stiff shape. Yellow wool piping to top and sides with double grommet vents. Alum eagle and black leather chinstrap, brown leather sweatband and purple satin lining. Above avg. cond. $491

Cap, "Coffee Can," Germany, SA, 1930s. Entire cap has same brown wool construction, two grommet vents per side, twisted b&w piping around sides and dark silver twisted piping around top. Silver eagle, pebbled buttons and black leather chinstrap. Leather sweatband and orange waterproof lining with inked "30.B.245." Avg. cond. $1350

Cap, "Coffee Can," Germany, SA, WWII. Tan twill body. Double grommet vents to yellow wool sides. Gray wartime eagle, nickel button and brown chinstrap. Leatherette sweatband with oilcloth RZM tag. Orange waterproof top lining with inked size "57." Above avg. cond. $550

Cap, EM, Naval, Germany, Navy, WWII. "Donald Duck" style. Removable blue wool top has blue satin lining sewn inside. Blue wool band with leather sweatband and front stiffener inked "56 HFT." Gold bevo "Kriegsmarine" tally. Gold-painted eagle pin lacks cockade. Avg. cond. $365

Cap, Fatigue, EM, M1910, Imperial Germany, Army, WWI. Field gray wool body with red wool band and piping. With Reichs rosette and cotton duck lining. Some moth damage. Below avg. cond. $46

Imperial Germany Model 1910 Fatigue Cap

Cap, Field, Camo, Germany, Waffen SS, WWII. Center seam. 2nd variant with reversible summer/spring oak leaf design to outside and fall/winter design inside. Small sweatband and two grommet vents per side. Exc. cond. $788

Cap, Field, EM, Prussian, Germany, Army, Reservist, WWI. Pillbox style. Field gray body with red wool piping on crown and red band around base. Off-white lining with well-marked maker stamps and size 53. National colors cockade over reservist with IC center. Avg. cond. . $177

Cap, Field, M43, Officer, Germany, Waffen SS, WWII. Gray-green twill wool and alum piped top. Missing both gray bevo insignia. Gray satin lining has inked out areas and large Russian museum number. Avg. cond. ... $375

Cap, Foul Weather, Naval, Germany, Navy, WWII. Gray-brown rubberized cloth body, off-white tie-strings and white inked "Willy Sprengpfeil etc U29." Early U-Boat item. Exc. cond. $90

Cap, Overseas, EM, Germany, Army, Panzer, 1941. Black wool body with grommet vent on each side. Gray bevo eagle on black is hand sewn on as is bevo cockade on green. Pink soutache is machine sewn on. Gray lining inked "Lago Berlin 1941 56 B. 40." Exc. cond. .. $1050

Cap, Overseas, EM, Germany, Army, WWII. Gray wool body with grommet vents. Gray lining and maker name. Below avg. cond. $30

German Infantry EM (M1938) Overseas Cap

Cap, Visor, EM, Flak, Germany, Luftwaffe, 1937, Robert Lubstein. Blue-gray wool body, red wool piping and black mohair band. Down-tail alum eagle and wreath/cockade. Black leather chinstrap and visor with trim. Leather sweatband. Orange lining with diamond maker mark "Robert Lubstein etc 1937 57." Avg. cond. $292

Cap, Visor, EM, Flak, Germany, Luftwaffe, 1938. Blue-gray twill wool body, red wool piping and black band. Gray eagle, alum wreath and cockade. Black chinstrap, visor with trim, leather sweatband, orange lining and diamond with maker mark "Franz Ritter etc 1938 55½." Avg. cond. $225

Cap, Visor, NCO, Prussian, Imperial Germany, Army, WWI. Field gray wool body with red wool band and piping. Prussian Land and Reichs rosettes. Molded fiber visor and patent leather chinstrap. Light brown oilcloth sweatband and cotton liner. Minor wear and some blemishes. Avg. cond. $230

Cap, Visor, Officer, Prussian, Germany, Army, Hussar, WWI. Black wool with white piping. Officer Reichs and Prussian rosettes. Silvered skull and bones between rosettes. Custom purchase silk and leather liner. Exc. cond. $225

Cap, Visor, Officer, Prussian, Imperial Germany, Army, Infantry, WWI. Stiff tall saddle body with stone gray wool body, red piping and band. Complete with officer Reichs and Prussian rosettes. Leather visor. Made without chinstrap. Full deluxe lining with celluloid moisture shield. Exc. cond. $334

Cap, Visor, NCO, Baden, Imperial Germany, Army, Infantry, WWI. Standard course field gray wool top with red wool piping and band. Baden Land rosette and Reichs rosette. Black molded fiber visor. Tan oilcloth sweatband and cream silk lining. Above avg. cond. $230

Cap, Visor, NCO, Bavarian, Imperial Germany, Army, Chevauleger, WWI. Dark green with burgundy band and piping. Deluxe NCO kokarden. Fancy leather liner and blue silken top with silver eagle maker logo and Nurnberg address. Near mint cond. $326

Fez, Germany, Waffen SS, WWII. Maroon. Black tassel. Bevo eagle over skull. Leather sweatband. Avg. cond. $387

Fez, Germany, Waffen SS, WWII. Maroon. Black tassel on back and bevo gray eagle over skull on front. Leather sweatband and inked size "57." Above avg. cond. . $588

German Medical Service Visor Cap

Waffen SS Fez

Caps—Other

Cap, Spain, Army, 1980s. OD wool, square cut with red piping and button-strap side panels, cotton lined and red tassel front. Near mint cond. $45

Cap, Badge, Naval, CPO, Poland, Navy, c1950. Gold and silver bullion. Above avg. cond. $50

Cap, Badge, Royal Air Force, Officer, England, Royal Air Force, WWII. Embroidered gold bullion and brass, padded, on dark blue wool. Above avg. cond. $25

Cap, Brimmed, Officer, Italy, Army, Alpine Infantry, WWII. Field gray wool, two-toned hand-embr gold bullion front eagle insignia, central cockade with brass unit number "2." Complete with 2nd Lieut gold bullion side chevron, gilded plume holder and side feather, field gray grosgrain band, braided cord, grosgrain brim binding, black cotton interior lining and leather sweatband. Above avg. cond. $247

Cap, Eagle, Army, General, Poland, Army. Silver bullion. Above avg. cond. $40

Cap, Eagle, Naval, Poland, Navy, c1960. Gray eagle insignia on blue wool field. For field uniform cap. Exc. cond. $20

Cap, Eagle, Naval, NCO, Poland, Navy, c1960. Silver bullion eagle with gold bullion wreath on blue wool field. Above avg. cond. $75

Cap, Eagle, Naval, NCO, Poland, Navy, c1960. Silver and gold bullion on cloth. Above avg. cond. $50

Cap, Eagle, Naval, Warrant Officer, Poland, Navy, c1960. Silver and gold bullion. Above avg. cond. . . $50

Cap, EM, Naval, France, Navy, 1982. Dark blue wool, red pom-pons, "Marine Nationale" on ribbon, fouled anchor insignia and leather sweatband, dated "1/82." Above avg. cond. $24

Cap, Fatigue, Soviet Union, Army, c1980. Brimmed "Boonie" style. Khaki twill with red Soviet star insignia. Exc. cond. $20

Cap, Field Service, Arty, Officer, Austria, Army, c1917. Field gray poplin wool with two brass Arty buttons. High-relief bullion rosette with brass cipher. Black composition visor with leatherette edging. Gray leather sweatband, sateen lining and label inside marked "Alexander Sohn/...etc." Above avg. cond. $127

Cap, Folding Side, Greece, Air Force. White cotton twill crown. Black mohair band, chinstrap, sweatband, and moisture shield. Hand-embr gold bullion wreath having Greek shield and eagle cockade. Exc. cond. $225

Austrian Officer's Field Service Cap, c1917

Cap, Folding Side, EM, Greece, Air Force, 1970s. Blue-gray twill with dark blue piping, gilded laurel wreath Air Force front insignia, satin lining and leather sweatband. Dates from the military dictatorship era. Exc. cond. $25

Cap, Folding Side, Officer, Greece, Army. Khaki twill, light khaki green piping, gilded laurel wreath insignia with white-blue shield device, satin lining and leather sweatband. Above avg. cond. $25

Cap, Folding Side, Officer, Soviet Union, Army, 1990. Khaki wool, red piping, with enameled and gilded cockade, lining of khaki cotton, and gray oilcloth sweatband. Exc. cond. $20

Cap, Folding Side, Officer, Soviet Union, Army, 1991. Khaki wool, red piping, with enameled and gilded cockade, lining of gray cotton, and blackoil cloth sweatband. Exc. cond. $20

Cap, Folding Side, Officer, Naval, Soviet Union, Navy, 1991. Blue wool, white piping, enameled and gilded cockade, lining of black cotton, and gray oilcloth sweatband. Exc. cond. $21

Cap, Side, General Officer, Italy, Army, Fascist Militia, WWII. Field gray wool. Hand-embr gold and silver bullion eagle and fascist insignia on rose wool field, with gold bullion crown cording. Grosgrain ribbon sweatband. Above avg. cond. $121

Cap, Visor, Poland, Air Force, WWII. Gray wool twill having dark blue wool piping, dark blue band with four hand-embr gold bullion stars, silvered eagle front badge, and black leather chinstrap with eagle side buttons. Visor has red-yellow trim, liner, and replacement sweatband. Exc. cond. $450

Cap, Visor, Sweden, Army, 1950s. Field gray wool, two-button front, black piping, and cotton lining. Above avg. cond. $15

Cap, Visor, Camo, Soviet Union, Army, 1980s. Cotton. Exc. cond. $20

Cap, Visor, General, Soviet Union, Air Force, 1980. Service style. Dark blue twill with bright blue piping and band, interior with moisture shield, sweatband, and satin lining. Hand-embr gold bullion winged star and wreath insignia, with Soviet star cockade, gold bullion chincord, and front visor with hand-embr gold bullion laurel leaves. Exc. cond. $250

Cap, Visor, Medical Admiral, Naval, Italy, Navy, WWII. Dark blue wool complete with chinstrap, silk lining with Italian eagle motif, and leather sweatband. Hand-embr gold bullion wreath with crown and fouled anchor device surmounted by red enamel cross and two-toned hand-embr gold bullion frieze band piped in gold bullion and dark blue. Exc. cond. $287

Cap, Visor, Medical Officer, Italy, Army, 1950. Khaki wool twill, khaki woven band with oak leaf frieze, gold bullion chinstrap, hand-embr bullion crown, medical insignia, yellow satin lining, moisture shield and leather sweatband. Rome maker's trademark. Above avg. cond. $40

Cap, Visor, Officer, Imperial Russia, Army, WWI. White cotton body with red wool band. Red and green cloisonné rosette. Black molded fiber visor. Leather sweatband and patterned silk lining. Above avg. cond. $316

Imperial Russian Officer's Visor Cap

Cap, Visor, Officer, England, Army, WWI. Khaki twill wool with bronze 5th BN, South Lancashire Regiment, Prince of Wales Volunteers cap badge. Complete with brown leather chinstrap, leather sweatband and moisture shield. Exc. cond. $225

Cap, Visor, Officer, Italy, Army, WWI. Field gray wool, black chinstrap, silk lining partially intact and leather sweatband. Silver bullion captain rank bands with hand-embr silver bullion infantry officer front insignia and silver infantry side buttons. Above avg. cond. $367

Cap, Visor, Officer, Poland, Army, 1992. Khaki twill square crown with silver bullion band and visor piping, blue wool band, three silver hand-embr rank stars, Polish eagle front insignia, black leather chinstrap, black visor, leather sweatband and twill lining. For Lieut. Exc. cond. . . . $350

Cap, Visor, Officer, Soviet Union, Army, 1983. Khaki wool, cloth visor, detachable ear protectors, khaki cotton lining and gray oilcloth sweatband. Exc. cond. $26

Cap, Visor, Officer, Soviet Union, Army, 1980s. Khaki twill, subdued Soviet star cockade, khaki visor and chinstrap, satin lining, and sweatband. Above avg. cond. $30

Cap, Visor, Officer, Italy, Army, WWII. Field gray wool twill. Hand-embr gold bullion winged flaming grenade front insignia, 2nd Lieut gold bullion rank band, black leather chinstrap, gray silk lining, and leather sweatband. Above avg. cond. $150

Cap, Visor, Officer, Naval, Soviet Union, Navy, 1990. White cotton cover, black band, gilded and enameled insignia, gold bullion chincord, black composition material visor and oilcloth sweatband. Manufacturer's label inside. Exc. cond. $34

Cap, Winter Fur, Admiral, Soviet Union, Navy, 1980s. Black fleece with black leather crown, Soviet star front badge, gold bullion wreath, visor with gilded laurel leaf trim, and quilted lining. Unissued. Near mint cond. $175

Caps, Visor, Camo, Syria, Army, Commando, 1970s. Green and brown camo pattern. Number One Commando Battalion black shield insignia, featuring grinning white skull on crossed swords. Above avg. cond. $15

Hat, Bush, Israel, Army, 1980s. Quilted khaki cotton twill with Israeli markings. Above avg. cond. $20

Hat, Fatigue, Camo, South Vietnam, Army, Vietnam War. "Boonie" hat. Cotton twill composite construction and ARVN jungle camouflage pattern. Above avg. cond. $42

Headdress, Feathered, England, Army, Scottish Regt, Late 1800s. "Bonnet" style with black ostrich feathers throughout. Complete with 4" red-white knit wool dicing, black grosgrain cockade, white feather plume, leather chinstrap with roller buckle, four ostrich feather tails, leather sweatband, and faded red silk lining. No cap badge. Above avg. cond. $867

Chapeaus and Hats—U.S.

Chapeau, Dress, Officer, USA, New York Guard, 1890s. Black beaver body trimmed in wide-ribbed black satin gold bullion, tassel on each end, and heavy bullion eagle crested NY state shield on bullion border ribbon-trimmed oval. Small ostrich plume in crown. Satin lined. Avg. cond. $196

Chapeau, Dress, Officer, Naval, USA, Navy, WWI. Chapeau in black beaver with woven silk trim, gold wire tassels, panel with gilt button and black rosette. Silk lined with English coat-of-arms. Size 7¼. Comes in fitted black lacquered tin carrier with interior compartment. Includes dress boards with fouled anchor ornamentation. Above avg. cond. $292

Chapeau, Dress, Officer, Naval, USA, Navy, Early 1900s. Purchased at Midshipman's Store-USNA. Black beaver body trimmed in wide, fancy woven black satin. Heavy bullion tassel on each end with early gilt eagle button on gold wire panel on side. Size 7⅜, USNA marked on satin lining, oilcloth sweatband. Avg. cond. $160

Chapeau, Dress, Officer, Naval, USA, Navy, WWI, Horstmann. Black beaver-covered body with wide, ornate woven satin trim and early gilt eagle button on bullion trim panel on side. Horstmann maker marked on satin lining. Below avg. cond. $187

Hat, Baseball, USA, USMC, 1970. Blue wool felt body with stitched bill, woven Japanese maker's label. Has Japanese-made fully embr sqdn patch and embr design on front which reads "'70–'71/VMFA-115/Iwakuni/Da Nang/Chu Lai." Above avg. cond. $72

Hat, Baseball, USA, Army, 1970. Dark OD cotton with 1970 dated spec label. Has cb Lieut Col leaf attached to front. Size 7⅝. Avg. cond. $11

Hat, Baseball, USA, Navy, 1980s. Marked for USS Voge (FF-1047). Navy blue knit body. Adjustable size. Has patch stitched to front with surface warfare badge (frosted silver finish) pinned on front. Exc. cond. $20

Hat, Baseball, USA, Army, Aviator, Vietnam Era. Locally manufactured in OD cotton with black aviator wing and captain's bar embr on the front of the cap. Small size. Avg. cond. $36

Hat, Baseball, Camo, USA, Army, 1980s. Issue in six-color desert camo with stitched brim. Size 7¼. Avg. cond. $23

Hat, Baseball, Officer, USA, Army, Vietnam War. OD green vented ball cap with elasticized sweatband and embr white 1½" eagle on front. Saigon tailors hmk on sweatband. Near mint cond. $125

Hat, Bush, USA, USAF, Vietnam War. OD cotton with wide stitched brim that snaps up on each side. Red cotton lining marked size 57. Has locally made color "Nakhon Phanom" tab sewn to front. Above avg. cond. $53

Hat, Bush, USA, Army, Vietnam Era. Overall stitched OD cotton body with wide brim that snaps up on both sides, blue cotton lining, black vinyl sweatband and parachute cord chinstrap. Ink stamped size "8" inside crown. Above avg. cond. $38

Hat, Bush, USA, Army, Vietnam Era. Overall stitched in dark OD poplin with wide brim that snaps up on one side. Matching chinstrap with all-leather slide. Insect net inside pocket in top of crown. Size 7¼. Exc. cond. $90

Hat, Bush, USA, Army, Vietnam Era. Faded OD cotton body. With wide brim that snaps up on one side, wire-covered large metal grommet vents and brown vinyl sweat-

band. Has "Viet-Nam" tab, cb para wing applied to one side of brim and locally made five-point star device attached to front. Size small. Avg. cond. $23

Hat, Bush, USA, Army, Vietnam Era. Theater made. OD cotton with wide brim that snaps up on both sides, large brass grommet vents, holes covered in nylon mesh, red oilcloth sweatband and pale red lining. Small size. Above avg. cond. $20

Hat, Bush, USA, Army, Vietnam Era. Theater made. OD cotton with wide brim that snaps up on one side, large alum grommet wire vents, brown vinyl sweatband and chinstrap. Has color Vietnamese-made insignia, hand embr on red cotton, "Bien-Hoa/Viet-Nam" tab on brim, "Viet-Nam" patch on front of crown and US and SVN flags. Small size. Avg. cond. $45

Hat, Bush, Camo, USA, Army, Vietnam War. Tiger stripe camo pattern cotton with wide brim that snaps up on both sides, metal grommet vent holes, lt blue lining and blue vinyl sweatband. Size 7. Above avg. cond. $69

Hat, Campaign, USA, USMC, WWI. OD fur felt body with brim edge folded under and double stitched, ribbed satin band, leather chinstrap, leather sweatband and dark bronze finish EG&A device on front of crown. Size 6⅞. Above avg. cond. $198

Hat, Campaign, Officer, USA, Army, WWI. Private purchase in OD fur felt with ribbed satin band. Hat cord shows age. Leather sweatband is hmkd Meyer. Size 7. Avg. cond. $35

US Army Campaign Hat

Hat, Cold Weather, USA, Navy, WWII. Blue twill with wool lining and straps to hold goggles in place. Neck flap and chinstrap. Above avg. cond. $24

Hat, Fatigue, USA, Army, WWII. "Daisy Mae" style. Dark blue denim with soft crown and stitched brim. Size 6⅞. Above avg. cond. $30

Hat, Fatigue, USA, Army, WWII. "Daisy Mae" style. Dark blue denim with "beachball" crown, stitched brim and Qm label. Size 6⅝. Above avg. cond. $25

Hat, Fatigue, Female, USA, USMC, WWII. "Daisy Mae" style. Distinctive green cotton with wide stitched brim, "beachball" crown and Knox maker markings on ribbed green satin sweatband. Named. Size 21½. Has bronze plastic EG&A device on front. Exc. cond. $135

Hat, Survival Sun, USA, Army, Vietnam Era. Reversible from dark OD to brilliant orange poplin with stitched brim, soft crown and adjustable headband. Well marked. Exc. cond. $30

Hat, Tropical, USA, Army, 1969. "Boonie" hat. Issue pattern in OD ripstop. With insect net. Dated 1969. Size 7. Avg. cond. $12

Hat, Tropical, USA, Army, 1969. Issue pattern in OD ripstop. With insect net. Dated 1969. Size 6¾. In issue bag. Near mint cond. $11

Hat, Tropical, USA, Army, Vietnam Era. Theater made. OD ripstop resembling issue pattern with soft crown and stitched brim. Size 7¼. Has subdued metal S/Sgt rank on front crown. Above avg. cond. $28

Hat, Tropical, USA, Army, 1968. Issue pattern in OD poplin. With insect net. Size 6⅞. Dated 1968. In issue bag. Near mint cond. $28

Hat, Tropical, Camo, USA, Army, 1969. "Boonie" hat. Issue in ERDL pattern camo ripstop. Dated 1969. Size 6⅝. In issue bag. Near mint cond. $11

Hat, Tropical, Camo, USA, Army, 1968. "Boonie" hat. Issue pattern in ERDL pattern camo ripstop. Size 6⅝. 1968 dated. Exc. cond. $21

Chapeaus and Hats—Germany

Chapeau, Admiral, Naval, Imperial Germany, Navy, WWI. Fore and aft pattern with black leather sweatband and refolded-style white silk liner. Size 59. Black stiff fur-covered body with 1¾" of gold braidwork, heavy gold wire "rope" over national color cockade with large gold high relief naval button. Case is of black patent leather with carrying handle, side straps and black japanned tin lock, yellow padded silk interior. Near mint cond. $856

Chapeaus and Hats—Other

Cap Insignia, Army, Officer, Bersaglieri, Italy, Army, WWII. Gold bullion on field gray backing. Above avg. cond. $20

Cap Insignia, Army, Officer, Carbinieri Reali, Italy, Army, WWII. Silver bullion on black wool field. Above avg. cond. $20

Chapeau, Cavalry, France, Dragoons, c1805. Large chapeau of the type used by the heavy Cav. Retains four strands of braided bullion. Interior label states that the chapeau was used by the Dragoon Regt of Neufchatel. Shows some wear and minor tears. Avg. cond. . . . $1150

Chapeau, Officer, France, Army, Infantry, c1816, Paris. Front of chapeau has single strip of silver lace. With leather sweatband and white silk lining. Label on lining marked "Rue de Fosses Saine/Germanin des Pres No. 28 Lallerman/ a Paris." Some wear and tear to body and lining. Avg. cond. $460

Chapeau, Officer, England, Navy, c1830. Standard-style chapeau with black lacing, gold lace strip, and gilt brass button with original black silk ribbon. Black paper cockade on obverse. Some wear and a few tears. Avg. cond. .
. . . . $920

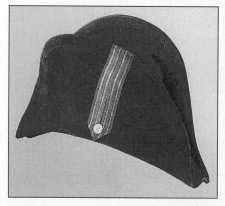

British Naval Officer's Chapeau, c1830s

Hat Band, French, Navy, France, Navy, c1950. Black silk, inscribed "MARINE NATIONALE" in gold. Above avg. cond. $20

Combat Helmets—U.S.

Chincup, Paratrooper, USA, Army, Airborne, WWII. Leather with fur-lined padded chincups and hooks to connect to helmet. Avg. cond. $21

Cover, Helmet, M1, Camo, USA, USMC, 1943, Australia. Reversible from green to tan spot pattern camo canvas with ink stamped EG&A device on front (green side only). USMC, Australian maker marked and dated 1943. Near mint cond. $165

Cover, Helmet, M1, Camo, USA, Army, WWII. Cord net tied in 2" squares. Laced with burlap scrim in shades of olive and dark tan. Avg. cond. $28

Cover, Helmet, M1, Camo, USA, USMC, WWII. Reversible from green to tan spot pattern camo on HBT. Avg. cond. $59

Cover, Helmet, Camo, USA, Army, 1980s. Unissued

desert pattern camo Kevlar helmet cover. Size medium/large. Mint cond. $22

Helmet, Armor, Crewman, USA, Army, Vietnam War. Domed fiber shell in OD sand finish with dark OD webbing, padded earcups wired with receivers and "boom" mike with lead wire and plug. Avg. cond. $24

Helmet, Combat Vehicle Crewman (CVC), DH-132, USA, Army, 1986, Gentex. Gentex Kevlar model. Sealed in original box dated 2/86. Exc. cond. $30

Helmet, Combat Vehicle Crewman (CVC), DH-132, USA, Army, 1988, Gentex. Gentex Kevlar model. In original box and inner bag, dated 1/88. Size small. Near mint cond. $34

Helmet, Combat Vehicle Crewman (CVC), DH-132, USA, Army, 1980s, Gentex. Reinforced plastic (Kevlar) construction with OD sand textured surface. Ear cutouts and fitted inserts with padded earphones and boom mike. Electronics included. Size medium. Above avg. cond. $35

Helmet, Combat, Kevlar "Fritz," USA, Army, 1983. OD sand finish shell with dark OD nylon webbing, chinstrap and leather sweatband. Large size. Early production dated 1983. Exc. cond. $65

Helmet, Combat, Kevlar "Fritz," USA, Army, 1989. OD sand finish shell with dark OD webbing and chinstrap. Includes sweatband in issue bag and instruction booklet. Dated 1989. Small size shell. Near mint cond. $48

Helmet, Combat, Kevlar "Fritz," USA, Army, 1980s. OD sand finish shell with dark OD nylon webbing and chinstrap. Medium size. Fitted with woodland camo cover with subdued Specialist 4 rank patch on front and covered in "Desert Shield" graffiti. Above avg. cond. $76

Helmet, Combat, Kevlar "Fritz," USA, Army, 1985. OD sand finish shell with dark OD nylon webbing, chinstrap and leather sweatband. Woodland camo cover. Size small shell. Dated 1985. Above avg. cond. $50

Helmet, Combat, Kevlar "Fritz," USA, Army, 1980s. Olive sand finish shell with dark OD nylon webbing, chinstrap and sweatband. Medium size shell. With woodland camo cover. Above avg. cond. $84

Helmet, Combat, Kevlar "Fritz," USA, USMC, 1980s. Kevlar shell in OD sand finish with dark OD nylon webbing, chinstrap and leather sweatband. Size small shell. Fitted with woodland camo cover with EG&A stencil on front of crown area and OD elastic helmet band. Exc. cond. $42

Helmet, Combat, M1, USA, Army, WWII. Steel shell in OD sand refinish with lt OD web chinstraps on fixed bales. M1 liner has lt OD webbing, nape strap, leather

chinstrap and sweatband. Has neatly painted 87th Div large patch design on front of crown with smaller S/Sgt chevron painted below. Fitted with camo net in ¼" squares. Above avg. cond. $124

Helmet, Combat, M1, USA, Army, WWII. OD finish shell with chinstrap. No liner. Avg. cond. $22

Helmet, Combat, M1, USA, Army, Vietnam Era. Helmet in OD refinish shell with dark OD web chinstraps on metal swivels. Includes thick fiber liner with dark OD webbing and fitted with early Vietnam era camo cover and OD helmet band. Avg. cond. $20

Helmet, Combat, M1, USA, Army, WWII. OD sand finish shell with lt OD web chinstraps. With rare pressed paper liner. Lt OD cloth covering, clean lt OD webbing and leather chinstrap. Above avg. cond. $276

Helmet, Combat, M1, USA, USMC, WWII. Dark olive sand finish shell with dark OD web chinstraps and fiber liner with dark OD webbing. With badly tattered USMC HBT spot pattern camo cover. Avg. cond. $35

Helmet, Combat, M1, USA, Army, WWII. OD sand finish shell with dark OD web chinstraps. With sand finish shell with lt OD webbing and leather chinstrap. Above avg. cond. $40

Helmet, Combat, M1, USA, Army, WWII. OD sand finish shell with lt OD web chinstraps on fixed bales. Fiber liner with lt OD webbing, nape strap, leather sweatband and chinstrap. Above avg. cond. $100

Helmet, Combat, M1, USA, Army, WWII. OD sand finish steel shell with lt OD web chinstraps on foxed bales. With M1 liner with lt OD webbing and leather sweatband. Avg. cond. $53

Helmet, Combat, M1, USA, Army, WWII. OD sand finish shell with lt OD web chinstraps. OD finish fiber liner with good lt OD webbing, leather chinstrap and replacement sweatband. Avg. cond. $49

Helmet, Combat, M1, USA, Army, WWII. OD sand refinish shell with lt OD web chinstraps on fixed bales. With 1952 dated M1 fiber liner with olive webbing and dark brown leather chinstrap. Avg. cond. $45

Helmet, Combat, M1, USA, Army, Medic, WWII. OD finish fiber shell with large red cross in white circle painted on all four sides. Lt OD webbing and chinstrap. Avg. cond. $132

Helmet, Combat, M1, USA, Army, WWII. OD sand finish shell with lt OD web chinstraps on fixed bales, fiber liner with dark OD webbing, nape strap, leather sweatband and chinstrap. Fitted with string net in 2" squares. Avg. cond. $53

Helmet, Combat, M1, USA, USMC, WWII. OD sand finish shell with lt OD web chinstraps, M1 helmet liner with lt OD webbing, nape strap, leather chinstrap and sweatband. Fitted with reversible from green to tan spot pattern camo HBT cover with large EG&A stencil on front. Above avg. cond. $82

Helmet, Combat, M1, USA, Army, WWII. OD sand finish shell with dark OD web chinstraps. Fiber M1 liner with lt OD webbing, nape strap, leather sweatband and chinstrap. Front of helmet crown has 2nd Armored Div design neatly painted on. Above avg. cond. $93

Helmet, Combat, M1, USA, Army, WWII. Dark OD sand finish shell with lt OD web chinstraps on flexible swivels. With M1 liner with lt OD webbing, nape strap and leather chinstrap. Faint traces of once having Sgt chevron design on front crown. Avg. cond. $37

Helmet, Combat, M1, USA, Army, WWII. Dark OD sand finish shell with lt OD web chinstraps on fixed bales. Faint white vertical stripe painted on back of shell crown. Also, M1 liner with lt OD webbing, nape strap and leather sweatband. Above avg. cond. $82

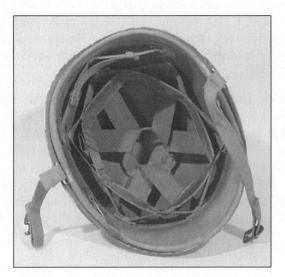

US Army M1 Helmet with Early War Inner Liner

Helmet, Combat, M1, USA, Army, Vietnam Era. OD refinish shell with nylon chinstraps on snap-on swivels. Includes Vietnam era liner with dark OD webbing, leather sweatband and fitted with reversible leafy pattern camo cover and two OD elastic helmet bands. Includes extra M1 helmet liner. Avg. cond. $20

Helmet, Combat, M1, Camo, USA, Army, WWII. OD sand finish shell with unusual splotchy camo pattern in red and dark blue. Has lt OD web chinstraps on fixed bales. With pressed fiber M1 liner with white webbing and nape strap. Avg. cond. $216

Helmet, Combat, M1917, USA, Army, WWI. Retains 95% of original rough dark olive finish. With black painted 35th Div emblems on both sides. Liner intact but chinstraps are gone. Avg. cond. $28

Helmet, Combat, M1917, USA, Army, WWI. OD sand finish shell with good liner and chinstrap. Has faint unit design painted on front of crown. For 103rd MG BN. Avg. cond. $51

Helmet, Combat, M1917, USA, Army, WWI. Semi-smooth olive sand finish steel shell with small dark 5th Div design (red diamond with thin black border and "5" in center) handpainted on front of crown. Fair liner and chinstrap. Avg. cond. $76

Helmet, Combat, M1917, USA, Army, WWI. Semi-smooth olive finish shell with 89th Div patch design with blue insert neatly painted on each side of crown. Fair liner. Lacks most of chinstrap. Avg. cond. $45

Helmet, Combat, M1917, USA, Army, WWI. Dark OD sand finish with small handpainted 33rd Div design on front of crown. Fair liner. No chinstrap. Avg. cond. . $55

Helmet, Combat, M1917, USA, Army, WWI. OD sand finish shell with handpainted 33rd Div design on front of crown, fair liner and chinstrap. Avg. cond. $38

Helmet, Combat, M1917, USA, Army, WWI. OD sand finish shell with 78th Div design neatly painted on one side of crown. Good liner and chinstrap. Above avg. cond. $40

Helmet, Combat, M1917, USA, Army, WWI. Semi-smooth dark olive sand finish shell with handpainted unit design on front of crown. With liner and broken chinstrap. Remains of insignia and "101" at top. For 101st Field Arty Regt. Avg. cond. $60

Helmet, Combat, M1917, USA, Army, WWI. Semi-smooth OD sand finish shell made with no rim. Has large handpainted insignia of cavalier-type figure riding Arty shell through the air on white oval background with white border. Fair liner and chinstrap. Avg. cond. $48

Helmet, Combat, M1917, USA, Army, WWI. Sand finish shell overall finished in erratic camo pattern in shades of yellow, black and green with thin orange borders. Has handpainted 225 Inf, France, Worlds War, USA AEF 1918–19, etc., lettering. No liner or chinstrap. Avg. cond. $45

Helmet, Combat, M1917, USA, Army, WWI. Semi-smooth olive finish steel shell with large 145th Arty ("145" above large crossed cannons) unit design handpainted on front of crown. Fair liner. No chinstrap. Avg. cond. $75

Helmet, Combat, M1917, Camo, USA, Army, WWI. Semi-smooth sand finish shell with overall handpainted design of geometric designs in shades of orange, yellow, lt blue and green. 3rd Army design painted on front of crown. Leather chinstrap intact. Liner missing. Avg. cond. $91

Helmet, Combat, M1917, Camo, USA, Army, WWI. OD sand finish shell with faint erratic camo design in shades of red, brown and lt green. 87th Div design on front of crown. Good liner and leather chinstrap. Dent on one side of crown. Avg. cond. $85

Helmet, Combat, M1917, Camo, USA, Army, WWI. Sand finish shell with large geometric shape camo pattern in shades of orange, green and dark brown separated by black lines. 27th Div patch design painted on front of crown. Good liner. No chinstrap. Avg. cond. $60

Helmet, Combat, M1917, Camo, USA, Army, WWI. Sand finish shell with erratic design in green and dark tan separated by thin black borders. One side of shell has dark rectangular-shaped design. Liner and chinstrap missing. Above avg. cond. $80

Helmet, Combat, M1917, Camo, USA, Army, WWI. Semi-smooth sand finish shell painted in erratic camo design in shades of dark yellow and lt blue-green. 35th Div design painted on each side of crown with all white quadrants and borders. No chinstrap or liner. Avg. cond. $69

Helmet, Combat, M1917A1, USA, Army, WWII. Thick OD sand finish shell with dark tan leather-covered sheet metal liner, dark tan web chinstraps. Above avg. cond. $65

Helmet, Combat, M1917A1, USA, Army, WWII. OD sand finish shell with leather-covered sheet metal liner, dark tan web chinstraps. Avg. cond. $40

Helmet, Combat, M1917A1, USA, Army, WWII. Improved version of M1917 helmet, also called the Gilley

US Army M1917A1 Combat Helmet

helmet. In OD sand finish shell with oiled leather-covered sheet metal liner, dark tan web chinstraps. Avg. cond. $27

Helmet, Combat, M1917A1, USA, Navy, WWII. Smooth dark olive finish domed steel shell with many neatly hand-painted designs of naval life and subjects all around crown. "USN" on front of crown with stylized crow above, sailor on shore leave, Wildcat fighter plane, "US Navy" life ring, fouled anchor, crow atop skull and crossbones, "Iceland" polar bear, flying tiger design with "Roaring Rosa" below, firing warship with "Morton's Raiders," Nazi submarine periscope and more. Underside brim and interior painted in blue-gray, dark tan web chinstraps and leather-covered liner in worn gold finish. Avg. cond. $219

Helmet, Combat, M1C, USA, Army, Airborne, 1950s. Exterior paint job with white field, black wing-like shapes on either side, metal jump wings on center front over painted name and small heraldic emblem above all. Open chin cup and web chinstrap. Air guard labeled head restraint and top cushion. Above avg. cond. $195

Helmet, Combat, M1C, USA, Army, Airborne, WWII. Paratroop version of M1 helmet. Fiber shell in dark olive finish with lt OD webbing, nape strap, leather sweatband and riveted dark OD web yoke straps. No chincup. Name and service number painted in white on underside of lip. Avg. cond. $50

Helmet, Dress, USA, Army, New York State Militia, 1850s. For New York State Militia. 'Tarbucket' style with wool sides. Patent leather crown and lower band. Parade visor with crazed leather. Gilded brass device with large spread wing eagle with italicized cipher initials on chest and motto banner at bottom reading "EXCELSIOR." Small pompon at front top with two shades of green darker on top. Avg. cond. $118

Helmet, Dress, M1872, USA, Army, 1870s. Black felt covered body with black trim band, arty side buttons, leather sweatband and vent at top of crown. With fluted spike and oak leaf base. Above avg. cond. $111

Helmet, Dress, M1872, USA, Army, 1870s. Black dubbed canvas-covered fiber body with green lining, leather sweatband on cork spacers, vent at top of crown with acorn and oakleaf base, fluted spike and Inf side buttons. Has 1872 pattern stamped brass eagle frontplate. Avg. cond. $187

Helmet, Dress, M1881, USA, Army, 1880s. Canvas covered body in black finish. With stamped brass acorn/oak leaf base with fluted spike, large stamped brass eagle frontplate with crossed cannons. Green lining. Remains of sweatband on cork spacers. No side buttons or chinstrap. Avg. cond. $145

Helmet, Dress, M1881, USA, Army, 1880s. Black wool-covered cork body. With gilt brass fittings, 1881 inf eagle frontplate with silver "2" applied to shield (small hole visible in shield above "2"), Inf side buttons with hooks for chinscales and set of brass chinscales. Poor cond. $149

Helmet, Dress, M1881, USA, Army, 1880s. Navy blue wool-covered cork body with gilt brass fittings and 1881 Inf eagle frontplate (has holes in shield for numeral but none remains). Satin lined with leather sweatband. Avg. cond. $132

Helmet, Dress, M1881, USA, Army, New York State, 1881. For New York State troops. White wool-covered fiber shell with stamped brass Inf side buttons with hooks, stamped brass "Excelsior" frontplate with appliqué "2" numeral and fluted spike at brass vent at top of crown. Avg. cond. $105

Helmet, Dress, M1881, USA, Army, New York State Militia, 1880s. White cotton-covered cork body with long rear visor, tall crown, NY State frontplate with "14" applied to shield. Has 1872 spike base with unusual tapered brass plume holder and long black horsehair plume. Inf side buttons with hooks. Green cotton lined. Cork spacers on leather sweatband. Size 6⅞. Avg. cond. $370

Helmet, Flight Deck Crew, USA, Navy, 1975. Tan cotton with 1975 dated spec label. Size 7¼. Green plastic cranial plates painted dark red with reflective tape sections and red finished earcups. Avg. cond. $20

Helmet, Vehicle Crewman, USA, Army, 1988, Gentex. Unissued helmet in original cardboard box. 1988 maker date. Ballistic shell. Mint cond. $75

Combat Helmets—Germany

Helmet, Combat, M16, Camo, Imperial Germany, Army, WWI. Dark leather liner band has folded cloth cushions tied to band behind each black oilcloth pad. Leather chinstrap has steel end lugs and both buckles are nickel-plated brass. Shell has thick green painted inside. Size 64 marked by vents. Camo design has 13 geometric panels with narrow black divider lines. Colors in red, green, yellow, brown, white and black. Avg. cond. $160

German Combat Helmet M1916 Camo

Helmet, Combat, M35, Camo, Germany, Luftwaffe, WWII. North African camo helmet with pinkish tan paint.

Camo paint was applied over base blue-gray rough texture paint. Eagle decal painted over. Dark blue-gray interior shell marked "SE62." Leather liner. Avg. cond. . . . $643

Helmet, Combat, M35, Camo, Germany, Luftwaffe, WWII. Shell marked "Q66" with blue-gray interior. Thick camo repaint with sprayed green and tan design. Faint traces of painted-over Eagle decal. 1939 alum band marked "66/58." Leather liner. Full chinstrap. Avg. cond. $370

Helmet, Combat, M35, Camo, Germany, Army, WWII. Shell marked "EF66" shows many period repaints. Last gray-brown coat peeling and shows traces of whitewash. Gray rough texture below with traces of Eagle decal. Leather liner. 1940 steel band. Shortened chinstrap fits over visor. Fair cond. $160

Helmet, Combat, M35, Camo, Germany, Army, WWII. Leather liner with inked size "57." Shell marked "EF64." Gray rough texture painted finish is over decal and base paint with five green brushed splotches. Avg. cond. $310

Helmet, Combat, M35, Camo, Germany, Army, WWII. Shell marked "NS64" with original gray inside. Outside was painted with glossy battleship gray and black central camo band. Decal area painted around and sanded. Leather liner. 1940 steel band and size inked "64/56." Below avg. cond. $110

Helmet, Combat, M35, Camo, Germany, Army, WWII. Shell marked "EF64" with original gray rough texture base paint covered with tan, green and reddish camo paint. Decal removed before camo paint applied. Leather liner. Steel liner band marked "64/56." Avg. cond. $502

Helmet, Combat, M35, Camo, Germany, Luftwaffe, WWII. Shell marked "ET68" with blue-gray repainted rim and body. Painted-over Eagle decal with traces scratched out. 1939 alum liner band marked "60/68." Leather liner. Avg. cond. $147

Helmet, Combat, M35, Double Decal, Germany, Luftwaffe, WWII. Shell marked "Q62" with blue-gray paint. Second pattern Eagle decal. National decal. Red painted owner's name "Frowen Kron" on rim with white "5/26." Alum 1937 band with leather liner. Below avg. cond. $221

Helmet, Combat, M35, Double Decal, Germany, Army, WWII. Shell marked "ET64" with green inside and gray brush-stroked exterior. Eagle decal affixed over gray paint. National decal painted over. 1938 alum liner band with leather liner with name "Kolbe." Includes camo string net covering with union ring at top, ¾" net spacing and attached liner band. Above avg. cond. $454

Helmet, Combat, M35, Double Decal, Germany, Luftwaffe, WWII. Dark combat finish. Eagle and national decals. Alum framed leather liner. Avg. cond. $210

Helmet, Combat, M35, Double Decal, Germany, Army, WWII. Shell marked "ET62" with gray rough texture paint inside and out. Both decals are painted over. Steel liner band. Leather liner inked size "54." Full chinstrap. Avg. cond. $196

Helmet, Combat, M35, Double Decal, Germany, Luftwaffe, WWII. 1938 alum band marked "64/57." Shell marked "EF64." Blue-gray paint. Second pattern Eagle decal and National decal. Leather liner. Avg. cond. $337

Helmet, Combat, M35, Double Decal, Germany, Luftwaffe, WWII. 1937 alum band marked "57/64" and leather liner. Full chinstrap with alum fittings. Smooth blue-gray paint exterior. Eagle and National decals. Avg. cond. ...
.... $356

Helmet, Combat, M35, Double Decal, Germany, SS Allgemeine. Shell marked "EF64." Original green top with inked oval mark, black painted rim and body. First style runes decal and party decal. 1939 alum band to liner inked "57." Shortened chinstrap fits over visor. Exc. cond. ...
.... $2369

Helmet, Combat, M35, Double Decal, Germany, Waffen SS, WWII. Leather liner inked "56." Full chinstrap. Shell marked "Q64." Gray rough texture finish. SS runic decal and party decal. Avg. cond. $716

Helmet, Combat, M35, Double Decal, Germany, Army, WWII. Shell marked "Q64" with green paint. Eagle and National decals. Inked "1939" oval to inside top. 1937 alum band with leather liner inked "57." Full chinstrap with 1938 date and maker name. Exc. cond. $1750

Helmet, Combat, M35, Double Decal, Germany, Army, WWII. Shell marked "EF62." Green paint. Eagle and National decals. 1937 alum band marked "62/54." Below avg. cond. $175

Helmet, Combat, M35, Double Decal, Germany, Army, WWII. Shell marked "Q68" with thin gray brush-stroked coat over original green. Eagle decal, painted-over National decal has been uncovered. Leather liner. 1937 dated band and inked size "58/61." Full chinstrap has RB-NR. Avg. cond. $433

Helmet, Combat, M35, Double Decal, Germany, Army, WWII. Shell marked "Q66." Green period repaint. Eagle and National decals. 1939 alum band marked "66/58." Leather liner. Avg. cond. $375

Helmet, Combat, M35, Double Decal, Germany, Army, WWII. Shell marked "SE62" with green paint. Eagle and

National decals. Rim marked with owner's name in white "S.Schenk." 1937 alum band with leather liner. Full chinstrap by "gxy 42." Avg. cond. $662

Helmet, Combat, M35, Double Decal, Germany, Luftwaffe, WWII. Shell marked "ET66" with blue-gray paint. First model straight-leg Eagle decal and National decal. Leather liner. Alum band and size 66/59. Shortened chinstrap fits over visor. Avg. cond. $406

Helmet, Combat, M35, Double Decal, Germany, SS, WWII. Shell marked "Q62." Has original green top, sprayed gloss black rim and body. First style SS runes decal and party decal. 1937 alum liner band marked "54/62." Leather liner. Shortened chinstrap fits over visor. Above avg. cond. $3150

Helmet, Combat, M35, Double Decal, Germany, Luftwaffe, WWII. Shell marked "EF64" with smooth blue-gray paint. Early "snake-leg" down-tail Eagle decal and National decals. National inked rectangle wording to inside top. 1935 alum liner band. Leather liner. Leather chinstrap with alum fittings and 1936/maker. Avg. cond. .
.... $399

Helmet, Combat, M35, Double Decal, Germany, Army, WWII. Shell marked "SE62." Green paint. Eagle and National decals. 1940 steel band and leather liner. Full chinstrap with alum fittings is dated 1937 and maker marked. Avg. cond. $343

German M1935 Combat Helmet

Helmet, Combat, M35, Double Decal, Germany, Luftwaffe, WWII. Shell marked "EF64." Dark blue-gray paint. Eagle and National decals. 1939 alum band marked "64/57." Leather liner. Shortened chinstrap fits over visor. Avg. cond. $225

Helmet, Combat, M35, Double Decal, Germany, Luftwaffe, WWII. Shell marked "ET64" with blue-gray paint. First pattern Eagle and National decals. Leather liner. 1936 alum band marked "64." Avg. cond. $300

Helmet, Combat, M35, Double Decal, Germany, SS Allgemeine, WWII. Shell marked Q64. Black painted rim and original green on top. First pattern runes decal and party decal. Owner's name "Hefer" on rim in white Gothic letters. 1939 alum band. Leather liner. Above avg. cond. $2300

Helmet, Combat, M35, Double Decal, Camo, Germany, Luftwaffe, WWII. 1936 alum band size 66. Smooth gray finish shows traces of tan camo finish. Second pattern Eagle decal and National decal. Below avg. cond. . $118

Helmet, Combat, M35, Double Decal, Camo, Germany, Army, WWII. Liner marked "NS66." Gray camo finish. Traces of Eagle and National decals. Below avg. cond. $50

Helmet, Combat, M35, Double Decal, Naval, Germany, Navy, WWII. Leather liner with inked "58." Shell marked "ET66" with painted white owner's name "Bruhn" on top. Smooth green paint. Gold Eagle decal shows repairs. Oversize painted tri-color National decal. Avg. cond. . . . $298

Helmet, Combat, M35, Double Decal, Reissue, Germany, Waffen SS, WWII. Has SS reissue decal. Shell marked Q62 with gray rough texture paint. Originally combat-issued as Police double decal helmet. First style SS runes decal covers original eagle/wreath decal. Original party decal to right side. Leather liner, inked "55" and faint owner name. Avg. cond. $750

Helmet, Combat, M35, Double Decal, Reissue, Germany, Luftwaffe, WWII. "Q68" marked shell with blue-gray interior and white painted rim marked "1400" with triangle over bar. Smooth blue-gray painted exterior. Painted over National decal. Eagle decal on left. Below avg. cond. $165

Helmet, Combat, M35, Double Decal, Reissue, Germany, Luftwaffe, WWII. Shell marked "Q66" with rough texture blue-gray paint. Both decals were painted around. Second pattern Eagle and National decals. 1943 steel band, tan liner inked "58" and lt brown chinstrap with RB-NR. Above avg. cond. $308

Helmet, Combat, M35, Double Decal, Reissue, Germany, Army, WWII. Shell "NS64" with gray rough texture paint. Eagle decal is painted around. Covered National decal has been exposed. Steel liner band marked "64/56." Leather liner. Avg. cond. $387

Helmet, Combat, M35, Double Decal, Reissue, Germany, Army, WWII. Shell "Q64" with original green finish inside. Green base finish outside shows reissue gray paint. Double decals affixed over gray finish. Alum liner band with dark leather liner. Chinstrap. Below avg. cond. $225

Helmet, Combat, M35, Double Decal, Reissue, Germany, Luftwaffe, WWII. 1942 steel band and leather inked "54" and red inked "N.F.A/S." Blue-gray repainted interior has white painted rim with owner's name "Schwenke." Blue-gray rough texture paint applied over both decals. Eagle side sanded to show outline. Chips and sanding on National decal. Avg. cond. $160

Helmet, Combat, M35, No Decal, Germany, Army, WWII. Shell marked "ET62" with green paint inside and out. Both decals removed. 1940 alum band. Leather liner. Shortened chinstrap with alum fittings fits over visor. Avg. cond. $93

Helmet, Combat, M35, No Decal, Germany, Army, WWII. Shell marked "Q64." Gray rough texture paint exterior. Below avg. cond. $30

Helmet, Combat, M35, No Decal, Reissue, Germany, Army, WWII. "Q64" marked shell shows double decals were removed from the original texture gray finish. Reissued in dark green paint inside and out. 1943 steel liner band marked "57/64." Pigskin liner. Avg. cond. $80

Helmet, Combat, M35, Single Decal, Germany, Luftwaffe, WWII. Shell marked "ET 64." Blue-gray rough texture paint. Eagle decal. Tan leather liner inked "56." Full chinstrap. Avg. cond. $245

Helmet, Combat, M35, Single Decal, Germany, Luftwaffe, WWII. Leather liner. 1941 alum band marked "56/64." Back rim with worn white painted owner's name "Zogl.Matziuk." Dark blue-gray paint. Eagle decal. Avg. cond. $145

Helmet, Combat, M35, Single Decal, Germany, Luftwaffe, WWII. Shell marked "EF62" with blue-gray rough texture paint. Eagle decal. Tan leather liner inked "55." Exc. cond. $709

Helmet, Combat, M35, Single Decal, Germany, Luftwaffe, WWII. Shell marked "ET64" with blue-gray paint. Eagle decal. Leather liner. 1940 steel band marked 56/64. Avg. cond. $217

Helmet, Combat, M35, Single Decal, Germany, Luftwaffe, WWII. Shell marked "NS 62." Blue-gray rough texture paint. Eagle decal. Liner inked "54." Full pigskin chinstrap. Above avg. cond. $225

Helmet, Combat, M35, Single Decal, Germany, Army, WWII. Shell marked "ET64" with gray rough texture paint exterior. Eagle decal. Leather liner inked size "56." Full pigskin chinstrap with faint 1941 date and maker name. Avg. cond. $350

Helmet, Combat, M35, Single Decal, Germany, Army, WWII. Shell marked "ET66" with gray rough texture paint finish. Eagle decal. Steel liner band with liner inked "58." Avg. cond. $317

Helmet, Combat, M35, Single Decal, Germany, Army, WWII. Shell marked "hkp60" with gray rough texture paint. Eagle decal. Liner inked "53." 1942 steel band. Above avg. cond. $279

Helmet, Combat, M35, Single Decal, Germany, Luftwaffe, WWII. Shell marked "SE64" with blue-gray rough texture paint. Eagle decal. Steel liner band marked "57/64." Avg. cond. $195

Helmet, Combat, M35, Single Decal, Germany, Army, WWII. Shell marked "Q62" with gray rough texture paint. Eagle decal. 1940 steel band marked "54/62." Leather liner inked "54." Avg. cond. $229

Helmet, Combat, M35, Single Decal, Camo, Germany, Army, WWII. Shell marked "EF64" with pea-green brushed camo over base gray. Eagle decal painted over but visible. Leather liner. Avg. cond. $237

Helmet, Combat, M35, Single Decal, Camo, Germany, Army, WWII. Shell marked "ET62" with gray rough texture base paint covered with whitewash that lets some gray show through. Eagle decal painted around. Leather liner and steel band marked "62/55." Avg. cond. $250

Helmet, Combat, M35, Single Decal, Camo, Germany, Army, WWII. Shell size painted over. Gray painted inside. Flat white painted exterior. Eagle decal painted around. 1943 steel liner band marked "64/56." Leather liner. Avg. cond. $565

Helmet, Combat, M35, Single Decal, Reissue, Germany, Waffen SS, WWII. Shell marked "ET66" with gray rough texture paint. First runes decal. Steel 1943 liner band marked "66/59." Leather liner. Below avg. cond. . . $748

Helmet, Combat, M35, Single Decal, Reissue, Germany, Army, WWII. Leather liner. 1939 band inked "66/58." Gray repainted rim and body over original green finish. Eagle decal. Avg. cond. $160

Helmet, Combat, M35, Single Decal, Reissue, Germany, Army, WWII. Shell marked "ET62" with gray rough texture paint inside and out. Eagle decal. 1943 steel liner band inked "62/54" with leather liner. Above avg. cond. $440

Helmet, Combat, M35, Single Decal, Reissue, Germany, Army, WWII. Shell marked "ET64" has original green inside and reissue gray rough texture outside. Eagle decal. 1940 steel liner band. Chinstrap dated 1938 and maker marked. Below avg. cond. $101

Helmet, Combat, M35, Single Decal, Reissue, Germany, Army, WWII. Shell marked "NS66" with owner's name

"Uffz.Meyer" painted in white on rim. Gray rough texture paint exterior. Covered Eagle decal. Steel liner band. Leather liner. Avg. cond. $145

Helmet, Combat, M42, Camo, Germany, Army, WWII. Shell marked "64" with gray inside. Thick rough texture tan spray painted overall with green and reddish splotches. Leather liner inked "57." Full chinstrap. Above avg. cond. $712

Helmet, Combat, M42, Double Decal, Germany, Army, WWII. Shell marked "ckl66" with gray inside having inked wording on top. Gray rough texture paint exterior. Eagle and National decals. 1943 steel liner band marked "58/66" and leather liner. Early full chinstrap has alum fittings. Avg. cond. $608

Helmet, Combat, M42, No Decal, Germany, Army, WWII. Liner marked "ckl64." Gray paint inside and out. Inked oval to inside top. Avg. cond. $55

Helmet, Combat, M42, No Decal, Germany, Army, WWII. Shell marked "ET62." Gray rough texture paint. Leather liner band. Chinstrap with alum fittings is dated 1937 and maker marked. Avg. cond. $164

Helmet, Combat, M42, No Decal, Germany, Army, WWII. Shell marked "hkp66." Gray rough texture paint. Steel band marked "66/59." Tan pigskin liner with inked "59" and owner's name "Kan. Schwarzmueller." Full chinstrap with stamped "44." Exc. cond. $282

Helmet, Combat, M42, No Decal, Germany, Army, WWII. Shell marked "ckl66." Gray rough texture paint exterior. Steel and leather liner inked "59." Below avg. cond. $93

Helmet, Combat, M42, Single Decal, Germany, Waffen SS, WWII. Shell marked "EF68." Gray rough texture paint. Second pattern runes decal. Dark pigskin liner has 1943 steel band. Size 60. Avg. cond. $643

Helmet, Combat, M42, Single Decal, Germany, Army, WWII. Shell marked "EF64" with owner's name "Uffz. Nolte" painted in white on rim. Gray rough texture paint. Eagle decal. Steel liner band. Below avg. cond. . . . $118

Helmet, Combat, M42, Single Decal, Germany, Luftwaffe, WWII. Leather liner. 1942 dated steel liner band marked "58/66." Blue-gray rough texture paint. Eagle decal. Avg. cond. $175

Helmet, Combat, M42, Single Decal, Germany, Luftwaffe, WWII. Shell marked "ckl64" with blue gray rough texture paint. Blue Eagle decal. Leather liner inked "57." Avg. cond. $292

Helmet, Combat, M42, Single Decal, Germany, Luft-

waffe, WWII. Shell marked "SE64" with blue-gray rough texture paint. Eagle decal. Tan liner inked "57." Avg. cond.
. . . . $275

Helmet, Combat, M42, Single Decal, Germany, Luftwaffe, WWII. Shell "NS64" with blue-gray rough texture paint. Eagle decal. Tan liner and inked "57." Avg. cond. .
. . . . $183

Helmet, Combat, M42, Single Decal, Germany, Luftwaffe, WWII. Leather liner inked "56." Shell marked "NS64." Blue-gray rough texture paint. Eagle decal. Avg. cond. $214

Helmet, Combat, M42, Single Decal, Germany, Navy, WWII. Shell marked "ET66." Gray rough texture paint. Gold eagle decal. Steel liner band. Below avg. cond. . . .
. . . . $171

Helmet, Combat, M42, Single Decal, Germany, Waffen SS, WWII. Shell size is on steel liner band 66/59. Gray rough texture paint. Runic decal. Leather liner. Fair cond.
. . . . $420

Waffen SS Marked M42 Helmet

Helmet, Combat, M42, Single Decal, Germany, Waffen SS, WWII. Shell marked "hkp66." Gray rough texture paint. Second pattern runes decal. Leather liner. 1940 steel band marked "64/56." Full chinstrap. Avg. cond. . . $626

Helmet, Combat, M42, Single Decal, Germany, Navy, WWII. Shell marked "ckl64" with gray rough texture paint. Bullet hole enters near back rivet, through band and glances off visor. Gold eagle decal. Below avg. cond. . .
. . . . $190

Helmet, Combat, M42, Single Decal, Germany, Army, WWII. Shell marked "ckl64" with gray rough texture paint. Eagle decal. Liner size inked "56." Inked procurement stamp to shell. Full chinstrap with 1942 date and maker name. Avg. cond. $177

Helmet, Combat, M42, Single Decal, Germany, Luftwaffe, WWII. Light use to liner with inked "55." Shell marked "NS62." Blue-gray rough texture paint. Eagle decal. Avg. cond. $190

Helmet, Combat, M42, Single Decal, Germany, Army, WWII. Liner marked "NS62." Gray rough texture paint. Eagle decal. Below avg. cond. $40

Helmet, Combat, M42, Single Decal, Germany, Army, WWII. Shell marked "64" with gray rough texture paint. Eagle decal. Steel liner band marked "64/57." Avg. cond.
. . . . $110

Helmet, Combat, M42, Single Decal, Germany, Army, WWII. Shell marked "ckl64" with gray rough texture paint. Bullet dent to top left side. Eagle decal. Inked procurement label to top. Liner dark from use and inked "56." Shortened chinstrap. Avg. cond. $250

Helmet, Combat, M42, Single Decal, Camo, Germany, Army, WWII. Shell marked "64" with gray inside. Tan camo over base gray shows age. Eagle decal painted. Bullet hole entered front and exited rear. Below avg. cond. .
. . . . $260

Helmet, Combat, M42, Single Decal, Camo, Germany, Army, WWII. Shell marked "EF66" with base gray paint covered by green and splotches of tan and brown. Eagle decal mostly painted over. Leather liner. Below avg. cond.
. . . . $175

Helmet, Combat, M42, Single Decal, Naval, Germany, Navy, WWII. Shell marked "ET62." Gray rough texture paint. Gold eagle decal. Tan liner inked "55." Full chinstrap by "gfg42." Exc. cond. $544

Helmet, Combat, Model 1916, Imperial Germany, Army, WWI. Shell marked "ET60." Gray paint. Below avg. cond.
. . . . $70

Helmet, Combat, Model 1916, Imperial Germany, Army, WWI. Shell marked "Q66," 50% of original green paint remains. Leather liner band has two pads. Below avg. cond. $29

Helmet, Combat, Model 1916, Imperial Germany, Army, WWI. Shell marked "ET64." Green paint. Steel liner band with three-pad liner. Below avg. cond. $88

Helmet, Combat, Model 1916, Germany, Army, WWI. Shell marked with size "BF64." Dull gray period repaint inside and out. Avg. cond. $32

German Combat Helmet M1916

Helmet, Combat, Model 1916, Imperial Germany, Army,

WWI. Matte field gray finish. Leather liner band. Avg. cond. $90

Helmet, Combat, Model 1916, Imperial Germany, Army, WWI. Marked "Q66." Green paint inside and out. Early leather liner band with three pads. Avg. cond. $125

Helmet, Combat, Model 1916, Imperial Germany, Army, WWI. Shell marked "BF64" with green paint. String plugs on each grommet/vent. Steel liner band with two leather pads. Avg. cond. $100

Helmet, Combat, Model 1916, Imperial Germany, Army, WWI. Shell marked "ET64," 70% of original green paint finish remains. Steel liner band has three-pad liner. Avg. cond. $131

Helmet, Combat, Model 1916, Imperial Germany, Army, WWI. Shell marked "L64" with bell trademark. Green paint finish. Leather liner band and three brown pads with cushions intact. Avg. cond. $250

Helmet, Combat, Model 1916, Austrian, Imperial Germany, Army, WWI. Shell marked "CAS66" with brown paint inside and out, 85% of original finish remains. Three-pad leather liner, grommets and cushions intact. Faint inked owner name on pads on steel band. Web chinstrap with grommets and roller buckles. Exc. cond. $378

Helmet, Combat, Model 1916, Austrian, Imperial Germany, Army, WWI. Steel band with three-pad liner. Brown leather chinstrap. No size marked. Tan-brown paint inside and out. Above avg. cond. $210

Helmet, Combat, Model 1916, Austrian, Imperial Germany, Army, WWI. White three-pad leather liner. Grommets and two cushions intact. Gray cloth chinstrap with gripper buckle. Brown paint inside and out. Above avg. cond. $210

Helmet, Combat, Model 1916, Camo, Imperial Germany, Army, WWI. Steel liner band with three-pad liner. Shell marked "ET64." Geometric camo design with black divider lines. Three brown, three darker brown and four gray-green panels. Avg. cond. $177

Helmet, Combat, Model 1916, Camo, Imperial Germany, Army, WWI. Shell marked "ET64" with green paint inside. Dark leather band and three-pad liner with cushions intact. Large geometric camo design with black divider lines. Green, brown and reddish brown colors used. Avg. cond. $279

Helmet, Combat, Model 1916, Camo, Imperial Germany, Army, WWI. Shell marked "W66." Dark green-brown paint with black melon stripes. Below avg. cond. ... $84

Helmet, Combat, Model 1916, Camo, Austrian, Imperial Germany, Army, WWI. Shell size 68. Brown paint-

ed inside. Ten-stripe camo design with black and brown brush strokes. Watermelon design. Steel band with three pads. Web chinstrap. Avg. cond. $218

Helmet, Combat, Model 1916, Transitional Double Decal, Germany, Army, WWII. Shell marked "Q62" with green paint inside and out. Eagle and National decals. 1939 alum liner band. Tan leather liner inked "54" and owner "Heinlin." Black leather chinstrap with roller buckle. Exc. cond. $1326

Helmet, Combat, Model 1916, Transitional Double Decal, Germany, Army, WWII. Riveted chinstrap loops. M31 liner inked "59." Alum 1939 liner band marked "66n.A.59." Thin gray brush-stroked paint covers original green finish. Eagle and National decals. Avg. cond. $495

Helmet, Combat, Model 1916, Transitional Double Decal, Germany, Army, WWII. Shell marked "Si66" with green rim stenciled in black "66 57-58." M18 steel liner band, three-pad leather liner, chinstrap loops and chinstrap with clip is dated 1918 and maker marked. Green brush-stroked paint. Eagle and National decals. Early transition. Avg. cond. $200

Helmet, Combat, Model 1916, Transitional Double Decal, Germany, Army, WWII. Variant with black finish. Shell marked "Si66" with original vent lugs and chinstrap lugs. Black painted inside and out. Eagle and National decals. WWI leather three-pad liner on leather band is 1939 dated. Avg. cond. $585

Helmet, Combat, Model 1916, Transitional No Decal, Germany, Army, WWII. Original brown paint to shell with chinstrap loops, steel liner band and three-pad liner. Cloth red-yellow maneuver band with buckle and three hook straps. Early example. Above avg. cond. $252

Helmet, Combat, Model 1916, Transitional Single Decal, Germany, Army, WWII. Shell marked "Si66." Green painted inside and outside. Eagle decal. 1940 steel band, marked "58/66" and leather liner. Avg. cond. $322

Helmet, Combat, Model 1916, Transitional Single Decal, Germany, Army, WWII. Shell shows removed vent lugs and chinstrap lugs. Thick rough texture paint inside and out. Eagle decal. Steel band with leather liner inked "56." Avg. cond. $282

Helmet, Combat, Model 1918, Transitional Double Decal, Germany, Luftwaffe, WWII. Shell marked "L64" with bell trademark. Battleship gray paint inside and out. First pattern straight-leg Eagle decal and National decal. M31 liner. Inked "56" and owner's name "Markert." 1939 alum band and inked procurement oval to inside top. Above avg. cond. $1200

Helmet, Combat, Model 1918, Transitional Double Decal, Germany, Army, WWII. Special variant of Model 1916 with earhole cutouts to allow field telephone use. Few issued during WWI but saw use postwar. Steel shell with vent lugs shows brush-stroked gray rim and exterior. Eagle and National decals. Rim marked "Uffz.Jung 8/13" in white paint. 1939 alum band, "66 n.A. 59" and leather liner. Full chinstrap. Avg. cond. $403

Helmet, Combat, Model 1918, Transitional No Decal, Germany, Army, WWII. Special variant of Model 1916 with earhole cutouts to allow field telephone use. Shell marked "W66" with traces of green paint. M31 steel liner band. Avg. cond. $90

Helmet, Combat, Model 1918, Transitional Single Decal, Germany, Army, WWII. Leather liner on steel 1941 band marked "68/61." Shell marked "TJ68." Worn gray rough texture paint to inside and out. Eagle decal. Avg. cond. $260

Helmet, Combat, Paratrooper, West Germany, Army, 1950s. Early "West German" style retaining 95% of field gray finish with liner and full chinstrap rigging. Mint cond. $275

Helmet, Motorcycle, Germany, NSSK, WWII. First type. Black leather body with ridged pads, metal grommet vents, brass eagle, neckflap and earflaps with roller buckle strap. Nine-finger leather liner with oilcloth RZM tag and inked "55." Leather pad at top has inked NSKK unit and "Berolina" color maker decal. Above avg. cond. . . .
. . . . $437

Helmet, Paratrooper, Camo, Germany, Luftwaffe, Paratrooper, WWII, Heisler/Muller. Shell marked "ET68" with gray rough texture base paint, Eagle decal painted over in gray and 11 brushed tan splotches. Two chicken-wire lengths are wrapped over helmet with four hooked ends at rim. Leather liner with inked maker "Heisler/Muller etc. 57/68." Gray chinstrap/harness has friction clip with strap. Four spanner bolts. Above avg. cond. $4187

Helmet, Paratrooper, No Decal, Germany, Luftwaffe, Paratrooper, WWII. Shell marked "ET68." Gray rough texture paint. Three solid and one vented alum liner bolts. Liner with inked RB-NR and size 56/58. Couple inked owner initials on liner. Chinstrap/harness still intact. Avg. cond. $1600

Helmet, Paratrooper, Single Decal, Germany, Luftwaffe, Paratrooper, WWII. Shell by "ET71" with blue-gray rough texture paint. Eagle decal. Variation steel liner bolts are vented and slotted. Early tan leather liner with maker name and size 60/71. Leather chinstrap/harness with friction clip and strap. Above avg. cond. $2700

Helmet, Paratrooper, Single Decal, Camo, Germany, Luftwaffe, Paratrooper, WWII. Shell marked "ET68" with gray base showing thick sawdust camo repaint. Tan and green sprayed design. Painted-over Eagle decal and spanner bolts, Eagle is slightly visible. Alum liner band on leather with faint maker and size 57/68. Gray leather chinstrap/harness and friction clip with strap. Italian front camo pattern. Avg. cond. $3161

Combat Helmets—Other

Helmet, "Jingasa" Style, Japan, Mid-19th Century. Open helmet having black lacquered exterior with gold leaf dragon motifs throughout and obverse having stylized four-diamond moon worked in gold leaf highlights. Complete with red lacquered interior, two-pad lining with silk-wrapped lining coils, bronze top floral finial and brass lace loops throughout. Some lacquer losses around edges. Above avg. cond. $704

Helmet, Combat, Thailand, Army, Post-WWII. Originally a WWII Japanese steel combat helmet. Helmet repainted and reissued by Thailand post-war. Thai insignia mounted on front. Retains 70% OD finish. Now lacking chinstrap and liner. Some surface discoloration. Poor cond. . . $36

Japanese Marine Combat Helmet

Helmet, Combat, North Vietnam, Army, Vietnam War. Viet Cong. Eleven-inch diam. Woven bamboo with string chin ties. Above avg. cond. $75

Helmet, Combat, Poland, Army, 1920s. Blue finish. French "Adrian"-style helmet. Probably surplus French helmet transferred after WWI. Has Polish eagle insignia, tattered liner and chinstrap. Avg. cond. $800

Helmet, Combat, Greece, Army, WWII. Exterior retains 90% of khaki finish. With chinstrap, liner with Greek inscription and hallmark. Above avg. cond. $70

Helmet, Combat, Greece, Army, WWII. Retains 90% of original khaki finish. With leather chinstrap and liner having Greek inscription and issue mark. Exc. cond. . . $70

Helmet, Combat, Yugoslavia, Army, WWII. Adrian pattern. Obverse mounted double-headed eagle and crest, reverse comb lacking one attachment rivet and no liner. Avg. cond. $256

Helmet, Combat, Greece, Army, WWII. Retains 95% of original khaki finish. With leather liner and chinstrap. Above avg. cond. $80

Helmet, Combat, M1916, England, Army, WWI. Also known as the MKI or "Brodie" pattern. Rimmed specimen retains 80% of the original khaki finish. Interior complete with oilcloth liner, leather chinstrap, and nickeled buckle. Chinstrap inscribed with soldier's name. Avg. cond. $44

Helmet, Combat, M1916, Canada, Army, WWI. British MKI pattern. Retains 50% of original OD sand finish. Side has painted green oak leaves surmounted by yellow painted "236" on gray field with scrolled red ribbon beneath and gold letters "N-Q-K S I A-S-O." Top has Canadian flag outlined in gold. Liner and chinstrap missing. Some surface discoloration and a small dent. Fair cond. $130

Helmet, Combat, M1926, France, Army, WWII. Retains 70% of original khaki finish. With Arty frontplate, liner and chinstrap. Some surface discoloration. Above avg. cond. $37

French M1926 Combat Helmet

Helmet, Combat, M1926, Thailand, Army, WWII, France. Originally a French contract M1926 helmet. Retains 90% of original OD finish. With painted brass Thai (Siam) national insignia, liner and chinstrap. Above avg. cond. $140

Helmet, Combat, M1931, Poland, Army, WWII. M1931 steel helmet. Khaki sand or "salamander" finish. Obverse with nickeled eagle insignia. Complete with liner and chinstrap. Above avg. cond. $970

Helmet, Combat, M1933, Spain, Army, Spanish Civil War, Italy. Originally an Italian M1933 helmet. Reissued

by Spanish Army. Retains 90% of brown field-applied camo paint, with brass Spanish Army insignia, complete with liner and chinstrap. Above avg. cond. $65

Helmet, Combat, M1933, Italy, Army, WWII. Retaining 50% of original brown khaki finish. Lacks liner. Chinstrap present. Avg. cond. $20

Italian M1933 Combat Helmet

Helmet, Combat, M1936, Soviet Union, Army, WWII. Retains 70% of dark field gray finish. With mildly flared brim shape, small top comb, chinstrap and part of inner sweatband. Lacks liner. Some surface discoloration. Avg. cond. $167

Helmet, Combat, M1940, China, Army, Korean War (originally 1939), Soviet Union. "Battlefield Relic." Originally a Soviet M1940 helmet. Retains 80% of OD finish, slightly flared rim, small off-center painted red star on front, four shrapnel holes and one large fracture near top of helmet, incomplete liner and broken web chinstrap. Interior inscribed with Chinese stamp in blue. Soviet manufacturing date of "3/39" still visible. Some surface discoloration. Below avg. cond. $220

Helmet, Combat, M35, Hungary, Army, WWII. Similar to German M35 except has riveted loop to back rim. Green painted inside top with gray rim and outside. Leatherette-covered steelband with leather three-pad liner with black rubber pads. Leather chinstrap. Avg. cond. $126

Helmet, Combat, M35, Camo, Hungary, Army, WWII. Similar to German M35 design but has riveted loop to back. Shell marked "DE66." Thick green painted inside has leather liner band, three pads, cushions and leather chinstrap. Thick green painted exterior shows faint airbrushed brown camo design. Above avg. cond. $95

Helmet, Combat, MK III, England, Army, WWII. MK III "tortoise"-shaped steel combat helmet. Retains 90%

of original khaki finish. Complete with webbed chinstrap, liner, and black rubber crown tab. Above avg. cond. $85

British WWII MKII Combat Helmet

Helmet, Combat, Model 1940, Portugal, Army, 1940s. Steel helmet with 70% of field gray finish remaining. Interior complete with three-pad leather liner and chinstrap attached with brass rail buckles. Avg. cond. .. $51

Helmet, Combat, Model 69, Sweden, Army. Model 69 steel helmet. Gray matte finish with tan leather sweatband and chinstrap. Above avg. cond. $30

Helmet, Combat, Pro-Nazi Reissue, Czechoslovakia, Army, 1930s. Steel helmet with green paint was reissued with white Slovak double cross stenciled to both sides and blue band at rim. Five-pad leather liner. Brown leather chinstrap. Avg. cond. $381

Helmet, Combat, Tropical, France, Army, 1958. Khaki cotton construction, stitched brim and crown, khaki twill band and snap holding upturned brim. Interior with "58" date stamp, khaki web chinstrap and slide knot. Unissued. Exc. cond. $38

Helmet, Dispatch Rider, France, Army, 1950. Composition helmet retaining 90% of original OD finish. With rear neck visor, interior having OD suspension, brown leather sweatband and leather chinstrap. Above avg. cond. $0

Helmet, Dispatch Rider, England, Army, WWII. Exterior retains 95% of original khaki finish. Unissued example with pristine liner, brown leather havelock and chinstrap. Exc. cond. $150

Helmet, Dispatch Rider, England, Army, WWII. Retaining 90% khaki finish. With liner, brown leather neck havelock and chinstrap. Avg. cond. $150

Helmet, Dispatch Rider, England, Army, 1944. Retains 90% of original OD sand finish. With wool and leather interior shock absorber, dark brown leather havelock,

chinstrap and leather sweatband hmkd "BMB 1944." Above avg. cond. $60

Helmet, Dispatch Rider, England, Army, 1943. Retains 90% of original khaki finish, complete with brown leather padded liner marked "BMB" and chinstrap. Exc. cond. $35

Helmet, Other Ranks, M1808, Prussia, Army, Cuirassier, c1810. Standard pattern helmet with high crown and crest. With long horsehair plume, brass helmetplate, brass peakmount and chinscales and leather liner. Above avg. cond. $3450

Helmet, Other Ranks, M1815, France, Army, Dragoons, c1820. Brass skull with tall crest decorated with oak leaves and bearing the regimental number (3). With black horsehair plume, brown leather turban, brass chinscales and black leather lining. Some small dents and tears. Avg. cond. $2300

Helmet, Paratrooper, Poland, Army, WWII. British pattern paratrooper helmet retaining 80% of khaki finish. With painted white lower identification band, bronze front Polish eagle insignia, leather liner, brown leather havelock and chinstrap. Above avg. cond. $700

Helmet, Spanish WWII Era Army, Spain, Army, WWII. Spanish WWII-era helmet retaining 50% khaki finish, lacking front metal insignia, with liner and chinstrap. $39

Helmet, Tank Crewman, Italy, Army, WWII. Domed helmet of black leather with leather havelock, chinstrap, and crown tab. Complete with interior lining, mounted with Italian crest. Exc. cond. $400

Helmet, Tank Crewman, Spain, Army, WWII. Black padded leather, with havelock, chinstrap with nickeled rail buckle, brown wool and black leather lining and manufacturer's label. Insignia missing. Avg. cond. $34

Flight Caps—U.S.

Cap, Aviator, USA, Navy, WWI. Black wool tam style with "US NAVAL AVIATION" around band. Owner's name written in ink on inside. Above avg. cond. ... $82

Cap, Flight Nurse, K-1, USA, AAF, WWII, Knox. Dark tan cotton with ribbed sweatband, AAF marked woven spec label and AAF/Knox maker markings on satin lining. Size 22. Above avg. cond. $48

Cap, Flying, A-1, USA, AAF, WWII. OD green fatigue cloth with short bill and headband loop above bill. Ear flaps store inside but are used when cap is converted into flying helmet. Below avg. cond. $40

Cap, Flying, A-3, USA, AAF, WWII. Multi-piece dark

OD HBT construction with stitched bill. Has printed oil-cloth spec label inside. Size 7½. Large AAF ink stamp on back. Exc. cond. $86

Cap, Flying, A-3, USA, AAF, 1942. Lt OD HBT with "beachball" crown, stitched visor and 1942 dated Qm tag. Size 7½. Well marked. Above avg. cond. $86

Cap, Flying, A-3, USA, AAF, WWII. Ball-cap style with multi-piece top, printed AAF spec label with inspector's stamp and stitched bill. Size 7½. Above avg. cond.   . $54

Cap, Flying, A-3, USA, AAF, WWII. Dark shade OD HBT. Size 7½ on printed spec label inside. Large AAF ink stamp on the outside. Has large stitched bill. Above avg. cond. $65

Cap, Flying, A-3, USA, AAF, WWII. LT OD-tan shade HBT cotton in multi-piece construction. Stitched bill with printed AAF spec tag inside. Has large, dark blue ink AAF stamp inside and out. Exc. cond. $55

Cap, Flying, A-3, USA, AAF, WWII. Lt OD HBT with long stitched bill and printed spec label inside. Size 7½. Exc. cond. $75

Cap, Flying, A-3, USA, AAF, WWII. Size 7½ on sewn label. HBT fatigue material with crudely stamped AAF logo on back. Exc. cond. $124

Cap, Flying, Summer, B-1, USA, AAF, 1942. OD green herringbone fatigue cloth with sewn bill. Size 7½ marked on cloth tab on inside rear. 1942 dated spec label. Above avg. cond. $139

Cap, Flying, Summer, B-1, USA, AAF, 1942. Lt OD gabardine soft crown with covered semi-stiff visor, leather sweatband and AAF marked/1942 dated Qm tag. Well marked. Size 6⅞. Above avg. cond. $150

Cap, Flying, Winter, B-2, USA, AAF, WWII. Dark brown leather body with semi-soft leather bill, fold-down earflaps. Size 7⅛. Above avg. cond. $103

Cap, Flying, Winter, B-2, USA, AAF, WWII. Leather body. Fleece-lined with fleece lined earcovers. Size 7½. Above avg. cond. $145

Cap, Flying, Winter, B-2, USA, AAF, WWII. Dark brown leather with fleece lining, semi-soft bill, fold-down earflaps and woven AAF spec label. Above avg. cond. $150

Cap, Flying, Winter, B-2, USA, AAF, WWII. Dark brown leather with fleece lining, fold-down earflaps, semi-soft leather bill and woven AAF marked spec label. Size 7¼. Exc. cond. $174

Cap, Flying, Winter, B-2, USA, AAF, WWII. Brown leather with sheepskin earflaps and inside lining. Sewn

spec tag. Size 7¼. Avg. cond. $100

Cap, Visor, Officer, USA, AAF, WWII. "Crush" style. Soft-form OD gabardine top with woven band, oversize gilt eagle device, glove-soft russet brown leather visor and chinstrap. Approx. size 7. Above avg. cond. $97

US Army Air Corps Officer's (Crush) Flight Cap

Cap, Visor, Officer, USA, AAF, WWII. "Crush" style. Tan worsted wool with woven band, soft leather visor and chinstrap and original gilt eagle device. Plastic sweat-shield in crown is still pliable. Size 7¼. Exc. cond. $116

Cap, Visor, Officer, USA, AAF, WWII. "Crush" style. Soft OD gabardine top with light OD woven band, glove-soft russet brown leather visor, front and rear chinstraps and oversize gilt eagle device. Approx. size 7. With offi-cer's name and serial number written on the underside of bill. Avg. cond. $97

Flight Caps—Other

Flight Cap, Italian WWII Air Force Visor Hat and Briefcase Ensemble, Italy, Air Force, World War II. White cotton twill summer-style visor hat, embr crown and eagle, moisture shield, leather sweatband. briefcase of desert tan canvas with exterior pockets. Ensemble includes pilot's flight jacket and tan twill flight trousers. Above avg. cond. $3000

Flight Helmets—U.S.

Helmet, Flak, M3, USA, AAF, WWII. OD flocked finish shell with pivoting protective earcups lacking felt pads. Lt OD webbing with headband, adjustable lt OD web chin-strap. Exc. cond. $65

Helmet, Flak, M3, USA, AAF, WWII. OD flocked finish shell with pivoting earcups, lt OD web chinstrap and lt OD webbing. Faint captain's bar design on front of crown. Avg. cond. $49

Helmet, Flak, M3, USA, AAF, WWII. OD flocked finish steel shell with lt OD webbing and headband, hinged protective earcups and lt OD web chinstrap. Above avg. cond. $53

Helmet, Flight, USA, Army, WWI. Classic pattern in black leather with multi-piece "beachball" crown and side skirts with pierced diamond-shaped ear panels and integral chinstraps with snaps. Brown wool lining, has diamond on top of crown with small strap for streamer. Avg. cond. $65

Helmet, Flight, USA, Army, WWI. Four-piece brown leather body is chamois lined with woven name label inside. Has snap-down goggle straps in back. Avg. cond. $50

Helmet, Flight, USA, Navy, 1950s, Centex. Small Centex football-style helmet with gold finish and white-orange reflective tape on exterior. Gold Navy wing decal on center front. One-piece goggles with clear lens rest above forehead. Boom mike attached on right side. Avionics installed. Padded inner lining with web and leather head restraints. Tan twill helmet liner with padded earphones and leather-mounted snaps for mask. Leather chinstrap included. Sewn label. Above avg. cond. $101

Helmet, Flight, USA, Navy. Gold finish with Day-glo bands. Single visor with wings and "NAVY" on shield. Nylon chin and neckstrap. Leather tabs with snaps for mask and padded earphones. Avionics and comfort pads. Avg. cond. $94

Helmet, Flight, USA, Navy, 1950s. Ribbed exterior with white finish and red shape painted at top. WWII-type Pioneer one-piece goggles with amber lens. Mike boom mount on right side. Helmet and inner liner both size medium. Helmet interior has leather and web fit/comfort restraints. Green twill skull cap with earphone receptacles. Sewn label in back. Chinstrap and snaps for mask. Exc. cond. $294

Helmet, Flight, A-11, USA, AAF, WWII. Chamois lined and with sewn label showing specs and medium size. Padded earpieces with earphones installed. Chinstrap and snaps for oxygen mask and throat mike. AAF emblem on side and earphone cords pass through goggle headband straps. Above avg. cond. $124

Helmet, Flight, A-11, USA, AAF, WWII. Dark brown leather with chamois lining, woven AAF marked spec label, large rubber oval earcups, chinstrap, snaps and clip for oxygen mask and AAF inkstamp markings. Medium size. Avg. cond. $79

Helmet, Flight, A-11, USA, AAF, Air Force, WWII. Modified for Korean War usage. Soft brown leather chamois lined. Has large woven AAF spec label inside. Medium size. Has been fitted with type H79/A1C metal receivers and external wire loom and socket for mike. Has never been fitted with boom mike bracket. Exc. cond. $145

Helmet, Flight, A-11, USA, AAF, WWII. Dark brown leather exterior with hard rubber mounts for earphones, straps for goggles, snaps for oxygen mask and chinstrap. Chamois lined interior with pads for ears and sewn label with medium size and also stamped with AAF emblem. Above avg. cond. $65

Helmet, Flight, A-4, USA, AAF, WWII. Lt OD gabardine body with woven AAF marked spec label, fleece earpads and leather chinstrap with fleece pad. Above avg. cond. $20

Helmet, Flight, A-9, USA, AAF, WWII. OD green twill helmet with web straps and hooks for mask and goggles, etc. Interior has sheepskin pads for ear comfort and sewn label with size large. Leather chinstrap. AAF emblem on forehead. Avg. cond. $20

Helmet, Flight, A-9, USA, AAF, WWII. Lt OD cotton with fleece earpads, adjustable leather chinstrap with fleece pad and AAF marked woven spec label. Large size. In issue carton. Near mint cond. $37

Helmet, Flight, A-9, USA, AAF, WWII. Lt OD cotton twill body with lt OD trim, fleece earpads, leather chinstrap and woven AAF marked spec label. Medium size. Exc. cond. $50

Helmet, Flight, A-9, USA, AAF, WWII. Size large in lt OD cotton with woven AAF marked spec label, fleece earpads and adjustable leather chinstrap with fleece pad. Exc. cond. $25

Helmet, Flight, AN-H-15, USA, AAF, WWII. Tan twill material with padded leather chinstrap and goggle headband restraints. Left inner earpiece pad missing. Size large. Avg. cond. $34

Helmet, Flight, AN-H-15, USA, AAF, WWII. Tan cotton poplin with leather straps to hold goggles and mounts for earphones. Snaps for oxygen mask and mike. Missing chinstrap. Interior has sewn label and chamois-lined earpads. Above avg. cond. $20

Helmet, Flight, AN-H-15, USA, AAF, WWII. Tan poplin cloth with leather straps to hold goggles and wires. Hard rubber mounts for earphones. Padded leather chinstrap. Chamois-lined pads for ears. Sewn label showing size as medium. Above avg. cond. $25

Helmet, Flight, AN-H-15, USA, AAF, WWII. Tan cotton body with AF marked woven spec label, adjustable leather chinstrap with pad, large oval rubber earcups and snaps for oxygen mask. Medium size. Avg. cond. $20

Helmet, Flight, APH-1, USA, Army. Matte black finish on exterior with dual visor and boom mike on left side. Padded web chinstrap and floating earpieces with snaps for oxygen mask. Custom black leather-covered fit and comfort pads. Exc. cond. $250

Helmet, Flight, APH-5, USA, Army, 1960s. Exterior painted in blue with gold and white pattern. Over each ear is dark blue star and name "BLUE STAR." Single center-pull visor with cover. List of names and units in Nam apparently supported by pilot. Left side boom mike and floating padded earpieces. Leather and web head restraint/comfort pads. Medium size. Above avg. cond. $244

Helmet, Flight, APH-6, USA, Navy, 1970s. With horse-shoe bayonet fittings. Red and white reflective tape pattern on outside. Hand-written VP-92 on one side. Single visor clear. Avionics included. Padded blue web chin- and neckstrap. Padded headphones installed. Limited fit/comfort padding. Avg. cond. $145

Helmet, Flight, APH-6, USA, Navy, 1970s. With horse-shoe bayonet fittings. White finish. Navy wing and "Navy" on visor cover. Single clear visor. Blue web padded chin- and neckstrap. Padded earpieces and internal avionics. White Styrofoam liner. Exc. cond. $210

Helmet, Flight, APH-6, USA, Navy. White fiberglass shell with NAVY decal on front. Army-style foam pads glued inside. With cloth inner helmet. Avg. cond. . $158

Helmet, Flight, B-5, USA, AAF, WWII. Fleece-lined, brown finish body with fleece-covered chinstrap and metal fittings. Size X-large with woven spec label inside. Hole punched in each side at ear for gossport or receiver access but never had earcups applied. Exc. cond. . $196

Helmet, Flight, B-6, USA, AAF, WWII. Dark leather exterior with earcups, snaps and hooks. Metal shows rust. Padded leather chinstrap. Sheepskin lined with sewn label and size tab (medium). Below avg. cond. $51

Helmet, Flight, B-6, USA, AAF, WWII. Dark brown leather outside and sheared fleece inner lining with sewn manufacturer's label. Some insect damage to exterior leather and fleece. Straps for the goggles. Padded chinstrap. Avg. cond. $84

Helmet, Flight, B-6, USA, AAF, 1942. Dark brown leather exterior with padded chinstrap. Sheared sheepskin inner lining and sewn size tab (small) and label dated 1942. Exc. cond. $175

Helmet, Flight, HGU-2A/P, USA, USAF, 1970s. Exteri-

or covered with camo tape. Center-pull tinted single visor. Bayonet receptacles. Padded chin- and neckstrap. Thin tan edge roll. Interior with gray plastic padded earpieces and custom-padded black leather comfort/ fit pads. MBU-5/P oxygen mask (dated 1980), with complete avionics and offset bayonets. Hose has single QR connector. Exc. cond. $256

Helmet, Flight, HGU-34, USA, Navy. With bronze finish and single visor. Navy wings and "Navy" on shield. Rt side boom mike assembly and avionics. Chin- and neck-strap. Tabs for mask snaps have snaps missing. Padded earphones and leather-wrapped foam comfort/fit pads. Above avg. cond. $158

Helmet, Flight, HGU-34, USA, Navy. Exterior covered in white reflective tape with orange trim. Single center pull visor missing pull. Bayonet receptacles at cheeks. Blue web chinstrap. Earpieces missing padded covers. Some comfort padding in top. User's name in pencil in several locations. Avionics intact. Above avg. cond. $100

Helmet, Flight, HGU-39P, USA, USAF, 1974. Flyer Chemical Warfare. White exterior. No visor or alligator clips. Green web chinstrap with pad. Earpiece assemblies with leather tabs and snaps, leather pad and web comfort fit assembly. Helmet dated 1974 on back. External label and last service date Oct. 1986. Exc. cond. $91

Helmet, Flight, HGU-39P, USA, USAF, 1980. Flyer Chemical Warfare. White exterior. No visor or alligator clips. Green web chinstrap. Earpiece assemblies with leather tabs and snaps and leather pad and web comfort fit assembly. Helmet dated 1980 on internal manufacturer's label and last service date Sept. 1985. Excellent . . . $75

Helmet, Flight, HGU-7P, USA, USAF, 1960s. With detachable white visor. White plastic helmet with notches at sides for earphones and boom mike. Safety warning label at back. White nylon padded chinstrap. Earphones suspended by white nylon webbing and rt side supports mike. Compression pads front and rear and no other head restraints. Above avg. cond. $93

Helmet, Flight, M-450, USA, Navy, WWII. Summer style with tan twill shell, goggle straps and leather chinstrap with cup. Sewn label inside and size 7¼. Exc. cond. . $72

Helmet, Flight, Model H-4, USA, Navy, Korean War Era. Ridged top pattern with gold finish. Decaled pilot wing on front and gothic initials. Boom mike on rt side and fit-adjustable straps on outside. Padded leather headband, web restraints and shock pad liners. Gentexite label with hand-written names and 1954 date on ear covers. Avg. cond. $86

Helmet, Flight, Model H-4, USA, Navy, Korean War Era.

Black finished exterior. No avionics. Mount for boom mike on rt side. Interior with leather and web head restraints. Size large. Above avg. cond. $50

Helmet, Flight, NAF-1092, USA, Navy, WWII. Brown leather exterior. Fleece-lined interior with no labels. Padded chinstrap. Avg. cond. $40

Helmet, Flight, NAF-1092, USA, Navy, WWII. Dark brown leather with chamois lining, woven NAF marked spec label, embossed brown leather chinstrap with embossed fleece-lined chincup. Size 7⅛. Exc. cond. . . . .
. . . . $133

Helmet, Flight, P-1B, USA, USAF. Personal helmet of named M-Sgt. White finish. USAF emblem decal and spring-actuated tinted visor. White web chinstrap. Net covers over earpieces. Web and leather head restraint and comfort set. AF emblem at top of inside. Exc. cond. . . .
. . . . $525

Helmet, Flight, SPF-4, USA, Army, 1970s. OD finish shell with single visor and Velcro tabs on cover. Elastic tube across back. Boom mike on left side. Web chin strap, floating padded earpieces and web and leather head restraint. Avionics intact. Avg. cond. $160

Helmet, Flight, SPH-3, USA, Coast Guard, Late 1960s. White exterior with reflective tape pattern and Coast Guard wings on visor cover. Dual ram's-horn visors. Boom mike on left side with complete avionics and chinstrap. Floating padded earphones. Leather and web head restraints. Above avg. cond. $177

Helmet, Flight, SPH-4, USA, Army, 1970s. Single clear visor under shield. OD finish on exterior. Avionics installed and boom mike on left side. Padded earphones, leather head comfort/restraints and Styrofoam pads in shell. Avg. cond. $114

Helmet, Flight, SPH-4, USA, Army, 1970s. OD finish with wear. Single center-pull clear visor and cracked shield. Boom mike on left side. Interior with comfort pads and head restraints. Earphones loose in padded receptacles. Avg. cond. $139

Helmet, Flight, SPH-4, USA, Army, 1980s. Exterior covered in reflective tape. Dual visors with ram's horn controls. Sophisticated electronics with high security interlocking connectors. Custom-fitted black leather-covered comfort fit pad. Padded chin- and neckstrap. Floating padded earpieces/boom/mike snaps for mask. Exc. cond. $100

Flight Helmets—Germany

Helmet, Flight, LKp W 101, Germany, Luftwaffe, WWII. Winter pattern. Brown leather body with fleece lining.

Oval bakelite throat mikes. Soiled bevo label by "Deutsche Telephonwerke etc." and inked size 61. Avg. cond. $140

Helmet, Flight, LKp W 101, Germany, Luftwaffe, WWII. Winter pattern. Brown leather body with fittings intact, oval bakelite throat mikes and long cord with plug. Fleece inside with bevo tag "Siemens etc" and inked size 55. Exc. cond. $200

Flight Helmets—Other

Helmet, Flight, Ensemble, Soviet Union, Air Force, 1980s. Black leather with fleece lining, chamois earphone pads, plug-in cords and goggles with clear glass lens. Exc. cond. $66

Pith Helmets—U.S.

Helmet, Fiber, USA, Army, WWII. Also called the sun helmet. CBI made. Thick fiber body is covered in tan cotton twill with several small metal grommet vent holes, matching adjustable chinstrap. Underside of brim lined with green cotton. Fully lined inside crown with Calcutta's maker label. Has captain's name and serial number inked inside. Size 7. Avg. cond. $32

Helmet, Summer, M1889, USA, Army, 1890s. Canvas-covered cork shell with vent at top. Extended rear for sun protection. Web band where crown blends into brim. Lined interior with leather sweatband. Avg. cond.
. . . . $90

Helmet, Summer, M1889, USA, Army, 1880s. White cotton-covered cork body with threaded vent cap in crown, green cotton lining and cork spacers on leather sweatband. Size 6⅞. Hooks for chinstrap but none remains. Above avg. cond. $150

Helmet, Tropical, USA, Army, Vietnam War Era. Tan cotton-covered fiber shell with green lining, adjustable sweatband and web chinstrap. Metal grommet vents. DSA contract markings. Exc. cond. $13

US Navy/USMC Tropical Pith Helmet

Helmet, Tropical, Fiber, USA, USMC, 1940. CBI-made helmet. With white cotton-covered thick cork body, brown leather chinstrap and trim, vent in top of crown, and underside of brim lined in dark green cotton. Reverse side of sweatband named to a Lieut with serial number and "Manila 1940." Has hand-written name label under sweatshield. 1937 pattern EM EG&A device affixed to front of crown. Above avg. cond. $93

Pith Helmets—Germany

Helmet, Tropical, M1940, Germany, Army, WWII. Second pattern felt model. Green felt body with early dark brass shields. Leather sweatband. Red felt liner. Below avg. cond. $81

Helmet, Tropical, M1940, Germany, Army, WWII. First pattern canvas model. Tan canvas body, green leather trim and chinstrap. Painted gray metal side shields. Leather sweatband inked size "53" and red lined top. Above avg. cond. $175

Helmet, Tropical, M1940, Germany, Army, WWII. First pattern canvas model. Tan body with green leather trim and chinstrap. Eagle and tri-color metal shields. Leather sweatband with maker trademark and inked "57" on red lining. Avg. cond. $140

Helmet, Tropical, M1940, Germany, Army, 1942. Second pattern felt model. Eagle and tri-color alum shields. Leather sweatband marked "JHS" and "1942 57." Red felt interior. Above avg. cond. $51

Helmet, Tropical, M1940, Germany, Army, WWII. First pattern canvas model. Alum National shield and gray Eagle shield. Fair cond. $30

Helmet, Tropical, M1940, Germany, Army, 1942. Second pattern felt model. Green body with green leather trim and chinstrap. Brass Eagle shield and alum National shield. Leather sweatband with underside inked "APN 1942 56." Above avg. cond. $181

German Tropical Pith Helmet

Helmet, Tropical, M1940, Germany, Navy, 1941. First pattern canvas model. White canvas-covered cork body with white leather trim and brown chinstrap. Gold finished gray metal eagle to front. Green canvas lining with leather sweatband. Embossed "Erel" maker mark and inked "1941 58." Above avg. cond. $1096

Pith Helmets—Other

Cover, Helmet, Tropical, Britain, Army, WWII. White cotton with ventilation hole on top and size marked inside. Exc. cond. $10

Helmet, Tropical, England, Army, WWII. Tan khaki pith helmet with sweatband and chinstrap. With Bombay maker's label. Above avg. cond. $61

Spike Helmets—U.S.

Helmet, Spike, Chinstrap Retainer, U.S.A. stamped brass buttons with Inf crossed rifle emblem, double prongs soldered at back. Near mint cond. $15

Spike Helmets—Germany

Chinscales, Spiked Helmet, Officer, Imperial Germany, Army, Infantry, WWI. Brass. Avg. cond. $158

Chinscales, Spiked Helmet, Officer, Imperial Germany, Army, WWI. Dark brass flat scales with black leather backings. Avg. cond. $145

Cover, Spiked Helmet, Imperial Germany, Army, WWI. Two-part main body with red painted "104" on front. Fittings for visors with front inked "vorn." Five straps to spike cover. Avg. cond. $171

Cover, Spiked Helmet, Imperial Germany, Army, Kurassier, WWI. Wartime expediency gray cloth cover with reinforced front and rear panels. Bag for spike. Body extended by extra cloth panel at rear to fit down and over lobster tail. Avg. cond. $180

Cover, Spiked Helmet, Camo, Imperial Germany, Army, WWI. Rush green camo. Two-part sewn body with attached spiked cover held by four cloth straps. Five brass hooks on rim. Exc. cond. $210

Eagle Crown, Spiked Helmet, EM, Imperial Germany, Army, Garde Du Corps, c1890. Beautifully made with open vaulting and cross on top. Metric threaded. Designed for M1889 pattern spiked helmet. In brass. Near mint cond. $82

Helmet, Spike, EM, Prussian, Imperial Germany, Army, Garde Inf., WWI. Black leather body and visors. Gray trim, spine, removable spike with dented tip and eagle frontplate having attached star. Clean kokardes. Ten-finger black leather liner. Inked Army issue stamp inside. Above avg. cond. $387

Helmet, Spike, EM, Prussian, Imperial Germany, Army, Jager Zu Pferde, WWI, Helbing Sackewitz. Blued steel body with tail and gray metal trim. Stamped size "57" and maker "Helbing Sackewitz." Gray spike. Avg. cond. $342

Helmet, Spike, EM, Prussian, Imperial Germany, Army, Kurassier, WWI. Wartime. Steel body, lobster tail, rivets, trim and spike. Steel line eagle with loops. Below avg. cond. $292

Helmet, Spike, EM, Prussian, Imperial Germany, Army, WWI. Black leather body and visors. Gray metal trim, spine, removable spike and line eagle frontplate. Black leather liner with three-pad liner. Avg. cond. $229

Helmet, Spike, EM, Prussian, Imperial Germany, Army, WWI. Black leather body and visors. Dark brass trim, spine, spike and line eagle frontplate. Ten-finger brown leather liner with felt pad on top. Reichs kokarde. Inked names on liner and stenciled front visor underside "R.v.d.H Berlin-Sch No.7 ???" Exc. cond. $538

Helmet, Spike, EM, Prussian, Imperial Germany, Army, WWI. Black leather body and visors. Gray metal trim, spine, removable spike and line eagle. Black leather chinstrap with gray fittings and kokardes. Nine-finger black leather liner. Avg. cond. $240

Helmet, Spike, EM, Prussian, Imperial Germany, Army, WWI. Black leather body and visors. Gray metal trim, spine, removable spike and line eagle. Eight-finger black leather liner. Avg. cond. $176

Helmet, Spike, EM, Prussian, Imperial Germany, Army, 1916. Black leather body and visors. Gray metal trim, spine, side posts and base. Nine-finger leather liner. Inked 1916 date, maker name and size "57." Avg. cond. . $137

Helmet, Spike, EM, Prussian, Imperial Germany, Army, Garde Du Korps, 1915. Inside stamped "CE Juncker 1915." Tombak body, matching chinscales, silvered Garde star and black eagle with motto "Suum Cuique" (To each his own). Silver trim and large kokardes. Avg. cond. $2785

Helmet, Spike, EM, Prussian, Imperial Germany, Army, WWI. Black leather body and visors with back inked "B.A.IV." Gray metal trim, spine, removable spike and eagle frontplate. Nine-finger leather liner. Inked "55" and "B4." Below avg. cond. $237

Helmet, Spike, EM, Prussian, Imperial Germany, Army, Jager Zu Pferde, 1913, C.E. Juncker. Blued steel body and lobster tail. Silver trim and rivets with backrim stamped

"56 7.J.z.P. 1913 3.I." Silver spike with fittings. Nickel eagle with attached nickel star. Eight-finger black leather liner. Stamped top "C.E.Juncker 1913." Avg. cond. $559

Helmet, Spike, NCO, M1857, Prussian, Imperial Germany, Army, Dragoon, Pre-1898. Tall solid black leather body and visor. Brass trim, spike with pearl band and cruciform base. FWR device to eagle frontplate and flat chinscales with Prussian kokarde. Nine-finger black leather liner. Exc. cond. $1000

Helmet, Spike, NCO, M1857, Prussian, Imperial Germany, Army, Dragoon, Pre-1898. Tall black leather body with cruciform base spike having NCO pearlring. Large eagle frontplate with FWR device. Single large Prussian kokarde (the Reichs kokarde was not introduced until Dec. 1898). Large convex dragoon chinscales. Partial lining. Exc. cond. $1210

Helmet, Spike, Officer, Prussian, Imperial Germany, Army, Grenadier, c1890. Marked "L.G.1890." Black leather visors to body with stamped title inside. Brass trim, spine, pearl ring on spike and eagle frontplate. Prussian kokarde with silver ring. Nine-finger leather liner. Avg. cond. $550

Prussian EM Spike Helmet, M1867

Helmet, Spike, Officer, Prussian, Imperial Germany, Army, Garde Du Korps, WWI. Marked "GKR.3E." Body, ridged visor and tail have silver trim. Stamped title to tail with black leather to underside. Front visor trim stamped "Wilh. Jager." Below avg. cond. $825

Helmet, Spike, Officer, Prussian, Imperial Germany, Army, WWI. Black leather body. Brass line eagle with pierced crown. Brass spike, pearl ring and cruciform base. Both kokardes. Below avg. cond. $327

Helmet, Spike, Reserve Officer, Prussian, Imperial Germany, Army, WWI. Black leather body and visors. Brass trim, spine, spike with pearl ring, four star bolts, chinscales and line eagle with nickel cross on chest. Prussian and Reichs kokardes. Below avg. cond. $350

Helmet, Spiked, EM, M1867, Prussian, Imperial Germany, Army, Cuirassier, 1870s. Standard configuration with regulation spike base, two-hole vent, spike and stepped visor. Early pattern helmetplate and kokarde. Flat chinscales with slotted screwback rosettes. Leather sweatband and liner. A few dents in shell. Rt chinscale broken. Liner torn and incomplete. Above avg. cond. $1150

Helmet, Spiked, EM, M1889, Prussian, Imperial Germany, Army, Cuirassier, 1890s. Standard pattern copper helmet with white metal spike base, regulation spike, leather liner and two-hole vent. White metal visor edging. One-piece silver EM helmetplate. Above avg. cond. ...
.... $3162

Helmet, Spiked, EM, M1897, Bavarian, Imperial Germany, Army, 1897. With circular spike base held by four domed retainers. Wrong pattern spike. Brass edging on beak. Leather liner and neckguard. Marked "J.R.97/Hel.J.R./ED./Comp." Avg. cond. $690

Helmet, Spiked, EM, M1897, Prussian, Imperial Germany, Army, Grenadier, WWI. Standard pattern helmet with round spike base attached with domed retainers. Five-hole vent but missing ball finial. Brass peakmount. Gold-washed Grenadier helmetplate. One-piece Reichs Kokarde and chinstrap. Nine-finger leather liner. Avg. cond. $748

Helmet, Spiked, EM, M1900, Prussian, Imperial Germany, Army, WWI. Standard pattern spike base, spike, kokarde and liner. Correct pattern helmetplate. Chinscales missing. Avg. cond. $575

Helmet, Spiked, EM, M1900, Prussian, Imperial Germany, Army, WWI. Standard pattern helmet with double tiered spike pedestal, vent holes, regulation spike, helmetplate and chinstrap. Nine-finger leather liner. Helmet stamped "7.K.R.I.E.46.23." Above avg. cond. $805

Prussian EM Spike Helmet

EM Spike Helmet, M1915

Helmet, Spiked, EM, M1915, Imperial Germany, Army, Cuirassier, 1916. Standard configuration with field gray base and spike. Silver-plated helmetplate. Regulation chinstrap. Ten-finger helmet liner. Hmkd "Helbing O. Sakewitz/1916." Above avg. cond. $690

Helmet, Spiked, EM, Prussian, Germany, Army, Arty, WWI. Large black leather body and visors. Gray line eagle, visor trim and spine. Brass base and ball top. Leather liner. Below avg. cond. $235

Helmet, Spiked, Officer, M1867, Prussian, Imperial Germany, Army, Kurassier, c1890. Steel shell with "step" visor and deep lobster tail. Silvered spread-winged Early 1860 Garde eagle on front having officer Garde star. Interior enamel ring missing. Convex chin-scales cloverleaf base on spike ventilator in cross pattern with fluted steel spike. Single Landes kokarde is present and correct. Kreeblatten or side lugs appear to be 1897-issue screw mounts proper for M1867. Below avg. cond. $1440

Helmet, Spiked, Officer, Model 1897, Prussian, Imperial Germany, Army, Pioneer, WWI. Standard form helmet with circular spike base, four-hole vent, leather sweatband and silk liner. With removable 6" trichter with horsehair parade plume. Above avg. cond. $1093

Kokarde, Spiked Helmet, EM, Prussian, Imperial Germany, Army, c1900. 49mm stamped black body with white ring and 20mm-diam hole. Near mint cond. $29

Kokarde, Spiked Helmet, EM, Wurttemberg, Imperial Germany, Army, WWI. Small hole pattern with silver round retainer. Avg. cond. $40

Kokarde, Spiked Helmet, NCO, Reichs, Imperial Germany, Army, c1890. M1887 pattern. Avg. cond. $66

Kokarde, Spiked Helmet, Officer, Prussian, Imperial Germany, Army, WWI. 50mm black with white metal ring and black center. Small hole in center. Near mint cond. $45

Kokarde, Spiked Helmet, Officer, Prussian, Imperial Germany, Army, c1900. For M1897 spiked helmet. Avg. cond. $56

Kokarde, Spiked Helmet, Officer, Reichs, Imperial Germany, Army, WWI. Post-1915. 52mm. 8½mm-diam hole to fluted center. Avg. cond. $35

Spike Helmets—Other

Helmet, Spike, NCO, England, Army, Life Guard, 1950s. Nickeled metal body, brass furniture, red plume and spine of floral acanthus leaf ornamentation. Frontplate presents Saint Edward's crown with oak leaf and laurel wreath and contrasting nickel starburst. Complete with brass chain chinstrap, floral oversize cockades and pristine leather lining. Exc. cond. $1800

Individual Equipment and Field Gear

Chapter Four covers the equipment and gear used by the officers and men in the field to fight and survive on the battlefield. It covers a vast assortment of the equipment that was issued, from ammunition pouches to Walkie-Talkies.

The extensive listings are not totally comprehensive, however, since only objects that were sold over the past two years are listed.

The equipment listed is heavily American and German. This does not tell the full story, however, since it should be remembered that millions of combatants from other countries such as England, Poland, France, and the Soviet Union were also equipped with American-made equipment. So, in that sense, American equipment is the standard for the Allies in World War Two.

As is true for this entire book, every effort has been made to positively identify each piece of equipment listed. This is often difficult given the cryptic wording of many auction house listings.

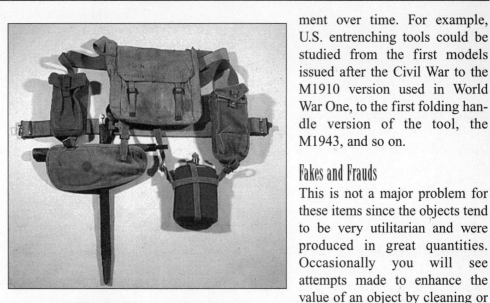

British Pattern 1937 Field Gear

Collecting Tips

One method of organizing a collection of field equipment is to collect the same items for several different countries. This gives the collector the opportunity to contrast and compare the design, technology, and manufacturing capability of various combatants in a conflict.

Another interesting way to collect field equipment and gear is to trace the evolution of a particular type of equipment over time. For example, U.S. entrenching tools could be studied from the first models issued after the Civil War to the M1910 version used in World War One, to the first folding handle version of the tool, the M1943, and so on.

Fakes and Frauds

This is not a major problem for these items since the objects tend to be very utilitarian and were produced in great quantities. Occasionally you will see attempts made to enhance the value of an object by cleaning or refurbishing, but these are usually easy to detect.

Collectors Clubs

Karabiner Collector's Network, High Point, NC, (910) 884-5566, Newsletter, German Militaria

Museums

The US Army Quartermaster Museum, Ft. Lee, VA, (804) 734-4203

The US Navy Supply Corps Museum, Athens, GA

The US Marine Corps Museum, Washington, DC, (202) 433-3534

The US Navy Museum, Washington, DC, (202) 433-4882

The Frontier Army Museum, Ft. Leavenworth, KS, (913) 684-3191

The US Cavalry Museum, Ft Riley, KS

Ammo Belts and Cartridge Boxes—U.S.

Ammo Carrier and Belt, USA, Army, c1880, Metcalf. Exact pattern unclear. Leather belt with four attached brass loops for saber, straps and holster carrier. Leather ammunition carrier has Mills superposed webbed cartridge strap and brass single tongue frame buckle. Good cond. $500

US M1880 Cartridge Belt

Ammo Pouch, Shotgun, USA, Army, WWII. Lt OD canvas body with twin liftdot closure flap, stitched web shell loops and stitched web loops on back. US marked and dated 1942. Avg. cond. $177

Ammunition Bag, M2, USA, Army, WWII. One-piece lt OD canvas body that slips overhead. Large pocket on each side. Dark OD trim. Well marked. Above avg. cond. $20

Cap Box, USA, Army, Civil War Era, E. Grossman Co., Newark, NJ. Has both maker's and inspector's stampings on front flap. "E.-Grossman Co., Newark, N.J." and "US Ord. Dept. Sub Inspector." Size: 3½" x 3¾". Good cond. $165

Cartridge Belt, USA, Army, c1900, Mills. Exact pattern unclear. Variant has loops for 40 rounds. 2.5"-wide tan web body with brass T-closure, stamped brass adjustments and marked "Mills etc. May18.15." 1⅜"-tall loops with black border stripes for .30 cal. Exc. cond. $69

Cartridge Belt, Assistant Automatic Rifleman, USA, Army, WWI. For Browning Automatic Rifle (B.A.R.). Four B.A.R. magazine pockets. Dark tan canvas and web with riveted metal buttcup. Built-in .45 clip pouch and metal fittings. 1918 dated. Above avg. cond. $27

Cartridge Belt, M1887, USA, Army, c1890. For .45–70 Springfield breechloading rifle. Dark tan web with 50 stitched loops that have three thin rows of black horizontal stripes. Brass fittings. Avg. cond. $133

US M1887 Cartridge Belt

Cartridge Belt, M1887, USA, Army, Spanish American War, Mills. 50 loops for .30–40 Krag cartridges and six handgun ammo loops. Unit mark on back of belt. Brass fittings. Above avg. cond. $244

Cartridge Belt, M1887, USA, Army, Spanish American War. Rifle ammo loops, brass fittings and brass "US" buckle plate. Above avg. cond. $98

Cartridge Belt, M1887, USA, Army, Spanish American War. 3"-wide black web belt with 45 stitched web ammo loops and brass fittings. For .30–40 Krag cartridges. Above avg. cond. $56

Cartridge Belt, M1903, With Magazine Pockets, USA, Army, c1903, Mills. Nine-magazine pouch belt. Back labeled "2nd 10 105/10-2-105." Avg. cond. $60

Cartridge Belt, M1903, With Magazine Pockets, USA, Army, Post 1906, Mills. Manufactured with reinforced puckers at pocket bottom. Hmkd to Mills at each end. Patent dates present. Above avg. cond. $120

Cartridge Belt, M1903, With Magazine Pockets, USA, Army, c1903, Mills. Tan canvas with nine magazine pouches sewn into the belt. For Springfield M1903 .30 cal rifle. Leather saber strap with metal loop. Avg. cond. $20

Cartridge Belt, M1903, With Magazine Pockets, USA, Army, Post 1906, Mills. Manufactured with reinforced puckers at pocket bottom. Hmkd at each end with Mills. Patent dates present. Above avg. cond. $60

Cartridge Belt, M1910, USA, Army, WWI, Mills. Ten magazine pockets. Dark tan web with faint Mills markings and date with dark bronze-colored fittings also Mills marked. Avg. cond. $30

Cartridge Belt, M1910, USA, Army, WWI, Mills. Ten magazine pockets. Dark tan web with Mills markings and 1918 date with dark bronze-colored fittings also Mills marked. Above avg. cond. $20

Cartridge Belt, M1910, USA, Army, WWI, Mills. Blackened brass fittings with Mills hallmark on brass tips. Stenciled on inside, "56/(crossed cannons)/ E/US." Exc. cond. $68

Cartridge Belt, M1910, USA, Army, WWI, Mills. Ten magazine pockets. Dark tan web with Mills markings and 1918 date with dark bronze-colored fittings also Mills marked. Above avg. cond. $38

Cartridge Belt, M1910, USA, Army, WWI. Non-Mills variant. Nine magazine pouches. Tan canvas web. Exc. cond. $87

M1910 Cartridge Belt

Cartridge Belt, M1910, USA, USMC, WWI, Mills. Mills hmkd on brass tip. M1910 for Marine Corps. Has US bronze button on rt side of buckle. Avg. cond. $103

Cartridge Belt, M1910, USA, Army, WWI, Mills. Ten magazine pockets attached. Lt olive web with rimless eagle snap on each pocket flap. Brass fittings. Faint date. Mills marked. One-half of front has replacement section of 1943 dated OD web riveted in place. Avg. cond. . $75

Cartridge Belt, M1910, Naval, USA, Navy, WWI, Mills. Nine magazine pouches. Tan canvas with Navy buttons on the pouches. Mills hallmark on ends of belt. Avg. cond. $129

Cartridge Belt, M1910, With Magazine Pockets, USA, Army, WWI. Nine attached magazine pockets. Dark tan web with rimless bronze eagle snap closure on flaps and bronze-colored fittings. Name stenciled on reverse side. Above avg. cond. $69

Cartridge Belt, M1910, With Magazine Pockets, USA, Army, WWI, Mills. Nine attached magazine pockets. Mills marked. Tan canvas and web with brass fittings. Above avg. cond. $35

Cartridge Belt, M1914, USA, Army, Cavalry, WWI, Mills. M1914 mounted cartridge belt set with 1918 date on back and brass Cav tag marked "2B36." Nine cartridge pouches. M1912 US .45 cal auto pistol holster. "US" in large oval on flap. Swivel frog hmkd "Rock Island/1913" on back. Leather strap wrapped around base. Above avg. cond. $200

Cartridge Belt, M1918, USA, Army, WWI. Nine magazine pouches. In olive web and canvas with brass fittings. Small attachment for pistol ammo pouch. Avg. cond. $25

Cartridge Belt, M1918, USA, Army, WWI. Nine magazine pouches. Tan canvas and web with brass fittings. Well marked and 1918 dated. Also has one .45 clip pouch. Above avg. cond. $38

Cartridge Belt, M1923, USA, Army, Korean War. Dark OD web with brass fittings. Includes two dark OD web Carlisle bandage pouches. Dated 1952 and 1945. Above avg. cond. $20

Cartridge Belt, M1923, USA, Army, 1944. Ten magazine pockets. Dark OD web with metal fittings. US marked and 1944 dated. Above avg. cond. $30

Cartridge Belt, M1923, USA, Army, WWII. Ten magazine pockets. Lt OD web with black finish metal fittings. US marked, dated 1943. Near mint cond. $93

Cartridge Belt, M1923, USA, Army, WWII. Ten magazine pocket style. Lt OD and dark tan web with metal fittings. "US" marked. Avg. cond. $19

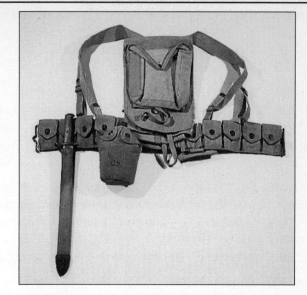

US M1923 Cartridge Belt Shown with Backpack, M1910 Canteen, Suspenders and M1905 Bayonet

Cartridge Belt, M1923, USA, Army, 1942. Ten magazine pockets. Lt OD and dark tan web with metal fittings. US marked and dated 1942. Above avg. cond. $20

Cartridge Belt, M1923, USA, Army, 1943. "US" inked pocket with nine others and faint 1943 date and maker name. Snap straps inside each pocket. Avg. cond. .. $20

Cartridge Belt, M1923, USA, Army, 1942, Boyt. Ten magazine pockets. Lt OD web with metal fittings. US/Boyt marked and 1942 dated. Avg. cond. $30

Cartridge Belt, Mk-1, Naval, USA, Navy, 1943. Lt OD web belt with two thin black lines running length of body. Many stitched web loops and metal fittings. USN marked and dated 1943. Above avg. cond. $37

Cartridge Box, USA, Army, Cav, Civil War. Cav issued. For percussion revolver. Flap cover secures at bottom with two belt loops in back. Single chamber for rounds. No marks apparent. Black finish. Above avg. cond. ... $95

Cartridge Box, USA, Army, NY Guard, c1880s. By Frazier. Patented 1872. Apparently saw only limited usage. Black finished leather with top latch and lower hinged front. Brass oval with "NY" in italic style. Wooden holder insert has 18-round capacity. Above avg. cond. $150

Cartridge Box, M1874, USA, Army, c1875. McKeever 20-round box for .45–70 Springfield cartridges. Black leather. Serviceable. Avg. cond. $28

McKeever M1874 Cartridge Box

Cartridge Box, M1885, USA, Army, c1890s, Watervliet Arsenal, NY. McKeever box. Dark brown leather with "US" in oval on front. Watervliet Arsenal marked. Canvas loops for .45–70 inside. Above avg. cond. $47

Cartridge Box, M1903, USA, Army, 1908, Rock Island Arsenal, IL. McKeever box. Rock Island Arsenal made and 1908 dated. Leather with "US" in oval on front. Canvas ammo loops inside for .30–40 ammo. Below avg. cond. $27

Cartridge Box, M1903, USA, Army, 1909, Rock Island Arsenal (RIA), IL. McKeever box. Dark brown leather with "US" embossed in oval on body. Twenty stitched dark tan web loops for .30–40 Krag ammo. Brass stud closure flap. RIA marked and 1909 dated. Avg. cond. $27

Cartridge Pouch M1889, USA, Navy, 1890s. Dark leather with "USN" embossed in oval on flap, fitted wooden block insert and two leather belt loops on back. Below avg. cond. $35

Cartridge Pouch, Revolver, M1917, USA, USMC, WWI, 1918. Three-pocket design. Each pocket held two three-round "half moon" .45 cal clips. Dark tan canvas with lift-the-dot (LTD) closure flaps. USMC marked and 1918 dated. Above avg. cond. $71

Device, Ammo Pouch, USA, Civil War. Unofficial badge for a division of the Union 6th Corps. Made of curved brass plate with cross device attached to face. Mounted by loop and lug. Above avg. cond. $75

Haversack, USA, Army, Spanish American War, Rock Island Arsenal, Illinois. Dark tan canvas. Flap measures approx. 14" x 14". US/RIA marked. Brass loops for sling. Above avg. cond. $24

Haversack, USA, Army, Spanish American War. Tan canvas with straps. Marked on outside of flap "TROOP C, 55" and hand-written name. Three storage pouches on underside of flap and two side pouches under main storage area. Above avg. cond. $55

Magazine Bag .45 Cal, USA, Army, 1942. For Thompson SMG. Canvas pouch dated 1942 and marked "US" on front. With carry straps. Exc. cond. $37

Magazine Belt, B.A.R., USA, Army, 1942, Boyt. Six-pocket design. Lt OD canvas and web with metal fittings. US/Boyt marked and dated 1942. Avg. cond. $28

Magazine Belt, B.A.R., USA, Army, 1952. Six-pocket version. Dark OD canvas and web with metal fittings. US marked and 1952 dated. Above avg. cond. $24

Magazine Belt, B.A.R., USA, Army, 1942. Six pockets. Lt OD canvas and web with dark finish metal fittings. "US" marked and dated 1942. Above avg. cond. . . . $30

Magazine Pouch .45 Cal, USA, USMC, 1942. For Thompson SMG. Five-pocket type. Dark tan web with lift-dot closures on individual flaps and wide belt loop on back. USMC marked and 1942 dated. Avg. cond. . . $29

Magazine Pouch .45 Cal, USA, USMC, 1944. For Thompson SMG. Three-pocket version. Clip carrier with snap flaps. Belt loop and dated 1944. Unused, well marked. Near mint cond. $42

Magazine Pouch .45 Cal, USA, USMC, 1944. For Thompson SMG. Three-pocket version. Individual flap cover with snap. Belt loop for ammo belt. Marked USMC and dated 1944. Exc. cond. $38

Magazine Pouch, Pistol, USA, Navy, WWI, Mills. Stenciled with Navy emblem on back. Light green canvas pouch for two .45 M1911 pistol clips. Above avg. cond. $37

Pistol Belt, M1912, USA, Army, Cavalry, WWI. Dark tan web with dark bronze finish fittings and saber "D" ring. Above avg. cond. $65

Pistol Belt, M1912, USA, Cavalry, WWI. Lt OD web with brass fittings and saber ring. Avg. cond. $16

Pistol or Revolver Belt, M1936, With Magazine Pouches, USA, USMC, WWII. Light OD web M1936 pistol or revolver belt with black finished metal buckle and belt tab. Holds five M1 carbine magazine pouches. Unissued condition. Near mint cond. $17

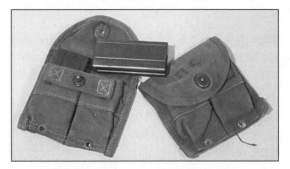

US Magazine Pouch for M1 Carbine

Suspenders, Belt, M1936, USA, USMC, WWII. For many pattern pistol and revolver or cartridge belts. OD web straps with brass fittings. Some green patina from age and soiling to the web. Avg. cond. $20

Suspenders, Field Combat Pack, M1956, USA, USMC, Vietnam Era. Dark OD web pair of adjustable suspenders with black finished metal fittings. Minor green patina to painted brass fittings. Unissued. Near mint cond. . . $14

Ammo Belts and Cartridge Boxes——Germany

Ammo Belt, MG08, Imperial Germany, Army, WWI. Off-white body with brass fittings and unmarked starter tab ends. One end inked in red "Top." Above avg. cond. $100

Ammo Belt, MG08, Germany, Army, 1932. 250 round. White web belt with brass fittings and leather endtabs. Inked numbers up to "250" and stamped brass "1932" with maker trademark. Good cond. $105

Ammo Pouch, Imperial Germany, Army, WWI, Loh Sohne, Berlin. 2" x 4" x 5" black leather body with belt loop and large flap with attached brass Garde star and four flaming cannon balls. Divided inside and maker stamped "Loh Sohne Berlin." Exc. cond. $538

Ammo Pouch, Saxon, Imperial Germany, Army, Cav, 1870. Pre-dates German unification. Large black leather body, 4" x 6" x 2½" with large crowned nickel cipher in front. Two interior compartments. Maker marked. Straps on the box to hook to the cross belt. Above avg. cond. $295

Pouch, Ammo, Three Pocket, Germany, Army, WWII. Black leather with RB-NR. Above avg. cond. $44

Ammo Belts and Cartridge Boxes—Other

Ammo Belts, China, Army, c1970s. Five unissued Chinese SKS ammo belts. Canvas ten-pocket belts complete with shoulder straps, buckles and wooden torpedo flap buttons. Type carried by Viet Cong in Vietnam War. Near mint cond. $25

Bandoleer, Ammunition, SKS, China, Army, 1980s. Green canvas with straps. Above avg. cond. $20

Pouch, Ammo, England, Army, WWII. Light OD single-pocket pouch with brass press stud on flap belt hooks. Avg. cond. $14

Pouch, Ammo, M1907, Italy, Army, WWII. Two-pocket leather ammo pouch, gray finished leather pouches in box shape with flap and leather closure tab and black finished metal fastener, loop to each on back for wear on belt and square ring on tab at center to back. Avg. cond. $10

Pouch, Ammo, M1907, Italy, Army, WWII. Two pockets, field gray leather with flap tabs, tab posts and rear belt loops. Above avg. cond. $20

Pouch, Cartridge, Denmark, Army, WWII. Brown leather with white metal tab finials, waistbelt straps and twisted wire interior divider. Above avg. cond. $40

Pouch, Dress, England, Army, Artillery, Victorian Era. Black leather strap with gold bullion obverse lace, gilded rail buckle with floral scrollwork ornamentation, matching floral slide and flaming grenade ornament. Rectangular black leather pouch with flap tab, brass tab post, black wool reverse, reverse flap hand embr in gold bul-

lion embr having royal arms, laurel and oak leaf ornament, gold lace border and gilded Art insignia. Above avg. cond. $400

Pouches, Grenade, Soviet Union, Army, WWII. Two WWII Russian grenade pouches, 5" x 5" burlap fabric, webbed belt loops and black leather strap. Above avg. cond. $17

Backpacks, Haversacks, and Knapsacks—U.S.

Backpack, Combat, M1943, USA, Army, 1942. Lt OD canvas body with lt OD web straps and metal fittings. US marked and 1942 dated. Above avg. cond. $61

Backpack, Combat, M1943, USA, Army, 1942. Medium shade OD canvas body with lt OD web straps, metal fittings. US marked and 1942 dated. Above avg. cond. $59

US M1943 Backpack

Backpack, Combat, M1943, Camo, USA, Army, 1943. Also called the jungle pack. Spot pattern camo on lt green background canvas with lt OD web straps and brass fittings. "US" marked and 1943 dated. Above avg. cond. $145

Backpack, Combat, M1943, Camo, USA, Army, 1943. Spot pattern camo on green background. Canvas body with lt OD web straps and metal fittings. US marked and 1943 dated. Above avg. cond. $145

Backpack, M1941, USA, USMC, 1942. Lt OD canvas body with different shade lt OD trim and web straps. Dated 1942–43. Above avg. cond. $27

Backpack, M1941, USA, Navy, WWII. USMC pattern. Lt OD canvas body with lt OD web straps and sliding pads on shoulder straps. USN marked. Avg. cond. $22

Backpack, M1944, USA, Army, 1945. British made and US marked. 1945 dated. Exc. cond. $28

Bag, Field (Musette), M1936, USA, Army, 1941. Lt OD canvas body with lt OD web straps. US marked and 1941 dated. Avg. cond. $21

Bag, Field (Musette), M1936, USA, Army, 1943. Lt OD canvas body with web straps and sling. US marked and 1943 dated. Avg. cond. $25

Bag, Field (Musette), M1936, USA, Army, 1940. Lt OD canvas with lt OD web straps. US marked and 1940 dated. Includes web sling. Above avg. cond. $59

Bag, Field (Musette), M1936, USA, Army, 1944. Lt olive canvas with tan trim and straps and metal fittings. British made and marked with broad arrow proofs. Dated 1944. Avg. cond. $45

Blanket, USA, Army, WWI. OD wool with two darker stripes on side and stenciled outline of "US" over Ordnance bomb emblem. Below avg. cond. $59

Cargo Bag, USA, Army, 1945, Boyt. For M1945 field pack. Waterproof lined single chamber, flap top with canvas handle and two security buckles. Web straps and stowage rings on bottom. Hmkd Boyt with 1945 date. Above avg. cond. $24

US Army M1945 Field Pack

Cargo Pack, USA, Army, WWII. For M1944 or M1945 field pack. British made. Lt olive canvas with dark OD web straps. US and broad arrow marked. Avg. cond. $20

Dispatch Rider Bags, USA, Army, WWII. For motorcycle use. Brown leather with triple strap closure flaps that are marked with "US" in an oval. Top leather section has been shortened and riveted back together. Avg. cond. $40

Drop Bag, For "Walkie-Talkie," USA, Army, Paratrooper, WWII. Felt-padded and canvas-covered zipper close bag with reinforced web straps and hangers. For

delivering "Walkie-Talkies" (BC-611) with paratroops. Avg. cond. $19

Haversack, USA, Army, Spanish American War. Tan canvas with "US" stenciled on front of pouch and on underside of flap. Avg. cond. $30

Haversack, M1910, USA, Army, WWI. Dark tan canvas body with dark tan web straps, dark metal fittings and matching mess kit (meat can) carrier. "US" marked and 1918 dated. Includes tan canvas lower half that is "B.2nd/65" unit marked. Avg. cond. $12

Haversack, M1910, USA, Army, WWI. Dark tan canvas body with dark OD web and dark bronze finish fittings. "US" marked and dated 1918. Includes matching mess kit (meat can) carrier. Above avg. cond. $30

Haversack, M1910, USA, Army, WWI, Rock Island Arsenal, Illinois. Dark tan canvas body with tan trim. Brass hooks for sling. US/RIA marked. Flap approx. 14" x 14". Stencil marked "C/Inf/3/Ore" and "2." Avg. cond. $24

Haversack, M1910, USA, Army, 1918, Rock Island Arsenal, Illinois. Tan canvas with tan web straps and brass fittings. "US/RIA" marked and dated 1918. Above avg. cond. $12

Haversack, M1910, USA, Army, 1914, Rock Island Arsenal, Illinois. Lt OD canvas body with lt OD web straps and matching mess kit (meat can) carrier. "US/79" marked on flap. Lot includes RIA marked, 1914 dated mess kit with stamped markings on handle. Avg. cond. $27

Haversack, M1928, USA, Army, 1942. Lt OD canvas body with matching mess kit carrier, lt OD web straps and metal fittings. US marked and 1942 dated. Exc. cond. $27

Haversack, M1928, USA, Army, 1942. Lt OD canvas body with lt OD web straps, dark metal fittings and mess kit carrier. US marked and 1942 dated. Above avg. cond. $29

Knapsack, USA, Army, Civil War. Black treated cloth and black leather straps. Below avg. cond. $132

Map Case, M1918, USA, Army, WWI. Dark tan canvas with twin lift-the-dot (LTD) fasteners on flap. Web carrying strap. "US" marked and 1918 dated. Exc. cond. $23

Pack Board, Yukon Type, USA, Army, WWII. Yukon pattern pack board with dark OD canvas padding and web straps. Large canvas pack attached by metal snap hooks and "D" rings. Flap marked "US-CE-C." Allowed individual soldiers to transport heavy awkward loads such as mortars. A wide variety of accessories were available for attaching various types of loads. Replaced in 1944 by a plywood model. Avg. cond. $20

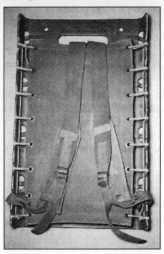

US Army WWII Packboard

Suspenders, Combat, M1936, USA, Army, 1942. Lt OD web with metal fittings. US marked and 1942 dated. Above avg. cond. $37

Suspenders, Combat, M1936, USA, Army, 1942. Lt OD web with metal fittings. US marked and 1942 dated. Exc. cond. $49

Suspenders, Combat, M1936, USA, Army, 1943. Dark OD web with dark finish metal fittings. British made with broad arrow proof marks and 1943 date. Above avg. cond. $37

Wool Blanket, USA, Army, WWI. Dark gray wool with green stripe at either end. Marked "U.S." and also has woven maker's label. Above avg. cond. $38

Wool Blanket, USA, Army, WWI. Lt OD wool with OD stripe at either end. "US" in center and dark tan stitch reinforced edges. Above avg. cond. $72

Wool Blanket, USA, Army, 1884. Blue-gray coarse wool blanket. Dark blue stripe on one side. Dated 1884. Above avg. cond. $93

Wool Blanket, USA, Army, WWI. Lt OD wool with brown stripe at either end. Avg. cond. $35

Wool Blanket, USA, Army, 1935. OD brown wool with "US" in center. Philadelphia Qm depot tag on side. Tag dated 8-12-35. Avg. cond. $23

Backpacks, Haversacks, and Knapsacks—Germany

Assault Pack, Pioneer, Germany, Army, Pioneer, WWII. Green canvas body is divided and has four snap flaps to side ammo pockets. Gray leather closure straps to flap, green web belt loops and one D-ring. Above avg. cond. $113

Assault Pack, Pioneer, Germany, Army, Pioneers, WWII. Green canvas body with two side openings and mess kit pocket to top flap. Web fittings and hooks for Y-strap use. Avg. cond. $118

Backpack, Imperial Germany, Army, WWI. 13" x 15". 1915 dated. Maker marked. Complete with straps and roller buckles. Cloth compartments. Dark olive gray ersatz pebbled leather body. All loops present. Avg. cond. . $60

Backpack, Imperial Germany, Army, WWI. Tan/gray canvas body with fur backing. Dark leather fittings. Maker and 1917 marks on back. Field repaired leather straps. Avg. cond. $35

Backpack, Imperial Germany, Army, WWI. Gray canvas flap with brown leather fittings. Thin brown fur to back. Gray canvas inside with large owner inked "Reinhardt Wittenberg/E" and some issue stamps. Stamped 1915 date and maker name. Black leather shoulder straps. Below avg. cond. $50

Backpack, Imperial Germany, Army, 1915, Franz Cobau, Berlin. Gray canvas flap, fur back, wood frame, brown leather fittings and straps. Reddish canvas inside. Maker "Franz Cobau Berlin 1915." Below avg. cond. $36

Backpack Cover, Camo, Germany, Army, WWII. 22"-long white cotton body resembles large helmet cover. Double tie-strings on one end, single tie-string on the other. Covers backpack. Exc. cond. $38

Backpack, Assault, Germany, Army, DAK, WWII. This is the pack that goes with the DAK canvas "A" frame. OG canvas. Avg. cond. $125

Backpack, Cable Layer, Germany, Army, 1940, IBB, Berlin. Field gray metal tubular frame and reel. Chain drive reel with wire guide. Crank handle is stored in brown leather pouch with leather pad on back, canvas back panel, brown leather shoulder straps and leather brake strap. Alum maker tag "IBB Berlin 1940." Above avg. cond. $264

Backpack, Pony Fur, Germany, Army, 1943. Two-tone brown fur flap, green canvas body and leather fittings. 1943 date and maker name. Black leather shoulder straps. Avg. cond. $50

Backpack, Pony Fur, Germany, SS, 1938. Fur on back and flap. Gray canvas body with wooden frame and black leather fittings. "RZM Tornister" oilcloth tag has large inked SS runes in circle at side. Black leather stamped "RZM L3/9/38." Black leather straps. Below avg. cond. $55

Backpack, Pony Fur, Germany, Army, 1942. Two-tone brown pony fur covered flap with olive green canvas body. Well marked and 1942 dated. Named on back in ink. Avg. cond. $20

Backpack, Pony Fur, Germany, Army, 1937. Reddish brown fur flap and sides. Brown leather trim, gray canvas inside. Inked "AD ABt 4/152 AD Gau XV." Wooden frame. Dated 1937 and maker named. Shoulder straps unit stamped "AD Abt.4/152." Avg. cond. $50

Backpack, Pony Fur, Germany, Army, 1941. Two-tone brown fur, green canvas body and black leather straps. Maker marked "bdl41" and owner's name inked "Sperl K." Avg. cond. $40

Backpack, Pony Fur, Germany, Army, WWII. Brown fur flap. Green canvas body. Maker marked and dated. Black leather shoulder straps. Avg. cond. $35

Backpack, Pony Fur, Germany, Army, 1940. Brown fur flap, green canvas body and black leather fittings. Stamped with 1940 date and maker name. Avg. cond. . .
. . . . $35

Backpack, Pony Fur, Germany, Army, 1940, Wittkopp & Co., Bielefeld. Green canvas body and flap with black leather fittings. Hooks for Y-strap use. By "Wittkopp & Co. Bielefeld 1940." Above avg. cond. $45

Backpack, Pony Fur, Germany, Army, 1940, Gebruder Klinge, Dresden. Green canvas body, brown fur and brown leather fittings. Maker "Gebruder Klinge Dresden 1940." Black straps. Avg. cond. $40

Backpack, Pony Fur, Germany, Army, WWII. Two-tone brown fur flap, black leather trim and green canvas body. Black leather shoulder straps. Avg. cond. $30

Backpack, Pony Fur, Germany, Army, 1942. Two-tone brown fur flap to green canvas body. Black leather shoulder straps and fittings with 1942 date and maker name. Avg. cond. $50

Backpack, Pony Fur, Germany, Army, Signalman, 1941. Brown fur on all sides and leather number 1 on front. Brown leather fittings. Gray canvas inside with dividers. Stamped "fft/41 WaA136." Avg. cond. $66

Backpack, Pony Fur, Germany, RAD, 1937. Brown fur flap and sides. Olive canvas body, wood frame and alum fittings. Roller buckle missing one prong. Inked "RAD etc." Black leather shoulder straps. Dated 1937 and maker marked. Avg. cond. $65

Battlepack, A-frame, Germany, Army, 1944. Olive web body inked "epf1944." Four steel hooks and three black leather straps. Exc. cond. $271

Bread Bag, Germany, Army, WWII. Late-war olive canvas body with black leather and steel fittings. Rifle cleaning kit pocket has canvas closure strap. Exc. cond. . $75

Bread Bag, Germany, Army, WWII. Green canvas body with three sewn loops at top. Black leather and steel fittings. Canvas pocket for rifle cleaning kit. Exc. cond. $177

Bread Bag, Imperial Germany, Army, WWI. Brown-tan body with brown leather and alum buttons and fittings. Fair cond. $34

Bread Bag, Germany, Luftwaffe, WWII. Blue-gray canvas, black leather and steel fittings. Exc. cond. $47

Bread Bag, Germany, SA, 1930s. Dark brown bag. Exc. cond. $203

Bread Bag, Germany, Army, WWII. Green canvas body, black leather and steel fittings. With shoulder strap. Avg. cond. $40

Bread Bag, Germany, SA, 1930s. Tan cloth. Alum buttons. Avg. cond. $20

Bread Bag, Germany, Army, DAK, WWII. Olive canvas body has web fittings to outside and stiff leather straps inside. Below avg. cond. $24

Bread Bag, Germany, Luftwaffe, WWII. Blue-gray canvas body, black leather and steel fittings. Inside flap inked black "B.B.1648.2." Avg. cond. $50

Bread Bag, Imperial Germany, Army, WWI. Gray canvas body with inked Army issue to inside. Avg. cond. . . $21

Bread Bag, Imperial Germany, Army, WWI. Reddish brown canvas body with brown leather and gray metal fittings. Inked "B.A.XV.1913." Shoulder strap. Above avg. cond. $75

Bread Bag, Germany, Army, 1942. Gray canvas with black leather and alum fittings. Inside flap inked "1942 Ferdinand Brenner etc." Divided pouch. Exc. cond. . $35

Bread Bag, Germany, Luftwaffe, 1941. Blue-gray canvas with gray leather and alum fittings. Inked inside flap "WL 41 etc." and Luftwaffe eagle. Exc. cond. $35

Duffle Bag, Naval, Germany, Navy, WWII. Bag is of field green color and is complete. Lock has anchor logo, maker marks, etc. Above avg. cond. $51

Pouch, Assault Pack, Tropical, Germany, Army, WWII. For A-frame use. Small olive canvas body with black leather and web fittings. Inked maker name. Above avg. cond. $141

Ration Bag, Germany, Army, 1941. 26" x 44" Off-white woven body with two blue stripes. Black inked eagle and marked "H.Vpfl. 1941." Above avg. cond. $21

Ration Bag, Germany, Army, 1944. Gray woven body with two blue stripes. Black inked eagle and "H.Vpfl 1944." Avg. cond. $28

Ration Bag, Germany, Army, 1941. 26" x 41". Off-white woven body with two blue stripes. Black inked eagle side and "H.Vpfl. 1941" side. Avg. cond. $20

Ration Bag, Germany, Army, 1937. 28" x 42". Off-white woven bag with two blue stripes, black inked party eagle and "H.Vpfl.1937." Avg. cond. $20

Y-straps, Combat, Germany, Army, WWII. Black leather. D-rings. RB-NR present. Avg. cond. $120

Y-straps, Combat, Germany, Army, WWII. Black leather. D-rings. RB-NR present. Above avg. cond. $202

Y-straps, Combat, Germany, Army, WWII. Brown leather. D-rings, steel fittings and stamped RB-NR. Exc. cond. $162

Y-straps, Combat, Germany, Army, WWII. Variation. Brown leather straps, D-rings and steel fittings. Above avg. cond. $125

Backpacks, Haversacks, and Knapsacks——Other

Backpack, Hungary, Army, WWII. Rigid frame, field gray canvas with brown leather fittings and straps. With buckles. Above avg. cond. $45

Knapsack, Italy, Air Force, WWII. Blue cotton canvas with cargo pockets, blue finished leather retaining and equipment straps and blanket roll straps. Above avg. cond. $30

Knapsack, Switzerland, Army, 1940. Brown fur with brown leather trim and straps. Interior lining of field gray linen. Dated "40." Above avg. cond. $34

Binoculars and Telescopes——U.S.

Binoculars, USA, Army, Civil War, France. French made with hmk on eyepiece. Leatherette covered barrels. Brass construction. String cord neckstrap. Below avg. cond. $23

Binoculars, USA, Army, 1870s, France. French-made field glasses hmkd on lens frame. Extension tubes marked "Field/Marine extra powerful." Leather-covered optic tubes. Avg. cond. $40

Binoculars, USA, Army, Civil War, France. French made and marked on eyepiece. Also marked "Army Navy Extra Powerful" on tube. Black finished brass tubes. Leather-wrapped barrels. Lenses good. Avg. cond. $45

Binoculars, USA, Army, Civil War. Gray metal body with black wrinkle finish. Steel lens frames and black hard

rubber eyecups. Two hanging loops on side. 4 ½" x 8" extended. Avg. cond. $66

Civil War Binoculars (5 x 8)

Binoculars, 5 x 8, USA, Army, Civil War. Heavy brass body with black finish. Cord-wrapped handholds. Avg. cond. $82

Binoculars, 6 x 30, USA, Army, WWII, England. Hmkd on barrel. British broad arrow marked on barrel end. Cloth neckstrap. Avg. cond. $40

Binoculars, 6 x 30, USA, Army/Navy, WWII. Army Signal Corps and Naval Gun Factory marked. Tan leatherette cover on tubes and carry strap. Adjustable prismatic lenses. Rt lens broken. Avg. cond. $30

US WWII Binoculars (6 x 30)

Binoculars, M15a1, 7 x 50, With Case, USA, Army, WWII. With M1924 case. OD color, coated optics and conventional design. Leather carry case. Avg. cond. $51

Binoculars, Mark 21, 7 x 50, With Case, USA, Navy, WWII. BuAero model. Black textured finish on tubes. Specs and hmkd (SARD) on base plates. Adjustable focus lenses with soft rubber formed eyepieces. Black leather case. Avg. cond. $120

Binoculars, Mark 28, 7 x 50, USA, Navy, 1943. Navy marked Mod. 0. 1943 dated. Avg. cond. $25

Binoculars, Naval, USA, Navy, WWI, France. 8¼"-long brass bodies. Paris maker hmk on eyepieces. Covered in black leather. Optics are clear. Comes in matching fitted leather case. Attached oval dog tag reads "Donated to U.S. Navy." Avg. cond. $102

Binoculars, Naval, USA, Navy, Civil War, France. French made. Binoculars hmkd "Junelle marine" on each eyepiece. Leatherette-covered barrels. Brass rings at large end. Avg. cond. $34

Binoculars, Naval, 6 x 30, With Case, USA, Navy, WWI, U.S. Naval Gun Factory. Black finish metal bodies covered in brown grain leather. Eyepieces can be rotated to amber tint. "USN/Bureau of Navigation/U.S. Naval Gun Factory" marked. Serial numbered. Includes fitted leather carrying case. Avg. cond. $45

Binoculars, Naval, 6X, USA, Navy, WWI, Bausch & Lomb. Hmkd "Bausch & Lomb." Also marked "Marine" on front of barrel. OD finish over brass and black leatherette barrels. Russet leather case. OD green finish carry strap. Avg. cond. $44

Binoculars, Naval, 6X, USA, Navy, WWI, Bausch & Lomb. Black finish brass bodies. Hmkd "Bausch & Lomb/U.S. Navy." Serial numbered. Brown crinkle texture leather covered. Includes leather neckstrap. Adjustable eyepieces with filters. Above avg. cond. $40

Binoculars, Naval, 7 x 50, USA, Navy, WWII, Square D Co. Binoculars made by Square D Co. Black crinkle on barrels. Leather strap. Fair cond. $50

Binoculars, Trench, USA, Army, WWI. Leather carrier and tripod. OD finish with leather covers for eyepieces. Accessories included in carrier. Labeled on face. Original straps included. Tri-pod has wooden legs with metal extensions and pivoting/swiveling base for binoculars. Lockable azimuth ring. Adjustable for height and stability. Exc. cond. $212

Case, Periscope, Trench, M1917, USA, Army, WWI. Stitched brown leather body with stud closure, hinged lid and stitched belt loop on back. Inspector marked. Above avg. cond. $35

Sextant, Mark I, Mod 0, USA, Navy, WWII. Calibrated at US Naval Observatory and dated Oct. 27, 1944. Mergenthaler made in black and brass. Wooden carry case. Exc. cond. $192

Sight, Panoramic, USA, Army, 1917, Warner Swazey Co. Brass and steel construction with two prismatic lenses. Multiple calibrations. Hmkd "Warner Swazey co." and dated 1917. Exc. cond. $125

Spyglass, Naval, 16X, USA, Navy, 1942. Qm spyglass. 32" long with black leatherette covering on metal tube and adjustable optics. 1942 dated at viewing end. In oak box with felt padded braces inside. Metal spec plate. Exc. cond. $250

Telescope, M-120, USA, Army, WWII. Original packing. Rubber eyepiece, OD finish and spec plate. Exc. cond. $85

Telescope, M-17, USA, Army, WWII. Elbow style. Prismatic optics in OD finished metal telescope. Specs. Four-position lens selection, power input and rubber eyepiece. Mounted to 6¼" wood disk with 6½" x ¾" rod. Above avg. cond. $223

Telescope, M-17, USA, Army, 1943. 1943 dated with view lens and focus ring, sight lens with clear, neutral, red and amber lenses. Spec plate on side. Pedestal mount. OD finish. Avg. cond. $45

Telescope, M-1915A1, USA, Army, WWI. Binocular viewing with prismatic lenses and adjustments for elevation and azimuth. Leather case with accessories and spares. Above avg. cond. $145

Telescope, M-38A2, USA, Army, WWII. Brass case with black finish, prismatic optics and mounting studs. Avg. cond. $26

Telescope, M-84, USA, Army, WWII. Optics clear. Black finish metal tubular body with rubber eyepad and adjustable dials and mount. Dark OD canvas carrying case. Exc. cond. $400

Telescope, M84 with Case

Telescope, M-86F, USA, Army, WWII. OD finished metal tube with optics and scale on one lens. Two brackets for mounting clamps and M76 carrying case. Above avg. cond. $23

Binoculars and Telescopes—Germany

Binoculars, 10 x 50, Germany, Army, WWII. 6½"-tall bodies with black rough texture finish. Maker "blc etc." Optics clear with scale on rt side. Below avg. cond. $72

Binoculars, 10 x 50, Germany, Army, WWII. 7"-tall gray painted body with black finished fittings. By "rln Dienstglas 10x50 etc." Leather neckstrap. Below avg. cond. $98

Binoculars, 1908 Pattern, Imperial Germany, Army, WWI, Carl Zeiss, Jena. "Carl Zeiss Jena etc." marked on green rough textured bodies. Heavy leather neckstrap. Clear optics. Avg. cond. $66

Binoculars, 1908 Pattern, Imperial Germany, Army, WWI, Carl Zeiss, Jena. Green bodies. By "Carl Zeiss etc." Optics clear. With neckstrap. Avg. cond. $45

Binoculars, 1908 Pattern, Imperial Germany, Army, WWI, Spindler and Hoyer, Gottingen. Green rough texture bodies, maker "Spindler&Hoyer Gottingen." Optics clear. Fair cond. $55

Binoculars, 1908 Pattern, With Case, Imperial Germany, Army, WWI, Emil Busch. Black leather case by "Emil Busch etc." with brass fittings and straps intact. Smooth green-gray painted bodies by same maker as case. Avg. cond. $50

Binoculars, 1908 Pattern, With Case, Imperial Germany, Army, WWI, Emil Busch. Green textured bodies by "Emil Busch etc." Brass fittings and Bakelite eyecups. Leather neckstrap. Optics clear. Black burlap-covered case with leather stamped "Emil Busch etc." Paper instructions on lid. Fair cond. $34

Binoculars, 6 x 30, Germany, Army, WWII. Late war. Tan finish. 4½"-tall body with end only stamped "6x30." Leather neckstrap. Avg. cond. $95

Binoculars, 6 x 30, Germany, Army, DAK, WWII. Tan painted body with alum ends by "cag 6x30 etc." Optics fogged with scale on rt side. Leather neckstrap. Avg. cond. $100

Binoculars, 6 x 30, Germany, Army, WWII, Dienstglas. Black texture paint on body. By "ddx Dienstglas etc." Optics dirty. Scale to rt-side. Leather neckstrap. Avg. cond. $54

Binoculars, 6 x 30, Germany, Army, WWII, Hensoldt Wetzlar. 4½" tall heavy body. Black leatherette covers. Black painted brass ends marked "Hensoldt Wetzlar etc." Optics fogged. Below avg. cond. $45

German WWII Binoculars (6X)

Binoculars, 6 x 30, With Case, Germany, Army, WWII. By "Busch Rathenow A Solluxon 6x30 etc." with black textured bodies. Optics clear. No scale. Leather neck strap. Brown leather case with strap. Avg. cond. $40

Binoculars, 6 x 30, With Case, Germany, Army, WWII. 4½" tall. Painted body by "cag etc." Optics dirty with scale on rt side. Black leather neckstrap and commercial brown leather case with shoulder strap. Avg. cond. $130

Binoculars, 6 x 30, With Case, Germany, Army, WWII, Carl Zeiss. Early. 4½" tall, black leather-covered bodies and black painted gray metal fittings. By "Carl Zeiss etc.." Optics a little fogged. Black painted wood and leatherette case. Below avg. cond. $28

Binoculars, 7 x 40, Germany, Army, WWII, G. Rodenstock, Muenchen. 6" tall heavy gray metal body. Brass fittings and marked "G. Rodenstock Muenchen Euclar 7x40 etc." Leather neckstrap. Below avg. cond. $33

Binoculars, 7 x 56, With Case, Germany, Army, WWII, Hensoldt-Wetzlar. 9"-tall bodies. Rough black texture bodies. Marked "Hensoldt-Wetzlar Nacht-Dialyt." Optics clear. Black leather neckstrap and black leatherette case. Avg. cond. $286

Binoculars, 8 x 24, Germany, Army, WWII, C.P.Goerz. 4½"-tall black textured body. Stamped "8x C.P.Goerz etc." Optics fogged. Below avg. cond. $35

Binoculars, 8 x 24, With Case, Germany, Army, WWII, Hensoldt. 4"-tall black leather bodies. Black finish to brass fittings. Title marked and "Wacht Wetzlar." Single adjustment knob. Optics clear. Brown leather case. Below avg. cond. $20

Binoculars, Anti-Aircraft, 12 x 60, Germany, Luftwaffe, Flak, WWII, Zeiss. 11½"-long green painted body. Optics clear with scale. Rubber face pads on hinged assembly. Metal cover on eyecups on leather strap with spring latch. Filter knob "Farbglaser," title plate and scale use plate. Avg. cond. $160

Binoculars, Naval, 7 x 50, Germany, Navy, WWII, Carl Zeiss, Jena. 7" tall. Black leatherette-covered main body marked with owner's name. Black finished alum fittings with stamped Eagle-M IV/1 and "Carl Zeiss Jena D.F. 7x50 etc." Avg. cond. $116

Binoculars, Naval, 7 x 50, With Case, Germany, Navy, WWII, Carl Zeiss, Jena. 7"-tall bodies show remains of leatherette covering and black texture paint. Marked "Carl Zeiss Jena D.F.7x50 etc." and Eagle-M IV/1. Optics fogged. Leather neckstrap and leather eyecup cover present. Commercial brown leather case with shoulder strap. Avg. cond. $250

Binoculars, Naval, 7 x 50, With Case, Germany, Navy, WWII, Case 1942. 8 ½"-tall bodies with black leatherette covering. Optics clear. Leather neckstrap. Black leatherette case with Eagle M on lid and "beh 1942" at front. Four filter caps inside. Avg. cond. $339

Camera, Germany, Luftwaffe, WWII. Black leatherette-covered metal body is stamped "Luftwaffen-Eigentum." Nameplate on back. Lens missing. Avg. cond. $158

Carrying Case, Binocular, Germany, Army, WWII. For 6 x 30 binoculars. Brown Bakelite body with black leather belt loops. Black leatherette tab on spring latch stamped "frn44." Above avg. cond. $132

Carrying Case, Binocular, Germany, Army, WWII. Brown Bakelite body with belt loops. For 6 x 30 binoculars. Avg. cond. $72

Carrying Case, Binocular, 1908 Pattern, Imperial Germany, Army, WWI, Carl Zeiss, Jena. Dark leather body. By "Carl Zeiss Jena" and paper instructions inside. Below avg. cond. $20

Carrying Case, Binocular, Naval, Germany, Navy, 1943. 11½"-tall black leatherette body by "1943 beh." Lid has stamped Eagle-M. Leather tab on spring closure. Avg. cond. $50

Periscope, Trench, Imperial Germany, Army, WWI. 21" long overall, ⅞"-diam tan painted metal tube. Optics clear with rubber eyecup and by "dow." Avg. cond. $80

Binoculars and Telescopes—Other

Binoculars, Japan, Army, WWII. Black enameled binoculars, clear glass lenses and black plastic adjustment knob. Marked with "4 x 10," "60," and "70," manufacturer's stamps and crown-shaped designation. Complete with pliable brown leather carrying strap and rubber-treated khaki canvas carrying case. Above avg. cond. $20

Binoculars, Field, Poland, Army, WWII. Lacquered finish binoculars with excellent optics, leather neckstrap and brown leather carrying case. Good cond. $350

Carrying Case, Binoculars, England, Army, 1916. Brown leather, complete with belt loops, flap tab, brass rail buckle and maker's stamp. Above avg. cond. . . . $25

Canteens—U.S.

Canteen and Cover, USA, USMC, WWII. Dark tan canvas with wire belt hanger device stitched near top of body. Includes M1910 canteen and cup both dated 1918. Avg. cond. $40

Canteen and Cover, M1910, USA, Army, 1918. Canteen dated 1918. Includes dark tan canvas cover with wire belt hanger. Cover "US" marked and 1918 dated. Below avg. cond. $11

Canteen and Cover, M1910, USA, Army, 1917. 1917 dated canteen. Includes tan canvas cover with wire belt hanger. "US" marked and 1917 dated. Stenciled "63/Inf/C" markings. Above avg. cond. $20

Canteen and Cover, M1910, USA, Army, 1918. 1918 dated canteen and tan canvas cover also dated 1918. Includes cup. Below avg. cond. $11

Canteen and Cover, M1910, USA, Army, WWI. Canteen "US" marked and dated 1918. Includes 1918 dated tan canvas cover. Avg. cond. $20

Canteen and Cover, M1910, USA, Army, 1915, Rock Island Arsenal, IL. Inside of cover dated 1915 and marked "RIA." Outside of cover is stenciled NA (National Army) on side. Avg. cond. $38

Canteen and Cover, Various Models, USA, Army, WWII. 1918 dated M1910 canteen. Dark tan canvas M1917 cover with adjustable leather strap with metal snap hook at top. "US" marked and dated 1935. Avg. cond. $39

Canteen Cover, M1910, USA, Army, WWI. Lt olive canvas cover with rimless bronze finish eagle snaps and wire belt hanger. "US" marked. Above avg. cond. $87

Canteen Cover, M1910, USA, Army, 1918. Tan canvas cover with wire belt hanger. Dated 1918. Avg. cond. $25

Canteen Cover, M1910, USA, Army, NY Guard, WWI. Dark tan canvas body with wire belt hanger. Stenciled "N.Y.G." on front. Avg. cond. $28

Canteen Cover, M1910, USA, Army, 1917, Rock Island Arsenal, IL. Lt OD canvas cover with dark tan bottom panel and trim and wire belt hanger. Marked "US/RIA/1917." Above avg. cond. $40

Canteen Cover, M1941, USA, Army, 1944, England. Lt olive canvas with dark tan trim and wire belt hanger. British made with broad arrow marks and dated 1944. Avg. cond. $25

Canteen Cup, USA, Army, WWII. Dark blue porcelain over metal. Metal hinged handle. Above avg. cond. . $75

Canteen Rig, M1910, USA, Army, WWI, Rock Island Arsenal, IL. 1918 dated canteen with cup. Dark tan canvas cover marked "US/RIA" and dated 1917. Above avg. cond. $97

Canteen Rig, M1910, USA, Army, WWI. Includes 1918 dated canteen. Cup marked "2 D/16" on handle. Canvas cover dated 1918 with US Inf equipment ID disc. Avg. cond. $33

Canteen Rig, Various Models, USA, Army, WWII. M1942 canteen and cup both dated 1944. M1941 OD canvas cover dated 1942. Avg. cond. $13

Canteen Rig, Various Models, USA, Army, WWII. M1942 canteen and cup dated 1945. In M1941 dated lt OD canvas cover dated 1943. Above avg. cond. $20

Canteen Rig, Various Models, USA, Army, WWII (Complete Rig). M1942 metal canteen dated 1943. M1910 cover in lt OD canvas with dark tan trim and wire belt hanger. Initials inked on cover front. Dated 1917. Also includes, M1942 canteen cup dated 1942. Above avg. cond. $37

Canteen Rig, Various Models, USA, Army, WWII. M1917 "US" marked canvas cover with adjustable brown leather strap with heavy metal snap hook at top. Dated 1934. Includes M1910 alum canteen and cup. Above avg. cond. $75

Canteen Rig, Various Models, USA, Army, WWII. M1942 canteen and cup. "US" marked and dated 1942. In M1941 lt OD canvas cover dated 1942. Above avg. cond. $37

Canteen, Collapsible, USA, USMC, 1945. Dark OD canvas cover with dark OD web straps. Soft inner bladder with threaded cap. Both pieces USMC stenciled. Dated 1945. Above avg. cond. $33

Canteen, M1858, USA, Army, Civil War. M1858 pattern smooth-sided canteen. Solder repair on bottom quarter. Old paint covers entire surface and owner's name painted on "J.B. Cp. D. 74th N.Y." Old leather carrying strap present. Avg. cond. $275

Canteen, M1858, USA, Army, Civil War. 7½" diam. Has pewter spout with chain and stopper. Some dents. Avg. cond. $110

Canteen, M1858, USA, Army, Civil War, J.C. Johnson & Co. M1858 pattern smooth-sided canteen. Spout marked "J.C. Johnson & Co/Feb. 6.65." Original brown wool cover with original linen strap, stopper and chain. Avg. cond. $225

Canteen, M1879, USA, Army, Coastal Arty, Spanish American War. Canvas-covered canteen with stopper on chain. Faint marks of Coastal Arty unit includes crossed cannons emblem on side. Avg. cond. $53

Canteen, M1879, USA, Army, Spanish American War. Khaki cotton cover. Has "US" on one side, Signal Corps emblem on the other with "13" above and "USV" below. Stenciled "54" on bottom of side. Exc. cond. $120

Canteen, M1879, USA, Army, Kansas National Guard, Spanish American War. Circular tin body with dark tan

canvas cover. Front side has faint unit stencil over "U.S." and "K.N.G." below. Also stenciled "17/32" on opposite side. Avg. cond. $57

Canteen, M1879, USA, Army, Spanish American War. Circular tin body with tan canvas cover and cork stopper on safety chain. U.S. marked. Includes correct pattern dark leather sling with brass hooks at each end. Avg. cond. $101

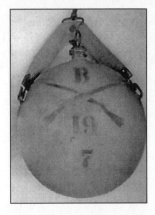

US M1887 Canteen, similar to the M1879 Canteen

Canteen, M1879, USA, Army, Spanish American War. Tan canvas-covered circular metal body with cork stopper on safety chain and shoulder strap attachment loop on each side of body. "US" marked. Other side is stenciled "US VOL/K/Inf/44/93." Avg. cond. $60

Canteen, M1942, USA, Army, WWII. Metal canteen with threaded cap on safety chain. "US" marked and dated 1945. Paper wrapping with contract markings. Near mint cond. $34

Canteen, Private Purchase, USA, Army, Civil War. Tin construction, cylindrical, 6" diam and 2" wide. Soldered seams and three soldered strap loops. Man's leather belt used as strap. Avg. cond. $72

Canteen, Water, USA, Army, 1964. One-quart capacity. OD polyethylene plastic. Dated 1964. Avg. cond. . . $11

Flotation Bladder, Collapsible, USA, Army, 1968. Five-quart capacity. Comes in sealed cardboard carton dated 1968. Near mint cond. $48

Water Bucket, Field, Collapsible, USA, Army, WWI. 11.5" diam. Tan canvas with covered rope handle. "US" marked and dated 1918. Above avg. cond. $11

Canteens—Germany

Canteen, Imperial Germany, Army, WWI. Alum body and cap. Both stamped "H.A.Schmidt 13." Leather strap with attachment clip and felt cover. Avg. cond. $93

Canteen, Germany, SS, SA, WWII. Alum body and cap stamped "RZM M6/43/39." Gray wool cover, black leather strap and steel clip. Above avg. cond. $74

Canteen, Imperial Germany, Army, 1917. Gray painted metal body, gray corduroy cover, clip-on leather strap and cork stopper with leather strap. Dated 1917 and maker marked. Avg. cond. $40

Canteen, Imperial Germany, Army, 1915. Gray painted steel body. Maker tag dated 1915. Cork stopper with leather strap and clip. Avg. cond. $50

Canteen, Imperial Germany, Army, WWI. Gray porcelainized body with gray corduroy cover. Cork stopper has leather loop and clip. Avg. cond. $26

Canteen, Imperial Germany, Army, 1916. Gray metal body with metal-topped cork stopper. Gray corduroy cover with inked maker name and 1916 date. Broken leather strap with metal clip. Below avg. cond. $20

Canteen, Imperial Germany, Army, 1917. Includes harness and cup. 1917 maker tag on gray steel body. Cork stopper with cap attached to brown leather skeleton straps. Brown corduroy cover. Silver-gray finish on metal cup with same maker and 1917 date. Avg. cond. $32

Canteen, M1931, Germany, Army, 1938. 1938 alum body, 1939 cap, felt cover, black strap and black painted alum cup dated 1940. Avg. cond. $25

Canteen, M1931, Germany, Army, WWII. Red steel body and black cap. Gray cloth cover and black leather strap with clip. Black painted cup dated 1940. Avg. cond. $30

Canteen, M1931, Germany, Army, WWII. Red steel body and cap. Gray cloth cover, black leather strap and gray painted "CFL44" steel cup. Near mint cond. $243

Canteen, M1931, Germany, Army, WWII. Red steel body, black plastic cap, gray cover, pigskin strap and black painted alum cup by "FWBN42." Avg. cond. $66

Canteen, M1931, Germany, Army, WWII. Alum body and cup made by "HRE41." Padded gray cover, black leather skeleton strap with shoulder strap and black alum cup. Above avg. cond. $85

Canteen, M1931, Germany, Army, 1938. Alum body by "CFL 38" with 1937 dated cap. Padded gray felt cover. Leather skeleton strap is missing shoulder strap. Below avg. cond. $20

Canteen, M1931, Germany, Army, 1936. 1936 alum body and black cap. Felt cover, brown strap and green painted steel cup dated 1943. Avg. cond. $35

Canteen, M1931, Germany, Army, 1936. Alum body and cap by "G&CL 36." Gray felt cover and black leather strap. Avg. cond. $20

Canteen, M1931, Germany, Army, WWII. Dark blue wool cover. Leather straps with black painted alum cup.

Unissued. Near mint cond. $40

Canteen, M1931, Germany, Army, WWII. Alum body and cap by "VAL 39." Felt cover, black leather strap with repair on buckle and captured foreign alum cup with leather strap. Below avg. cond. $28

Canteen, M1931, Germany, Army, WWII. Alum body and cup by "CFL43." Black cap, gray felt cover and black leather strap. Exc. cond. $196

Canteen, M1931, Germany, Army, WWII. Alum body, black plastic cap, padded gray cover, pigskin strap and 1944 dated black cup. Avg. cond. $50

Canteen, M1931, Germany, Army, WWII. Red steel body and cap. Gray cloth cover and brown leather strap with clip. Near mint cond. $35

Canteen, M1931, Germany, Army, 1940. Alum body and cap by "ESB 40." Gray felt cover, black leather strap, alum clip and black painted alum cup by same maker. Exc. cond. $139

Canteen, M1931, Germany, Army, 1942. 1942 alum body, felt cover, black leather strap and OG painted steel cup dated 1943. Above avg. cond. $40

Canteen, M1931, Germany, Army, WWII. Gray steel body, black cap, gray cover, black strap and gray steel cup dated 1943. Below avg. cond. $45

Canteen, M1931, Germany, Army, 1939. Alum body and cap by "SSL39." Gray felt cover, black leather strap and green painted steel cup with 1943 date. Avg. cond.   . $30

Canteen, M1931, Germany, Army, WWII. Red steel body, black cap, felt cover, black strap and steel cup dated 1943. Above avg. cond. $41

Canteen, M1931, Germany, Army, WWII. Red steel body, black cap, felt cover, brown leather strap and black Bakelite cup. Avg. cond. $35

Canteen, M1931, Germany, Army, 1938. Body and cap with different 1938/1939 makers. Gray wool cover, black leather strap and alum clip. Avg. cond. $30

Canteen, Medic, Imperial Germany, Army, WWI. Gray painted steel body with silver painted cup. Gray woven and padded cover with faint inked "J.R.18 E.H.17." Brown leather skeleton harness with leather shoulder strap. Hook on back with leather stamped "E.Hecker.Aue.1917." Avg. cond. $50

Canteen, Medic, Imperial Germany, Army, WWI. Gray painted steel body and cup. Cup marked "Mussbach 1915." Gray padded twill cloth cover. Brown leather skeleton harness with shoulder strap having red web body. Cover marked in ink "JR 18. EF 17." Avg. cond. ... $63

Canteen, Tropical, Germany, Army, DAK, 1941. Bakelite/wood-covered body by "HRE 41." Olive web skeleton strap with clip and roller buckle. Black Bakelite cup. Exc. cond. $60

Canteen, Tropical, Germany, Army, DAK, WWII. Alum body with black cap. Felt cover with unsewn web loop, web strap and steel clip. Avg. cond. $25

Canteen, Tropical, Germany, Army, DAK, 1943. Bakelite-covered body by "HRE 43." Web skeleton strap and green steel cup. Avg. cond. $40

Canteen, Tropical, Germany, Army, DAK, 1942. Alum body by "KCL 42." Padded olive felt cover, olive web strap with clip, black cap and Bakelite cup. Exc. cond. $155

Canteen, Tropical, Germany, Army, 1941. Brown Bakelite body marked "HRE 41 etc." Web skeleton strap. 1943 dated black Bakelite cup. Missing buckle on leather strap at neck and no metal tip on web closure strap. Below avg. cond. $90

Canteen, Tropical, Germany, Army, DAK, 1942. Bakelite/wood-covered body by "HRE 42." Olive web skeleton strap on alum cap with 1943 date. Avg. cond. $50

German Tropical (Africa Corps) Canteen

Drinking Cup, Austrian, Imperial Germany, Army, 1917. Thick green porcelain outside with two loops and white maker disc dated 1917. Blue and white swirl inside. Above avg. cond. $30

Drinking Cup, Canteen, Imperial Germany, Army, WWII. Porcelainized. Oval shape with gray handle. Above avg. cond. $20

Drinking Cup, Canteen, Imperial Germany, Army, WWI. Porcelainized. Oval shape with gray handle. Above avg. cond. $20

Canteens——Other

Canteen, Italy, Army, WWII. Alum canteen with field gray wool cover and screw top with chains. Complete

with rough wool twill carrying strap. Above avg. cond. $30

Canteen and Cover, South Vietnam, Army, 1969. Vietnamese-made ARVN Qm item. Patterned after U.S. issue plastic canteen. Molded in dark olive plastic. 1969 marked. OD canvas cover, South Vietnamese made and patterned after U.S. snap flaps and wire belt hanger. Above avg. cond. $84

Carriers, Water Bottle, 1937 Pattern, England, Army, WWII. Two water bottle carriers, 1937 pattern. Open darkened webwork and darkened metal fittings. Above avg. cond. $20

Water Bottle, M1937, England, Army, WWII. Dark blue enamel, webbed harness and wood stopper. Felt cover missing. Above avg. cond. $20

Compasses——U.S.

Compass, USA, Army, WWI, Wittnaur . Alloy case in pocket-watch form. Hmkd Wittnaur on face. Black leather pouch. Below avg. cond. $37

Compass, USA, AAF, 1941, Longines-Wittnaur Watch Co. Pocket-watch style in alloy case with slip cover and box. Box labeled "COMPASS ASSEMBLY POCKET TYPE" with specs and hmkd "Longines-Wittnaur Watch Co. 1941." Exc. cond. $129

Compass, Engineer, USA, Army, WWII. Lensatic type in black metal case. Canvas pouch with belt clips. Above avg. cond. $45

Compass, Engineer, USA, Army, WWII. Army engineer (lensatic) compass in black metal case. Dated 5-45 and canvas belt carrier pouch. Above avg. cond. $80

Compass, Engineer, USA, Army, WWI. Brass case with windowed lid and index line. Sight and compass inside. Safety ring for carrying. Avg. cond. $35

Compass, Engineer, USA, Army, WWII. Black case with lensatic sighting slots. Labeled on rim. Pouch with belt loop and clip. Above avg. cond. $40

Compass, Engineer, USA, Army, 1966. 1966 dated army topographical compass with map x-ref capability. Lanyard included. Above avg. cond. $33

Compass, Engineer, M-2, USA, Army, WWII. Steel case with brass fittings. Mirror under lid with sighting hole at bottom. Plastic belt-mounted case. Avg. cond. $40

Compass, Lensatic, USA, Army, 1952. Folding OD finish body is "US/1952" marked. Above avg. cond. .. $40

Compass, March, USA, Army, WWI, Sperry Gyroscope Co. By Sperry Gyroscope Co. Olive finished metal body.

Hmkd Mark VII Mod. E. Brown leather carrying case with wire belt hanger device. Above avg. cond. $45

US Army March Compass

Compass, Pocket, USA, Army, WWII, Waltham. Brass body with flip cover. Face hmkd Waltham. Jeweled bearing and actuating safety lever. "U.S." marked. Dark blue pressed paper box with label. Above avg. cond. ... $145

Compass, Pocket, USA, Army, WWI. Dull nickel finished body. Hinged lid marked "Eng. Dept./U.S.A. 1918." Face marked "USA Nite." Above avg. cond. $30

Compass, Pocket, USA, Army, Civil War. Eight-point azimuthal ring with floating pointer and locking lever. Glass cover with brass case. Kept in octagonal box with blue velour lining and blue satin interior padded top. Above avg. cond. $164

Compass, Pouch, USA, Army, WWII. Dark OD canvas with lt OD trim, twin lift-the-dot closures on flap, and wire belt hanger device. Above avg. cond. $23

Compass, Survival, USA, Army, WWII. Escape and evasion compass. 18mm across and easily hidden. Avg. cond. $26

Compass, Wrist, USA, Army, WWII, Taylor. Taylor model. Brown Bakelite body. Well marked on back. Leather adjustable wrist band. Above avg. cond. ... $42

Compass, Wrist, USA, Army, WWII, Taylor. Taylor model. Liquid filled. OD Bakelite body well marked on reverse. Leather wrist band. Above avg. cond. $55

Compass, Wrist, USA, Army, 1949, Waltham Watch Co. Dry type. Dated 1949 and hmkd "Waltham Watch Co." OD plastic case with full hinged cover and green web strap. Avg. cond. $39

Compass, Wrist, USA, Army, WWII. OD plastic body. Corps of Engineers marked. Brown leather wrist band. Above avg. cond. $33

Compass, Wrist, USA, Army, WWII. Plastic body with rotating bezel and leather wrist strap. Below avg. cond. $20

Compass, Wrist, USA, Army, Airborne, Korean War. Brass case with plastic rotatable lens with compass rose and fixed indices. Floating pointer. Leather wrist strap. Exc. cond. $40

Compasses—Germany

Compass, Imperial Germany, Army, WWI. 1.75" diam. Crystal top with functional compass and stop. Complete with carrying ring and hook for attachment to equipment or belt. Exc. cond. $41

Compass, March, Germany, Army, WWII. Bakelite body by "cxn." With scale, black lid with mirror and string and leather neckstrap. Avg. cond. $40

Compass, March, Germany, Army, WWII. Bakelite body with hinged brass cover. Berlin maker marked. Avg. cond. $25

Compass, March, Germany, Army, WWII. Bakelite body with scale, white "A" stenciled on black lid with mirror and black neck string. Above avg. cond. $40

Compass, March, Germany, Army, WWII. Scale on side and maker marked "fxn." White "A" painted on black lid with mirror. Above avg. cond. $26

Compass, March, Germany, Army, WWII. Black krinkle painted lid with mirror. Bakelite body with scale. Avg. cond. $24

Compass, March, Germany, Army, WWII, Busch. Black painted body with scale, lid and mirror. Marked "Busch etc." Avg. cond. $33

Compasses—Other

Compass, March, China, Army, 1970s. Green lacquered finish, face marked with Chinese characters and red star emblem and reddish brown leather carrying case with belt loop. Unissued. Above avg. cond. $29

US Wrist Compass, M1949

Entrenching Tools—U.S.

Carrier, Entrenching Tool, M1943, USA, Army, WWII. OD green canvas with flap and snap. "US" marked on front, hmkd and dated 1943 inside. Exc. cond. $20

Cover, Entrenching Tool, M1910, USA, Army, WWII, England. Dark tan web with matching straps and wire belt hanger. US/British made marked. Broad arrow proofed. Above avg. cond. $45

Cover, Entrenching Tool, M1910, USA, Army, WWI. Dark tan web with wire belt hanger. US marked and dated 1918. Avg. cond. $29

Entrenching Tool, USA, c1890, Springfield Armory. 8½" single-edged spear-point blade with brass crossguard and turned oak grip. Crossguard marked "Springfield/ Armory" and on obverse "U.S./1892," leather scabbard marked "Rock Island/Arsenal/ W.T.G./R.H.S." with riveted brass belt hook. Above avg. cond. $700

Entrenching Tool, USA, Army, c1890s. Bright metal blade inset to reinforced metal hilt. Turned ribbed oak handle with "US" stamped at guard end. Hard leather scabbard with brass throat and belt ring. Stamped "US" near throat. Above avg. cond. $276

Entrenching Tool, M1910, USA, Army, WWI. Entrenching tool with spade blade and T-handle. Marked US on shaft. Shovel painted dark red with black grip. Avg. cond. $35

Entrenching Tool, M1910, USA, Army, WWI. Metal throat of spade and wooden handle. US marked. Olive finish. Lt OD and dark tan canvas web cover with wire belt hanger. US marked and dated 1918. Above avg. cond. $76

Entrenching Tool, M1910, USA, Army, WWII. T-handled M1910 tool with "US" on metal reinforcing strap. OD finish is worn. M1943 tan canvas belt carrier dated 1943. Avg. cond. $49

Entrenching Tool, M1943, USA, Army, WWII. US marked and 1945 dated. Avg. cond. $24

Entrenching Tool, M1943, USA, Army, 1944, Wood. "US/Wood/1944" marked. OD finish. 1945 dated dark OD canvas cover with wire belt hanger. Avg. cond. $24

Entrenching Tool, M1943, USA, Army, 1945, Ames. Dark OD finish. "US/Ames/1945" marked on blade. Lt OD canvas cover with dark OD trim and wire belt hanger. Above avg. cond. $30

Entrenching Tool, M1943, USA, Army, WWII. Dated 1945 on blade. Solid wooden handle. Above avg. cond. $25

Entrenching Tool, Model 1872, USA, Army, c1870s. Large spade-like entrenching knife with reinforced top edge, 8" long x 3½" wide. Mounted on walnut ribbed handle stamped "US" at base. Brown leather scabbard with brass throat and iron attachment mount on reverse. Top left-hand corner of scabbard stamped "US." Exc. cond. . $300

Shovel, Picket Pin, USA, Army, 1845. Breakdown shovel head with picket pin for handle. Handle has hammer end with claws and shovel head is curved point spade type. Dated on back "1845 USA." Avg. cond. $70

Entrenching Tools—Germany

Shovel Carrier, Germany, Army, WWII. Black leather. 9½" x 10" body with three-strap closure, steel clip and stamped "evg41 WaA101." Above avg. cond. $124

Shovel, Entrenching, Germany, Army, WWII. Black steel blade, Bakelite nut and wood handle. Black leatherette carrier stamped "ggu 1942." Avg. cond. $140

Shovel, Entrenching, Germany, Army, WWII. The carrier is marked Berlin 1940 and "WaA286." Black painted pointed steel folding shovel with large Bakelite nut and wooden knobbed handle. Above avg. cond. $196

Shovel, Entrenching, Germany, Army, WWII. Black painted steel blade stamped "VBW WaA727," Bakelite nut and wooden handle. Black leather carrier by "cgn41 WaA47." Above avg. cond. $342

Shovel, Entrenching, Germany, Army, WWII. Unmarked black repainted steel blade, Bakelite nut and wood handle. Black paper and leather carrier with stamped "1943 jml Muenchen" on belt loop. Above avg. cond. $150

Entrenching Tools—Other

Entrenching Tool, Soviet Union, Army, 1940. Field gray finish with Finnish Army reissue markings. Good cond. $35

Entrenching Tool, M1937, England, Army, WWII. Model 1937 head dated 1943. Khaki canvas carrier broad arrow marked and dated 1923. Above avg. cond. $65

Gas Masks—U.S.

Gas Alarm, USA, Army, WWI. Multi-piece wooden construction. Has handle that acts as a ratchet and when turned against body makes sharp "clicking" sound. Avg. cond. $34

Gas Alarm, USA, Army, WWI. Manually operated by swinging green painted wood handle. Copper-plated steel bell with clapper and "GAS" painted on two sides. Avg. cond. $50

Gas Mask, USA, Army, WWI. Tan canvas carrier with tan web straps. Mask is soft with "butterfly" valve. Includes anti-dim stick and plaster repair envelope. Faint ink markings on side of carrier. Above avg. cond. $82

Gas Mask, USA, Army, WWI. With good lenses, intact "butterfly" valve and soft flexible hose. In canvas carrier named to an EM in HQ Co. 69th Arty CAC AEF. Avg. cond. $34

Gas Mask, USA, Army, WWI. In dark tan canvas carrier with owner's name inked on body. Plastic lenses and soft connector tube. Includes anti-dim stick and plaster repair envelope. Avg. cond. $28

Gas Mask, For Dogs, USA, Army, WWII. Black rubberized material with elongated face mask to accommodate snout and special curved eyepieces. Two side filter canister mounts and lower exhalator valve. Straps intact. Exc. cond. $330

Gas Mask, Lightweight, Model M3, USA, Army, WWII. 1941 mold dated rubber mask with "butterfly" valve and rectangular metal filter unit. In well-marked dark tan canvas carrier with anti-dim stick. Above avg. cond. ... $34

Gas Mask, Mark III, USA, Navy, WWII. Mask, hose and canister in canvas bag with carry straps. Above avg. cond. $20

Gas Mask, Mark IV, USA, Navy, WWII. Navy Department Mark IV in gray canvas carrier with straps. Mask eyepieces clear, rubber soft and canister intact. Above avg. cond. $28

Gas Mask, Training, Model M2A1, USA, Army, WWII. 1942 mold dated rubber mask with elastic harness and rectangular metal filter unit. OD canvas carrier with anti-dim stick. Above avg. cond. $33

Gas Mask, Training, Model M2A1, USA, Army, 1941. Molded rubber mask dated 1941 with elastic harness and rectangular metal filter unit. Well-marked lt olive canvas carrier with dark tan web straps and anti-dim stick. Exc. cond. $49

Protective Mask System, CBR, Model M25A1, USA, Army, 1960s. Unit in case, with mask, single faceplate, mike, straps, hose, canister and accessories. Green canvas bag. Above avg. cond. $55

Gas Masks—Germany

Canister, Gas Mask, Imperial Germany, Army, WWI. 6½" tall. Blue-gray painted body with black inside. Gray woven shoulder strap. Avg. cond. $35

Carrier, Gas Mask, East Germany, Army, 1970s. Dark OD canvas, leather strap and roller buckle flap bag closure with several interior compartments. Above avg. cond. $25

Gas Mask, Imperial Germany, Army, WWI. Pliable brown leather body with all straps and strings intact. Clear lenses and metal base marked "M2." Metal filter inked "1.Feb.18." Exc. cond. $110

Gas Mask, M1930, Germany, Waffen SS, WWII. With canister. White hand-painted "SS-K??? Kaufind 22????" on inside lens lid. Below avg. cond. $125

Gas Mask, M1930, Germany, Army, WWII. Black rubber mask with "FE47" marked filter, amber lenses and replacement lenses in lid. Includes canister with hinged lid. Below avg. cond. $35

Gas Mask, M1930, Germany, Army, WWII. Dated 1940 on inside lid. Mask includes respirator. Extra lenses in holder. Shoulder strap present. Below avg. cond. ... $48

Gas Mask, M1930, Germany, Army, WWII. Gray fluted canister with maker's name and dated 1940. Includes extra lens packets. Tan web hook strap and shoulder strap. M1930 mask with straps and "FE41" marked filter. Avg. cond. $92

German M1930 Gas Mask and Canister

Gas Mask, M1930, Germany, Army, WWII. M1930 mask with straps and "40" marked on nose. Gray painted D-canister with lens packet and 1942 dated lid. Above avg. cond. $60

Gas Mask, M1930, Germany, Army, WWII. M1930 mask with straps, "44 btc" marked nose and "FE41" marked filter. Gray D-canister with empty extra lens holder stamped "eph 44" and inked "WaA??." With shoulder strap. Above avg. cond. $135

Gas Mask, M1930, Germany, Army, WWII. Includes gray painted fluted D-canister marked "bsm 42." Shoulder strap with rivet. Extra lens packet. Gray rubber mask marked "41 bmw." Caps on "FE41" marked filter. Above avg. cond. $82

Gas Mask, M1930, Germany, Army, 1944. M1930 mask with 1944 dated blue metal fittings. Filter marked "FE41." Includes 1942 dated fluted D-canister with gray paint and missing straps. Extra lens packet included. Avg. cond. $50

Gas Mask, M1930, Germany, Army, 1940. Includes 1940 dated fluted metal canister with all straps, maker's label and extra lens packet. White painted owner's name on bottom. Filter marked "FE37." Bevo name tag on strap of M1930 mask. 1940 dates overall. Above avg. cond. $127

Gas Mask, M1938, Germany, Army, WWII. M1938 mask with straps and "FE37R" marked filter with plug. Green painted D-canister is missing the rubber seal and straps. Inked "WaA145" on lid of holder with 1943 date. Above avg. cond. $50

Gas Mask, M1938, Germany, Army, WWII. Gray canvas cover on body and lid with web trim. Web shoulder and hook strap on gray painted canister with paper name tag on lid with two extra lens packets. M1938 mask with straps and "Auer-1942" marked filter with cap. Above avg. cond. $171

Gas Mask, M1938, Germany, Army, WWII. Gray fluted canister marked "pfk44" and with three extra lens packets. Web hook strap and shoulder strap. M1938 mask with straps and "FE41" marked filter. Avg. cond. $79

Gas Mask, With Canister, Imperial Germany, Army, WWI. Dark leather body is pliable and straps intact. 1917 dated filter. 7"-tall metal body with gray paint. Four extra lens packets. Avg. cond. $93

Gas Mask, With Canister, Imperial Germany, Army, WWI. Stiff gray mask with straps having inked owner's name tag. Gray metal filter canister marked "M2 AGFA 11.Apr.18 etc." Loose paper instructions in gray painted metal can with woven straps. Avg. cond. $100

Gascape Pouch, Germany, Army, WWII. Gray cloth with two snap flap. Exc. cond. $20

Gascape Pouch, Germany, Army, WWII. Gray rubberized cloth. Two snaps on flap inked "gdv 251/1940." No cape. Above avg. cond. $34

Gascape Pouch, Germany, Army, WWII. Gray rubberized. Two gray glass buttons to flap inked "apn 1942." No cape. Avg. cond. $20

Glasses, Gas Mask, Germany, Army, WWII. Gray metal case with black stenciled title "masken-brille." Blue divider inside. Glass lenses loose from wire frame with gray cloth ear loops. Avg. cond. $27

Glasses, Gas Mask, Germany, Army, WWII. Gray metal box with black title "masken-brille." Lenses in nickel frames with cloth ear loops. Avg. cond. $30

Gas Masks——Other

Gas Mask, Soviet Union, Army, 1970s. Gray rubber with filter in paper wrapping. Includes khaki cotton carrying bag and shoulder sling. Unissued. Exc. cond. $45

Gas Mask, North Vietnam, Army/Viet Cong, 1960s. Khaki plastic with clear plastic eyepieces and gauze covered breathing aperture. Includes carrying case. Above avg. cond. $54

Gas Mask, Switzerland, Army, WWII. Field gray finish with shoulder straps, clear eyepieces, mask with filter and headstrap. Above avg. cond. $35

Gas Mask, Belgian, Army, 1976. Rubber gas mask with alum filter canister and printed paper instructions. Gray painted storage canister with OD painted lid, tan web strap, marked with raised letters on lid "L.702," paper sticker with "III 1976." Exc. cond. $20

Gas Mask, Model ARS, France, Army, WWI. Hmkd model "ARS." Complete with filter and shoulder strap. Avg. cond. $43

Goggles——U.S.

Goggles, USA, Army, 1988. One-piece clear lens and one-piece frame. Conformal face mask with headband. Dated 1988. Exc. cond. $22

Goggles, All Purpose, USA, Army, WWII, Polaroid. One-piece gray rubber frame with plastic lens and black elastic headband. Oilcloth case with spare lens. Avg. cond. . $20

Goggles, M-1938, USA, Army, WWII. "Resistol." Nickel frames with clear glass lenses, rubber face pad and black elastic headband. Left lens shows clouding. In Strauss and Buegeleisen marked alum oval case with hinged lid. Avg. cond. $72

Goggles, M-1944, USA, Army, WWII, Polaroid. In N-2 goggle box. Avg. cond. $28

Goggles, M-1944, USA, Navy, WWII, Polaroid. One-piece black rubber frame with clear plastic lens and OD elastic headband. USN marked and dated 1945. Above avg. cond. $20

Goggles, Ski, USA, Army, WWII. Dark lenses, fur-trimmed cloth eye protectors and narrow headband. Leatherette pouch. Exc. cond. $20

Goggles, Ski, USA, Army, WWII. Green-tinted laminated lenses with metal frames, padded lt OD surrounds and elastic headband. Avg. cond. $10

Goggles——Germany

Goggles, Germany, Army, WWII. Brown leatherette pouch with snap flap. Brown leather body, round clear lenses and elastic headband. Above avg. cond. $45

Goggles, Dust, Throwaway, Germany, Army, WWII. Rubber body marked "Auer Neophan" with round lenses and elastic headband. Gray cloth pouch with metal button closure. Avg. cond. $37

Goggles, Dust, Throwaway, Germany, Army, WWII. Gray cloth pouch with four pockets is inked "ang WaA??." Holds two clear and two tinted goggles. Above avg. cond. $46

Goggles, Dust, Throwaway, Germany, Army, WWII. Gray leather pouch, round lenses and elastic headband. Brown leatherette pouch with snap flap and inside inked "Ultrasin 75%." Above avg. cond. $40

Goggles, Dust, Throwaway, Germany, Army, WWII. Black rubber body with round red lenses, gray elastic and cloth straps. Marked "Auer" and "Neophan" above nose area. Includes gray canvas pouch with button. Exc. cond. $55

Goggles, Dust, Throwaway, Germany, Army, WWII. Gray woven case with inked "WaA??" and "gng." Holds two clean tinted and two clear goggles with straps. Unused. Exc. cond. $46

Goggles, Dust, Throwaway, Germany, Army, WWII. Variation. Green cloth pouch with snap-on flap. Orange tinted lenses, screens on sides, brown velvet frames and elastic headband. Exc. cond. $20

Goggles, Mountain Troop, Germany, Army, WWII. Variation. Stamped deep alum ovals with four slashes for viewing. Leather-padded rims and elastic headband. Above avg. cond. $25

Goggles, Mountain Troop, Germany, Army, WWII. Yellow tinted oval glass lenses. Gray metal frames with vent holes. Leather nose bridge, gray velvet padding on frames and white elastic band. Green painted metal can with bottom inked "8/44." Exc. cond. $61

Goggles——Other

Goggles, Dust, England, Army, WWII. Dust goggles in small tin. Stamped brass oval bodies with clear lenses. Above avg. cond. $16

Map Cases——U.S.

Dispatch Case, USA, Army, WWI. All leather with brass fittings. Stamped "SERVICE CO/113TH INF." Avg. cond. $35

Dispatch Case, USA, Army, WWI, Horstmann Co, Philadelphia. Leather with OD wool blanket material covering. Leather strap and metal hooks for carrying. Single chamber with full-length flap on front. Embossed "Horstmann Co, Philadelphia" hmk on inside of flap. Avg. cond. $78

Map Case, USA, Army, WWI. Light OD canvas construction with celluloid protected map pocket, pencil slots and carry case. Has map of the trench fortifications used for training at Camp Wadsworth in Spartanburg SC. Avg. cond. $82

Map Case, M1938, USA, Army, WWII. Also called a dispatch case. Tan canvas folding body with plastic grid covers for maps, pen/pencil slots and detachable sling. Exc. cond. $28

Map Case, M1938, USA, USMC, 1941. Lt OD canvas with dark tan trim. Several pockets, plastic grid map cover and sling. Marked "US" and dated 1941. Also has stenciled EG&A design. Avg. cond. $32

Map Case, M1938, USA, Army, WWII, Boyt. Dark tan canvas with lt OD trim. Marked "US/Boyt" and dated 1943. Stenciled "14th Signal Center" on flap. Avg. cond. $20

Map Case, M1938, USA, Army, 1942. Lt OD canvas with several pockets, stitched pencil/pen slots and detachable lt OD web sling. Includes plastic map grid protective cover. Marked "US," "HOW Co 107" and dated 1942. Above avg. cond. $40

Map Case, Officer, USA, Army, 1921. 5½" x 11" lt brown fold-up leather case. Stitched slots for pens/pencils on one side. Other side unfolds to show plastic grid. Qm marked and dated 1921. Includes adjustable leather shoulder strap. Exc. cond. $63

Map Cases——Germany

Briefcase, Officer, Germany, Waffen SS, 1942, R.Larsen, Berlin. Black leather. 6" x 13" x 16" body with handle on top. Two straps on flap with roller buckles and latch. Inside inked "R.Larsen Berlin 1942." B&w painted panel on flap "SS III A 97 Hauptamt SS Gericht (B) Sturmbannfuhrer D.Muller." Sturmbannfuhrer was the equivalent of a major in the U.S. Army. Above avg. cond. $244

Map Case, Germany, Army, WWII. Brown leather. With snap pouch side and fold open side. Clear plastic on one side of map viewing area. Includes riveted carrying strap. Avg. cond. $26

Map Case, Germany, Army, WWII. Dark brown leather body, full flap, alum closure adjustment and empty tool fittings. Dated 1936 and maker stamped. Three inked owner names. Avg. cond. $40

Map Case, Germany, Luftwaffe, WWII. 1½" x 8" x 10" blue/gray canvas body, snap flap covers grid pouch, two pocket main pouch, snap flap cover on tool area with some pencils intact. Avg. cond. $113

Map Case, Germany, Army, WWII. Black leather. Dark pebbled body. Half-flap with roller buckle strap and tool pouches on front. Divided main body. Two roller buckle straps on back. Avg. cond. $35

Map Case, Germany, Luftwaffe, 1940. Dark brown leather body with alum roller buckle straps. Maker marked and 1940 dated. Also marked "LBA." Avg. cond. . . $55

Map Case, Imperial Germany, Army, WWI. Half-flap with roller buckle and tool pouches. Divided pouch. Stamped "A.R.5" on underside of flap with inked owner's name. Two roller buckle loops on back. Avg. cond. . $25

Map Case, Germany, Army, WWII. Brown leather, pebbled body, half flap, roller buckle and tool pouches. Dated 1938 and maker marked. Inked owner's name "Oblt. Wehner." Two belt straps with alum fittings, roller buckles. Avg. cond. $66

Map Case, Germany, Army, WWII. Black pebbled leather body, half-flap, steel roller buckles and empty tool fittings. Avg. cond. $45

Map Case, Germany, Luftwaffe, WWII. Dark brown pebbled body, half-flap with roller buckle strap, tool pouches and divided main pouch. Stamped "LBA(S)" with inked maker name. Includes eraser and color map paper packet showing "Die Westfront" and "Afrikan Kolonien." Avg. cond. $108

Map Case, Germany, Luftwaffe, WWII. Full-flap style with metal loop and three position fittings. Maker marked and dated 1937. Stamped "LBA.B.36" and inked "Fl.Horst-Kdtr. Fritzlar 1.St. II." Tool pouches hold wooden 20cm ruler and two pencils. Two roller buckle straps at back. Avg. cond. $82

Map Case, Imperial Germany, Army, WWI. Three-color camo design inside. About 2½" x 8" x 11" size. Two gray leather roller buckle straps at back D-rings. Gray canvas body has latch closure on flap. Avg. cond. $75

Map Case, Germany, Army, WWII, Anton Schnell, Dresden. Brown leather. Pebbled body with half-flap and roller buckle strap. Tool pouches with wooden ruler. Inked maker name "Anton Schnell Dresden etc." Two roller buckle straps on back. Shows use and late war style but is not dated. Avg. cond. $69

Map Case, Germany, Army, WWII. Brown leather. Peb-

bled body. Long leather straps on back. Roller buckles. Two compartments. Pencil holders. Avg. cond. $30

Map Case, Germany, Army, WWII. Brown leather. Pebbled body with full flap and US-style closure. Tool pouches, lacks divider on main body and belt loops on back with D-rings. RB-NR on flap. Below avg. cond. $32

Map Case, Germany, Army, WWII. Black leather. Pebbled body, half flap, tool pockets, roller buckle strap and two back roller buckle straps. Avg. cond. $45

Map Case, Germany, Army, WWII. Brown leather. Pebbled body. Three alum roller buckles and empty tool pouches, Maker marked. Below avg. cond. $23

Map Case, Germany, Army, WWII. Variation. 1" x 8" x 11" green leatherette body, brown leather trim and full flap with closure strap. Divided inside pouch and empty tool pockets on front. Two belt loops with D-rings and leather lace shoulder strap. Avg. cond. $65

Map Case, Germany, Army, WWII. Black leather. Pebbled body with full flap having US-style "Tuck-Tite" closure missing loop. Tool pouches on front. Inked owner name on flap with snap pouch on back and two RZM D-rings. Large 1938/1940 dated color map of French coast labeled "Strassenkarte von Sudwestfrankreich Blatt 29 La Rochelle-Bordeaux." Avg. cond. $36

Map Case, Germany, Army, WWII. Brown leather. Variation. 7½" x 10" body with shoulder strap, snap flap to fold-open grid area with felt divider and unsewn pouch/cover on tool side. Below avg. cond. $50

Map Pouch, Imperial Germany, Army, WWI. 1" x 7" x 8½" dark brown body with half-flap, two roller buckle belt loops and tool pockets inside. Inked eagle stamp disc on flap and paper owner label marked "Chevauleger Philipp 5.Eskadron k.b.3.Chevauleger-Regiment." Above avg. cond. $76

Scale, Map, Germany, Army, WWII. 20cm (8½")-long wooden ruler with hanger hole and black scale. Avg. cond. $20

Map Cases—Other

Map Case, Officers, Soviet Union, Army, 1980. Brown leather with nickeled fittings and issue markings. Exc. cond. $24

Personal Items and Equipment—U.S.

Armband, Invasion, USA, Army, WWII. White oilcloth body with printed U.S. flag design. Safety pin adjustable back (pins still intact). Unissued cond. Near mint cond. $61

Armband, Medic, USA, Army, WWII. White cotton twill body with red cotton red cross appliqué. Marked with maker proof. Light yellowing but unused. Above avg. cond. $23

Bandage, USA, USMC, WWI. Paper-wrapped bandage with printed EG&A design on front. Dated 1917 and shows USMC Qm markings. Avg. cond. $72

Barracks Bag, USA, Army, WWII. Lt OD cotton body with rope draw closure opening and 1942 dated Qm tag. Above avg. cond. $21

Blanket, Medical Department, USA, Army, WWII. Hospital blanket in white wool with maroon details. Stamped 1944 on blanket and 1943 dated spec tag. Above avg. cond. $12

Body Bag, USA, Various, 1965. Large OD rubberized body with six reinforced integral carry handles with heavy OD web straps. "US" marked. 1965 dated. Zipper opening. Above avg. cond. $85

Brassard, M.P., USA, Army, Vietnam War. Vietnam made. 9"-tall glossy black vinyl body with applied white vinyl "MP" letters and machine-made color patch above. Snap closures at back. 18th M.P. Bde. Avg. cond. .. $80

Bugle, USA, Army, WWII. Brass with nickel-plated mouthpiece. Constructed with two loops before the bell. Marked "US REGULATION" on throat of horn. Avg. cond. $50

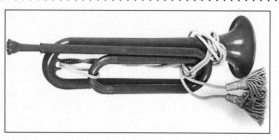

US Army WWII Bugle

C Ration, USA, Army, WWII. Biscuit, confection and beverage. 3" x 3½" cylindrical can with opener on bottom. Dated 5-43 in black on top of can. Above avg. cond. $80

Carlisle Bandage, USA, Army, WWI. Olive finish sealed tin. Well marked and dated 1918. Avg. cond. $40

Drop Case, Equipment, Paratroop, USA, Army, Airborne, WWII. Heavily padded canvas-covered body approx. 13" in diam and 26" tall. Strap closure opening and heavy tan web carry handle. Avg. cond. $265

Drum, USA, Army, Civil War Era, Randl. Painted walnut drum. Sticker inside reads "Randl." Painted image on side of drum depicts eagle with flag shield on breast under stand of 13 stars. Eagle clutches banner in beak: "Regular

U.S. Infantry" and "Company B" and "3rd Inf." Eagle appears to be 9" x 6½". Appears to have been retouched. Top rim broken, but repairable. Skins on both heads damaged and separated. All hardware present, but not attached. Size: 11" high x 15" across and 49" in circumference. Below avg. cond. $748

Drumstick, USA, Army, Civil War, 1861. Oak drumstick with leather padded tip. Marked "US/1861" near grip. Exc. cond. $87

Flute, USA, Civil War. Piccolo. Wooden with nickel silver keys and bands. Dated 1862. Exc. cond. $147

Foot Locker, Officer, USA, Army, WWII. 30½" x 16" x 12" dark olive finish fiber box with riveted metal edges, corner plates, leather carrying handles and dual latch closure hinged lid with hasp lock (no key included). Stenciled with owner's name and has Alaskan Defense Command patch decal on lid (some wear). No inner tray. Avg. cond. $26

Hammock, USA, Navy, WWII. White canvas shipboard hammock. Metal grommets with rope and rod to shape included. Avg. cond. $34

Hammock, Jungle, USA, Army, WWII. With cloth netting, waterproof cover and rigging lines. Above avg. cond. $40

K Ration, USA, Army, WWII. Sealed K ration dinner unit made by Kellogg of Battle Creek, MI. In waxed cardboard box. Below avg. cond. $50

K Ration

Life Preserver, M1926, USA, Various, WWII. Invasion life belt. Dated 1942. Waistbelt style with manual and auto inflation. Exc. cond. $40

Life Vest, Model AN-6519-1, USA, AAF, WWII. Former model B-4. Bright yellow rubberized cotton construction marked with both designations. All straps intact. Dated Feb.1945 and marked with "832nd AAF Specialized Depot" inspector stamps and AAF acceptance markings. Exc. cond. $75

Life Vest, Model AN-6519-1, USA, Army, WWII. Bright yellow canvas body with all straps. Well marked with dual designation B-4 and AN6519–1. Bears "AN" and one other inspector mark and two large, dated inspection stamps from the 832nd AAF Specialized Depot. Exc. cond. $164

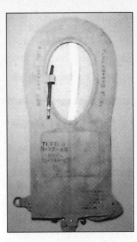

Model AN-6519-1 Life Vest

Life Vest, Model AN-V-18, USA, Navy, WWII. Dark blue-gray cotton body with matching web straps and manual inflation tubes. "USN" marked and dated 1944. Above avg. cond. $88

Medical Bag, Corpsman, USA, Navy, WWII. Dark tan canvas body with lt OD web straps. Red cross printed on flap and "U.S.N." below. Above avg. cond. $30

Medical Instruments, USA, Army, Civil War. Set of glass drawing cups for bleeding patients and wood gripped veining knife. Exc. cond. $80

Medical Kit, USA, Army, WWII. Complete medical kit in metal box. With labeled lid and Army Medical logo. Contents complete. Above avg. cond. $44

Mess Container, USA, Army, WWI. Tin box 16½" x 10" x 8" with snap-on lid. Marked "USQMC" and hmkd. Avg. cond. $25

Mess Kit, USA, Army, 1944. Dated 1944. Contains fork and spoon. Above avg. cond. $20

Mess Kit, USA, Army, WWI. Stamped name and number on lid. Includes utensils. Avg. cond. $12

Mess Kit, USA, Army, WWII. Dated 1944 on handle. With utensils. Exc. cond. $15

Mess Kit, USA, Army, Civil War. Includes 8"-diam shallow bowl and dish of steel construction with rolled edges. Also has fork and spoon with "US" stamped on handles. Avg. cond. $91

Mess Kit, M1906, USA, Army, WWI. Traces of silver finish on magnetic gray metal body and cover. Handle marked "U.S." Avg. cond. $20

Mosquito Net, Camo, USA, Army, WWII. Spot pattern camo on lt green background. Fine mesh and cotton construction. Above avg. cond. $25

Pack Roll, Medical Department, USA, Army, c1900. Dark tan canvas body with lt OD trim and olive web straps. Interior has several stitched olive web loops for instruments and snap pockets covered by flap with rimless dark bronze eagle snaps. "US/Med. Dept." marked. Above avg. cond. . . . $20

Parachute, Model B-10, USA, AAF, WWII. By Pioneer Parachute Company. Harness set with canvas case for canopy, shrouds and supporting accessories. Shrouds, risers and wires remain. Dated 1945. Above avg. cond. . . . $520

Paratroop Weapon Bag, USA, Army, Airborne, WWII. Quilt padded canvas bag with zipper closure and alum clip. For M1 carbine or Thompson sub-machine gun. Label on one side. Exc. cond. $203

Pipe, USA, Army, Civil War. 6" white clay. Bowl with design of cannon and crossed rifles on either side. Avg. cond. $30

Poncho, USA, Army, 1968. Dark OG rubberized material with metal snaps. 1968 spec markings. Above avg. cond.
. . . . $23

Pouch, First Aid, M1910, USA, Army, WWI. Dark tan canvas with wire belt hanger and two-snap closure flap. Dated 1918. Exc. cond. $32

Pouch, First Aid, M1910, USA, Army, WWI. Tan canvas pouch with snap flap. Complete contents. Marked "US" on front and dated "10-18" inside. Web strap and belt clip. Above avg. cond. $40

Pouch, Red Cross, USA, Army, WWI. OD tan twill with red crosses on front and back. Red silk lining. One-piece with handle. Multi-purpose utility bag. Avg. cond. . $12

Raft, Parachute, Model AN-R-2, USA, AAF, WWII. One-man seat pack life raft. Dated 1943. In canvas container with clips for chute harness. Air pump with two outlet hoses. Below avg. cond. $143

Razor, USA, Army, WWII. Gem razor kit in original box with instructions and bar of soap. Above avg. cond. $24

Sleeping Bag, USA, Army, WWII. OD wool with zipper entry and web ties. Above avg. cond. $100

US Army WWII Sleeping Bag

Stove, USA, Army, Civil War. Tin stove with refillable kerosene burner and ventilated cook tower. 6" high. With metal base and folding wire handles. Avg. cond. . . . $90

Stove, Field, USA, Army, WWII. Large OD finished cylindrical fuel tank with black enamel framework and two separate burners. Instructional label intact. "US" marked and dated 1945. Comes with "US" marked and 1944 dated alum carrying case with hinged lid and carrying handle. Avg. cond. $105

Stove, Medical Service, USA, Army, WWII. Coleman-type white gas two-burner stove in stainless steel case with Medical Service emblem on lid. Avg. cond. $69

Straight Razor, USA, USMC, WWII. Marked "USMC" on shank of blade. Black plastic cover for blade and box for storage. Above avg. cond. $59

Swagger Stick, USA, USMC, WWII. 22" long. High quality brown wooden body with nickel tip and handle with EG&A appliqué. Exc. cond. $66

Table Cloth, USA, Navy, WWII. White with embr eagles in center. Above avg. cond. $59

Tent, Shelter Half, Camo, USA, Army, 1944. Reversible from green to tan spot pattern camo. Canvas with OD finish ribbed metal buttons and 1944 dated spec tag. No lines, pegs or pole. Avg. cond. $94

Thermometer, USA, Army, WWII. Black Bakelite case with threaded cap. Well-marked thermometer. Exc. cond. $40

Toiletry Kit, Field, USA, Army, WWI. Dark tan cotton roll-up case with several pockets. Contains field mirror, package of sewing needles, leather razor strop, small olive finished canister containing thimble and buttons, two soap dishes with lids, two "Handy Grip" shaving sticks in metal canisters and pocketsize sewing kit with contents. Avg. cond. $65

Tray, Mess Hall, USA, Army, WWII. Six-compartment design. "US" marked and dated 1943. Avg. cond. . . $20

Water Bag, USA, USMC, WWI. Portable with canvas strap and crossed ropes on bottom. Hmkd and dated 1918 on bottom. Also stenciled "CO G/131st Inf" and with commander's name. Above avg. cond. $20

Whistle, Bosuns, USA, Navy, WWII. Bright finished white metal with braided black cord. Has some age patina to the metal finish. Above avg. cond. $36

Personal Items and Equipment—Germany

Belt Pouch, Medical, Germany, Red Cross (DRK), WWII. 3" x 4" x 6½" black leather body stamped "DRK

Sanitatslager Babelsberg 10." Above avg. cond. $30

Belt Pouch, Medical, Germany, Army, 1942. Brown leather. 3" x 3½" x 6½" body. Marked "dny 1942." Alum fittings. 1940 dated paper contents label. Avg. cond. $23

Belt Pouch, Medical, Germany, Army, WWII. Black leather. 3" x 4" x 6½" size. Inked "WaA65" inside lid. Above avg. cond. $20

Belt Pouch, Medical, Germany, SS, 1930s. Brown leather. 4" x 4½" x 8" body with belt loops and alum rivets. Stamped title maker mark and smaller SS runes in circles above. May have been added later. Same inked maker mark on inside of lid with leather fitting for missing equipment. Above avg. cond. $85

Bugle, Infantry, Prussian, Imperial Germany, Army, c1900. Brass. Silver border on bell. Large Prussian raised eagle on neck. 10½"-tall brass hanging loops. Mouthpiece present. Below avg. cond. $107

Bugle, Prussian, Imperial Germany, Army, WWI. 11"-tall coiled brass body with flared nickel ring. Has owner's name engraved on it. Tri-color twisted yarn rope with tassel. Leather shoulder strap. Attached brass eagle disc at top. Below avg. cond. $425

Crampons, Mountain, Germany, Army, Mt. Troops, WWII. Ten-point-steel bodies. Metal toe loop and rings for straps. Marked "Eckenstein Made in Austria." Above avg. cond. $165

Drum Hanger, Prussian, Imperial Germany, Army, WWI. 3½"-tall brass casting with swivel loop, crowned eagle and two hooks. Black leather riveted hook. Gold finish. Exc. cond. $80

Fife, Bandsman, Naval, Imperial Germany, Navy, WWI. Black wood. Marked "Sonora" and with maker mark on body and silvered fittings. Complete with black leather and brass carrying case with belt loop and marked with "crown and M" mark for Imperial Navy. Above avg. cond. $115

Heater, Ration, Germany, Army, WWII. Marked "esbit-kocher Mod.9." Folding gray metal body with stamped title and illustrated instructions. Above avg. cond. . . $26

Knee Pads, Paratrooper, Germany, Luftwaffe, Paratrooper, WWII. Brown cloth. About 11"-long bodies have six sewn link pads. Two metal corner rivets on each for hook-up. Above avg. cond. $588

Lantern, Carbide, Germany, Army, WWII. Bakelite. 11"-tall body with handle and alum hook chain. Stamped "WaA38" on alum hook. Three clear lenses with side covers. Above avg. cond. $100

Lantern, Carbide, Germany, Army, WWII. Bakelite. Maker's code "efv." 9" tall, 4" x 4½" body with three clear lenses. Alum hook on back. Avg. cond. $75

Lanterns, Carbide, With Case, Germany, Army, WWII. Set of two with spare parts in box. 6" x 12" x 14½" gray painted metal case with black stenciled title on both sides having metal handles. Two latches on removable lid. Contains two standard Bakelite lamps, one has broken Bakelite side lens area and mirrored reflector. The other lamp is missing its Bakelite cover and handle. Many spare parts in box with two tan painted metal containers with contents, glass lenses, metal covers, Bakelite fittings and small tool box with burner fittings. Paper booklet "Merkblatt etc." and has typed contents list on lid. Above avg. cond. $360

Mess Kit, Imperial Germany, Army, WWI. 7½"-tall body and lid with handle. With leather strap. Both pieces marked with owner's name. Wire handle. Above avg. cond. $87

Mess Kit, Imperial Germany, Army, WWI. Porcelainized steel. Blue-gray finished body and lid. Wire handle. Avg. cond. $36

Mess Kit, Germany, Army, 1970s. Alum mess kit with black painted finish and traces of field gray finish. Complete with bid, bail, and handle. Above avg. cond. $20

Mess Kit, M1931, Germany, Army, 1944. Alum. Gray paint. Lid by "HRE 44." Wire handle. Above avg. cond. $23

Mess Kit, M1931, Germany, Army, 1944. Alum. Green paint. Handle stamped "FWBN 44." Wire hanger. Avg. cond. $20

Mess Kit, M1931, Germany, Army, WWII. Alum. Green paint. 1941 lid and 1940 body with wire handle. Owner's name hand engraved "Lorenz." Black strap with roller buckle, maker marked and dated 1938. Avg. cond. . $20

Mess Kit, M1931, Germany, SA, 1934. 7"-tall alum body and lid with black paint. Stamped "RZM FA.1/34." Wire handle. Avg. cond. $50

Mess Kit, M1931, Germany, Army, WWII. Green painted alum body by "KCL 39." Wire handle. Avg. cond. . . $25

Pack, Medical, Germany, Army, WWII. Brown leather. 4½" x 8½" x 10½" body with top flap having two stud straps and fold-open back. Leather handle on top, shoulder strap and belt loops. Cardboard divider tray inside. Avg. cond. $60

Parachute Storage Bag, Germany, Luftwaffe, Paratrooper, WWII. Green burlap body with green woven

straps and all snaps intact. Exc. cond. $263

Parachute, Camo, Germany, Luftwaffe, Paratrooper, WWII. This is the packed chute with riser lines and two connector lines with clips. Lacks harness and back pack. Inked 1941 date and other maker marks. No static line. Above avg. cond. $683

Pick/Hammer, Mountain, Germany, Army, Mt. Troops, WWII. 11"-long wood handle stamped "G.J.R.137" and "WaA??." Leather wrist loop. Steel head by "WG" in crown. Avg. cond. $53

Pouch, Medical, Germany, Army, WWII. Brown leather. 4" x 8½" x 9" fold-open body with handle on top. Marked "bla 1944 WaA159." Below avg. cond. $35

Pouch, Musician, Germany, Army, 1939. Black leather. 3" x 8" x 8½" body with half-flap and roller buckle. Maker marked and dated 1939. Marked "WaA389." Two belt loops and D-rings on back. Avg. cond. $32

Pouch, Tent Pole, Germany, Army, WWII. Three Swiss-style white painted wooden poles with alum cups. Gray canvas pouch with two alum buttons and two leather loops. Avg. cond. $36

Pouch, Tent Pole, Camo, Germany, Army, WWII. Camo splinter pattern. 4½" x 17"-long pouch with two alum buttons and brown leather loops. Inked "A.S.L.39" and with cross in shield design. Avg. cond. $35

Pouch, Tent Pole, Camo, Germany, Army, WWII. Splinter pattern camo. Two leather loops and alum buttons on pouch. Inked maker name, 1942 date and cross in shield design on flap. Three white painted wooden poles, alum sockets and gray galvanized stamped stakes. Above avg. cond. $145

Shelter Quarter, Germany, SA, 1930s. Brown canvas. Alum grommets and all buttons. Ink stamped to an SA unit "SA Sturm 34/95." Owner' name inked at other corner. Exc. cond. $120

Shelter Quarter, Germany, TENO, 1939. Military cut gray canvas body with alum grommets and buttons. Inked maker mark and dated 1939. TENO cogged wheel logo present. Below avg. cond. $75

Shelter Quarter, Camo, Germany, Waffen SS, WWII. Oak leaf camo pattern. Spring and fall sides with inked RB-NR. Gray grommets and buttons. Avg. cond. . . $450

Shelter Quarter, Camo, Germany, Army, WWII. Italian three-color camo print to one side, head slash at center, alum buttons and sewn corner grommets. Exc. cond. $195

Shelter Quarter, Camo, Germany, Army, WWII. Splinter

pattern. Light and dark printed sides, gray grommets and steel buttons. Inked 1944 date and RB-NR. Wooden stake and pole with steel fittings. Avg. cond. $91

Shelter Quarter, Camo, Germany, Army, WWII. Splinter pattern. Light and dark printed sides, alum grommets and buttons. Some buttons missing. Avg. cond. $58

Shelter Quarter, Camo, Germany. Splinter pattern. Light and dark printed sides, gray grommets and buttons. Maker marked and dated 1941. Avg. cond. $75

Shelter Quarter, Camo, Germany, Waffen SS, WWII. Oak leaf camo pattern. Spring and fall sides. Gray grommets. Below avg. cond. $375

Shelter Quarter, Camo, Germany, Army, WWII. Splinter pattern. Light and dark sides about same shade with grommets and most buttons intact. Avg. cond. $67

Utensils, Folding, Officer, Germany, Army, WWII. Fork, knife and large spoon all have folding wire handles. Stamped "DRGM" and knife blade stamped "Solingen Stahl." Nickel-plated ends. Avg. cond. $38

Utensils, Mess Kit, Germany, Army, WWII. All Rostfrei parts with eagle stamp on each. Marked Star-A "Rostfrei" to knife, "GAG" fork and "C&C.W." on spoon and holder. Above avg. cond. $93

Utensils, Mess Kit, Germany, Army, 1970s and 1980s. Knife, fork, and spoon with 1974 and 1982 coded dates. Above avg. cond. $20

Utensils, Mess Kit, Germany, Army, WWII. Eagle stamp only on silver-plated holder/opener. Also includes plated knife, alum fork and spoon. Avg. cond. $25

Utensils, Mess Kit, Germany, Army, WWII. Fork and spoon only. Alum. Pivoting handle. Marked "O.H.W.38 WaA??." Avg. cond. $20

Utensils, Mess Kit, Germany, Army, WWII. Four-piece set. All except knife marked Rostfrei "WSM 41" with party eagle. Avg. cond. $25

Utensils, Mess Kit, With Pouch, Germany, Army, WWII. Large alum spoon and fork. Gusstahl knife and holder/opener has Eagle stamp/5266. Felt pouch. Near mint cond. $108

Personal Items and Equipment—Other

Mess Kit, Switzerland, Army. Gray lacquered alum, with MB 51 manufacturer's stamp and turned oak handle. Above avg. cond. $20

Mess Kit, Officer, Soviet Union, Army, WWII. Includes demitasse cup and silver spoon. Hmkd and has hammer and sickle insignia. Above avg. cond. $65

Radios and Electronics—U.S.

Beacon, RT-37 PPN, USA, Army, Airborne, WWII. For Army paratroop pathfinders. Used to guide paratroopers to drop zones. Eureka-Rebecca beacon. In drop bag. Exc. cond. $1250

Flashlight, USA, Army, WWII. OD green plastic case. Model MX944/U. Uses 3 D cell batteries. Above avg. cond. $29

Headphones, ANB-H-1, USA, Army, WWII. By Utah-Chicago with leather padding on headband and soft rubber on earpieces. Male connector. In original storage box. Exc. cond. $150

Lamp Assembly, Aerial Delivery Container, A-1, USA, Army, Airborne, WWII. 6¼"-long black plastic body with domed amber-tinted plastic lens on each end. Well marked. Attached to drop bundles to allow easier location in the dark or poor weather. Above avg. cond. $20

Radio, AN-URT-33B-1, USA, Army, 1984. Unit in OD finish with large 1984 dated spec/instruction decal. Includes power unit, both in issue heavy plastic bags. Near mint cond. $72

Radio, AN/PRC-9, USA, Army, 1960s. Man portable. OD metal case with electronics. Hand-held-telephone type receiver, whip antenna and magnesium battery in separate pack. Last inspection date Oct. 1, 1969. Above avg. cond. $117

Radio, Emergency, AN-CRT-3, USA, AAF, WWII. Also called the "Gibson Girl." Padded case with antenna segments and accessories. Waterproof exterior with straps and clips. Exc. cond. $187

Radio, Emergency, AN-CRT-3, USA, AAF, WWII. Also called "Gibson Girl." In yellow canvas case with carry straps. Radio in yellow metal case with all switches on top and accessible. Heavy web strap for securing while cranking. Generator powered. Continuous signal or hand keyed. Exc. cond. $124

Radio, Field, RT-176, USA, Army, 1950s. Radio and battery pack latched together as a unit with independent labels. Dated 1963. Canvas accessory pack with two pouches, headset/mike and antenna sections. Good cond. $40

Telegraph, M1914, USA, Army, WWI. Signal corps system with battery powered telegraphy key and buzzer circuit with control switch. Portable leather case with stenciled legend on lid. Instructions inside lid. Above avg. cond. $65

Telephone, Field, EE-3B, USA, Army, WWI. Wooden

case with metal top and phone inside with terminal mounts and wires. Power crank on back side. Above avg. cond. $44

Telephone, Field, EE-8B, USA, Army, 1945. Black Bakelite handset and side handcrank in heavy dark OD web carrier with dark OD web carrying straps. Well marked. Issue carton with 1945 mfg date and 1951 repacking date. 1945 dated manual. Exc. cond. $70

Telephone, TA-312/PT, USA, Army, 1962. OD finish metal unit with side power handcrank and 1962 dated spec tag and handset. Avg. cond. $20

Transmitter, BC-604-DM, USA, Army, 1943. Signal corps issue with 1943 date. Includes TM-11-600 dated 1943 with instructions on machine. Enclosed metal case with external controls and four spring-actuated locks for mounting. Above avg. cond. $50

Walkie-Talkie, RT-196/PRC-6, USA, Army, 1960s. OD finish metal body with riveted spec tag, antenna and dark OD web wrist strap. Some wear to finish. Avg. cond. $28

Walkie-Talkie, BC-611, USA, Army, Airborne, WWII. In drop bag. Reinforced canvas with heavy duty zipper. Interior lined with shock pads. Exc. cond. $300

Walkie-Talkie, BC-611-F, USA, Army, WWII. Smooth dark OD finish metal body with telescoping antenna and rubber-covered talk push button. Signal Corps marked and 1945 dated. Dark OD web strap. Avg. cond. $51

Walkie-Talkie, BC-611-F, USA, Army, WWII. 1945 dated. Carry strap and one-hand operation. OD crinkle finish case with speaker and earphone on one side. Exc. cond. $51

Walkie-Talkie, BC-611-F, USA, Army, WWII. Smooth OD finish metal body with telescoping antenna, waterproofed talk button and 1945 dated metal spec plate. Avg. cond. $55

Radios and Electronics—Germany

Flashlight, Germany, Army, WWII. Personal size marked "daimon 2233." Black metal case, large glass lens, title front with "Made in Germany," two slides for green and red lenses. Switch side and two leather buttonhole tabs. Above avg. cond. $36

Flashlight, Germany, Army, WWII. Personal size marked "artas." Black painted metal body with raised title, glass lens and three slides for green, red and blue. Two leather buttonhole tabs. Avg. cond. $44

Flashlight, Germany, Army, WWII. Personal size marked "pertrix #656." Green painted metal case with title front,

hinged metal cover on bulb and wire loop to back. Avg. cond. $25

Flashlight, Germany, Army, WWII. Personal size marked "hassia." Gray metal case with stamped title, round glass lens and rounded top. Leather buttonhole tab to back. Avg. cond. $23

Flashlight, Germany, Army, WWII. Personal size marked "artas." Black painted metal body with raised title, glass lens and three slides for green, red and blue. Two leatherette buttonhole tabs. Avg. cond. $42

Reel, Telephone Cable, Germany, Army, WWII. 6"-long black painted metal body with wooden handle and bar socket with lock. Stamped metal "Heimschutz Berlin 36 WaA315." Above avg. cond. $50

Reel, Telephone Cable, Germany, Army, WWII. 10"-diam gray metal spool with wooden grip on side crank/handle. Frame stamped "D.Z.43 WaA5" with large wooden handle. Exc. cond. $150

Reel, Telephone Cable, Germany, Army, WWII. With backpack frame. 11"-diam green painted metal ends on 10"-wide reel with old cloth-covered wire to center. Center shaft has affixed cogged wheel logo to one side with square end for crank. Riveted alum frame with canvas-covered pad and web shoulder straps with wool pads on leather. Avg. cond. $200

Switchboard, Telephone, Germany, Army, 1940. For desk. Bakelite body with stamped "WaA304," metal maker plate marked "1940 Heliowatt AG" and alphabet chart. Handcrank on side and Bakelite receiver. Wired Bakelite switchbox with five lines and empty battery area. Exc. cond. $114

Telegraph Key, Germany, Army, WWII. For field radio. Black rubber cover on Bakelite base with body having hinged cover marked "vor dem Offnen Stecker herausziehen" and signal blitz. Two-prong plug to cord. Avg. cond. $114

Telephone, Field, Germany, Army, WWII. Bakelite. Dark case with dated works. 1944 dated receiver. Avg. cond. .$50

Telephone, Field, Germany, Army, 1937. Bakelite. 1937 dated works and broken black receiver. Crank intact. Avg. cond. $40

Telephone, Field, Germany, Army, WWII. Dated works, receiver, 1939 crank, 1944 battery and Bakelite box. Avg. cond. $129

Telephone, Field, Germany, Army, WWII. Tan painted works, crank, receiver, battery box and eight extra speakers from receiver. One drilled hole on Bakelite front. Above avg. cond. $76

Radios and Electronics—Other

Telephone, Field, Austria-Hungary, Army, WWI. About 4½" x 8" x 11" oak hinged case that folds open. Side loops for missing shoulder strap. Ground stack stored inside front door with metal maker plate "Ericsson Budapest etc." Works intact with four line hook-ups, alum and black leather receiver from same maker. Exc. cond. $487

Tools and Equipment—U.S.

Engineering Tool, USA, USMC, WWII. Leather belt pouch. Black crinkle finish with calibrated ring, mirror and view port. Brass pins on outside control action. Used for elevation readings. Case marked USMC and tool marked Leitz. Above avg. cond. $38

Handles, Ax, Hand, M1910, USA, Army, WWII. Six handles. Some dated 1944. Army green. Good cond. . . $18

Shovels. Swiss shovel, squared metal blade on wood handle, 21½" long, unmarked. Avg. cond. $15

Wire Cutter Pouch, M1936, USA, Army, WWII. Dark tan web with lift-dot closure flap and wire belt hanger device. US/British made marked. Dated 1944. Broad arrow proofed. Above avg. cond. $54

Wire Cutters, USA, Army, WWI. Compound cutter with heavy rubber insulated grips and 5000-volt limit stamped on cutting head. Avg. cond. $90

Wire Cutters, M1910, USA, Army, WWI. Marked on one arm and dated 1918. Wooden grips. Above avg. cond. $93

Wire Cutters, M1936, USA, Army, WWII. 1945 dated cutters in canvas carrier with snap closure. Avg. cond. . . $35

Tools and Equipment—Germany

Pouch, Wire Cutter, Germany, Army, WWII. Black leather. 16"-tall body. Roller buckle closure on flap. Hmkd "hjh 41." Avg. cond. $46

Pouch, Wire Cutter, Germany, Army, WWII. Black leather. 16"-long body with roller buckle strap closure on flap. Two belt loops. Inside inked "bcy 41 WaA??." Avg. cond. $100

Tool, Wire Sizing, Germany, Army, 1934. 9" long with wood handle and steel fitting for 5mm sizes, 1 through 3. Screw toggle closure. Stamped 1934/maker and "WaA134." Above avg. cond. $40

Cavalry Equipment—U.S.

Bit, Cavalry, USA, Army, Cavalry, WWI, Rock Island Arsenal. Full bit with rings on rear extensions. Marked "RIA" and "4" on mouthpiece. Small clip on rt front ring. Avg. cond. $25

Bugle, Cavalry, USA, Army, Cavalry, WWI. Mouthpiece and double loop to horn. Below avg. cond. $100

Carbine Socket, Cavalry, USA, Army, Civil War. Dark leather cylindrical tube 3" high with strap for cavalry saddle. Holds carbine barrel down. Above avg. cond. . . $48

Pack/Saddle Covers, USA, Army, Cavalry, WWII. Tan canvas with US at bottom and dated 1942. Trimmed in heavy leather. Avg. cond. $59

Rifle Ring, Cavalry, M1912, USA, Army, Cavalry, 1918, Rock Island Arsenal. For McClellan saddle and M1903 rifle. Hmkd Rock Island Arsenal, 1918. Heavy leather cup for rifle butt and leather pad to protect horse and strap to secure to saddle. Exc. cond. $347

Saddle Bags, Cavalry, USA, Army, Cavalry, 1917. Military saddle bags with oval and raised "US" on flap of each pouch. Three-strap security. Pebble grain leather exterior and removable white canvas liner. Dated 1917 on cross shoulder band. Above avg. cond. $295

Saddle Pack, Gatling Gun, USA, Army, c1870s. Brown leather saddle with steel side panel reinforcement plates, cast grass carriage mounted on top with canvas-covered saddle pad and harness with four brass US marked rosettes. Above avg. cond. $1300

Saddle, Cavalry, USA, Post-Civil War. Morgan style. Russet leather with accessories. One covered stirrup and straps. Woven horsehair cinch with three leather positioning disks. Mounting straps. Above avg. cond. $180

Saddle, Cavalry, USA, Army, Pre-WWI. McClellan style. 12" seat, brass fittings, woven hemp cinch, leather adjustments, side pads and metal stirrups, pair of stamped brass US eagles with loops from rigging. Above avg. cond. $160

Scabbard, Carbine, M1895, USA, Army, Cavalry, Early 1900s, Rock Island Arsenal. Saddle mounted and hmkd Rock Island Arsenal. Dark leather with curved brass plate at top. Straps for securing included. Exc. cond. . . . $198

Spurs, USA, Army, 1912, Rock Island Arsenal (RIA). Army issue cavalry spurs, nickel steel with solid rowel. Hmkd "RIA 1912" at back. Leather boot strap. Good cond. $101

Cavalry Equipment—Germany

Saddle Bags, Cavalry, Germany, Army, WWII. Brown leather. Smooth leather 1940/maker on left side. Marked "gjl" pebbled rt side with shoulder straps. Avg. cond. $30

Saddle Bags, Cavalry, Imperial Germany, Army, 1870. One pair. Brown leather with full flaps, double tongues. Roller buckles. Each approx. 12" x 15" in size. Avg. cond. . . . $68

Saddle Blanket, Cavalry, Saxony, Imperial Germany, Army, Pre-WWI. 4½" diam, eight-pointed silver rayed metallic star with red cloth center having large frosted silver royal crown. Looped back for securing through cloth of blanket or shabraque. Exc. cond. $252

Saddle, Cavalry, Germany, Army, WWII. Dark brown leather body by "eqr 43 WaA750" and size 5. Green canvas-covered cushions to underside. Metal stirrup on both leather straps. Exc. cond. $650

Saddle, Cavalry, Imperial Germany, Army, WWI. Dark brown leather body with rear edge stamped "4B 1.Esk.1908" and "5.Ch.R.1908." Avg. cond. $325

CHAPTER FIVE

Firearms, Explosives, and Field Pieces

Firearms, unlike the other categories in the book, are sold according to age and functionality. Typically, all firearms made before 1898 are over 100 years old and are considered antiques. This makes them exempt from Federal Firearms Regulations. To purchase weapons made after that date you must typically be a Federal Firearms Licensed (FFL) Dealer or you must apply for permits and be subject to a waiting period of some duration. Also, most auctions make no warranties about the condition of the weapons they sell. All are classified as war relics in as/is condition. Make sure you have a professional gunsmith thoroughly check out any weapon before it is fired.

Buyers must also be sure of the condition of ammunition and other explosive items, such as grenades. In some cases, live examples of these items have unknowingly gotten to auction. Some dealers will tell you in their catalogs if ammunition being sold is live. Only experts should handle these types of dangerous munitions.

Certain other types of former military equipment like recoilless rifles and cannons must be demilitarized according to ATF regulations before they can be sold.

There are hundreds of gun shows every year in this country. While not expressly militaria shows, military handguns and rifles are well represented at these events. Frequently large quantities of accessories and general militaria are available at these events.

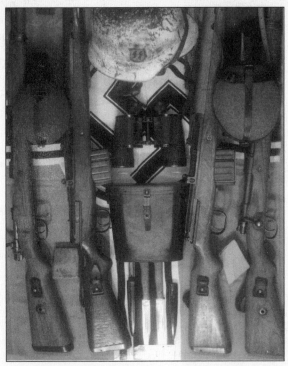

Late WWII German Rifles Including Two 98K Rifles and Two Gewehr 43 Rifles

Collecting Tips

When collecting firearms the first decision to be made is whether the weapons you collect will be fired or not. Then you need to consider if you want to specialize in one country's weapons, one type of weapon, or the weapons from one time period or war.

Fakes and Frauds

Most weapons were assembled when manufactured with matching numbered parts. Often examples of various weapons will be for sale with non-matching part numbers. Is this simply a weapon that has been repaired or is it one that was assembled from a pile of parts? Depending on your collecting criteria, this may or may not make a difference.

Periodicals

Magazine: *Man at Arms, The Official Arms Collecting Publication of the NRA,* (401) 726-8011

Museums

The US Army Ordnance Museum, Aberdeen Proving Ground, MD, (410) 278-3602

Rock Island Arsenal Museum, Rock Island, IL, (309) 782-5021

Springfield, Armory National Historic Site, Springfield, MA, (413) 734-6477

Anti-tank and Anti-aircraft Weapons——U.S.

Anti-tank Gun, 37mm, USA, Army, WWII. Single barrel towed weapon. Widely used as anti-tank weapon in early stages of WWII. Many were used on armored vehicles including the M3 Stuart light tank. This example has been restored. Good cond. $11,500

3-Inch Anti-Tank Gun

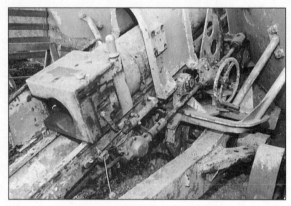

3-Inch Gun, Breech Detail

Bazooka Bag, Camo, USA, Various, WWII. Army/ Marine camo bag with carry strap for two-piece M9 bazooka weapon. Exc. cond. $280

Bazooka Round Bag, USA, Army, 1945. Dark OD canvas body with dark OD web straps. "US" marked and 1945 dated. Avg. cond. $28

Bazooka Round Carrier, USA, Army, 1944. WWII canvas carrier dated 1944 with web shoulder strap. Avg. cond. $20

Gun Mount, M45, USA, Army, WWII. Anti-aircraft gun mount. Originally mounted four.50 cal.-machine guns. This example is mounted on an M17 towed trailer. Avg. cond. $8500

Gun, 3", USA, Army, 1942, Pullman Standard. Three-inch single barrel towed gun. The weapon has been de-militarized and the breech removed. Widely used as an anti-tank weapon later in the war. This unit (Serial Number 276), is complete and original. Good cond. . . . . . .
. . . . $15,500

Gun, 40mm Bofors, USA, Army, 1942. Single barrel towed weapon. Demilitarized per ATF specifications. Widely used anti-aircraft weapon during WWII. This example was last used by the Norwegian Army. The gun is mounted on a four-wheel M2A1 carriage. It includes a canvas cover, tool box and tools, parts box and parts, and cleaning rods. Good cond. $8000

Recoilless Rifle, 57mm, M18, USA, Army, c1946. Demilitarized for use as a display or prop only. This anti-tank weapon designed in 1943–44 arrived too late for war service and has long been phased out by US forces. It measures 61" overall and weighs 46 lbs. This price is for the rifle, telescope and case, bipod, front handle, canvas breech and muzzle covers and bore brush. Avg. cond. . .
. . . . $975

Recoilless Rifle, 75mm, M20, USA, Army, 1950s. Demilitarized for use as a display or prop only. This anti-tank weapon has long been phased out of US service. It measures 82" overall and weighs 115 lbs. This example includes the rifle, tripod, sight and mounting bracket and canvas breech and muzzle covers. The tri-pod can be modified to fit the M151 quarter-ton 4 x 4 truck. Avg. cond.
. . . . $4500

Recoilless Rifle, 75mm, M20, USA, Army, 1950s. Demilitarized for use as a display or prop only. This anti-tank weapon has long been phased out of US service. It measures 82" overall and weighs 115 lbs. This example includes the rifle, tri-pod, sight and mounting bracket and canvas breech and muzzle covers. Avg. cond. . . . $1750

Recoilless Rifle, 105mm, M27, USA, Army, 1950s. Demilitarized for use as a display or prop only. This anti-tank weapon has long been phased out of US service. Was replaced in US service in the Late 1950s by the M40 106mm recoilless rifle. This example includes a mount for M38 or M38-A1 jeeps. Avg. cond. $5500

Rocket Launcher Tube, Dragon, USA, Army, 1980s. 40"-long tube in OD finish. Has endcaps, OD web sling and trigger. Above avg. cond. $78

Rocket Launcher, AT-4, USA, Army, 1980s. 40" long with instructions on outside, web carry strap and fire/safe controls. No weapon internally and port covers are miss-

Rocket Launcher, Anti-Tank AT-4

ing. Exterior shows much training use and retapes of components has been done with black electric tape. Replaced the LAW missile in the mid-1980s. Avg. cond. . . . $100

Rocket Launcher, LAW, USA, Army, 1972. 1972 dated weapon shows some wear and tear. US instructions are readable on sides. Inert rocket has black finished warhead and brass engine exhaust. Above avg. cond. $85

Searchlight, USA, Army, WWII, General Electric. 60" anti-aircraft searchlight. Mounted on trailer (not a military model). Also includes complete original generator. Good cond. $9500

Searchlight, USA, Army, WWII, Sperry. 60" anti-aircraft searchlight. Complete and also includes original generator. 800-million candlepower and 20-mile range. Good cond. $8000

Anti-tank and Anti-aircraft Weapons—Germany

Computer, Range-finder, Anti-aircraft, Naval, Germany, Navy, WWII, Dennert and Pape Hamburg. 4" x 4" x 13" blue-gray painted metal body has rounded back with two mounting clamps. Flat front facing has clear lens on scale, dial-scale knob at end and slide knob at bottom for setting "Schiffsgeschw.Vs sm/h." Front metal is stamped "TF Schu Re1," "Dennert & Pape Hamburg-Altona Werk Nr. 81698" and Eagle-M "Mar.Nr.551" issued. Rotating drum inside has lost paper cover with scale marks. Dial setting has red and green halves with moving outer scale ring. Above avg. cond. $125

Panzerfaust, Germany, Army, WWII. Steel tube has tan paint and red stenciled instructions. Sight and firing device intact. Tan painted head has paper firing instructions. Above avg. cond. $483

Panzerfaust, Germany, Army, WWII. Marked "8.8cm Raketenpanzerbuchse 54." Deactivated tube with large hole cut into side and welded rods inside. 64½" long with recent camo paint of tan-green-reddish brown. Comes with protective shield and only lacks sling. Above avg. cond. $750

Rifle Round, Anti-tank, Imperial Germany, Army, WWI. 13mm. Brass case had stamped "PM." FMJ projectile. Above avg. cond. $110

Shell, Anti-tank, 20mm, Imperial Germany, Army, WWI. Trench engraved lettering on side of shell body. "German Anti-Tank Shell/A.B.-S.C.J./Aug 11-19." Avg. cond. $61

Grenades and Mortars—U.S.

Grenade, USA, Army, WWI. Safe, intact with arm, fuse and safing pin. Case marked MO. Age patina and light rust. Above avg. cond. $130

Grenade, M68, USA, Army, 1973. Dated 1973 on fuse assembly. Complete with pin and arm. Smooth case. OD finish. Above avg. cond. $12

Grenade, MK-II A1, USA, Army, USMC, WWII. Safe grenade but complete with arm, pin and fuse assembly. Some residual pale green paint remains. Above avg. cond. $63

Grenade, MK-II A1, USA, Army, USMC, WWII. Complete with arm, fuse and safety pin. Case is serrated and shows finishing in OD green paint. No rust. Above avg. cond. $87

Grenade, MK-II A1, USA, Army, USMC, WWII. Silver finished fragmentation grenade with pin and arm in place on fuse. Bottom drilled out. Avg. cond. $20

Grenade, MK-II A1, USA, Army, USMC, WWII. Complete with arm, fuse and safety pin. Case is serrated and shows some residual paint signs. Avg. cond. $50

Grenade, MK-II A1, USA, Army, WWII. Complete with pin, arm and fuse case. Some rust in spots. Avg. cond. $20

Grenade, Smoke, Colored, M18, USA, Army, Vietnam War Era. Dummy grenade with all components present. Painted red at top below fuse. Labeled on side "M18/SMOKE/RED." Exc. cond. $22

Grenade, Smoke, Colored, M18, USA, Army, Vietnam War Era. Dummy grenade with all components present. Painted violet at top below fuse. Labeled on side "M18/SMOKE/VIOLET." Above avg. cond. $20

Grenade, Smoke, Colored, M18, USA, Army, WWII. Green smoke grenade with lt green painted top and pin in fuse. Bottom drilled out. Above avg. cond. $20

Rifle Grenade Launcher, M-1, USA, Army, 1944. For Springfield Model 1903. Parts still in protective wrapping. Includes instruction sheet. In 1944 dated dark OD canvas carrying case. Some soiling to case. Near mint cond. $20

Rifle Grenade Launcher, M-7, USA, Army, WWII. For M1 Garand. Well marked. Avg. cond. $20

Rifle Grenade Launcher, M-7, USA, Army, WWII. For M1 Garand. 8"-long gray metal body. Well marked. Avg. cond. $20

Grenades and Mortars—Germany

Grenade, "Ball" Style, Imperial Germany, Army, WWI. Cast-iron ball with three ridges upper and lower around a central serrated band. Fuse is inserted. Avg. cond. $90

Grenade, "Disc" Style, Imperial Germany, Army, WWI. Pancake shaped with safing pin in fuse and threaded access points around perimeter. Avg. cond. $140

Grenade, Anti-personnel, Germany, Army, WWII. Rifle-launched style. 5½" long with four-part dug body. Black and yellow repaint on pitted metal sections. Bakelite fuse and grooved tail. Below avg. cond. $37

Grenade, Anti-personnel, Germany, Army, WWII. Marked "wurfkorper 361." Style used with flare pistol that required smooth bore liner. 10" long with metal egg grenade, Bakelite tube and head stamped "43 1a." Above avg. cond. $175

Grenade, Anti-personnel, Germany, Army, WWII. Rifle launched style. 5½"-tall four-part body, yellow painted steel body, gray metal tip, Bakelite fuse and grooved tail. Marked "mne St 44 etc." Avg. cond. $93

Grenade, Anti-tank, Germany, Army, WWII. Rifle-launched style. 7"-tall cone-shaped metallic body. Bakelite stem with grooved end. Avg. cond. $105

Grenade, Anti-tank, Germany, Army, WWI. Rifle-launched style. 13mm. About 5½" tall with slug. Brass case head is stamped "18 T67 P 6." Avg. cond. . . $39

Grenade, Anti-tank, Imperial Germany, Army, WWI. 2" long overall with wooden nose and tail. 10½" sheet-metal body with four-wire rod framework. Above avg. cond. $100

Grenade, Anti-tank, Imperial Germany, Army, WWI. Rifle-launched style. 13mm. Dark brass case with primer intact. Slug shows pull marks from gunpowder removal. Head stamped "T67 P 4 18." Avg. cond. $34

Grenade, M1924, Germany, Army, WWII. "Stick" style with turned wooden handle stamped "RR 1939 WaA???." Green metal head with white stenciled wording, "WaA560" and top stamped "RR 1939." End cap and donut with pull-string. Exc. cond. $345

Grenade, M1924, Germany, Army, WWII. "Stick" style with wooden handle stamped "HR791 1940 WaA136." Gray painted metal head with gray smooth fragmentation sleeve. Avg. cond. $175

Grenade, M1924, Germany, Army, WWII. "Stick" style with white donut on white string with wire from fuse intact. Avg. cond. $38

Grenade, M1924, Germany, Army, WWII. "Stick" style with "WC1944" marked on metal head and turned wooden handle with drilled center. Done before fuse change to

head mount. "WaA" on end cap and pull-cord is missing. Avg. cond. $140

Grenade, M1924, Germany, Army, WWII. "Stick" style grenade with turned wooden handle is stamped "bab 43 WaA??." Steel end cap with loose white donut. Gray metal head by "RR 1940." Force fit gray metal smooth with fragmentation sleeve. Avg. cond. $175

Grenade, M1939, Germany, Army, WWII. "Egg" style. Cast body with serrated band and maker marked "HE H." Above avg. cond. $27

Grenade, M1939, Germany, Army, WWII. "Egg" style. Gray painted two-part body. Gray wings on blue painted fuse cover marked "efy 43" and string intact. Avg. cond. $220

Grenade, M1939, Germany, Army, WWII. "Egg" style. Small gray body with fragmentation band around center. Avg. cond. $24

Grenade, Smoke, Germany, Army, WWII. 5"-tall clear glass lightbulb-shaped body with glass tube inside and crack on fiber cap. Marked "m2h." Avg. cond. . . . $145

Grenade, Training, M1924, Germany, Army, WWII. "Stick" style. Turned wooden handle stamped "Ub 44 brb" inked "WaA." End cap. Red painted steel head with eight holes and stamped "44brb." Exc. cond. $282

Mine, Anti-personnel, Germany, Army, WWII. Complete example of "glasmine 43" type. Heavy glass body, shear plate, glass top, metal inside disc and M-44 pressure igniter. Above avg. cond. $177

Mortar Round, Germany, Army, WWII. 50mm mortar round, 9" tip to fin with well-defined Bakelite nose. Above avg. cond. $145

Mortar Round, Germany, Army, WWII. 50mm mortar round. 9" tip to fin with well-defined Bakelite nose. Avg. cond. $132

Mortar Round, Minenwerfer, Imperial Germany, Army,

German WWII Rifle Grenade Launcher Pouch

WWI. 11" long overall with fuse and threaded four fin tail on cast-iron segmented body. Avg. cond. $265

Pouch, Rifle Grenade Launcher, Germany, Army, WWII. Black leather body marked "dkk 43 WaA195." Gray web shoulder strap. Above avg. cond. $30

Pouch, Rifle Grenade Launcher, Germany, Army, WWII. Black leather body marked "cxb 42 WaA210." Olive web shoulder strap. Avg. cond. $25

Storage Box, Grenades, Germany, Army, WWII. Holds 15 M1924 "stick" grenades. Stamped steel body by "kho43" with original gray paint and white band around center. Wooden handle intact as is metal rack inside. Avg. cond. $240

Storage Box, Grenades, Germany, Army, WWII. Holds 15 M1924 "stick" grenades. Hinged stamped metal body with wooden handle still intact. Avg. cond. $95

Storage Box, Grenades, Germany, Army, WWII. Holds 15 M1924 "stick" grenades. Stamped steel hinged body with wooden handle. Avg. cond. $98

Grenades and Mortars—Other

Grenade, Type 99, Japan, Army, WWII. Steel cylindrical grenade with brass fuse. Inert. Above avg. cond. $100

Handguns—U.S.

Revolver, Colt, 1851 Navy Model, Cased, USA, Various, 1853, Colt. .36 cal. Stamped blued octagonal sighted barrel, cylinder with naval engagement scene, silvered trigger guard, grip strap engraved "Captn J.S.A. Herford" and walnut grips. In fitted oak case with green velvet lining, directions for loading and cleaning printed on lid. Exc. cond. $4370

Revolver, Colt, New Model Army, USA, Various, Civil War Era, Colt. Also called Model 1860. .44 cal, six-shot cylinder, 8" octagonal barrel, iron frame, brass trigger guard and two-piece walnut grips. Also includes three cap tins, one civilian powder flask, one shot flask and two single-cavity bullet molds, all in an oak box. Above avg. cond. $1000

Revolver, Colt, New Model Army, USA, Various, Civil War, Colt. Also called the Model 1860. Six-shot round cylinder, .44 cal, 8" octagonal barrel, iron frame with brass trigger guard and two-piece walnut grips. Exc. cond. $1000

Handgun, Pistol, Percussion, USA, Navy, 1842, NP Ames, Springfield, MA. .54 cal, 6" barrel and brass furniture on walnut stock. Above avg. cond. $625

Pistol, Colt, Model 1911A1, USA, Various, WWII, Remington Rand. .45 cal automatic. Standard issue government model with commercial shoulder holster, military magazine pouch and two military issue magazines. Serial numbered. Exc. cond. $550

Revolver, Starr, Double-action, USA, Various, Civil War Era, Starr Arms Co. .44 cal, six-shot cylinder, 6" round barrel and one-piece walnut grips. Serial numbered. Above avg. cond. $1700

Revolver, Starr, Double-action, USA, Various, Civil War Era, Starr Arms Co. .44 cal, six-shot cylinder and 6" round barrel and one-piece walnut grips. Serial numbered. Good cond. $375

Revolver, Colt, M1917, USA, Army, WWI, Colt. Rechambered for .45 cal. Standard issue has 5½" barrel, parkerized finish, fixed sights and checkered walnut grips. Serial numbered. Exc. cond. $300

US S & W Model 1917 .45 Cal Revolver

Revolver, Colt, New Model Army, USA, Various, Civil War Era, Colt. .44 cal, six-shot cylinder, 8" round barrel, one-piece walnut grips, U.S. government inspectors marks on barrel and back strap, and cartouche in grips. Exc. cond. $800

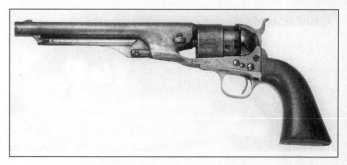

Colt New Model Army, .44 Caliber

Revolver, Colt, New Model Army, USA, Various, Civil War Era, Colt. Also called the Model 1860. .44 cal, six-shot cylinder, 8" barrel, and walnut grips. Above avg. cond. $750

Revolver, Remington, Army, USA, Various, Civil War Era, Remington. .44 cal, six-shot cylinder, 8" octagonal barrel, two-piece walnut grips and barrel marked "patented Sept 14, 1858/E. Remington & Sons, Ilion, New York, USA." Above avg. cond. $700

Revolver, Remington-Beals, Navy, USA, Various, Civil War Era, Remington-Beals. .36 cal. Standard model. Serial numbered. Good cond. $350

Revolver, Colt, Navy Model 1851, USA, Various, Civil War Era, Colt. .36 cal. Octagonal barrel, brass trigger guard and back strap and one-piece walnut grips. Serial numbered. Good cond. $600

Revolver, Remington, Army, USA, Various, Civil War Era, Remington. .44 cal, six-shot cylinder, 8" octagonal barrel, iron frame, brass trigger guard and two-piece walnut grips. Fair cond. $500

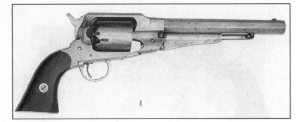
Remington Army Revolver, .44 Caliber

Revolver, Colt, Navy Model 1851, Cased, USA, Various, 1855, Colt. Blued octagonal barrel with London address, blued cylinder with naval engagement scene, blued frame, blued trigger guard and back strap. With original fitted oak case with blue velvet lining and accessories. Above avg. cond. $2098

Revolver, Colt, Dragoon, Model 1849, USA, Various, 1858, Colt, Hartford. .44 cal. Third model. Blued barrel with New York address, folding leaf back sight, blued cylinder, brass trigger guard, iron back strap and walnut grips. Avg. cond. $1224

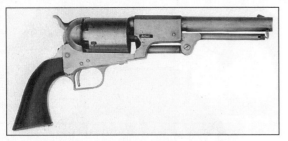
Colt Dragoon Model 1849, .44 Caliber

Pistol, Colt, Model 1911A1, USA, Various, 1944, Remington Rand. .45 cal automatic. Fully engraved. Mother-of-pearl grips. Slide and frame professionally engraved with beautiful floral work. Engraving also appears on front

bar of grip and trigger. Clean bore. Tight action. Colt letter accompanying piece notes it was shipped by Remington Rand in 1944. Full blued finish. Above avg. cond. $1055

Remington Manufactured M1911A1, .45 Caliber

Pepperbox, Bacon, Percussion, Underhammer, USA, Various, c1852, Thomas K. Bacon, Norwich, CT. .31 cal. Six shot. Floral engraving on the action. Plain wooden grips. White finish with some spot and lt pits. Avg. cond. $300

Pistol, Bacon, Percussion, Underhammer, USA, Various, 1850s, Thomas K. Bacon, Norwich, CT. .34 cal. Single shot. Barrel is half-round at the muzzle and octagonal at the back. Floral engraving on the action. Plain wooden cane handle grip. Smooth bore. White finish with wear and some age patina. Avg. cond. $200

Pistol, Colt, Model 1911, USA, Various, WWI, Colt. .45 cal automatic. 75% original blue finish, good bore, walnut checkered diamond grips and early two-tone magazine with no lanyard. Serial number range 304500. Above avg. cond. $400

Pistol, Colt, Model 1903, USA, Army, c1930s, Colt. .32 cal. Blue finish. Black hard rubber grips. Serial number range 525xxx and indicates commercial version converted to military use. With 8" x 10" b&w photo of O.S.S. officer wearing this gun in shoulder holster. Above avg. cond. $450

Pistol, Flintlock, Model 1816, USA, Army, 1817–20, Simeon North, Middletown CT. .54 cal. smoothbore flintlock pistol. 19,374 produced. Iron hardware with carved walnut stock that has "DCo" and "27." Age cracks and frizzen is missing. Length 15½". Avg. cond. $880

Pistol, Flintlock, Thomas French Contract Type, USA, Army, c1812, Thomas French, Canton, MA. .64 cal with 13¼"-inch round barrel. Lock shows faint eagle stamp with US, signature and Canton. Walnut stock with barrel bands. Some repairs. Below avg. cond. $330

Pistol, Training, USA, Army, 1980s. 9mm Beretta. Cast hard rubber with all details complete, no moving parts but same size as real weapon. Above avg. cond. $40

Pistol, Training, USA, Various, WWII. M1911A .45 automatic pistol in cast hard rubber. All details complete, some of casting is crude around butt and rear of grip. Needs cleaning. Avg. cond. $72

Pistol, I.N. Johnson, Percussion, USA, Army, 1853, I.N. Johnson, Middleton, CT. "US" marked. .54 cal single shot. 1853 date stamped on lockplate. Brass guard, tang buttcap and combination band/sideplate. Steel ramrod. Metal shows age and lt pitting. A few cracks on dark walnut stock. Faint cartouche. Action works. Avg. cond. $125

Revolver, Starr, Single-action, Army Model 1863, USA, Army, Civil War Era, Starr Arms Co., NYC. .44 cal. Finish is white but mostly patina and pitting. Single action works fine. Fair cond. $175

Revolver, Colt, New Model Army, USA, Army, Civil War Era, Colt. Also called the Model 1860. Six-shot round cylinder, .44 cal. Appears to be all matching numbers and condition, metal parts are all white, may have been bead blasted, has some pits, bore pitted and action is loose. Below avg. cond. $350

Revolver, Colt, Navy Model 1861, USA, Navy, Civil War Era, Colt. .36 cal, six-shot cylinder with 7½" barrel. Appears to be all matching numbers and condition, metal parts are all white, may have been buffed, bore pitted and action is loose. Avg. cond. $350

Revolver, Colt, Navy Model 1851, USA, Various, Civil War Era, Colt, Hartford, CT. .36 cal. Model manufactured from 1850 to 1873. Fourth model with signature, address plus "US America." Engraved cylinder with battle scene. Small areas of pitting. Serial numbered. Good cond. $1155

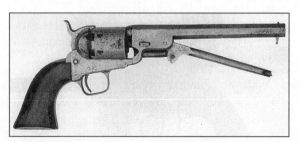

Colt Model Navy, .36 Caliber

Revolver, Colt, Navy Model 1851, USA, Various, Civil War Era, Colt, Hartford, CT. .36 cal with 7½" octagonal barrel. Early fourth model with Hartford address. Traces of engraved cylinder. Some pitting. Serial numbered. All serial numbers match. Avg. cond. $880

Handguns—Germany

Pistol, Luger, P08, German, Army, 1916, DWM. Semi-automatic, 9mm cal. 4" barrel with chamber date "1916" and "DWM" on toggle link. Serial numbered. Exc. cond. $625

Luger P08

Pistol, Luger, Parabellum P08, Germany, Army, WWII, Various. Semi-automatic, 9 mm cal. 4" tapered round barrel, fixed sights, checkered wood grips, blue magazine with alum bottom. Serial numbered. Above avg. cond. $475

Pistol, CZ, Model 1927, Germany, Army, WWII, Ceska Zbrojovka, Czechoslovakia. Semi-automatic, 7.65mm cal. Nazi marked late war production, manufacturers code "FNH" and "Pistole Modell 27 Kal. 7.65" stamped to left side of slide, brown composition CZ logo wrap around grips and black leather belt holster with spare magazine. Serial numbered. Above avg. cond. $350

Pistol, Astra, Model 600, Germany, Army, 1944–45, Astra, Spain. 9mm version. Nazi proofed. With black military pattern leather holster. 85% original blue, all matching numbers and checkered wooden grips. Bore has some minor pitting. Avg. cond. $275

Pistol, Browning, Model GP, Germany, Army, WWII, Fabrique Nationale, Belgium. Also known as the Model 35

Browning Model GP35 or "High Power"

or High Power. 9mm automatic pistol. Swastika stamped Nazi Occupation. Serial number range 98000. Standard proof marks have been removed and small swastikas stamped in their place. 97% original wartime finish, fine bore (slightly dark), wooden grips and one grip screw slightly loose. Exc. cond. $1000

Pistol, Browning, Model GP, Germany, Army, WWII, Fabrique Nationale, Belgium. Also known as the Model 35 or High Power. 9mm automatic pistol. Nazi Proofed, 70% original polished blue, all matching numbers, range 188700, checkered wooden grips and bore is pitted. Includes holster in poor condition. Avg. cond. $275

Pistol, Browning, Model 1922, Germany, Army, WWII, Fabrique Nationale, Belgium. Nazi marked. 7.65mm automatic pistol. With brown leather holster. 85% original blue, all matching numbers, range 188700, checkered wooden grips and bore is good. Holster is correct pattern made of ersatz leather and has a repaired flap in the back. Avg. cond. $175

Pistol, CZ, Model 1927, Germany, Army, WWII, Ceska Zbrojovka, Czechoslovakia. Semi-automatic, 7.65mm cal. Nazi proofed. With correct leather holster. 90% original polished blue, all matching numbers, range 90900, dark brown plastic grip, bore mirror perfect and extra magazine. Holster marked and dated 1942. Exc. cond.   . $150

CZ Model 1927

Pistol, Luger, P08, Germany, Army, 1912, DWM. 9mm. Matching numbers. Wooden bottom magazine not numbered. Bore good. About 85% original blue with some wear at muzzle. Small chip missing from left grip. Avg. cond. $600

Pistol, Radom, P-35, Germany, Army, WWII, Radom, Poland. 9mm automatic pistol. Nazi proofed. With correct holster, 70% original blue, all matching numbers, wartime production, no stock slot, dark reddish plastic grips, with "FB" in triangle on the grips, bore is good and serial number range F6500. Holster is Nazi pattern military, flap

strap has been changed and a leather tie-down added. Avg. cond. $150

Pistol, Luger, S/42, Germany, Army, 1937. 9mm. All matching numbers except clip. Wooden checker grips, one small edge chip on front rt grip, clean bore, dark anodized finish 90%, some small pitting on both sides and white highlights to number. Clip is alum grip and unmarked. Early Waffen stamped right side. Dated 1937 on top of barrel. Above avg. cond. $650

Pistol, Mauser, Model 1912, Germany, Army, WWI, Waffenfabrik Mauser, Oberndorf. Cal 7.63mm. Waffenfabrik Mauser Oberndorf marked. Blue has faded but action is strong and tight. Serial number 216xxx range. Matching bolt. Above avg. cond. $280

Pistol, Mauser, Model HSc, Germany, Army, WWII, Mauser. 7.65mm. Produced for Luftwaffe and Navy service. In rare original hardshell holster and in almost unfired condition. Wartime production with wooden grips, minor scuffs to blued finish, mirror bore and serial number range 847300. Holster is Nauser HSc hardshell marked "Wirsa 1941 Munchen," strings are white and leather is lt tan. Exc. cond. $375

Pistol, Radom, P-35, Germany, Army, WWII, Radom, Poland. Nazi proofed. With correct holster. 95% original blue, only holster wear and all matching numbers. Early piece slotted for stock. Black plastic grips, with "FB" in triangle on the grips, bore is good and serial number range D1400. Holster is Nazi pattern military with Nazi army Eagle added to flap. Above avg. cond. $250

Pistol, Walther, P38, Germany, Army, 1943, Walther. 9mm. 75% original blue, some spotting. All matching numbers, black plastic grips and bore is good. Holster is Nazi proofed military pattern dated 1943. Avg. cond. $250

Pistol, Walther, P38, Germany, Army, WWII, Walther. 9mm cal. Matching holster and extra magazine. 85% original blue, only holster wear, all matching numbers, extra magazine number does not match, black plastic grips, bore is good, holster is Nazi proofed military pattern dated 1942. Avg. cond. $425

Pistol, Walther, P38, Germany, Army, 1944, Walther. 9mm. 95% original blue, marked "BYF 44," only holster wear, all matching numbers, black plastic grips and bore is good. Holster is Nazi proofed military pattern dated 1944. Exc. cond. $375

Pistol, Walther, P38, Germany, Army, 1940, Walther. 9mm. 90% original blue, marked "CYQ," only holster wear, all matching numbers, black plastic grips and bore is good. Holster is Nazi proofed military pattern dated 1940. Above avg. cond. $375

Pistol, Walther, P38, Germany, Army, WWII, Walther. 9mm. Early example marked "AC-41," serial numbered, dark reddish brown plastic grips, has pitting in lands of bore, 70% original blue, some spots of pitting on surface and all numbers match. Avg. cond. $375

Walther P38

Handguns—Other

Pistol, Beretta, Model 1934, Italy, Army, 1942, Beretta. Semi-automatic, 9mm cal. Marked "M" with two bars stamped over it at left rear frame, finger-rest magazine and black logo composition grips, serial #491xxx. Exc. cond. $250

Pistol, Beretta, Model 1934, Italy, Various, 1944, Beretta. Semi-automatic, 9mm pistol. Made during RSI Fascist period under German occupation, marked with crown over a lion in a circle at left rear frame, finger-rest magazine and black logo composition grips. Serial #4132BB. Exc. cond. $400

Pistol, Flintlock Blunderbuss, Officer, France, Navy, c1805. Has 6¾" .62 cal. brass barrel, with flared muzzle. Rounded brass lockplate. Varnished walnut stock with brass furniture and iron ramrod. Barrel shows light marks. Hammer cleaned and its screw replaced. Some wear to stock and lt chipping at ramrod hole. Good cond. $2588

Pistol, Flintlock, Military, Belgium, Various, c1820s. Has 7½" .70 cal. barrel with octagonal breech section. Walnut stock. Ramrod missing. Metal shows deep pitting. Some wear to stock. Avg. cond. $489

Pistol, Flintlock, Model AN XIII (1805), France, Various, 1811, St. Etienne. Has 8" .68 cal. barrel, marked "1811" at breech and "Mle An 13" at breech (No. I). Lockplate marked "Mre. imp de St. etienne." Varnished walnut stock marked "C.B. 1811." Ramrod present. Barrel shows lt brown patina. Cock and plate has some pitting. Some marks on wooden grip. Good cond. $1265

Pistol, "Baby" Nambu, Japan, Army, WWII, Arsenal Tokyo Gas & Electric. Cal 7mm. Serial number range 6100. All matching and clip. 90% original finish. Checkered wooden grips. Bore excellent. Exc. cond. $500

Pistol, Nambu, "Papa" M1904, Japan, Army, WWI, Arsenal Kayoba Tokyo. Caliber 8mm. Serial number range 2200. All matching numbers and clip. 90% original finish, checkered wooden grips and clip button. Bore shows little wear except for some pitting near the muzzle. Has slot for shoulder stock. Above avg. cond. $4500

Pistol, Nambu, "Papa" M1904, Naval, Japan, Navy, WWI, Arsenal Tokyo Gas & Electric. Caliber 8mm. Serial number range 3000. All numbers matching except alum bottom clip. Has anchor on the rt side. 90% original finish. Checkered wooden grips. Bore excellent. No slot for shoulder stock. Has white painted characters on the left grip. Exc. cond. $500

Pistol, Nambu, "Papa" M1904, Japan, Army, WWI, Arsenal Tokyo. Caliber 8mm. Serial number range 7000. All matching except alum bottom clip. 80% original finish remains. Checkered wooden grips. Bore has pitting. No slot for shoulder stock. Has white painted characters on the left grip. Above avg. cond. $500

Pistol, Nambu, Type 14, Japan, Army, 1943, Nagoya Arsenal, Nambu Factory. 8mm cal. Large trigger guard version. Serial number range 12100. All numbers match. Dated 17,12 (Dec. 1943). 90% finish remains. Grips good. Shows scoring from safety lever. Bore good. Above avg. cond. $150

Pistol, Nambu, Type 14, Japan, Army, 1944, Nagoya Arsenal. 8mm cal. Large trigger guard version. Serial number range 91100. All numbers match. Dated 18,9 (Sept. 1944). 85% finish remains. Grips excellent. Bore good. Firing pin tip broken. Above avg. cond. $100

Pistol, Nambu, Type 14, Japan, Army, 1940, Nagoya Arsenal, Nambu Factory. Cal 8mm. Serial number range 70500. All matching numbers. Dated 14,11 (Nov. 1940).

Flintlock Pistol, Model ANXIII

85% finish remains. Grips and bore good. Avg. cond. $150

Pistol, Nambu, Type 94, Japan, Army, 1939, Nagoya Arsenal, Toriimatsu Factory. Cal 8mm. Serial number range 4700. Magazine number matches. Dated 13,2 (Feb. 1939). 95% of original commercial blue finish remains. Excellent hard rubber grips. Bore good. Above avg. cond. $150

Pistol, Nambu, Type 94, Japan, Army, 1945, Nagoya Arsenal, Nambu Factory. Cal 8mm. Serial number range 66000. Magazine matches. Dated 19,12 (Dec. 1945). 90% finish remains. Wooden grips and bore good. Above avg. cond. $150

Pistol, Nambu, Type 94, Japan, Army, 1943, Nagoya Arsenal, Toriimatsu Factory. Cal 8mm. Serial number range 31000. Both magazines match. Dated 17,10 (Oct. 1943). 95% of finish remains. Excellent plastic grips. Bore good. With holster, spare magazine and cleaning rod. Above avg. cond. $200

Pistol, Nambu, Type 14, Japan, Army, 1932, Kokura Arsenal. Cal 8mm. Small trigger guard version. Serial number range 21200. All matching. Dated 6,6 (June. 1932). 90% finish remains. Grips excellent. Bore shows some wear. Above avg. cond. $150

Nambu Type 14 Pistol

Pistol, Nambu, Type 14, Japan, Army, 1929, Nagoya Arsenal. Cal 8mm. Small trigger guard version. Serial number range 2400. All matching. Dated 3.4 (April 1929). 90% finish remains. Grips and bore excellent. Above avg. cond. $150

Pistol, Nambu, Type 14, Japan, Army, 1928, Nagoya Arsenal. Cal. 8mm. Serial number 8xx range. Matching bolt. Dated 2,7 (July. 1928). Grips good. Finish worn off barrel. Surface pitting to barrel and receiver area. Avg. cond. $125

Pistol, Glisenti, Model 1910, Italy, Army, WWII. Cal. 9mm. Double action. Side gate loading and ejection. Dark reblued finish. Action works fine. Chambers and bore

need to be cleaned. Wooden grips worn. Avg. cond. $40

Revolver, Nagant, Model 1895, Soviet Union, Army, 1941. Cal is the obsolete 7.62mm nagant. Checkered wooden grips, 75% original blue finish and all matching numbers. Double-action hammer link is missing and bore shows wear but doesn't look pitted. Holster is standard WWII Russian officer's pattern, except the two small belt loops in the back have been changed to one large loop. Avg. cond. $85

British Webley-Scott Mk. VI.455 Cal Revolver. Standard British Sidearm of WWI and WWII

Flare Guns—U.S.

Flare Gun, USA, Army, WWII. Gray metal body with tip over barrel and integral checkered grips. Marked "Sklar Signal Pistol." Above avg. cond. $67

US 37mm Flare Pistol

Flare Gun, USA, Navy, WWII, England. Break breech model for loading and single shot. Hmkd on side and USN marked on each grip. Avg. cond. $32

Flare Gun, Penlight, USA, Army, WWII. Black metal tube with lanyard and thumb-operated trigger. Avg. cond. $25

Flare Pistol, M8, USA, Army, WWII, Canada. Single shot, break barrel loading and black plastic grips. Metal parts show some rust patina. Holster of tan leather with alum plate on side and hmkd "Made in Canada." Above avg. cond. $70

Signal Flare Gun, Mark 5, USA, Navy, 1942. Break

US WWII Flare Pistol

front loading, single shot. USN on checkered grips. Black finish. Above avg. cond. $65

Flare Guns—Germany

Flare Pistol, Germany, Army, WWII. Black finished alum alloy body by "ac 1940." Bakelite grips. Black leatherette holster by "fsx 41 WaA445." Avg. cond. $180

Flare Pistol, Germany, Various, WWII. Black finished alum alloy body by "duv 42" with eagle proofs. Bakelite grips and lanyard ring. Exc. cond. $161

Flare Pistol, Germany, Various, WWII. Black finish to alum alloy body with Bakelite grips. By "ayf 43" with proofs. Exc. cond. $200

Flare Pistol, Germany, Various, WWII. Black finished alum body by "ayf 42." Bakelite grips and lanyard ring. Above avg. cond. $145

Flare Pistol, Germany, Various, WWII. Black finished alum body by "ac 42." Bakelite grips and lanyard ring. Avg. cond. $100

Flare Pistol, Germany, Various, WWII. Black finished alum body by "ac 41." Bakelite grips and lanyard ring. Avg. cond. $150

Flare Pistol, Germany, Various, WWII. Worn black finish to alum alloy body. Stamped "S/237 1938" and many eagle proofs. Bakelite grips. Lanyard ring. Avg. cond. $91

Flare Pistol, Germany, Various, WWII. Black finished alum body by "ayf 42" and large "Z" to barrel. Bakelite grips and lanyard ring. Avg. cond. $475

Flare Pistol, Imperial Germany, Army, WWI. 15"-long steel body by "Gebr.R." Wood grips and lanyard rings. Avg. cond. $110

Flare Pistol, Walther, Germany, Various, WWII. Early blued steel body/barrel with stamped maker and scroll. Many crown proofs and Eagle-4. Wooden grips. Black paper holster has leather closure strap stamped "dla 44." Avg. cond. $207

Flare Pistol, Germany, Army, WWII. Reworked to 1". Gray metal body with "euh" and mismatched numbers. Bakelite grips. Dark rust to sleeved barrel stamped "1"/m25." Avg. cond. $40

Flare Round, "fallschirmleuchtpatrone," Germany, Various, WWII. 5"-tall alum case with stenciled title. Avg. cond. $133

Flare Round, Smoke, Germany, Various, WWII. 5½"-tall three-part body, Bakelite tip, grooved alum body and steel case. Below avg. cond. $91

Holster, Flare Pistol, Germany, Army, 1941. Black leatherette body has leather fittings and area for missing cleaning rod. Stamped maker to flap "fuq 1941 WaA14." Flat from storage. Above avg. cond. $150

Machine Guns and Rifles—U.S.

Carbine, Maynard, Second Model, USA, Army, Civil War Era, Massachusetts Arms Co., Chicopee Falls, MA. .50 cal. Wood intact. Action crisp. Barrel has black pitted finish throughout. Nipple has been completely mashed from old dry firing. Hammer mechanism functional. Bore black with age. Lettering still visible. Good type example of a weapon not overly popular with CW cavalrymen because of blow-back during firing. Saddle ring and bar present. Below avg. cond. $345

Carbine, Krag-Jorgensen, M1896, USA, Army, 1896, Springfield Armory. Cal.30. 90% original blue with some fading. Wood excellent. Above avg. cond. $600

Browning Automatic Rifle (BAR), Model 1918A2, the Standard US Squad Automatic Weapon of WWII

Carbine, Sharps & Hankins, Model 1862, USA, Army, Civil War, Sharps & Hankins, Philadelphia. For Spencer rimfire cartridge. Single-shot sliding barrel action. Works fine. Graying metal. Stock has scuff or two. Leather barrel cover about 25% gone. Avg. cond. $660

Musket, Enfield, P1853, USA, Army, CSA, 1863, Enfield, England. .577 cal. Uncleaned with brass dark but not damaged. European walnut full stock. Original nipple, no burning marks. No ramrod. Lockplate bears crisp VR crown with "Tower 1863" date. No lower sling swivel. "B" carved on left side of stock. Complete rear sight. Percussion hammer has full and half cock. No safety plug for nipple. Bore shows wear to grooves at crown from use. Avg. cond. $150

Musket, Percussion, Model 1861, USA, Army, 1864, Trenton Locomotive and Machine Co. .58 cal. Lockplate has "1864 U.S. Trenton." Rare contract issue. Full stock with three iron bands, spring present. Finish is in white metal. Inspector marks on barrel. Percussion hammer functional, original issue nipple. Clean-out screw on bolster. Wood still bears clear inspector marks. Weapon lacks metal ramrod but has old period-made trumpet-style wooden replacement. Lower sling swivel loop gone, no swivel remains on band. Fittings of weapon are clean with minimal corrosion. Above avg. cond. $450

Musket, Enfield, P1853, USA, Army, CSA, Civil War. Some used by Confederate troops during CW. .58 cal. All parts are in the white and have been cleaned. The stock has been cleaned and refinished. Side plate shows wear to the markings. Above avg. cond. $375

Musket, Percussion, Model 1861, USA, Army, 1864, Wm. Muir & Co. .58 cal. Lock has 1864 date. With good signature, US and eagle motif. Missing rear sight. Length 56". Good cond. $605

Musket, Percussion, Model 1861, USA, Army, 1864, Providence Tool Co. .58 cal. Lock has 1864 date, US and eagle stamp. Missing rear sight. Stock shows usual wear and faint inspectors mark. Length 55½". Good cond. . . .
. . . . $770

Musket, Percussion, Model 1861, USA, Army, 1861, Springfield Armory. .58 cal. Lock stamped "US Springfield" and "1861" date. Pitted bayonet included. Lt pitting on lock and breech. Length 56". Good cond. . . . .
. . . . $1320

Musket, Percussion, Model 1861 Contract, USA, Army, 1865, Providence Tool Co. .58 cal. Providence, RI maker marks on lockplate with US Federal eagle and 1865 date. M61 style screw in holster. Tulip ramrod of first pattern. Maker is Providence Tool Co. who produced over 70,000 muskets under contract. Nipple replaced. Wood clean and intact with no burning. Polished down to bright. Uniform mild pitting from age. All clean and tight. Action clean and crisp. Grooves and lands in tact with only normal wear. Above avg. cond. $450

Carbine, Krag-Jorgensen, M1898, USA, Army, 1898, Springfield Armory. Springfield Armory rifle that has been cut down to carbine size. Has Redfield peep sight on rear and ramp front sight. Bore is dirty but looks good. Metal missing most the finish, stock looks good. Above avg. cond. $184

Musket, Percussion, Model 1861, USA, Army, 1865, Providence Tool Co., RI. .58 cal, maker marks on lockplate with U.S. Federal eagle and 1865 date. M61-style screw in bolster. Above avg. cond. $450

Musket, Percussion, Model 1861, USA, Army, 1861, Savage R.F.A. Co, Middletown, CT. Marked on lockplate, 40" round barrel with iron mountings on walnut stock. Exc. cond. $2700

Rifle, Springfield, Model 1903, US, Army, SA 05. Bolt-action service rifle. With sling. Barrel dated "SA 05." Serial number range 62900. All parts are proper to piece and have original high polish blue. Excellent bore. Only minor scratches to the stock. Inspector's proof clear on the stock. Exc. cond. $350

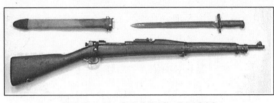

US Springfield Rifle M1903

Rifle, Garand, M-1, USA, Army, 1953, International Harvester. .30 cal gas-operated semi-automatic. Eight rounds in block clip. Stock is dark and shows age. Barrel dated "53." Serial number range 4533800. 65% original finish. Bore good. Avg. cond. $200

Rifle, Krag-Jorgensen, Model 1898, USA, Army, c1899, Springfield Armory. 30-40 cal, side box magazine, original blue finish, serial number range 206200 and 80% original finish. Avg. cond. $160

Rifle, Winchester-Lee, Model 1895, USA, Navy, 1895–97, Winchester. US Navy Model with 28" (Musket)-length barrel. Straight pull bolt action. Was first clip-loaded (five rounds) official rifle. 6mm (.236) cal Lee cartridge. Only 15,000 made. Serial number range 8200. 65% original finish. Wood shows some scratches and stains. Above avg. cond. $500

Thompson Sub-Machine Gun, M1928 M1A1. Powerful .45 Cal Weapon Widely Used in All Theaters in WWII

Rifle, Krag-Jorgensen, Model 1898, USA, Army, c1899, Springfield Armory. 30-40 cal. Side box magazine. Stock has been sporterized, but the original blue finish is good. Serial number range 206200. 80% original finish. Bore has some pitting. Avg. cond. $175

Rifle, Krag-Jorgensen, Model 1898, USA, Army, c1899,

Springfield Armory. 30-40 cal. Side box magazine. Inspector marks clear in the stock. Serial number range 198700. Bore has some lt pitting. 65% original finish. Avg. cond. $150

Rifle, Krag-Jorgensen, Model 1898, USA, Army, c1900, Springfield Armory. 30-40 cal. Side box magazine. Stock has been sporterized, barrel shortened and rear sight removed, replaced with peep sight. Serial number range 259200. 50% original finish. Bore good. Poor cond. $50

Rifle, Springfield, Model 1903, USA, Army, cWWI, Rock Island Arsenal, Rock Island, IL. Barrel rework dated RIA 9-44. Serial number range 214300. Rework has early and late parts. Bore has wear and some pits. Finger groove stock shows some age. Inspector's proof is faint. Avg. cond. $150

Rifle, Enfield, Model 1917, USA, Army, 1918, Remington Arms Co. of Delaware, Eddystone, PA. .30 cal. Mauser-type bolt action. Five-shot magazine. Barrel dated "R 10-18." Serial number range 851700. Rework has mixed parts, which is common. Bore is excellent. Inspector's proof is sharp and clear. Above avg. cond. . . . $125

Rifle, Enfield, Model 1917, USA, Army, WWI, Remington Arms Co. of Delaware, Eddystone, PA. 30-06 cal. Serial number range 4xxx. 95% original blue. Refinished stock. Above avg. cond. $150

Rifle, Enfield, Model 1917, USA, Army, WWI, Remington Arms Co. of Delaware, Eddystone, PA. 30-06 cal. Serial number range 339xxx. 90% original blue. Refinished wood. Dark bore. Above avg. cond. $150

Rifle, Enfield, Model 1917, USA, Army, WWI, Remington. 30-06 cal. Serial number range 409xxx. 95% original blue. Refinished wood. Bore dark. Above avg. cond. $100

Rifle, Enfield, Model 1917, USA, Army, WWI, Remington Arms Co. of Delaware, Eddystone, PA. 30-06 cal. 35xxx serial number range. 95% blue. Refinished stock. Above avg. cond. $100

Rifle, Garand, M-1C, USA, Army, WWII, Springfield Armory. Sniper version with M-82 scope. Stamped parts. Leather sling and cheek rest. Excellent wood and metal finish. With Anniston Arsenal release papers. Serial number range 3372xxx. Complete. Above avg. cond. $3500

Rifle, Garand, M-1D, USA, Army, WWII, Winchester. 30 cal. Sniper version with M-84 scope and detachable flash hider. Canvas sling with leather cheek rest. Stamped metal parts. Excellent wood and metal finish. Serial # 2493xxx range. With Anniston Arsenal release papers. Above avg. cond. $2500

Rifle, Springfield, Model 1903 A4, USA, Army, WWI (original), Springfield Armory. Sniper version of Model 1903 A1. Bolt action. 30-06 cal. Stamped trigger guard, bands and floor plate. Pistol-grip-style stock. M-84 scope and carrying case. Anniston Arsenal release papers and original TM. Small chip on stock near buttplate. Serial number range 3414xxx. Above avg. cond. $1200

Rifle, Springfield, Model 1873, USA, Army, c1870s, Springfield Armory. 45-70 cal. "Trapdoor" style. About 70% original finish, correct buttplate with cleaning rod door and breechblock marked 1873. Rear sight is early pattern 1877, rear band has notch for later style rear sight, bore is dirty, has inspector proof marks in wood and missing firing pin. Avg. cond. $200

Rifle, Springfield, Model 1873, USA, Army, c1870s, Springfield Armory. 45-70 cal. "Trapdoor" style. 70% original finish, good bore and early cleaning rod. Avg. cond. $200

Rifle, Springfield, Model 1873, USA, Army, c1870s, Springfield. 45-70 cal. Has early ramrod. Bore is good. Stock show normal age except for burnt spot on top of the butt. Ladder is missing from the rear sight. 60% original finish with patina. Avg. cond. $100

Rifle, Training, M16A1, USA, Army, c1960s. Lifesize in molded hard rubber with metal barrel. Above avg. cond. $250

Rifle, Training, Mk. 1, USA, Navy, cWWI, Parris-Dunn Corp., Clarenda, IA. Resembles Model 1903. Bolt opens and closes. Not made for firing. Above avg. cond. . . $50

Rifle, Enfield, Model 1917, USA, Army, WWI. .30–06 cal. Clean wood with nice finish. Serial numbered. Minor storage wear to stock. Bore needs cleaning. Above avg. cond. $150

Machine Guns and Rifles—Germany

Carbine, Kar 98K, Germany, Army, 1940, Mauser. Receiver ring bears 1940 date with "42" Mauser maker marks. Weapon is a mixture of early war, late war parts with mismatched bolt and floor plate and laminated body. Pitting on bolt and finish turning brown from age. Lacks rear receiver screw. Bore is dirty and pitted. Bolt lacks safety mechanism. Fair cond. $116

Machine Gun, MG34, Germany, Army, 1940. With monopod, wooden stock and dark bluing. Early war production with wooden buttstock and 1st pattern bipod. Has a made-up solid dummy receiver, marked "bpr 1940" all Nazi proof marks. 98% original blue. No registration papers needed as it is considered not a gun because of the solid receiver. All external parts present. Also includes original MG-34 ammo box with full belt of chain link clips for feeder. Also has belt with about 30 rounds, of which 10 are live, others shot. OD painted with post-war SA Finnish arsenal painted letters. All metal parts profusely waffenamt stamped with clear 1940 date on receiver. Trigger engages and all sights present. Exc. cond. $1200

Machine Gun, MG34, Germany, Army, 1945. Dummy receiver. Dated 1945. Late war with "dot" maker marks on receiver. Weapon has both Nazi Waffenamt stamps and post-war Czech for later reissue to Czech forces. 98% of original blue remains. Comes with original bandoleer, bolt, recoil spring and ejection cover, etc. Weapon has wooden butt with large WaA Waffenamt stamps. 2nd pattern bipod with rocket feet and many excellent issue stamps on bolt, barrel, front, rear sights, charging handle guide rail, barrel jacket charing handle latch, buttstock assembly and wooden buttstock. Exc. cond. $1200

German MG34

Machine Gun, Training Model, Uzi Paratrooper, West Germany, Army, 1970s. Used by West Germans. Has folding stock. Black composition body. Non-functional. Above avg. cond. $150

Musket, Potsdam, Germany, Army, 1832. With bayonet. Approx. .75 cal smoothbore. Percussion converted from flint. Excellent wood, only a few dings. Brass buttplate with regimental markings. Brass bands and nosecap. Original steel finish has aged to lt gray. Complete with steel ramrod and socket bayonet. Action works. Above avg. cond. $375

Rifle, Mauser, M 98k, Germany, Army, 1944. Cal 7.92mm. With sling. Laminated stock, marked Nazi eagle "H," 85% original blued finish, has sight hood, no cleaning rod, stamped magazine floor plate, and barrel bands, bore is dirty but does not look pitted. Above avg. cond. $275

Rifle, Gewehr 98, Imperial Germany, Army, 1915, DWM, Berlin. 7.92mm cal. DWM maker marked: Berlin, 1915. Matching bolt. Clean wood. Firing pin intact. Bore needs some cleaning. Receiver ring bright, no cleaning rod, and lower sling swivel is missing. Avg. cond. $150

Rifle, Mauser, Gewehr 41(M), Germany, Army, WWII, Mauser. Rarely seen as only Walther version went into wide production. 7.92mm cal self-loading rifle. All matching, serial number range 3200. Waffen proofed. 95% blue, excellent bore, has cleaning rod, sight hood and leather sling. Wood has only a few dents. Exc. cond. $6500

Rifle, Walther, Gewehr 41(W), Germany, Army, WWII. All matching serial numbers. 90% original finish, excellent bore, 6500 serial number range, has sight hood, cleaning rod and leather sling. Wood has some minor dents. Has original finish. Above avg. cond. $2750

Machine Guns and Rifles—Other

Carbine, Mauser, Model 1889, Belgium, Army, WWI. 7.65 cal. European walnut stock. Sling present. Faint Birmingham and Belgian markings on receiver. All matching. Turn-down bolt. Bore clean. Avg. cond. $225

Carbine, Arisaka, Type 38, Japan, Army, Arsenal Mukden. 6.5mm cal. Serial number range 620700. 50% original. Bore is pitted. Stock is dark and is scratched and dented. Has cleaning rod and sliding bolt cover. Avg. cond. $175

Carbine, Cavalry, Type 44, Japan, Army, Kokura Arsenal. Serial number range 23200. Mum ground. Usual wear, age and stock dents. First type bayonet housing. Has bolt cover, matching numbers except bolt cover. Avg. cond. $240

Carbine, Type 22, Japan, Army, Arsenal Tokyo. Serial number range 82800. Matched numbers. Cal 11mm. Blue finish is 70% with graying but not pitted. Stock has some dents. Bore is pitted. One screw missing from the buttplate. Avg. cond. $625

Carbine, Type 30, Japan, Army, Arsenal Koishikawa Tokyo. 6.5mm cal. Serial number range 8400. Bore is pitted. Stock is dark, scratched and dented. Has brass cleaning rod. Avg. cond. $250

Carbine, Type 30, Japan, Army, Arsenal Tokyo. Serial number 35100 range. Number not matching. 6.5mm cal. Blue finish is 75%. Stock has slight dents. Bore is sharp but dark. Receiver has chrysanthemum. Original cleaning rod. Above avg. cond. $225

Carbine, Arisaka, Type 38, Japan, Army, WWII, Nagoya Arsenal. Serial number 3xx range. Bolt not matching. 5th series. Cal 6.5mm. Finish 90%. Stock slight dents. Stock modified for paratroop. Hinge missing screws. Bore good. Cleaning rod. Dust cover. Chrysanthemum intact. Above avg. cond. $600

Carbine, Arisaka, Type 38, Japan, Army, WWII, Tokyo Arsenal. Serial number 11300 range. Bolt number matching. Caliber 6.5mm. Finish 95%. Stock slight dents. Bore excellent. Cleaning rod. Dust cover. Chrysanthemum ground. Above avg. cond. $150

Carbine, Arisaka, Type 38, Japan, Army, WWII, Nagoya Arsenal. Serial number 99000 range. Bolt number matching. 5th series. Cal 6.5mm. Finish 95%. Stock slight dents. Bore excellent. Cleaning rod. Dust cover matching. Chrysanthemum intact. Above avg. cond. $150

Carbine, Cavalry, Type 44, Japan, Army, WWII, Tokyo Arsenal. Serial number 58000 range. Bolt number matching. 6.5mm cal. Finish 95%. Stock some dents. Bore excellent. Dust cover matches. Second variation bayonet housing. Mum intact. Exc. cond. $250

Carbine, Cavalry, Type 44, Japan, Army, WWII, Kokura Arsenal. Serial number 04000 range. Bolt number matching. 1st series. 6.5mm cal. Finish 95%. Stock has some dents. Bore excellent. Dust cover. Cleaning rod. Third variation bayonet housing. Mum intact. Above avg. cond. $225

Carbine, Cavalry, Type 44, Japan, Army, Tokyo Arsenal. Serial number 12800 range. Bolt number not matching. 6.5mm. Finish 75%. Stock some dents. Bore dark. First variation bayonet housing. Mum defaced. Above avg. cond. $70

Carbine, Type 44, China, Army, 1960, Factory 26. Cal 7.62 mm. Serial number C91xx. Matching bolt. With sling and clamp-on grenade launcher. Metal graying. Wood shows wear. Bore dark. Avg. cond. $200

Carbine, Type 44, China, Army, 1955, Factory 26. Cal 7.62mm. Serial number 303xxx. Matching bolt. Nice blond varnished stock has only a few scuffs near buttplate. Deep blue finish to barrel, receiver and bayonet. Bore excellent. Exc. cond. $150

Carbine, Jungle, Lee Enfield, No. 5 Mark I, England, Army, Late WWII. .303 cal. Serial number range 5300. 75% original finish. Bore pitted. Missing front sling swivel. Avg. cond. $100

Carbine, Type 44, China, Army, 1955, Factory 296. 7.62 x 54mm. Serial number 1312xxx range. Dark wood shows use and some nicks. 95% original blue with blued bayonet. Avg. cond. $85

Musket, Brown Bess, 3rd Pattern, England, Army, American Rev/Napoleonic Era. .75 cal. Type used late in American Revolution. Dark iron barrel. Flintlock mechanism with dark age wear and corrosion. Remains of word "Tower" appears on lockplate as "T.er." Brass buttstock with matching trigger guard. Brass sideplate. Dark iron trumpet pattern ramrod. Most often used in Napoleonic campaigns and the last of the famous Brown Besses as used from the reign of Queen Anne to George III. Iron has turned black from age. European walnut stock. Tiny uneven area to crown of barrel. Bayonet stud present. Above avg. cond. $950

Musket, Flintlock, Model 1777, France, 1813, Charleville. 45" barrel of .70 cal. marked at breech "1813." Lockplate marked "Manufre. Imple. de Charleville." Varnished walnut stock marked "453" at cheekrest, "138/138" at butt and "*R" at counterplate. Barrel has lt gray patina and pitting. Stock has marks. Ramrod present. Good cond. $3450

Musket, Flintlock, Model 1777 Dragoon, France, 1811, St. Etienne. 40½" barrel of .70 cal. marked at breech "1811." Lockplate marked "Mre. Imple. St. etienne." Varnished walnut stock. Ramrod present. Barrel has medium brown patina and pitting near breech. Lockplate has some lt gray staining. Stock poor, shows much wear, worm holes and cracks at butt. Below avg. cond. $1610

Musketoon, Enfield, England, Army, c1857. .577 cal. Walnut stock with brass buttplate, trigger guard, endcap and iron thimble ramrod. Lockplate shows great age with no markings. Trigger guard bears rack number "32 3F." Iron barrel has "SAS 679" markings. Stock shows age storage: all metallic parts in black with old oxidization. Bayonet lug for sword bayonet present as is front sight with fixed rear sight. Type purchased in quantities by US, CSA agents for distribution in CW. Above avg. cond. $175

Musketoon, Tower, M1810, England, Army, c1820s. 500mm round barrel, .975 cal., has brass fittings. Crown proof on the side plate, walnut stock, swivel ramrod, age patina on the iron parts with some pitting. Avg. cond. $750

Rifle, Lee Enfield, No. 4 Mark I, England, Army, 1944, Fazakerly, England. .303 cal bolt-action service rifle. Serial number range 13400. 60% original finish. Bore is good. Stock is refinished. Avg. cond. $125

Rifle, Lee Enfield, No. 1 Mark III, England, Army, WWI. Cal 303. Serial number range 36100L. 75% original finish. Bore is good. Stock has two sections repaired with copper wire wrapping. Below avg. cond. $75

Rifle, Lee Enfield, No.1 Mark III, England, Army, WWI. .303 cal. Marked with crest of three lions. Serial number range 93800. 60% original finish remains. Bore has some wear and pits. Stock shows much wear. Avg. cond. $50

Rifle, Steyr-Mannlicher, M1895, Austria, Army, 1916, Steyr. 8mm cal. 29" barrel with full stock. All metal is gray, wood is a bit dark and dingy. All visible numbers match. Avg. cond. $200

Rifle, Martini-Henry, England, Army, 1886, Enfield. Breechloading. .45 cal. Bore is pitted, no original finish with some surface rust. Wood shows age, has cleaning rod. Serial number range a9500. Fair cond. $75

Musket, Flintlock, Brown Bess, England, Army, c1800. .75 cal, India pattern with 39" barrel and brass furniture. Above avg. cond. $1753

Musket, Flintlock, Brown Bess, England, Army, c1812. .75 cal, lockplate marker with George III crown and "GR" stamp forward of hammer. Includes socket bayonet having "Deskin" ricasso mark, with black leather scabbard having brass throat and drag. Above avg. cond. $2055

Carbine, Flintlock, Brown Bess, England, Army, Napoleonic Era. .69 cal, Yeomanry style with brass furniture. Above avg. cond. $490

Rifle, British Military Percussion Musket, England, Crimean War Era. Model 1839 Brown Bess conversion from flintlock action, .75 cal, complete with ramrod and sling swivels. Above avg. cond. $680

Rifle, Lee Enfield, No. 3 Mark I, England, Army, WWI, Enfield. Or 1914 Pattern. .303 cal. Marked ERA on the receiver. Bore is pitted. Stock shows normal age and wear, is dark. Avg. cond. $75

Rifle, Short Magazine Lee Enfield (SMLE), No. 1 Mark III, England, Army, 1918. .303 cal bolt-action service rifle. The standard British Inf weapon of WWI. Serial number range 51000. 70% original finish. Bore is good. Avg. cond. $95

Rifle, Type 56, China, Army, Vietnam War Era. Cal 7.62mm. Chinese version of the SKS. Stock is crude and refinished blade-style folding bayonet. Serial number range 2380400. 70% original finish. Bore good. Avg. cond. $125

Rifle, Type 56, China, Army, Vietnam War Era. Cal 7.62mm. Chinese version of SKS. Stock is crude. Spike-style folding bayonet serial number range 10077800. 65% original finish. Bore good. Avg. cond. $125

Musket, Flintlock, Model 1822, France, Army. .69 cal Model 1822 musket with lock, barrel and all metal surfaces of black lacquered finish, lockplate with crown and "M" proofmark. Good cond. $365

Rifle, Steyr-Mannlicher, M1895, Austria, Army, 1909, Budapest. 8mm cal. Bore is good. 75% original finish. Small crack in the stock at the wrist. Mismatched numbers. Serial number range 12600. Avg. cond. $50

Rifle, Type 13, Japan, Army, c1880s, Arsenal Koishakawa. Developed in 1880. 11mm cal. Single-shot bolt action. 20% original finish on metal parts some with patina. Wood is sound but dark with some scratches and dents. Bore is good. Numbers do seem to match. Avg. cond. $575

Rifle, Type 22, Japan, Army, c1900, Arsenal Tokyo.

Developed in 1895. 8mm cal. 65% original finish on metal parts, some with patina. Wood is sound but some crude hand checkering has been added. Bore is pitted. Numbers do not seem to match. Avg. cond. $550

Rifle, Type 18, Japan, Army, Arsenal Koishakawa. Developed in 1880. 11mm cal. Single-shot bolt action. 20% original finish on metal parts, some with patina. Wood is sound but dark with some scratches and dents. Bore is pitted. Numbers seem to match. Avg. cond. $525

Rifle, Type 13, Japan, Army, Arsenal Tokyo. Serial number range 14200. 11mm cal. Blue finish is 70% with graying but not pitted. Stock has some dents and has been arsenal-repaired at the wrist. Bore is dirty but should clean. Receiver chrysanthemum overstamped with a circle. Avg. cond. $500

Rifle, Type 22, Japan, Army, Paratroop, WWII, Nagoya Arsenal. Modified Type 99. Serial number 6400 range. Bolt number matches. Take-down block numbers match. 7.7mm cal. Finish 95%. Stock very good. Bore excellent. Cleaning rod. Dust cover matches. Anti-aircraft sight. Mum intact. Above avg. cond. $400

Japanese Type 22 Paratrooper Rifle

Carbine, Arisaka, Type 38, Japan, Army, WWII, Arsenal Tokyo. Serial number 37000 range. Bolt number matches. 6.5mm cal. Blue finish is 80%. Stock has slight dents and bore is dark. Original cleaning rod. Has replacement dust cover. Above avg. cond. $125

Rifle, Type 97, Japan, Army, Nagoya Arsenal. Sniper rifle with scope. Serial number 7800 range. Bolt number matches. Caliber 6.5mm. Finish 95%. Stock very good. Monopod attached. Bore excellent. Cleaning rod. Dust cover matches. Mum intact. Above avg. cond. $500

Rifle, Type 97, Japan, Army, Kokura Arsenal. Sniper rifle with scope. Serial number 3900 range. Bolt number matches. Caliber 6.5mm. Finish 95%. Stock very good. Monopod attached. Bore excellent. Cleaning rod. Dust cover matches. Mum ground. Above avg. cond. . . . $500

Rifle, Type 99, Long Version, Japan, Army, WWII, Nagoya Arsenal. Serial number 100 range. Bolt number matching. Cal 7.7mm. Finish 90%. Stock some dents. Monopod moved. Bore good. Cleaning rod. Dust cover. Aircraft sight. Mum ground. Above avg. cond. . . . $200

Rifle, Type 99, Short Version, Japan, Army, WWII, Nagoya Arsenal. 7.7mm cal. 78xxx serial number range.

Cleaning rod and aircraft sight wings missing. Avg. cond.
.... $85

Japanese Type 99 Short Model Rifle

Rifle, Sniper, Type 99, Japan, Army, WWII, Nagoya Arsenal. With scope. Serial number 6600 range. Bolt number not matching. Cal 7.7mm. Finish 90%. Stock some dents. Bore good. Cleaning rod. Dust cover. Mum ground. Above avg. cond. $500

Rifle, Sniper, Type 99, Japan, Army, Nagoya. With scope. Serial number 2400 range. Bolt number matches. Cal 7.7mm. Finish 85%. Stock very good. Bore excellent. Cleaning rod. Dust cover. Scope has rubber eyepiece. Mum defaced. Above avg. cond. $500

Rifle, Type 99, Japan, Army, WWII, Toyo Kogyo, Hiroshima Prefecture Arsenal. 7.7mm. Series 35. Serial number 22xx range. Matching bolt. 90% blue with some lt pitting to magazine floor plate. Mum intact. Avg. cond. ..
.... $75

Rifle, Mosin-Nagant, M1917, Imperial Russia, Army, WWI, Remington Armory. 7.62 cal. Serial number range 564000. Matching bolt. Converted to single shot for training. Finish 70% with lt pitting. Stock smooth with slight dents. Has Japanese characters painted and stamped. Bore excellent. Cleaning rod. Imperial Russian stamp on receiver and barrel. Above avg. cond. $250

Russian Moisin Nagant Rifle

Musket, Percussion, Holland, Army. .69 cal. 40"-round barrel, bayonet lug underneath mounted on black walnut stock with heavy brass furniture. Dutch proof marks "K" surmounted by crown on various parts, number "234" appears on various metal parts and tang engraved "2N/W91." Good cond. $600

Rifle, Mosin-Nagant, M1891, Russia, Army, 1941. 7.62mm cal. Receiver drilled. Finish has patina. Bore poor. Fair cond. $28

Rifle, Mauser, M1896, Sweden, Army, 1917, Carl Gustaf State Rifle Factory. 6.5mm cal. All numbers match. Stock few dings. Brass disc. Four holes where plaque was removed. Most original blue. Bore excellent. Includes bayonet and scabbard. Above avg. cond. $95

Rifle, Vetterli, M81, Switzerland, Army, 1870s. 10.4mm (.41) cal. Bolt action. Heavy surface rust. Action sluggish. Dark wood needs major repair to wrist. Fair cond. .. $35

Rifle, Vetterli, M78, Switzerland, Army, 1870s, Swiss Waffenfabrik Bern. 10.4mm cal. Tube-fed bolt action. Action tight and functional. Wood has been sporterized. Avg. cond. $60

Rifle, Type 99, Japan, Army, WWII, Nagoya Arsenal. 7.7mm. Two-digit serial number. Very fine blued finish. Minor arsenal dents to wood. Complete. Above avg. cond.
.... $450

Rifle, Vietminh Handmade Copy of French MAS Model 1936, North Vietnam, Army, 1950s. Smoothbore product of jungle workshops takes unknown cartridge. Rarely seen example of how guerrilla fighters armed themselves before Russians and Chinese stepped in to supply modern weapons. Stock has knot holes and metal is a little rusty but it works. Avg. cond. $800

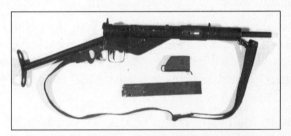

British Sten MKII Sub-Machine Gun. Widely Used 9mm, 32-round Capacity Sub-Machine Gun

Firearms-related Accessories—U.S.

Holster, Belt, USA, Air Force, 1991. Late-issue GI holster for air crew, for .38 revolver, marked with embossed US in oval on front, original sealed package dated 1991, black leather construction with snap fastener and metal hanger for web belt. Near mint cond. $16

Cartridge Box, Spencer Carbine, USA, Army, 1864, Gaylord, Chicopee, MA. Hexagonal leather-covered tin cartridge box with wooden block insert made for ten tin tubular magazines. Box is 12" high and 3½" wide with hinged lid with closure strap, two carrying rings and belt loop at bottom. Front of box embossed "U.S" below "Blakeslee's Cartridge Co," in arch over "Pat'd Dec 20, 1864/E. Gaylord/Chicopee/MASS," with original shoulder strap. Above avg. cond. $3250

Holster, M1916, US, Various, 1942, Boyt. For Colt M1911A1. Brown leather, embossed flap. Avg. cond. $20

Holster, Shoulder, M1911A1, USA, Army, 1943, U.S. Sears Saddlery Co. Brown leather body. Avg. cond. $35

Holster, USA, Army, 1883. Black leather holster with full flap and belt loop on reverse, face of holster embossed with "US" in oval, inside flap stamped "TR.B.N.Y.37," and belt loop stamped "B37." Above avg. cond. . . $475

Holster, Colt, New Model Army, USA, Army, Civil War, J.S. Storm. Leather holster for Colt Army revolver with percussion cap pouch. Avg. cond. $325

Holster, Colt, M1897 Revolver, USA, Various, 1918. Dark brown leather with "US" embossed in oval on body. Brass stud closure half-flap. Avg. cond. $28

Cover, Pistol, USA, Army, WWII. Unissued, waterproof, .45 pistol cover, transparent vinyl bag with roll-up top, blue printed instructions and press stud fastener on safety strap. Near mint cond. $8

Grips, Pistol, M1911A1, USA, Various, WWII. Pair. Brown plastic with gnarled pattern on grips. Unmarked. Near mint cond. $10

Holster, Shoulder, USA, USMC, WWII, Boyt. Shoulder holster with modifications. Dated 1943 on back. Appears to be modified WWII Navy/Marine .45 auto holster with leather-trimmed and resewn snap latch removed. Avg. cond. $20

Holster, Shoulder, USA, Various, 1990. Black leather shoulder holster for .38 revolver, same design as WWII Navy issue, lift-dot closure, embossed US in oval on front, original plastic package and dated 1990. Mint cond. $20

Cartridge Box, Spencer Carbine, USA, Army, Civil War Era. 8" x 4" leather with interior implement pouch and inserted wooden cartridge block. Avg. cond. $375

Ammunition, .45 cal, USA, Various, 1943. .45 cal. 56 rounds. Live. Steel cased by "CES 43" with copper FMJ slugs. Above avg. cond. $30

Anti-personnel Mine Bag, M18A1, USA, Army, Vietnam War Era. For "Claymore" mine. M18A1 mine carry bag with cord on winder and 1966 dated detonator and instructions. Two-pouch canvas bag with flap and strap. Above avg. cond. $76

Forearm, Replacement, BAR, USA, Various, WWII. Mint wooden forearm with original wrapping. Exc. cond. $25

Bolt Housing, M1 Carbine, USA, Army, WWII, Rock Island Arsenal (RIA), IL. RIA marked. Above avg. cond. $20

Parts Lot, M1 Carbine, USA, Army, WWII. Includes four-part take-down cleaning rod, piston wrench and web sling. Above avg. cond. $25

Cartridge Box Plate, USA, Army, c1881. For New York State troops. Stamped brass. Wire loop attachments on reverse. 57mm wide. Above avg. cond. $23

Cartridge Box Plate, USA, Army, c1840s. Brass lug back 3½"-wide oval with US in center. Filled back and shows light wear. Above avg. cond. $111

Cartridge Pouch Plate, USA, Army, Civil War. 86mm-wide stamped brass oval body with embossed "US." Reverse is lead filled with two wire loops for attachment. Above avg. cond. $107

Cartridges, Pistol, USA, Army, Civil War. .44 cal. Blue pressed paper carton with label that reads "R.Bartholow's Solid Water Proof Cartridge for Army Holster Pistol/ Patented, May 21st, 1861." Contents remain. Avg. cond. $205

Chart, "Gun, Submachine, CAL. .45, M3A1," USA, Army, 1952. 28" x 38" white plastic sheet with black illustrations. Shows parts of M3A1 "grease gun." Near mint cond. $20

Clips, Speed, M1917 Revolver, USA, Army, 1917. Bag of .45 ACP speed clips, approx. 50. Above avg. cond. $20

Cover, Gun, USA, Army, Vietnam War Era. In 1967 dated issue package. Near mint cond. $13

Cover, Thompson, M1A1, USA, Army, WWII. Dark OD canvas with leather trim and zippered opening. Well marked. Above avg. cond. $95

M1A1 Carbine Carrier

Dummy Land Mine, USA. Arty delivered mine dummy test and training device. Blue with metal vanes all around. Avg. cond. $25

Flash Hider, M1 Carbine, USA, Army, 1953. Unissued in 1953 dated issue carton. Near mint cond. $160

Grips, Pair, Colt, Single Action, USA, Army, WWII. Black checkered plastic with horse and US eagle loop. Screw intact. Near mint cond. $20

Grips, Pair, Military, For High Standard Pistol, USA, Various, WWII. Checkered walnut. Above avg. cond. $20

Handguards, Lot of Four, USA, Army, WWI, Springfield. For M1903 Springfield Rifle. Mint walnut with official paperwork from manufacturer. Avg. cond. $20

Holster, Shoulder, M3, USA, Army, WWII. For M1911A1 pistol. All straps present. Black leather supple but shows age and wear. Embossed US on front. Above avg. cond. $45

Holster, Colt, M1911, USA, USMC, 1914, Mills. Tan canvas web with brass barrel bottom. Marked inside flap with Mills hmk and 1914 date. Inked name on back. Shows light use. Exc. cond. $250

Holster, M1917, USA, Army, 1917. For M1917 revolver. Dark brown leather body. Two adjustment holes on flap with faint stamped numbers and belt loop stamped "G&K. 1917 A.G." with numbers. Avg. cond. $50

Holster, M1916, USA, Army, 1918, G.&K. Brown leather body with embossed "US" on flap. By "G.&K. 1918." Shows use. Avg. cond. $40

Holster, Hip, USA, Army, 1942, Sears. Brown leather body shows use, wire fitting and "Sears 1942" maker marked. Has been polished. Avg. cond. $50

Holster, Leather, M1, US, Army, 1942, Boyt. For M1911A1. Brown leather that has been dyed black on frontal surfaces. US embossed in oval on stud closure flap. Wire belt hanger. Boyt/42 marked. Little use. Above avg. cond. $32

Holster, Colt, M1917 Revolver, USA, Army, WWI, Colt. Dark leather with US embossed in oval on body plus brass stud closure half-flap. 1918 dated. Lacks small leather panel at bottom that holds lanyard. Avg. cond. $28

Holster, M1916, USA, Army, 1917, Sears. Brown leather with embossed US in oval on flap, Sears marked under flap, dated 1917, G.W.M. wire belt clip and loops. Shows some wear. Avg. cond. $29

Holster, M1916, USA, Army, 1917, Boyt. With US embossed in center of oval. Worn but fully serviceable. Avg. cond. $20

Holster, Shoulder, M7, USA, USMC, 1945, Boyt. Dark brown leather holster for M1911A1 with all straps. Has

embossed "US" in oval on front and marked "USMC/BOYT/45" on back. Shows wear but clean. Avg. cond. $45

Holster, M1917, USA, Army, 1917. For M1917 revolver. Brown leather hip holster, faint US oval, three rivets to belt loop with faint "?&K 1917?G." Solid body showing use. Above avg. cond. $50

Holster, M7, USA, USAF, 1963. Black with embossed "US" on face. All straps present; dated 1963 on back below hmk. Above avg. cond. $45

Holster, Shoulder, Colt, M1911A1, USA, Army, 1943, Enger-Kress. 43 dated by Enger-Kress and US in embossed oval on front. Some wear and darkening of leather. Above avg. cond. $45

Holster, Leather, Colt, M1911A1, USA, Army, 1944. Black leather 1944 dated and hmkd on back. Some wear. Avg. cond. $50

Holster for M1911A1 .45 (Sears Marked)

Holster, M1917, USA, Army, WWII. For .38 cal S&W or Colt M1917 revolver. Tan leather with large flap and single belt loop in back. Stamped with signal corps emblem over "SIGNAL CORPS." Near mint with storage wear. Exc. cond. $24

Holster, M1916, USA, Army, 1942, Boyt. Has "US" inside embossed oval on flap plus Boyt hmk on back with 1942 date. Dark russet leather construction. Above avg. cond. $45

Kit, Parts, Springfield M1903, USA, Army, WWII. Sealed cardboard box with photocopy of packing list showing 29 listed parts with quantity of 2 through 15 of each. Near mint cond. $100

Lanyard, Pistol, USA, Army, WWI. Dark tan cord with metal slide and snap hook. Near mint cond. $10

LAW Weapon, Dummy, USA, Army, 1960s. Covers on firing tube. Some wear signs but definitely a display quality piece. Avg. cond. $45

Missile Launcher, M-222, USA, Army, 1980s. 40" long, 5"-diam Kevlar tubular body. Has 1985 dated spec plate on side. Has folding stand assembly, etc., intact. Includes 1979 dated manual for M74 model. Shows some age. Avg. cond. $95

Sling, M1 Carbine Sling, USA, Army, 1944. Green web with metal fittings and dated 1944. Avg. cond. $23

Sling, M1 Carbine, USA, USMC, 1943, F-S Co. Mint tan web body by "F-S Co. 1943." Near mint cond. $30

Sling, Springfield, M1903, USA, Army, 1905, Rock Island Arsenal (RIA). Dark brown leather, brass fittings and double dated "Rock Island etc. 1908," "1905 etc." Pliable. Above avg. cond. $25

Sling, Rifle, Springfield M1903, USA, Army, WWI. Dark leather with brass fittings. Avg. cond. $20

Scope, Sniper, USA, Army, WWII. 11½" blued body with sliding metal sunshade and large rubber eyecup. Two-point adjustable crosshairs. On dovetail ramp with twin tension levers. Some surface rust, optics dirty. Lacks both protective caps for crosshair adjustment. Marked only with serial number. Avg. cond. $75

Tool, Rifle, USA, Army, WWI, Springfield. Pivot rivet to US stamped. Two-part body. Avg. cond. $20

Firearms-related Accessories—Germany

Grips, P38, Germany, Army, WWII. Bakelite construction. Dark brown. Above avg. cond. $35

Holster, Luger, Imperial Germany, Army, WWI. Brown leather hardshell body, inked "B.A.XI" to flap, stamped "Crown-I" on reverse. Avg. cond. $60

Holster, PO8, Germany, Army, 1936, Fr & K Vogels. Brown leather construction. Marked "Fr & K Vogels Koin-Deutz 1936 WaA387." Above avg. cond. $150

Holster, Luger, P08, Germany, Army, 1939. Brown holster for 4" Luger, marked on back "Vogels/Kuln/1939." Exc. cond. $300

Scope, Sniper, 4X, Cased, Germany, Army, WWII. Green painted metal storage case by "jvb," 12" blued metal body by "bek Dialytan 4x etc" Ring mounts and front band stamped "1-172," brown leather lens caps inked "WaA156." Exc. cond. $725

Scope, Sniper, ZF41, Cased, Germany, Army, WWII. Green painted metal case with olive web straps, lid stamped "jvb WaA???," blue metal scope by "cxn," metal

sun shades and blued metal mount by "duv WaA214," engraved serial number 7806 H and hold-down brackets stamped "511." Avg. cond. $425

Ammo Magazine, Basket Style, MG08, Imperial Germany, Army, WWI. Hinged steel body stamped "Feuer! Kurbelhoch." Crank handle on side with drum inside. Above avg. cond. $207

Ammunition, 9mm, Germany, Army, 1945. 9mm cal. Live rounds. Box with label marked steel cased and by "rfo 45 etc." Exc. cond. $20

Ammunition, 8mm, Germany, Army, 1938. Two boxes 8mm "M.30." 20 live rounds. Well-marked angled cardboard boxes, clean rounds and stripper. Near mint cond. $20

Ammunition, 9mm, Germany, Army, WWII. Three boxes of 9mm. 16 rounds per box. Above avg. cond. $50

Armored Frontshield, MG08, Imperial Germany, Army, WWI. 6"-tall green painted heavy metal fitting with barrel hole. Above avg. cond. $145

Bolt, 98K Rifle, Germany, Army, WWII. No blued finish to steel body. Stamped "6187 b" and mismatched numbers. Some rust spots. Below avg. cond. $20

Carrier, Spare Barrel, MG, Germany, Army, WWII. Dark gray painted body with web shoulder strap. By "bpr43" and "Laufschutzer 42." Above avg. cond. $76

Case, Sniper Scope, ZF41, Germany, Army, WWII. Battleship gray repainted body with olive web belt loop. Stamped maker "jvbWaA1?" and faint gun number "8965." Black repainted inside with no contents. Avg. cond. $200

Cleaning Kit, MG, Germany, Army, WWII. Dark gray painted tin with stamped lid "64 WaA20." Contains metal

German K98 Rifle Cleaning Kit

oiler both brushes, chain and spring-loaded tool. Above avg. cond. $100

Cleaning Kit, Rifle, Model 98K, Germany, Army, WWII. Gray finish to "tobacco-tin"-style canister by "arr 43 WaA20." Includes chain, two brushes and Bakelite oiler. Above avg. cond. $20

Cleaning Kit, Rifle, Model 98K, Germany, Army, WWII. Blue-gray finish on "Tobacco-Tin"-style canister with lid stamped "64 WaA20." Contains metal oiler and large brush. Avg. cond. $20

Clip Loading Tool, MP38/40, Germany, Army, 1941. Blued body with stamped title and "98E 41 WaA815." Shows use. Avg. cond. $60

Container, Spare Barrel, MG, Imperial Germany, Army, WWI. 2" x 4" x 32" gray painted steel-covered wood body with hinged end caps. Burlap shoulder strap. Avg. cond. $165

Grips, MP38/40, Germany, Army, WWII. Bakelite. Well marked. Matched. Above avg. cond. $25

Gun Cleaning Kit, Cased, Germany, Army, WWII. With Nazi proof. 2½" x 4" x 10½" body unfolds to reveal various cleaning parts. Four-part wooden rod has shotgun and rifle barrel fittings. Plus screwdriver, oil bottle, vaseline tin with rust holes and cloth. Broken snap on one flap and buckle broken from closure strap. Blurred eagle proof with wording. Shows its age. Avg. cond. $175

Holster, Luger, Imperial Germany, Army, 1916. Black polished hardshell body with all fittings intact except for removed belt loops. Faint stamped 1916/maker. 4½" x 8" machine sewn-on black leather tab with belt loops along top edge. Above avg. cond. $300

Holster, Leather, P08, Imperial Germany, Army, 1916, Otto Sindel, Berlin. Stiff body has both belt loops broken at back and lacks pull-up strap inside. By "Otto Sindel Berlin 1916." Small hole cut to tip. Plus early black velvet tab with brass eagle holding horn with lightning bolts and three brass star devices. Fair cond. $28

Holster, Leather, P08, Imperial Germany, Army, 1918, Nurnberg. Solid body with all fittings intact. 1918 Nurnberg maker stamp on flap and back has Swedish-style crown over "III." Closure strap shows age. Above avg. cond. $150

Holster, Leather, P08, Germany, Army, 1936, Voegels, Koln. Black leather hardshell body with all fittings intact. Crazed finish to front. Marked "FR&K. Voegels Koln-Deutz 1936 WaA234." Above avg. cond. $90

Holster, Leather, P08, Germany, Army, 1937, Gebruder

Klinge, Dresden. Hardshell leather body is dark brown and all fittings are intact. By "Gebruder Klinge Dresden 1937 WaA 142." Shows use, never cleaned and hole in flap for take-down tool. Avg. cond. $90

Holster, Leather, P08, Germany, Army, 1938. Plus tool. All fittings intact on black body showing use. By "E.K.St.WaA101." Blued tool Eagle-63 stamped. Avg. cond. $50

Holster, Luger, P08, Germany, Army, 1938, Genschow and Co., A-G Berlin. Good black leather hardshell body. All leather fittings intact with only one belt loop coming unsewn. Stamped by "Genschow and Co. A-G Berlin 1938 WaA268." Past owner penciled "SS.H.J." on inside near empty tool pouch. Avg. cond. $149

Holster, Leather, P08, Germany, Army, 1942. Black leather hardshell body with all fittings intact. By "bmd42 WaA? P08." Shows use and couple of dry areas. Avg. cond. $135

Holster, Leather, P08, Germany, Army, 1942. All fittings intact on black body showing use. By "bml/42 WaA23." Avg. cond. $60

Holster, Leather, P38, Germany, Army, 1942. Hardshell black body with all fittings intact. By "dkk 42 WaA 195 P38." Shows light use. Above avg. cond. $100

Holster, Leather, HSc, Germany, Various, 1944. Black leather breakaway style. Fittings intact to body by "jng 44 WaA41." Closure strap shows most age. Above avg. cond. $95

Holster, Leather, P38, Germany, Army, 1944. Breakaway style. Black leather body with fittings intact. By "gxy 1944 P38." Light use only. Exc. cond. $115

Holster, Leather, P38, Germany, Army, 1944. Good black leather body. Fittings intact and stamped "jwa44 WaA706 P38." Light use. Exc. cond. $90

Holster for Walther P38

Holster, Leather, P38, Germany, Army, 1944. Black polished front with brown leather back stamped "gxy 1944 P38." Faint scratched owner names. Fittings intact. Above avg. cond. $135

Holster, Leather, P38, Germany, Army, 1944. Brown hardshell body shows use but fittings are intact. By "ndk44 WaA77 P38." Avg. cond. $75

Holster, Leather, Baby Luger, Imperial Germany, Army, 1916, Steinmetz, Breslau. 6" x 7" hardshell body with flap having strap for roller buckle closure. Clip pouch to edge and two belt loops to back. Stamped inside "Steinmetz Breslau 1916" and inked "BAVII 1916." Has inside pull-strap but lacks pouch to loading tool. Above avg. cond. $225

Holster, Leather, Browning High Power, Germany, Army, 1944. Leather. "CLG 44" dated and marked. Storage age. Exc. cond. $75

Holster, Shoulder, P08/P38, Germany, Army, WWII. 5.5" x 9" brown leather body fits P38 or P08 with extra clip pouch. Shoulder strap and back strap with roller buckle. Unmarked. Above avg. cond. $40

Holster, Leather, Browning High Power, Germany, Army, 1941. Brown body shows use with fittings intact but side flap coming unsewn. By "jor 41 WaA90." Avg. cond. $75

Holster, Leather, Browning High Power, Germany, Army, 1944. Near mint brown body is flat from storage. By "cig44." Never cleaned. Exc. cond. $99

Holster, Leather, Browning Model 1922, Germany, Army, c1930s, Krieghoff. 5½"-wide black leather flap with drop straps and brown leatherette body. Extra clip pouch at edge and large "HK," Krieghoff trademark on belt loop that is riveted. Avg. cond. $85

Holster, Leather, P08, Germany, Luftwaffe, 1940. Extremely rare tan P08 holster. For Luftwaffe ground troops. Item marked "DLU 1940/WaA727." Clip pouch on end of holster with top covered by flap. Exc. cond. $315

Holster, Leather, Walther PP, Germany, Army, WWII, Akah. Breakaway style. Black leather body with faint "Akah" maker stamp, resewn belt loop for narrow belt and blued magazine with title scroll. Avg. cond. $75

German Walther PPK Holster

Holster, Leather, Walther PPK, Germany, Army, WWII. 5½"-wide and 6½"-tall body. Brown leather softshell style. Shows use and stamped Party Eagle-L on back. Above avg. cond. $75

Kit, Cleaning, MG 34/42, Germany, Army, WWII. Blue-gray painted tin box contains two brushes, chain, metal oiler, 98K floorplate tool and spring-loaded tool. Also stamped "BSW" Eagle-4 proofed open-end wrench plus "BSW" WaA4 proofed wrench with hammer end. Above avg. cond. $125

Magazine, Walther, PPK, Germany, Army, WWII. 7.65mm. Dark blue body with stamped title and faint Eagle proof with numbers. Exc. cond. $45

Magazine, MP38/40, Germany, Army, 1943. Blued steel body by "ayf 43 WaA280." Above avg. cond. $20

Magazine, MP38/40, Germany, Army, 1944. Dark patina, blue steel body by "ayf 4 WaA280." Avg. cond. $20

Magazine, P38, Germany, Army, WWII. Blued body by "jvd." Above avg. cond. $30

Magazine, P38, Germany, Army, WWII. Blued body stamped "P.38v WaA135." Above avg. cond. $35

Magazine, P08, Germany, Army, WWII. Blued body with alum, base stamped "2153k" and with Eagle-655 proof. Above avg. cond. $65

Magazine, Walther, PP, Germany, Army, WWII. 7.65mm. Blued metal body with stamped title. Above avg. cond. $55

Magazine, P08, Germany, Army, WWI. Steel body shows use. Dark wood base. Above avg. cond. $50

Magazine, P08, Germany, Army, WWI. Steel body shows use. Wood base stamped "4991 2" and "3" on side. Avg. cond. $50

Magazine, P08, Germany, Army, WWII. Lt wear to nickel-plated body. Alum base stamped "9857h +" and Eagle-63 proof. Above avg. cond. $50

Magazine, P08, Germany, Army, WWII. Patina to nickel-plated body. Alum base stamped "5372f +" and Eagle-63 proof. Avg. cond. $50

Magazine, P38, Germany, Army, WWII. Blued body stamped "P.38v." Lt use. Above avg. cond. $20

Rifle Bolt, 98K, Germany, Army, WWII. Wartime blued matching numbered body "239c." Appears complete. Above avg. cond. $30

Muzzle Covers, Rifle, Germany, Army, WWII. Made of

gas mask anti-gas sheet fabric. Unissued. Draw-strings. Near mint cond. $29

Sling, Rifle, Model 98K, Germany, Navy, 1937, Leo Schmidt, Muenchen. Dark oiled leather body with loop, no leather to steel buckle and three adjustment holes. Leather covered stud loop is stamped Eagle-M and "Leo Schmidt etc. Muenchen 1937." Shows use. Avg. cond. $125

Scope, Sniper, "Dialytan 4X," Germany, Army, WWII. 11¾" blued tube body with title marks and by "bek." Optics clear with three-point cross-hair. Plus black leather cups on strap starting to come unsewn. Stamped "WaA414" to one end. Above avg. cond. $300

Sight, Anti-Aircraft, MG34, Germany, Army, WWII. Over 4"-diam blued metal with mount. Exc. cond. . $50

Sling, Leather, MG34/42, Germany, Army, 1943. Double straps with sewn pads, steel clip and steel buckle with stamped "WaA892." Leather stamped "bia 1943 WaA159." Above avg. cond. $100

Sling, Mauser, M1898 Rifle, Imperial Germany, Army, WWI. Dark brown leather body, steel rectangle end, buckle with rivet and wire loop. Avg. cond. $20

Scope, Sniper, "Cad" (Kahles) 4x, Germany, Army, WWII, "Cad" (Kahles). Scope in blued finish with maker code "cad" has correct solder-mounted rings with rifle serial number "465xx" on front ring. Fitted with rare detachable sun shield. Has eight-point cross-hair with good optics. Some surface rust and wear/minor dings. Above avg. cond. $350

Tool, Nazi P08 Loading, Germany, Army. Blued steel with faint eagle proof. Above avg. cond. $40

Tool, Take-Down, P08, Germany, Army, WWII. Natural steel stamped "WaA9?" Shows use with bent end. Avg. cond. $24

Top Receiver Cover, MG34, Germany, Army, 1944. Gray finished steel with stamped "2730." Vendor states 44 dated but no Nazi stamps seen, just serial number. Above avg. cond. $50

Firearms-related Accessories—Other

Bandoleer, AK-47, North Vietnam, Army, Vietnam War Era. Khaki canvas with web straps, three magazine and four accessory pouches and wooden toggle closure. Complete with Chinese double spout-oil can. Above avg. cond. $48

Cartridge Belt, China, Army, 1980. Green canvas with nickeled buckle, eight magazine pouches and four

grenade fittings, with shoulder slings. Good cond. . $20

Holster, Mauser, Machine Pistol, China, Army, c1950s. Hollow wood stock, blued metal fittings and Chinese character hallmark. Good cond. $115

Holster, CZ, Model 1927, Czechoslovakia, Army, WWII. 5" x 6½" black leather holster with clip pouch on front. Avg. cond. $46

Pistol Holder, England, Army, 1942. Khaki webbing with broad arrow hallmark, brass flap snap and belt attachment device. Above avg. cond. $100

**English Khaki Canvas Service Holster
(Pistol Holder) for Webley Revolver**

Round Clip, MG Type 92, Japan, Army, WWII. Boxed 7.7mm. 30-round clip, live rounds on brass clip in tan cloth-covered cardboard box. Avg. cond. $22

Holster, Tokarev, TT 33, Soviet Union, Army, c1978. Brown leather, interior issue markings, complete with brown leather pistol lanyard. Exc. cond. $20

Holster, Tokarev, TT 33, Soviet Union, Army, 1970. For the Tokarev pistol, dark brown leather with brass fittings, interior issue marks. Above avg. cond. $20

Holster, Makarov, PM, Soviet Union, Army, 1980. Black leather construction. Flapped. Above avg. cond. . . . $35

Holster, Tokarev, TT 33, Soviet Union, Army, WWII. Brown leather with brass fittings. Compartment for extra magazine. Above avg. cond. $20

Holster, Nagant, M1895, Soviet Union, Army, WWII. For Nagant Model 1895 revolver. Brown pebble grained rubber with leather trim, unissued. Above avg. cond. $20

Bandoleers, SKS, North Vietnam, Army, Vietnam War Era. First unit is a ten-pocket khaki canvas pattern with web straps, wooden toggle straps and steel D-ring, the

other has numerous holes and worn areas. Good cond. .
.... $44

Ammunition, Arisaka, 6.5mm, Japan, Army, WWII. Ten rounds of Arisaka 6.5mm. Rounds each on two stripper clips. Above avg. cond. $0

Ammunition, 8mm, Denmark, Army, 1947. 8mm. Live. 1947 Danish label on box. Holding approx. 100 brass cases with wooden tips. Various dates. Exc. cond. .. $20

Carrying Case For Rifle, England, Army, WWII. Tan webbing, 46" in length. Has side pouch. Ink stamped. Also includes magazine filler for SMG. For Austin submachine gun. Above avg. cond. $20

Cartridges, 9mm, Italy, Army, WWII. Carton of 50. 9mm. Original carton shows age. Ammo is clean, head-stamped M-38, carton is also marked for M-38. Above avg. cond. $20

Cleaning Rod, Nambu, Type 14, Japan, Army, c1930s. Early nickel-plated steel rod. Above avg. cond. $40

Gun Clip, Bren, Light Machine Gun, England, Army, WWII. 30-round curved magazine. Gray metal finish. Above avg. cond. $0

Hand Guard Assemblies, Lot of 10, England, Army, WWII. For .30 cal rifle 1917 model Eddystone. In original sealed delivery box. Exc. cond. $20

Holster, Type 26 Revolver, Japan, Army, 1939. High quality brown leather body with fittings intact. Brass closure fittings and steel D rings. Inked 39 date and arsenal inside flap. Lt use only. Exc. cond. $132

Holster, Browning, High Power, Canada, Army, 1944, Inglis. 1st model clam shell. Tan canvas construction with ink-stamped markings and dated 1944. Includes cleaning rod. Above avg. cond. $65

Holster, Radom P35, Poland, Army, WWII. Dark brown soft-shell body with clip pocket at front and two belt loops. Shows use. One belt loop is coming unsewn and no marks. Avg. cond. $48

Holster, Nagant, M1895, Soviet Union, Army, WWII. Black leather soft-shell body lacks ammo pouch and has added tool pouch at edge. Avg. cond. $35

Holster, Tokarev, TT 33, Soviet Union, Army, WWII. Dark brown soft-shell leather body, magazine pouch and resewn back loops into short belt loops, no D-rings. Avg. cond. $40

Holster, Nambu, Type 14, Japan, Army, WWII. Dark brown leather body, brass closure, ammo pouch pocket for firing pin and steel square rings at back. Avg. cond. .
.... $65

Magazine, Nambu, Type 14, Japan, Army, WWII. 8mm. Blued metal body stamped "55" and alum base. Shows use. Above avg. cond. $25

Magazine, Nambu, Type 14, Japan, Army, WWII. 8mm. Blued metal body stamped "417" and alum base. Above avg. cond. $25

Muzzle Cover, Military Rifle, Japan, Army, WWII. Brass finish tin unit for Type 99 or 38-style rifle. Shows some age. Avg. cond. $25

Stock Assembly, Short Magazine Lee Enfield (SMLE), England, Army, WWI. Dark, oil-rubbed walnut stock. Has "A.A.F.3Gm-K" stamped in left side of stock. Has nose band, center band, buttplate, sling swivels and hand guard intact. Above avg. cond. $35

Artillery-related Accessories—U.S.

Artillery Drill Round, 57mm, USA, Army, WWII. 23" overall length with drill cartridge warhead, some polish remaining. Avg. cond. $20

Artillery Dummy Round, Wooden, USA, Army, WWII. Laminated wooden dummy shell for loading training. Avg. cond. $20

Artillery Dummy Training Round, 105mm, USA, Army, 1969. Dated 1969. Designated Comp-B, Heat-T for Gun M68. In black cardboard transport container. Above avg. cond. $60

Artillery Projectile, 37mm, USA, Navy, 1898. Safed, appears 37mm solid with copper compression band. Dated 1898. Avg. cond. $20

Artillery Round, 37mm, USA, Army, WWI. With solid projectile. Dated 1916 on bottom. Safed. Intact and was a display item. Avg. cond. $20

Artillery Round, 37mm, USA, Navy, 1899, Winchester. 1899 dated Winchester-made 8½"-tall round with polished brass case and polished projectile with wide copper drive band. Ready for display. Above avg. cond. $20

Artillery Round, 40mm Mk 2 Mod 1, USA, Various, WWII. 12½"-tall brass shell. Marked. Avg. cond. ... $20

Artillery Round, 40mm, M25 Saluting Shell, USA, Army, 1944. 8¾" length. Brass casing. 1944 dated. Well marked. Avg. cond. $10

Artillery Round, 5", USA, Navy, WWII. 26½" tall and 5¼" wide. Marked on bottom. Sides show stains and splashed paint. Possible display. Below avg. cond. ..
.... $33

Artillery Round, 75mm, USA, Army, WWI. Brass shell

with projectile and adjustable fuse in nose. Fuse is taped in place. Good copper driving band and lt tarnish on case. Above avg. cond. $38

Artillery Round, 75mm, USA, Army, WWI, England. With fused projectile. Nose dented in several places but driving band is good. Shell has stamped partially obscured values on side. Specs on bottom. 23½" high. Avg. cond. $38

Artillery Shell, 37mm, USA, Army, 1917. Marked and dated 5-17 on base. Good brass and complete with copper compression ring. Avg. cond. $12

Cannon Ball, USA, Army, Civil War. Battlefield retrieval. 3¼" diam with pitted surface. Mounted on 6¾" x 8" wooden base. Below avg. cond. $45

Cannon Ball, USA, Army, Civil War. 10"-circumference cast-iron ball. 4" diam with surface rust and cast marks. Avg. cond. $40

Cannon Round, 20mm, USA, AAF, 1944. 1944 dated and marked "Mk4." Solid projectile. Case empty. Avg. cond. $20

Cannon Round, Vulcan, 30mm, USA, Air Force, 1960s. In OD tan paint with brown fused tip and base. Avg. cond. $22

Clinometer, Artillery, USA, Army, WWII. Blackened brass and metal with bubble level and attachable accessory. Scaled angulation indicators. Wood and leather box with strap. Above avg. cond. $60

Dummy Artillery Round, 37mm, USA, Army, WWII. 5¾"-tall brass casing is 1940 dated and marked "Mk III-A2." Has M50 "dummy" projectile with 1941 dated driving band. Avg. cond. $25

Dummy Round, 3", USA, Navy, WWII. 34"-tall turned oak and gray metal unit. Well marked and 1943 dated on metal base plate has simulated fuse assembly with metal base ring. Avg. cond. $30

Fuse Setter, Artillery, M26, USA, Army, WWII. Massive circular body with rotating numeral grids and heavy folding grip. Well marked. Avg. cond. $21

Fuze Setter, Artillery, Model XM63, USA, Army, 1960s. Model XM63, battery powered with finger switch and view screen. Two-handed use. Avg. cond. $20

Lock, Ordnance Ammo Box, USA, Army, WWII. Brass. Heavy duty hasp lock with key entry on bottom and crossed cannon emblem on face. Above avg. cond. $45

Machine Gun Round, .30 cal, USA, Army, WWI. Safed round with brass case and copper jacketed projectile. Base

indicates 1918 production date, otherwise unremarkable. Minor tarnish. Avg. cond. $38

Mortar Round, 60mm, USA, Army, WWII. OD body with black warhead and alum impact fuse. No propellant in motor section. No marks visible. Above avg. cond. $69

Mortar Round, 60mm, USA, Army, 1943. Safed but complete. Fused nose with safing wire. Label printed on side and 1943 date stamped in case. Above avg. cond. $37

Mortar Round, 60mm, USA, Army, WWII. Wired fuse with black band, yellow shell and brown painted fins. Details printed on sides. Avg. cond. $55

Mortar Sling, 60mm, M2, USA, Army, WWII. Heavy dark OD web strap with brown leather and metal fittings. Avg. cond. $11

Range Finder, Hand Held, USA, Navy, 1943. Black plastic with center viewer and adjustable vertical calibration wires. Positioned 24" from eye, placing wires on wing tips of approaching aircraft will give range to target. Multiple scales cover most WWII enemy fighters. Spec plate on rear and dated 1943. Above avg. cond. $44

Sight, Mortar, M4, USA, Army, WWII. M4 mortar sight with azimuth and elevation controls in leather case with metal belt clip and rings for carry strap and securing strap. For 60mm M2 mortar. Above avg. cond. $71

Sight, Mortar, M4, USA, Army, WWII. For 60mm M2 mortar. Black metal case with mounting flange, two calibration knobs and two bubble levels. Above avg. cond. $37

Sighting Device, Artillery, USA, Army, WWII. Brass with OD finish, bubble level, elevation scales in red and black. Mounting flanges to mate to weapon. Plywood case. Above avg. cond. $50

Slide Rule, Artillery, M23, USA, Army, 1945. In original box dated May 18,1945. With canvas carrycase. Two rules with supporting materials. Near mint cond. $25

Wrist Watch, Ordnance, USA, Army, WWII, Bulova. Bulova made, 12-hour dial and small second dial. Stem set and wound. One-piece band. Above avg. cond. ... $250

Artillery-related Accessories—Germany

Artillery Fuse, Germany, Army, WWII. 4½"-tall three-part cone shaped body stamped "Zt.Z.3/3UFg jqc 1943 etc." Container marked 1939 with Bakelite lid on body with end marked "Zunderbuchse 1." Avg. cond. $37

Artillery Panoramic Sight, Imperial Germany, Army, WWI, Karl Zeiss, Jena. 4½" x 5½" x 6" black painted steel box, hinged lid with rivets, handle and front latch. Rubber sealed lid, wood block and leather inside fittings. 6"-tall blued metal body, three scale dials, black rubber eyecup, optics oil fogged and maker marked "Nedinsco s Gravenhage Systeem Karl Zeiss Jena." Avg. cond. $110

Artillery Round, 30mm, Germany, Army, WWII. 7¾"-tall brass-colored steel case with rusted primer area and "44 awt etc." Crack at opening. Avg. cond. $51

Artillery Round, 37mm, Germany, Army, WWII. 13½" long overall. Dark brass case head stamped "3.7cm Flak18 P 1939 WaA406 etc." Black painted metal projectile with copper band stamped "WaA534 etc." 1939 stamped lower rim with no threaded plug. Above avg. cond. $139

Artillery Round, 37mm, Germany, Army, WWII. 14" long overall. Dark brass finish to magnetic case head-stamped "3.7cm Pak arx42 WaA270 etc." Two-part high explosive head with alum fuse stamped "AZ39 eox 1942 etc." Steel projectile with pitted band and stamped "gax 14a etc." Above avg. cond. $187

Artillery Round, 37mm, Germany, Navy, WWII. 20½" long with two-part projectile having alum tip on steel body. Brass-colored magnetic case is pitted. Head stamped "aux 3.7cm 30 St 5 41" and Eagle-M present. Avg. cond. $244

Artillery Shell Case, Germany, Army, 1917, Patronenfabrik, Karlsruhe. Brass. Cut down. 8½" diam on 9"-tall dark body. Head stamped "Juni 1917 Patronenfabrik Karlsruhe 90 Sp255." No primer. Avg. cond. $75

Artillery Shell Case, Imperial Germany, Army, WWI. Brass. 9"-tall dark body with title head stamp and "Berndorf 411 W-n18v." Avg. cond. $20

Artillery Shell Case, Imperial Germany, Army, 1916, Patronenfabrik, Karlsruhe. Brass. Cut down to 9" tall, 8½"-diam. head stamped "Patronenfabrik Karlsruhe Nov. 1916 SP255." Avg. cond. $75

Artillery Shell Case, 25mm, Germany, Various, 1940. 6½"-tall brass body. Title head stamped and marked "LUM.S 13g 42" and "2.5cm H." With "WaA550." 1940 dated primer. Avg. cond. $30

Artillery Shell Case, 40mm, Germany, Navy, 1941. 12"-tall body lacks primer. Head stamped "enz 1941 4cm 28 38" and Eagle-M V/2. Above avg. cond. $95

Artillery Shell, 150mm, Imperial Germany, Army, 1918. 19¾"-tall body with head stamped "Aug. 1918 Polte

Karth 538 Magdeburg Sp406." Avg. cond. $87

Artillery, Slide Ruler, Germany, Army, WWII. With field-made splinter pattern camo pouch sewn from shelter-quarter material. 9"-long wooden rule with alum scale facing and clear slide. Above avg. cond. $45

Binoculars, 7x50, Coastal Artillery, With Case, Germany, Navy, Coastal Arty, WWII, Carl Zeiss, Jena. Complete cased set for Coastal Flak use. 7"-tall binoculars with black rough texture finish, brown rubber eyecups and leather neck-strap with leather cover. Marked "Carl Zeiss Jena Flak.(Kuste) etc." and "Eagle-M IV/1." Optics clear. Crosshair scale reading "10-20 through 50." With two sets of lens tint/filters still intact. 8½"-tall black leatherette case with all fittings intact except for shoulder strap. Stamped "blc" and "Eagle-M IV/1." Exc. cond. $500

Binoculars, Artillery, 10x80, Germany, Army, WWII. 11" long. Gray painted. Title and "dkl" marked. No sun shields but has both dovetails and top fitting for missing headpad. Optics are clear. With crosshair and four-position filter knob. Exc. cond. $292

Binoculars, Artillery, 10x80, Germany, Army, WWII. 15" long. Gray painted 45-degree bodies with sun shields on ends. Marked "beh D.F.10x80 etc." Dove-tail mount to base and gray rubber head pad. Optics clear. With crosshair and filter knob stuck. Above avg. cond. $281

Binoculars, Artillery, 10x80, Germany, Army, WWII. 13" long. Body painted battleship gray over original base tan. Metal sun shields on ends. Maker "cxn etc." Chip to Bakelite filter knob. Optics clear. Rubber head pad with stud. Avg. cond. $196

Binoculars, Artillery, 8x24, Captured French, Germany, Army, WWII. 10½"-tall tan painted bodies with pivot hinge and small movable handle. Marked "8x24 Decigrades M.G. S.R.P.1 etc." Avg. cond. $100

Binoculars, Artillery, 8x24, With Case, Germany, Army, WWII, Hensoldt. Black leather-covered bodies, brass fittings with worn paint and stamped title. Marked "8x24 Hensoldt." Single focus knob to clear optics. Leather neckstrap. Black leather case. Avg. cond. $90

Binoculars, Artillery, Rabbit-Ear Style, Germany, Army, WWII. 20" tall, tan painted body with pivot socket base. Optics little dirty. Grid on rt side. Marked "bmk etc" and "s.f.14z.gi." Below avg. cond. $282

Cleaning Rod, Imperial Germany, Army, WWI. 14½"-long wood body with cut on tip for cloth. Avg. cond. $20

Fuze, "sp Bu.37" Timer-style, Germany, Army, WWII. Bakelite. 3" tall body marked "RhS Zt.S.f. SpBu.37." and inked date. Avg. cond. $22

Quadrant, Artillery, Imperial Germany, Army, WWI. 10". Brass with eye adjuster for setting range. Cassel maker marks. In waterproof carrier. Exc. cond. . . . $131

Artillery-related Accessories—Other

Training Round, 18-Pdr, England, Army, WWI. 22" tall with fused projectile. Can be separated for study. Shows dents from use. Bottom has specs marked. Avg. cond. $66

CHAPTER SIX

Edged Weapons

This chapter examines the broad category of military edged weapons. The most widely used edged weapons of the 20th century are bayonets and combat knives. Combat knives evolved from the trench warfare on the Western Front in World War One. Initially, a variety of privately purchased hunting knives, daggers, and cut-down bayonets were used. By the end of the war, both US and French forces had developed specialty combat knives. The French version was the M1915 pattern. The US trench knives were designated the M1917 and the M1918. These were the first officially recognized patterns of knives adopted for combat.

The bayonet has continued to be a primary weapon for the modern infantryman. During World War One, the bayonet was widely used both as a weapon and as a tool for a wide variety of tasks, including, but not limited to, cutting firewood, opening ration cases, and as an eating utensil. The typical allied bayonets of the first World War were twelve to seventeen inches long, depending upon the model. The American Springfield and the British Enfield bayonets were cut-and-thrust weapons, while the French M1886 and M1915 bayonets were thrust-only types. German and Austrian bayonets of the period tended to be shorter, cut-and-thrust style weapons.

Swords, in contrast, by World War One were mostly used for ceremonial purposes. This continued to remain the case, except for the Japanese combat usage of swords in World War Two.

Daggers and dirks still saw some ceremonial usage through World War One, being carried particularly by

US Fighting Knives of WWII, Western (left) and M3 Imperial (right)

naval officers. With the establishment of the Nazi regime in Germany, daggers were adopted as a ceremonial replacement for swords across all military and governmental agencies and institutions. For example, even the forestry service and fire department personnel carried ceremonial daggers. These civilian weapons are outside the scope of this book, but may be found in other sources on Third Reich weaponry.

Collecting Tips

The most common ways of organizing edged weapons collections would be by type, by country, or by time period or war.

Fakes and Frauds

German daggers are one of the most frequently forged edged weapons. Often lesser weapons are etched or inscribed to resemble more valuable pieces. Fortunately, the quality of the etching is usually never as good as the originals. Another common problem is daggers assembled from miscellaneous parts of other daggers. Some of these examples are now almost fifty years old and must be examined thoroughly to be detected. Other frequently forged weapons include the U.S. M1918 trench knife and the British Fairbairn-Sykes (F-S) fighting knife.

Collectors Clubs

Military Knife and Bayonet Club, Richmond, VA, Magazine: *The Military Blade Journal*
National Knife Collector's Association, Chattanooga,TN, (800) 548-1442, magazine: *National Knife Magazine*

Axes and Machetes—U.S.

Axe, Crash, USA, AAF, WWII. For aircraft use. Green painted metal head with spiked and conventional ends. Black rubber composition high-voltage resistant handle with checkered grip. Marked "RP4" on head. Above avg. cond. $72

Axe, Crash, USA, AAF, WWII. For aircraft use. Metal head has pick end and trade ax end. Handle is metal covered with dense rubberized material capable of withstanding up to 20,000 volts of electricity. Avg. cond. $39

Bolo Knife, Collins, Model 1005, USA, Army, Engineers, WWI, Collins & Co. Bright curved blade, marked with partially stamped manufacturer logo and model number 1005. Tang tapers toward butt of green horn grips with copper rivets. Regulation sheath. Avg. cond. $50

Bolo Knife, Collins, Model 1005, USA, Army, WWI. Heavy coarse blade. Hmkd near hilt. Tan leather scabbard with brass throat and tip. Embossed decorations on one side and "Collins & Co." is embossed just below the throat. Exc. cond. $130

Bolo Knife, Collins, Model 1005, USA, Various, WWI, Collins & Co. 15" curved heavy steel blade, maker marked. Coco Bolo wood grip with four brass rivets. Leather sheath embossed with pattern on one side, brass at tip and throat. Avg. cond. $60

Machete (Collins 1005 Bolo)

Knife, Bolo, USA, Army, Special Forces, Vietnam War Era. 9½" thick blade with blunt end and sharp cutting edge. Steel ferrule with black finish. One-piece curved wood grip. OD alum-covered wood scabbard with leather belt loop. Exc. cond. $451

Knife, Bolo, USA, Army, Special Forces, Vietnam War Era. 11" parkerized blade with one-piece light wood grips held by three brass screws. Green canvas sheath with metal reinforcement at throat and belt loop. Above avg. cond. $370

Knife, Bolo, M1910, USA, Army, 1917, Plumb, Philadelphia, PA. 14" steel blade hmkd "US/55758" and "Plumb/Phila/(ord bomb)/1917" on ricasso. Black finished steel guard. Walnut grip held by 3 rivets. Brass pommel. Russet leather scabbard with blackened brass throat and catch. Brass swivel ring at tip. Belt loop on back and hmkd "Rock Island Arsenal/1911/HEK." Exc. cond. $191

Knife, Bolo, M1910, USA, Army, 1912, Springfield Armory (SA). 14" polished steel blade hmkd "US/15378" and "SA/(ord bomb)/1912" on ricasso. Black finished guard. Walnut grips held by three brass rivets with brass pommel. Leather sheath with blackened brass throat and latch pin. Belt loop and hmkd "LADEW/ /HJB." Exc. cond. $256

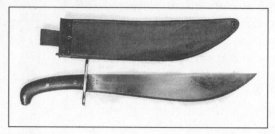

Bolo Knife, Model 1910, with Sheath, Springfield Armory

Knife, Bolo, M1910, USA, Army, 1910, Springfield Armory (SA). 14" bright steel blade marked "SA/(ord bomb)/1910" and "US/5688." Two-piece wood grip. Brass pommel. Above avg. cond. $98

Knife, Bolo, M1917, USA, Army, 1918. Dark blade hmkd "US MOD 1917/CT" and "AC CO. 1918." Wood ribbed grips. 1918 dated scabbard. Exc. cond. $118

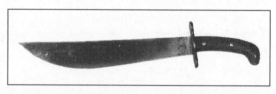

Bolo Knife, Model 1910, Springfield Armory

Knife, Bolo, M1917, USA, Army, 1918, Plumb, Philadelphia. Hmkd "Plumb/Phila 1918" and "US/Mod 1917." Blued blade. Type II scabbard. Above avg. cond. $100

Knife, Bolo, M1917, USA, Army, 1918, Plumb, Philadelphia. Hmkd on ricasso "Plumb/Phila./1918" and "US MOD 1917." Blade is pitted and scratched. Scabbard is canvas over wood and is dated 1918 on leather tip. Avg. cond. $45

Machete, USA, Army, Vietnam War Era. Private purchase Bolo style. 13" blade. Two-piece wooden grip with four metal rivets. Design is in Vietnam era Special Forces style. Canvas scabbard with brass throat and web belt loop and metal clip. Above avg. cond. $223

Machete, USA, Army, 1966, Collins & Co., Mexico. 18" blade dated 1966 on throat. Blade has Collins & Co. logo. Paper Mexican licensee tag. Black plastic grip held by four rivets. Plastic scabbard. Avg. cond. $34

U.S. Marine Corps noncommissioned officer's dress blue tunic and pants, 1888–1910 model.

U.S. Army Air Corps captain's summer service uniform. Second Air Force patch and captain's bars remain; insignia and wings have been removed.

German Army Infantry captain's 1936 pattern tunic. Notice marksmanship lanyard and ribbon bar.

British Artillery captain's tropical dress blouse (jacket).

U.S. Army Technician's (Fifth Grade) dress uniform with wool field ("Ike") jacket, trousers, and garrison cap. Note Seventh Army patch ("A"), 19th Corps patch, collar discs, overseas service bars on left sleeve, and "ruptured duck" honorable discharge emblem.

German Army mountain soldier's "splinter" pattern camouflage tunic. Note Edelweiss armband and Army pattern national emblem.

U.S. Army WWI trench boots.

U.S. Army WWII combat service boots M1943. Also called double buckle combat boots.

U.S. Army WWII M1 ("steel pot") helmet.

U.S. Marine Corps M1 helmet with 1941 pattern cloth camouflage cover.

German paratrooper's model 1937 helmet. Notice Luftwaffe decal.

British Army WWII helmet with camouflage net.

U.S. Army officer's service (dress) cap.

German Army Infantry officer's service cap.

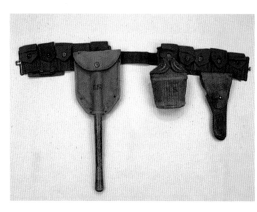

U.S. Army model 1923 dismounted cartridge belt with ten single ammo pockets. Also note the attached M1916 leather holster (hallmarked US), M1943 entrenching tool, and canteen cover.

British Army pattern 37 web belt and gear in khaki. Also note the haversack, entrenching tool, and canteen.

German Army model 34 field gear. Note the gas mask canister, canteen, and shovel.

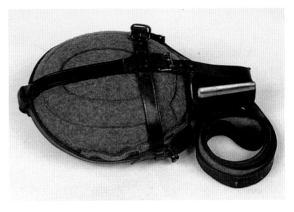

German Army Medical Corps canteen, dated 1944.

U.S. Army portable field radio model number BC611B.

Assorted German hand and rifle grenades.

German Luger model P08, 9mm automatic pistol. Shown with holster, magazine, and tool.

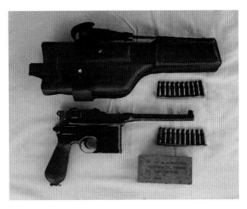

German Mauser Broomhandle 9mm automatic pistol. Shown with leather carrying rig, wooden handle/holster, cleaning rod, and ammo.

(*Top*) U.S. M1 Garrand 30 cal. semi-automatic rifle with boxes of armor piercing and ball ammunition and accessory pouch; (*bottom*) U.S. M1 carbine 30 cal. semi-automatic rifle with bayonet and scabbard, extra magazine, and attached buttstock magazine pouch.

(*Top*) British Enfield #1 MK III, .303 bolt action rifle with ammunition bandoleer and extra magazines; (*bottom*) Enfield .303 MK V bolt action jungle carbine with bayonet and scabbard.

(*Top*) German G43 semi-automatic 8mm rifle with extra magazine; (*bottom*) German K98 bolt action 8mm rifle with bayonet and scabbard.

U.S. fighting knives (*from left to right*) USMC MK II fighting knife marked KaBar with USM8 scabbard; USMC smachett with scabbard; M1 carbine bayonet with scabbard.

U.S. Army shoulder patch, 82nd Airborne Division (All-American Division). Removed from a uniform.

War Order of the German Cross medal (DK) in case. This is the German cross in gold.

U.S. Purple Heart medal in case with ribbon.

WWI trench art shell.

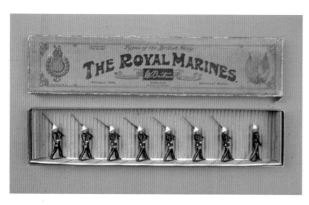

Toy soldiers. Britains #35, Royal Marines marching, circa 1935.

Japanese silk, rising sun, flag.

Machete, USA, Various, WWII. 21" blade. Dark blade with "Collins & Co." logo on side, modified to give saber-like curved cutting edge. Hand-decorated black plastic grip. Pommel area chipped. Below avg. cond. $11

Machete, Engineers, Type 3, USA, Army, Engineers, c1920s. Type number 3 with metal ferrule. Coco bolo grips held by three rivets. Leather and brass scabbard. Avg. cond. $25

Machete, M1942, USA, Army, 1943, Disston. 18" blade. Hmkd "DISSTON/US/1943" at ricasso. Black plastic grips held by four rivets. Green canvas sheath, marked on back with 1943 date. Above avg. cond. $35

Machete, M1942, USA, Army, 1942, Collins and Co., Hartford, CT. U.S. marked with Collins logo. Dated 1942. 18" blade. Black composition grips. Remains of paper label on side of blade. In "US/Boyt/44" marked OD canvas sheath. Above avg. cond. $66

Machete, M1942, USA, Army, 1944, Collins & Co. 18" blade. Collins marked. 1944 dated. Plastic grip. Canvas scabbard. Avg. cond. $24

Machete, M1942, USA, Army, 1943. Dark blade. Ricasso marked "US/1943/SWI." Black plastic grips held by rivets. Avg. cond. $19

Machete, M1942, USA, Army, WWII, England. Dark 18" blade with English maker on side. Wood grips. Incorrect canvas scabbard is for Navy Mark 2, 22" machete. Avg. cond. $20

Machete, Mk 1, USA, Navy, 1942. Hmkd "Collins & Co." on ricasso "USN MK1/1942." 26" blade. Canvas scabbard with "USN/MK1" at throat. Above avg. cond. $33

Machete, Mk 2, USA, Navy, 1944, Collins & Co. Dated 1944. Collins hmkd blade with logo at ricasso. 22" blade. Black plastic grip held by four rivets. Tan canvas sheath marked "USN/Mk 2." Avg. cond. $35

Machete, Mk 2, USA, Navy, 1941, Collins and Co. Steel blade. Hmkd on ricasso and dated 1941. 22" blade. Black plastic grip. Tan leather sheath. Avg. cond. $35

Machete, Survival, USA, AAF, WWII, Camillus. Folding model. Hmkd Camillus on blade. Two-piece black plastic grip. Avg. cond. $28

WWII AAF Survival Machete, Folding Model

Machete, Survival, USA, AAF, 1945, England. Folding model. English made and marked on ricasso, dated 1945. Black plastic handle. Avg. cond. $150

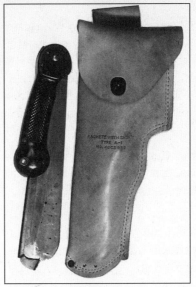
Machete, Folding Survival

Machete, Survival, Case Model XX, USA, AAF, WWII, Case. Non-folding version. Has blued 10" blade. Dark stained wood grips with four rivets. Above avg. cond. $50

Machete, Survival, Case Model XX, USA, AAF, WWII, Case. Blue blade. Black blade guard. Marked "CASE XX." Walnut grip held by four blued metal rivets. Avg. cond. $35

Woodsman's Pal, Model LC/14B, USA, Army, WWII, Victor Tool Co., Reading, PA. Black finished machete-style blade with brush hook. Hmkd "WOODMANS PAL/784" on side of blade. Black finished steel knuckle guard and leather grip. Canvas sheath with sharpening stone and zipper closure. Exc. cond. $115

Woodsman's Pal, Model LC/14B, USA, Army, WWII, Victor Tool Co., Reading, PA. WWII era. Hmkd on blade "Victor Tool Co." Leather grip. Canvas scabbard with instructions. Above avg. cond. $105

Woodsman's Pal, Model LC/14B, USA, Army, WWII, Victor Tool Co., Reading, PA. Hmkd on blade "Victor Tool Co." Leather grip. Canvas sheath with instructions and sharpening stone. Above avg. cond. $120

Woodsman's Pal, Model LC/14B, USA, Army, WWII, Victor Tool Co., Reading, PA. Combination fighting knife and machete. Blued 12" blade. Hmkd "WOODMANS PAL/284" on side of blade. Knuckle guard. Avg. cond. $50

Axes and Machetes—Germany

Machette, Survival, Germany, Luftwaffe, WWII, Alcoso

ACS Solingen. Maker marked "Alcoso ACS Solingen." 21½"-long overall. 16" steel blade. Brass crossguard and hilt with removable wood grips. Blued steel scabbard. Above avg. cond. $750

Pickaxe, M1887, Imperial Germany, Army, WWI. Heavy combat-ready weapon with 18½" wavy wood handle. 10½"-long gray painted ax head with pick. Affixed to wood by two metal straps and band. Brown leather carrier with two belt loops, roller buckle strap, handle loop with extra loop and stamped "II.Grt." Above avg. cond. $221

Pickaxe, M1887, Imperial Germany, Army, WWI. 9½"-long steel head and 18" wooden handle. Black leather carrier with roller buckle loop, snap strap and elastic. Avg. cond. $107

Trench Mace, Imperial Germany, Army, WWI. 22" overall with 3" iron warhead having conical/triangular spikes. Knob at end of handle. Avg. cond. $140

Trench Mace, Imperial Germany, Army, WWI. 22" overall with wooden shaft. 3" spiked head. Swift and brutal weapon of the trenches as used in WWI for silent killing or taking of prisoners in night operations. Avg. cond. $155

Axes and Machetes—Other

Machete, England, Army, 1952, S&J Kitchin LTD. Sheffield No. 2640. 20¼" in length, large heavy curving blade, black riveted handle, leather thong, broad arrow marked and blade inscribed with maker's name. Above avg. cond. $75

Machete, England, Army, 1944. Black blade, black grip with copper rivets. Brown leather scabbard with belt loop and top grip strap, having broad arrow proof marks. Exc. cond. $90

Bayonets—U.S.

Bayonet, Krag, USA, Army, c1898. All metal with chrome plating. Wood grips. Scabbard with belt clip and black leather pad. Exc. cond. $42

Bayonet, Krag, USA, Army, 1898. Dated 1898 on ricasso and "US" on reverse. Bright steel blade. Wood grips. Blued scabbard. Above avg. cond. $74

Bayonet, Krag, USA, Army, 1898. Bright blade. Hmkd "US" and "1899" on ricasso. Wood grips. Avg. cond. $34

Bayonet, M1, USA, Army, WWII. Hmkd "UC/US" with ord bomb. Exc. cond. $66

Bayonet, M1, USA, Army, WWII. Hmkd "UFH/U" ord

bomb "S" on ricasso. Blued blade. Green fiber scabbard. Exc. cond. $82

Bayonet, M1, USA, Army, WWII. Hmkd "AFH/US" with ord bomb. Above avg. cond. $66

Bayonet, M1, USA, Army, WWII. For M1 rifle. Anodized blade. Hmkd "AFH/U (ORD BOMB)S" on ricasso. Steel guard and pommel. Avg. cond. $40

Bayonet, M1, USA, Army, WWII. For M1 rifle. Unmarked. 6½" parkerized blade. Cut-down model. M1 hilt fully functional. Avg. cond. $20

Bayonet, M1, USA, Army, WWII. Hmkd "AFH/U ord bomb S" on ricasso. Bright blade. Ribbed brown plastic grips. Green fiber scabbard. Avg. cond. $34

Bayonet, M1905 E1, USA, Army, WWII. WWII-era modification of M1905 (cut from 16" long to 10"). With saber tip. Parkerized blade. Exc. cond. $48

Bayonet, M1905 E1, USA, Army, 1906, Rock Island Arsenal. 1942 modification of M1905 (cut from 16" long to 10"). Also given knife-point blade. Original manufacture in 1906 at Rock Island Arsenal. Standard scabbard shows lt wear. Above avg. cond. $41

Bayonet, M1905 E1, USA, Army, WWII. WWII-era modification of M1905 (cut from 16" long to 10"). Bowie-point gray blade, hmkd "SA/(ord bomb)/1908." Black plastic grooved grips. Green fiber scabbard. Avg. cond. $35

Bayonet, M1905, USA, Army, 1906, Rock Island Arsenal (RIA), Rock Island, IL. For M1903 rifle. Hmkd on ricasso "RIA/(ord bomb)/1906" and "US." Below avg. cond. $38

Bayonet, M1905, USA, Army, 1906, Springfield Armory (SA), Springfield, MA. For M1903 rifle. Blued blade. Hmkd "SA/(ord bomb)/1906" on ricasso. Above avg. cond. $60

Bayonet, Model 1905

Bayonet, M1905, USA, Army, 1908. For M1903 rifle. Bright steel blade. "US" on obverse, "1908" on reverse of ricasso. Wood grips. Avg. cond. $40

Bayonet, M1905, Variant, USA, Army, WWI. For M1903 rifle. With bolo-style bright metal blade. Marked "US/14517" on ricasso. Steel guard with muzzle ring and pommel. Wood grips. Exc. cond. $280

Bayonet, M1917, USA, Army, 1918, Remington Arms Co., Eddystone, PA. For US M1917 Enfield rifle. Gray blade. Ricasso hmkd "1918" and "Remington stamp." Grips with well-defined twin vertical notches. Green leather sheath with metal tip and throat. Heavy leather frog for wire belt loop. Exc. cond. $107

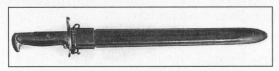

Bayonet, Model 1942, in Fiber Scabbard

Bayonet, M1917, USA, Army, 1917. For US M1917 Enfield rifle. Ricasso obverse with "1917" over "circled W," reverse with "(ord bomb)/US." Avg. cond. $51

Bayonet, M1942, USA, Army, 1942. For M1 and M1903 rifles. 16" steel blade. Hmkd on ricasso "UC/(ord bomb)" and "US/1942." With brown fiber scabbard. Avg. cond. $55

Bayonet, Model 1942, in Canvas Scabbard

Bayonet, M1942, USA, Army, 1942. For M1 and M1903 rifles. 16" blade. Parkerized blade. Canvas scabbard cover with leather tip. Avg. cond. $55

Bayonet, M4, USA, Army, WWII, Camillus. For M1 carbine. Marked Camillus on guard. Parkerized blade. Grooved leather washer grip. Dark metal hilt. Exc. cond. $48

Bayonet, M4, USA, Army, WWII, Camillus. For M1 carbine. Blued blade. Hmkd on guard "US M4/Camillus." Polished leather grip. USM8A1 scabbard. Exc. cond. $75

Bayonet, M4, USA, Army, WWII, Imperial. For M1 carbine. Imperial hmkd on guard. Anodized blade. Brown leather sheath. Exc. cond. $100

Bayonet, M4, USA, Army, WWII, Imperial. For M1 carbine. Blued blade. Hmkd "US M4/IMPERIAL" on guard. USM8 scabbard. Above avg. cond. $50

Bayonet, M4, USA, Army, WWII, Camillus. For M1 carbine. Hmkd "Camillus" on guard. Parkerized blade. Ribbed grip. Avg. cond. $34

Bayonet, M4, USA, Army, WWII. For M1 carbine. Parkerized blade. Black plastic checkered grip. Gray plastic Mark II scabbard. Avg. cond. $23

Bayonet, M5, USA, Army, c1950, Imperial. Adopted post war for M1 Garand rifle. Gray parkerized finish on all metal. Imperial maker marked. Black checkered Bakelite grips. Exc. cond. $31

Bayonet, M5A1, USA, Army, c1950, Imperial. Blued blade. Hmkd guard "USM5A1/IMPERIAL." With "USM8A1" marked scabbard. Above avg. cond. . . . $35

Bayonet, M6, USA, Army, 1962, Milpar, Co. For M14 rifle. Vietnam era. Sealed delivery pouch with bayonet and scabbard inside. Dated April 1962. Hmkd Milpar. Near mint cond. $53

Bayonet, M6, USA, Army, c1958, Milpar, Co. For M14 rifle. Parkerized blade. Hmkd on guard "MILPAR." Checkered black plastic grips. Green fiber scabbard. Above avg. cond. $37

Bayonet, M6, USA, Army, c1958, Milpar, Co. For M14 rifle. Anodized blade. Hmkd on guard "MILPAR CO." With "US M8A1" marked scabbard. Avg. cond. . . . $30

Bayonet, M7, USA, Army, c1970, England. For M16 rifle. British made under US contract. M3 trench knife blade parkerized finish. Marked on guard "M7" and British long arrow. Checkered black plastic handle. Light green plastic scabbard with web belt loop and clip. British long arrow on throat and specs on back. Exc. cond. $66

Bayonet (M7), English

Bayonet, M7, USA, Army, 1960s. For M16 rifle. Hmkd "US M7/BOC" on guard. Anodized blade. Black hard rubber checkered grips. "M8A1" marked scabbard. Avg. cond. $23

Bayonet, M7, USA, Army, 1960s, Imperial. For M16 rifle. Hmkd on guard Imperial. Parkerized blade. Checkered black hard rubber grips. Green fiber scabbard. Avg. cond. $30

Bayonet, M7, USA, Army, c1970, Milpar. For M16 rifle. Parkerized blade. Hmkd "US M7/MILPAR" on guard. Black plastic checkered grips. Avg. cond. $23

Bayonet, M9, USA, Army, c1980s. For M16 rifle. Adopted in 1980s. 7" steel anodized blade with saw back and slot for wire cutting. Hmkd "M9/LANCAY/USA" on ricasso. Steel guard/muzzle ring. Slotted, ribbed and checkered OD plastic grip. OD plastic scabbard with black metal wire cut assembly at tip. Nylon web frog with grip strap, plastic QR buckle and metal belt loop. Sharpening stone on back of scabbard. Near mint cond. $136

Bayonet, Socket, USA, Army, c1870s. For Model 1873 Springfield "trapdoor" cadet rifle. Triangular blued blade marked "US" at base of flute. 3" socket with functional compression ring. With steel scabbard. Below avg. cond. $22

Bayonet, Socket, USA, Army, c1870s. For Model 1873 Springfield "trapdoor" rifle. Marked "US" at base of top flute. Metal scabbard. Leather frog with swivel belt loop. Below avg. cond. $30

Bayonet, Socket, USA, Army, Civil War Era. For Model 1855 musket. Hmkd "US" at base of top flute. Compression ring operable. Below avg. cond. $34

Bayonet, Socket, USA, Army, c1870s. For Model 1873 Springfield "trapdoor" rifle. Marked "US" at base of blued blade. With leather scabbard. Below avg. cond. $27

Bayonet, Socket, USA, Army, c1820. For Model 1812 musket. Triangular blade with mark near base. Narrow fuller on top flute. Above avg. cond. $87

Bayonet, Socket, USA, Army, c1870s. For Model 1873 Springfield "trapdoor" rifle. 16" triangular blade with ordnance bomb on face. Large-bore muzzle ring with latch. Avg. cond. $38

Bayonet, Socket, USA, Army, Civil War. For Model 1841 musket. Marked "78" at base of top flute. Operable compression ring. Avg. cond. $45

Bayonet, Socket, USA, Army, c1820s. For Model 1816 musket. No latch or ridge at end of muzzle ring. Avg. cond. $30

Bayonet, Socket, USA, Army, c1820s. For Model 1816 musket. No latch or ridge at end of muzzle ring. Avg. cond. $40

Bayonets—Germany

Bayonet, Conversion, Imperial Germany, Army, c1870, France. Originally for French M1866 Chassepot Rifle. Converted after Franco-Prussian War. Hmkd "S" on ricasso. Wood grip. Avg. cond. $48

Bayonet, Crank Handle, Ersatz, Imperial Germany, Army, WWI. Demag. Has scabbard with original leather belt loop. 6" blade and 4" handle, well hmkd on both sides of the blade. All steel construction. Avg. cond. $175

Bayonet, Dress, Germany, Army, WWII, Wilhelm Wagner. Long model. Maker "Wilh. Wagner." Below avg. cond. $40

Bayonet, Dress, Germany, Army, WWII. Short model. Unmarked. Below avg. cond. $49

Bayonet, Dress, Germany, Army, WWII, Carl Eickhorn. Short model. Maker "Eickhorn." Brown leather Czech frog. Below avg. cond. $49

Bayonet, Dress, Germany, Army, WWII, Alcoso ACS Solingen. Short model. Maker "Alcoso ACS Solingen." Black patent leather frog. Exc. cond. $66

Bayonet, Dress, Germany, Army, WWII, Tiger. Long model. Maker "Tiger." Distributor marked "Georg Rieder Munchen." Above avg. cond. $48

Bayonet, Dress, Germany, Army, WWII, Carl Eickhorn. Maker "Eickhorn." Short model. Red wool plug in slot. Brown leather frog. Above avg. cond. $73

Bayonet, Dress, Germany, Army, WWII, Tiger. Short model. Maker "Tiger." Red wool plug in slot. Above avg. cond. $50

Bayonet, Dress, Germany, Army, WWII, Alcoso ACS Solingen. Long model. Maker "Alcoso ACS Solingen." Black leather frog. With knot with gray cloth strap, yellow slide, white stem, yellow cap and gray ball. Above avg. cond. $95

German 98K Dress Bayonet with Engraved Blade and Scabbard

Bayonet, Dress, Germany, Army, WWII, W.K.&C. Long model. Maker "WKC." Avg. cond. $32

Bayonet, Dress, Germany, Army, WWII, Alcoso ACS Solingen. Long model. Maker "Alcoso ACS Solingen." Avg. cond. $24

Bayonet, Dress, Germany, Army, WWII, E. Pack & Sohne. Long model. Maker "E. Pack & Sohne." Avg. cond. $40

Bayonet, Dress, Germany, Army, WWII, Carl Eickhorn. Long model. Maker "Eickhorn." Black leather frog. Avg. cond. $60

Bayonet, Dress, Germany, Army, WWII, Carl Eickhorn. Short model. Maker "Eickhorn." Black patent leather frog. Avg. cond. $27

Bayonet, Dress, Germany, Army, WWII, W.K.&C. Long model. Maker "WKC." Black leather frog. Avg. cond. $40

Bayonet, Dress, Germany, Army, WWII, Klittermann.

Short model. Maker "Klittermann." Red wool plug in slot. Avg. cond. $35

Bayonet, Dress, Germany, Army, WWII, Gustav Spitzer. Long model. Maker "Gustav Spitzer." With M1898 scabbard marked "S/173G." Avg. cond. $44

Bayonet, Dress, Germany, Army, WWII, W.K.&C. Short model. Maker "WKC." Avg. cond. $30

Bayonet, Dress, Germany, Army, WWII, Anton Wingen Jr. Short model. Maker "Anton Wingen Jr." Black patent leather frog. Avg. cond. $37

Bayonet, Dress, Germany, Army, WWII, Puma. Long model. Maker "Puma." Avg. cond. $37

Bayonet, Dress, Germany, Army, WWII, Carl Eickhorn. Long model. Maker "Eickhorn." Black patent leather frog. Avg. cond. $40

Bayonet, Dress, Germany, Army, WWII, Carl Eickhorn. Long model. Maker "Eickhorn." Black patent leather frog. Avg. cond. $35

Bayonet, Dress, Germany, Army, WWII, Puma. Short model. Maker "Puma." Red wool plug in slot. Black leather frog. Avg. cond. $45

Bayonet, Dress, Germany, Army, WWII. Long model. Unmarked. Black patent leather frog. Avg. cond. . . . $30

Bayonet, Dress, Germany, Army, WWII. Unmarked. Short model. Carved wood grips simulating stag. Red wool plug in slot. Black patent leather frog. With knot gray cloth strap, blue slide, red stem, blue cap and gray ball on knot. Avg. cond. $133

German WWII Dress Bayonet

Bayonet, Dress, Germany, Army, WWII, W.K.&C. Long model. Maker "WKC." Early version. Avg. cond. . . $48

Bayonet, Dress, Germany, Army, WWII, Robert Klaas. Long model. Maker "Robert Klaas." Avg. cond. . . . $48

Bayonet, Dress, Germany, Army, WWII. Special variant. Short model. Unmarked. With DE nickel blade with narrow center fuller. Avg. cond. $93

Bayonet, Dress, Germany, Army, WWII, Robert Klaas. Maker "Robert Klaas." Long model. Avg. cond. . . . $24

Bayonet, Dress, Germany, Army, WWII, F.W. Holler. Long model. Maker "FW Holler." Black leather frog. Avg. cond. $36

Bayonet, Dress, Germany, Army, WWII, Alcoso ACS Solingen. Maker "Alcoso ACS Solingen." Long model. Stag grips. Avg. cond. $32

Bayonet, Dress, Imperial Germany, Army, WWI. Carbine nickel blade. Black painted hilt with solid hilt having button. Black wood grips with brass crowned cipher. Black painted scabbard. Black leather frog. Above avg. cond. $280

Bayonet, Dress, Imperial Germany, Army, WWI, C. Eickhorn. Nickel carbine blade. By Eickhorn with trademark "C.E." with back-to-back squirrels. Black painted steel fittings with checkered wood grips. Black scabbard. Above avg. cond. $66

Bayonet, Dress, Imperial Germany, Army, WWI. Nickel carbide blade, black painted hilt and three rivets on black grips. Black scabbard. Avg. cond. $20

Bayonet, Dress, Imperial Germany, Army, WWI. Bright carbine blade with faint E. Pack-trademark man. Wood grips. Nickel fittings and scabbard. Solid button on hilt slot. Avg. cond. $55

Bayonet, Dress, Engraved, Germany, Army, WWII, FW Holler. Maker "FW Holler." Single engraved blade with vines on sides of "Zur Erinnerung an meine Dienstzeit Inft.Rgt.3 Mohrungen/Ostpr." Exc. cond. $725

Bayonet, Dress, Engraved, Germany, Army, WWII, FW Holler. Short model. Maker "FW Holler." Single engraved blade with scroll with oak leaves "Zur Erinnerung an meine Dienstzeit" with MG crew, Arty crew and small tank. Above avg. cond. $238

Bayonet, Dress, Engraved, Germany, Army, WWII, Carl Eickhorn. Long model. Maker "Eickhorn." Double engraved. Obverse with scroll with oak leaves "Zur Erinnerung an meine Dienstzeit," stylized eagle end and crossed rifles with helmet/oak leaf wreath. Reverse "Infanterie-Regiment No.119 Stuttgart." Avg. cond. $352

Bayonet, Dress, Engraved, Germany, Army, WWII, Carl Eickhorn. Short model. Maker "Eickhorn." Distributor marked "Militarwarenhaus Durbeck Wien IX." Single engraved with engraved stylized eagles, scroll "Zur Erinnerung an meine Dienstzeit" with oak leaves. Avg. cond. $235

Bayonet, Dress, Engraved, Germany, Army, WWII. Short model. Maker "Eickhorn." Single engraved blade with scroll "Zur Erinnerung an meine Dienstzeit" with oak leaves, stylized eagle and wreath with crossed rifles-steel helmet. Black patent leather frog. Avg. cond. $210

Bayonet, Dress, Miniature, Imperial Germany, Army,

WWI. About 9½" overall. 5½" steel wooled nickel blade with fuller. Black grips and polished bright steel fittings. Black scabbard with faint EK decal. Avg. cond. $44

Bayonet, Ersatz, Imperial Germany, Army, WWI. Emergency pattern for use on Mauser Model 1898 rifle. 11½" flat steel blade with Crown proof on spine. ¾" muzzle ring on crossguard stamped "1143" and steel hilt. With blued steel scabbard. Avg. cond. $30

Bayonet, Ersatz, Imperial Germany, Army, WWI. 17½" long overall and 12" steel blade with faint Crown proofs. Steel hilt and ¾" muzzle ring on crossguard. Steel scabbard. Avg. cond. $37

Bayonet, Ersatz, Imperial Germany, Army, WWI. 16" long overall and 9½" polished steel blade with fuller. Heavy cast hilt with ¾" muzzle ring, green paint and double-stamped crossguard numbers. Green painted steel scabbard with rounded frog stud. Avg. cond. $27

Bayonet, Ersatz, Imperial Germany, Army, WWI. 12¼" steel blade with wide fuller and Crown proof on spine. ¾" muzzle ring on crossguard is stamped "1371." Metal hilt stamped "3134." Steel scabbard with throat. Avg. cond. $24

Bayonet, M1871, Imperial Germany, Army, WWI. Steel blade. Spine marked with Crown-W, "74" and proof. Maker "P.D. Luneschloss etc." Steel crossguard marked "107.R.2.19." Avg. cond. $65

Bayonet, M1871, Dress, Imperial Germany, Army, Pre-WWI, W.K.&C. By "W.K&C" with heads. Engraved floral and military equipment. Nickel crossguard and solid brass hilt with fitted spring. Black leather scabbard. Avg. cond. $139

Bayonet, M1871/1884, Imperial Germany, Army, Pre-WWI. Bright blade hmkd on ricasso. Wood grips. Black leather scabbard with metal tip and throat. Avg. cond. $52

Bayonet, M1884/1898, Imperial Germany, Army, WWI. Polished bright steel blade and fittings. By "Rich. A. Herder etc.," Crown-W, "18" and proof. Wood grips. Polished bright blued scabbard. Small dress brown leather frog with three rivets. Exc. cond. $134

Bayonet, M1884/1898, Imperial Germany, Army, 1915. Nickel-plated blade by "Move-Werke etc." and spine stamped Crown-W, "15," proof. Wood grips to nickel hilt. Black painted scabbard. Avg. cond. $130

Bayonet, M1884/1898, Sawtooth, Imperial Germany, Army, WWI. Prussian 1915. By "Erfurt" and spine Crown W, 1915 and proof. Above avg. cond. $95

Bayonet, M1884/1898, Sawtooth, Imperial Germany, Army, WWI. By "Erfurt" with crown and "Gebr.Heller Marienthal." Crossguard stamped "3620." Wood grips. Black leather scabbard with steel fittings and stamped "B.8.R.R.9.176." Avg. cond. $66

Bayonet, M1898, Germany, Army, Waffen SS, 1944. Maker "cof 44" matching. Bakelite grips. SS-style black leather narrow frog with straps, stamped with RB-NR and "EZGJ1944." Exc. cond. $265

Bayonet, M1898, Germany, Army, 1940. Maker "fnj 40" matching. Bakelite grips. Below avg. cond. $40

German WWII Model 98 Bayonet

Bayonet, M1898, Germany, Army, 1937. Maker "S/176 37" matching. Wood grips. Black leather frog with strap. Above avg. cond. $72

Bayonet, M1898, Germany, Army, 1943. Maker "asw 43." Bakelite grips. Above avg. cond. $48

Bayonet, M1898, Germany, Army, 1944. Maker "sgx 44." Bakelite grips. Phosphate finish overall. Above avg. cond. $80

Bayonet, M1898, Germany, Army, 1939. Maker marked "Carl Eickhorn 39." Bakelite grips. Black leather frog with straps. Above avg. cond. $98

Bayonet, M1898, Germany, Army, 1944. Maker "asw 44." Bakelite grips. Late war variation. Above avg. cond. $105

Bayonet, M1898, Germany, Army, 1936. Maker "S/185 36." Wood grips. Avg. cond. $22

Bayonet, M1898, Germany, Army, 1941. Maker "41 cvl" matching. Bakelite grips. Black leather frog. Avg. cond. $40

Bayonet, M1898, Germany, Army, 1940, EuF Horster. Maker "EuF Horster 1940" matching. Bakelite grips. Black leather frog. Avg. cond. $45

Bayonet, M1898, Germany, Army, 1939. Maker "Durkopp 1939." Bakelite grips. Tropical OG web frog with straps. Avg. cond. $68

Bayonet, M1898, Germany, Army, 1938, Elite-Diamant. Maker "Elite-Diamant 38" matching. Bakelite grips. Avg. cond. $45

Bayonet, M1898, Germany, Army, WWII. Maker "J. Sch. 38" matching. Bakelite grips. Black leather frog maker marked and dated 42. Avg. cond. $72

Bayonet, M1898, Germany, Army, 1940, Mundlos. Maker "Mundlos 40" matching. Bakelite grips. Brown leather frog unit marked "5./Flak Rgt.62." Avg. cond. $48

Bayonet, M1898, Germany, Army, 1939, Carl Eickhorn. Maker "Carl Eickhorn 1939." Bakelite grips. Avg. cond. $30

Bayonet, M1898, Germany, Army, 1943. Maker "cof 43." Bakelite grips. Tropical tan web frog with straps. Avg. cond. $120

Bayonet, M1898, Germany, Army, 1944. Maker "ffc 44." Bakelite grips. Avg. cond. $40

Bayonet, M1898, Germany, Army, 1944. Maker "crs 44." Bakelite grips. Black leather frog. Avg. cond. $35

Bayonet, M1898, Germany, Army, 1943. Maker "cqh 43" matching. Bakelite grips. Black leather frog with straps. Avg. cond. $38

Bayonet, M1898, Germany, Army, 1943. Maker "cul 43." Wood grips. Unusual to see wood grips this late in the war. Avg. cond. $40

Bayonet, M1898, Germany, Army, 1942. Maker "cve 42." Wood grips. Avg. cond. $24

Bayonet, M1898, Germany, Army, 1943. Maker "fnj 43." Bakelite grips. Black leather frog. Avg. cond. $29

Bayonet, M1898, Germany, Army, 1940, W.K.&C. Maker "WKC 40." Bakelite grips. Black leather frog with straps. Avg. cond. $37

Bayonet, M1898, Germany, Army, 1944. Maker "crs 44." Bakelite grips. Avg. cond. $43

Bayonet, M1898, Germany, Army, 1939, F. Herder and Son. Maker "F.Herder A.Sn 39." Bakelite grips. Black leather frog. Avg. cond. $30

Bayonet, M1898, Germany, Army, 1939, W.K.&C. Maker "WKC 39." Bakelite grips. Black leather frog. Avg. cond. $37

Bayonet, M1898, Germany, Army, 1938, Coppel G.m.b.H. Maker "Coppel G.m.b.H. 38." Wood grips. Black leather frog. Avg. cond. $48

Bayonet, M1898, Germany, Army, WWII. Maker "S/175G" matching. Wood grips. Brown leather frog. Avg. cond. $73

Bayonet, M1898, Germany, Army, 1937, FW Holler. Maker "FW Holler 37." Wood grips. Avg. cond. . . . $49

Bayonet, M1898, Germany, Army, 1942. Maker "fnj 42" matching. Bakelite grips. Black leather frog. Avg. cond. $35

Bayonet, M1898, Germany, Army, 1938, FW Holler. Maker "FW Holler 38" matching. Bakelite grips. Black leather frog. Avg. cond. $45

Bayonet, M1898, Germany, Army, 1937, Carl Eickhorn. Maker "Carl Eickhorn 1937." Wood grips. Black leather frog with straps. Avg. cond. $45

Bayonet, M1898, Germany, Navy, 1939, Elite Diamant. Maker marked "Elite Diamant 39." Bakelite grips. Crossguard stamped "O.17983K." Black leather frog Eagle-M issue proofed. Above avg. cond. $160

Bayonet, M1898, Dress, Imperial Germany, Army, WWI, C. Eickhorn. Nickel blade by "C.E." with squirrels. Good wood grips on nickel hilt. Black leather scabbard with nickel fittings. Avg. cond. $87

Bayonet, M1898/1905, Imperial Germany, Army, 1918, Mauser. Blued blade by "Mauser etc." and spine marked Crown-W, "18" and proof. Crossguard and throat stamped "P.W.2862." Wood grips and blued steel scabbard. Avg. cond. $140

Bayonet, M1898/1905, Imperial Germany, Army, 1916, Deutsche Maschinenfabrik. Gray blade by "Deutsche Maschinenfabrik etc.," crown-W, "16" and proof. Wood grips. Metal scabbard. Avg. cond. $60

Bayonet, M1898/1905, Imperial Germany, Army, 1918, Waffenfabrik Mauser. Reissued. Bright steel blade by "Waffenfabrik Mauser etc.," spine marked Crown-W, "18" and proof. Crossguard stamped "6447." Replaced smooth wood grips and no flashguard. Olive painted steel scabbard. Avg. cond. $80

German WWII Model 1898/1905 Bayonet

Bayonet, M1898/1905, Imperial Germany, Army, 1915, O.Dietrich, Altenburg. Steel blade by "O.Dietrich Altenburg" and spine marked Crown-W, "15" and proof. Wood grips. Black finished scabbard. Avg. cond. . . $55

Bayonet, M1898/1905, Imperial Germany, Army, 1917, Pack Ohliger & Co. By "Pack Ohliger & Co. etc.," Crown-W, "17" and proof. Wood grips. Blued steel scabbard. Avg. cond. $58

Bayonet, M1898/1905, Imperial Germany, Army, 1918, P.D. Luneschloss. By "P.D. Luneschloss etc." and marked Crown W, "18" and proof. Wood grips. Avg. cond. . $90

Bayonet, M1898/1905, Bavarian, Imperial Germany, Army, 1917, Fichtel & Sachs. By "Fichtel & Sachs etc.,"

Crown-L, "17" and proof. Crossguard stamped "1920." Blued scabbard. Above avg. cond. $65

Bayonet, M1898/1905, Sawtooth, Imperial Germany, Army, WWI, W.K.&C. "SAXON 1907" by "WK&C etc.," Crown-FA, "07" and proof. Partial muzzle ring on crossguard stamped "22.P.2.97." Good wood grips without flashguard. Black leather scabbard with gray steel fittings and stamped "PKP 225." Exc. cond. $475

Bayonet, M1898/1905, Sawtooth, Imperial Germany, Army, WWI. By "Weyersberg etc." and Crown-W, "16" and proof. Wood grips. Blued scabbard. Above avg. cond. $105

Bayonet, M1898/1905, Sawtooth, Imperial Germany, Army, WWI, Alex Coppel Solingen. Dark blued blade by "Alex Coppel Solingen" with good teeth on spine stamped Crown-W, "15" and proof. Steel fittings with wood grips and no stamps on crossguard. Blued steel scabbard with dents and stamped "2204 Mauser etc." Avg. cond. . $110

Bayonet, M1898/1905, Sawtooth, Imperial Germany, Army, 1915, Deutsche Maschinenfabrik A-G Duisburg. By "Deutsche Maschinenfabrik A-G Duisburg," Crown-W, "15" and proof. Blued steel scabbard. Avg. cond. $82

Bayonet, Sawtooth Style, Dress, M1905, Imperial Germany, Army, WWI, A.Wingen Jr. Solingen. 10" bright nickel blade with sawteeth on spine and by "A.Wingen Jr. Solingen." Nickel fittings with working slot, two rivets on black horn grips. Black scabbard. Black patent frog. Above avg. cond. $100

Bayonets—Other

Bayonet, Sword Socket, Austria, Army, c1850s. Made for Austrian M1849 Augustine rifle. Has long fullered sword blade with muzzle locking ring. No scabbard. Above avg. cond. $150

Bayonet, Socket, England, Army, c1820, East India Co. For third model India pattern Brown Bess musket. With hallmark socket but no scabbard. Good cond. $71

Bayonet, Socket, 1876 Pattern, England, Army, c1870s. For the Martini-Henry rifle. Bright fullered blade, blued socket retaining muzzle locking ring and leather scabbard with brass fittings. Exc. cond. $76

Bayonet, Socket, 1876 Pattern, England, Army, c1870s. For Martini-Henry rifle. No scabbard or muzzle ring. Relic condition. Poor cond. $20

Bayonet, 1907 Pattern, England, Army, 1917. For Lee Enfield (SMLE) rifle. This was the standard bayonet for the British in WWI and many also saw service as late as WWII. 17" fullered blade with ricasso dated 1917, hilt

with grooved wood grips, scabbard of khaki leather and brass wire belt attachment device. Above avg. cond. $75

Bayonet, Socket, 1876 Pattern, England, Army, c1870s. For Martini-Henry rifle. Parade dress with nickel finish, with muzzle locking ring and brass-mounted leather scabbard. Good cond. $65

Bayonet, Socket, England, Army, c1775. For Brown Bess musket. DE blade with open-ended slot. Near relic condition. Poor cond. $59

Bayonet, Spike, No. 4 Mk. II, England, Army, WWII. For Lee Enfield No. 4 Mk I rifle. 8" circular section blade. With sheath. Above avg. cond. $20

Bayonet, France, Army, c1871. For M1866 Chassepot rifle. Brass ribbed grip, with scabbard. Good cond.   . $70

Bayonet, M1891, Italy, Army, WWII. For M1891 Carcano rifle. Fullered blade with wood grips. Scabbard is gray metal with leather frog with belt loop and top grip strap. Exc. cond. $125

Bayonet, Italy, Army, WWII. Modified crossguard, converted to folding-style bayonet. Blade and wood grips with heavy wear. Avg. cond. $100

Bayonet, Type 30, Japan, Army, WWII. For Arisaka Type 30 rifle. Fullered 15¾" blade, hilt with hooked quillion guard and wood grip. Steel scabbard. Avg. cond. . . . $37

Bayonet, Type 30, Japan, Army, WWII, Tokyo-Kokura Arsenal. Fullered blade, ricasso marked Tokyo-Kokura Arsenal, crossguard with hooked quillon, wood grips, shaped pommel, with scabbard. Above avg. cond. . . $40

Bayonet, Type 30, Japan, Army, WWII. Fullered, unsharpened blade, ricasso with Kokura Arsenal and hourglass manufacturer's stamps, hooked crossguard, wood grips and scabbard with light wear. Above avg. cond. $31

Bayonet, Type 30, Japan, Army, WWII, Nagoya Arsenal. Blade in excellent polish, ricasso with Nagoya Arsenal and star with "K" designation manufacturer's stamp, straight crossguard, wooden grips, contoured pommel and steel scabbard. Good cond. $55

Bayonet, Socket, England, Army, c1810, Osborn & Gunby. For Napoleonic-era Brown Bess musket. Semibright finish. No scabbard. Good cond. $54

Bayonet, M1929, Poland, Army, 1937. For M1929 Mauser rifle. Ricasso marked "PERKUN," wood grips, scabbard and black leather belt frog. Exc. cond. $250

Bayonet, Socket, England, Army, c1880, Providence Tool Co., Providence, RI. For Peabody-Martini rifle. Thousands of these rifles were manufactured under contract to

English government. Bayonet with cruciform blade and "L78" on socket. Working compression ring. Avg. cond. $17

Bayonet, Model 1969 CETME, Spain, Army, 1970s. 13¼" long with bolo-type blade and checkered grip. For Model 58 CETME rifle. OD scabbard with belt loop and leg strap. Exc. cond. $50

Bayonet, Model 1906, Switzerland, Army, WWI. For Schmidt-Rubin rifle. 23¾" in length, fullered sawtooth blade, ricasso with cross, straight crossguard, wood grips and iron pommel. Black lacquered scabbard and brown leather strap. Above avg. cond. $75

Bayonet, Model 1898/1905, Turkey, Army, WWI. Similar to German version but with shortened blade and scabbard. Turkish marks on crossguard. Below avg. cond. ... $25

Bayonet, AKM, Egypt, Army, 1970s. For Egyptian pattern AKM. 5¾" bright blade factory sharpened, black Bakelite grip and composition wire cutter scabbard and gray leather belt loop. Near mint cond. $20

Bayonet, Czechoslovakia, Army, 1960s. For 1st pattern AK-47. 7¾" gray parkerized blade, black Bakelite grip, blued metal scabbard and gray nylon webbing belt loop. Near mint cond. $20

Bayonet, Spike, China, Army, 1970s. Chinese bayonet for Type 56 (SKS) assault rifle. Unissued with cruciform blade and mounting screw. Near mint cond. $16

Combat Knives and Daggers—U.S.

Knife, Combat, USA, Army, Confederate, Civil War. Hand-forged knife. 21¼" long with 15¾" blade and iron crossguard forged with scalloped edges. Right side of blade engraved with "OUR," "Stars and Bars" Confederate flag, followed by "AND OUR RIGHTS." Complete with original black leather scabbard with hand-sewn seams. Avg. cond. $11,500

Knife, Trench, Model 1917, USA, Army, WWI. Blued triangular blade, 8⅞" long tapering to a needle point. Stamped iron "knuckle-duster" guard with protruding points and finger groove round wooden handle. In original green leather sheath with metal tip and throat marked "Jewell 1918." Above avg. cond. $250

Knife, Bowie, USA, Army, Confederate, Civil War. 15½" blade. One-piece brass D guard with two-piece walnut grip with hand-cut checker pattern. Avg. cond. ... $333

Knife, Bowie, USA, Army, Civil War, William WS/Swift. 15" blade with "William WS/Swift." "12" at ricasso. Tin D-guard with knuckle bow. Stag grip. Above avg. cond. $527

Knife, Combat, USA, Army, USMC, WWII, Case. Blued 6¾" blade. Hmkd "Case" at ricasso. Polished leather grip. Uncommon black plastic pommel. Unmarked russet leather sheath. Exc. cond. $213

Knife, Combat, USA, Army, USMC, WWII, Case. Case "Pig Sticker." Bright blade. Marked on distinctive ricasso "CASE." Riveted shaped walnut grip. Light brown stitched and riveted sheath. Exc. cond. $178

Knife, Combat, USA, Army, USMC, WWII, Case. Case "Pig Sticker." 6½" polished steel DE dagger blade with unusual ricasso marked "CASE." Tang runs length of hilt and is covered by two-piece wood grip held by three rivets. Cross cut several times at each end and center to give better grip. Above avg. cond. $200

Knife, Combat, USA, Army, USMC, WWII, Case. Case "Pig Sticker." Polished steel blade. Marked CASE "XX" on ricasso. Wood two-piece grip with three rivets and stamped "US." Leather scabbard. Above avg. cond. $250

Knife, Combat, USA, Army, USMC, WWII, Case. 6.9" polished DE blade. Hmkd "CASE" on ricasso. Steel guard curved toward point. Washer grip. Black plastic pommel. Sheath has brown frog and black finished cover. Avg. cond. $448

Knife, Combat, USA, Army, USMC, WWII, Kabar. 6" bright steel blade. Hmkd on ricasso. Brass guard. Leather grip custom notched and alum pommel with name engraved. Leather sheath hmkd. Avg. cond. $37

Knife, Combat, USA, Army, WWII, Gerber. 6½" DE blade with sawteeth on each edge. Hmkd on ricasso and serial number. One-piece black textured grip with lanyard at pommel. Black leather sheath with belt loop and retaining strap. Exc. cond. $76

Knife, Combat, USA, Army, Vietnam War Era, KaBar. KaBar Model 1207. Polished steel blade, narrow fuller and hmkd on ricasso. Leather washer grip notched along bottom. Tan leather roll-over-style sheath with logo at throat. Exc. cond. $108

Knife, Combat, USA, Army, WWII, Gerber. 6¾" steel DE blade with sawback on both edges. Hmkd on ricasso. One-piece black textured finish hilt, drilled at pommel for lanyard. Black leather sheath with lanyard at tip and guard strap. Above avg. cond. $97

Knife, Combat, USA, Army, WWII, Cattaraugus. Hmkd "Cattaraugus 225q" on ricasso. Bright blade. Leather sheath. Above avg. cond. $30

Knife, Combat, USA, Army, Vietnam War Era, Milpar. Developed from M6 bayonet by Milpar. Parkerized blade. Hmkd on guard. Knuckle bow welded to guard and mated to pommel and has three wide ribs on underside. Checkered black grips. With "US M8A1" scabbard. Above avg. cond. $145

Knife, Combat, USA, Army, WWII, KaBar. WWII era. 6" plated steel blade patterned after Mark II. Steel disc for pommel. Tan leather sheath. Marked on guard. Above avg. cond. $76

Knife, Combat, USA, Army, WWII. M1905 bayonet converted to fighting knife. Polished steel blade cut down from original. Guard made from old muzzle ring assembly. New wood grips added. Unmarked leather sheath. Above avg. cond. $75

Knife, Combat, USA, Army, WWII, John Ek. 6¾" DE steel blade with "John EK Knife/Hamden, Conn." Serial number on ricasso. "S"-curved steel guard and unusual shaped wood grip with three steel rivets. Tang extends beyond pommel and grip is drilled for lanyard. Leather sheath. Above avg. cond. $304

Knife, Combat, USA, Army, WWII, EGW. Marked. Oval steel half-guard. Contoured leather grip. Lanyard ring at pommel. Tan leather sheath. Avg. cond. $39

Knife, Combat, USA, Army, WWII, Cattaraugus. 6" nickel plated blade with "Cattaraugus" hmkd on ricasso. Steel guard and pommel. Russet scabbard. Avg. cond. $50

Knife, Combat, USA, Army, Vietnam War Era. 9" thin flexible blade. Brass ferrule secures wood grip with hand checkered sides. Has "Vietnam 1968" on top and "23 INF" on sides. Avg. cond. $48

Knife, Combat, USA, Army, WWII, Southern & Richardson, Sheffield England. 6½" DE dagger blade hmkd "Southern & Richardson/Sheffield England." Brass guard and pommel. Leather washer grip between plastic spacers. Brown leather sheath. Avg. cond. $81

Knife, Combat, USA, USMC, WWII, PAL. Hmkd on ricasso "PAL." Parkerized blade. Leather washer grip. Dark leather sheath w/hand carved pattern on front and name on back. Below avg. cond. $40

Knife, Combat, USA, USMC, WWII, East Bros., Sidney, Australia. 6" steel blade, hmkd "East Bros/Sidney" on ricasso. Hallmarked "US/1944" on blade side of guard. Wood grips with broad arrow inspection mark. Leather sheath. Exc. cond. $533

Knife, Combat, USA, USMC, WWII, Cutlers Co., Auckland, New Zealand. Theater made for US Marines. 5¾" long steel blade with "N Z/CUTLERS CO/AUCKLAND" on side. One-piece alum ribbed grip. Above avg. cond. $263

Knife, Combat, USA, USMC, WWII, Camillus. Hmkd "Camillus" on guard. Parkerized blade. Leather sheath. Avg. cond. $28

Knife, Combat, USA, USMC, WWII, Camillus. Camillus hmkd on guard. Dark blade. Russet leather sheath. Avg. cond. $45

Knife, Combat, USA, USMC, 1944, Whittingslove, Australia. Hmkd on guard "Whittingslove" and "US 1944." 5¾" blade. Wood grip with three rivets. Leather sheath hmkd "Sidney" on neck and dated "1944." Avg. cond. . . $196

Knife, Combat, USA, USMC, WWII. Similar to PAL RH-36. 6½" clip point, blued blade. Oval guard. Leather washer grip. Alum pommel stamped "USMC." Avg. cond. $35

Knife, Combat, USA, Various, WWII, Western, Boulder, CO. Western Shark model. 6" bright plated blade. Steel guard. Polished alum pommel. Two-piece leather grip. Tan leather sheath. Avg. cond. $135

Knife, Combat, M3, USA, Army, WWII, Case. Anodized blade. Hmkd "US M3 Case" on side. With scabbard. Below avg. cond. $76

Knife, Combat, M3, USA, Army, 1943, U. C. Parkerized blade hmkd "USM3-U.C.-1943." Grooved leather grip. Tan leather M6 sheath with metal plates at tip and belt clip, eight staples at throat and "US M6/Milsco/1943/S" marked. Near mint cond. $703

Fighting Knife (M3) in M6 Sheath, Hallmarked USM3-U.C.-1943. The Standard US Army Combat Knife of WWII.

Knife, Combat, M3, USA, Army, 1943, Kinfolks. Blued blade hmkd "US M3 Kinfolks 1943." Polished ribbed leather washer grip. 1943 dated M6 sheath with eight staples at throat and metal plates at tip. Exc. cond. $456

Knife, Combat, M3, USA, Army, WWII, Case. Dark gray parkerized finish on all metal. Hmkd on straight guard "Case." Smooth contoured leather grip. Step pommel. Tan leather sheath with hilt strap. Exc. cond. $196

Knife, Combat, M3, USA, Army, WWII, Imperial. Parkerized blade, guard and pommel. Grooved leather grip. Guard hmkd "US M3/Imperial." USM8 scabbard with frog. Exc. cond. $200

Knife, Combat, M3, USA, Army, WWII, Case. Parkerized blade hmkd "US M3 Case." Steel guard and pommel. Grooved leather washer grip. With USM8 scabbard. Exc. cond. $328

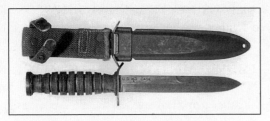

Fighting Knife (M3) with M8 Scabbard, Case

Knife, Combat, M3, USA, Army, WWII, Case. Anodized blade. Hmkd "CASE" on guard. With USM8A1 scabbard. Above avg. cond. $104

Knife, Combat, M3, USA, Army, WWII, Case. Hmkd on guard "Case." Leather grip. With "USM8A1" scabbard. Above avg. cond. $96

Knife, Combat, M3, USA, Army, WWII, Camillus. Blued blade hmkd "US M3 Camillus 1943." Ribbed leather grip. No scabbard. Avg. cond. $250

Knife, Combat, M3, USA, Army, WWII, Camillus. Anodized blade. Hmkd "US M3 CAMILLUS'" on blade. No scabbard. Avg. cond. $76

Knife, Combat, M3, USA, Army, WWII, Imperial. Anodized blade. Hmkd "US M3/Imperial" on guard. Scabbard stenciled with a name and USM8 on throat. Avg. cond. $78

Knife, Combat, M3, USA, Army, 1943, Camillus. Hmkd on blade "M3 Camillus 1943." Anodized blade. Leather grip. With unmarked M6 sheath. Avg. cond. $126

Knife, Combat, M3, USA, Army, 1943, R.C.Co. Blued blade. Hmkd "R.C.Co." Leather grip. Dark brown leather M6 sheath hmkd "Milsco/1943." Avg. cond. $249

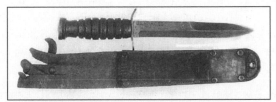

Fighting Knife (M3), R. C. Co., WWII Era

Knife, Combat, M3, USA, Army, WWII, Imperial. Parkerized blade hmkd "US M3 Imperial." The USM8 scabbard with lanyard at tip. Avg. cond. $125

Knife, Combat, M3, USA, Army, WWII, Utica. Anodized blade. Hmkd "M3-Utica" on blade and "US" on ricasso.

Grooved leather washer grip. With "USM8" scabbard. Avg. cond. $125

Knife, Combat, M3, USA, Army, WWII, H. Boker & Co. Blade hmkd "US M3 H. Boker & Co/USA." Leather washer grip. With USM8 scabbard. Avg. cond. . . . $100

Knife, Combat, M3, USA, Army, WWII, Case. Parkerized blade. Hmkd "US M3/CASE" on guard. 1943 dated M6 sheath. Avg. cond. $200

Knife, Combat, Mk I, USA, Navy, UDT, WWII. Special rust resistant bright blade. Hmkd on ricasso "USN/MK2" with manufacturer struck over. Smooth leather grip. Green plastic scabbard with nylon web frog and hilt strap. Exc. cond. $282

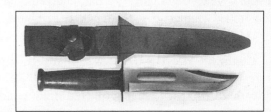

Fighting Knife (MK1, USN, UDT Version), WWII Era

Knife, Combat, Mk I, USA, Navy, WWII, Robeson Shuredge. "Robeson Shuredge" hmkd on ricasso with "USN" on rev. Parkerized blade. Mk 2 sheath. Below avg. cond. $40

Knife, Combat, Mk I, USA, Navy, WWII, Pal. "Pal RH-35" marked on ricasso and "USN/Mark I" on reverse. Steel blade. Smooth leather grip. Commercial "George Lawrence Co." fold-over leather sheath. Below avg. cond. $33

Knife, Combat, Mk I, USA, Navy, WWII, KaBar, Olean, NY. Hmkd on ricasso "KaBar, Olean NY." Blued blade. Half-guard. Leather fold-over sheath with "USN" on throat. Exc. cond. $75

Knife, Combat, Mk I, USA, Navy, WWII, Pal. Hmkd "Pal RH35" on ricasso. Mk I canvas scabbard. Above avg. cond. $65

Knife, Combat, Mk I, USA, Navy, WWII, Colonial, Providence, RI Gray unfullered blade marked "USN/Colonial/ Prov. R. I." on ricasso. Solid rubber composition half-guard, grip, and pommel. Grip is grooved for traction. Avg. cond. $20

Knife, Combat, Mk I, USA, Navy, WWII, Western. Blued blade. "Western" marked on ricasso. Leather sheath. Avg. cond. $34

Knife, Combat, Mk I, USA, Navy, WWII, Geneva Forge. Hmkd "Geneva Forge" on ricasso under "Mark I."

Smooth leather grip. Alum pommel. Mk 1 scabbard. Avg. cond. $49

Knife, Combat, Mk I, USA, Navy, WWII, Colonial, Providence, RI 5¼" gray blade. "USN" marked on one side of ricasso and "Colonial Prov. R.I." marked on the other side. One-piece black molded plastic grip/guard and pommel. Avg. cond. $85

Knife, Combat, Mk I, USA, Navy, WWII, Camillus. Steel blade. Hmkd "Camillus/New York" on ricasso. Leather grip. Black plastic pommel. Leather sheath with "Keep this knife well oiled" embossed on front. Avg. cond. $37

Knife, Combat, Mk II, USA, Navy, USMC, WWII, KaBar. Dark parkerized blade. "KaBar" marked on guard. Polished ribbed leather grip. With Mk II scabbard. Exc. cond. $110

Knife, Combat, Mk II, USA, Navy, WWII, KaBar. Parkerized blade. KaBar marked on guard. Polished ribbed leather grip. Mk 2 scabbard. Near mint cond. $120

Knife, Combat, Mk II, USA, Navy, WWII, Robeson Shuredge. Parkerized blade hmkd "ROBESON SHUREDGE." Tan leather roll-over sheath marked USN at throat. Exc. cond. $125

Knife, Combat, Mk II, USA, Navy, WWII, Kabar. WWII era. Hmkd "KABAR" on ricasso. Parkerized blade. Leather sheath with "USN" at throat. Exc. cond. $122

Knife, Combat, Mk II, USA, Navy, WWII, KaBar. Unmarked version of KaBar with fullerless steel blade and smooth leather grip. Gray Mk II scabbard. Exc. cond. $500

Knife, Combat, Mk II, USA, Navy, WWII, R C C. Parkerized blade. Hmkd "USN MK II/R C C" on guard. Grooved leather washer grip. Gray Mk 2 scabbard with web frog and protective paper around throat. Exc. cond. $128

Knife, Combat, Mk II, USA, Navy, WWII, KaBar. Fullerless blade. "KABAR" and "USN MK2" marked on ricasso. With Mk II scabbard. Above avg. cond. . . . $35

Knife, Combat, Mk II, USA, Navy, WWII, Camillus. "Camillus" hmkd on guard. Parkerized blade. Tan leather USN sheath. Avg. cond. $30

Knife, Combat, Mk II, USA, Navy, WWII, Camilus. Blued blade hmkd "US/Camillus" on ricasso. Dark sheath with initials carved in face. With lanyard. Avg. cond. $27

Knife, Combat, Mk II, USA, Navy, WWII, KaBar. Hmkd "Ka-Bar" on guard. Dark blade. Smooth ribbed leather grip. Gray fiber scabbard. Avg. cond. $44

Knife, Combat, Mk II, USA, Navy, WWII, Pal. Bright blade hmkd "US NAVY" and "PAL RH-37" on ricasso. Grooved leather washer grip. Russet leather sheath with "USN" at throat. Avg. cond. $49

Knife, Combat, Mk II, USA, USMC, WWII, Kabar, Olean, NY Parkerized blade hmkd "KA-BAR." Smooth grooved leather grip. Tan leather sheath. Above avg. cond. $102

Knife, Combat, Mk3, USA, Navy, SEAL, Vietnam War Era. All black with clip-point blade and sawtooth back. Checkered rubber grips. Black plastic and webbing scabbard. Marked "Mk3 modo." Exc. cond. $35

Knife, Combat, Murphy, USA, Army, WWII. 6" steel fullerless blade. One-piece alum grip with simulated stag finish. Hmkd "USA" and "Murphy Combat" on sides of grip. Exc. cond. $375

Knife, Combat, Murphy, USA, Army, WWII. All metal. Fullerless steel blade. One-piece alum grip, simulated stag surface. Hmkd "Murphy Combat Knive" on one side and "USA" on other. Leather sheath. Exc. cond. $380

Knife, Hospital Corp, USA, USMC, WWII, Chatillon. 11½" heavy metal blade. Hmkd "USMC/Chatillon, NY." Two-piece wood grip with brass rivets. Leather scabbard, hmkd "Boyt/43." Avg. cond. $82

Knife, Hospital Corp, M1887, USA, Army, Hospital Corps, c1890. 12" polished steel blade with "Hospital Corps/US Army" monogrammed on side. Initials NJ at ricasso. Steel guard and ribbed wood grip with steel ferrule and pommel. Black leather scabbard with brass throat and belt clip, marked Rock Island Arsenal on back. Exc. cond. $1026

Knife, Hospital Corp, Model 1904, USA, Army, 1914, Springfield Armory (SA). 12" blade and blunt end. Hmkd "SA/(ord emb)/1914" and "US/38188" at ricasso. Brass guard and notched wood grip. Scabbard of leather over wood, brass throat and belt loop. Avg. cond. $65

Knife, Medical Corp, USA, USMC, WWII, Chatillon. Hmkd "USMC/CHATILLON, NY" on blade. Wood grip held by three brass rivets. Russet leather scabbard with brass throat, leather lanyard and hmkd "BOYT/44" on belt loop. Above avg. cond. $76

Knife, Modified M7 Bayonet, USA, Army, c1970s. Converted to knuckle knife. Hmkd on guard "US M7/GEN CUT." Parkerized blade. One grip removed and black cast-iron four-finger (two-hole) knuckle guard added. With M8A1 scabbard. Above avg. cond. $125

Knife, Survival, USA, Air Force, 1967, Camillus. For downed pilots. Hmkd on pommel "Camillus/1967." Bright blade. Sheath has stone. Avg. cond. $35

Knife, Survival, USA, USAF, c1950s, Camillus. Early version by Camillus with 6" parkerized blade. Hmkd on ricasso. Leather sheath with stone pocket and stone. Avg. cond. $87

Knife, Survival, USA, Various, WWII, Case. Chrome-plated 5" blade. Marked "CASE" on ricasso. Nickel silvered half-guard. Smooth leather washer grip with pommel as threaded cap for equipment chamber. Dark brown leather sheath. Exc. cond. $680

Knife, Survival, USA, Various, WWII, Gerber. Polished steel DE blade with sawtooth sections on each side. Hmkd on ricasso. Blackened one-piece metal hilt. Black leather sheath with hmk. Exc. cond. $66

Knife, Survival, USA, Various, 1976, Ontario. For aircraft pilots and crew. Ontario marked and dated 10-76 on pommel. Gray blade. Above avg. cond. $25

Knife, Survival, M2, USA, Various, WWII, Geo Schrade Knife Co., Inc. Single blade. Marked "Presto/Pat Jan 30-40" and "Geo Schrade/Knife Co Inc" on ricasso. Simulated bone grips. OD green nylon lanyard tied to bail. Blade lock and release button on side. Exc. cond. $712

Survival Knife (M2), WWII Era

Knife, Survival, MC-1, USA, USAF, 1960s. With switch cutting blade and shroud cutter. Hmkd on ricasso. Controls on side. Day-glo grips. Exc. cond. $28

Knife, Survival, V-44, USA, Various, WWII, Western. Black composition grip held by three steel rivets. Dark leather sheath. "Western" engraved on blade by ricasso. Exc. cond. $350

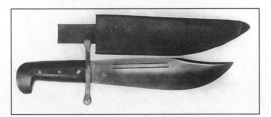

Survival Knife (V-44), WWII Era

Knife, Trench, USA, Army, Rangers, WWII. 9" broad steel blade. Unmarked. One-piece brass hilt with knuckle guard. Guard equipped with seven gear-type bumps. Dark leather sheath. Above avg. cond. $500

Knife, Trench, USA, Army, WWII, Everett. Green finish on hilt. Bright 6¾" DE dagger blade. One-piece hilt with four-hole knuckle guard. Marked on side below grip on both sides. Light tan leather sheath, patterned after M6, six staples at throat and grommet at tip. Exc. cond. $500

Knife, Trench, USA, Army, WWII, Everett. Black finish. 6¾" center fullered DE blade. Marked on knuckle guard. One-piece alum grip and four-hole knuckle guard. Leather sheath with six staples at throat. Above avg. cond. . $460

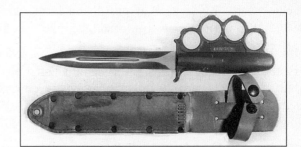

Trench Knife (WWII Everett)

Knife, Trench, USA, Army, WWII, New Zealand. 6" steel blade. Marked on blade. One-piece alum grip with knuckle bar. Dark leather scabbard. Avg. cond. $200

Knife, Trench, USA, Army, WWII, Australian. 10" parkerized, clip-pointed bowie blade, hmkd "Case XX" on side. One-piece brass grip with seven gear tooth knobs on knuckle guard. "US" stamped on one side of grip. Avg. cond. $345

Knife, Trench, USA, Army, WWII, English. Middle Eastern design. 7" dagger blade. One-piece brass hilt. Unmarked. Brass hilt has palm rest, two slots for fingers and four knuckle ridges. Avg. cond. $130

Knife, Trench, Mk I Model 1918, USA, Army, 1918, Landers, Frary and Clark, Philadelphia, PA. 7" blued blade. Hilt modified, loss of oval guard but four hole knucks guard intact. Marked on side "US 1918/LF&C-1918." Leather sheath. Below avg. cond. $160

Knife, Trench, Mk I Model 1918, USA, Army, 1918, French. Blued blade with "Au Lion" hallmark on ricasso. One-piece brass grip with four-finger knuckle grip and "US 1918" on side. Skull cracker at rear. With black finished metal scabbard. Exc. cond. $282

Knife, Trench, Mk I Model 1918, USA, Army, 1918, Landers, Frary and Clark, Philadelphia, PA. 6½" DE blade.

One-piece brass hilt has four-hole knuckle guard with four bumps and skull cracker. Hmkd "US 1918/LF&C 1918." 1918 dated scabbard. Avg. cond. $215

Knife, Trench, Mk I Model 1918, USA, Army, WWI, Henry Disston and Sons. 8" DE-style blade. One-piece brass hilt with four-hole knuckle guard and skull cracker. Hmkd on side "US 1918/HD&S." Avg. cond. $315

Knife, Trench, Mk I Model 1918, USA, Army, 1918, Oneida Community Limited. Modified with non-standard 8" DE steel blade with all brass hilt. Marked on side "US 1918/O. C. L. 1918." Knuckle spines are sharply pointed. Oval guard. Avg. cond. $420

Knife, Trench, Model 1917, USA, Army, 1917, Landers, Frary and Clark, Philadelphia, PA. Triangular blade. Knuckle guard. Blade side of guard hmkd "US/LF & C/1917." Wood grip. Below avg. cond. $82

Knife, Trench, Model 1917, USA, Army, 1917, Landers, Frary and Clark, Philadelphia, PA. Blued triangular blade. Walnut grip. Steel guard and knuckle bar with seven knobs including skull cracker. Hmkd on guard "LF&Co./1917." Below avg. cond. $175

Knife, Trench, Model 1917, USA, Army, 1918, Oneida Community Limited. Triangular blued blade. Dark steel guard and knuckle bow with double row of five knobs each. Walnut grip shows signs of cross-hatching. Marked on face of guard "US/OCL/1918." Custom leather sheath. Exc. cond. $450

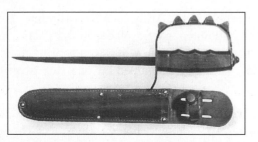

Trench Knife, Model 1917 OCL

Knife, Trench, Model 1917, USA, Army, 1917, AC Co. Blued triangular blade, unmarked. Walnut grip. Hmkd on knuckle guard "AC Co. 1917." Double row of knobs and skull cracker. Green finished leather scabbard with metal fittings. Exc. cond. $200

Knife, Trench, Model 1917, USA, Army, 1917, LF&C. Blued triangular blade. Heavy sheet metal D-shaped knuckle bow with pyramidal knuckle flares. Hmkd "U.S. L.F.&C. 1917." Finger notched black walnut grip. OD finish leather scabbard maker marked and dated 1918 with blued metal tip and throat. Exc. cond. $269

Knife, Trench, Model 1917, USA, Army, 1917, Landers, Frary and Clark, Philadelphia, PA. Blued triangular blade.

Pyramidal knuckles on sheet metal crossguard. Hmkd "LF&C" and dated 1917. Black walnut grip. With green leather scabbard with blued metal fittings. Above avg. cond. $160

Knife, Trench, Model 1917, USA, Army, 1917, Landers, Frary and Clark, Philadelphia, PA. Blued triangular blade. Hmkd on guard "US/LF&C/1917." Wood grip. Avg. cond.
.... $66

Knife, Utility, USA, Navy, SEAL, 1960s. Switchblade. 5¾" folded with 4" parkerized blade. Single release/latch pin and black plastic ribbed grips. Exc. cond. $135

Knife, Utility, USA, Navy, WWII, Camillus. Pocket style, single blade with "Camillus/cutlery" on ricasso. Wood grips. Oversize bail. Above avg. cond. $45

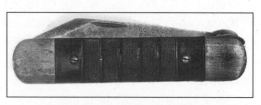

Utility Knife, USN, WWII Era

Knife, Utility, USA, Navy, WWII, Camillus. Camillus marked on ricasso of cutting blade. Includes can opener blade and oversized bail with simulated wood grips. Cotton cord lanyard. Above avg. cond. $21

Knife, Utility, USA, USMC, 1994, Camillus. Hmkd "Camillus" with 1994 date on ricasso. Checkered metal grips with "USMC" on one side. Four jackknife blades and bail. Exc. cond. $13

Knife, Utility, USA, USMC, WWII. Checkered metal grips with "U S MARINE CORPS" on side. Cutting blade, punch can, bottle openers and bail. Above avg. cond. $50

Smatchet, USA, OSS, WWII, England. Bright blade. Steel oval guard. Wood grip. Brass pommel marked with broad arrow and "13." Canvas scabbard with belt loop, broad arrow and 1942 date. OSS took up the smatchet and made it a major weapon for field operatives. Exc. cond. .
.... $710

Smatchet, WWII British

Smatchet, USA, OSS, WWII. Chrome-plated 11" blade with oval steel guard. Two-piece black plastic grip held by three steel rivets. Black dyed leather over wood sheath with belt loop and guard strap. Exc. cond. $460

Stiletto, USA, USMC, WWII. Polished steel unmarked blade. One-piece oval guard. Checkered grip in the F-S style. Brown leather sheath, similar to M6, 10 staples at throat and two metal reinforcing plates at bottom. Exc. cond. $800

Stiletto, USA, USMC, WWII, Case. Variant with blued blade and guard. Hmkd on ricasso "CASE." DE dagger blade. Steel guard. Contoured smooth leather grip. Marked black plastic pommel. Tan leather sheath. Exc. cond. $658

Stiletto, USA, USMC, WWII, Western. Polished steel blade. Hmkd on ricasso. Brass guard. Leather grip with multi-colored spacers at each end. Brown leather sheath. Exc. cond. $1062

Stiletto, V-42 Case, USA, USMC, WWII, Case. Blued blade with ribbed thumb rest. Hmkd "CASE" on ricasso below thumb rest. Forward curved guard, ribbed metal grip and skull cracker. Dark leather sheath. Exc. cond. $1500

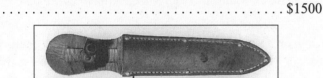

Stiletto (Case), WWII Era

Combat Knives and Daggers—Germany

Dagger, East Germany, Army, c1960s. Blade in excellent polish, hilt with recurved crossguard, push button release, stippled pommel and nickeled throughout. Throat with oak leaf and East German insignia. Exc. cond. . . . $275

Dagger, Luftwaffe, 1st Model, Germany, Luftwaffe, WWII, Tiger Solingen. Maker "Tiger Solingen." Alum fittings with gilt remaining on swastikas. Wire wrapped blue leather covered grip. Blue leather covered scabbard with alum fittings. Alum chain hanger with clip. Exc. cond. $538

Dagger, Luftwaffe, 1st Model, Germany, Luftwaffe, WWII, E&F Horster. Maker marked "E&F Horster." Nickel blade. Alum crossguard and pommel and gold swastikas. Alum wire wrap on blue leather grip. Blue leather scabbard with alum fittings. Chain hanger with clip. Avg. cond. $300

Dagger, Luftwaffe, 1st Model, Germany, Luftwaffe, WWII, Alcoso. Maker "Alcoso." Nickel blade, crossguard and pommel. Dark wire wrap on blue leather grip. Blue leather scabbard with nickel fittings. Avg. cond. . . $375

Dagger, Luftwaffe, 1st Model, Germany, Luftwaffe, WWII, P.D.Luneschloss Solingen. Maker "P.D. Luneschloss Solingen." Silver finished fittings with copper and brass mobile swastikas. Wire wrapped blue leather-covered grip. Blue leather-covered scabbard with silver finished fittings. Alum chain hanger with clip. Avg. cond. $387

Dagger, Luftwaffe, 1st Model, Germany, Luftwaffe, WWII, Puma Solingen. Maker "Puma Solingen." Silver finished fittings. Wire wrapped blue leather-covered grip. Blue leather-covered scabbard with silver finished fittings. Alum chain hanger with clip. Avg. cond. . . . $166

Dagger, Luftwaffe, 2nd Model, Germany, Luftwaffe, WWII, Alcoso ACS Solingen. Maker "Alcoso ACS Solingen." Gray alum fittings. Wire wrapped white celluloid grip. Steel scabbard. Below avg. cond. $140

Dagger, Luftwaffe, 2nd Model, Germany, Luftwaffe, WWII, WKC. Maker "WKC." Silver finished fittings. Yellow celluloid grip. Wire wrapped yellow celluloid grip. Steel scabbard. Short silver cord knot. Deluxe pattern hangers with oak leaves on fittings. Exc. cond. . . . $467

Luftwaffe 2nd Model (1937 Pattern) Dagger in Scabbard with Hangers and Knot

Dagger, Luftwaffe, 2nd Model, Germany, Luftwaffe, WWII, Rich. Abr. Herder Solingen. Maker "Rich. Abr. Herder Solingen." Gray alum fittings. Wire wrapped white celluloid grip. Steel scabbard. Short silver cord knot. Exc. cond. $380

Dagger, Luftwaffe, 2nd Model, Germany, Luftwaffe, WWII, Alcoso ACS Solingen. Maker marked "Alcoso ACS Solingen" with scale trademark. Gray alum crossguard and pommel. Dark bullion wrap on orange grip. With gray steel scabbard. Above avg. cond. $290

Dagger, Luftwaffe, 2nd Model, Germany, Luftwaffe, WWII, F.W. Holler Solingen. Maker "F.W. Holler Solingen." Gray alum fittings. Wire wrapped white celluloid grip. Steel scabbard. Above avg. cond. $250

Dagger, Luftwaffe, 2nd Model, Germany, Luftwaffe, WWII, Alcoso ACS Solingen. Maker "Alcoso ACS Solingen." Gray alum hilt. Wire wrapped white celluloid grip. Steel scabbard. Above avg. cond. $250

Dagger, Luftwaffe, 2nd Model, Germany, Luftwaffe, WWII, Carl Eickhorn. Maker "Eickhorn." Alum fittings. Silver wire wrapped yellow celluloid grip. Steel scabbard with hanger. Short silver cord knot. Avg. cond. . . . $285

Dagger, Luftwaffe, 2nd Model, Germany, Luftwaffe, WWII, SMF. Maker "SMF." Eagle-5 issue marked. Nickel blade by "SMF Solingen" with trademark and Eagle-5 proof. Alum fittings. Silver wire wrapped orange celluloid grip. Steel scabbard with hanger. Short silver cord knot. Avg. cond. $315

Dagger, Luftwaffe, 2nd Model, Germany, Luftwaffe, WWII. Unmarked. Gray alum fittings. Wire wrapped orange celluloid grip. Gray steel scabbard. Avg. cond. $190

Dagger, Luftwaffe, 2nd Model, Germany, Luftwaffe, WWII, Carl Eickhorn. Maker "Eickhorn." Eagle-5 issue marked. Alum fittings. Wire wrapped white celluloid grip. Steel scabbard. Avg. cond. $210

German Army Officer Pattern Dagger with Scabbard

Dagger, Luftwaffe, 2nd Model, Germany, Luftwaffe, WWII, Rich. Abr. Herder Solingen. Maker "Rich. Abr. Herder Solingen." Alum fittings. Wire wrapped orange celluloid grip. Steel scabbard. Silver cord knot. With "Army Deluxe Pattern Hanger." Avg. cond. $225

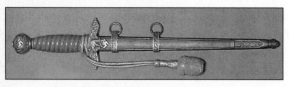

Luftwaffe 1937 Pattern Dagger

Dagger, Luftwaffe, 2nd Model, Germany, Luftwaffe, WWII, Rudolf Buchel. Maker "Rudolf Buchel etc." Dull alum fittings. Wire wrapped dark orange celluloid grip. Steel scabbard. Avg. cond. $218

Dagger, Luftwaffe, 2nd Model, Germany, Luftwaffe, WWII. Unmarked. Gray alum fittings. Gray alum crossguard and pommel. Wire wrap on white celluloid grip. No scabbard. Avg. cond. $116

Dagger, Luftwaffe, 2nd Model, Germany, Luftwaffe, WWII, Carl Julius Krebs. Maker "Carl Julius Krebs" with trademark. Silver finish. Yellow celluloid grip. Steel scabbard. Fair cond. $117

Dagger, Luftwaffe, 2nd Model, Damascus Blade, Germany, Luftwaffe, WWII, Echt Damascener C.W. Maker "Echt Damascener C.W." Rose pattern Damascus blade. Alum fittings. Wire wrapped yellow celluloid grip. Steel scabbard with hanger. Exc. cond. $1780

Dagger, Luftwaffe, 1st Model, Germany, Luftwaffe, WWII, Carl Eickhorn/Solingen. 10¼" DE blade marked "Carl Eickhorn/Solingen," sitting squirrel logo on obverse side of blade, yellow celluloid grip with oak leaf and acorn pattern band at bottom and grip cap, handguard is a spread eagle clutching wreath and swastika in its talons. Dagger is in an alum pebble finish scabbard with oak leaf pattern hanger bands and rings to which is attached silver braid and gold buckle hanger. Above avg. cond. $275

Dagger, Officer, Germany, Army, WWII, Carl Eickhorn. Maker "Eickhorn." Nickel fittings. Orange celluloid grip. Long alum knot. Hanger with alum fittings and some with oak leaves. "Johnson" black suede zipper case. Exc. cond. $455

Dagger, Officer, Germany, Army, WWII, Puma Soligen. Maker "Puma." Nickel blade, fittings and scabbard. Yellow celluloid grip. Long alum knot. Hangers with some oak leaf fittings. Above avg. cond. $300

German Army Officer Pattern Dagger in Scabbard with Hangers

Dagger, Officer, Germany, Army, WWII, WKC. Maker marked "WKC Solingen." Nickel fittings and scabbard. Dark yellow celluloid grip. Long silver cord knot. Above avg. cond. $292

Dagger, Officer, Germany, Army, WWII, Carl Eickhorn. Maker marked "Eickhorn." Nickel hilt and scabbard. Orange celluloid grip. Early example. Above avg. cond. $300

Dagger, Officer, Germany, Army, WWII, Carl Eickhorn. Maker marked "Eickhorn." Nickel hilt and scabbard. Yellow celluloid grip. Early example. Above avg. cond. $275

Dagger, Officer, Germany, Army, WWII, FW Holler. Maker "FW Holler." Nickel blade, fittings and scabbard. Dark yellow celluloid grip. Early example. Above avg. cond. $200

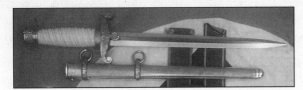

German Army Dagger, General Officer's Variant

Dagger, Officer, Germany, Army, WWII, Gustav Spitzer. Maker "Gustav Spitzer." Silver finished fittings. White celluloid grip. Silver finished scabbard. Above avg. cond. $270

Dagger, Officer, Germany, Army, WWII, WKC. Maker "WKC." Nickel blade, fittings and scabbard. Yellow celluloid grip. Above avg. cond. $219

Dagger, Officer, Germany, Army, WWII, Alcoso ACS Solingen. Maker "Alcoso ACS Solingen." Nickel fittings and scabbard. Orange celluloid grip. Above avg. cond. $327

Dagger, Officer, Germany, Army, WWII, SMF Solingen. Maker "SMF Solingen." Nickel fittings and scabbard. White celluloid grip. Above avg. cond. $215

Dagger, Officer, Germany, Army, WWII, WKC. Maker "WKC." Wartime gray metal fittings and scabbard. White celluloid grip. Avg. cond. $152

Dagger, Officer, Germany, Army, WWII, Alcoso ACS Solingen. Maker "Alcoso ACS Solingen" with scales trademark. De-Nazified. No swastika/wreath on eagle crossguard. Dark yellow grip. Avg. cond. $128

Dagger, Officer, Germany, Army, WWII, SMF Solingen. Maker "SMF." Alum hilt. Variation yellow celluloid grip with swirl. Nickel scabbard. Silver cord knot. Avg. cond. $330

German Army Officer Pattern Dagger in Scabbard with Sword Knot

Dagger, Officer, Germany, Army, WWII, E&F Horster Solingen. Maker "E&F Horster Solingen." Alum fittings.

Orange celluloid grip. Nickel scabbard. With hanger. Avg. cond. $185

Dagger, Officer, Germany, Army, WWII, Puma Solingen. Maker "Puma Solingen." Nickel fittings. Orange celluloid grip. Nickel scabbard. Long silver cord knot. Avg. cond. $270

Dagger, Officer, Germany, Army, WWII, Robt. Klaas Solingen. Maker "Robt. Klaas Solingen" with birds. Silver finished fittings. Orange celluloid grip. Fair cond. $147

Dagger, Officer, Naval, Germany, Navy, WWII, F.W. Holler. Maker "F.W.Holler." Nickel double fullered blade. Brass fittings. Wire wrapped orange celluloid grip. Lightning bolt scabbard. Below avg. cond. $570

Dagger, Officer, Naval, Germany, Navy, WWII. Bright nickel double fullered blade. Brass eagle pommel and crossguard with lock button. White grip with twisted brass wire. Brass lightning bolt scabbard with oak leaves on hanger bands. Exc. cond. $405

Dagger, Officer, Naval, Germany, Navy, WWII, ACS. Maker "ACS." Hmkd with naval Eagle-M and "N738." Double fullered blade. Gilt fittings. Wire wrapped white celluloid grip. Gilt lightning bolt scabbard with throat stamped "N738." Above avg. cond. $930

Dagger, Officer, Naval, Imperial Germany, Navy, WWI. 11½"-long fully engraved (on both sides) blade. No hmk. Gilded brass guard with naval emblems on each side. Gilded crown pommel and ivory grip. Brass scabbard with ritual engraved marks and emblems and two rings. Avg. cond. $850

Dagger, Officer, Naval, Imperial Germany, Navy, WWI. Double engraved blade with knight head logo. White handle with gold gilt crown pommel cap. Lighting bolt scabbard. Complete with original silver wire dagger knot with marine colors. Dagger is about 19¼" OA length and owner's name is on the throat. With blue cloth named dagger-hanger belt with clips and straps. Avg. cond. . $2200

Dagger, Officer, Naval, Double Engraved, Germany, Navy, WWII, ACS. Maker "ACS" with scale trademark. Looks to be a transitional dagger with added eagle pommel. Blade with fouled anchor, galleon and floral motif. Anchor on brass crossguard. Wire wrap on ivory grip. Hammered brass scabbard with knot hanger bands. Long tied alum knot. Below avg. cond. $538

Dagger, Officer, Naval, Double Engraved, Germany, Navy, WWII, WKC. Maker "WKC." Gilt finished brass crossguard, eagle pommel and lightning bolt scabbard. Twisted brass wire to white celluloid grip. Darkening to silver cord knot. Above avg. cond. $545

Dagger, Officer, Naval, Double Engraved, Germany, Navy, WWII, Carl Eickhorn. Maker "Eickhorn." Double engraved blade with fouled anchor motif with naval Eagle-M issue stamp. Brass crossguard with lock button and eagle pommel. Twisted brass wire wrap on white celluloid grip. Brass lightning bolt scabbard with tied knot hanger ring bands and stamped throat "O.929." The "O" stands for East Sea Division. Above avg. cond. $978

Dagger, Officer, Naval, Double Engraved, Germany, Navy, WWII, Carl Eickhorn. Maker "Eickhorn." Double engraved blade with naval motif. Brass eagle pommel and crossguard with button release. Twisted brass wire wrap on white grip. Lightning bolts on brass scabbard with oak leaf hanger bands. Avg. cond. $401

Dagger, Officer, Naval, Engraved, Damascus, Germany, Navy, WWII, WKC. Maker marked "WKC." Transition dagger; converted from WWI to Third Reich. 9" double fullered maidenhair Damascus blade, engraved 1914 at each end of initials "H.F. H.J. C.R." Brass crossguard with lock button. Wire wrapped ivory grip. Gilt finished Third Reich eagle pommel. Hammered brass scabbard. Above avg. cond. $2500

Knife, Combat, Germany, Army, WWII. 9" long overall. 4½" bright steel blade and two rivets on wood grip with grooves. Black painted steel scabbard with long spring/clip. Exc. cond. $319

Knife, Combat, Germany, Army, WWII. Steel blade stamped "W." Steel crossguard and three rivets on wood grips. Black scabbard with three-prong loop. Exc. cond. $123

Knife, Combat, Germany, Army, WWII, Puma. Maker "Puma." Gray crossguard and Bakelite grips. Black scabbard with spring clip. Above avg. cond. $125

Knife, Combat, Germany, Army, WWII. With four tool grip. 6" steel blade. Steel crossguard. Black composite grips, corkscrew, marlin spike, opener and screwdriver. Black scabbard with metal belt loop. Avg. cond. .. $276

Knife, Combat, Germany, Army, WWII. Maker "cof." Cast crossguard and tang. Three rivets on wood grips having owner carved "K." Black scabbard with long clip/spring. Avg. cond. $125

Knife, Combat, Germany, Army, WWII, Puma. Maker "Puma." Bakelite grips. Black painted scabbard with steel spring clip. Avg. cond. $107

Knife, Combat, Germany, Army, WWII, Puma. Maker "Puma." Bakelite grips. Black painted steel scabbard with spring clip. Avg. cond. $112

Knife, Combat, Germany, Luftwaffe Ground Forces,

WWII. Eagle-6 issue marked. Steel blade. Steel crossguard and three rivets on light wood grips. Black scabbard with three-prong loop. Exc. cond. $125

Knife, Combat, Germany, Luftwaffe Ground Forces, WWII. Eagle-5 issue marked. Steel crossguard, three rivet grips and three spring clips to black scabbard. Above avg. cond. $110

Knife, Combat, Germany, Luftwaffe Ground Forces, WWII. Eagle-5 issue marked. 6½"-long steel blade. Three rivets on wood grips. Black scabbard has three spring clips. Avg. cond. $149

Knife, Combat, Germany, Luftwaffe Ground Forces, WWII. Eagle-6 issue marked. Steel crossguard and three rivets on wood grips. Black scabbard with three spring clips. Avg. cond. $79

Knife, Combat, Imperial Germany, Army, WWI, W.K.&C. Weyersberg trademarked with king and knight heads. Wood grips. Black scabbard. Below avg. cond. $75

Knife, Combat, Imperial Germany, Army, WWI, Mercator. WWI folding style by Mercator. White metal frame with trademark of leaping cat and "K55K" lettering. Base of blade maker marked and also stamped "Solingen Germany" for export purposes. 8" OA length when extended. Complete with lock for blade and metal lanyard. Avg. cond. $45

Knife, Combat, Imperial Germany, Army, WWI, Anton Wingen. 5" steel blade with faint "Anton Wingen etc." Large stag grip with black steel fittings. Black steel scabbard. Avg. cond. $95

Knife, Combat, Imperial Germany, Army, WWI, Demag. Steel blade stamped "Demag," "Germany" and crown proof. Steel crossguard and wood grips with grooves. Black steel scabbard with leather belt loop and straps. Avg. cond. $72

Knife, Combat, Imperial Germany, Army, WWI. Ern style with gray steel blade, black painted steel crossguard and dark wood grips with three rivets. Steel scabbard with belt loop. Avg. cond. $40

Knife, Combat, M1845, Saxon, Imperial Germany, Army, Inf, WWI. 18¾" steel blade with faint crown. Solid brass hilt and crossguard with stamped "103. R.8.171." reissued. Black leather scabbard with mismatched stamped brass throat "104.R.10.229." Avg. cond. $145

Knife, Combat, M1845, Saxon, Imperial Germany, Army, Inf, WWI, P. D. L. About 19" steel blade by "P.D.L." and crowned "AR." Solid brass hilt and crossguard with stamped title and crown on tip. With unit marked "12. r.310." Avg. cond. $90

Knife, Combat, Stag Handle, Imperial Germany, Army, WWI. 8½" long overall. With 4½" gray steel blade stamped "Fein Stahl." Stag antler grip. Brown leather sheath with nickel throat. Avg. cond. $55

Knife, Diver, Naval, Germany, Navy, WWII. About 14" overall. Heavy brass body. Threads below handle with grooved grip, 6½" plain steel blade and scabbard. Avg. cond. $339

Knife, Gravity, Germany, Luftwaffe, Paratrooper, WWII, SMF Solingen. Maker "SMF Solingen." Blued finish. Wood grips. With 58"-long braided rope lanyard with sewn end loops having steel clips. Exc. cond. $750

Knife, Gravity, Germany, Luftwaffe, Paratrooper, WWII, Paul Weyersberg. Maker "Paul Weyersberg." Eagle-5 issue marked. Silver finish. Wood grips. Avg. cond. $75

Knife, Gravity, Germany, Luftwaffe, Paratrooper, WWII. Unmarked. Eagle-5 issue marked. Silver finish. Wood grips. Avg. cond. $175

Knife, Gravity, Germany, Luftwaffe, Paratrooper, WWII, Paul Weyersberg. Maker "Paul Weyersberg." Waffenampt proofed. Silver finish. Wood grips. Avg. cond. $130

Knife, Gravity, Germany, Luftwaffe, Paratrooper, WWII. Unmarked. Silver finish. Wood grips. Avg. cond. . $135

Knife, Gravity, Germany, Luftwaffe, Paratrooper, WWII. Eagle-5 issue marked. Blued finish. Wood grips with owner's initials. Still works. Avg. cond. $300

Knife, Trench, Imperial Germany, Army, WWI, Solingen-Foche. Bright steel blade shows sharpening, title maker "Solingen-Foche" and "Germany." Crown proof to other side of ricasso. Steel crossguard, wood grips, black scabbard and dry leather loop. Avg. cond. $81

Knife, Trench, Imperial Germany, Army, WWI. 6" spear-point blade. Black painted steel crossguard. Wood grips with grooves. Black scabbard with leather belt loop and straps. Avg. cond. $133

Combat Knives and Daggers——Other

Dagger, Officer, Bulgaria, Army, c1950. Blade with narrow center fuller, very good polish, hilt with recurved crossguard and white composition grip with obverse and reverse mounted by brass plate. Scabbard with nickel finish and contrasting throat with lion and rising sun motif. Above avg. cond. $200

Dagger, Cadet, Greece, Army, c1970. Narrow stiletto blade, ricasso with maker's hallmark, hilt with crossguard,

banded ferrule and white grip. Gilded scabbard with Greek shield and wreath motif, laurel leaf frieze and scabbard ring mounts. Exc. cond. $200

Dagger, Officer, Italy, Air Force, WWII. Narrow stiletto blade, brass furniture, winged crossguard and mother-of-pearl slabs on grip. With brass scabbard and pommel, both having eagle motif. Above avg. cond. $899

Dagger, "Field Made," Japan, Army, WWII. 14" long. Unusual specimen fashioned in the field from a c1875 American officer sword. Brass hilt, American eagle on pommel and wood grip remain intact. Avg. cond. $166

Dagger, Officer, Bulgaria, Army, WWII. Double engraved blade. Nickel crossguard with lion heads, lion shield and affixed cross. Nickel crown pommel. Dark wire wrap on orange grip. Army style scabbard has pebbled details. Hanger with brown straps, oakleaves on buckles and slides, pebbled clips and top clip. Avg. cond. $950

Dagger, Officer, Hungary, Air Force, WWII. Lock button on back of brass eagle crossguard. Eagle head pommel. Black fluted grip. Brass scabbard with crest on front. Avg. cond. $270

Dagger, Officer, Poland, Army, 1920s. Blade has "Honor i Ojczyzna" inscribed with Polish eagle, cruciform crossguard and yellow grip. Scabbard 100% black leather wrap. Above avg. cond. $1000

Dagger, Officer, Poland, Air Force, 1954. Silvered furniture, blade in exc condition and ivory grip. Scabbard with red-white checked throat insignia. Above avg. cond. $550

Dagger, Officer, Poland, Air Force, 1954. Nickeled furniture, blade in excellent polish, ivory grip and scabbard has throat with miniature pilot's badge. Above avg. cond. $650

Dagger, Officer, Poland, Army, WWII, G. Borowski. Stiletto blade with Polish eagle and floral scrollwork, inscribed "Honor i Ojczyzna," hilt has cruciform crossguard, orange grip and ferrule and pommel have laurel frieze. With black leather scabbard. Above avg. cond. $394

Dagger, Officer, Poland, Navy, WWII, G. Borowski. Blade engraved with Polish eagle "Honor i Ojczyzna" inscribed, silvered hilt, yellow grip, square pommel and ferrule in laurel frieze. Ricasso stamped with manufacturer name. Black leather scabbard. Above avg. cond. $459

Scabbard, Dagger, Poland, Navy, WWII. Silvered fittings

with black leather wrap, throat, idle band, and drag with laurel wreath frieze. Above avg. cond. $215

Dagger, Dress, Officer, Soviet Union, Air Force, 1986. DE blade, hilt having gilded crossguard, embossed pommel cap and yellow grip. With black leather scabbard. Exc. cond. $102

Dagger, Dress, Officer, Soviet Union, Army, 1979. DE blade, hilt with gilded crossguard and embossed pommel cap and yellow grip. With black leather scabbard. Exc. cond. $102

Kindjal, Cossack, Imperial Russia, Army, c1855, Crimean War Era. DE curved fullered blade and hilt with grips of molded brown horn. No scabbard. Above avg. cond. $268

Dagger, KGB, Soviet Union, KGB, c1950. Double sided blade, hilt with recurved crossguard, ferrule with spring lock button, yellow grip and engraved pommel. Obverse throat has star with hammer and sickle emblem, reverse has Kremlin motif. With black leather scabbard. Above avg. cond. $108

Dagger, Officer, Soviet Union, Navy, 1949. DE blade, ricasso dated, recurved crossguard, yellow grip and brass pommel with star motif. Black leather scabbard. Above avg. cond. $107

Dagger, Officer, Soviet Union, Navy, 1981. DE blade, hilt with gilded crossguard, embossed pommel cap, yellow grip and black leather scabbard. Exc. cond. $102

Dagger, Officer, Soviet Union, Navy, c1950s. DE blade, hilt with recurved crossguard, ferrule with spring-lock button, pommel with star motif, yellow grip and black leather scabbard. Above avg. cond. $88

Dirk, Dress, Scotland, c1880, Wilson and Sharp Edinburgh. 19" in length, narrow blade, wide fullers, silver furniture and stag grip hilt. Above avg. cond. $2250

Dirk, Officer, Artillery, France, Army, 1812, Klingenthal. Straight 11" blade of hollow triangular section with full-length blued and gilt panel engraved with panoplies of arms and scene of mortar. Marked at hilt "Klingenthal 1812." Simple recurved brass quillions. One-piece ivory grip attached with four rivets. Blade has dark patina and minor pitting. Grip with several age cracks. Good cond. $1955

Dirk, Officer, Naval, England, Navy, c1800. Straight 16" blade with full-length central fuller and engraved with florals and female figure. Recurved gilt brass quillions and pillow-form pommel. One-piece ivory grip of tapered octagonal section. Blade with gray metal and light pitting. Hilt with 50-60% gilt finish. Exc. cond. $690

Dirk, Officer, Naval, France, Navy, First Empire (1804–15). Narrow, stepped 7½" blade of diamond section with conventional blued and gilt panel. Gilt bronze mounted hilt with anchor on quillion block and acorn finials. Turned ivory grip. No scabbard. Blade with patches of light pitting and with traces of blued and gilt decoration remaining. Hilt mounts with 50–60% gilt finish. Grip with three age cracks. Good cond. $1265

Knife, Combat, Belgium, Army, WWI. Stiletto blade with blackened oval guard and shaped wooden grip with "76" designation. Scabbard with 90% black painted finish remaining and metal belt hook. Above avg. cond. $168

Knife, Combat, Belgium, Army, WWII. Narrow stiletto blade, hilt with shaped wood grip, oval crossguard and grip with "76" designation. Includes scabbard. Above avg. cond. $225

Knife, Fighting, Fairbairn-Sykes, England, Army, SAS, WWII, Wilkinson. Blued stiletto with double sided engraving, obverse with SAS winged dagger insignia "22nd Special Air Service Regiment," reverse with airplane and descending paratrooper. Elliptical crossguard, gray metal grip, leather scabbard with leg and top elastic strap and brass drag. Above avg. cond. $165

Knife, Fighting, Fairbairn-Sykes, England, Army, WWII, Wilkinson. Blade and ribbed grip with nickeled finish. Brown leather scabbard having leg and elastic grip strap and brass drag. Avg. cond. $150

Knife, Fighting, Fairbairn-Sykes, Second Model, England, Army, WWII, Wilkinson. Large domed top nut, cast ribbed brass grip and crossguard marked "England." With brown leather scabbard. Above avg. cond. $125

Knife, Fighting, Fairbairn-Sykes, England, Army, WWII, Wilkinson. Blade has 60% blued finish, heavy tip wear and finished gray metal ribbed grip. Brown leather scabbard and blued brass drag. Avg. cond. $125

Knife, Combat, Austria, Army, WWI. 8" modified dagger style blade with long false edge. Marked "KH" on ricasso. Steel diamond-shaped guard loose. Two-part wood grip held by three rivets. With metal scabbard. Avg. cond. $58

Knife, Combat, Austria, Army, WWI. 8" steel blade with faint "R" on ricasso. Green painted steel scabbard with two metal loops and web belt loop. Avg. cond. $87

Knife, Belt, Spain, 1853, Toledo. 13" in length, stiletto blade, iron hilt with cruciform crossguard and iron scabbard. Above avg. cond. $200

Swords—U.S.

Saber, Cavalry, Model 1912 "Patton," USA, Army, 1917, Springfield Arsenal. Bright steel DE fullered blade. Hmkd "Springfield Arsenal (emblem)/1917" on obverse and "US/32694" on reverse of ricasso. Deep curved guard and knuckle basket. Checkered composition grip, backstrap and thumb rest. Leather cord and knot. Steel scabbard with tan canvas cover. Exc. cond. $265

Saber, Cavalry, Model 1912 "Patton," USA, Army, 1913, Springfield Arsenal. Steel DE fullered blade. Hmkd "Springfield Arsenal (emblem)/1913" on obverse and "US/4134" on reverse of ricasso. Cutlass-style knuckle basket. Checkered composition grip, backstrap and thumb rest. Steel scabbard with canvas cover. Above avg. cond. $150

Cavalry Saber, Model 1912 Patton

Saber, Cavalry, Officer's, Model 1872, USA, Army, c1870s, Shannon, Miller and Crane, NY. Bright curved blade with engraved pattern on first third. Hmkd "Shannon, Miller & Crane of NY." Brass hilt with oval guard and eagle on arrows on side toward pommel. Phrygian helmet pommel. Wood grip, fishskin wrapped and wire bound. Steel scabbard with brass throat, drag and suspension rings. Above avg. cond. $450

Saber, Cavalry, USA, Army, Confederate, Civil War Era, C. Hammon. Brass three-branch hilt shows dark patina with most of the leather worn off, however wire remains. Blade measures 1¼" x 36" long with two fullers and a couple of areas of pitting near the tip. Avg. cond. $715

Saber, Heavy Cavalry (Dragoon), EM, Model 1840, USA, Army, Cavalry, Civil War. Curved steel blade. Unmarked. Brass hilt. Steel scabbard. Above avg. cond. $201

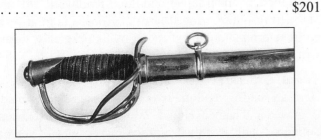

Cavalry Saber, Model 1840 Dragoon

Saber, Heavy Cavalry (Dragoon), Model 1840, USA, Army, Cavalry, Civil War. Nickel-plated steel blade with "US" on obv. Hmkd on reverse at ricasso. Brass hilt with oval guard, three-strand knuckle basket and bow, Phrygian helmet pommel and wood grip with leather and wire wrap. Nickel-plated steel scabbard with drag and two ring bands. Above avg. cond. $260

Saber, Heavy Cavalry (Dragoon), Model 1840, USA, Army, Cavalry, 1850, Ames. Heavy blade. Ames maker marked and dated 1850. Brass hilt with leather-wrapped grip. Heavy scabbard. Above avg. cond. $345

Saber, Heavy Cavalry (Dragoon), Model 1840, USA, Army, Cavalry, Civil War. Curved blade. Hmkd on ricasso with bow/arrow and initials "B. M." Brass guard and knuckle basket. Wood grip. Avg. cond. $275

Saber, Light Cavalry, Model 1860, USA, Army, Cavalry, 1864, Ames. Dark blade is 1864 dated and Ames marked. Above avg. cond. $300

Saber, Light Cavalry, Model 1860, USA, Army, Cavalry, Civil War, Francis/Saintietienne, France. French-made contract version. Bright curved blade. Hmkd "Manufacture Francis/Saintietienne." All brass hilt with two-strand knuckle guard and Phrygian helmet pommel. Wood grip is wire wound. Avg. cond. $289

Saber, Light Cavalry, Model 1860, USA, Army, 1865, ADK. Curved blade. "US/ADK/1865" on ricasso. Oval brass guard with three-strand basket and bow. Wood grip, leather wrapped and wire wound. Below avg. cond. $145

Saber, Light Cavalry, Model 1860, USA, Army, 1861, Ames. Curved steel blade. Hmkd "Ames Co, Chickapee, Mass" and "US/J T/1861" on ricasso. Polished brass hilt. Leather-covered and wire-wrapped contoured wood grip. Polished steel scabbard with two ring bands. Exc. cond. $125

Saber, Cavalry, Model 1860, USA, Army, 1863, Ames Mfg. Blade has faint Ames signature with "US" and "1863" stamps. Brass three-branch hilt with leather-covered handle and wire missing. Scabbard is pitted. Avg. cond. $523

Cavalry Saber, Model 1860 EM Light Cavalry

Sword, General and Field Officer, M1850, USA, Army, 1850, Tiffany & Co., NY. Imported and signed by Tiffany and so etched at the ricasso. 31" single edged blade with etched panels showing scrolls, military trophies, an eagle and U.S. blade maker "P.D.L." stamped in oval cartouche on obverse ricasso. Cast-brass basket guard with floral decoration and "U.S.," fishskin grip with twisted brass wire wrap. Steel scabbard with brass mounts. Exc. cond. $950

Sword, Foot Officer, Model 1850, USA, Army, Civil War. Curved etched blade. Hmkd at ricasso. Brass hilt with wood grip wrapped in fishskin and gilt brass wire. Part of guard is open pattern with floral design. Pommel is of Phrygian helmet design. Above avg. cond. $200

Saber, Light Cavalry, Model 1860, USA, Army, 1860, Mansfield & Lamb, Forestdale, RI. Manufactured on contract to U.S. government. Cast-brass three-branch guard with leather and twisted wire wrapped grip. 34½" single edged curved blade and steel scabbard. Exc. cond. $600

Sword, Musician, M1840, USA, Army, 1863, Roby. Straight fullered blade. Ricasso stamped with "U.S.," inspector's initials, and 1863 date. Brass hilt, wire-wrapped grip and ball pommel. No scabbard. Avg. cond. $145

Cutlass, Naval, USA, Navy, 1860, Ames Mfg Co, Chicopee, MA. Cast-brass hilt with large sheet-brass cup guard, leather grip and 26" slightly curved single edged blade. Hmkd and dated. No scabbard. Above avg. cond. $375

Sword, Presentation, Officer, Naval, USA, Navy, 1851, Wm. Read & Sons, Boston, MA. 29½" single edged blade with etched panels having military trophies, scrolls, and "U.S.N." and "G. Mumford" on reverse. Cast-brass guard with acorn motif and decorated pommel and fishskin grip with twisted brass wire wrap. With leather scabbard with brass mounts. Above avg. cond. $200

Sword, Naval Officer, Model 1852, USA, Navy, Civil War. 31½" polished blade with etched embellishments. Marked on ricasso "made USA." Brass guard with floral knuckle basket labeled "USN" on face. Knuckle guard extends to pommel with dolphin's head. Pommel is of

Naval Sword, Model 1852 Officer

Phrygian helmet style and has 13 stars around eagle. Quillon is in dolphin's head form. Grip is wire wound white fishskin over wood. Black leather scabbard has brass throat and tip. Suspension rings are done in knotted hawser design and tip drag is in dolphin design. Exc. cond. $225

Sword, Naval Officer, Model 1852, USA, Navy, Civil War, Wade and Co. Polished engraved blade. Hmkd "Wade & Co." on ricasso. Oval guard with dolphins head quillon and "USN" on floral pattern of guard. Knuckle bow with dolphin design and pommel. Wood grip is fishskin-wrapped and wire bound. Metal scabbard with leather cover. Ring bands of woven rope design. Avg. cond. $164

Sword, NCO, Model 1840, USA, Army, 1861, Ames. Straight fullered blade. Ricasso stamped with "US," inspector's initials, and 1861 date. Brass hilt, wire grip, double guard and ball pommel. No scabbard. Above avg. cond. $235

Sword, NCO, Model 1840, USA, Army, 1862, Emerson and Silver. Straight fullered blade, ricasso dated 1862, brass hilt with double guard, knuckle bow with inspector's initials, and ball pommel. No scabbard. Avg. cond. $275

Sword, NCO, Model 1840, USA, Army, Civil War. Straight blade. Hmkd on ricasso. Brass hilt with fixed langets on guard, single strand bow and ball pommel. Grip is ribbed. Steel scabbard. Avg. cond. $215

Sword, Officer, Cavalry, Model 1872, USA, Army, c1870s, Springfield Armory. Curved fullered blade. Ricasso stamped with "SPRINGFIELD ARMORY, SPRINGFIELD, MASS. USA." Double side engraved. Obverse with American eagle, ribboned "E PLURIBUS UNUM" inscription, floral scrollwork, and military trophies. Cast hilt in American eagle, stars and starburst motif. Fishskin-covered grip. Nickeled scabbard with brass fittings. Above avg. cond. $385

Sword, Officer, Model 1902, USA, Army, c1910, Springfield Armory. Hmkd on ricasso "SPRINGFIELD ARMORY." Double sided engraved blade, obverse with American eagle, "E PLURIBUS UNUM" ribboned inscription, national shield, and floral scrollwork. Hilt with nickeled furniture, banded ferrule, grooved horn grip and quillion terminating in ball finial. With nickeled scabbard. Avg. cond. $30

Sword, Officer, Model 1902, USA, Army, c1910, WKC. German-made version with Damascus steel blade. Engraved and named. Hmkd "Weyersburg & Kirschbaum, Solingen." Hilt is dulled nickel finished metal. Notched black finished wood grip. Polished steel scabbard with two ring bands and drag. Exc. cond. $450

Sword, Officer, Model 1902, USA, Army, c1910. Engraved bright blade. Three-strand knuckle basket and back strap blending into pommel. Ferrule secures notched wood grip. Scabbard with grip and two ring bands. Avg. cond. $70

Sword, Officer, Model 1902, USA, Army, cWWI, Ames. Nickel-plated engraved blade. Hmkd "The Ames Co." on ricasso. Alloy three-strand basket knuckle guard with slot for knot. Formed grip with notches under back strap. Hooked quillon. Metal scabbard with two ring bands and drag. Avg. cond. $95

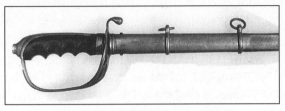

Army Sword, Model 1902 Officer

Sword, Foot Officer, Model 1850, USA, Army, Civil War Era, Ames Mfg. 30¼"-long blade is etched and engraved with eagle, "US" and stand of flags. Brass hilt is pierced with cast scrollwork and some gilding. Sharkskin grip is worn and missing wire. Leather scabbard with brass bands also marked Ames Mfg. and is broken just above the drag. Above avg. cond. $605

Swords—Germany

Sword, Artillery, NCO, Imperial Germany, Army, WWI, WK&C. 35" curved nickel blade by "WK&C" with heads. Engraved "Unteroffizier Dierkmann" with rose motif, horsehead and military equipment. Reverse has rose motif with five ovals of military equipment. Gold finish to brass fittings with crossed cannons to rectangular langet. P-guard with Knight head and faces. Lion hilt with two paws behind. Wire wrapped black grip. Black finished scabbard. Avg. cond. $400

Sword, Artillery, Officer, Imperial Germany, Army, WWI. 31½" curved heavy steel blade with traces of floral engraving under dark patina. Dark brass fittings with crossed cannons to langet, military equipment to P-guard and lion-head hilt with two paws behind. Sharkskin grip. Steel scabbard with two brass hanger rings. Below avg. cond. $148

Sword, Artillery, Officer, Bavarian, Imperial Germany, Army, WWI. 32½" curved nickel blade with different engraved "In Treue Fest!" panels having blued backings. Scroll has oak and laurel leaves to each side and extra crowned shield with five-panel Bavarian details to obverse. Nickel hilt fittings and black celluloid-covered grip. Black scabbard. Avg. cond. $106

Sword, Combat, Prussian, Imperial Germany, Army, WWI, WK&C. 29½" heavy curved steel blade by "Weyersburg etc." and spine Crown W, "05" and proof. Steel P-guard, stamped "8.A.F.1.64." Blued scabbard with matching unit. Avg. cond. $193

Sword, M1889, Prussian, Imperial Germany, Army, Cavalry, WWI, Weyersberg & Co., Solingen. Straight blade, polished steel. Hmkd "Weyersberg & Co./Solingen." Steel basket with eagle crest and bow back to pommel. Notched, ribbed, contoured Bakelite grip. Avg. cond. $80

Sword, NCO, Germany, Army, WWII, Anton Wingen Jr. 33½" nickel blade with maker and trademark. Nickel fittings. Wire wrapped black celluloid grip. Black painted scabbard. Avg. cond. $96

Sword, NCO, Germany, Army, WWII, G. Weyersberg. 29½" nickel blade with maker. Nickel fittings. Wire wrapped black grip. Black scabbard. Avg. cond. . . . $70

Sword, NCO, Eickhorn #40, Germany, Army, WWII, Carl Eickhorn. 32" bright nickel blade with title maker and squirrel logo. Gold-finished alum fittings. Brass wire wrap on black grip. Black scabbard. Avg. cond. $130

Sword, Officer, Alcoso Model 119, Lion Head, Germany, Army, WWII, Alcoso ACS. 32" nickel blade by "Alcoso ACS" with scales. Gold-finish brass P-guard with oak leaves, Party eagle langet/crossguard and ruby eyes on head. Dark silver wrap to black grip. Black scabbard. Above avg. cond. $292

Sword, Officer, Double Engraved, Bavarian, Imperial Germany, Army, Arty, WWI, CK Co. 32½" very curved nickel blade by "C K Co" with crossed swords and crown trademark. "In Treue Fest," flowers, shield and goddess. Nickel D-guard and fittings. Celluloid grip. Nickel scabbard. Avg. cond. $125

Sword, Officer, Double Engraved, Bavarian, Imperial Germany, Army, Cuirassier, WWI, WK&C. 33" straight nickel, double-fullered blade, with knight's head trademark. Same "In Treue Fest" scroll and floral design to each side. Nickel hilt fittings. Wire wrapped sharkskin grip. Blued scabbard. Avg. cond. $145

Sword, Officer, Double Engraved, Bavarian, Imperial Germany, Army, Inf, WWI, Carl Eickhorn. About 30½" nickel blade by "C.E." with two squirrels. Engraved panel "In Treue Fest" with oak tree and lion/shield on both sides. Black painted steel fittings with B-guard and wire wrapped black grip. Black scabbard. Above avg. cond. $160

Sword, Officer, Double Engraved, Bavarian, Imperial Germany, Army, Inf, WWI, Carl Eickhorn. 30¾" curved nickel blade by "C.E." with squirrel logo. Engraved "In Treue Fest" scroll and lion shield with oak trees on both sides. Nickel B-guard and fittings. Wire wrapped black grip. Black scabbard. Avg. cond. $125

Sword, Officer, Double Engraved, Naval, Imperial Germany, Navy, WWI. 29" nickel blade with crowned anchor having eagle, military equipment and sails. Reverse has fouled anchor, galleon and crossed cannons. Gold-finished steel fittings, folding crowned anchor guard with oak leaves, D-guard with oak leaves and lion head with green-red eyes. Ivory grip has dark wire wrap. Black leather scabbard has three hammered steel fittings with gold finish. Dark silver knot with red and black flecks. Avg. cond. $789

Sword, Officer, Double Engraved, Wurttemberg, Imperial Germany, Army, WWI, WK&C. 30½" steel blade with different military equipment to each side. Maker "WK&C" with heads. Gold finish on brass fittings, military equipment on P-guard, short lion head and langet has affixed silver star with enamel "Furchtlos und Trew." Steel scabbard. Below avg. cond. $385

Sword, Officer, Double Engraved, Prussian, Imperial Germany, Army, Cuirassier, WWI, Gebr. Baus & Cie Fabrikanten in Solingen. 32½" curved steel blade, faint floral motif and spine "Gebr. Baus & Cie Fabrikanten in Solingen." Dark brass three-branch guard. Bullion wrap black leather grip. Avg. cond. $98

Sword, Officer, Dove Head, Germany, Army, WWII, "Rich.a.Herder." 32½" nickel blade with maker and trademark. Gold finish to hilt fittings leaving copper shade. Party eagle on langet and crossguard. Oak leaves on back strap and P-guard. Wire wrap on black grip. Black painted scabbard. With knot. Avg. cond. $190

Sword, Officer, Eickhorn Model 1693, Wrangel, Dove Head, Germany, Army, WWII, Carl Eickhorn. 29½" bright nickel blade with title maker and squirrel sword. Bright gold-finished alum/alloy fittings with Party eagle langet crossguard. Black grip with wire wrap. Black scabbard. Avg. cond. $190

Sword, Officer, Eickhorn Model 1695, Leopard Head, Germany, Army, WWII. 33½" bright nickel blade with maker squirrel sword. Gold-finished alum fittings with crossguard stamped "Ges.Gesch." Leopard head with ruby eyes, oak leaves to P-guard, Party eagle langet and crossguard. Alum wire on black grip. Black scabbard. Above avg. cond. $289

Sword, Officer, Eickhorn Model 1714, Freiherr Von Stein, Dove Head, Germany, Army, WWII, Carl Eickhorn. 34" curved nickel blade with trademark and maker. Dark copper finish to all alum/alloy fittings with oak

leaves and stylized eagle langet. Black grip with wire wrap. Black scabbard. Avg. cond. $210

Sword, Officer, Eickhorn Model 1765, Prinz Eugen, Dove Head, Germany, Army, WWII, Carl Eickhorn. 32" nickel blade with title maker. Gold finish fittings. Party eagle to langet and crossguard. Back langet jeweler engraved "KHG." Stylized eagle to pommel. Alum wrap on black grip. Black scabbard. Above avg. cond. . . $430

Sword, Officer, Eickhorn Model 40, Dove Head, Germany, Army, WWII. About 32" bright nickel blade with squirrel sword and maker. Bright gold finish to brass fittings. Alum wrap on black grip. Black scabbard. Avg. cond. $158

Sword, Officer, Krebs 3, Dove Head, Germany, Army, WWII, Krebs. 33" unmarked blade. Party eagle on langet and crossguard. Oak leaves on P-guard that is bent at top and more leaves on back strap. Wire wrapped black celluloid grips. Black painted scabbard. Avg. cond. $131

Sword, Officer, Lion Head, Germany, Army, WWII, Carl Eickhorn. Gilted alum lion-head fittings with stylized eagle shield on crossguard. Wire wrapped black celluloid grip. Hmkd "Ges Gesch." Black painted scabbard. Above avg. cond. $205

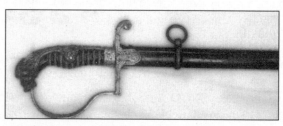

German Army Officer Lionhead Pattern Sword

Sword, Officer, M1889, Prussian, Imperial Germany, Army, WWI, O. Pack. 29" double-fullered steel blade by "O.Pack" with trademark man. Brass fittings with traces of gold finish and eagle on folding guard. Wire wrapped sharkskin grip with brass WII cipher. Black scabbard. Avg. cond. $229

Sword, Officer, M1889, Prussian, Imperial Germany, Army, WWI, WK&C. 30½" double-fullered steel blade by "WK&C" with heads. Brass hilt fittings with folding eagle guard. Wire wrapped sharkskin grip with brass crown-cipher. Nickel scabbard with two hanger rings. Avg. cond. $158

Swords—Other

Cutlass, Naval, Model 1833, France, Navy, c1840. Slightly curved 26" blade. Black painted hilt of standard pattern. Black leather scabbard with brass mounts. Blade with light spotting. Hilt with areas of pitting and repainted black finish. Scabbard scuffed. Good cond. $489

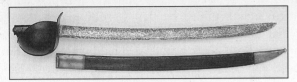

Cutlass, Naval, Model 1833

Saber, Hussar, Model 1811, Prussia, Army, c1820. Unmarked 34" blade with broad, shallow fuller. Brass stirrup hilt. Leather-wrapped grip. Brass-mounted black leather scabbard. Blade shows some light pitting. Above avg. cond. $747

Saber, Officer, Light Cavalry, France, Army, 1811, Chatellerault Armory. Curved 33½" blade with worn spine markings for the Chatellerault Armory and dated "1811." Simple brass D-form hilt with lion mask pommel. No scabbard. Blade with areas of pitting, nicks to blade and 5½" at the tip has been reattached. Hilt with minor blemishes. Above avg. cond. $345

Saber, Light Cavalry, Model An XI (1803), France, Army, 1813, Klingenthal. Curved 34½" blade marked on spine "Mfture Impale du Klingenthal Mars 1813." Bass three-bar hilt of standard pattern. Stamped on knucklebow "Versailles." Iron scabbard. Blade showing light spotting and minor pitting overall. Hilt with dark patina. Grip missing the wire and most of the leather wrapping. Scabbard showing light scratches and pitting. Avg. cond. ... $920

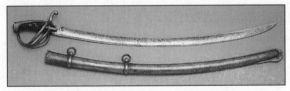

Saber, Light Cavalry, Model ANXI

Saber, Sapeur, France, Army, Infantry, 1840, Chatellerault Armory. Curved 26½" blade with broad shallow fuller and flat spine. Marked "Manufte Role de Chatellerault 9-1840." Bronze rooster-head hilt retaining leather spacer. Blade lightly pitted overall. Some restoration. Above avg. cond. $863

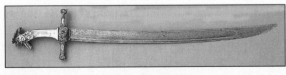

Saber, Sapeur's

Sword, General, Italy, Army, WWII, Milan. Straight double sided engraved blade, ricasso marked to Milanese manufacturer, obverse presents military trophies, floral scrollwork, and Italian heraldic crest rendered against frosted ground, reverse with Italian eagle, military trophies, and floral scrollwork against floral back strap with cross-hatched base pattern. Two-ring scabbard in asymmetrical drag, complete with gold bullion sword knot and complete hanger having two gold bullion straps, fire gilded rail buckles and swivel spring clips, and hanger chain with hook. Above avg. cond. $646

Sword, General, Italy, Air Force, WWII. Straight fullered blade, double sided engraving of military trophies and floral scrollwork, brass hilt with guard cast in feathered detail, eagle-head pommel with crown finial, wire wrapped wood grip with black lacquered finish and back strap with detailed feathering. With black leather scabbard with brass furniture having throat with Air Force insignia and floral scrollwork throughout. Above avg. cond. $262

Sword, Field Marshal, England, Army, 1890. Curved blade, brass furniture, cruciform crossguard with center wreath cast in sword and baton motif, scalloped floral side ornamentation, crossguard terminates in stepped oval finials and hilt with ivory grips having two floral bosses. With brass scabbard with scabbard ring mounts in the form of stylized crosses. Above avg. cond. $563

Sword, Officer, 1804 Pattern, England, Army, c1810. Double edged, tapered hollow ground spadroon blade, etched with spray of foliage and crowned double monogram of George III. Inscribed "Warrented Never To Fail 1790" stirrup hilt, with wooden scabbard covered with black leather with signed locket. Exc. cond. $787

Sword, Infantry Officer Pattern, England, Army, 1853, Hill Bros, Old Bond St., London. 32½" straight single edged blade with wide primary fuller, cast-brass basket hilt with Victorian cipher within oval cartouche, bird's-head pommel and back strap and fishskin grip wrap with twisted brass wire. With steel scabbard. Above avg. cond. $125

Dha, Burma, 1890s. 36"-long, double sided engraved blade having ornamentation comprised of nine panels depicting Burmese subjects, patriotic inscriptions and floral scrollwork rendered in silvered inlay. Silver furniture including hilt and matching scabbard rendered in intricate floral hand-wrought motifs. Above avg. cond. $300

Sword, EM, Cavalry, Model 71/29, Italy, Army, c1930s, Alex, Coppel Soligen, Germany. German manufacturer, ricasso marked to the Alex, Coppel firm of Soligen. Pierced half-basket guard with wood grip, cross-hatched pommel back strap and scabbard with one ring. Above avg. cond. $145

Cutlass, Naval, France, Navy, c1845. 26" single edged wide curved blade with an engraved anchor on each side. Mounted in heavy iron D-guard hilt with iron cup guard and iron grip. Back of blade dated 1845. Includes leather scabbard with brass mounts. Exc. cond. $250

Sword, Heavy Cavalry, France, Army, c1810. 36" straight single edged blade, cast-brass four-branch basket hilt with leather twisted brass wire grip wrap and steel scabbard with two ring mounts. Good cond. $300

Mameluk, France, Army, 1820. Curved unfullered blade with double sided engraving, iron hilt mounted by ivory grips. Complete with chain guard and hiltplate with engraving "A. d. C." Two-ring iron scabbard with throat having matching engraving. Above avg. cond. $650

Saber, Heavy Cavalry, France, Army, Cavalry, c1814. Straight blade with two fullers, back dated 1814, hilt with brass guard and wire wrapped grip. Includes iron two-ring scabbard. Above avg. cond. $518

Saber, Light Dragoon, 1788 Pattern, England, Army, c1800. Unmarked 31" blade with a broad, shallow fuller. Brass stirrup hilt. Leather-wrapped grip. Black leather scabbard with brass mounts. Blade shows some pitting and light spotting. Above avg. cond. $374

Katana, Japan, 19th Century. 34¼" overall blade length, deep cross-hatched engraved ornamentation over falling rain pattern, blade mounted in scabbard and grip of carved wood resembling natural tree bark. Above avg. cond. $450

Sword, Japanese, Japan, 19th Century. 38" overall length, carved ivory furnitures including hilt and scabbard. Hilt with massive ivory tsuba having dragon motif, grip with armored Samurai, phoenix birds, and terminating in dragon pommel. Samurai vignettes on scabbard and ring mounts with Phoenix bird motifs. Above avg. cond. $5776

Sword, Staff Officer, Model An XII (1804), France, Army, First Empire (1804–1815). Narrow 32" blade with 15" double fullers and with worn inscription for "Coulaux Freres." Gilt bronze hilt comprising shaped boatshell, quillion block with classical panoply and helmet-form pommel. Wire wrapped grip. Brass-mounted leather scabbard. Blade cleaned and showing some minor pitting. Hilt with 60–70% gilt finish. Scabbard broken above the chape. Good cond. $1150

Sword, Cuirassier, Model An XIII (1805), France, Army, 1812, Klingenthal. Straight 38" double fullered blade marked on spine "Manufre Imp du Klingenthal - 1812." Hilt of standard pattern. With iron scabbard. Smooth, clean gray metal showing some minor spotting. Grip has minor scuffs to leather. Good cond. $1955

Sword, Officer, 1803 Pattern, England, Army, Napole-

onic War Era. 28" curved blade, obverse engraved with floral motif, classical figures and crowned pierced symmetrical guard, gilded banded ferrule, gilded lion-head pommel and back strap, fishskin grip and gilded wire wrapping. With black leather scabbard with gilded throat, middle band, and asymmetrical drag, engraved banded decoration, complete with suspension rings. Good cond. $225

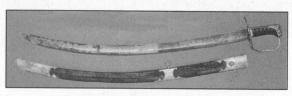

Sword, Officer's, 1803 Pattern

Sword, Officer, Naval, France, Navy, First Empire (1804–15). Narrow 31" blade engraved with conventional florals. Silver-plated copper hilt comprising oval shell pierced with grapevines, quillion block with anchor, lion head and acanthus quillions, knuckle bow with panel of wheat and ovoid pommel with panels of grapevines and wheat. Silver wire wrapped grip. Black leather scabbard with silver-plated mounts. Blade with patches of light pitting and traces of gilt decoration. Grip and scabbard mounts with 98% silver-plated finish remaining. Scabbard restored. Above avg. cond. $1495

Sword, Officer, Austria, Army, WWI. 25" nickel blade. Gold-finished brass D-guard with pierced crowned double headed eagle and floral design. Wire wrapped sharkskin grip. Black leather scabbard with three ornate brass fittings, throat has crowned FA cipher. Above avg. cond. $187

Sword, Officer, Double Engraved, Austria, Army, WWI, WK&C. 29" nickel blade by "Weyersberg etc." and distributor. Crown profile over crowned "FA" cipher and floral motif. Reverse has military equipment, etc. Gold-finished brass D-guard with pierced crowned double headed eagle and floral design. Wire wrapped sharkskin grip. Black leather scabbard with three ornate brass fittings, throat has crowned FA cipher. Avg. cond. $277

Saber, Light Cavalry, Austria, Army, c1820. The 32" clip-point, pipe-back blade is marked on the spine "Buchner." Gilt brass stirrup hilt with one-piece brass grip. Black leather scabbard with pierced brass mounts. Blade shows cleaning and light pitting. Above avg. cond. $805

Sword, Officer, Romania, Air Force, WWII. 39" sword with 32" blade, cast-brass hilt with eagle-head pommel and back strap, large basket knuckle bow with eagle feather motif cast over surface, patent leather grip with triple-strand brass wire wrap, single edged straight blade with etched panel over half surface, etched panel illustration of Romania Crest, square knot, military trophies, floral panels and an airplane. Includes leather scabbard with brass mounts. Above avg. cond. $350

Sword, Infantry, Poland, Army, WWI, J. Splichal-Pribram. Double edged 25½" blade with center rib, cast-brass hilt with single-branch knuckle bow and down-turned crossguard terminating in foliated ball finials, circular counterguard with double headed eagle crest cast center, etched panel on obverse reads "J. Splichal-Pribram" and on reverse "Gluck auf," horn with twisted brass wire wrap grip, leather with brass top mount and hook for frog and brass scabbard. Above avg. cond. $250

Shashka, Imperial Russia, Army, 1846. Mildly curved blade, obverse with light geometric engraving, hilt with horn grips carved in channeled ornamentation, pommel of silver with niello floral scrollwork and raised border with engrailed ornamentation, complete with silversmith's proofmark and pommel base presenting "84" designation. No scabbard. Above avg. cond. $1125

Sword, Short, Artillery, South America, Army, c1900, European manufacture. Fullered blade, hilt with crossguard of recurved finials, wood grip and iron pommel. With black leather scabbard. Above avg. cond. $51

Saber, Light Cavalry, Model 1796, England, Army, c1810. Curved 33" spear-point blade marked on the spine "Wooley." Iron stirrup hilt of standard pattern. Leather-wrapped grip. With iron scabbard. Some light pitting present and a few nicks. Avg. cond. $403

Sword, Officer, Spain, Army, Spanish American War Era, P.D.L. Clipped-point blade, fair polish, light pitting, ricasso with "P.D.L." and hilt with ribbed guard. Good cond. $65

Fascine Hook, Vietnam, Viet Cong, Vietnam War Era. Single edged blade, black finish, bamboo handle with five bronze ferrules. Above avg. cond. $48

Weapon Accessories—U.S.

Waist Belt and Plate, Infantry Officer, USA, Army, 1851. Sewn Russian leather waistbelt with exterior covered in wide ban of ribbed gilt cloth with three light blue stripes, U.S. Model 1851 pattern saber beltplate having eagle and wreath cast on face and retaining bar and wide tongue on reverse, "Made In U.S.A." cast into back of plate. Above avg. cond. $145

Waist Belt and Plate, Maryland, USA, Army, Civil War. Rectangular Maryland saber beltplate with narrow tongue,

on reverse having state seal within oval cartouche. .58-cal triangular socket bayonet mounted on belt, leather Civil War-period scabbard and Model 1875 McKeever cartridge box. Above avg. cond. $1750

Cover, Scabbard, M1910, USA, Army, 1918, Brauer Brothers. Dated 1918. Unissued. Exc. cond. $13

Belt, Sword, USA, Navy, WWII. Black leather body with both straps, brass fittings and eagle/anchor buckle. Stamped size 32. Avg. cond. $10

Belt, Sword, USA, Navy, WWII. Black leather body with both straps, brass fittings and eagle/anchor buckle. Marked maker "Hilborn-etc." and size 34. Avg. cond. $38

Belt, Sword, Dress, USA, USMC, c1960s. Leather belt with patent finish and brass buckle. Hanger has brass fittings and black corfam material for straps. Above avg. cond. $37

Hanger, Sword, USA, Army, c1920s. For black Sam Brown belt. Marked "Service Full Grain Bridle Leather" and inked to a 1st Lieut. Black leather cross-strap, gold-finished brass fittings, nickel hanger. Avg. cond. $22

Knot, Sword, USA, Army, Civil War Era. Leather. Complete with strap. Avg. cond. $40

Knot, Sword, USA, Army, WWI. For M1912 sword. Russet leather knot with fringe at one end and loop at other. Avg. cond. $30

Knot, Sword, USA, Navy, c1900. Gold brocade cord with woven knot and gold wiring. Avg. cond. $27

Knot, Sword, USA, Navy, WWI. Gold wire and brocade cord and knot. Avg. cond. $23

Knot, Sword, USA, USMC, WWI. Ornate bullion wire body. Above avg. cond. $100

Weapon Accessories—Germany

Frog, Bayonet, Germany, Army, WWII. Brown leather. Unissued with German Army eagle proofmark, grip strap. Exc. cond. $40

Belt Loop and D-ring, Germany, Army, WWII. Brown leather loop will fit 1¾"-wide belt. Nickel D-ring and rivet for release of loop. Leather shows moisture darkening. Avg. cond. $20

Belt, Sword, Under-the-Tunic, Germany, Army, WWII. Blue web body with brown leather loops, brass D-rings and roller buckle strap. About size 95. Above avg. cond. $50

Belt, Sword, Under-the-Tunic, Germany, Army, WWII. Blue web body with brown leather loops, nickel D-rings and roller buckle strap. About size 85. Above avg. cond. $45

Belt, Sword, Under-the-Tunic, Germany, Army, WWII. Purple web body with brown leather fittings and loops. Two D-rings. About size 90. Avg. cond. $20

Belt, Sword, Under-the-Tunic, Germany, Army, WWII. Blue web body. Brown leather fittings with sewn D-ring and movable D-ring. Avg. cond. $20

Dagger Knot, Naval, Imperial Germany, Navy, WWI. Silver cord with flecks, slide and stem also have flecks. Silver cap and ball with tri-color bullion on inset. Exc. cond. $120

Frog, 98k Bayonet, Germany, Army, 1940, Goch. Black leather. Maker "Goch 1940." Four steel rivets. Exc. cond. $29

Frog, 98k Bayonet, Germany, Army, WWII. Black leather, four rivets and faint maker marks. Above avg. cond. $27

Frog, 98k Bayonet, Germany, Army, 1942, Wittkop & Co. BieleFeld. Black leather with four steel rivets. Maker marked "Wittkop & Co BieleFeld 1942." Avg. cond. $25

Frog, 98k Bayonet, Germany, Army, 1937. Black leather with two broken alum rivets. Faint 1937 maker. Avg. cond. $20

Frog, 98k Bayonet, Germany, Luftwaffe, 1937, Gebruder Klinge, Dresden. Four alum rivets and sewn construction. Stamped "Gebruder Klinge Dresden 1937 LBA(S)." Exc. cond. $91

Frog, Bayonet, Germany, Army, WWII. Tropical style olive web body with straps. Inked maker. Above avg. cond. $76

Frog, Bayonet, Germany, Army, 1939. Brown leather with black polished front. Front alum rivets. Faint 1939 maker. Avg. cond. $20

Frog, Bayonet, Germany, Waffen SS, WWII. For 98k bayonet. Late-war SS style. Narrow black body with handle straps and four rivets. Avg. cond. $66

Frog, Bayonet, Imperial Germany, Army, WWI. M98/05-style black leather body. Four rivets of copper and brass. Avg. cond. $25

Frog, Bayonet, Imperial Germany, Army, WWI. 7½"-tall black leather body with belt loop and six rivets. Open hole for bayonet scabbard stud with buckle closure loose from loop. Avg. cond. $20

Frog, Dress, Bayonet, Germany, Army, WWII. Late war. Black imitation pigskin design. Avg. cond. $30

Hanger, 2nd Model Dagger, Deluxe Pattern, Germany, Luftwaffe, WWII. Facings on gray velvet straps. Oak leaves on all gray fittings with faint gold wash. Above avg. cond. $65

Hanger, 2nd Model Dagger, Deluxe Pattern, Germany, Luftwaffe, WWII. Brocade straps and velvet backings. Oak leaves on gray buckles, slides, top loop and clips. Avg. cond. $34

Hanger, 2nd Model Dagger, Deluxe Pattern, Germany, Luftwaffe, WWII. Facings on gray velvet straps. Oak leaves on all gray fittings. Avg. cond. $34

Hanger, Dagger, Germany, Army, WWII. Alum brocade on brown velvet. Alum buckles and slides with oak leaves. Silver painted gray pebbled clips and alum loop. Early. Above avg. cond. $55

Hanger, Dagger, Germany, Army, WWII. Oak leaves on buckles and slides. Gray pebbled clips. Alum brocade facings on gray twill cloth straps. Above avg. cond. $59

Hanger, Dagger, Germany, Army, WWII. Alum brocade facing on green velvet straps. Silver paint on buckles, slides and clips of gray metal with oak leaves. Avg. cond. $75

Hanger, Dagger, Germany, Army, WWII. Alum brocade facings on green velvet straps. Oak leaves on alum buckles and slides. Pebbled gray clips and nickel top loop. Avg. cond. $45

Hanger, Dagger, Germany, Army, WWII. Oak leaves to alum buckles and slides. Gray pebbled clips. Alum brocade facing on green velvet straps. Avg. cond. $40

Hanger, Dagger, Germany, SS, WWII. For M1933 dagger. Black leather strap. Gray buckle and clip. Maker "RZM M5/71 OLC." Avg. cond. $34

Hanger, Dagger, Germany, SS, WWII. For M1933 dagger. Black leather body, loop and roller buckle strap. Nickel clip. Maker marked "DRGMM5/8cRZM A." Avg. cond. $202

Hanger, Dagger, Deluxe Pattern, Germany, Army, WWII. Bright alum brocade facings on green velvet straps. Oak leaves on all frosted silver fittings. Exc. cond. $115

Hanger, Dagger, Deluxe Pattern, Germany, Army, WWII. Alum brocade facing on green velvet straps. Oak leaves on all gray metal fittings with silver frosted finish. Avg. cond. $82

Hanger, Sword, Germany, Army, WWII. 6½" long imitation pigskin body with gray pebbled clip, rivet and loop. Wartime example. Avg. cond. $20

Hanger, Sword, Officer, Germany, Luftwaffe, 1936, Paul Klopfer, Berlin. Blue leather 4"-tall tear-drop with two-position strap for rivet that lacks belt loop D-ring. Pebbled alum clip. Stamped "1936 Paul Klopfer Berlin" and blurred inked unit. Above avg. cond. $40

Hanger, Sword, Officer, Germany, Luftwaffe, 1936. 5"-tall blue leather tear-drop, silver painted pebbled clip and adjustment rivet. Stamped 1936/maker. Lacks belt loop with D-ring. Avg. cond. $55

Hanger, Sword, With Shoulder Harness, Germany, Army, WWII, Assmann. White cloth shoulder strap with buckle, black leather tab and pebbled silver painted clip. Maker marked "A DRGM" for Assmann. Avg. cond. $30

Knot, Bayonet, Germany, Army, WWII. Green strap with alum stripes, alum stem with green zigzags, green cap with silver flecks and alum ball. Above avg. cond. . $26

Knot, Bayonet, Germany, Army, WWII. Silver cord acorn with green cap with silver flecking. Green cloth strap with silver striping. Avg. cond. $30

Knot, Bayonet, Germany, Army, WWII. Green cord acorn with off-white cap and slider. Green cloth strap. Avg. cond. $24

Knot, Bayonet, Germany, Army, WWII. Gray cloth strap, red slide, yellow stem, red cap and gray ball. Avg. cond. $24

Knot, Bayonet, Germany, Luftwaffe, WWII. Gray pigskin strap, white slide, blue cap and gray ball. Exc. cond. $35

Knot, Bayonet, Germany, Luftwaffe, 1937. Gray leather strap with faint 1937 maker, white leather slide, red cap and gray ball. Avg. cond. $24

Knot, Bayonet, Imperial Germany, Army, WWI. Original tie-string on white cloth strap, blue slide, yellow stem, blue fuzz-ball and white tassels. Above avg. cond. . . $42

Knot, Bayonet, Imperial Germany, Army, WWI. Original tie-string to white cloth strap, yellow slide, blue painted stem, yellow fuzz-ball and white tassels. Avg. cond. $25

Knot, Bayonet, Imperial Germany, Army, WWI. Gray cloth strap with gray acorn, yellow neck and red base. Avg. cond. $20

Knot, Dagger, Germany, Army, WWII. Silver cord. Long model. Exc. cond. $66

Knot, Dagger, Germany, Army, WWII. Gold cord. Long model. Exc. cond. $37

Knot, Dagger, Germany, Army, WWII. Silver cord. Long model. Avg. cond. $20

Knot, Dagger, Germany, Army, WWII. Silver cord. Short model. Avg. cond. $20

Knot, Dagger, Naval, Germany, Navy, WWII. Gold cord. Long model. Avg. cond. $45

Knot, Sword, Germany, Army, WWII. Large size. Green leather strap with three double silver stripes, slide, stem, cap and ball. Exc. cond. $40

Knot, Sword, Germany, Army, WWII. Alum brocade strap with double black border stripes, braided slide, alum stem, black cap, black and alum ball. Exc. cond. $55

Knot, Sword, Germany, Army, WWII. Black leather strap with silver stripes showing darkening. Braided slide. Dark silver stem, cap and ball. Early example. Avg. cond. $54

Knot, Sword, Germany, Army, WWII. Green leather strap has silver stripes. Alum on the rest. Avg. cond. $20

Knot, Sword, Imperial Germany, Army, WWI. Large silver cord acorn with black leather strap with silver wire striping. Avg. cond. $20

Knot, Sword, Imperial Germany, Army, WWI. Dark tarnished silver strap with double black border stripes. Dark silver slide, stem, cap and ball. Faint b&w flecks to slide and stem. Avg. cond. $22

Knot, Sword, Bavarian, Imperial Germany, Army, WWI. Alum brocade strap has double blue line borders. Silver cap and ball. Avg. cond. $27

Knot, Sword, Naval, Imperial Germany, Navy, WWI. Darkening to silver cord with black and red flecks. Same zigzag flecks to slide and stem. Dark silver cap and ball with bullion tri-color inset. Has been on sword. Above avg. cond. $108

Knot, Sword, Naval, Imperial Germany, Navy, WWI. Very dark silver cord with black and red flecks. Same zigzag flecks on slide and stem. Very dark silver cap and ball with tri-color bullion inset. Avg. cond. $165

Knot, Sword, NCO, Germany, Army, WWII. Green cloth strap, alum border stripes, fixed slide to stem, green cap with silver flecks and alum ball. Avg. cond. $20

Knot, Sword, NCO, Germany, SS, WWII. 14" long overall with alum brocade strap having double black border stripes. Black and alum zigzag design to slide and stem. Black and alum cap and ball. Above avg. cond. . . $164

Weapon Accessories—Other

Frog, Bayonet, England, c1880. Buff leather with brass adjustment buckle. Missing two reinforcement rivets. Above avg. cond. $38

Frog, Bayonet, England, Army, 1953. Green web construction. Exc. cond. $20

Bayonet, frogs, Italy. Carcano bayonet frogs, gray-green leather, faint ink markings on reverse, unissued. ... $20

CHAPTER SEVEN
Military Vehicles

One of the most specialized collecting categories is military vehicles. The most commonly collected vehicles are of the unarmored wheeled type, such as jeeps and trucks. Gaining in popularity are the armored vehicles, including tanks, armored personnel carriers and armored cars.

Many surplus government vehicles are being lent to veterans groups and military reserve units as static displays on their grounds or property.

M4 Sherman Tank

Military vehicle collecting can be very expensive. Armored vehicles are particularly so. Restoring a vehicle to operating condition frequently requires a high financial investment, as well as hundreds of man hours of work. Due to the scale and weight of many of the component parts, heavy duty cranes and forklifts are needed to facilitate restoration work. Replacement parts are frequently difficult to obtain. This is especially true of the World War Two vintage armored vehicles. There is a limited pool of parts, since most of the vehicles have not been manufactured for over fifty years. Many collectors will buy multiple specimens of the same model of armored vehicle and cannibalize them to produce one fully restored vehicle.

Vehicle collecting is popular internationally, especially in Europe. Many surplus vehicles were used by post-war European armed forces. Another popular source for surplus vehicles is South America. Vehicles were used to support South American military forces throughout the 1950s and 1960s.

In addition, with the fall of the Eastern Bloc, 1950s and 1960s vintage Soviet vehicles are beginning to appear in the market.

Collectors Clubs
Military Vehicle Preservation Society, Independence, MO, (816) 737-5111, Newsletter

Periodicals
Magazine: *Military Vehicles,* Eagle Press, (908) 688-6015. A bimonthly magazine for military vehicles (wheeled and tracked).

Museums
American Military Museum, El Monte, CA, (818) 442-1776

Patton Museum of Cavalry and Armor, Fort Knox, KY, (502) 624-6968

U. S. Army Transport Museum, Ft. Eustis, VA, (804) 878-1182

Tracked Vehicles

Armored Personnel Carrier, M114, USA, Army, 1960s, Cadillac Div of General Motors, Cleveland, OH. Fully tracked and amphibious. Long out of service with US forces. Professionally restored and includes accessories such as tools, fire extinguisher, radios, first-aid kit, etc. Exc. cond. $38,000

Armored Personnel Carrier, M114

Armored Personnel Carrier, M114, USA, Army, 1960s, Cadillac Div of General Motors, Cleveland, OH. Older restoration. Good cond. $29,500

Cargo Carrier, M29 "Weasel," USA, Army, 1943, Studebaker Corp., South Bend, IN. Small tracked vehicle designed to haul cargo in snow. Improved version of the

M29 Cargo Carrier, Restored, $18,500 (Not Listed)

M29 Cargo Carrier, Restored, $10,500 (Not Listed)

Cargo Carrier, M28 which entered service in 1943. Wider tracks and engine moved to the front of the vehicle resulted in improved amphibious performance and greater cargo capacity. Kits allowed field conversion to an amphibious capability. Some remained in US Army service into the Late 1960s. Good cond. $7500

Gun Motor Carriage, M19, USA, Army, 1944, Cadillac or Massey Harris Co., Racine, WI. Stripped hull only. Formerly carried Bofors twin 40mm AA gun. The M19 arrived too late to see action in WWII but was used in the Korean War. Below avg. cond. $2500

M2 Half-track in Need of Restoration, $15,000 (Not Listed)

Half-Track, Model M16-A1, USA, Army, 1943, White Motor Co., Cleveland, OH. Modified White M3 half-track with quad .50-cal machine guns on powered mount for anti-aircraft use. The M16-A1 version of this vehicle had improved communications and weapons systems compared to the standard M16. Other changes included the elimination of the hinged armor section and rearrangement of the ammunition storage. This variant was not new production vehicles, but modifications of vehicles already in the inventory, usually M3s or M15's. This example (serial number 2150) has been completely restored and includes the quad mount with four dummy .50-cal machine guns. Also included are an extra engine and set of tracks. Above avg. cond. $30,500

Half-Track, Model M16, USA, Army, WWII, White Motor Co., Cleveland, OH. Modified White M3 half-track

M3 Half-track

with quad .50-cal machine guns on powered mount for anti-aircraft use. Changes from basic design included mount, generator to power mount, and 6" hinged armor sections that could be lowered on each side. Almost 2900 of this variant were made by the time production ended in 1944. This example has been completely restored and is drivable. Above avg. cond. $19,000

Half-Track, Model M16, USA, Army, WWII, White Motor Co., Cleveland, OH. Modified White M3 half-track with quad .50-cal machine guns on powered mount for anti-aircraft use. Changes from basic design included mount, generator to power mount, and 6" hinged armor sections that could be lowered on each side. Almost 2900 of this variant were made by the time production ended in 1944. This example needs some work and is missing the hinged armor section. Tracks are 85% and has front winch. Good cond. $14,500

Tank, M22 "Locust," USA, Army, WWII, Marmon-Herrington Co., Indianapolis, IN. Light tank designed for use by Army airborne forces. Ordered in April 1942 and 830 had been completed when the contract was canceled in Feb. 1944. Resembled a small M4 Sherman tank. Armed with a 37mm- and .30-cal machine gun in a turret. Never saw action with US forces although some saw limited service with the British. Main defects were lightness of armament and armor. Most were scrapped after the war. This example needs restoration and lacks the turret. Below avg. cond. $7500

M22 Locust Tank (Hull Only)

Tank, M4 "Sherman," USA, USMC, 1941. Early model. Serial number 45. Has flame thrower barrel in place of original 75mm gun. Has duckbill track extenders on both sides of each track for use in sand. Served in North African theater. Not running but price includes new original engine. Outside restored and retains original USMC markings. Avg. cond. $45,000

Tank, M4-A3 "Sherman," USA, Army, WWII. Medium tank. Most widely used medium tank of WWII, was used in combat by most Allied forces. Fully restored. Driven 65 miles since restoration. Good cond. $68,500

Tank, M47 "Patton," USA, Army, 1947, Detroit Tank Arsenal (Chrysler Corp.). Medium tank developed from the earlier M46. The M47 had an improved turret with a 90mm high-velocity cannon. This model was produced from 1951 to 1953 by Chrysler. A total of almost 8600 units were produced. This unit was delivered on May 27, 1952. It has been restored and is drivable. It is fitted with a new Continental V12 engine and rubber tracks. Was previously part of a military vehicle museum collection and had been stored inside. Above avg. cond. $150,000

Tank, M4-A3 "Sherman," USA, Army, 1943. Medium tank. Was used in combat by most Allied forces. The most widely produced variant of the M4 with 12,342 units manufactured. Fully restored and drivable. This unit is equipped with a Ford GAA V8 engine, T23 turret and 105mm gun barrel. Above avg. cond. $47,500

Tank, M5 "Stuart," USA, Army, WWII. Light tank. The M5 was an interim version of the M3 produced due to a shortage of radial engines. This model was fitted with two standard automotive V8 engines and an automatic transmission. Manufactured by three different companies in four locations, a total of 2074 units were produced from 1942–44. Another 22,447 units of other versions of this tank were also produced. This unit includes an engine and transmission but they need to be installed. It was recently painted. Was previously part of a military vehicle museum collection. Avg. cond. $40,000

M5 Stuart Light Tank

Wheeled Vehicles—U.S.

Ambulance, Model M43, USA, Army, 1953, Dodge Div of Chrysler Corp., Mound Park, MI. Three-quarter-ton truck. Modified version of the Dodge M37 series of trucks. The model was produced between 1950 and 1954. This example was delivered in Nov. 1953. The unit is drivable and has recent paint job. Avg. cond. $7500

Ambulance, Model WC18, USA, Army, 1941, Dodge Div of the Chrysler Corp., Mound Park, MI. Half-ton 4x4 ambulance. Over 6400 of this and its two similar variants (WC9 and WC27) were delivered between 1940 and 1942. This example runs well and has locking hubs and rare wheels. Also included are extra doors, original engine and PTO transmission. Good cond. $5000

Armored Car, M20, USA, Army, 1945, Ford Motor Co., St. Paul, MI. Six-wheeled vehicle. The M20 is a variant of the M8 armored car less the 37mm gun turret. In its place is a ring-mounted machine gun. This example has been rebuilt and is equipped with over 200 parts and accessories. Good cond. $26,000

Armored Car, V100 "Commando," USA, Army/USAF, 1960s, Cadillac Gage Co., Warren, MI. 4x4 multi-mission vehicle. Developed as a private venture in the early 1960s. Entered production in 1964 for the Army. Saw service with the Army (as the M706) and Air Force in Vietnam. Removed from US service in the mid-1970s. Many sold to foreign customers. This example is complete and operable. Avg. cond. $35,000

Armored Personnel Carrier, "Peacekeeper," USA, USAF, 1980, Cadillac Gage Company, Warren, MI. Body only. Can be refitted to a standard Dodge M880, 1¼-ton, 4x4 chassis. USAF version of Cadillac Gage Commando Ranger. Chosen in 1979 to meet a requirement for a security police armored response/convoy truck. Used to provide security at USAF bases worldwide. Avg. cond. . . . $5000

Dump Truck, Model M51, USA, Army, 1975, International Harvester Corp. 5-ton dump truck. Has 20,000 miles and 952 hours. Winch included. Above avg. cond. $6500

Scout Car, M3-A1, USA, Army, 1943, White Motor Co., Cleveland, OH. Armored car. Unrestored. This unit (serial number 297296), is 85–90% complete. Has uncut frame and new gauges. Below avg. cond. $8000

1943 M3-A1 Scout Car, Restored, $6,500 (Not Listed)

Scout Car, M3A1, USA, Army, WWII, White Motor Co., Cleveland, OH. Armored car. Fully restored. Has Beechwood canvas top and uncut armor. Above avg. cond. $20,000

Scout Car, M3A1, USA, Army, 1942, White Motor Co., Cleveland, OH. Armored car. Chosen for production by the US Army in June 1939. Was widely used by US and other Allied Forces and almost 21,000 were produced. This example features all original parts, rebuilt transmission and uncut armor. Above avg. cond. $23,000

Another View of the Same M3-A1 Scout Car

Scout Car, M3A1, USA, Army, 1942, White Motor Co., Cleveland, OH. Armored car. Restored. Early model with split armor, skate rail, two trolleys, six rear seats and radio antenna. Good cond. $25,000

Tractor, Model M2, USA, Army, WWII. M2 Cletrack, 7-ton high-speed tractor. Manufactured by Cleveland Tractor Co. or John Deere Co. from 1942 to 1945. Complete except for rear compressor. Below avg. cond. . . $12,500

Trailer, Model G-527 "Water Buffalo," USA, Various, 1945, Checker Cab Co. 1½-ton trailer with tank used to transport and dispense drinking water to troops in the field. Above avg. cond. $1250

Trailer, Model M101-A1, USA, Various, c1960s, Various. Three-quarter-ton cargo trailer. Manufactured from the early 1950s to the present. This example has sideboards and bows (to support canvas top). Good cond. $750

Trailer, Model M101-A1, USA, Various, c1960s, Johnson Corp. Three-quarter-ton cargo trailer. Manufactured from the early 1950s to the present. This example has sideboards. Avg. cond. $950

Trailer, Model M14, USA, Army, WWII, J.G. Brill Co.

1952 M101 Trailer

Large all-steel trailer used by Army anti-aircraft artillery units. The M14 transported fire control directors. This model had an insulated steel top, ventilation fan and gasoline-powered heater. This example (serial number 707) has a 9200# GVW but needs restoration. Avg. cond. $800

Trailer, Model M14, USA, Army, WWII, J.G. Brill Co. Complete and unrestored. 9600# GVW. Serial number 707. Avg. cond. $800

Trailer, Model M416, USA, Various, c1960s, Various. Third-generation quarter-ton general purpose trailer. Built by several manufacturers from the Early 1960s to the present. This example's body has been completely rebuilt. Tires in good condition and tailgate present. Good cond. $600

Trailer, Model M416, USA, Army, c1960s, Various. Completely rebuilt. Complete with tailgate and good tires. Good cond. $600

Truck, CCKW Gasoline Tanker, USA, Army, 1944, GMC. 2½-ton 6x6 truck. Over 412,000 cargo variants of this model and 60,000 of other versions were produced by GMC between 1941 and 1945. The most numerous military vehicle type produced in WWII. This tanker example is drivable and fitted with two oval alum tanks, working pump and meter. No body rust but needs paint job. Ex-Norwegian Army vehicle, only 2500 original miles. Good cond. $5500

Truck, CJ3A, USA, US Navy, 1952, Willys-Overland Motor Co., Toledo, OH. Post-war variant of the wartime jeep. Quarter-ton 4x4 truck. Commercial procured by the Navy in the Early 1950s to replace worn out WWII models. This example includes towbar and pushbars. Avg. cond. $3750

Truck, Dodge R2, USA, USAF, Early 1960s, Dodge Div (Chassis), ACF Brill Motors Co., Philadelphia, PA. Modified M37 chassis (or M56) for use as an airport fire and rescue vehicle. 4x4. This example retains the special body for rescue missions and a 10,000-lb. winch in front. Has been restored. Avg. cond. $6000

Truck, M26-A1 "Dragon Wagon," USA, Army, 1944, Pacific Car and Foundry, Renton, WA. 12-ton 6x6 semi-tractor truck. One of the largest trucks designed and used by the US Army in WWII. Primarily used to recover damaged armored vehicles from the battlefield. It was used in conjunction with a large trailer. The manufacturer produced 1400 units between 1943 and 1945. This unit has the removable canvas cab of the A1 variant. Needs restoration. Below avg. cond. $6500

Truck, M561 "Gamma Goat," USA, Army, 1970, Con-

dec Corp., Old Greenwich, CT. 1½-ton 6x6 amphibious truck. Vehicle consists of two light alloy bodies joined by a roll-articulated joint, allowing the two bodies to pitch and roll independent of each other. This gives the vehicle excellent all-terrain and cross-country performance. About 14,000 units were produced between 1969 and 1973. This example is drivable, has an arctic cab but lacks a tailgate. Avg. cond. $3900

Gama Goat, $9,000 (Not Listed)

Truck, MB, USA, Army, 1944, Willys-Overland Motor Company, Toledo, OH. Quarter-ton 4x4 truck. This is the original WWII jeep. This vehicle (serial number 375768) was manufactured in 1944. Restored and has Beechwood canvas, tools, accessories, radio set and many spare parts. Good cond. $10,000

Truck, MB, USA, USMC, 1943, Willys-Overland Motor Company, Toledo, OH. Quarter-ton 4x4 truck. This is the original WWII jeep. Restored to 1944–45 USMC specifications. New paint and wiring. Includes towbar and some spare parts. Avg. cond. $5200

Truck, MB, USA, Army, 1941, Willys-Overland Motor Company, Toledo, OH. Quarter-ton 4x4 truck. This is the original WWII jeep. This vehicle (serial number 100212) was delivered on Nov. 18, 1941. Solid but needs restoration. An early example of the type. Avg. cond.　. $10,000

Truck, Model 123-A1C "Dragon Wagon," USA, Army, 1960s, Mack Truck Co. 10-ton 6x6 semi-tractor truck. Primarily used to recover damaged armored vehicles from the battlefield. It was used in conjunction with an M15-A1 or M15-A2 trailer. Mack produced several versions of this truck between the mid-1950s and the late 1970s. This unit (serial number 1552), has a removable canvas top and fifth wheel. Avg. cond. $18,500

Truck, Model 123-A1C "Dragon Wagon," USA, Army, 1968, Mack Truck Co. 10-ton 6x6 semi-tractor truck. Primarily used to recover damaged armored vehicles from the battlefield. It was used in conjunction with an M15-A1 or M15-A2 trailer. Mack produced several versions of this truck between the mid-1950s and the late 1970s. This unit (serial number 2241–2157), has a hard top, winch and fifth wheel. Above avg. cond. $18,500

Truck, Model 151-A1, USA, Army, 1965, Ford Motor Corp., Highland Park, MI. Quarter-ton 4x4 truck. Replaced the M38 and M38-A1 jeeps in US military service. Produced from 1961 through 1969. This example has been restored. Includes new tires, top, side curtains and good seats. Good cond. $7000

M151-A2 Truck

Truck, Model 151-A2, USA, Army, 1974, Ford Motor Co. Quarter-ton 4x4 truck. Produced from 1961–69. Replaced the M38 and M38-A1 jeeps. This vehicle has a full enclosure, is outfitted for deep water fording and has a six-point roll cage. Includes an M 416 quarter-ton trailer. Good cond. $8750

M151-A2 Truck

Truck, Model CCKW-353, USA, Various, WWII, GMC. 2½-ton 6x6 long wheelbase truck. Over 412,000 cargo variants of this model and 60,000 of other versions were produced by GMC between 1941 and 1945. The most numerous military vehicle type produced in WWII. This example has an open cab and a winch. Complete and original. Avg. cond. $6200

Truck, Model GPW, USA, Various, 1942, Ford Motor Co. Quarter-ton 4x4 truck. Ford Motors version of the original jeep. This vehicle (serial number 51767) was

delivered on July 27, 1942. Needs to be restored. Runs and drives but needs wiring, body work and tires. Below avg. cond. $5000

Truck, Model GPW, USA, Various, 1942, Ford Motor Co., Detroit, MI. Quarter-ton 4x4 truck. Ford Motor's version of the original jeep. This vehicle has been restored and features many accessories. Price includes an extra motor and other spares. Above avg. cond. $9500

Truck, Model GPW, USA, Various, 1942, Ford Motor Co. Quarter-ton 4x4 truck. Ford Motor's version of the original jeep. This vehicle (serial number 60620) has been completely restored. All part numbers match, frame, body, engine. Has new summer top, tires, brakes and seats. Good cond. $11,000

Truck, Model M135, USA, Army, 1952, GMC Truck Div, Pontiac, MI. 6x6 2½-ton truck. Same basic truck as the M211 but had single 11.00 x 20 tires and wheels rather than the dual 9.00 x 20s used on M211. This resulted in better off-road performance. Mass produced by GMC from 1950–55. Replaced the GMC CCKW series of WWII. Avg. cond. $4500

Truck, Model M151-A1, USA, Army, 1965, Ford Motor Corp., Highland Park, Michigan. Quarter-ton 4x4 truck. Replaced the M38 and M38-A1 jeeps in US military service. Produced from 1961 through 1969. This example is 100% original and has only 2400 miles. Includes new tires. Above avg. cond. $7200

Truck, Model M151-A2, USA, Army, 1970, A.M. General Corp., Wayne, MI. Quarter-ton 4x4 truck. Replacement model for the original jeep which was first placed in service in 1960. This example (serial number NB017U28072) has been restored and has 23,100 miles on it. Includes new vinyl enclosure kit, roll-over protection system, water fording kit, radio mount and antenna setup for PRC-25 radio system. Has been modified with civilian off-road 700 x 16 tires. Above avg. cond. $7500

Another Example of an M151-A2 Truck, $6,500 (Not Listed)

Truck, Model M211, USA, Army, 1952, GMC Truck Div, Pontiac, MI. 6x6 2½-ton truck. Mass produced by GMC from 1950–55. Replaced the GMC CCKW series of WWII. Avg. cond. $3500

Truck, Model M274-A2 "Mule," USA, Army, 1960s, Bowen McLaughlin Co. Also called the Mechanical Mule. 4x4½-ton platform truck. Used by inf units to transport cargo and soldiers over all types of terrain. Produced from the Late 1950s into the Early 1970s, over 11,000 units of all versions were produced. This unit includes three spare engines, eight spare tires and various other parts. Avg. cond. $4500

M274 Mechanical Mule

Truck, Model M274-A5 "Mule," USA, Army, Late 1960s. Also called the Mechanical Mule. 4x4 half-ton platform truck. This unit includes spare parts, manuals and various other accessories. Avg. cond. $1800

Truck, Model M37, USA, USAF, 1954, Dodge Division of Chrysler Corp., Mound Park, MI. Three-quarter-ton truck. Improved version of the Dodge WWII WC series of trucks. Over 47,000 were produced between 1950 and 1954. This ex-USAF example is fitted with an Arctic cab. New brakes and has no rust. Avg. cond. $3000

M37 Truck, Restored, Diesel Engine, $10,000 (Not Listed)

Truck, Model M37, USA, Army, 1951, Dodge Div of Chrysler Corp., Mound Park, MI. Three-quarter-ton truck. Improved version of the Dodge WWII WC series of trucks. Over 47,000 were produced between 1950 and 1954. This example runs well, has 45,000 original miles,

is well maintained, body in good condition and includes front winch. Avg. cond. $4500

1952 Dodge M37

Truck, Model M38-A1, USA, USMC, Late 1950s. Former USMC jeep. Produced by Willys or Kaiser Jeep International. Over 80,000 were produced. This vehicle was recently overhauled and includes 24-volt electrical system, new OD paint, full enclosure and new canvas. Above avg. cond. $6500

Another Example of an M38-A1 Truck, $6,500 (Not Listed)

Truck, Model M38-A1, USA, Various, 1954, Willys-Overland Motor Co., Toledo, OH. Quarter-ton 4x4 truck. This is an improved version of the M38. The model was produced for US forces from 1952–57 and was released as the commercial CJ5 in 1955. This vehicle (serial number 72805), shows 40,880 miles on its odometer. Has new tires, top and seats. Avg. cond. $5500

Truck, Model M38, USA, Various, 1950s, A M. General Corp., Wayne, MI. Quarter-ton 4x4 truck. Militarized version of the Willys' CJ-3 post-war civilian version of the jeep. Featured strengthened suspension and 24-volt electrical system. This example (serial number 26606) was fully restored in 1991 and repainted again in 1996. Price includes a spare rebuilt engine. Good cond. $7000

Restored M38 Truck, $7,500 (Not Listed)

Truck, Model M38, USA, Various, 1954, Willys-Overland Motor Company, Toledo, Ohio. Quarter-ton 4x4 truck. This is the militarized version of the post-war CJ3A jeep. This vehicle, (Serial Number 80633), shows 42,700 miles on its odometer. Olive drab finish. Has new summer top, civilian mud and snow tires, modified seats, bumpers and 12-volt system. Avg. cond. $2300

M38 Truck

Truck, Model M422-A1 "Mighty Mite," USA, USMC, 1960, American Motors Corp., Detroit, MI. Quarter-ton 4x4 truck. Original model was 43" shorter and 1300 lbs. lighter than the original jeep. A1 version had 6" longer body and wheelbase. Fully restored. This vehicle (serial number 485) has 7192 miles. Water fording kit is included. Above avg. cond. $12,500

Truck, Model M422-A1 "Mighty Mite," USA, USMC, 1960, American Motors Corp., Detroit, MI. Quarter-ton 4x4 truck. Restored 1996. Repainted, engine overhauled, 12-volt electrical system, seats reupholstered and all five new non-military recap tires. Good cond. $4500

Truck, Model M880, USA, Army, 1976, Dodge Motor Corp. 1¼-ton 4x4 truck. Vehicle has 68,700 miles. New transmission and cargo cover. Good cond. $3500

1977 M886 Ambulance, $3,850 (Not Listed)

Truck, Model M968-A, USA, Army, 1942, Diamond T Motor Co., Chicago, IL. 6x6 4-ton truck. Fully restored. Hard cab model with winch. Above avg. cond. . $10,500

Truck, Model M968-A, USA, Army, 1942, Diamond T Motor Co., Chicago, IL. 4-ton 6x6 truck. New paint. Hard cab model with winch. This model was produced from 1940–45 and almost 9800 were made. Avg. cond. $7000

Truck, Model WC51, USA, Army, 1942, Dodge Motor Co. Three-quarter-ton 4x4 truck. Rebuilt in 1996. This example has new canvas, paint and exhaust. Swiss tires. Good cond. $7000

Truck, Model WC51, USA, Army, WWII, Dodge Div of Chrysler Corp., Mound Park, MI. Three-quarter-ton 4x4 truck. Over 123,000 of this model were produced by Dodge between 1942 and 1945. This example is Norwegian Army surplus. Complete. Good cond. . . . $6200

1943 WC51 Truck

Truck, Model WC51, USA, Army, 1942, Dodge Motor Co. Three-quarter-ton 4x4 truck. This example (serial number 81560119) has a full canvas top and cargo cover. Former Norwegian Army vehicle. Good cond. . . . $7500

Truck, Model WC51, USA, Army, 1953, Dodge Motor Corp. Three-quarter-ton 4x4 truck. This model was widely produced during WWII and used by all arms of the US military. It was returned to production from 1950–55 for the Korean War. This example has a cargo cover, winch, data plates and new top. Good cond. $5500

Wheeled Vehicles—Other

Amphibious Scout Vehicle, BRDM-1, Soviet Union, Army, 1950s (1951). Formerly known as BTR-40. Widely used by Soviet, Eastern Bloc and client state forces. This 4x4 vehicle was captured by the Israelis during the Six Day War in 1967. Converted in the Late 1960s to standard US Army Dodge M37, T-245 engine and transmission and a 12-volt ignition. Renovated with new paint and seats but still has original radio mounts, gun mounts and ammo racks. Street legal. Above avg. cond. $12,500

Armored Car, AML-90, France, Army, 1960s-70s, Panhard, Paris. Fully restored interior and exterior. Engine included but needs to be reinstalled. Large low turret is fitted with 90mm (3.54") gun. First production models were delivered in 1960. Over 4000 have been produced including licensed versions in South Africa. Above avg. cond. $15,500

AML 90 Armored Car

Armored Car, Ferret Mk 2/3, England, Army, 1950s and 1960's, Daimler Ltd., Coventry, England. Small two man armored car. Over 4400 were produced between 1953 and 1971. The Mk2/3 featured a one-man turret with a 7.62 mg. Has only 2000 miles since MoD refit. Also features pioneer kit, spotlight, fire extinguishers, first-aid kit, camo net, tools and spares. Good cond. $12,000

Ferret Mk 2/3

Armored Car, Saladin Mk 2, England, Army, 1958, British Leyland (Alvis Ltd.), Coventry, England. 6x6, three-man armored car. Accepted into British Army service in 1959. Manufactured from 1958 to 1971, a total of 1171 units were produced. Many of this total were produced for foreign sales. The vehicle is no longer in service with the British Army. This unit is drivable and has been restored. The unit has an operational turret with dummy 76mm gun, new periscopes, radios, tools, fire extinguishers, spotlight and hatch covers. Above avg. cond. $22,000

Armored Personnel Carrier, BTR-152, Soviet Union, Army, 1952. First seen in 1951 although the model was probably in service for some years earlier. Widely used by Soviet, Eastern Bloc and client state forces. This 6x6 vehicle still has original radio mounts, tool racks, gun mounts and ammo racks. Winch included. Street legal. Above avg. cond. $15,500

1955 Soviet BTR-40 Armored Car, $12,500 (Not Listed)

Truck, GAZ Model 69, Soviet Union, Army, 1950s. Soviet version of the jeep. Produced from 1952–65 to replace worn-out wartime Lend-Lease vehicles. Still remains in service in Russian and client states forces. This example is a former East German Army vehicle. Running condition with less than 1000 kilometers. Good cond. $7500

Truck, Stalwart Mk II, England, Army, 1967, Alvis, Coventry England. 6x6 cargo truck. Has full amphibious capability. Adopted by the British Army in the Late 1960s. This unit has a Rolls-Royce engine and winch. Above avg. cond. $18,000

Vehicle Accessories—U.S.

Boat, PBR Mk II, Hull Only, USA, Navy, 1960s, United Boatbuilders, Bellingham, WA. This is the stripped 31' hull of a 1960s vintage Patrol Boat River (PBR). Hundreds of PBRs were operated by US and South Vietnamese forces on the rivers and waterways of South Vietnam. Originally powered by a GM diesel truck engine and Jacuzzi waterjets. This combination produced a top speed of 28 knots. Manned by a crew of four, they were originally armed with machine guns and grenade launchers. Below avg. cond. $6000

US Patrol Boat, River (PBR), Hull Only

Optical Viewer, Sherman Tank, USA, Army, WWII. Anodized finished metal frame with prismatic lens behind glass plate. Above avg. cond. $20

Periscope, Tank, USA, Army, WWII. For M5 light tank. 7" x 11" x 2" with handle for removal. Metal case with compression springs for snug fit and wide viewing angle. Bakelite case around prism. Above avg. cond. $20

Periscope, Tank, M-38, USA, Army, WWII. Black case. Mirrored optics with floating reticle in center. Mounted on brass base with spring controlled positioning. Avg. cond. $20

Periscope, Tank, M-70H, USA, Army, WWII. 30" steel tube. Direct optic coated lens scope used on tanks. Rubber goggle style viewer with monocular vision allowed. Above avg. cond. $56

Tachometer, Jeep, USA, Army, WWII. 4" diam with dash chrome trim. Includes odometer function and hmkd on rear. Above avg. cond. $27

Telescopic Sight, Tank, USA, Army, WWII. OD finish on steel barrel with coated optics. Full-fit goggle-style viewing end with one eye masked. Above avg. cond. . . . $69

Tire Tool, Jeep, USA, Army, WWII. OD finished with two sizes of lugs and holes for torque rods. Above avg. cond. $13

Vehicle Accessories—Germany

Eagle, Railway Car, Germany, Army, WWII. Alum 27" wingspan. Avg. cond. $199

Headset, Radio, Panzer, Germany, Army, WWII. Black leather-covered steel band, black rubber earcups and brown cloth-covered cord with two-prong plug. Avg. cond. $345

ID Disc, Vehicle License Plate, Germany, Army, WWII. 1¾" alum with raised party eagle, "Der Oberburgermeister Kreispolizeibehorde Bonn" border and red background. Swastika rivet at center has been on license plate. Above avg. cond. $87

Medical Box, Vehicle, Germany, Army, WWII. White stenciled title "verbandkasten" on lid with Red Cross. Tan paint over base gray with rust on bottom. Handle at end and two latches to hinged lid with paper contents label. Below avg. cond. $66

Medical Box, Vehicle, Germany, Army, WWII. Gray lid with white disc having red cross. Metal handle on end, two latches on hinged lid, metal splint inside and five other contents remain. Avg. cond. $68

Periscope, Tank, With Case, Germany, Army, Armor, WWII, Zeiss. "SA" stamped green painted wooden storage box with leather handle on hinged lid and three latches. 4½" x 4½" x 48". White painted "T.Z.M.G.3a" on lid. 45"-long black finished periscope has 1½" diam. Optics clear with "7.62" and "37mm" scales. Marked "1.75 x 30 Zeiss" and includes spanner wrench. Avg. cond. . . $225

Periscope, Tank, With Case, Germany, Army, Armor, WWII, Zeiss. "SA" stamped green painted wooden box. White painted "T.Z.M.G.3a" on lid. With leather handle and three-latch front. 4½" x 4½" x 48" box has metal reinforced corners. 35" black painted periscope has clear optics with "7.62" and "37mm" scales. Marked "1.75 x 30 Zeiss." Spanner wrench included. Avg. cond. $216

Radio, Headset, Panzer, Germany, Army, WWII. Black rubber earcups on 1943 dated speakers. Black leather-covered steel headband. Brown cloth-covered cord with two-prong plug. Exc. cond. $683

Radio, Throat-mike Set, Panzer, Germany, Army, WWII. Black leather-covered steel band with Bakelite mikes, cloth-covered cord, Bakelite switch with clip and two-prong plug. Above avg. cond. $184

Sights, Optical, Tank, With Case, Germany, Army, Armored, WWII. 10½" x 12" x 22" gray painted metal storage box. Box has two handles, two latches, one broken hook and a hinged lid. Lid marked "pz.b.w.f.8 2,5x19." Storage rack inside for three sights and a small empty wooden box. Both sights are title marked by "gwr" and "bvf" respectively. Optics clear with crosshair inside and scaled numbers. 18"-long L-shaped bodies with 9"-long end with eyecup. Avg. cond. $433

Vehicle Heater, Germany, Army, WWII. Black painted sheet-metal body has stamped title, wire hanger and removable burner works. Marked "auto Union DRGM." Paper instruction sheet is rolled and inserted in burner. Above avg. cond. $72

Vehicle License Plate, Germany, Luftwaffe, WWII. 3½" x 18" stamped metal body with mounting tab along bottom. Numbered on plate "wl 592188." B&w painted details show peeling and inked eagle stamp. Six mounting holes. Above avg. cond. $160

Vehicle License Plate, Germany, SS, WWII. 4" x 19" stamped steel rectangle with b&w paint showing age. Number "ss-201652." With three bullet holes and rust. Two mounting holes. Avg. cond. $565

CHAPTER EIGHT

Aviation-related Militaria

Aviation-related militaria is frequently overlooked. It does not get the same attention that is given to the more traditional infantry and armored units.

Because of the major role Air Forces played in World War Two, the aviation militaria of that period has become an important collectors' market. At its peak in 1944, the US Army Air Force had a strength of close to 2.4 million members and over 230,000 aircraft. US naval aviation aircraft numbered over 40,000.

The most highly prized aviation collectibles from other countries come from the German Luftwaffe and the English Royal Air force (RAF). Flight suits, flight helmets and other flight gear are the most commonly collected items.

Certain aviation militaria, such as decorated and undecorated leather jackets, have been highly prized for a long time. Other types of aviation militaria that became popular collectibles include flight helmets, flight suits, and other leather flight clothing.

Flight clothing from the post-World War Two period also gained popularity, particularly items related to the early

Taylorcraft L2M Grasshopper—"The Ultimate Aviation Collectible"

jet era. Pressurized flight suits, flight helmets and Anti-G suits are several examples of sought after collectibles.

Recently, interest has turned to aircraft as a collecting category. Highly publicized expeditions have been undertaken to recover aircraft from jungles in the Pacific, from glaciers in Greenland and from undersea crash sites. Short of owning an entire aircraft, many collectors are content to own instruments and other aircraft component parts.

Objects that can be traced back to actual combat in Korea or Vietnam also attract the interest of collectors.

Museums

Air Force Armament Museum, Eglin AFB, FL, (904) 872-5371

National Museum of Naval Aviation, US Naval Air Station, Pensacola, FL, (904) 452-3604

US Air Force Museum, Wright-Patterson AFB, OH, (513) 255-3286

US Army Aviation Museum, Ft. Rucker, AL

USMC Air Ground Museum, Quantico, VA, (703) 640-2606

Aircraft Equipment—U.S.

Gauge, Oxygen, USA, AAF, 1944, Autopoint. Blinker oxygen flow indicator, 2¼" x 2¼" black Bakelite body with brass fittings and dated factory plate on back. Above avg. cond. $8

Aircraft, L2M "Grasshopper," USA, AAF, 1943, Taylorcraft Aviation, Alliance, OH. High-wing, single-engine, two-seat liaison aircraft. Widely used in WWII as a trainer and observation aircraft. Approx. 900 of this model were procured during 1943 and 500 of other versions were procured earlier in the war. Originally powered by a Continental O-170–3 engine, the top speed was around 95 mph. Of the 900 examples only 150 are known to have survived. This example has been restored and is one of the approx. 50 in flyable condition. Good cond. $29,000

Blackout Lamp Assembly, Aircraft, USA, AAF, WWII. In issue box with AAF marked spec label. Model scr-573/src-643-a. Avg. cond. $28

Bomb, Aerial, USA, AAF, WWII. Small, 250-lb standard configuration bomb with boxed fins at rear and provisions for nose and tail fuse. Either two or one lug suspension. Dark green finish. Much rust on fins. Avg. cond. . $250

Bomb, Aerial, USA, Army, Aero Service, WWI. Small 20/25-lb bomb with vanes, serrated casing and fusing device on nose. Fuse has safety pin installed. Casing pitted and rusty. Below avg. cond. $145

Bomb, Aerial, USA, Army, Aero Service, WWI. Aerodynamic shape with four fins for control. Appears to have fused nose and used three suspension lugs for hanging from aircraft (two are missing.) Currently has alum finish but surface shows signs of many paint jobs. Evidence of past repairs and a few surface rust spots. Avg. cond. $100

Camera, Aircraft, F-8, USA, Navy, WWII. Hmkd Keystone Mfg Co. Magazine loaded and pre-set lens values with 15" focal length. Aircraft powered. Stored with accessories in reinforced box with labels. Exc. cond. $250

Camera, Aircraft, Model K-25, USA, Air Force, c1960s. Modified to K-25B standards. Uses film pack and pre-set lens settings. Black case with controls. Original box with maintenance tag. Last use date 1989. Above avg. cond. $23

Clock, Aircraft, Eight Day, USA, AAF, WWII, Elgin. Elgin brand. Black dial and Bakelite body. Above avg. cond. $75

Clock, Aircraft, Eight Day, USA, AAF, WWII, Wittnaur. Hmkd Wittnaur on back. Black face with 12-hr dial and sweep second hand. Fully operational. Above avg. cond. $38

Directional Gyro, Aircraft, USA, AAF, WWII, Sperry. Serial numbered in 3700 range. Rotating azimuthal bar with center indices for read out. Knob at lower front of instrument. Shows wear and lacks mil spec plate. Avg. cond. $13

Display, Gauge, Bank and Turn Indicator, Aircraft, USA, AAF, WWII. Unit with black finish. Well marked (b-17 I-101-c). Mounted in wooden display frame for table top or desk display. Plate engraved "B-17 Flying Fortress" at bottom. Exc. cond. $72

Display, RPM Indicator, Aircraft, USA, AAF, WWII. Solid oak display with RPM gauge center mounted with red fuel shut-off knob set above. Engraved plate below shows for B-17 aircraft. Near mint cond. $93

Driftmeter, Aircraft, USA, AAF, WWII, Bendix Corp. Model B-3 by Bendix Corp. Gyro-stabilized optics for determining wind drift effect. Used rectangular reticule grid on viewplate to observe rate of drift. A 360-degree azimuth ring allowed accurate measurement. Timing device, solar shade, spare lens all with original equipment. 67" long and mounted through aircraft floor at navigator station. Exc. cond. $200

External Periscope, Driftmeter, Aircraft, USA, AAF, WWII. The fuselage-mounted periscope and optics for the driftmeter at the navigator station. At one end is gearing for motors and mounting plate, at the other is glass dome over prismatic mirror system to pass view to navigator. Black metal tube protects the components. Above avg. cond. $150

Film Pack, Gun Camera, Aircraft, USA, Navy, WWII. Spring powered for use on Mark VI, Mod 2 and Mark VII gun cameras. External gear drive, winding key and test switch on side. Avg. cond. $25

First Aid Kit, Aircraft, USA, AAF, WWII. Tan canvas container with red cross emblem and title. Zipper and snap closures and full set of first-aid gear for airborne emergencies. Avg. cond. $25

Gauge, Directional Gyro Indicator, Aircraft, USA, AAF, WWII. Model AN-5735–1. 4½"-deep black finish housing with 3"-diam dial and adjustment knob below. Riveted metal spec plates on back with 1943 AC contract markings. Decal on top with 1964 overhaul date. Above avg. cond. $20

Gauge, Engine Oil Temp, Aircraft, USA, AAF, WWII. Includes line and transducer. 2"-diam gauge with 100 to 250 temperature range. Above avg. cond. $20

Gauge, Gyro Horizon Indicator, Aircraft, USA, Various, 1943. Model AN-5736–1. Dated spec plate. Black dial with white indicators. Displays degrees of bank angle left or right. Avg. cond. $20

Gauge, High Pressure Hydraulics, Aircraft, USA, AAF, 1943. 2½"-diam face with 0 to 2000 lb/sq inch range. 1943 dated on spec plate in back. Avg. cond. $25

Gauge, Pressure Altimeter, Aircraft, USA, AAF, WWII, Kollsman. Black face with 0 to 1000 feet on dial and both 1000 ft and 10,000 ft indicators. Adjustable Kollsman window is functional. Connecting plug on back has been cut. Avg. cond. $55

Gun Camera, Aircraft, USA, AAF, 1942, Bell & Howell. Dated and marked Bell & Howell. Mountable to aircraft frame. 35mm lens with pre-settable values based on mission. Film cartridges used. Avg. cond. $72

Gun Camera, Aircraft, USA, Various, 1944. Type AN-N-6 magazine fed with pre-set conditions and lens. Aircraft-powered unit. Dated. Amber outer lens filter shattered. Below avg. cond. $47

Propeller Assembly, Aircraft, USA, AAF, WWII. Two halves of propeller with mounting hubs for attaching to engine shaft. Each piece dark wood with metal protective trim on leading edge. Could be part of variable pitch assembly. Above avg. cond. $150

Propeller Blade and Hub, Aircraft, USA, Army, Aero Service, WWI. Wood blade with metal reinforced leading edge, black finish with yellow tip and 10% missing. Nicks and cuts on trailing edge. Below avg. cond. $54

Aircraft Equipment—Germany

Bomb, Aerial, Imperial Germany, Air Force, WWI. 7" long overall, 3½" cast body with green paint. Gray fuse and sheet-metal four-fin tail. Avg. cond. $35

Bomb, Aerial, Incendiary, Germany, Luftwaffe, WWII. About 14"-long body with silver paint and many stamped maker numbers. Red and green sheet metal tail. Typed paper label reads "Hyde Park, London Dec. 29th, 1940 etc." Above avg. cond. $200

Compass, Aircraft, Germany, Luftwaffe, WWII. 3" diam Bakelite body with four mounting tabs. Dark fluid filled inside, alum ID plates marked "FL 23233 etc." and "fuhrerkompass Fk 38." Exc. cond. $91

Compass, Aircraft, Germany, Luftwaffe, WWII. 3" diam Bakelite body with four mounting hole tabs and 4" long metal frontplate marked "fk38 Fl.23233" and inked "nfe." Chipped Bakelite socket at bottom. Dark fluid filled body with luminous compass. Above avg. cond. $160

Electric Motor, Aircraft, Germany, Luftwaffe, WWII. For Fw190. 4½"-long body with about 3" diam with no cover. Metal maker tag "eoa EM1-20K 24V 24 WL etc." Base has four holes to mount and wire with two metal end loops. Avg. cond. $35

Gauge, Air-speed, Aircraft, Germany, Luftwaffe, WWII. Marked "fahrtmesser Fl 22234." 3"-diam Bakelite body with four mounting tabs, luminous needle and numbers on scale. Two cut hose fittings at back with maker decal. Exc. cond. $177

Gauge, Air-speed, Aircraft, Germany, Luftwaffe, WWII. Marked "fahrtmesser Fl 22230." 3"-diam Bakelite body with four mounting tabs, luminous needle and numbers on scale. Two cut hose fittings at back with maker decal. Avg. cond. $53

Gauge, Aircraft, Germany, Luftwaffe, WWII. 3"-diam Bakelite body with four mounting tabs, dial below face with luminous needle and scale. Metal spec plate marked "stat. Variometer Fl22381–10" and two cut hose fittings. Exc. cond. $93

Gauge, Aircraft, Germany, Luftwaffe, WWII. 3"-diam Bakelite body with four mounting hole tabs. Luminous needle and scales "0-5-10-20-30." Title decal on back marked "variometer Fl.22386" and by "oeq." Two fittings at back for missing hoses. Exc. cond. $164

Gauge, Aircraft, Germany, Luftwaffe, WWII. 2¼"-diam gray finished alum case with four mounting hole tabs. Metal maker tag by "bwz etc." and "o2-wachter Fl30489." Broken-off tube at back nut. Luminous four rectangles on face with title. Above avg. cond. $339

Gauge, Aircraft, Germany, Luftwaffe, WWII. Marked "fl20723 X100." 2¼"-diam black finished metal case with four mounting hole tabs. Luminous needle and "X100" scale "1234." Corrosion on stenciled wiring diagram with rest intact. Three prongs on socket with wire loop. Above avg. cond. $117

Gauge, Aircraft, Germany, Luftwaffe, WWII. Marked "vorrats-anzeiger Fl20723." 2"-diam black metal body with four mounting lugs and numbered scale with needle "x100." Three prongs on socket with wire loop. Above avg. cond. $370

Gauge, Aircraft, Germany, Luftwaffe, WWII. 2¼"-diam black alum body with four mounting hole tabs. Two luminous needles and "nahe Ln 27002" marked on front. Above avg. cond. $164

Gauge, Aircraft, Germany, Luftwaffe, WWII. 2¼"-diam

black alum body with four mounting tabs. Two luminous needles and "nahe Ln27002" marked. Stenciled instructions near empty back socket with wire loop. Above avg. cond. $60

Gauge, Altimeter, Aircraft, Germany, Luftwaffe, WWII. Marked "fl 22320." 3"-diam Bakelite body with four mounting tabs. Dial adjustment knob moves scales and needle. "E" and "F" marked clips move red indicators at edge. Luminous numbers on scale. Maker decal at back with cut hose. Exc. cond. $139

Gauge, Altimeter, Aircraft, Germany, Luftwaffe, WWII. Marked "hohenmesser Fl.22322." 3"-diam Bakelite body with four mounting hole tabs and 3½" long. Dial adjustment knob moves on scales, three red marks on rim, two metal clips "E" and "F" marked. Hose stem to back with title decal. Above avg. cond. $97

Gauge, Artificial-horizon, Aircraft, Germany, Luftwaffe, WWII. 7" tall, 4" diam, with four mounting lugs. Worn decal marked "Fl.22411/1." Plug on cord with socket intact and cut cord. Luminous painted detail and bubble level to face with dial adjustment. Above avg. cond. $145

Gauge, Artificial-horizon, Aircraft, Germany, Luftwaffe, WWII. Model "FL22412." Black ball in curved tube with vertical pointer. Black metal case and spec label in back. Above avg. cond. $120

Gauge, Bank and Turn Indicator, Aircraft, Germany, Luftwaffe, WWII. 2½"-diam black crinkle finished metal body with four mounting tabs, ball level on face with "L & R" and needle. Metal maker plate marked "wendezeiger Fl22402" with specs. Many metal fittings at back connector. Exc. cond. $122

Gauge, Gyroscope, Aircraft, Germany, Luftwaffe, WWII, Siemens-LGW. 4½' x 5" black metal box is 5" long with large socket on back. Maker plate marked "Siemens-LGW etc." and "Fl.22561." Four mounting holes on front, ball level, two adjustment knobs and two scales "N-3-6-thru-33." Above avg. cond. $180

Gauge, Manifold Pressure, Aircraft, Germany, Luftwaffe, WWII. 3"-diam Bakelite body with four mounting hole tabs and 4" long. Luminous needles and numbered scale by "ata." Marked "doppel-ladedruckmesser Fl.20556" on back with two threaded fittings having cut-off hose ends. Exc. cond. $87

Gauge, Manifold Pressure, Aircraft, Germany, Luftwaffe, WWII. 55mm-diam Bakelite body with four mounting lugs. Marked "FL. 20516-4." Luminous numbers on gauge "kg/cm2." Original cap on brass fitting. Exc. cond. $145

Gauge, Manifold Pressure, Aircraft, Germany, Luftwaffe, WWII. Marked "ladedruckmesser Fl.20555." 3"-diam Bakelite body with four mounting hole tabs and 4" long. Luminous needle and numbered scale by "ata." Title decal on back with threaded stud. Avg. cond. $135

Gauge, Voltmeter, Aircraft, Germany, Luftwaffe, WWII. Model "FL 32502-7." Black metal case with specs stamped on side. Center 0 indicator with plus and minus values to 40 volts. Single pointer. Exc. cond. $80

Propeller, Aircraft, Imperial Germany, Air Force, WWI, Mercedes. About 103" long and 8" wide. Light and dark wood laminated construction. Center hub has six mounting holes and two metal wall hangers. Marked "100 PS, Mercedes, D270, St175." Above avg. cond. $800

Propeller, Aircraft, Imperial Germany, Air Force, WWI, Mercedes. 59" tall, single blade on hub with opposite side blade cut away, leaving flat side that allows remaining blade to stand upright off hub on the floor. Laminated wood construction. Hub is impressed "Nofan Propeller/Berlin O/100P Mercedes/27000143S/Zug/No. 2411" and "Stand 13300 Geppert P&W." Avg. cond. $288

Radio, Aircraft, Germany, Luftwaffe, WWII. Model K42 Nora, multi-band. 4½" x 11" x 19" blue-gray painted wood body with handle on top and hinged door in front. Two stenciled white LW eagles. Paper instruction sheet on door, multi-band adjustment knob and works appear intact with some extra tubes. Exc. cond. $227

Radio, Aircraft, Germany, Luftwaffe, WWII, Siemens. Siemens Model K32 Gwb, multi-band. 7½" x 12" x 18" blue-gray painted wood case with large white stenciled eagle on back and two smaller eagles on front doors. Handle on top, speaker multi-band adjustments in front. Shows some tube rework inside with paper parts illustration and couple of extra tubes and fittings. Above avg. cond. $464

Swastika, Aircraft, Germany, Luftwaffe, WWII. 16" square painted black swastika with gray border and on gray finished fabric. Framed. Above avg. cond. . . . $555

Transformer, Electrical, Aircraft, Germany, Luftwaffe, WWII. Gray metal case with spec plate on top. Model "FL22420." Attached to four-bolt mounting frame. Exc. cond. $120

Window, Aircraft, Germany, Luftwaffe, WWII. Right-hand side window for Ju-88 bomber. Gray alum frame with multiple screws on mount. Sliding window without glass. Inside view shows rusted ventilation tubes around frame and wiring and mount for cockpit lighting. Brackets at bottom may have held additional wiring for cockpit or tubing. Above avg. cond. $360

Wing Camera, Aircraft, Germany, Luftwaffe, WWII, Siemens. 3½" x 5½" x 6½" green painted metal case, shade on lens, leather handle at top and plug-in cord with two-hole socket. Marked "FL32601." Includes "Siemens" marked film cartridge inside. Exc. cond. $700

Aircrew Equipment and Gear—U.S.

Aviation Chart, Cloth, USA, AAF, WWII. Two sided. Color on rayon. Includes Sheet A (43/A) France, Belgium and Holland and Sheet B (43/B) German-Swiss Frontier/France and Spain. Folded. Exc. cond. $105

Aviation Chart, Cloth, USA, AAF, 1943. Color printed on white rayon. Two sided. No. 4, Tyrol and No. 6, Balkans. 1943 dated. Some fraying on edges. Above avg. cond. $133

Aviation Chart, Cloth, USA, AAF, WWII. No. 30, South Burma and No. 31, North Burma. Two sided. Color on white rayon. Some light fraying to edges and yellowing. Avg. cond. $23

Aviation Chart, Cloth, USA, AAF, WWII. Multi-color on white rayon. Two sided. Cyrenaica and Anglo-Egyptian-Sudan. Avg. cond. $100

Blood Chit, USA, AAF, WWII. Printed US flag at top and foreign language phrases. Many Island languages used. Very clean. Some fraying. Exc. cond. $135

Blood Chit, USA, AAF, WWII. Used by US bomber crews on shuttle missions. Has American flag at top, Russian phrases and phonetic pronunciation. Folded as a pamphlet. Undated. Exc. cond. $150

Blood Chit, USA, AAF, WWII. Well worn and stained but all languages are readable. Done on silk and now edges are fraying. Avg. cond. $55

Blood Chit, USA, Army, Aviator, 1951. Printed on white rayon with large US flag printed at top and message in ten different languages below. Dated 1951 and serial numbered. Avg. cond. $25

Blood Chit, USA, USAF, 1961. 1961 dated with US flag at top and language phrases below. Appears to be for European operations. Sealed in cellophane. Near mint cond. $30

Blood Chit, USA, USAF, 1962. 1962 dated with 50-star flag at top and message displayed in 14 languages. Nylon cloth. Exc. cond. $35

Blood Chit, USA, USAF, 1951. 1951 dated with US flag at top and six oriental and four European languages below. Above avg. cond. $28

Blood Chit, CBI, USA, AAF, WWII. 7" x 9½" hand-embroidered silk on white silk panel. With Chinese flag cross stitched above several black embroidered characters. Exc. cond. $121

Blood Chit, CBI, USA, AAF, WWII. 8" x 10" color printed on white silk. With Burmese peacock flag over several rows of Burmese characters. White muslin backing. Exc. cond. $379

Blood Chit, CBI, USA, AAF, WWII. Has Chinese flag at top and Chinese characters below and Kumontang stamp at bottom. Silk 10" x 8½" one side. Exc. cond. $150

Blood Chit, CBI, USA, AAF, WWII. All leather construction, multi-piece using 16 pieces. Has US and Chinese flags, CBI emblem and Chinese characters. Taken from jacket, two minor tears on side. Above avg. cond. $282

Blood Chit, CBI, USA, AAF, WWII. 9½" square leather 16-piece construction. With US and China flag, CBI emblem and Chinese characters. Some small stains on leather. Above avg. cond. $195

Blood Chit, CBI, USA, AAF, WWII. Serial numbered. With US flag at top and seven languages shown below. On rayon with some discoloration on edges. Avg. cond. $79

Blood Chit, CBI, USA, AAF, WWII. 9" x 9" white silk body backed in off-white muslin. Color printed with US flag across the top and small blue serial number stamped below. With five-language plea below-none of them in English. Soiled muslin backing loose along one edge. Avg. cond. $100

Blood Chit, CBI, First Type, USA, AAF, WWII. Chinese flag at top and Chinese characters below. Kumontang stamp visible on front and back. Serial number 404 stamped on lower left. Sewn on cloth, may have been removed from uniform. Worn but presentable. Avg. cond. $387

Camera, Aerial, F-56, USA, AAF, 1943, Bauch & Lomb. 24"-long body with large shield assembly around lens. Bauch & Lomb marked with detachable yellow glass filter. Flip-up glass sight assembly. 1943 dated spec plate. Avg. cond. $49

Camera, Aerial, Model K-20, USA, AAF, 1942, Fairchild Aircraft. Hand held. Adjustable lens settings, magazine film, manually operated. Hmkd Fairchild Aircraft and dated 1942 on spec plate. Stored with accessories in reinforced fiber box. Box exterior shows age and wear. Exc. cond. $250

Computer, Aircrew, Mark 8 (Hand Held), USA, Navy, WWII, G. Felsenthal & Sons. Circular slide rule format for time, speed and distance computations, etc. White plastic and black lettering. Marked G. Felsenthal & Sons. Avg. cond. $20

Emergency Light, Life Raft, USA, AAF, WWII. Battery powered with red and white lens and cord with safety clip. Avg. cond. $27

First-Aid Kit, Aeronautic, USA, AAF, WWII. Dark tan canvas impregnated body with zippered sides, pockets and snaps for bulkhead. Well marked with painted red cross design. Includes several contents, bandages, gauze, tourniquet and more. Avg. cond. $37

Foot Locker, USA, Army, Aero Service, WWI. 13" x 17" x 31" fiberboard foot locker in regulation pattern with metal trim and triple hasps on lid. Hand-painted with 2nd Army and Air Service cockade motifs and "Lt. R.S. Barker/Air Service/American E.F." and large rendition of 100th Aero Sqdn. insignia (devil riding downward-falling bomb). Complete with inner tray. Above avg. cond. $440

Gloves, Flight, USA, AAF, WWII. For Type F-2 and F-3 flight suit. Electrically heated. Dark brown leather. Five-finger design. Woven AAF marked spec labels. Size 11. Above avg. cond. $116

Haversack, USA, Army, Aero Service, WWI, Rock Island Arsenal (RIA). Light OD canvas body with 12" x 12" flap and metal snap hooks for sling. RIA marked and 1914 dated. Flap stenciled "24th/Aero. Sqdn./KANS." Inside also stenciled with unit. Avg. cond. $30

Headset, Aircrew, USA, AAF, WWII. Twin spring metal headbands with russet leather covers support two padded earphones. Boom mike mounted on exterior of one earphone. Twist wire cord with male connector. Avg. cond. $40

Headset, Model HS-37, USA, AAF, WWII. Web-covered headbands and chamois-covered earpads. Avg. cond. $37

Load Adjuster, Aircraft, USA, Air Force, c1960s. For B-57b aircraft. In leather carrier. Slide rule style with payloads. Avg. cond. $24

Load Adjuster, Aircraft, USA, Army, c1960s. Slide rule style with instructions and leather carry case. For Army CU-2B Caribou light transport aircraft. Exc. cond. . $28

Navigation Kit, Pilot, USA, AAF, WWII. Brown leather exterior with gilt lettering. Brass zipper with flex web panels. Interior compartment with multiple document and equipment pockets. Above avg. cond. $93

Octant, Aircraft, Model A-7, USA, AAF, 1941. Dated. Battery-powered optical sighting celestial observation device. Hand held or suspended, allowed time-controlled observations with collimation and preserved readouts.

Stored in wooden box with accessories and spares. Above avg. cond. $34

Oxygen Mask, A-13A, USA, AAF, WWII. With avionics. Nylon web snap mounts in place. "Y" mount QR fitting on hose. Used on high-altitude aircraft such as B-29s. Type standardized on Aug. 28, 1944. Below avg. cond. $48

Oxygen Mask, A-14, USA, AAF, 1945. Sized medium and dated May 1945. With headstrap and hose. Avionics. Avg. cond. $35

Oxygen Mask, A-14, USA, AAF, WWII. Size small. Web straps and supple ribbed hose with connector. Widely used model which was standardized on July 1, 1943. Avg. cond. $35

Oxygen Mask, A-14B, USA, AAF, 1957. In original box. Still sealed. AAF stock number and dated July 3, 1957. Expiration date of Oct. 1960. Exc. cond. $91

Oxygen Mask, MBU-5/P, USA, USAF, 1961. Plastic shell with nylon web and bayonet catches, soft rubber mask with all components, mike and avionics. Flex hose with wrap-around mike cord and single QR fitting. Exc. cond. $92

Radio, Emergency, Model AN/CRT-3, USA, AAF, WWII. AN/CRT-3 or "Gibson Girl" survival radio for 5-20-man life rafts. Crank arm and wrench on back. Last model issued late in the war. Avg. cond. $66

Radio, Emergency, Model SCR-578B, USA, AAF, 1943. Model SCR-578B "Gibson Girl" hand-cranked transmitter. Dated 1943. For use in multi-place life rafts. Size 9" x 11" x 12". Copper wire antenna on reel. Below avg. cond. $59

Sextant, A-10, USA, AAF, 1942. Optical sextant, battery powered, drum recording, celestial observation device. Original wooden box with accessories and spares. Dated 1942 and last inspection 1945. Above avg. cond. $60

Sextant, AN-5851-1, USA, AAF, WWII. Black Bakelite case with 10" x 10" x 11" hinged lid with instruction and nomenclature plates on lid. Massive, hand-held unit. Includes hanger bracket for inside of the aircraft. Avg. cond. $38

Sextant, Bubble, AN-5851-1, USA, AAF, WWII. Celestial sighting device with automatic collimator to give accurate read-outs. Pre-settable and capable of multiple shots without leaving station. Stored in black Bakelite case with hanger, battery pack and accessories. Leather carry strap broken. Above avg. cond. $75

Sextant, Model A-10a, USA, AAF, 1943. Dated 1943.

Sextant with collimating optics, adjustable bubble and battery powered. Stored in wood case with provisions for power supply and other accessories. Case in wood with padded braces in lid. Includes maintenance and surplus disposition tags. Near mint cond. $125

Sextant, Model A-10a, USA, AAF, WWII. Bubble collimator, optics, elevation control and power supply all in single unit. Case stores spares and dome hanger. Exc. cond. $96

Stop Watch, Navigator, Model A-8, USA, AAF, WWII, Elgin. Elgin brand. Nickel case is well marked on back. Crystal in nice shape. Works. Comes in worn issue carton with 1943 dated and AAC marked spec label. Above avg. cond. $135

Stop Watch, Navigator, Model A-8, USA, AAF, 1944, Elgin. Pocket style hmkd "Elgin" on specs. Ten-second dial and five-minute inner dial. Stem wound. Hinged rear for maintenance. Dated 1944. Above avg. cond.   . . . $77

Stop Watch, Navigator, Type B, Class 7, USA, Navy, WWII, Elgin. Elgin brand. Nickel body is BuOrd and serial numbered on reverse. Black numbers on white-faced dial that is marked "Elgin Timer." Bezel loose but included. Comes in protective cotton bag and in thick pressed paper box with USN spec label. Works. Avg. cond. $135

Sunglasses, Aviator, USA, AAF, WWII. Thin metal wire frames with dark tinted lenses and plastic-coated wrap-around ear pieces. In cotton-lined brown leather case. Avg. cond. $20

Sunglasses, Aviator, USA, Navy, WWII. Cushion wire glasses with green tinted windows, nose and forehead pads. Exc. cond. $54

Survival Pack, Ejection Seat, USA, Navy, 1974. From Navy A-6 aircraft. Green plastic container with survival pack, raft and lanyard to deploy pack prior to landing. Seat pad in place as are O2 lines. Includes beacon radio and a lot of survival items from kit, all stored inside. This model dated April 1974. Exc. cond. $221

Throat Microphone, Aircrew, Model T-30, USA, AAF, WWII. Black elastic strap to hold against vocal cords and two mikes on flexible strap to press against throat. Avg. cond. $20

Watch, Bombardier/Navigator, USA, AAF, WWII, Elgin. Elgin model. Black face with dual-dial 24-hr ability and sweep second hand. Stem-wound pocket-watch style. Nickel-plated case. Above avg. cond. $165

Wrist Watch, Navigator, Model A-11, USA, AAF, WWII, Elgin. Elgin brand. Nickel body is AAF marked on re-verse. Works. Crystal intact. On dark OD poplin adjustable wrist band. Government inspection tag still attached. Near mint cond. $223

Wrist Watch, Navigator, Model A-7A, USA, AAF, WWII. 12-24-hour dial, sweep second hand and stem set and wound. Two-piece band. Avg. cond. $223

Aircrew Equipment and Gear—Germany

Compass, Pilot, Wrist Style, Germany, Luftwaffe, WWII. Clear dial with Bakelite body and black numbered inside. Bakelite by "AK39 Fl. 23235 Armbandkompass etc." Fluid filled. Works. Three leather straps for wrist or leg use. Exc. cond. $112

Compass, Pilot, Wrist Style, Germany, Luftwaffe, WWII. Bakelite body stamped "Armbandkompass AK39 etc." Fluid filled. Dark dial/scale still works. Two-piece gray leather wrist strap. Exc. cond. $134

Compass, Pilot, Wrist Style, Germany, Luftwaffe, WWII. Clear dial with Bakelite body and movable white bottom marked "AK39 Fl. 23235-1." Operable. Avg. cond.   . $80

Compass, Pilot, Wrist Style, Germany, Luftwaffe, WWII. Bakelite body stamped "Armbandkompass AK39 etc." Dark dial/scale still works. Gray leather wrist strap. Avg. cond. $78

Flight Computer, Hand Held, Germany, Luftwaffe, WWII. It is Fl. marked and is made to fit. 6"-diam black alum rim on b&w plastic body with scales on both sides. Marked with maker name, date and "Fl.23825." 1" x 7" x 8" tan painted alum holder has indented side with clips to hold computer. Other side has 6"-diam movable scale with yellowed plastic lens over paper grid. Six screws on cover for adjusting paper. Above avg. cond. $271

Flight Computer, Hand Held, Germany, Luftwaffe, 1941. 6" diam. Maker marked and dated 1941. Avg. cond. $79

Flight Computer, Hand Held, Germany, Luftwaffe, WWII. 6" diam black finished alum rim. B&w plastic centers with scales on each side. Marked with maker name, date and "Fl.23825." Avg. cond. $72

Goggles, Aviation, Germany, Luftwaffe, 1943. Dated 1943. RB-NR inked on green tin storage case. White rubber pads on oval nickel frames with plastic lenses and elastic headband. Exc. cond. $72

Goggles, Aviation, Germany, Luftwaffe, 1943. White rubber pads on nickel oval frames with plastic lenses and elastic headband. Green painted can with inked 1943 RB-NR. Exc. cond. $50

Luftwaffe Pilot Goggles

Goggles, Aviation, Germany, Luftwaffe, WWII. Tan cardboard box holds goggles, "Auer" lens cloth and cloth pouch with clear and tinted glass lens. Stiff gray rubber pads on gray metal oval frames with adjustable nose bridge, title marked and elastic headband. Exc. cond. $219

Luftwaffe Pilot Goggles

Goggles, Aviation, Germany, Luftwaffe, WWII. About 2½" x 2½" x 4½" metal case with area inside for extra gray elastic headband. Four clear plastic lenses in gray pouch. Rectangular brown painted brass frames with brown leather pads, tinted plastic lenses and elastic headband. Above avg. cond. $212

Goggles, Aviation, Germany, Luftwaffe, WWII. Gray metal can with marked goggles "MW 41." Green oval frames, light green rubber pads, fogged lenses "MW 41" and elastic headband. Extra clear glass lenses in pouch, fogged and one cracked. Avg. cond. $145

Goggles, Aviation, "Auer 295," Germany, Luftwaffe, 1940. Tan cardboard box with maker label on lid and inked "4.Apr.1940." Contents label on underside listing six items. Full gray rubber face pad with maker, gray finished oval alum frames with stamped numbers and tinted lenses. Green elastic headband and extra band and "Auer" suede cleaning section. Two sets of extra lenses, clear and tinted. Good cond. $250

Goggles, Flight, Imperial Germany, Air Force, WWI. Brown leather body, round steel frames, clear glass lenses and elastic headband. Above avg. cond. $78

Message Container, Germany, Luftwaffe, WWII. For aircraft drops to ground troops. 2"-diam x 14½"-long red painted metal tube. Removable end cap and other end has grenade-style blue cap igniter. Above avg. cond. $124

Navigation Instrument, Flight, Germany, Luftwaffe, WWII. Marked "fl.#23750." 5½" x 9" x 12" brown repainted wooden case with white painted "P.A.Z." on each side.

Leatherette handle on hinged lid with two latches and metal-capped corners. 12"-long tan finished metal body with many adjustment fittings and scales. Metal ID plate at side reads "Libellen-Oktant etc." All spare parts appear to be intact with rubber eyecup, brush and bulbs. Exc. cond. $280

Sextant, Hand Held, Germany, Luftwaffe, WWII. 5½" x 9" x 13" blue-gray painted alum storage box with handle on each end. Two-part lid with alum operating instructions and contents list. About 12"-long main body with tan crinkle paint, alum tag "Libellen-Oktant etc. Fl.23750." Maker "De Te We." Comes with extra fittings. Above avg. cond. $347

Sextant, Hand Held, Germany, Luftwaffe, WWII. 12" long, tan crinkle finish metal unit with large rotating dials on each side, precision optics with flip-in filters, etc. In fitted wooden case. Above avg. cond. $315

Aircrew Equipment and Gear——Other

Pilot Headband, Japanese, Air Force, WWII. White cotton cloth headband with red ball and black characters motif in center. Above avg. cond. $95

Flight Clothing——U.S.

Trousers, Flight, A-11C, USA, USAF, Korean War Era. Size 32 in dark blue nylon with woven spec label, USAF ink stamp markings and well marked correct detachable suspenders. Above avg. cond. $72

Trousers, Flight, A-11C, USA, USAF, WWII. Dark blue nylon with woven spec label and knit cuffs. Good zippers. Size 32. Above avg. cond. $80

Trousers, Flight, D-1A, USA, USAF, c1950. Dark blue nylon body with dark blue nylon lining, woven spec label, correct detachable suspenders, good original zippers, early USAF patch design ink stamp markings and blue knit cuffs. Size 38. Above avg. cond. $75

Trousers, Flight, D-1A, USA, USAF, c1950. Dark blue nylon with woven spec label, detachable suspenders and knit cuffs. Well marked. Size 32. Avg. cond. $45

Trousers, Flight, F-1A, USA, USAF, c1950. Dark blue nylon with woven spec label. Size 28. Avg. cond. . . $45

Flight Shirt, Aviator, USA, Army, 1971. Size medium/long in OD Nomex with zipper front, 1971 dated spec label and epaulet added to each shoulder in matching material. Has subdued insignia direct machine embr senior pilot and basic para wing and "U.S. Army" on left chest, name on rt chest, major and aviation (winged prop) collar devices. Also, 7th Div patch with Ranger tab above on left shoulder. Above avg. cond. $25

Flight Shirt, Aviator, USA, Army, c1960s. Size small/long in OD Nomex with zipper front, US-made color 101st Airborne Div patch on left shoulder and woven nylon US Army subdued pocket tape. Avg. cond. $23

Boots, Flying, Winter, A-10, USA, AAF, WWII. Molded black rubber corded soles, natural color roughout hightop bodies with brown leather trim and fleece lining and woven spec labels. Size large. Avg. cond. $282

Boots, Flying, Winter, A-6, USA, AAF. Dark brown leather bodies with fleece lining, woven AAC marked spec labels, good original zipper fronts, leather retaining straps across front and molded black rubber soles. Medium size. Above avg. cond. $187

Inserts, Flight Boot, Heated, USA, AAF, WWII. OD with woven AAF spec labels and snap fasteners. Felt construction. Size medium. Avg. cond. $20

Flight Boots, A-1, USA, USAF, c1947. Size XXL. Dark brown leather with fleece lining, molded black rubber soles, good original zipper fronts with leather retaining straps across front, woven spec labels and early USAF decal on side of each. Above avg. cond. $53

Flight Boots, A-1, USA, AAF, WWII. Fleece lined. Size XL in dark brown leather with molded black rubber soles, woven spec labels, good zipper fronts with dual leather retaining straps across front. Well marked. Above avg. cond. $54

A-1 Flight Boots

Flight Boots, A-6, USA, AAF, WWII. Dark brown leather bodies with fleece lining, brown finish molded rubber-soles, AAF marked woven spec labels, good original zipper front and AAF patch design decal markings. Size large. Exc. cond. $201

Flight Boots, A-6, USA, AAF, WWII. Fleece lined, brown finish bodies with cleated rubber soles and zipper front. Early example. Exc. cond. $130

Flight Boots, A-6, USA, AAF, WWII. Dark brown leather bodies with shearling lining, molded black rubber soles, good original zipper fronts with leather retaining straps across front of each and woven AAF marked spec labels. Size small. Exc. cond. $282

Flight Boots, A-6, USA, AAF, WWII. Fleece lined. Dark brown leather with woven AAF marked spec labels, molded black rubber soles, zipper fronts with two leather retaining straps across front of each. Medium size. AAF ink stamp markings. Avg. cond. $70

Flight Boots, A-6A, USA, AAF, WWII. Size XL. Dark brown leather with fleece lining, woven AAF marked spec labels, good original zipper fronts, molded black rubber soles, AAF patch design ink stamp markings and twin adjustable leather straps across front of each. Above avg. cond. $150

A-6 Flight Boots

Flight Boots, USA, USAF, 1974. Black leather bodies with lace fronts, rubber soles with beveled heels and 1974 dated spec markings. Size 8½R. Above avg. cond. . . $40

Flight Boots, USA, USAF, 1967. Size 11R in black leather with beveled heels and laced-in zipper-front closures. 1967 dated markings. Avg. cond. $20

Flight Shirt, A-1A, USA, USAF, c1950. Size XL. In early USAF shade blue wool serge with woven spec label. Button front and four front pockets. Above avg. cond. $48

Flight Shirt, A-1B, USA, USAF, c1950s. Sage green serge with woven spec label, button front, faint color early USAF patch design printed on rt chest and four pocket front. Medium size. Above avg. cond. $38

Trousers, Flight, A-10, USA, AAF, WWII. Size 40 in dark OD cotton with alpaca lining, woven AAF marked spec label and AAF ink stamp markings. No suspenders included. Avg. cond. $22

Trousers, Flight, A-11, USA, AAF, WWII. Size 32 in dark OD nylon with alpaca lining, woven AAF marked spec label and detachable suspenders. Above avg. cond. $72

Trousers, Flight, A-11A, USA, AAF, WWII. Dark OD cotton with alpaca lining, detachable suspenders and woven AAF marked spec label. Size 34. Avg. cond. . $37

Trousers, Flight, A-11B, USA, USAF, c1950. Dark blue nylon with knit cuffs and detachable suspenders. Medium size. Above avg. cond. $118

Trousers, Flight, A-3, USA, AAF, WWII. Dark brown leather with AAF marked woven spec label and built-in suspenders. Zipper front needs some work. Fleece lined. Avg. cond. $40

Trousers, Flight, A-5, USA, AAF, WWII. Size 42R in dark brown leather. With AAF marked woven spec label (white with black lettering), built-in suspenders and good original zippers. Fleece lined. Above avg. cond. . . $129

AAF A-5 Flight Trousers

Trousers, Flight, A-8, USA, AAF, WWII. Size 38 in dark OD cotton with quilted lt OD cotton lining, woven AAF marked label and detachable suspenders. AAF ink stamp markings. Above avg. cond. $72

Trousers, Flight, A-8, USA, AAF, WWII. Dark OD cotton with quilted lining, zipper fly, adjustable strap across rear and two front patch pockets. With simple printed label "A-8 Type/Size Small." Avg. cond. $25

Trousers, Flight, A-9, USA, AAF, WWII. Size 38 in OD cotton with alpaca lining. AAF marked woven spec label and detachable suspenders. Above avg. cond. $70

Trousers, Flight, A-9, USA, AAF, WWII. Dark OD cotton with alpaca lining, zipper fly, two front patch pockets, knit cuffs and simple printed label marked "A-9 Type/Size Small." Avg. cond. $27

Trousers, Flight, AN-T35 (AN6554), USA, AAF, WWII. Fleece lined. Size 40R in dark brown leather with brown woven on white spec label, built-in suspenders and large AAF patch design decal on front. Above avg. cond. . $63

Trousers, Flight, E-1, USA, USAF, c1950s. Size 38 in olive wool serge with woven spec label, zip fly and knit cuffs. Above avg. cond. $50

Trousers, Flight, E-1A, USA, USAF, c1950s. Size 42 in USAF shade blue wool serge with woven spec label and USAF ink stamp markings. Still has paper Qm inspector tag stapled to body. Above avg. cond. $28

Trousers, Flight, E-1A, USA, USAF, c1950s. Size 36 in USAF shade blue wool serge with woven spec label and USAF ink stamp markings. In original issue carton. Above avg. cond. $25

Trousers, Flight, E-1B, USA, USAF, c1950s. Size 28 in sage green wool serge with woven spec label, USAF ink stamp markings, knit cuffs and adjustable strap across rear waist. Avg. cond. $25

Trousers, Flight, F-3A, USA, AAF, WWII. Electrically heated. Size medium/regular. In original paper envelope with GE marked spec label. Above avg. cond. $36

Trousers, Flight, M-446A, USA, Navy, WWII. Fleece lined. Size 38. Dark brown leather, built-in suspenders, BuAero marked woven spec label and leather insteps. "NAVY" marked. Above avg. cond. $70

Trousers, Flight, A-9, USA, AAF, WWII. Size 40 in OD cotton with alpaca lining, AAF marked woven spec label and detachable suspenders. Above avg. cond. $55

Gloves, Flight, B-3a, USA, USAF, c1950s. Pair dark brown leather Five finger gloves. Well marked. Size 10. With knit inserts and some snags. Well marked leather mittens with sage green knit inserts. Avg. cond. . . . $21

Gloves, Flight, D-2, USA, AAF, WWII. Yellow-tan leather five-finger bodies with dark OD knit wrists and printed AAF marked spec labels. Size 10. Above avg. cond. $160

Mittens, Flight, USA, AAF, WWII. Fleece lined. Dark brown leather bodies with separate trigger finger. Above avg. cond. $50

AAF WWII Flight Mittens

Mittens, Flight, USA, Navy, WWII. With trigger finger.

Dark brown leather with fleece lining and faint NAVY markings. Above avg. cond. $72

Mittens, Flight, N-2, USA, USAF, c1950. Dark brown leather with early USAF ink stamp markings on each. Contract markings. Above avg. cond. $25

Mittens, Flight, N-4B, USA, USAF, c1950s. Sage green nylon with tan leather palms and alpaca facings. Tri-strap adjustable gauntlets and woven spec labels. With OD wool liners with woven spec labels. Both well marked. Exc. cond. $35

Flight Shirt, Aviator, USA, USAF, c1970. Size large/regular. Army issue Nomex shirt mint but has Asian-made cloth insignia, name, USAF pocket tapes, USAF command pilot wing and USAF major leaves on collar. Vietnamese Air Force patch on left chest winged dragon, Vietnamese Air Force unit patch on left shoulder with eagle head and "III." Above avg. cond. $196

Flight Clothing—Germany

Boots, Flight, Germany, Luftwaffe, WWII, Paul Hoffmann & Co. Brown leather and suede. 14"-tall bodies. Fleece lined, two adjustment belts and brown leather lowers. Inked maker labels "Paul Hoffmann & Co. Stadtilm 37." Original "Wilop" black rubber soles. Below avg. cond. $244

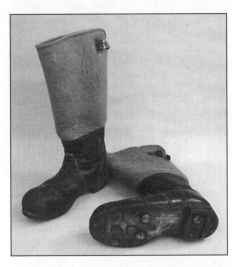

Luftwaffe Aircrew Felt Boots with Wooden Lug Sole

Gaiters, Germany, Luftwaffe, WWII. Blue-gray canvas and brown leather fittings with roller buckles. Above avg. cond. $40

Trousers, Flight, Summer Pattern, Germany, Luftwaffe, WWII. Made from same tan-brown material as the flight suit. Reinforced seat, metal zippers by "Zipp," equipment pockets with snaps on flaps and built-in waistbelt with suspender fittings. Inked RB-NR and "Ia." Exc. cond. $538

Trousers, Flight, Winter Pattern, Germany, Luftwaffe,

WWII. Natural suede body with fleece-lined inside. Five metal zippers are intact and hidden waistbelt with button closure. Above avg. cond. $292

Trousers, Flight, Winter Pattern, Germany, Luftwaffe, WWII. Gray cloth body. Dark thick fur/fleece lining. Waist has belt loops and inked RB-NR with size "2A." Avg. cond. $108

Flight Clothing—Other

Boots, Flight, 1936 Pattern, England, RAF, WWII. Black leather, high-top flight boots are sheep wool lined with adjustment strap across the top in front. Well marked, size 5, RAF markings inside have been over-stamped with mail stamp, probably an effort by owner to conceal them. Shows use. Above avg. cond. $381

Scarf, Aviator, Japan, Air Force, WWII. White silk aviator's scarf with one character. Good cond. $145

Flight Jackets—U.S.

Jacket, Flight, G-1, USA, Navy, c1950. Dark brown leather body with real fur collar, satin lining, good original zipper front, replacement knit cuffs and waistband. Large size. Avg. cond. $150

Jacket, Flight, B-15C, USA, USAF, c1950. Size 38 in dark blue nylon with large fur collar, woven spec label, good original zipper front, small pocket on left sleeve, slash pockets with snap tab above each, knit cuffs and waistband. Above avg. cond. $979

Jacket, Flight, B-15C, USA, USAF, c1950. Size 40 in dark blue nylon with large fur collar, woven spec label, zipper front, knit cuffs and waistband, pocket on left sleeve, slash pockets with snap tab above each. Above avg. cond. $1840

Jacket, Flight, B-15D, USA, USAF, c1950. Dark blue nylon body with dark blue nylon lining, woven spec label (some wear to lettering), good original zipper front, large fold-over fur collar, good navy blue knit cuffs and waistband, pocket on left sleeve, slash pockets with snap nylon tab above each and faint color printed early USAF patch design on left shoulder. Size 38. Avg. cond. $1155

Jacket, Flight, L-2A, USA, USAF, c1950s. Dark blue nylon body and lining with woven spec label, slash pockets with snap closure flaps, pocket on left sleeve, epaulettes, good original knit collar and waistband with snap tab. Replacement zipper and cuffs. Avg. cond. $1168

Jacket, Flight, N-2A, USA, USAF, c1950s. Size large in dark blue nylon with woven spec label, built-in hood trimmed in real fur ruff, good original zipper button/zipper front, snap closure slash pockets, pocket on left sleeve, knit cuffs and waistband, faint color early USAF patch design printed on left shoulder. Exc. cond. $696

Jacket, Flight, N-2A, USA, USAF, c1950. Dark blue nylon lining with woven spec label, real fur-trimmed built-in hood, dark color early USAF patch design decal on left shoulder (near 100%), zipper/button closure front, several pockets and blue knit cuffs and waistband. Name and "19th BSA 22 BWG" inked. Medium size. Above avg. cond. $1420

Jacket, Flight, N-2A, USA, USAF, c1950. Size large. In dark blue nylon with woven spec label, built-in fur-lined hood, good original zipper, pocket on left sleeve, slash pocket with snap tab above each, original knit cuffs and waistband, color printed early USAF patch design on left shoulder. Avg. cond. $277

Jacket, Flight, N-3, USA, USAF, c1950. Dark blue nylon body with real fur ruff trimmed built-in hood, zipper/button front, several pockets, faint printed color early USAF patch design on left shoulder. Medium size. Avg. cond. .
.... $368

Jacket, Flight, N-3B, USA, USAF, c1950. Dark blue nylon with built-in hood trimmed in real fur, "Talon" replacement zipper front, several pockets, faint USAF decal on left shoulder and woven spec label. Size small. Avg. cond. $380

Flight parka, N-3B

Jacket, Flight, G-1, USA, USMC, Korean War Era. WWII-era jacket. Size 38 in dark brown leather with real fur collar, woven "BuAero/NAVY" marked spec label, good original zipper front, original knit cuffs and waistband and satin lining. Zipper pull has Korean coin added to pull. Has 5"-diam fully embr VMF(N) 513 Sqdn patch stitched to rt chest. Above avg. cond. $1210

Jacket, Flight, A-2, USA, USMC, c1950. Dark brown

leather, size 40 with woven maker's label. Has Asian-made "Marine Aircraft Group 11" on left shoulder, large Asian-made red and yellow name tag on left chest with winged USMC device over name, serial number and USMC. Has 5" x 7" USMC VMJ-1 Sqdn patch on rt chest which appears to be Japanese made. Large, diamond-shaped USMC 1st Marine Air Wing patch on rt shoulder. Size 40. Above avg. cond. $500

Flying Coat, Aviation, USA, Army, Aero Service, WWI. Three-quarter-length in brown leather with large vegetable buttons on double-breasted front, brown wool lining, slash pockets, matching belt and button tabs at cuffs. "Classic" pattern associated with WWI flyers. Avg. cond. ... $375

Jacket, Flight, CWU-36/P, USA, USMC, c1970s. Sage green flame resistant body with zipper front, several pockets and knit cuffs and waistband. Has large embr on cotton VMA(AW) 242 Sqdn patch on rt chest, Velcro-attached name tag on left chest with golden-yellow embr name and naval aviation wing design on scarlet. Lacks spec label. Size large. Above avg. cond. $187

Jacket, Flight, CWU-36/P, USA, USCG, 1991. Large size in sage green polyamide with 1991 dated spec label, zipper front, several pockets, knit cuffs and waistband and Velcro panel on left chest. Has Velcro-attached USCG Lieut's name tag with embossed design of naval aviation wing, large embr on twill USCG Search and Rescue, CGAS Elizabeth City, NC patch on rt chest. Above avg. cond. $150

Jacket, Flight, CWU-36/P, USA, Navy, c1980s. Sage green polyamide with zipper front, knit cuffs and waistband and several pockets. Has US flag patch on left shoulder, Tomcat "Grim Reapers" patch on rt shoulder, Velcro-attached brown vinyl nametag on left chest with gold embossed naval aviator wing over man's name and "LT USN." No spec label. Above avg. cond. $160

Jacket, Flight, CWU-45/P, USA, Navy, 1980. Large size in sage green nylon with zipper front, 1980 dated spec label, slash pockets, pocket on left sleeve, Velcro panel on left chest, knit cuffs and waistband. Has twill Attack Sqdn 216 patch on left chest, fully embr "Strike Fighter/NAVY Hornet" patch on rt chest, fully embr "Corsair II" patch on left chest. Exc. cond. $240

Jacket, Flight, CWU-45/P, USA, Navy, c1980s. Sage green polymide body with zipper front, knit cuffs and waistband, slash pockets with Velcro closure flaps and pocket on left sleeve. Has large embr on cotton "Hawk-eye" patch stitched to left chest, large embr on twill Miramar Naval Air Station patch stitched to rt chest. Lacks spec label. Size medium. Above avg. cond. ...
.... $402

Jacket, Flight, CWU-45/P, USA, Navy, 1986. Sage green polyamide with zipper front, large 1986 dated spec label, knit cuffs and waistband and several pockets. Has classic "Tomcat" patch on left shoulder, embr on twill "F-14" patch on rt shoulder, twill Navy Fighter Weapons School patch on left chest and USS Midway patch on rt chest. Avg. cond. $100

Jacket, Flight, G-1, USA, Navy, 1967. Size 36 in dark brown leather with fur collar, 1967 dated spec label, good lining, good original zipper front and original knit waistband. Above avg. cond. $184

Jacket, Flight, G-1, USA, Navy, 1977. Size 38 in dark brown leather with simulated fur collar, good original zipper front, original knit cuffs and waistband and good lining. Printed 1977 dated spec label. Above avg. cond. $145

Jacket, Flight, G-1, USA, Navy, 1986. Size 40 in dark brown leather with simulated fur collar, printed 1986 dated spec label, original zipper front, good nylon lining and original knit cuffs and waistband. Above avg. cond. $171

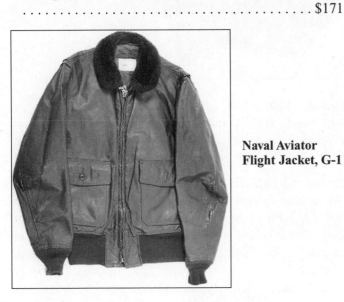

Naval Aviator Flight Jacket, G-1

Jacket, Flight, G-1, USA, Navy, c1950s. Dark brown body with real fur collar, woven BuAero marked spec label, good original zipper front and original knit cuffs and waistband. Good lining. Size 36. Faint trace of name tag on lower left chest. Has had section of zipper flap removed. Avg. cond. $376

Jacket, Flight, G-1, USA, Navy, 1962. Size 40 in dark brown leather with real fur collar, 1962 dated/BuAero marked spec label, good original zipper front, original knit cuffs and waistband and satin lining. Avg. cond. . . $185

Jacket, Flight, L-2B, USA, Army, 1970. Size large in sage green nylon with orange nylon lining, zipper front, knit collar, cuffs and waistband and several pockets. 1970

dated spec label. Has subdued insignia, plastic sealed captain bars, Air Defense Center and School patch on left shoulder, Americal Div patch on rt shoulder, CIB, aviator wing and US Army and name pocket tapes. Above avg. cond. $250

USAF Jacket, L-2B

Jacket, Flight, MA-1, USA, Army, 1968. Sage green nylon with orange nylon lining, zipper front, knit collar, cuffs and waistband, several pockets and 1968 dated spec label. Has subdued 7th Corps patch on left shoulder, subdued pilot wing and name tape on left chest and color captain rank patches. Size small. Above avg. cond. . . . $485

Jacket, Flight, MA-1, USA, Army, 1967. Size medium. Sage green nylon jacket with orange nylon lining, zipper front, several pockets, knit collar, cuffs and waistband and 1967 dated spec label. Has large fully embr "U.S. Army Silver Eagles" patch with silver bullion tinsel detail on rt chest and Velcro attached major's name tag with embossed design of cmd pilot wing and reads "Silver Eagles/Exec. Officer." Above avg. cond. $387

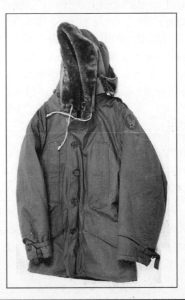

AAF Jacket, L-2B

Jacket, Flight, A-11, USA, AAF, WWII. Size 34 in dark OD cotton with woven AAF marked spec label in neck, fur-lined built-in hood with real fur trim, alpaca lining, zipper/button front, several pockets, adjustable tab at cuffs, epaulettes, color printed AAF patch design decal on left shoulder and AAF ink stamp markings. Exc. cond. $643

Jacket, Flight, A-2, "War Art," USA, AAF, WWII. Size 40R in dark brown leather with woven spec label in neck. Has 8th Air Force patch on left shoulder and 6"-diam Sqdn patch on left chest comical likeness of wolf in flight clothing riding a camouflage bomber with bomb under his arm. Back has large likeness of same wolf riding bomber with eight-ball under his arm, "Section Eight" with clouds and 31 mission bombs below. Exc. cond. $1575

Jacket, Flight, A-2, "War Art," USA, AAF, WWII. Dark brown leather with 5"-diam, English-made, felt Bomb Sqdn patch on left chest has stylized view of B-17 in flight with falling bombs, flak guns shooting back and small stylized geometric caricature of Hitler's face—motto "Potestas Accuratioque." Has large red and white block letters "Yank" on rt chest. Size 40 with woven Rough Wear AAF spec label in neck. Above avg. cond. $2330

Jacket, Flight, A-2, "War Art," USA, AAF, WWII. 8th Air Force. Light brown leather. Size 42 with woven Aero Leather spec label in neck. Good original zipper, excellent cuffs and waistband. Has gold leaf impressed name tag on left chest, silver painted leather Lieut's bars on shoulder straps and 11"-diam painted rendition of the 8th Air Force patch in center of back with 30 large painted silver mission bombs superimposed over the 8th Air Force patch design. Avg. cond. $1650

Jacket, Flight, A-2, "War Art," USA, AAF, WWII. Size 38 with large Rough Wear AAF spec label in neck. Couple of nips in waistband old replacement cuffs (correct color) and zipper. Has 6"-diam patch on left chest "Alone – Unarmed – Unafraid?" Blackbirds around the edge, likeness of comical magpie in center, star and moon in background, bomb in one hand and camera in the other, he wears a red bowler and smokes a cigar. Above avg. cond. $1150

Jacket, Flight, A-2, USA, AAF, WWII. Brown leather body with period replacement "Talon" zipper front, dark tan cotton lining and original knit cuffs and waistband. About size 40. Above avg. cond. $683

Jacket, Flight, A-2, USA, AAF, WWII. Size 40 in dark brown leather with woven AAF marked spec label in neck, good original zipper front and original knit cuffs and waistband. Cotton lining. Avg. cond. $1000

Jacket, Flight, A-2, USA, AAF, WWII. Size 38 in dark brown leather with AAF marked woven spec label in neck, original knit cuffs and waistband and good cotton lining. Period "Talon" replacement zipper front. Avg. cond. $660

Jacket, Flight, A-2, USA, AAF, WWII. Size 44 in dark brown leather with woven AAF marked spec label in neck, original zipper front, good replacement knit cuffs and waistband, good cotton lining. Has Air Service CMD patch stitched to left chest and applied decal design on 5"-diam leather disc. Avg. cond. $685

AAF Flight Jacket, A-2

Jacket, Flight, AL-1, USA, Navy, WWII. OD cotton body with woven BuAero marked spec label, alpaca lining, zipper/button front, several pockets and zippered expansion panels at cuffs. Size 38/40. Above avg. cond. $223

Jacket, Flight, AN-J-4 (AN6553), USA, AAF, WWII. Winter flight jacket. Replacement for the B-3 beginning in mid-1943. Fleece lined. Size 38 in dark brown leather with large fleece collar, woven AAF marked spec label, good original zipper front and adjustable leather tabs at waist. Exc. cond. $1420

AAF Flight Jacket, AN-J-4

Jacket, Flight, AN-J-4 (AN6553), USA, AAF, WWII. Fleece lined. Size 40 in dark brown leather with large fleece collar, good original zipper front, AAF marked woven spec label, color AAF patch design decal on left shoulder (approx. 65%) and adjustable leather tabs at waist. Well marked. Above avg. cond. $380

Jacket, Flight, B-10, "War Art," USA, AAF, WWII. Size 34 in dark OD cotton with real fur collar, woven AAF marked spec label in neck, period "Conmar" replacement zipper front, original knit waistband and replacement knit cuffs, epaulettes and color AAF patch design printed on left shoulder. Has "USA" painted in large red letters above left pocket and Sgt chevron inked on left sleeve. Avg. cond. $525

Jacket, Flight, B-10, USA, AAF, WWII. Size 36 in dark OD cotton with real fur collar, good original zipper, woven AAF marked spec label in neck, front epaulettes, color AAF patch design decal on left shoulder and original knit cuffs and waistband. Avg. cond. $935

Jacket, Flight, B-13, USA, AAF, WWII. Size 40 in dark OD gabardine with woven AAF marked spec label in neck and satin lining and concealed chest pockets with buttoned flaps, slash pockets below, concealed button front, button adjustable cuffs and waist tabs and 9th Air Force patch on left shoulder. Avg. cond. $384

Jacket, Flight, B-14, USA, AAF, WWII. In OD wool, cut like an "Ike jacket." Satin lined with flap-top-concealed chest pockets and slash pockets near waist. Has 9th Air Force patch on left with Staff Sgt's chevrons, three o/s bars, Engr specialty triangle, 3" sterling Air Gunner wing, three-place ribbon bar with oak leaf cluster on Air medal ribbon, discharge patch and DUC ribbon. Size 36 with woven AAF spec label in neck and man's name and serial number neatly ink stamped in neck. Avg. cond. $328

Jacket, Flight, B-15, USA, AAF, WWII. OD cotton body with large real fur collar and alpaca lining, good original zipper front, snap closure slash pockets, original knit cuffs and waistband, printed AAF patch design on left shoulder and pocket on left sleeve. About size 40. Above avg. cond. $492

Jacket, Flight, B-15, USA, AAF, WWII. OD cotton body with large real fur collar, alpaca lining, good original knit cuffs and waistband, snap closure slash pockets and pocket on left sleeve. About size 40. Avg. cond. $310

Jacket, Flight, B-15D, USA, USAF, c1950. Size 42, sage green nylon with sage green nylon lining, woven spec label, large fur collar, zipper front, knit cuffs and waistband, printed color early USAF patch design on left shoulder, pocket on left sleeve, slash pockets with small snap

tab above each. Has faint gold embossed on black leather rank tabs. Above avg. cond. $825

USA Jacket, B-15D

Jacket, Flight, B-3, USA, AAF, WWII. Fleece lined. Size 38 in dark brown leather with AAF marked spec label in neck, corroded original zipper front, large fleece collar, blank leather rank tab on each shoulder and adjustable waist straps. Avg. cond. $559

Jacket, Flight, B-5, USA, AAF, WWII. Fleece lined in dark brown finish with large fleece collar and fleece cuff trim. Size 38R with woven spec label in neck and 90% and AAF decal on left shoulder. Exc. cond. $3160

Jacket, Flight, CWU-36/P, USA, USAF, 1980. Sage green flame resistant jacket with zipper front, 1980 dated spec label, pocket on left sleeve, slash pockets and knit cuffs and waistband. Velcro-attached US flag patch on left chest. Plastic sealed captain bars. Medium size. Avg. cond. $164

Jacket, Flight, CWU-36/P, USA, USAF, 1987. Medium size in sage green Nomex with 1987 dated spec label, zipper front, knit cuffs and waistband and several pockets. Avg. cond. $136

Jacket, Flight, CWU-45/P, USA, USAF, 1989. Sage green polyamide with zipper front, 1989 dated spec label, several pockets, knit cuffs and waistband and Velcro panel on left chest. Medium size. Avg. cond. $93

Jacket, Flight, L-2B, USA, USAF, 1961. Size X-large in sage green nylon with orange nylon lining, zipper front, 1961 dated printed spec label, epaulettes with plastic sealed Lieut Col leaf on each, knit collar, cuffs and waistband and several pockets. Has US flag patch on left shoulder, twill 9th MAS patch on rt shoulder, fully embr Military Airlift CMD patch on rt chest, Velcro-attached sage green nylon panel on left chest. Has color pilot wing stitched to panel over web name tape. Above avg. cond. $450

Jacket, Flight, L-2B, USA, USAF, 1966. Size X-large. In sage green nylon with orange lining, 1966 dated printed spec label, zipper front and knit collar, cuffs and waistband. Avg. cond. $138

Jacket, Flight, L-2B, USA, USAF, 1972. Size medium. In sage green nylon with orange nylon lining, zipper front, knit collar, cuffs and waistband, epaulettes, several pockets and 1972 dated spec label. Has Thai machine embr on blue cotton "T-33 Frustrated Fighter Pilot" patch on left shoulder and Velcro panel on left chest. Faint traces of other removed insignia. Avg. cond. $165

Jacket, Flight, M-422A, USA, Navy, WWII. Dark fleece collar, soft brown leather, good cuffs and waistbands with Edmund T. Church label and size 42. Above avg. cond. $685

Jacket, Flight, M-422A, USA, Navy, WWII. Dark brown leather with real fur collar, woven BuAero/US Navy/M-422A marked spec label, "Talon" replacement zipper front, original knit waistband, replacement cuffs and original satin lining. Size 40. Has faint remains of large Sqdn decal patch on left chest. Avg. cond. $175

Jacket, Flight, MA-1, USA, USAF, c1960s. Sage green nylon with orange lining, zipper front, slash pockets, pocket on left sleeve, knit collar, cuffs and waistband and printed spec label. Size medium, zipper broken. Avg. cond. $24

Jacket, Flight, MA-1, USA, USAF, 1961. Size X-large, sage green nylon with orange nylon lining, good original zipper front, 1961 dated printed spec label, knit collar, cuffs and waistband and several pockets. Has plastic sealed Col eagles, large fully embr Military Airlift CMD patch on rt chest, silver embossed on black leather name tag in clear plastic pocket on left chest with likeness of CMD pilot wing, name and USAF. Above avg. cond. $425

Jacket, Flight, MA-1, USA, USAF, 1958. Medium size in sage green cotton with 1958 dated woven spec label. Zipper front, pocket on left sleeve, slash pockets with snap tab above each, knit collar, cuffs and waistband. Above avg. cond. $1473

Jacket, Flight, MA-1, USA, USAF, 1969. Size X-large in sage green nylon with orange lining, zipper front, knit collar, cuffs and waistband, pocket on left sleeve, slash pockets and 1969 dated printed spec label. Above avg. cond. $305

Jacket, Flight, MA-1, USA, USAF, 1971. Sage green nylon body with orange nylon lining, zipper front, 1971 dated spec label, knit collar, cuffs and waistband and several pockets. Some signs of removed insignia and age. Size small. Avg. cond. $177

Jacket, Flight, N-2A, USA, USAF, 1963. Size medium. In sage green nylon with 1963 dated woven spec label, real fur-trimmed built-in hood, good original zipper/button front, several pockets and original knit cuffs and waistband. Above avg. cond. $409

Jacket, Flight, N-2B, USA, USAF, 1982. Size large with sage green nylon body, printed 1982 dated spec label, built-in collar trimmed in real fur ruff, zipper/button front, several pockets and good knit cuffs and waistband. Avg. cond. $59

Jacket, Flight, N-3B, USA, USAF, 1962. Size large in sage green nylon with real fur trimmed built-in hood, printed 1962 dated spec label, dark (near 100%) patch design decal on left shoulder, zipper/button front and several pockets. Exc. cond. $369

Parka, Flight, A-9, USA, AAF, WWII. Dark OD cotton with built-in collar lined in real fur, quilted lining, woven spec label in neck, button and original zipper front, knit cuffs, epaulettes and four front pockets. About size 38. Avg. cond. $300

Parka, Flight, B-11, USA, AAF, WWII. Size 40 in dark OD cotton with real fur-lined built-in collar, woven AAF marked spec label in neck, epaulettes, good original zipper/button front, several pockets and adjustable tab at each cuff. Exc. cond. $538

Parka, Flight, B-11, USA, AAF, WWII. Size 36 in dark OD cotton with fur-lined built-in hood, woven AAF marked spec label in neck, alpaca lining, several pockets, epaulettes and adjustable strap at each cuff. Avg. cond. $100

Flight Parka, B-11

Parka, Flight, B-9, USA, AAF, WWII, Eddie Bauer. Dark OD cotton with quilted satin lining, fur-lined built-in hood, replacement zipper front and several pockets. AAF/Eddie Bauer marked woven spec label in neck. Size 38. Below avg. cond. $36

Parka, Flight, B-9, USA, AAF, WWII. Dark OD cotton body with fur-lined built-in hood, zipper/button front, woven spec label in neck, quilted green satin lining, several pockets and adjustment tabs at cuffs. Small size 14 tag in neck. Exc. cond. $185

Parka, Flight, D-2, USA, AAF, WWII. Size large with lt OD poplin body with snap-in alpaca, built-in hood trimmed in real fur, zipper neck, drawcord at neck and slash chest pockets with lower patch pockets. Above avg. cond. $500

Flight Jackets—Germany

Jacket, Flight, Winter Pattern, Germany, Luftwaffe, WWII. Dark blue-gray body with dark brown fleece lining and collar. Plastic "Ri-Ri" white front zipper and metal "Zipp" cuff zippers. Three slash pockets and hidden waistbelt with snap closure. Avg. cond. $556

Jacket, Flight, Winter Pattern, Germany, Luftwaffe, WWII. Dark gray suede body with large brown fleece collar. "Ries" metal zipper front, waistbelts and two-snap closure lacks one stud. Two slash pockets with snap strap closures. Full white fleece inside. "Zipp" metal zipper at each cuff with snap closures. Avg. cond. $430

Flight Suits—U.S.

Flight Suit, USA, Navy, WWII, Colvinex. Electrically heated. Size 36 in dark brown leather with real fur collar, built-in leather belt, woven "Colvinex" and printed NAVY spec labels in neck and several pockets. Zipper on rt leg needs some work. Some overall aging but solid suit. Avg. cond. $158

Flight Suit, A-4, USA, AAF, WWII. Size 46. In OD gabardine with woven AAF marked spec label in neck, matching belt, zipper front and several pockets. Above avg. cond. $126

AAF A-4 Flight Suit

Flight Suit, A-4, USA, AAF, WWII. Size 36 in OD gabardine with woven AAF marked spec label in neck, zipper front, matching belt and several pockets. Has AAF patch on left shoulder. Above avg. cond. $164

Flight Suit, A-4, USA, AAF, WWII. Size 38 in OD gabardine with woven AAC marked spec label in neck, matching belt, several pockets and zipper front. Avg. cond. $37

Flight Suit, A-4, USA, AAF, WWII. OD gabardine with matching belt, zipper front and several pockets. About size 38. Avg. cond. $35

Flight Suit, AN-6550, USA, AAF, WWII. OD gabardine with zipper front, woven AAC marked spec label, matching belt and several pockets. Faint AAF ink stamp markings on left shoulder. Below avg. cond. $35

Flight Suit, AN-6550, USA, AAF, WWII. Size 40 in OD gabardine with matching belt, woven spec label with AAC contract markings, zipper front, several pockets and AAC patch design ink stamp in neck. Exc. cond. $145

Flight Suit, AN-6550, USA, AAF, WWII. OD gabardine with zipper front, woven spec label, matching belt, several pockets and faint AAF ink stamp markings in neck. Size 42. Avg. cond. $50

Flight Suit, AN-S-31, USA, AAF, WWII. Size 42 in dark OD gabardine with woven spec label, zipper front and matching belt. Above avg. cond. $101

AAF AN-S-31 Flight Suit

Flight Suit, AN-S-31, USA, AAF, 1944. Size 40M in OD gabardine with woven 1944 dated spec label, matching belt, zipper front and several pockets. AAF ink stamp markings in neck. Avg. cond. $45

Flight Suit, AN-S-31, USA, AAF, WWII. Size 36M in OD gabardine with zipper front, several pockets and woven spec label. No belt. Avg. cond. $40

AAF AN-S-31 Flight Suit

Flight Suit, AN-S-31, USA, Navy, WWII. Size 36S in tan cotton with woven spec label, matching belt, zipper front and several pockets. USN marked below spec label. Avg. cond. $70

Flight Suit, AN-S-3A, USA, AAF, WWII. Size 38 in OD gabardine with woven AAF marked spec label, zipper front and matching belt. Above avg. cond. $66

Flight Suit, AN-S-3A, USA, AAF, WWII. Lighter weight version of AN-S-3. Size 38M in dark OD gabardine with woven AAF mark spec label, zipper front, matching belt and several pockets. Avg. cond. $37

Flight Suit, Anti-G Pressure, USA, USAF, 1950s. 1950s. Sage green nylon body with zipper front, lace panels, pressure hose and color printed early USAF patch design on left chest. Above avg. cond. $100

Flight Suit, Anti-G Type II, USA, Navy, c1950. OD nylon one-piece with diagonal zipper across front pressure tube off left waist. Has woven spec label. Size 36. Exc. cond.   . $40

Flight Suit, CWU-1/P, USA, USAF, 1958. Size large/regular. Insulated sage green nylon with 1958 dated woven spec label, hood in zippered collar, zipper front and several pockets. Above avg. cond. $76

Flight Suit, CWU-1/P, USA, USAF, 1958. Size small/short. Insulated sage green nylon, 1958 dated woven spec label, hood in zippered collar and several pockets. Above avg. cond. $82

Flight Suit, CWU-1/P, USA, USAF, 1960. Size small/regular. Insulated sage green nylon with 1960 dated woven spec label, zipper front, hood in zippered collar and several pockets. Above avg. cond. $50

Flight Suit, CWU27/P, USA, USAF, c1980s. Size 44L in sage green aramid with zipper front, several pockets and several Velcro attachment panels. Above avg. cond.   . $35

Flight Suit, CWU27/P, USA, USAF, 1985. Size 38S in sage green aramid with zipper front, several pockets and 1985 dated spec label. Some traces of removed insignia. Avg. cond. $30

Flight Suit, K-1, USA, AAF, WWII. Size medium/regular. Lightweight tan cotton with zipper front, several pockets, woven AAF marked spec label in neck and color printed AAF patch design on left shoulder. Avg. cond. $72

AAF K-1 Flight Suit

Flight Suit, K-2A, USA, USAF, c1950. Size medium/short. Dark blue nylon with woven spec label, zipper front and several pockets. Near mint cond. $59

USAF K-2A Flight Suit

Flight Suit, K-2A, USA, USAF, c1950. Size medium/short. Dark blue nylon with woven spec label and ink stamp markings, dark (near 100%) patch design decal on

left shoulder, zipper front and several pockets. Exc. cond.
....$161

Flight Suit, K-2A, USA, USAF, c1950. Size medium/long. Dark blue nylon with woven spec label, zipper front and several pockets. Above avg. cond. $139

USAF K-2A Flight Suit

Flight Suit, L-1, USA, AAF, WWII. Size medium/long in OD gabardine with zipper front, AAC marked woven contract label and several pockets. Above avg. cond. ..
....$48

Flight Suit, L-1, USA, AAF, WWII. Size medium/regular. OD gabardine with woven AAF marked spec label in neck, zipper front and several pockets. Above avg. cond.
....$90

USAF L-1 Flight Suit

Flight Suit, L-1A, USA, USAF, c1950. Size medium/regular. Dark blue gabardine with woven spec label and faint USAF ink stamp markings, zipper front and several pockets. Above avg. cond. $114

Flight Suit, L-1A, USA, USAF, c1950. Size large/long. Dark blue gabardine with woven spec label, zipper front and several pockets. Left chest has four female snap ends for name tag (not included), two female snap ends on each shoulder. Above avg. cond. $125

L-1A Flight Suit

Flight Suit, Z-2 Anti-blackout, Navy, c1950. OD nylon with diagonal zipper up front. Has woven spec label size 40/long. Never had pressure hoses installed. Near mint cond. $85

Navy Z-2 Anti-Blackout Flight Suit, Korean

Flight Suit, Z-2 Anti-blackout, USA, Navy, WWII. Size 38-L in OD nylon with woven spec label, diagonal zippered front, several pockets and pressure hose. Above avg. cond. $55

Flight Suits—Germany

Flight Suit, For Maritime Flying in Winter, Type KW s/34, Germany, Luftwaffe, WWII. Brown body has dark brown fleece collar and full lining. Button closure front with various metal zippers to pockets. Oilcloth maker tag has wording. Above avg. cond. $325

Flight Suit, Summer Pattern, Type K So/34, Germany, Luftwaffe, 1941. Tan body with 13 metal zippers by "Rapid" and "Rheinnadel." All leather pull tabs intact. Emergency escape has bevo Berlin maker tag. Inked 1941/maker and " Above Average." Above avg. cond. $381

Flight Suit, Summer Pattern, Type K So/34, Germany, Luftwaffe, 1940. Tan cotton. Emergency escape to left side. Bevo maker tag "Bekleidungsfabrik Habelt Crailsheim Wrttbg. 1940 Grosse I." Above avg. cond. $375

Flight Suit, Summer Pattern, Type K So/34, Germany, Luftwaffe, WWII. Tan cotton body with 15 metal zippers by "Zipp" and "Elite." Emergency escape to side. Above avg. cond. $360

Flight Suit, Summer Pattern, Type K So/34, Germany,

Luftwaffe, 1936, Hermann Frank, Berlin. Tan/brown cloth body with bevo maker tag "Hermann Frank etc. Berlin" with inked script owner numbers and "April 1936." Bevo size 10 tag. Metal zipper by "Ri-Ri." Fair size and pre-emergency escape style. Above avg. cond. $355

Flight Suit, Summer Pattern, Type K So/34, Germany, Luftwaffe, 1941. Tan-brown cloth body with inked maker, "1941" and size "Ib." Metal zippers. Emergency escape seam intact. Avg. cond. $256

Flight Suit, Winter Pattern, Type KW 1/33, Germany, Luftwaffe, WWII. Heavy gray cloth body with thick brown fleece collar and white fleece lining. Metal zippers and buttons all appear intact. Above avg. cond. . . . $384

Flight Suit, Winter Pattern, Type KW 1/33, Germany, Luftwaffe, WWII. Gray-brown body with thick brown fleece lining and collar, eight gray resin button front. Metal zippers by "Zipp" and various pockets. Avg. cond. $276

CHAPTER NINE

Cloth Insignia

The collecting of cloth badges and insignia has been popular since the nineteenth century. Embroidered badges have long been used in place of metal insignia for distinguishing rank, for unit identification and for indicating the specialty or trade of the wearer.

Around 1900, service or field uniforms began to replace more formal dress uniforms for general wear and the use of cloth insignia became more widespread. The English and American armies' adoption of khaki uniforms hastened the introduction of similarly subdued cloth insignia.

Many countries used cloth chevrons to distinguish rank. Often specialty or trade badges were used in conjunction with chevrons to not only denote the rank of the wearer, but also his trade or job.

World War One marked a turning point in the development and use of cloth insignia as cloth divisional badges and patches were authorized for the first time. Although some units had worn divisional identification patches as early as the American Civil War, the World War One era marked the first official adoption of these identifying emblems.

World War Two marked the pinnacle of development for

Second Army Shoulder Patch (WWII)

American shoulder patches. Designs were created for each of the hundreds of newly formed units during the war. Designs were created using popular cartoon characters of the World War Two era, including those created by Walt Disney and Warner Brothers.

Cloth insignias for German forces took the form of shoulder boards, shoulder straps, specialty badges, national emblems, cuff titles and collar pips.

Fakes and Frauds

The problem with embroidered insignia is dating the items. There is basically no reliable way of dating older pieces. A recently manufactured patch can be made to look the same as a World War One vintage patch. Be conscious of original materials, designs, and colors used during the era. Look for wear and signs of removal from uniforms. Make sure that the location of the wear makes sense. Examine pieces carefully. The market has been flooded over the past thirty years with thousands of reproductions, especially Third Reich era cuff titles.

Collectors Clubs

American Society of Military Insignia Collectors, Palmerton, PA, (610) 826-5067, Newsletter

Breast Eagles

Breast Eagle, Coastal Artillery, EM, Germany, Navy, WWII. Golden bevo on tan. Avg. cond. $88

Breast Eagle, Coastal Artillery, Officer, Germany, Navy, WWII. Three-tone hand embr gold bullion on green wool. Avg. cond. $97

Breast Eagle, Luftwaffe, EM, Germany, Luftwaffe, WWII. Bevo. White on dark blue. Uncut. Exc. cond. $71

Breast Eagle, Luftwaffe, EM, Germany, Luftwaffe, WWII. Machine embr on reed-green HBT twill. Exc. cond. $183

Breast Eagle, Luftwaffe, EM, Germany, Luftwaffe, WWII. Machine embr. Silver-gray on blue-gray wool. Above avg. cond. $37

Breast Eagle, Luftwaffe, EM, Germany, Luftwaffe, WWII. Machine embr silver-gray on blue-gray wool. Avg. cond. $20

Breast Eagle, Naval, EM, Germany, Navy, WWII. Golden-yellow machine embr on dark blue wool. Exc. cond. $37

Breast Eagle, Naval, EM, Germany, Navy, WWII. Golden-yellow machine embr on dark blue wool. Avg. cond. $20

Breast Eagle, Naval, Officer, Germany, Navy, WWII. Hand embr three-tone celleon details on blue wool. Avg. cond. $66

Breast Eagle, Naval, Officer, Germany, Navy, WWII. Gold bullion hand embr on dark blue wool. Avg. cond. $86

Breast Insignia, EM, Germany, Luftschutz, WWII. 5" wide gray bevo Luftschutz winged swastika. Uncut gray. Exc. cond. $25

Chevrons and Sleeve Insignia—U.S.

Chevron, 6th Class Spec, Mechanic, USA, Army, c1930s. Lt OD felt on black felt base. Above avg. cond. $19

Chevron, Armor, 2nd Design, USA, Army, WWI. Tan embr on OD wool base. Above avg. cond. $30

Chevron, Band Senior Sgt, USA, Army, WWI. OD embr design of lyre with five-point star above and wreath below on OD wool. Above avg. cond. $20

Chevron, CAC, Engineer, USA, Army, CAC, WWI. Embr on OD wool. Exc. cond. $25

Chevron, Chief Plotter, Dress, USA, Army, CAC, WWI.

2¾" diam navy blue felt base with golden-yellow felt border and two-piece red felt design. Above avg. cond. $22

Chevron, Color Sgt, USA, Army, Infantry, c1899. Single chevron. Three white twill stripes separated by black twist thread with tan insert and sewn circle in center. For the field service blouse. Above avg. cond. $20

Chevron, Ferrier, USA, Army, Cavalry, WWI. Rectangular white cotton base with applied yellow felt specialty design. Exc. cond. $13

Chevron, Ferrier, USA, Army, Cavalry, WWI. Rectangular white cotton base with applied yellow felt specialty design. Above avg. cond. $16

Chevron, First Sgt, USA, Army, Infantry, c1899. Single chevron. Three white twill stripes separated by black twist thread with tan insert and sewn diamond in center. For the field service blouse. Above avg. cond. $20

Chevron, Gunner 1st Class, CAC, USA, Army, CAC, WWI. Tan twill base with applied dark tan felt design. Above avg. cond. $10

Chevron, Gunner 1st Class, Mine Co., CAC, USA, Army, CAC, WWI. Tan twill base with applied dark tan felt design. Above avg. cond. $10

Chevron, Gunner 2nd Class, Mine Co., CAC, USA, Army, CAC, WWI. Tan twill base with applied dark tan felt design. Exc. cond. $10

Chevron, Hospital Corps, USA, Army, Hospital Corps, c1872. Pair of chevrons. Three green felt stripes outlined by white twisted thread and black center and green-over-white patee cross. Above avg. cond. $32

Chevron, Master Qm, USA, Army, QMC, WWI. Color embr design on lt OD wool base. Above avg. cond. . $35

Chevron, Mine Planter Plotter, Dress, USA, Army, CAC, WWI. 2¾"-diam navy blue felt base with golden-yellow felt border and red felt design. Exc. cond. . . $20

Chevron, Musician Senior Sgt, USA, Army, WWI. OD wool base with embr lyre design in center with five-point star above and wreath below. Above avg. cond. $20

Chevron, Pfc, Armored Forces, USA, Army, Armor, WWI. 1st design embr in OD on OD wool base. Above avg. cond. $10

Chevron, Saddler, USA, Army, Cavalry, WWI. Rectangular white cotton base with applied yellow felt specialty design. Unused. Only lt soiling. Exc. cond. $11

Chevron, Senior Sgt, Armor, 1st Design, USA, Army, WWI. OD embr on OD felt base. Above avg. cond. . $30

Chevron, Sgt, Militia, USA, Army, Militia, Civil War. Single chevron. Sewn gold braid on black cloth in curved "V" style. Three stripes, showing some darkening and wear on finish. Avg. cond. $55

Chevron, Sgt, Signal Corps, USA, Army, Signal Corps, WWI. Dark tan applied felt stripes and brown hand-stitched branch device on tan twill. Exc. cond. $11

Chevron, Specialist 1st Class, USA, Army, c1930s. Pre-WWII. OD embr on black felt. Exc. cond. $30

Chevrons, 1st Sgt of Cavalry, USA, Army, Cavalry, WWI. Pair of chevrons, three gold felt stripes with twisted black thread to outline. Between arms is black wool piece with gold diamond centered. Above avg. cond. $51

Chevrons, 1st Sgt, USA, Army, Infantry, c1885. Pair of chevrons. Three white felt stripes outlined by black twisted thread and white diamond outlined in black wool field between arms of chevron. Above avg. cond. $61

Chevrons, Baker, USA, Army, WWI. Red felt appliqués on rectangular white cotton bases. Above avg. cond. $11

Chevrons, Corporal of Cavalry, USA, Army, Cavalry, WWI. Applied yellow felt stripes on white cotton bases. Off uniform but good. Above avg. cond. $14

Chevrons, Corporal of Cavalry, USA, Army, Cavalry, WWI. Applied yellow felt stripes on white cotton bases. Above avg. cond. $15

Chevrons, Corporal of Cavalry, USA, Army, WWI. Pair of chevrons. Two gold felt stripes outlined by black twisted thread. Avg. cond. $29

Chevrons, Corporal of Ordnance, USA, Army, Ordnance, WWI. Lt OD wool bases with applied black felt stripes with red cord borders and cord stitched flaming bomb device. Exc. cond. $34

Chevrons, Engineer, USA, Army, WWI. Red felt branch design on rectangular white cotton bases. Above avg. cond. $12

Chevrons, First Sgt of Cavalry, USA, Army, Cavalry, WWII. Applied yellow felt stripes on white cotton bases. Above avg. cond. $17

Chevrons, First Sgt of Cavalry, USA, Army, Cavalry, WWI. Applied yellow felt stripes on white cotton bases. Off uniform but good. Above avg. cond. $16

Chevrons, Lance Corporal of Cavalry, Dress, USA, Army, Cavalry, WWI. Pair of chevrons. Gold felt stripe with gold brocade cover. Some age darkening. Avg. cond. $55

Chevrons, Master Hospital Sgt, Medical Dept, USA,

Army, Medical Dept, WWI. Brown embr on OD wool. Unused. Near mint cond. $18

Chevrons, Master Sgt, USA, Army, Vietnam War Era. Vietnam made. Subdued. Hand-embr stripes on OD cotton bases. Off uniform. Above avg. cond. $20

Chevrons, Mechanic, USA, Army, WWI. Dark tan felt appliqués on brown cotton rectangular bases. Above avg. cond. $11

Chevrons, Mechanic, USA, Army, WWI. Rectangular white cotton bodies with applied red felt specialty design. Good cond. $10

Chevrons, Medical, USA, Army, c1902. Rectangular dark tan cotton twill bases with burgundy and white felt inserts. Exc. cond. $19

Chevrons, Pioneer Specialty, USA, Army, Pioneer, c1872. Dark blue wool with crossed ax cutout filled from white wool. Above avg. cond. $20

Chevrons, PO 2nd Rate, USA, Navy, WWII. Winter red chevrons on black wool with embr eagle and crossed anchors for Boatswains mate. Above avg. cond. ... $24

Chevrons, S/Sgt, USA, AAF, WWII. Matched pair. Unofficial. Olive embr on dark felt with winged prop design. Above avg. cond. $24

Chevrons, Saddler, USA, Army, Cavalry, WWI. Rectangular white cotton base with applied yellow felt specialty design. Exc. cond. $24

Chevrons, Saddler, USA, Army, Cavalry, WWI. Rectangular white cotton base with applied yellow felt specialty design. Above avg. cond. $12

Chevrons, Sgt of QMC, USA, Army, QMC, WWI. Applied buff felt stripes on white linen base with beautiful cord stitched branch design. Above avg. cond. $17

Chevrons, Sgt of QMC, USA, Army, QMC, WWI. White linen bases with applied buff felt stripes and beautiful cord stitched branch design. Above avg. cond. $34

Chevrons, Sgt, Dress Blue, USA, USMC, WWI. Pair with applied golden-yellow tape stripes on red felt. Three chevrons with three curved rockers. Above avg. cond. ..
.... $28

Chevrons, Sgt. Major, USA, USMC, c1950s. Forest green embr on tan twill. Above avg. cond. $20

Chevrons, Stable Sgt of Cavalry, USA, Army, Cavalry, c1872. Single chevron. Three gold felt stripes outlined by black twisted thread. Black center and gold horse's head. Above avg. cond. $56

Rate, PO 2nd Class, Chemical Warfareman Rate, USA,

Navy, WWII. Navy blue wool serge with applied red felt stripes. Some sporadic nips. Avg. cond. $12

Service Stripes, Cavalry, USA, Army, Cavalry, Spanish American War. Gold wool with white wool stripe in center. Defined SAW service. Above avg. cond. $28

Sleeve Rank, PO, USA, Navy, Civil War. Shows eagle perched on fouled anchor, perimeter outlined in dots. Above avg. cond. $35

Chevrons and Sleeve Insignia—Germany

Sleeve Chevron, Army, Germany, Army, WWII. Large black wool field with double silver taped "V"s. Exc. cond. $23

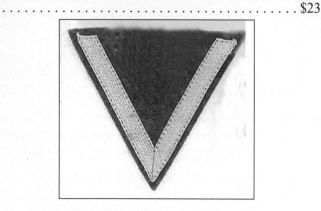

Gefrieter (Lance Corporal) Chevrons

Sleeve Chevron, EM, Naval, Imperial Germany, Navy, WWI. Red, white and black double cord "V"s. Above avg. cond. $37

Sleeve Chevron, SA Old Fighter, Germany, SA, WWII. Bevo alum with black stripes white borders. Near mint cond. $450

Sleeve Chevron, SA Old Fighter, Germany, SA, WWII. Bevo alum with black stripes with black borders. Near mint cond. $160

Sleeve Chevron, SA Old Fighter, Germany, SA, WWII. Brownish-gray wool with silver bevo stripe with two brown center stripes sewn on. Has blue paper RZM tag on back. Above avg. cond. $50

Sleeve Chevron, SS, Germany, Waffen SS, WWII. Black wool with silver braid "V." Exc. cond. $27

Sleeve Chevron, SS, Germany, Waffen SS, WWII. Black wool with two silver braid "V"s. Avg. cond. $33

Sleeve Diamond, EM, SS, Medical, Germany, Waffen SS, WWII. Black wool base black snake with silver white outline. Exc. cond. $35

Sleeve Diamond, EM, SS, Signal, Germany, Waffen SS, WWII. Black wool diamond with silver-white embr blitz. Backed. Near mint cond. $32

Sleeve Diamond, EM, SS, Signal, Germany, Waffen SS, WWII. Silver-gray machine embr blitz on black wool diamond. Backed. Near mint cond. $32

Sleeve Diamond, EM, SS, Signal, Germany, Waffen SS, WWII. Black wool base with silver white lightning blitz. Exc. cond. $32

Sleeve Diamond, EM, SS, Veterinarian, Germany, Waffen SS, WWII. Black wool base with silver white snake embr. Avg. cond. $28

Sleeve Diamond, NCO, SS, Germany, Waffen SS, Ordnance, WWII. Black wool with silver-gray embr of crossed rifle and MG, cut and folded on mat back. Near mint cond. $90

Sleeve Diamond, NCO, SS, Ordnance, Germany, Waffen SS, WWII. Black wool base with silver white embr crossed weapons. Near mint cond. $72

Sleeve Diamond, Officer, SS, Motorized, Germany, Waffen SS, WWII. Alum hand-embr spoked wheel on black wool. Bevo cloth tag "St.159/35 SS." Avg. cond. $175

Sleeve Diamond, SS "sd," Germany, SS, WWII. Silver-gray embr SD to black wool diamond. Paper RZM/SS tag. Near mint cond. $247

Sleeve Diamond, Volkssturm, "standschutzen Bataillon Bruneck," Germany, Volkssturm, WWII. Green wool diamond with color embr Tirol eagle and title. Avg. cond. $61

Sleeve Diamond, Volkssturm, "standschutzen Bataillon Innsbruck," Germany, Volkssturm, WWII. 4½"-tall green felt diamond with embr yellow border, red Tirol eagle and green title. Near mint cond. $111

Sleeve Eagle, EM, SS, Germany, Waffen SS, WWII. Embr. Near mint cond. $79

Sleeve Eagle, EM, SS, Germany, Waffen SS, WWII. Embr. Above avg. cond. $51

Sleeve Eagle, EM, SS, Germany, Waffen SS, WWII. Machine embr. Above avg. cond. $80

Sleeve Eagle, EM, SS, Germany, Waffen SS, WWII. Bevo. Gray eagle on black is zigzag machine sewn to gray wool. Cut from tunic and trimmed close. Avg. cond. $91

Sleeve Eagle, EM, SS, Germany, Waffen SS, WWII. Gray machine embr on black wool. Avg. cond. $67

Sleeve Eagle, EM, SS, Germany, Waffen SS, WWII. Gray machine embr on black wool. Avg. cond. $139

Sleeve Eagle, EM, SS, 1st Type, Germany, Waffen SS,

WWII. Gray embr "dipped-wing tips" eagle on gray wool. Exc. cond. $250

SS Sleeve Eagle, 1st Pattern

Sleeve Eagle, Officer, SS, Germany, Waffen SS, WWII. Three-tone silver bullion hand-embr details with black highlights, black wool and black paper backing. Above avg. cond. $412

Sleeve Eagle, SS, Camo, Germany, Waffen SS, WWII. Bevo. Tan on black. Uncut. Near mint cond. $72

Sleeve Eagle, SS, Camo, Germany, Waffen SS, WWII. Light golden-tan bevo on black with black wool backing. Near mint cond. $35

Sleeve Eagle, SS, Camo, Germany, Waffen SS, WWII. Light golden-tan bevo on black. Uncut. Near mint cond. $35

Sleeve Eagle, SS, Tropical, Germany, Waffen SS, WWII. Light tan bevo on black. Uncut. Exc. cond. $40

Sleeve Edelweiss, SS, Mt. Troop, Germany, Waffen SS, WWII. Black wool oval base with silver white border and edelweiss with yellow stamens. Near mint cond. ... $33

Sleeve Edelweiss, SS, Mt. Troop, Germany, Waffen SS, WWII. Embr 2¾"-tall brown wool oval with green border, gold seeds and white flower/stem center. Late war item. Near mint cond. $342

Sleeve Edelweiss, SS, Mt. Troop, Germany, Waffen SS, WWII. Black oval, gray embr edelweiss with gold seeds and gray border. Above avg. cond. $50

Sleeve Edelweiss, SS, Mt. Troop, Germany, Waffen SS, WWII. Silver-gray flower and oval border on black wool. Yellow flower center. Above avg. cond. $87

Edelweiss Badge of Mountain Troops

Sleeve Edelweiss, SS, Mt. Troop, Germany, Waffen SS, WWII. Machine embr on black wool. Avg. cond. .. $26

Sleeve Pip, Private, SS, Germany, Waffen SS, WWII. Silver-gray machine embr on black wool. Near mint cond. $20

Sleeve Rank Bar, General-obergruppenfuhrer, SS, Germany, Waffen SS, WWII. About 2½" x 4" black wool rectangle with yellow embr oak leaves and acorns over three bevo tape bars. Exc. cond. $93

Sleeve Rank Bar, General-obergruppenfuhrer, SS, Germany, Waffen SS, WWII. 2½" x 4" black wool body with yellow embr oak leaves/acorns over three bevo bars. Exc. cond. $200

Sleeve Rank Bar, Lieutenant, Luftwaffe, Germany, Luftwaffe, WWII. Off flight suit. 3" x 4" gray flight suit rectangle with two white wool gulls and bar below. Above avg. cond. $39

Sleeve Rank Bar, Luftwaffe Lieutenant

Sleeve Rank Bar, Oberfuhrer, SS, Germany, Waffen SS, WWII. Embr black wool rectangular, double green embr oak leaves/acorns and four green tape stripes. Near mint cond. $79

Sleeve Rank Bar, Oberfuhrer, SS, Germany, Waffen SS, WWII. 3½" x 4" black wool body with double green embr oak leaves/acorns over four green bevo bars. Above avg. cond. $150

Sleeve Rank Bar, Officer, SS, Germany, Waffen SS, WWII. For a hauptsturmfuhrer. Green printed on black with oak leaf bar over three straight bars. Avg. cond. $40

Sleeve Rank Bar, Officer-major, SS, Germany, Waffen SS, WWII. Black wool base with two dark green embr oak leaf bars with sewn four-celleon bar tress with three bars of black separating bars, bevo construction 90mm x 100mm. Near mint cond. $190

Sleeve Rank Bars, Officer, Luftwaffe, Germany, Luftwaffe, WWII. Dark blue wool with two white gulls over two white bars. Still stapled together and with original price tag. Near mint cond. $34

Sleeve Rank Bar, Luftwaffe Unterfeldwebel

Sleeve Rank Pip, Private, Germany, Army, WWII. Bullion. Dark green wool with hand-embr silver bullion pip. Above avg. cond. $23

Sleeve Shield, Army Standardbearer, Jager, Germany, Army, WWII. Bevo. Alum details, green standards, b&w eagle and uncut green backing. Near mint cond. . . $641

Sleeve Shield, Army Standardbearer, Pioneer, Germany, Army, WWII. Bevo. Alum details, black standards, b&w eagle and uncut green backing. Exc. cond. $391

Sleeve Shield, Army Standardbearer, Recon, Germany, Army, WWII. Bevo. Alum details, copper brown standards, b&w eagle and uncut green backing. Exc. cond. $496

Sleeve Shield, Army Standardbearer, Signal, Germany, Army, WWII. Bevo. With flat silver, bright yellow and white details. Near mint cond. $295

Sleeve Shield, Army, Foreign Vol "armenien," Germany, Army, WWII. Printed. Exc. cond. $40

Sleeve Shield, Army, Foreign Vol "aserbaidschan," Germany, Army, WWII. Bevo. Field gray cloth with bevo design of black border with red lettering over blue-red-green shield. Above avg. cond. $35

Sleeve Shield, Army, Foreign Vol "bergkaukasien," Germany, Army, WWII. Bevo. Black border shield with all bevo three stylized horse heads on wheel. Uncut field gray cloth. Above avg. cond. $61

Sleeve Shield, Army, Foreign Vol "bulgarian," Germany, Army, WWII. Bevo. Exc. cond. $167

Sleeve Shield, Army, Foreign Vol "georgien," Germany, Army, WWII. Bevo uncut field gray cloth with black border and white lettering over red field with black and white corner. Exc. cond. $50

Sleeve Shield, Army, Foreign Vol "hungarian," Germany, Army, WWII. Bevo. Hmkd "Bevo Wuppertal." Exc. cond. $63

Sleeve Shield, Army, Foreign Vol "idel Ural," Germany,

Army, WWII. Bevo. Color bevo shield on uncut gray with "Bevo Wuppertal." Exc. cond. $55

Sleeve Shield, Army, Foreign Vol "latvian," Germany, Army, WWII. Bevo. White diagonal stripe on maroon shield with ornate black border and on uncut gray. Near mint cond. $160

Sleeve Shield, Army, Foreign Vol "poa," Germany, Army, WWII. Bevo. Dark green cloth, yellow bevo POA over bevo red border shield with white field and blue cross center. Exc. cond. $55

Sleeve Shield, Army, Foreign Vol "turkistan," Germany, Army, WWII. Bevo. With pink and blue shield with white bow and arrow. Dark green border with blue lettering. Field gray background. Uncut. Exc. cond. $58

Sleeve Shield, SS, Foreign Vol Albania, Germany, SS, WWII. Black embr Albanian eagle on red shield on black wool. Above avg. cond. $75

Sleeve Shield, SS, Foreign Vol Albania, Germany, SS, WWII. Black machine-embr double headed eagle on red shield on black wool. Avg. cond. $45

Sleeve Shield, SS, Foreign Vol Croatia, Germany, SS, WWII. Black wool base with straight-top red and white checkerboard shield. Exc. cond. $30

Sleeve Shield, SS, Foreign Vol Croatia, Germany, SS, WWII. Red and white machine-embr checkerboard shield on black wool. Avg. cond. $20

Sleeve Shield, SS, Foreign Vol Denmark, Germany, SS, WWII. Black wool base with red shield with white cross center. Embr. Exc. cond. $44

Sleeve Shield, SS, Foreign Vol Estonia, Germany, SS, WWII. Black wool body with embr blue, black and white. Exc. cond. $50

Sleeve Shield, SS, Foreign Vol Estonia, Germany, SS, WWII. Black wool base with blue-black and white shield embr. Above avg. cond. $28

Sleeve Shield, SS, Foreign Vol France, Germany, SS, WWII. Horizontal embr red, white and blue shield on black wool. Above avg. cond. $237

Sleeve Shield, SS, Foreign Vol Holland, Germany, SS, WWII. Black wool base with orange-white-blue center. Embr. Near mint cond. $48

Sleeve Shield, SS, Foreign Vol Holland, Germany, SS, WWII. Black wool base with orange-white-blue center. Embr. Exc. cond. $42

Sleeve Shield, SS, Foreign Vol Italy, Germany, SS, WWII. Black wool base with golden-yellow bundle of sticks with ax head and outlined in red. Exc. cond.   . $30

Sleeve Shield, SS, Foreign Vol Italy, Germany, SS, WWII. Embr yellow fasces with red highlights, yellow shield outline and on black wool. Exc. cond. $50

Sleeve Shield, SS, Foreign Vol Italy, Germany, SS, WWII. Black wool with gold and red detailed fasces. Exc. cond. $25

Sleeve Shield, SS, Foreign Vol Italy, Germany, SS, WWII. Black wool with yellow machine-embr fasces with red highlights in yellow outlined shield. Exc. cond.   . $45

Sleeve Shield, SS, Foreign Vol Latvia, Germany, SS, WWII. Black wool base with "Latvija" on a red and white shield. Near mint cond. $30

Sleeve Shield, SS, Foreign Vol Latvia, Germany, SS, WWII. Red and white machine-embr shield on black wool. Near mint cond. $45

Sleeve Shield, SS, Foreign Vol Latvia, Germany, SS, WWII. Red and white machine-embr shield on black wool. Exc. cond. $35

Sleeve Shield, SS, Foreign Vol Norway, Germany, SS, WWII. Black wool body, red embr shield with blue and white cross. Near mint cond. $105

Chevrons and Sleeve Insignia——Other

Sleeve Insignia, Army, Machine Gunner, France, Army, WWI. Embr guns and grenades on horizon blue wool field. Above avg. cond. $20

Collar Tabs——U.S.

Collar Insignia, Nurse Corps, USA, Navy, WWII. Heavy bullion devices direct embr into uncut section of navy blue felt. Exc. cond. $25

Collar Tabs, Aviation Officer, USA, Army, Aero Service, WWI. Pair of OD twill with bullion embr "US" over bullion winged prop. Exc. cond. $102

Collar Tabs, Hospital Steward, USA, Army, c1900. Sb Patee crosses in metal. Shows age and tarnish. Avg. cond. $16

Collar Tabs——Germany

Collar Tab, Army, Admin Official (pair), Germany, Army, WWII. Green felt piping on three sides of light gray cloth body having yellow celleon center. Paper "DRGM 1477996" tag. Above avg. cond. $40

Collar Tab, Army, Admin Official (pair), Germany, Army, WWII. Light gray wool base. Dark green piping border except one end and gold wire litzen bar with gold

wire braided cord center on both. Matted back. Avg. cond. $40

Collar Tab, Army, Artillery EM (pair), Germany, Army, WWII. Parade dress. Red wool base with silver wire bevo litzen with white centers. Matted back. Avg. cond. $20

Collar Tab, Army, Artillery Officer (pair), Germany, Army, WWII. Bevo pattern. Green cloth bases, gray bevo litzen and twisted red cords. Inked DRGM etc. Near mint cond. $91

Collar Tab, Army, Artillery Officer (pair), Germany, Army, WWII. Silver-gray bullion hand-embr bars with red litzen on dark green wool. Matte backings. Near mint cond. $66

Collar Tab, Army, Artillery Officer (pair), Germany, Army, WWII. Gray embr litzen with twisted red centers and green wool bases. Above avg. cond. $58

Collar Tab, Army, Artillery Officer (pair), Germany, Army, WWII. Parade dress. Silver bullion hand-embr bars on red wool. Matte backings. Above avg. cond. $50

Collar Tab, Army, Cavalry EM (pair), Germany, Army, WWII. Parade dress. Alum tape litzen on yellow wool. Near mint cond. $20

Collar Tab, Army, Cavalry EM (pair), Germany, Army, WWII. Parade dress. Bright silver braid bars on golden-yellow wool. Matte backings. Exc. cond. $20

Collar Tab, Army, Cavalry Officer (pair), Germany, Army, WWII. Green wool bases, gray litzen and twisted yellow cords. Exc. cond. $78

Collar Tab, Army, Cavalry Officer (pair), Germany, Army, WWII. Silver-gray embr bars with yellow cord centers. Green felt bases. Above avg. cond. $50

Collar Tab, Army, General (pair), Germany, Army, WWII. Red wool bodies with yellow celleon embr designs and matte backings. Above avg. cond. $197

German Army General Collar Tabs

Collar Tab, Army, Infantry Officer (pair), Germany, Army, WWII. Alum litzen with white twisted cord centers and green wool bases. Above avg. cond. $45

Collar Tab, Army, Infantry Officer (pair), Germany,

Army, WWII. Alum litzen with white cord centers and green wool bases. Avg. cond. $35

Collar Tab, Army, Infantry Officer (pair), Germany, Army, WWII. Alum litzen with faded gray bullion centers and green wool bases. Avg. cond. $35

Collar Tab, Army, Infantry Officer (single), Germany, Army, WWII. Parade dress. Alum litzen on white wool. Avg. cond. $20

Collar Tab, Army, Medical Officer (pair), Germany, Army, WWII. Parade dress. Bright silver bullion hand-embr bars on dark blue wool. Matte backings. Above avg. cond. $38

Collar Tab, Army, Mt. Troop Officer (single), Germany, Army, WWII. Alum litzen, twisted green cords and green base. Exc. cond. $20

Collar Tab, Army, Panzer EM (pair), Germany, Army, WWII. Dark green wool base with matted backs. Gray bevo with pink bars and dark green centers. Exc. cond. $45

Collar Tab, Army, Panzer EM (pair), Germany, Army, WWII. For wrap-around tunic. Black felt bodies with pink felt piping and attached alum skulls. Exc. cond. . . $181

Collar Tab, Army, Panzer EM (pair), Germany, Army, WWII. Pink stripes to gray bars sewn to dark green felt. Above avg. cond. $50

Collar Tab, Army, Panzer EM (single), Germany, Army, WWII. For wrap-around tunic. Black wool body with pink wool piping and silver finish skull. Below avg. cond. $75

Collar Tab, Army, Panzer Officer (pair), Germany, Army, WWII. Embr gray litzen with twisted pink centers and green cloth bases. Still tied together. Inked "DRGM 1477996." Near mint cond. $80

Collar Tab, Army, Panzer Officer (pair), Germany, Army, WWII. Dark green wool with silver bullion and pink cord centers. Avg. cond. $37

Collar Tab, Army, Pioneer Officer (pair), Germany, Army, WWII. Dark green wool base with silver bullion litzen with black cord centers. Avg. cond. $41

Collar Tab, Army, Propaganda Officer (pair), Germany, Army, WWII. Parade dress. Bright silver bullion hand-embr bars on gray wool. Matte backings. Near mint cond. $30

Collar Tab, Army, Recon Officer (pair), Germany, Army, WWII. Parade dress. Bright silver bullion hand-embr bars on brown wool. Matte backings. Near mint cond. $101

Collar Tab, Army, Recruiting Officer (pair), Germany, Army, WWII. Parade dress. Bright silver bullion hand-embr bars on orange wool. Matte backings. Near mint cond. $37

Collar Tab, Army, Signal Officer (pair), Germany, Army, WWII. Parade dress. Bright silver bullion hand embr bars on lemon yellow wool. Matte backings. Above avg. cond. $38

Collar Tab, Army, Signal Officer (pair), Germany, Army, WWII. Thick alum litzen with yellow centers and dark green backing. Avg. cond. $30

Collar Tab, Luftwaffe, Admin Official (pair), Germany, Luftwaffe, WWII. Green wool body, twisted alum piping, bullion wreath and pip. Near mint cond. $55

Collar Tab, Luftwaffe, Admin Official (pair), Germany, Luftwaffe, WWII. Green body, bullion embr half-wreath, three pips and twisted alum piping. Above avg. cond. $36

Collar Tab, Luftwaffe, Engineer Officer (single), Germany, Luftwaffe, WWII. Left-hand side. Twisted alum piping on pink body with hand-embr half-wreath and propeller. Above avg. cond. $32

Collar Tab, Luftwaffe, Engineer Officer-hauptmann (pair), Germany, Luftwaffe, WWII. Black bodies with twisted alum piping, hand-embr half-wreath and three gulls. Near mint cond. $38

Collar Tab, Luftwaffe, Engineer Officer-major (pair), Germany, Luftwaffe, WWII. Black wool bodies, twisted alum piping, alum wreath and gull. Near mint cond. $97

Collar Tab, Luftwaffe, Engineer Officer-oberstlt (pair), Germany, Luftwaffe, WWII. Black wool bodies, twisted alum piping, alum wreath and two gulls. Exc. cond. $50

Collar Tab, Luftwaffe, Flak EM (pair), Germany, Luftwaffe, WWII. Red wool. Blank. Avg. cond. $23

Collar Tab, Luftwaffe, Flak Officer-hauptmann (pair), Germany, Luftwaffe, WWII. Red wool bodies, twisted alum piping and hand-embr alum half-wreath and three gulls. Exc. cond. $38

Collar Tab, Luftwaffe, Flak Officer-Lieut (pair), Germany, Luftwaffe, WWII. Alum embr gull over half-wreath on red wool with gray piping. Above avg. cond. $40

Collar Tab, Luftwaffe, Flak Officer-major (pair), Germany, Luftwaffe, WWII. Hand-embr alum bullion on red felt. Near mint cond. $50

Collar Tab, Luftwaffe, Flak Officer-oberlt (pair), Germany, Luftwaffe, WWII. Red felt bodies, twisted alum piping, hand-embr half-wreath and two gulls. Late war example. Avg. cond. $20

Collar Tab, Luftwaffe, Flak Officer-oberst (pair), Germany, Luftwaffe, WWII. Red wool bodies, twisted alum piping, alum wreath and three gulls. Exc. cond. $65

Collar Tab, Luftwaffe, Flight EM (single), Germany, Luftwaffe, WWII. Golden yellow wool with two gray metal gulls. Matte backing. Avg. cond. $24

Collar Tab, Luftwaffe, Flight NCO (pair), Germany, Luftwaffe, WWII. Golden yellow wool with silver braid "L" border. Single alum gull device on each. Matte backings. Above avg. cond. $55

Collar Tab, Luftwaffe, Flight Officer-major, Germany, Luftwaffe, WWII. Yellow wool bodies, twisted alum piping and hand-embr wreath with gull center. Near mint cond. $93

Collar Tab, Luftwaffe, Flight Officer-oberst (pair), Germany, Luftwaffe, WWII. Yellow wool bases with silver bullion details. Avg. cond. $139

Collar Tab, Luftwaffe, General Staff Officer-major (single), Germany, Luftwaffe, WWII. Left-hand side. Crimson wool body, twisted alum piping, alum hand-embr wreath and one gull. Near mint cond. $68

Collar Tab, Luftwaffe, General Staff Officer-oberst (single), Germany, Luftwaffe, WWII. Right-hand side. Crimson wool body, twisted alum piping, alum hand-embr wreath and three gulls. Near mint cond. $77

Collar Tab, Luftwaffe, Herman Goring Div EM (single), Germany, Luftwaffe, WWII. Right-hand side. White wool body, red wool piping and two attached alum gulls. Above avg. cond. $56

Collar Tab, Luftwaffe, Herman Goring Div Flak EM (single), Germany, Luftwaffe, WWII. Left-hand side. White wool body with red wool piping and two alum gulls. Above avg. cond. $50

Collar Tab, Luftwaffe, Herman Goring Div Officer-hauptmann (single), Germany, Luftwaffe, WWII. Left-hand side. Hand-embr alum bullion work on white wool. Above avg. cond. $75

Collar Tab, Luftwaffe, Herman Goring Div Panzer, Germany, Luftwaffe, WWII. For wrap-around tunic. Black wool twill with white piping and matted backing, gray metal skulls with two fold prongs each. Avg. cond. $559

Collar Tab, Luftwaffe, Medical Officer-hauptmann (pair), Germany, Luftwaffe, WWII. Blue wool body, twisted alum piping, hand-embr alum half-wreath and three gulls. Near mint cond. $34

Collar Tab, Luftwaffe, Medical Officer-hauptmann (pair), Germany, Luftwaffe, WWII. Brown felt bodies, twisted alum piping and hand-embr half-wreath with gulls. Exc. cond. $59

Collar Tab, Luftwaffe, Medical Officer-major (pair), Germany, Luftwaffe, WWII. Blue wool bodies, twisted gray piping, alum wreath and gull. Near mint cond. $48

Collar Tab, Luftwaffe, Medical Officer-oberlt (pair), Germany, Luftwaffe, WWII. Blue wool body, twisted alum piping, hand-embr alum half-wreath and two gulls. Exc. cond. $32

Collar Tab, Luftwaffe, Signal Officer-hauptmann (pair), Germany, Luftwaffe, WWII. Brown wool body, twisted alum piping, hand-embr alum half-wreath and three gulls. Avg. cond. $32

Collar Tab, Luftwaffe, Signal Officer-lieut (pair), Germany, Luftwaffe, WWII. Brown wool body, twisted alum piping, hand-embr alum half-wreath and gull. Near mint cond. $40

Collar Tab, Luftwaffe, Signal Officer-major (pair), Germany, Luftwaffe, WWII. Brown wool bodies, twisted celleon piping, alum wreath and one gull. With tie-string at corner. Exc. cond. $50

Collar Tab, Luftwaffe, Signal Officer-oberlt (pair), Germany, Luftwaffe, WWII. Brown wool body, twisted celleon piping, hand-embr alum half-wreath and two gulls. Near mint cond. $34

Collar Tab, SA, Brigadefuhrer (pair), Germany, SA, c1930s. Red wool bodies, twisted white celleon piping and hand embr alum two oak leaves, three acorns and pip. Paper RZM tag. Near mint cond. $300

Collar Tab, SA, Cavalry (pair), Germany, SA, c1930s. Blue wool bodies. Unit side with silver affixed crossed lances and number 6. Rank with silver pip and RZM tag. Above avg. cond. $25

Collar Tab, SA, EM (pair), Germany, SA, c1930s. Both in yellow. Unit side with chain stitched "28/110." Rank blank. Matted backs. Above avg. cond. $118

Collar Tab, SA, EM (pair), Germany, SA, c1930s. Blue wool with yellow cord piping. Unit side with white embr "22/99." Rank side blank. Paper "RZM" tag on each. Above avg. cond. $70

Collar Tab, SA, EM (pair), Germany, Sa, c1930s. Both sides orange-yellow wool with right black chain stitched "28/110" and other side blank. Matted. Above avg. cond. $77

Collar Tab, SA, Obergruppenfuhrer (pair), Germany, SA, c1930s. Wine-red velvet bodies, twisted gray piping, three affixed silver metal oak leaves and pip to each. Exc. cond. $250

Collar Tab, SA, Unit (single), Germany, SA, c1930s. Dark blue wool body with white chain stitched "37/R224." Above avg. cond. $30

Collar Tab, SA, Unit (single), Germany, SA, c1930s. Dark brown with white chain stitched "4/M58." Above avg. cond. $72

Collar Tab, SS Allgemeine, #9 Signal Unit (single), Germany, SS, WWII. Right-hand black wool body with off-white embr blitz and "#9." Near mint cond. $748

Collar Tab, SS Allgemeine, Reserve #26 Scharfuhrer (pair), Germany, SS Allgemeine, WWII. Light gray wool bodies, twisted black and alum piping, black embr "26" and two bronze pips. Black bevo "RZM 38/38 SS" cloth tag. Exc. cond. $790

Collar Tab, SS, Brigadefuhrer (single), Germany, SS, WWII. 1933/42 pattern. Left-hand side. Black velvet body, twisted alum piping, two hand-embr alum oak leaves with four acorns and pip. Exc. cond. $300

Collar Tab, SS, Camp Guard (single), Germany, SS, WWII. Silver-gray embr double armed swastika on black wool. Exc. cond. $79

Collar Tab, SS, Camp Guard, EM (single), Germany, SS, WWII. Black wool body with gray embr swastika. Exc. cond. $50

Collar Tab, SS, EM (single), Germany, SS, WWII. Black wool. Blank. Near mint cond. $50

Collar Tab, SS, EM (single), Germany, SS, WWII. Black wool. Blank. Above avg. cond. $114

Collar Tab, SS, EM, Runic (single), Germany, SS, WWII. Gray bevo runes on black twill. Near mint cond. $124

Collar Tab, SS, EM, Runic (single), Germany, SS, WWII. Bevo. Gray runes on black twill with white mesh backing. Exc. cond. $110

Collar Tab, SS, EM, Runic (single), Germany, SS, WWII. Bevo. Gray runes on black twill with cardboard backing. Exc. cond. $135

Collar Tab, SS, EM, Runic (single), Germany, SS,

WWII. Gray bevo runes on black twill right-hand tab. Exc. cond. $108

Collar Tab, SS, EM, Runic (single), Germany, SS, WWII. Gray bevo runes on black twill wool. Right-hand tab. Exc. cond. $102

Collar Tab, SS, EM, Runic (single), Germany, SS, WWII. Gray bevo runes on black twill. Above avg. cond. $91

Collar Tab, SS, EM, Runic (single), Germany, SS, WWII. Bevo. Gray runes on black wool. Tattered paper RZM/SS tag. Avg. cond. $387

Collar Tab, SS, EM, Totenkopf (single), Germany, SS, WWII. Horizontal pattern. Black wool body with embr silver-gray death head. Paper RZM tag. Near mint cond. $250

Collar Tab, SS, EM, Totenkopf (single), Germany, SS, WWII. Horizontal style, gray embr death head on black wool and matte backing. Near mint cond. $276

Collar Tab, SS, EM, Totenkopf (single), Germany, SS, WWII. Horizontal pattern. Gray embr death head on black wool. Exc. cond. $202

Collar Tab, SS, EM, Totenkopf (single), Germany, SS, WWII. Horizontal pattern. Right-side black wool tab with silver-gray embr death head. Above avg. cond. ... $125

Collar Tab, SS, Foreign Volunteer 11th Div Nordland (single), Germany, SS, WWII. Black wool body with gray embr mobile swastika. Avg. cond. $115

Collar Tab, SS, Foreign Volunteer 15th Div Latvian (single), Germany, SS, WWII. Black wool body with gray embr sun and stars. Near mint cond. $58

Collar Tab, SS, Foreign Volunteer 15th Div Latvian (single), Germany, SS, WWII. Silver-gray embr sun and stars on black wool. Exc. cond. $125

Collar Tab, SS, Foreign Volunteer 18th Div Horst Wessel (single), Germany, SS, WWII. Silver-gray embr. SA logo on black wool. Exc. cond. $67

Collar Tab, SS, Foreign Volunteer 18th Div Horst Wessel (single), Germany, SS, WWII. Silver-gray embr. SA logo on black wool. Exc. cond. $100

Collar Tab, SS, Foreign Volunteer 21st Div Skanderbeg (single), Germany, SS, WWII. Black wool body with gray embr helmet. Avg. cond. $100

Collar Tab, SS, Foreign Volunteer 23rd Div Nederland (single), Germany, SS, WWII. Gray embr wolf-angel on black wool. Right-hand tab. Exc. cond. $145

Collar Tab, SS, Foreign Volunteer 24th Gebirgs Div (pair), Germany, SS, WWII. Black wool bodies. Unit-gray embr flower. Rank-two attached gray pips. Near mint cond. $495

Collar Tab, SS, Foreign Volunteer 25th Div Hunyadi (single), Germany, SS, WWII. Silver-gray embr "H" on black wool. Avg. cond. $125

Collar Tab, SS, Foreign Volunteer 27th Div Langenmarck (single), Germany, SS, WWII. Black wool base with matted back and silver-white embr of three-armed swastika. Near mint cond. $55

Collar Tab, SS, Foreign Volunteer 29th Div Italian (single), Germany, SS, WWII. Silver-gray machine embr fasces with red trigger on black wool. Matte backing. Above avg. cond. $45

Collar Tab, SS, Foreign Volunteer 29th Div Russische #1 (single), Germany, SS, WWII. Silver-gray embr Maltese cross with swords on black wool. Avg. cond. $75

Collar Tab, SS, Foreign Volunteer 30th Div Tarters (single), Germany, SS, WWII. Silver-gray embr wolf head on black wool. Exc. cond. $85

Collar Tab, SS, Foreign Volunteer 36th Div Dirlewanger (single), Germany, SS, WWII. Silver-gray embr crossed rifles and stick grenade on black wool. Near mint cond. $150

Collar Tab, SS, Foreign Volunteer 7th Div Prinz Eugen (single), Germany, SS, WWII. Silver-gray embr. Odal rune on black wool. Avg. cond. $125

Collar Tab, SS, Foreign Volunteer Florian Geyer (single), Germany, SS, WWII. Silver-gray embr cornflower on black wool. Near mint cond. $100

Collar Tab, SS, Foreign Volunteer Italian (single), Germany, SS, WWII. Black wool base with matted back and silver-white embr of fasces (bundle of sticks and ax head). Near mint cond. $45

Collar Tab, SS, Officer Odalrune (single), Germany, SS, WWII. Hand-embr alum rune on black wool with twisted alum piping. Above avg. cond. $381

Collar Tab, SS, Totenkopf Sturmbann-v Officer (single), Germany, SS, WWII. Black wool body, twisted alum piping, hand-embr skull and "V" below. Avg. cond. $250

Collar Tabs—Other

Collar Tab, Officer, Czechoslovakia, Army, c1940. For a Lieut. Embr pair, gold six-point star on brown wool and gold cord border. Above avg. cond. $43

Collar Tab, Unit Insignia, France, Army, WWI. Pair.

Having "90" unit designations embr bullion on black wool fields. Above avg. cond. $20

Collar Tab, Motor Transport Insignia Set, Italy, Army, WWII. One pair of light and dark blue wool with star device. Above avg. cond. $35

Collar Insignia, Italian Waffen SS Volunteer, Italy, Waffen SS, WWII. Black wool field with Italian fasces motif. German made. Exc. cond. $50

Collar Tab, Private 1st Class, Japan, Army, WWII. Uncut woven design. Above avg. cond. $19

Collar Tabs, Leading Private, Japan, Army, WWII. Japanese leading private collar insignia, uncut woven design. Above avg. cond. $19

Collar Tabs, Officer, Soviet Union, Army, Armored, c1980s. Ten Soviet armored officers collar tab pairs, wrapped in brown paper with gilt metal base and black wool centers. Near mint cond. $15

Cuff Titles—Germany

Cuff Bar, Army, General (single), Germany, Army, WWII. Embr on red wool and has been sewn on. Above avg. cond. $80

Cuff Title, Army, DAK "Afrika," Germany, Army, WWII. 17"-long brown body with gray embr title and palm trees, off-white cord borders. Below avg. cond. $165

Cuff Title, Army, DAK "Afrika," Germany, Army, WWII. 14½" brown doeskin body, gray cord piping and gray embr title with palm trees. Below avg. cond. $114

Cuff Title, Army, DAK "Afrika," Germany, Army, WWII. 18"-long tan body, gray cord piping, gray embr title and palm trees. Inked RB-NR. Near mint cond. $370

Cuff Title, Army, DAK "Afrikakorps," Germany, Army, WWII. 16½"-long tan and green body with flat-silver bevo details. Avg. cond. $143

Cuff Title, Army, Officer "Grossdeutschland," Germany, Army, WWII. 15" black doeskin base with silver wire script lettering and silver wire cord borders. Avg. cond. $750

Cuff Title, Luftwaffe, EM "Geschwader General Wever," Germany, Luftwaffe, WWII. 20"-long blue wool body with gray embr title. Above avg. cond. $300

Cuff Title, Luftwaffe, EM "Legion Condor," Germany, Luftwaffe, WWII. 12" blue felt body with gray embr title. Above avg. cond. $374

Cuff Title, Luftwaffe, Officer "Geschwader Boelcke," Germany, Luftwaffe, WWII. 15"-long dark blue wool. Hand-embr alum title. Above avg. cond. $400

Cuff Title, Luftwaffe, Officer "Jagdgeschwader Richtohofen," Germany, Luftwaffe, WWII. 17½"-long blue wool body with alum hand-embr title. Above avg. cond. $750

Cuff Title, Luftwaffe, Officer "Jagdgeschwader Richtohofen," Germany, Luftwaffe, WWII. 10"-long blue wool body. Silver hand embr title. Avg. cond. $480

Cuff Title, Luftwaffe, Paratrooper, EM "Fallschirm-Jager Rgt. 2," Germany, Luftwaffe, WWII, L. Kargl & Sohne. 19"-long green doeskin body with gray embr title. Inked paper tag "L.Kargl & Sohne etc." Exc. cond. $830

Cuff Title, Luftwaffe, Paratrooper, EM, "Fallschirm-Division," Germany, Luftwaffe, 1944. 19"-long dark green doeskin body with gray embr title. Paper tag with inked RB-NR and dated 1944. Near mint cond. .. $1319

Cuff Title, SA, "schlageter," Germany, SA, c1930s. Bevo. 18" black body with gray Gothic title. Exc. cond. $100

Cuff Title, SS Allgemeine, Officer Motorized Unit #9-sturm, Germany, SS Allgemeine, WWII. RZM pattern. 19" black body with sewn ends, seven-strand alum edges and hand-embr alum #9 with black cloth backing. Both paper RZM/SS tags. Above avg. cond. $265

Cuff Title, SS, EM "Adolf Hitler," Germany, SS, WWII. Bevo pattern. 19"-long black body with sewn ends and "Bevo Wuppertal." Gray borders and title. Salt and pepper back. Near mint cond. $597

Cuff Title, SS, EM "Adolf Hitler," Germany, SS, WWII. 13½"-long black body with frayed ends, seven-strand alum borders and gray embr Sutterlin script title. Exc. cond. $492

Waffen SS Cuff Title

Cuff Title, SS, EM "Das Reich," Germany, SS, WWII. RZM pattern. 17"-long black body with sewn ends, seven-strand alum borders and gray embr title. Near mint cond. $397

Cuff Title, SS, EM "Prinz Eugen," Germany, SS, WWII. RZM pattern. 15"-long black body with frayed ends,

seven-strand alum edges and gray title. Above avg. cond. $450

Cuff Title, SS, EM "Reinhard Heydrich," Germany, SS, WWII. Bevo pattern. 19"-long black body, sewn ends and "Bevo Wuppertal." Gray title and borders. Salt and pepper back. Near mint cond. $486

Cuff Title, SS, Officer "Thuringen," Germany, SS, WWII. RZM. Full-length uncut black cloth with correct silver wire thread border and silver bullion lettering. Has folded ends and RZM paper tag. Near mint cond. . $542

Cuff Title, SS, Officer Totenkopf, Germany, SS, WWII. Alum hand-embr skull on 13½"-long black band with seven-strand alum borders. Shows tunic use. Avg. cond. $1200

Cuff Titles, German Air Force, Germany, Air Force, c1960s. Blue-gray embr wings, gray side stripes and full length. Above avg. cond. $20

Cuff Titles——Other

Cuff Rank Insignia, Army, General, Italy, Army, WWII. Pair. General of Div rank. Silver bullion on field gray wool backing. Above avg. cond. $64

Cuff Rank Insignia, Army, General, Italy, Army, WWII. Pair. For dress parade uniform. General of Div rank. Bullion on black wool field. Above avg. cond. $75

Cuff Rank Insignia, Army, Major, Italy, Army, WWII. Pair. Gold braid on black and red wool field. Above avg. cond. $23

Patches——U.S.

Patch, 5th Air Force, USA, AAF, WWII, Australian. 3" diam. Australian machine embr in silk on blue cotton. Avg. cond. $20

Patch, 8th Air Force, USA, AAF, WWII. English made. 2¾" diam. Mach silk embr on felt base. Above avg. cond. $35

US 8th Air Force Shoulder Patch

Patch, 8th Air Force, USA, AAF, WWII. Theater made. 2½"-diam blue felt base with silk mach-embr design with short, stubby wings. Some light soiling and fading. Avg. cond. $20

Patch, 8th Air Force, USA, AAF, WWII, England. English made on dark blue wool, upswept wings with some tarnish. Removed from uniform. 100% original. Above avg. cond. $114

Patch, 9th Air Force, USA, AAF, WWII. Theater made. 2½"-wide dark blue felt base with nice hand-embr design. Above avg. cond. $20

Patch, 9th Air Force, USA, AAF, WWII. Theater made. Heavy bullion, cord and appliqué design on 2½" x 3" blue satin base. Light age. Above avg. cond. $33

Patch, 10th Air Force, USA, AAF, WWII. CBI made. 2¾"-diam mach-embr design on cotton. Cotton backed. Avg. cond. $25

Patch, 12th Air Force, USA, AAF, WWII. 4" triangle with wings of gold bullion and gold ribbon and star of silver bullion. Silver bullion has darkened. Above avg. cond. $145

Patch, 12th Air Force, USA, AAF, WWII. Theater made. 3½"-wide blue felt base with heavy bullion design. Above avg. cond. $39

Patch, 15th Air Force, USA, AAF, WWII. Italian made. 2½"-diam black felt base with heavy bullion design. Some tarnish. Avg. cond. $35

Patch, 15th Air Force, USA, AAF, WWII. Gold and silver bullion design with pink embr center on the star. 2½" diam, some wear and patina to the bullion. Avg. cond. $24

Patch, 15th Air Force, USA, AAF, WWII. Gold bullion on blue velvet. Nice detailing, slight darkening of bullion. Above avg. cond. $40

Patch, 20th Air Force, USA, AAF, WWII. 5½"-diam brown leatherette border with ribbed cotton center. Heavy cord stitched center design. Above avg. cond. $45

Patch, 11th Airborne Div, USA, Army, c1950s. Japanese made. 2¾" x 4" blue felt base with heavy silver bullion design and attached Airborne tab. Some light tarnish and age. Exc. cond. $105

Patch, 82nd Airborne, USA, Army, WWII. Airborne tab at top. On coarse twill cloth. Avg. cond. $21

Patch, 101st Airborne, USA, Army, WWII. Famous screaming eagle patch with airborne tab. This variant has the white tongue vs the usual red tongue. Fully embr. Above avg. cond. $60

Patch, 101st Airborne Div, USA, Army, Vietnam War Era, Vietnam. Vietnam made. 2½" x 3" black twill with hand-embr design and attached airborne tab. Exc. cond. $40

Patch, 101st Airborne Div, USA, Army, WWII, England. English made. 2½" wide with mach-embr design on black felt. Includes matching Airborne tab with hand-embr letters on black felt. Above avg. cond. $35

Patch, 1st Allied Airborne, USA, Army, WWII. Theater made. 2¼" x 3¼" o/a size. Mach-embr design on medium blue felt with attached matching tab. Avg. cond. $28

Patch, 1st Army, USA, Army, WWI. Three-piece construction. Black wool "A" with red and white bars between legs. Avg. cond. $15

Patch, 3rd Army, USA, Army, WWI. 1½"-diam blue felt base with two-piece felt appliqué design. Several small nips. Avg. cond. $30

Patch, 3rd Army, USA, Army, WWII. Embr on OD wool. With paper tag. Near mint cond. $20

Patch, 6th Army, USA, Army, WWII. Standard fully embr patch on tan twill with heavy silver bullion and stitches applied over original design. Above avg. cond. $37

Patch, 8th Army, USA, Army, Korean War Era, Korea. Korean made. 2¾" wide. Pinkish red felt base with heavy silver bullion design. Light even tarnish. Off uniform. Avg. cond. $20

Patch, 828th Bomb Sqdn, USA, AAF, WWII. Embr design of covered wagon on white felt. 4¾" diam. Exc. cond. $76

Patch, 84th Bombardment Sqdn, USA, AAF, WWII. Embr design of devil with bomb on orange twill. 4" diam. Above avg. cond. $75

Patch, 614th Bombardment Sqdn, USA, AAF, WWII. 5" disc, fully embr with red devil's face with gold wings and green bomb below. Blue field. Above avg. cond. $87

Patch, 1st Cav Div, USA, Army, c1930s. Pre-WWII. Three-piece felt constr. Approx. 3½" x 5" size. Off uniform but good. Above avg. cond. $72

Patch, 2nd Cav Div, USA, Army, c1930s. Pre-WWII. Shield in yellow felt with blue chevron and two eight-point stars. Above avg. cond. $19

Patch, 1st Cav Sniper, USA, Army, Vietnam War Era. Subdued 1st Cav patch with sniper ring and weapon emblem in center. Weapon embr in blue. Above avg. cond. $139

Patch, 2nd Chemical Battalion, USA, Army, WWI. 2"

with embr emblem in brown, red and blue. Above avg. cond. $108

Patch, 1st Corps, USA, Army, WWI. Black wool disc with embr white ring. Some moth nips. Avg. cond. . $30

Patch, 2nd Corps, USA, Army, c1930s. Pre-WWII. 2½" wide. Mach-embr design on OD wool base. Some nips to base. Above avg. cond. $28

Patch, 1st Div, USA, Army, c1930s. Pre-WWII. 2" x 3¾" dark tan twill base with silk mach-embr "1." Avg. cond. $20

Patch, 2nd Div, USA, Army, c1930s. Pre-WWII. 3¼" x 3¾" size. Two-piece felt with embr Indian head design. Off uniform but good. Avg. cond. $24

Patch, 2nd Div, USA, Army, WWI. Large square blue felt base measures approx. 4". Has multi-piece felt appliqué five-point star and Indian head design. Shows mothing but original example. Avg. cond. $66

Patch, 4th Div, USA, Army, WWII. Fully embr US-made patch with"ivy" design bordered in bullion. Avg. cond. $16

Patch, 9th Div, USA, Army, Vietnam War Era, Vietnam. Vietnam made. 2½"-diam dark OD cotton base with three-piece velveteen and cotton panel design. Off uniform. Avg. cond. $25

Patch, 28th Div, USA, Army, c1930s. Pre-WWII. 2½"-diam OD wool base with silk mach-embr "Keystone" design. Above avg. cond. $20

Patch, 28th Div, USA, Army, WWI. Yellow felt keystone in 28th Div shape and size. Avg. cond. $28

Patch, 30th Div, USA, Army, WWII. English made. 1½" x 2¼" size. Fully silk mach embr. Avg. cond. $20

Patch, 31st Div, USA, Army, WWII. Theater made. 2⅜"-diam white felt base with cord stitched design. Avg. cond. $20

Patch, 36th Div, USA, Army, c1930s. Pre-WWII. 2½" diam dark tan twill base with lt OD embr border and applied lt blue felt design. Avg. cond. $20

Patch, 36th Div, USA, Army, WWII. Italian made. Fully embr with tan colored T in center. Above avg. cond. $39

Patch, 36th Div, USA, Army, c1930s. Pre-WWII. 3"-diam dark shade OD wool serge base with lt blue silk machine-embr design. Exc. cond. $24

Patch, 42nd Div, USA, Army, WWI. 2¾" wide. Three-piece felt "rainbow" design on OD wool base. Avg. cond. $24

Patch, 43rd Div, USA, Army, c1920s. Fully embr patch

design on brown felt. Has been removed from uniform and has some lt wear and soiling from use. 3¼" wide. Avg. cond. $26

Patch, 45th Division, USA, Army, WWII. 60 x 60mm red felt base with thunderbird design woven in fine gold wire. European made. Exc. cond. $68

US Army 45th Division Shoulder Patch

Patch, 83rd Div, USA, Army, WWI. 3"-wide black felt triangular base with silk mach-embr design. Off uniform. Avg. cond. $38

Patch, 89th Div, USA, Army, WWI. 2¾"-diam dark tan felt base with black silk mach-embr four-quadrant border with "W" in center and blue insert. Couple nips but good. Avg. cond. $55

Patch, 89th Div, USA, Army, c1930s. Pre-WWII. 2¼"-diam OD wool base with applied yellow felt sunflower design and mach-embr center. Glue/paper remains on back but front nice. Avg. cond. $24

Patch, 13th FIG, USA, USAF, c1950s. Embr design on orange twill with scroll at bottom. 3¾" wide, in unissued cond. Exc. cond. $42

Patch, 507th Fighter Group, USA, USAF, c1960. 3¾" x 4¼" embr on twill. Avg. cond. $23

Patch, 335th Fighter Sqdn, USA, USAF, c1950. 3¾" x 4" fully embr. Above avg. cond. $402

Patch, 179th FIS, USA, USAF, c1960s. Full embr 5" with junkyard dog laying on MG, -reads "179th FS CAVE CANUM." Avg. cond. $21

Patch, 199th Infantry Bde, USA, Army, Vietnam War Era, Vietnam. Vietnam made. Subdued. 2" x 3" OD poplin base with mach-embr design that has red embr heart design. Remains of paper backing. On the crude side. Avg. cond. $35

Patch, 1st Infantry Div, USA, Army, WWI. Red felt "1" on OD wool. 2¼" wide. Some damage to the "1." Below avg. cond. $11

Patch, 18th Infantry Regt, USA, Army, WWII. Bevo style. Unit emblem with motto on thin silk cloth. Avg. cond. $27

Patch, 704th Marine Raider BN, USA, USMC, WWII. Shield fully embr with death's head on red diamond in center. Avg. cond. $19

Patch, Air Training Command, USA, AAF, WWII. Gold and silver bullion design on blue felt. 2½" diam. Unissued. Near mint cond. $22

Patch, Alaskan Def CMD, USA, Army, WWII. Mach-embr design on white felt. Early style with seal design and "ADC" above. Avg. cond. $32

Patch, Aviator VA-212 "Rampant Raiders" Sqdn, USA, Navy, c1970s. Japanese made. Fully mach-embr 4½" x 5½" size. Above avg. cond. $55

Patch, CBI GHQ, USA, Army, WWII. Theater-made embr with blue velvet field and white chain stitch and backs with tan cloth. Off the uniform. Avg. cond. $136

Patch, CBI, USA, Army, WWII. Theater made. 2¼" x 3¼" size with heavy silver bullion suns, cord and wire stripe field on uncut dark blue wool base. CBI made. Above avg. cond. $20

Patch, Coastal Arty Brigade, USA, Army, CAC, WWI. White embr triangle on OD wool triangle, 4" a side. For 59th Coastal Arty Regiment, 31st Brigade. Exc. cond. $45

Patch, Desert Storm, USA 4½" x 5¼", Bomb Saddam. $8

Patch, ETO Adv Base, USA, Army, WWII. English made. 2¼"-wide dark blue felt base with cord stitched design. Avg. cond. $16

Patch, Flying Tiger Squadron, USA, AAF, WWII. Cut off leather jacket. Embr on brown wool. Shows tiger jumping through Chinese star hoop wearing Uncle Sam top hat and ripping Japanese flag. Soiled and leather worn. Avg. cond. $315

Patch, Jungle Expert, USA, Army, Vietnam War Era. Asian made. Subdued. Approx. 3" x 2¾" mach embr on dark OD twill with attached tab. Avg. cond. $18

Patch, OSS, USA, OSS, WWII, England. English-made example of yellow-gold cord stitched design on 2½" x 3½"

oval black wool disc. Above avg. cond. $145

Patch, USS Galveston (CLG-3), USA, Navy, c1960s. 4" diam. Mach embr on twill. Avg. cond. $16

Patch, WMEC-620 Resolute, Astoria, Oregon, USA, USCG, c1970s. 4½" x 5¾" size. Fully embr with design and reads "SAR/MLE/Fisheries Conservation." Avg. cond. $10

Patch, Technical Representative, USA, AAF, WWII. 67mm-round blue embr with winged prop and wording around border. Mint cond. $12

Shoulder Tab, USA, Army, Vietnam War Era, Vietnam. Subdued tab reads "LRRP" black on OD green. Above avg. cond. $50

Patches—Germany

Patch, Qualification, Army, Signal, Imperial Germany, Army, WWI. 85mm diam, issue stiff blue wool patch with mach-sewn "V" stitching on yellow wool signal flag poles and the white and red flags with blue linen backing. Avg. cond. $34

Specialist Patch, Army, Armor, Mechanic 1st Class, Germany, Army, WWII. Pink mach-embr cogwheel on field gray wool with pink twisted cord piping. Avg. cond. $30

Specialist Patch, Army, Boatswain, Germany, Army, WWII. Bullion. Dark green wool oval with hand-embr anchor with boat wheel in center. Above avg. cond. . $40

Specialist Patch, Army, Medical, Imperial Germany, Army, WWI. Field gray oval with sewn-on golden-yellow snake on pole. Avg. cond. $25

Specialist Patch, Army, Smoke Troop, Gunner, Germany, Army, WWII. Silver-gray mach-embr shell in oak leaf wreath on dark green wool. Above avg. cond. $34

Specialist Patch, Naval, Diver, Germany, Navy, WWII. Hand-embr red and blue hand-embr diver helmet on dark blue wool oval. Above avg. cond. $65

Specialist Patch, Naval, Engineering, CPO, Imperial Germany, Navy, WWI. White cloth body, blue sewn circle with crown, banner above anchor and steering wheel. Above avg. cond. $63

Specialist Patch, Naval, Engineering, EM, Germany, Navy, WWII. White cloth body, blue border with anchor and steering wheel for Engineering Div. Above avg. cond. $65

Patches—Other

Patch, Artillery Unit, South Vietnam, Army, Vietnam War

Era. "34" artillery patch, full size, black and OD bevo woven. Above avg. cond. $15

Patch, Artillery Unit, South Vietnam, Army, Vietnam War Era. "62" artillery patch, full size, black and OD bevo woven. Above avg. cond. $15

Cap Insignia, Army, EM, Pioneer, Italy, Army, WWII. Enlisted, black embr on wool twill ground, with "60" unit designation. Exc. cond. $20

Shoulder Insignia, Army, EM, Machine Gun Specialist, Italy, Army, WWII. Red embr machine gun and star motif on black wool background. Above avg. cond. $20

Patch, Army, EM, Soviet Union, Army, c1980s. Mint, unissued red wool shield with yellow shield and center of wreath with star and hammer and sickle and cloth backed. Mint cond. $15

Patch, Army, EM, Armored Troops, Soviet Union, Army, Armored, c1980s. Mint black wool base with yellow applied shield and red star emblem over tank, maker marked on back. Mint cond. $15

Patches, Army, Unit Insignia, France, Army, WWII. Woven. For the "22 CJF." Exc. cond. $0

Pocket Insignia, Vichy Garde Du Marechal, France, Army, WWII. Unissued specimen of Marshall Petain's personal body guard. Exc. cond. $76

Shoulder Insignia, Air Force, Italy, Air Force, c1970s. Triangular shaped with eagle and mountain, blue sky field, red scroll inscribed "NAF SIGONELLA." Above avg. cond. $20

Patch, Unit, South Vietnam, Army, Vietnam War Era. 2/2 "Soi Than" unit patch, shield shape in red bevo with black woven head design in center and white figures. Avg. cond. $15

Patch, Unit, South Vietnam, Army, Vietnam War Era. Ben Hai unit patch, black and OD bevo woven shield with three stars in chief and motto below. Avg. cond. $15

Shoulder Straps—U.S.

Banjo Boards, USA, USMC, c1880s. Red knotted cord board with bright metal USMC emblems on red wool field and brass trim. Pair of Cols bullion dress shoulder pieces with gold trim and dark green background. Exc. cond. $43

Epaulets, USA, Army, State Militia, Civil War Era. Gold-colored metallic thread with gilded brass plates. Probably state militia. Edges worn and one button missing. Avg. cond. $220

Shoulder Rank Tabs, Slip-on, General Grade, USA, USAF, c1980s. USAF shade blue knit with silver tinsel

embr stars. Includes 1-, 2-, 3- and 4-star general pairs. Above avg. cond. $24

Shoulder Rate, CPO, USA, Navy, WWI. Rt shoulder 1918 period CPO Qm rate. Above avg. cond. $17

Shoulder Rate, PO1, USA, Navy, WWII. Black on tan PO1 turret captain rate. For rt shoulder. Exc. cond. . $27

Shoulderboards, 2nd Lieut, USA, Army, Civil War Era. For 2nd Lieut. Bullion trimmed and checked brocade center. Appear unused but bullion has darkened. Above avg. cond. $250

Shoulderboards, Full Dress, Officer, Major, USA, Army, WWII, Vangard. Boxed by Vangard and cellophane sealed inside. Color coded for field arty. Above avg. cond. $20

Shoulder Straps—Germany

Aiguillette, Adjutant, Bavarian, Imperial Germany, Army, WWI. Double braided cords with shoulder loops, silver needles with open crown caps blue-white coloration. Designed to secure to shoulder strap with large braid "board." Avg. cond. $72

Aiguillette, Prussian General, M1914, Imperial Germany, Army, WWI. Double looped. Gold bullion wire with gilt gold needles. Near mint cond. $475

Shoulder Strap, Army, Anti-tank, EM (single), Germany, Army, WWII. Sew-in green wool body, pink wool piping and pink chain stitched "P." Avg. cond. $60

Shoulder Strap, Army, Anti-tank, Officer-hauptmann (single), Germany, Army, WWII. Sew-in style. Gray cords, pink wool base, gold "P 560" and two pips. Avg. cond. $101

Shoulder Strap, Army, Artillery, EM (single), Germany, Army, WWII. Sew-in style. 4½"-long gray wool body, red wool piping and chain stitched red "6." Avg. cond. . . $30

Shoulder Strap, Army, Artillery, NCO (pair), Germany, Army, WWII. Sew-in dark green wool bodies, red wool piping, red chain stitched "60" and alum tape stripe border. Avg. cond. $59

Shoulder Strap, Army, Artillery, Officer-hauptmann

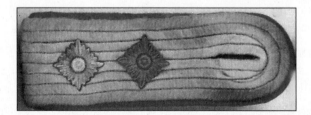

Shoulder Strap, Artillery Captain

(pair), Germany, Army, WWII. Slip-on style. Gray cord bodies, red wool bases and gilt "39." Above avg. cond. $61

Shoulder Strap, Army, Artillery, Officer-oberlt (single), Germany, Army, WWII. Sew-in style. Gray cords, red wool base, gold "242" and pip devices. Avg. cond. . $30

Shoulder Strap, Army, Cavalry, EM (pair), Germany, Army, WWII. Slip-ons with field gray wool tops and golden yellow piping with chain stitched "17" on both. Above avg. cond. $69

Shoulder Strap, Army, Cavalry, NCO (single), Germany, Army, WWII. Sew-in style. Green wool body, yellow wool piping, alum tape and hand-embr yellow "5." Above avg. cond. $40

Shoulder Strap, Army, Cavalry, Officer-major (pair), Germany, Army, WWII. Silver-gray plaited cords on golden yellow wool. Removable. Above avg. cond. . . . $139

Shoulder Strap, Army, Early EM (single), Germany, Army, WWII. Early pointed style. Slip-ons. Gray wool pointed body, black chain-stitched "55" and black twisted cord loop sewn near end. Exc. cond. $35

Shoulder Strap, Army, Early EM (single), Germany, Army, WWII. Early pointed style. Slip-ons. Gray wool pointed body and yellow chain stitched "4." Avg. cond. $34

Shoulder Strap, Army, Early NCO (pair), Germany, Army, WWII. Early pointed style. Slip-ons. Pointed green wool bodies, alum tape and gray pip on each. Avg. cond. $60

Shoulder Strap, Army, Early NCO (single), Germany, Army, WWII. Early pointed style. Slip-on green wool pointed body, alum tape, frosted silver "S4" cipher and pip. Exc. cond. $25

Shoulder Strap, Army, Infantry School, NCO (single), Germany, Army, WWII. Slip-on green wool body, white wool piping, alum tape, alum "AS," frosted silver "S" and two alum pips. Near mint cond. $35

Shoulder Strap, Army, Infantry, EM (pair), Germany, Army, WWII. Sew-in. Dark green wool bodies, white wool piping, white chain stitched "87" and stone gray backs. Above avg. cond. $77

Shoulder Strap, Army, Infantry, NCO (pair), Germany, Army, WWII. Dark green wool base slip-ons with silver litzen and white piping. Two bronze pips and "480." Good cond. $88

Shoulder Strap, Army, Infantry, Officer-hauptmann (pair), Germany, Army, WWII. White wool base and eight silver cord tops and two gilt alum pips. Slip-on. Above avg. cond. $68

Shoulder Strap, Army, Infantry, Officer-major (pair), Germany, Army, WWII. Silver-gray plaited cords on white wool. Sew-in. Avg. cond. $28

Shoulder Strap, Army, Infantry, Officer-oberst (single), Germany, Army, WWII. Sew-in style. Gray plaited cords on white wool. Gilt "12" and two pip devices. Blue wool slip-on loop to hide numbers. Below avg. cond. $1217

Shoulder Strap, Army, Medical, Officer-hauptmann (single), Germany, Army, WWII. Slip-on style. Gray cords, blue wool, gold snake/staff and lacks one pip device of two. Below avg. cond. $25

Shoulder Strap, Army, Medical, Officer-oberstlt (single), Germany, Army, WWII. Sew-in style. Gray plaited cords, blue wool, gold pip and snake/staff devices. Above avg. cond. $40

Shoulder Strap, Army, Motorcycle, NCO (single), Germany, Army, WWII. Slip-on green felt body, lime-green wool piping, alum tape, alum "K" and gray "6." Avg. cond. $25

Shoulder Strap, Army, Mt. Troop, EM (pair), Germany, Army, WWII. Slip-ons with dark green body, green wool piping and chain stitched "15." Two bars of gray tress sewn together and at the base of each strap. Near mint cond. $223

Waffen SS Oberstumbannfuhrer Shoulder Straps

Shoulder Strap, Army, Panzer, EM (single), Germany, Army, WWII. Leather. 4½"-long black slip on body and pink/red leather piping. Style used on leather greatcoat. Above avg. cond. $150

Shoulder Strap, Army, Panzer, NCO (pair), Germany, Army, WWII. Slip-on type with field gray wool bases and pink braid piping with silver wire bevo tress borders. Exc. cond. $166

Shoulder Strap, Army, Panzer, Officer-major (pair), Germany, Army, WWII. Silver-gray plaited cords on pink wool. Avg. cond. $85

Shoulder Strap (Single), Army Panzer Major

Shoulder Strap, Army, Pioneer, NCO (pair), Germany, Army, WWII. Dark green wool with silver braid borders and black piping. Field gray wool backings. Removable. Above avg. cond. $53

Shoulder Strap, Army, Pioneer, Officer-lieut (pair), Germany, Army, WWII. Slip-ons with black wool base and eight silver wire tops. Avg. cond. $50

Shoulder Strap, Army, Recruiting, NCO (single), Germany, Army, WWII. Sew-in green felt body, white felt piping, alum tape, frosted silver "W VII" and pip. Avg. cond. $25

Shoulder Strap, Army, Signal, EM (pair), Germany, Army, WWII. Sew-in style. Green wool body, yellow wool piping and hand-embr yellow "48" on each. Near mint cond. $35

Shoulder Strap, Army, Signal, Officer-oberstlt (single), Germany, Army, WWII. Sew-in style. Gray plaited cords, yellow wool base, gold "56" and pip device. Above avg. cond. $40

Shoulder Strap, Army, Smoke Troop, Officer-hauptmann (single), Germany, Army, WWII. Slip-on style lacks tongue. Gray cords, Bordeaux wool, two gold pips and "5." Above avg. cond. $59

Shoulder Strap, Coastal Artillery, EM (single), Germany, Navy, WWII. 4½"-long pointed gray wool body, slip-on style, affixed gray "15" and gold anchor devices. Avg. cond. $20

Shoulder Strap, Luftwaffe, EM (pair), Germany, Luftwaffe, WWII. Blue gray wool with pink piping. Field gray wool backing. Removable. Near mint cond. $255

Shoulder Strap, Luftwaffe, Flak, NCO (pair), Germany, Luftwaffe, WWII. Blue-gray wool with silver braid and red piping. Single silver alum pip. Removable. Above avg. cond. $28

Shoulder Strap, Luftwaffe, Flak, Officer-hauptmann (pair), Germany, Luftwaffe, WWII. Sew-in. Bright alum cord body on red felt. Two gold pips and "#25." Avg. cond. $50

Shoulder Strap, Luftwaffe, Flight, EM (pair), Germany, Luftwaffe, WWII. Slip-on style. Blue-gray wool with yellow piping. Above avg. cond. $87

Shoulder Strap, Luftwaffe, Flight, NCO (pair), Germany, Luftwaffe, WWII. Sew-in style blue-gray twill body, yellow cord piping and alum tape. Above avg. cond. $66

Shoulder Strap, Luftwaffe, Flight, Officer-hauptmann (pair), Germany, Luftwaffe, WWII. Slip-on style. Alum cords on yellow wool and two gold pips each. Avg. cond. $78

Shoulder Strap, Luftwaffe, Flight, Officer-oberst (pair), Germany, Luftwaffe, WWII. Bright silver plaited cords on golden yellow wool. With two gilt metal pips. Sew-in. Avg. cond. $50

Shoulder Strap, Luftwaffe, Signal, Officer-hauptmann (pair), Germany, Luftwaffe, WWII. Brown wool base and eight silver cord tops with two gilt alum pips. Avg. cond. $27

Shoulder Strap, Naval, CPO (pair), Germany, Navy, WWII. Dark navy blue wool with golden yellow tape border and gilt metal crossed anchors and silver-gray metal rank star. Sew-in pattern. Above avg. cond. $45

Shoulder Strap, Naval, Officer-lieut (pair), Germany, Navy, WWII. Removable wing-tip style. Early silver cords show darkening and white felt bases. Grommet on button holes. Above avg. cond. $65

Shoulder Strap, SA, EM (single), Germany, SA, c1930s. 4½"-long twisted b&w four-cord body on brown wool. Sewn-in. Above avg. cond. $50

Shoulder Strap, SS, EM (pair), Germany, SS, WWII. Slip on, black wool bodies and light green cord piping. Near mint cond. $125

Shoulder Strap, SS, Infantry, NCO (pair), Germany, SS, WWII. Black wool with silver-gray braid and white piping. With silver finished "N" cipher and single pip. Field gray wool backing. Removable. Above avg. cond. $526

Shoulder Strap, SS, Infantry, Officer-obersturmfuhrer (pair), Germany, SS, WWII. Sewn-in style. Gray-alum cords, white wool piping, black wool bases and gold pip on each. Near mint cond. $174

Shoulder Strap, SS, Infantry, Officer-untersturmfuhrer (pair), Germany, SS, WWII. Sewn-in style. Gray-alum cords, white wool piping and black wool bases. Exc. cond. $150

Shoulder Strap, SS, Medical, NCO (pair), Germany, SS, WWII. Black wool bases with field gray wool lining and dark blue piping and tan tress, slip-on tongues. Exc. cond. $111

Shoulder Strap, SS, NCO, Cipher "D" (pair), Germany, SS, WWII. For "Deutschland." Stamped silver Latin "D" and two prongs each. 10 x 12mm. Near mint cond. $219

Shoulder Strap, SS, NCO, Cipher "G" (pair), Germany, SS, WWII. For "Germania." Stamped alum Latin "G" and two prongs each. 14 x 18mm. Exc. cond. $244

Shoulder Strap, SS, Panzer Grenadier, Officer-lieut (pair), Germany, SS, WWII. Black wool base with light green braid piping with eight silver wire cords and are sewn-in type. Exc. cond. $255

Shoulder Strap, SS, Panzer, EM (pair), Germany, SS, WWII. Slip-on style, black wool bodies with pink cord piping. Above avg. cond. $265

Shoulder Strap, SS, Transport, EM (pair), Germany, SS, WWII. Slip-on style. Black wool bodies, light blue cord piping and gray wool backs. Above avg. cond. $244

Shoulder Straps, Artillery, EM, M1915 (single), Imperial Germany, Army, WWI. Yellow field red crossed cannons with flames. Red embr "16." Includes single metallic flying AA bomb for board. Avg. cond. $26

Shoulder Straps, Flieger, EM (pair), Imperial Germany, Army, Flieger (Pilot), WWI. Field gray wool bodies with red embr winged propellers. Sew-ins with pointed ends. Avg. cond. $61

Shoulderboards, Army, Lieut, Bavarian (pair), Imperial Germany, Army, WWI. Sew-in style. Silver field blue flecking. White base. Exc. cond. $30

Shoulderboards, Army, Lieut, Prussian (pair), Imperial Germany, Army, WWI. Red wool base silver wire field with single brass rank star. Black flecking. Above avg. cond. $24

Shoulderboards, Captain, Saxon (single), Imperial Germany, Army, WWI. Sew-in pattern. Red base silver field with green flecking. Gilt double rank pips with "108" numbers. Flat brass button. Avg. cond. $25

Swallow Nest, Bandsman (pair), Germany, Army, WWII. Green wool bodies, eight gold diagonal tape stripes and lower strip with 1"-long gold fringe. Sew-in style. Above avg. cond. $79

Swallow Nest, Bandsman (pair), Germany, Army, WWII. Sew-in style. Green wool bodies, dark silver vertical tape stripes and lower strip. Above avg. cond. $65

Swallow Nest, Bandsman, Imperial Germany, Army, WWI. Pair. Subdued silver braid on tan cloth backing. Avg. cond. $25

Swallow Nest, Bandsman, Imperial Germany, Army, WWI. Pair. Wartime. Feldgrau backing subdued white tressing with red bars. All hooks present. Avg. cond. $25

Swallow Nest, Cavalry, Bandsman, Imperial Germany, Army, WWI. Golden yellow wool body with seven diagonal bands of gold bullion (line cavalry unit), NCO tape (Tresse) and one horizontal bar. Yellow wool backing, all machine sewn, sewn-in type. Avg. cond. $25

Swallow Nest, Infantry, Bandsman, M1910, Imperial Germany, Army, WWI. Pair. Field gray body and backing, red wool piping, gold bullion NCO tape. Exc. cond. $63

Shoulder Straps—Other

Aiguillette, Prussian General, Prussia, Army, c1810. Napoleonic era. Heavy gold double braided loops with shoulder woven planchet for securing on uniform. Cords have proper brass "needles" on ends–actually turned and pointed. Below avg. cond. $59

Shoulder Straps, KGB, Soviet Union. White KGB SKS/AK-47 parade sling, 60", white nylon on coated fabric with metal fittings and buckles. Above avg. cond. $13

Shoulder Straps, Armored Division, Officer, Poland, Army, WWII. For Army in exile. Printed item with winged armored arm and sword. Above avg. cond. $70

Shoulder Straps, Artillery Regiment, Officer, Poland, Army, WWII. For Army in exile. Embr, dark blue wool field. Above avg. cond. $75

Shoulder Straps, Infantry Div, Officer, Poland, Army, WWII. Brown embr buffalo on tan field, khaki wool shield-shaped ground. Above avg. cond. $70

Shoulderboards, Army, EM, Soviet Union, Army, 1980. Pair of wine red wool shoulderboards on khaki field. Exc. cond. $20

Shoulderboards, Army, Major General, Soviet Union, Army, c1960. Pair of shoulderboards with hand-embr silver bullion star on gold bullion braid field, with red wool underlay. Above avg. cond. $45

CHAPTER TEN

Metal Insignia

Metal insignia to distinguish units from one another have been used since the 1700s. In the modern era, metal insignia break down into buttons, collar devices, cap devices, helmet frontplates, distinctive insignia (DI's), ID badges and wings.

The English military has a long, distinguished history of using metallic insignia. Compared to other countries, the English insignia are distinctively attractive and varied. However, English insignia are not highly collected in the United States.

The metal insignia of the United States are the most highly desirable collectibles in this category. The wide variety of metal wings produced during the war years are among the most sought after and collected metallic insignia.

Distinctive insignia (DI's) and collar discs were widely used between the wars, evolving into elaborate and detailed forms of unit identification. The demands

English Officer's Gorget

on resources during World War Two led to a simplification of these items, but they continued to be worn by various army organizations.

Fakes and Frauds

Metal insignia are often manufactured using original dies and stampings. World War Two era dies from the Meyer Company, a wing and other insignia manufacturer, were sold and are currently being used to produce reproduction wings which are identical to World War Two Meyer Company specimens. Wear should be a recognizable characteristic, indicating age, but processes can be applied to give the appearance of an aged or original piece.

Collectors Clubs

American Society of Military Insignia Collectors, Palmerton, PA, (610) 826-5067, Newsletter

Buttons, Plates and Gorgets—U.S.

Button, Cavalry, USA, Army, Civil War. Shows crossed sabers with "A" above cross. Some light surface spotting. Avg. cond. $20

Button, North Carolina Unit, USA, Army, Confederate, Civil War. From a North Carolina uniform. 22mm bronze button with state image on face. Avg. cond. $43

Button, Shako (1851 Pattern), USA, Army, Civil War. 41mm-diam stamped brass body with design of early spread-wing eagle and wreath border. Prong back. Avg. cond. $30

Buttons, Plates and Gorgets—Germany

Gorget, Reichs-Luft-Aufsicht, 1st Model, Germany, Luftwaffe, WWII, C.E. Juncker, Berlin. 6"-wide half-moon body shows worn frosted silver finish. Heavy brass winged swastika affixed over brass title. Green leatherette-covered back with center hook stamped "C.E.Juncker Berlin." Corner loops to silver linked chain. Above avg. cond. $675

Gorget, Reichs-Luft-Aufsicht, 2nd Model, Germany, Luftwaffe, WWII. Alum half-moon body with affixed gold finished title and winged swastika. Green leatherette backing, center hook and alum chain. Above avg. cond. $616

Gorget, SA, Germany, SA, c1930. Bright nickel heart-shaped body with wear to silver finished brass roundel having early mobile swastika. Gold finished brass star-burst backing on roundel. Brass corner domes with design on each. Blue wool backing has large metal RZM disc affixed. Two hooks and one corner loop. Avg. cond. $248

Buttons, Plates and Gorgets—Other

Gorget, Officer, England, Army, c1805. Gilt brass gorget engraved with the Royal cipher and crown. A few minor blemishes present. Above avg. cond. $863

French Officer's Gorget

Gorget, Officer, France, Army, c1810. Gilt brass gorget backed with green wool and applied with silvered Imperial eagle. Some small dents and scratches present. Above avg. cond. $1035

Gorget, Officer, France, Army, c1860. Gilt brass gorget with silver Imperial eagle. Some light tarnish. Above avg. cond. $288

Gorget, Officer, Light Infantry, France, Army, c1815. Brass gorget with silver plate of Infantry horn with Royal coat of arms. Dark patina and some minor blemishes present. Avg. cond. $230

Shoulder Belt Plate, Officer, England, Army, c1805. Oval gilt brass plate engraved with the Royal crown and cipher and spray of oak leaves. A few minor blemishes and discoloration. Above avg. cond. $575

Cap Devices—U.S.

Cap Device, 7th Cavalry, USA, Army, c1870. 2¾" wide. Gilt brass. Open catch pb. Some corrosion. Avg. cond. $45

Cap Device, Army, Scout, USA, Army, c1870s. Handsome silver crossed arrows with USS in upper cross, four wire loops LB. Great detail on feathers. Classic piece of Indian war's history. Exc. cond. $250

Cap Device, Cavalry, USA, Army, c1870s. For Cavalry Kepi. Lug-back brass crossed sabers in gilded brass. Appear mint. Near mint cond. $32

Cap Device, Cavalry, USA, Army, Civil War Era. Bronze. Crossed sabers with safety pin-type fastener. Above avg. cond. $36

Cap Device, Cavalry, USA, Army, Civil War. Large stamped brass crossed saber design with four wire loop attachments on back. Has been finished in matte black. Avg. cond. $72

Cap Device, Cavalry, Officer, USA, Army, c1880. Appears 1880 period, Sb brass, crossed sabers with five above and four F below cross. Above avg. cond. . . . $62

Cap Device, Cavalry, Officer, USA, Army. Brass and lead filled crossed sabers for officers full brimmed hat. Needs some polishing. Above avg. cond. $58

Cap Device, CPO, USA, USCG, WWII. Multi-piece. Pb. Above avg. cond. $14

Cap Device, EM, USA, USMC, WWI. EG&A device. Dark bronze finish. Sb. Above avg. cond. $32

Cap Device, EM, USA, USMC, WWII, H-H. 1937 pattern. Dark bronze finish. Sb. H-H hmkd. Avg. cond. $14

Cap Device, EM, USA, USMC, c1890s. Sb. Bronze finish over gilt EG&A device. Avg. cond. $27

Cap Device, Infantry, USA, Army, Civil War. Stamped brass image of rooster for 7th Ohio Infantry. Prong-mounted on cap or coat. Excellent detail but some age showing. Above avg. cond. $195

Cap Device, Officer, USA, Army, WWI. Heavy cast-bronze design. Sb. Tiffany hmkd. Standard design and size, fair detail. Near mint cond. $50

Cap Device, Officer, USA, Army, WWII. Luxembourg. Stamped gilt brass. Sb. Hmkd. Near mint cond. $20

Cap Device, Officer, USA, Army, WWII, J.R. Gaunt, England. English made. 50mm wide. Sb. J.R. Gaunt/Made in England hmkd. Above avg. cond. $30

Cap Device, Officer, USA, Army, WWII, Smilo, Co. Gilt brass. Sb. On Smilo Co. maker card. Above avg. cond. $18

Cap Device, Officer, USA, Army, WWII, Luxembourg. Dull gilt finished brass with single Sb post. Hmkd on reverse on star field. Good cond. $42

Cap Device, Officer, USA, Army, WWII, Luxembourg. Gilt finish, SB, Luxembourg maker marked. Some wear to the finish. Avg. cond. $31

Cap Device, Officer, USA, Navy, WWI. Heavy bullion on dark felt sew-on backing. Some tarnish. Avg. cond. $25

Cap Device, Officer, USA, USMC, c1950. 1937 pattern EG&A. Multi-piece. Sb. 211 hmkd. Exc. cond. $45

Cap Device, Officers, USA, Navy, WWII. Pb closed clasp. Sterling silver two-piece device 23mm high. Exc. cond. $56

Cap Device, Submariners, USA, Navy, WWII. Dolphin-shaped device. Gold-filled pb, nice finish. Above avg. cond. $20

Cap Device, WAAC, USA, WAAC, WWII. Gilt brass. Multi-piece. Sb. Above avg. cond. $30

Cap Emblem, Naval, USA, Navy, c1890s. 1890s era stamped brass emblem 2¼" x 2", comprised of leafed wreath with diagonal fouled anchor in center. Prong back for mounting. Exc. cond. $90

Cap Insignia, Infantry, USA, Army, Civil War. 3½"-wide stamped brass infantry horn design with wire attachment loops on reverse. Above avg. cond. $24

Cap Wreath, NCO, USA, Army, c1902. 48mm-wide gilt wreath with nickel "DKH" in center. Sb. Above avg. cond. $20

Cap Devices——Germany

Cap Edelweiss, Mt. Troop, Germany, Army, WWII. Gray metal. By "G.B.42." Five holes. Above avg. cond. .. $28

Cap Devices——Other

Cap Eagle, Naval, Officer, Poland, Navy. Gold bullion and Sb. Above avg. cond. $100

Cap Badge, Royal Air Force, England, Air Force, WWII. Brass RAF, reverse loops. Above avg. cond. $25

Beret Badge, England, Army. British beret badge, silver finish, airborne unit, eagle with wreath. Near mint cond. $15

Cap Badge, Royal Horse Artillery, England, Army, WWI. Silver planchet, George VI cipher and loop back. Above avg. cond. $90

Cap Badge, Royal Flying Corps, England, Royal Flying Corps, WWI. Brass RFC with reverse loops. Above avg. cond. $45

Cap Badge, Infantry, EM, England, Army, WWI. Silvered metal, The Cameronians, pb. Above avg. cond. $25

Cap Badge, Women's Auxiliary Corps, England, Army, WWI. Bronze, solid version Queen Mary's Army Auxiliary Corps. Above avg. cond. $35

Cap Badge, Army, England, Army, WWII. Silvered metal, inscribed "Liverpool Scottish," The Queen's Own Cameron Highlanders and loop back. Below avg. cond. $20

Cap Badge, Army, England, Army, WWII. Silvered metal, inscribed "London Scottish," 14 Battalion and loop back. Above avg. cond. $20

Cap Badge, Machine Gun Corps, England, Army, WWII. Brass. Above avg. cond. $20

Cap Badge, Mine Clearance Service, Naval, England, Navy, WWII. Silvered metal, wreath with crown and floating mine. Loop on back. Above avg. cond. .:..... $25

Cap Badge, Ordnance, England, Army, WWII. Gilded flaming bomb with silvered ribbed inscription "Ubique," red wool ground, rear loop attachments. Above avg. cond. $20

Cap Badge, EM, Canada, Army, WWI. Brass medallion inscribed "Maclean Kilties of America" raised in Canada and the United States in 1916, lower stars border, reverse loops. Became Canadian 236th Infantry Battalion. Good cond. $75

Cap Badge, Training Corps, Officer, Canada, Army, WWI. Bi-metal. For Officer Training Corps. Above avg. cond. $20

Cap Badge, Infantry, EM, Canada, Army, WWII. Brass, depicting Canadian maple leaf and beaver and scroll inscribed "British Americans." Above avg. cond. . . . $40

Cap Badge, Royal Canadian Air Force, Canada, RCAF, WWII. Brass planchet. Pb style. Above avg. cond. . $20

Cap Badge, Royal Canadian Air Force, Canada, RCAF, WWII. Brass construction. Above avg. cond. $20

Cap Badge, Paratrooper Proficiency, Cuba, Army, c1975. Lot of five different enameled specimens. SB style. Exc. cond. $34

Badge, Visor Cap, EM, Hungary, Army, c1960s. Brass cockade with silvered wreath having national colored enamel trim with red enamel star and reverse prongs. Above avg. cond. $25

Cap Badges, Naval Cadet, Japan, Navy, WWII. Gilded brass planchet with anchor and roped circular border. With reverse prongs. Above avg. cond. $58

Cap Eagle, Air Force, Poland, Air Force, 1950s. Large pattern, with one reverse prong. Above avg. cond. . . $25

Cap Eagle, Air Force, Officer, Poland, Air Force, 1950s. Silvered eagle. Reverse prongs. Above avg. cond. . . $40

Cap Eagle, Legion, Poland, Army, 1914. Bronze, missing reverse screw post. Good cond. $70

Cap Eagle, Naval, EM, Poland, Navy, 1950s. Silvered eagle with gilded anchor, reverse prongs. Above avg. cond. $50

Cap Badge, Woman's Corps Auxiliary Territory Service, England, WWII. Brass. Above avg. cond. $20

Collar Devices—U.S.

Collar Brass, Officer, Winged Eagles, USA, Army, c1930s. Matched set with Sbs, only worn for a short period. Wear to darken finish. Avg. cond. $100

Collar Device, 1st Corps, Officer, USA, Army, c1930s. Cb. Black plastic, two lots each consisting of "US" and "ASC" devices. Exc. cond. $20

Collar Device, 4th Cavalry, Officer, USA, Army, WWII. Even finished bronze metal crossed swords with "4" above. Pb with simple catch. Exc. cond. $20

Collar Device, Adj General Field Clerk, Officer, USA, Army, WWI. Open catch pb. Bronze finish. Avg. cond. $11

Collar Device, Air Corp, Officer, USA, Army, c1930.

Winged prop pb brass collar device. Near mint cond. $30

Collar Device, Air Service, Officer, USA, Army, Aero Service, WWI. Winged prop. Pb. Obverse matches, but reverse has different sized rivets and colored pins. Above avg. cond. $133

Collar Device, Airborne, Arty, EM, USA, Army Airborne, c1950s. Domed style. Gilt brass. Has crossed cannon over basic para wing design. Multi-piece. Cb. Above avg. cond. $20

Collar Device, Airborne, Engr, EM, USA, Army Airborne, c1950s. Domed style. Gilt brass. Has Engr castle over basic para wing design. Multi-piece. Cb. Above avg. cond. $20

Collar Device, Armor Forces, Officer, USA, Army, WWII. Gilt brass. Cb. WWI tank design. Above avg. cond. $13

Collar Device, Arty, Officer, USA, Army, WWII. Marked "816/Arty." Gilt brass. Cb. On maker card. Above avg. cond. $20

Collar Device, Arty, Officer, USA, Army, WWII. Marked "320/Arty." Gilt. Cb. In maker carton. Above avg. cond. $39

Collar Device, Arty, Officer, USA, Army, WWII, Meyer. Hawaiian Defense Sector 4 C. Arty. "Audacia" motto disc are multi-piece. Pb. Meyer hmkd. "4/C.Arty" devices are Cb. Meyer/Rolled plate hmkd. Above avg. cond. . . . $30

Collar Device, Band, Officer, USA, Army, WWI. Bronze finish lyre design with appliqué "6" in center. Open catch Pb. Avg. cond. $20

Collar Device, Cavalry, USA, Army, c1872. 2¾" wide. Stamped brass. Wire loop attachments. Exc. cond. . $20

Collar Device, Cavalry, USA, Army, c1870s. Marked "1/Cav/I." 60mm wide. Gilt brass. Has had Cb fasteners soldered to saber tips. Avg. cond. $40

Collar Device, Cavalry, Officer, USA, Army, WWI. Marked "1/Cav." Shirt size. 30mm wide. Open catch. Pb. Exc. cond. $20

Collar Device, Cavalry, Officer, USA, Army, WWII. Marked "8/Cav/E." Gilt brass. Twin Sb posts. Wear to gilt. Avg. cond. $27

Collar Device, Cavalry, Officer, USA, Army, WWI. Marked "4th Cav." Bronze. Avg. cond. $23

Collar Device, Chemical Corps, EM, USA, Army, WWII, Gemsco. All cb and on original Gemsco card. All type IV polished brass. Near mint cond. $20

Collar Device, Chemical Corps, Officer, USA, Army, WWI. Pb. Bronze finished officer blouse collar devices. Above avg. cond. $50

Collar Device, Commissary, Officer, USA, Army, WWI. Dark finished bronze, pb with simple catch. Appears unissued. Exc. cond. $26

Collar Device, Commissary, Officer, USA, Army, WWI. Bronze-toned pb commissary officer collar devices. Above avg. cond. $20

Collar Device, Dress, EG&A, Officer, 1937 Pattern, USA, USMC, WWII, Meyer. Sb. "Meyer/210" hmkd on reverse. In Meyer package. Near mint cond. $72

Collar Device, Dress, EG&A, Officer, 1937 Pattern, USA, USMC, WWII, Sterling. For left side of collar. Sb. "Sterling/Rolled Cold" hmkd. Avg. cond. $30

Collar Device, EG&A, EM, USA, USMC, c1898. Cap size in silver-colored finish. Prong back. Exc. cond. $28

Collar Device, EG&A, EM, USA, USMC, c1890s. Thin stamped metal body in dark bronze-colored finish. Prong back. Above avg. cond. $60

Collar Device, EG&A, EM, 1921 Pattern, USA, USMC, c1920s. For rt side of collar. In bronze finish. Sb. Above avg. cond. $25

Collar Device, EG&A, Officer, 1937 Pattern, USA, USMC, WWII, H-H. Sterling. H-H hmkd. Sb. In copper-colored finish. Above avg. cond. $40

Collar Device, Engineer Corps, Officer, USA, Army, WWI. 32mm wide. Pierced design. Dark bronze finish. Open-catch pb. Exc. cond. $37

Collar Device, General Staff, Officer, USA, Army, WWI. Multi-piece construction in dark bronze finish. Open-catch pb. Exc. cond. $55

Collar Device, Indian Affairs, Officer, USA, Army, c1900. Pb. Winged sheaf of arrows. Above avg. cond. $76

Collar Device, Infantry, Officer, USA, Army, WWII, Luke, Melbourne, Australia. Australian made. Smooth brass bodies are Luke/Melbourne hmkd. Cb. Above avg. cond. $20

Collar Device, Infantry, Officer, USA, Army, WWI. Marked "14/Inf." Above avg. cond. $51

Collar Device, Qm Corps, Officer, USA, Army, WWI. Single. Sew-on with loops to back and a pb type. All in dark finished bronze. Above avg. cond. $20

Collar Device, Qm Dept Service, Officer, USA, USMC, WWII, H-H/Imperial. Dark bronze finish. Pierced design.

Pb with "fall-in" catch. H-H/Imperial hmkd. Exc. cond. $28

Collar Device, Qm Dept, Officer, USA, USMC, WWII. Dark bronze finish. Open catch pb. Exc. cond. $29

Collar Device, Signal Corps Aviation, Officer, USA, Army, WWII. Bronze satin finish signal corps pattern device with appliqué silver-colored spread-wing design in center. Open-catch pb. Exc. cond. $45

Collar Device, Signal Corps, Officer, USA, Army, WWI, France. French made. Bronze finish. Open catch Pb. Above avg. cond. $24

Collar Device, Tank Destroyer Forces, EM, USA, Army, WWII, England. English made. Gilt brass. Sb. Design of half-track mounting anti-tank weapon. Avg. cond. . . $20

Collar Devices, Chemical Corps, Officer, USA, Army, WWI. Pb. Bronze finished officer shirt collar devices with "1" on top of benzene ring. Exc. cond. $82

Collar Devices, Dental Corps, Officer, USA, Army, WWI. Dark bronze pierced design with gilt brass "DC" appliqués. Open-catch pb. Above avg. cond. $45

Collar Devices, USR, USA, Army, c1898. Pb. Bronze finish. On original "Liberty Bronze" sales cards. Near mint cond. $37

Collar Disc, Air Service, EM, Type I, USA, Army, WWI. Dark bronze. Sb. Stubby, short prop design. Above avg. cond. $45

Collar Disc, Air Service, EM, Type I, USA, Army, WWI. Dark bronze finish with winged prop design with wide wings and short, stubby prop. Has horizontal line background. Sb. Avg. cond. $20

Collar Disc, Airborne, EM, USA, Army Airborne, c1950s. Domed brass body with miniature applied likeness of basic para wing over "U.S." Cb. Above avg. cond. $34

Collar Disc, Armor, USA, Army, WWI, France. Sb. Bronze post-1918 version showing Mark VIII tank over dragons. Appears to be French made. Above avg. cond. $52

Miscellaneous US Army Collar Discs

Collar Disc, Arty, EM, Type I, USA, Army, WWI. Marked "9/Arty/S." Bronze finish. Sb. Below avg. cond. $13

Collar Disc, Arty, EM, Type I, USA, Army, WWI. Mark "5/Arty/D." Bronze finish. Sb. Avg. cond. $23

Collar Disc, Arty, EM, Type I, USA, Army, WWI. Marked "18/Arty/A." Dark bronze finish. Sb. Avg. cond. $39

Collar Disc, Arty, EM, Type I, USA, Army, WWI. Marked "324/Arty/E." Bronze finish. Sb. Avg. cond. $24

Collar Disc, Arty, EM, Type II, USA, Army, c1930s. Pale red enamel finish. Avg. cond. $20

Collar Disc, Arty, EM, Type II, USA, Army, c1930s. Marked "C.Arty/A." Gilt brass. Sb. Avg. cond. $20

Collar Disc, Arty, Officer, Type I, USA, Army, WWI, BB&B. Marked "Arty/AT." Dark bronze. Pb. BB&B hmkd. Number removed from top. Avg. cond. $30

Collar Disc, Cavalry, EM, Type I, USA, Army, WWI. Marked "1/Cav/E." Bronze finish. Sb. Above avg. cond. $82

Collar Disc, EM, Type I, USA, Army, Pre-WWII. Bronze finish. Sb. Small "NA" in rectangle over US and applied "323" numerals. Above avg. cond. $72

Collar Disc, Engineer, EM, Type I, USA, Army, Pre-WWII. Dark bronze. Has appliqué "301" numbers on castle design. Sb. Above avg. cond. $25

Collar Disc, GHQ, EM, Type I, USA, Army, WWI. Dark bronze finish. Sb. Above avg. cond. $50

Collar Disc, Infantry, Type II, USA, Army, Pre-WWII. Sb (missing screw). For Company A. Bronze finish shows wear. Above avg. cond. $40

Collar Disc, Infantry, Bandsman, EM, Type II, USA, Army, c1930s. Marked "Inf/Musician." Gilt brass. Sb. Design of crossed rifles with lyre design below. Sb. Above avg. cond. $22

Collar Disc, Infantry, EM, Type I, USA, Army, WWI. Marked "27/Inf/B." Sb. Exc. cond. $60

Collar Disc, Infantry, EM, Type I, USA, Army, WWI. Marked "26/Inf/D." Bronze finish. Sb. Above avg. cond. $38

Collar Disc, Infantry, EM, Type I, USA, Army, Pre-WWII. Dark bronze finish. Sb. Marked mg/inf/b. Avg. cond. $20

Collar Disc, Infantry, EM, Type I, USA, Army, WWI. Gilt brass. Sb. Basic "3/Inf/M" design with center having circle with "2" in center. Avg. cond. $22

Collar Disc, Infantry, EM, Type I, USA, Army, WWI. Marked "332/Inv." Dark bronze finish. Numerals are appliqué. Sb. Avg. cond. $66

Collar Disc, Infantry, Officer, Type I, USA, Army, WWI. Marked "382/Inf." Dark bronze. Open-catch pb. Avg. cond. $20

Collar Disc, Machine Gun, EM, Type I, USA, Army, WWI. Marked "MG/Inf/A." Bronze finish. Sb. Above avg. cond. $12

Collar Disc, Machine Gun, EM, Type I, USA, Army, WWI. Marked "MG/Inf/A." Dark bronze finish. Sb. Above avg. cond. $25

Collar Disc, Medical, EM, Type I, USA, Army, WWI. Marked "Med/PC." Even dark bronze pendant with appliqué "P" and "C" numerals. Sb. Near mint cond. $213

Collar Disc, QMC, USA, Army, c1890s. Quill and key. Gilted brass. Wire prong back. Style obsolete in 1900. Above avg. cond. $32

Collar Disc, QMC, EM, Type II, USA, Army, c1930s. Experimental. Buff enamel finish. Above avg. cond. $20

Collar Disc, USV, EM, Type I, USA, Army, WWI. Dark bronze finish disc with appliqué "V" device in rectangle design over "US." Sb. Above avg. cond. $135

Collar Insignia, Sgt, USA, Army, c1950s. Gold filled. Cb. Above avg. cond. $20

Collar Pin, USA, Army, Civil War. Pb shows rifle and saber crossed behind knapsack with "NMA" on back. Bed roll at top and eagle resting on that. Red and blue enamel give color. Above avg. cond. $28

Insignia, Infantry, USA, Army, Civil War. US shield with Rhode Island Corps Anchor and "BAND OF HOPE" diagonally across shield. Stamped metal and pb. Avg. cond. $60

Rank Insignia, 2nd Lieut Bars, USA, Army, WWI. Textured "coffin lid" bodies with open-catch pb. Matched. Above avg. cond. $25

Rank Insignia, 2nd Lieut Bars, USA, Army, WWI. Stamped brass. Appear to be French made. Simulated bullion design. Full size for blouse wear. Above avg. cond. $19

Rank Insignia, Brig Gen Stars, USA, Army, WWI. 30mm wide. Textured surface. Loop on reverse of each for attachment. Some wear to silver finish. Above avg. cond. $49

Rank Insignia, Brig Gen Stars, USA, Army, WWI. Pair.

26mm wide. Dark bronze finish. Open-catch pb. Above avg. cond. $51

Rank Insignia, Col Eagle, USA, Army, WWII. 50mm size. Matched pair. Curve-formed pb. "Luxembourg" hmkd. Oversize pair. Some light tarnish. Above avg. cond. $67

Rank Insignia, Col Shoulder Eagle, USA, Army, Pre-WWII. Silver gilt over brass with open-catch pb. Shoulder size. Avg. cond. $30

Rank Insignia, Commissary Sgt, USA, Army, c1903. 1¾" wide. Multi-piece. Gilt wreath with nickel crescent moon design. Sb. Above avg. cond. $39

Rank Insignia, General Star, USA, Army, WWII, Luxembourg. 30mm heavy sterling. Cb. Luxembourg maker marked. Above avg. cond. $48

Rank Insignia, Major Leaves, USA, Army, WWI. Pair. Open-catch pb. Above avg. cond. $27

Rank Insignia, Major Leaves, USA, Army, WWII, BB&B. Shirt size. Gilt. Pb. BB&B and bronze hmkd. Avg. cond. $30

Collar Devices—Other

Sleeve Shield, Officer, Italy, Army, WWII. Stamped brass device, dark blue enamel finish, shield surmounted by gilded sword and oak leaf motif. Above avg. cond. $102

Sleeve Shield, Black Shirt, Anti-aircraft Unit, Italy, WWII. Stamped metal device having black painted finish, shield has gilded crossed cannon relief, surmounted by gilded fascist eagle, border inscription "Milizia Controaerei." Above avg. cond. $128

Collar Devices, Soviet Union, Army, c1980s. Ten Soviet armored officers collar tab pairs, wrapped in brown paper with gilt metal base and black wool centers. Mint cond. $15

Distinctive Insignia (DI's)

Beercan DI, 114th Aviation "Knights of the Air," USA, Army, Vietnam War Era, Vietnam. Vietnam made. 26mm wide. Thin stamped metal body with painted design. Cb. Above avg. cond. $28

Beercan DI, 145th Aviation BN, USA, Army, Vietnam War Era, Vietnam. Vietnam made. 22 x 31mm thin stamped metal body. Cb. Painted design. Above avg. cond. $28

Beercan DI, 173rd Abn Brigade, USA, Army, Vietnam War Era, Vietnam. Vietnam made. Cb. Enameled with

Casper the Ghost standing in front of chopper and unit particulars below. Above avg. cond. $32

Beercan DI, 29th FA, USA, Army, Vietnam War Era. Vietnam made. Thin stamped body with painted detail. Cb. Avg. cond. $22

Beercan DI, 32nd FA, USA, Army, Vietnam War Era. Vietnam made. Thin stamped metal body with painted details. Cb. Avg. cond. $22

Beercan DI, 3rd Tactical Fighter Wing, USA, USAF, Vietnam War Era. 27mm wide. Thin stamped metal body with painted detail. Cb. Above avg. cond. $17

DI, 11th Cavalry Regt, USA, Army, WWII, Meyer. Gilt brass and enamel finish pierced bodies. Pb. Meyer hmkd. Above avg. cond. $19

DI, 12th CAC Regt, USA, Army, WWII, Dondero. Sb. Pierced design. Gilt brass and enamel. Dondero hmkd. Above avg. cond. $28

DI, 12th Observation Grp, USA, AAF, WWII. Multi-piece. Pb. Above avg. cond. $30

DI, 12th Recon Sqdn, USA, AAF, WWII, Dondero. Pb. Gilt brass and enamel. Dondero hmkd. Avg. cond. . $19

DI, 14th Fighter Grp, USA, AAF, WWII, Meyer. Sb. Nickel and enamel. Meyer hmkd. Above avg. cond. $45

DI, 153rd Observation Sqdn, USA, AAF, WWII. Gilt brass and enamel. Pb. Above avg. cond. $34

DI, 15th Air Force, USA, AAF, WWII. Matched pair. Pb. Maker marked. Sterling. Above avg. cond. $25

DI, 16th Fighter Grp, USA, AAF, WWII. Pair. Pb. Enameled metal. One with mailed fist and lightning. Other has motto "PURGAMOUS COELUM." Above avg. cond. $22

DI, 16th Infantry Reg, USA, Army, WWII. Sb metal and enamel with blue and white inverted turret design. Above avg. cond. $20

DI, 17th Bomb Grp, USA, AAF, WWII, Meyer. Sb. Gilt brass and enamel. Meyer hmkd. Exc. cond. $44

DI, 181st Arty, USA, Army, WWII. Multi-piece. Gilt brass and enamel. Above avg. cond. $25

DI, 19th Bomb Grp, USA, AAF, WWII, Meyer. Sb. Gilt brass and enamel. Meyer hmkd. Above avg. cond. . . $30

DI, 1st Fighter Grp, USA, AAF, WWII, Amer. Metal Crafts, Attleboro. Sb. Gilt brass and enamel. Amer. Metal Crafts, Attleboro hmkd. Above avg. cond. $30

DI, 20th Fighter Grp, USA, AAF, WWII, Gemsco. Pb. Gilt brass and enamel. Gemsco hmkd. Avg. cond. . . $17

DI, 22nd Bomb Grp, USA, AAF, WWII, Meyer. Sb. Gilt brass and enamel. Meyer hmkd. Avg. cond. $20

DI, 252nd Arty, USA, Army, WWII. Gilt brass and enamel. Open catch pb. Avg. cond. $12

DI, 252nd Arty, USA, Army, WWII, Meyer. Gilt brass and enamel. Pb. Meyer hmkd. Avg. cond. $11

DI, 27th Bomb Grp, USA, AAF, WWII, Meyer. Hmkd "NS Meyer" on back. Metal and enamel shield with orange and blue diagonal field, closed fist and flower. Motto "INTELLIGENCE STRENGTH." Above avg. cond. $20

DI, 290 Engineer BN, USA, Army, WWII, Dondero. Sb. Nickel and enamel. Dondero/sterling hmkd. Above avg. cond. $20

DI, 2nd Bomb Grp, USA, AAF, WWII. Gilt and enameled metal design, Pb and Meyer marked. Some age patina. Above avg. cond. $20

DI, 302nd ORD Regt, USA, Army, WWII, Dieces & Clust. Multi-piece. Brass and enamel. Pb. Dieces & Clust hmkd. Above avg. cond. $25

DI, 310th Infantry Regt, USA, Army, WWII. Plastic Pb with blue shield and cross and tree separated by lightning flash. Motto at bottom reads "ALLONS MES ENFANTS." Exc. cond. $30

DI, 323rd Infantry Regt,, USA, Army, WWII, Sterling. Gilt brass and enamel. Pb. Sterling hmkd. Avg. cond. $27

DI, 33rd Fighter Grp, USA, AAF, WWII, Meyer. Pb. Gilt brass and enamel. Meyer hmkd. Above avg. cond. . . $28

DI, 34th Bombardment Group, USA, AAF, WWII, Sterling. Sterling hmkd. Gilt and enamel finish. Pb. Above avg. cond. $49

DI, 399th Infantry Regt, USA, Army, WWII, Sterling. Nickel and enamel. Pb. Sterling hmkd. Avg. cond. . . $20

DI, 3rd Wing, USA, AAF, WWII, Gemsco. Pb. Gilt brass and enamel finish. Gemsco hmkd. Above avg. cond. $14

DI, 4th Air Base Sqdn, USA, AAF, WWII, Amer. Metal Arts Co. Gilt brass and enamel. Pb. Amer. Metal Arts Co. hmkd. Above avg. cond. $30

DI, 54th Cavalry Bde, USA, Army, WWII, Meyer. Multi-piece construction. Sb. Meyer hmkd. Above avg. cond. $36

DI, 57th Fighter Grp, USA, AAF, WWII, Meyer. Pb. Gilt brass and enamel. Meyer hmkd. Above avg. cond. $20

DI, 5th Bomb Grp, USA, AAF, WWII, Meyer. Multi-piece construction. Pb. Meyer hmkd. Above avg. cond. $40

DI, 5th Bomb Grp, USA, AAF, WWII. Pb. Brass winged silver skull with motto "KIAIO KAIEWA" at bottom. Avg. cond. $18

DI, 6th Air Force, USA, AAF, WWII. ¾" wide. Enamel detail. Pb with "fall-in" catch. Above avg. cond. . . . $28

DI 6th Air Force

DI, 7th Bomb Grp, USA, AAF, WWII, Meyer. Sb. Gilt brass and enamel. Meyer hmkd. Above avg. cond. . . $21

DI, 7th Cavalry Regt, USA, Army, WWII. Brass and enamel with pierced center. Pb with open-loop catch. Some light enamel damage to sword blade. Below avg. cond. $10

DI, 88th Recon Sqdn, USA, AAF, WWII. Sb. Gilt brass and enamel. Above avg. cond. $30

DI, 91st Observation Sqdn, USA, AAF, WWII. Brass and enamel Pb on card. Shows knight chasing the devil. Exc. cond. $20

DI, 96th Signal Battalion, USA, Army, WWII. Sterling with enamel face and horse and rider in metal. Pb. Exc. cond. $40

DI, 9th Bomb Grp, USA, AAF, WWII. In plastic and on card. Pb. Enameled brass. Near mint cond. $28

DI, 9th Bomb Grp, USA, AAF, WWII. Pb enameled brass shield with band of iron crosses in center and coiled snake at top. Motto "SEMPER PARATUS." Avg. cond. $14

DI, AAF Gulf Coast Training Center, USA, AAF, WWII. Sb. 1¼" enameled shield. Avg. cond. $20

DI, Air Ferry CMD, USA, AAF, WWII. Pb. Gilt metal with enameled emblem. Displayed in box with clear lid. Exc. cond. $65

DI, Air Service CMD, USA, AAF, WWII, Amer. Metal Arts. Four-blade design. Pb. Metal Arts/sterling hmkd. Some even tarnish. Above avg. cond. $20

DI, Air Transport CMD, USA, AAF, WWII, LeVelle. Matched pair 30mm diam. In sterling and enamel. Cb. LeVelle hmkd. Avg. cond. $27

DI, G-2 Intelligence, USA, Army, WWII. Cb. Brass with

sphinx in center. Good detail. Near mint cond. $27

DI, Nurnburg War Crime Trials, USA, Army, 1946. 40mm alum shield with key over balance scales over flames and black eagle. Has Nurnberg hmk on back, painted but has some oxidation on eagle and flaking to color. Above avg. cond. $40

Helmet Frontplates—U.S.

Eagle Sideplate, Hardee Hat, Army, EM, USA, Army, Civil War. 48 x 68mm size. Stamped brass body. Lacks prong attachments. Above avg. cond. $60

Frontplate, Army, Arty, USA, Army, c1880s. Stamped brass. Lot includes another 1881 frontplate that has been reworked for what appears to be band usage. Below avg. cond. $14

Frontplate, Army, Eagle, USA, Army, c1890s. Stamped brass. Crossed rifles design with applied nickel "11" numerals on shield. Wire attachment loops in rear. Avg. cond. $23

Frontplate, Army, Infantry, USA, Army, c1880s. Stamped brass. Has "2" appliqué to shield. Avg. cond. $28

Helmet Device, Dress, EG&A, USA, USMC, c1880s. For M1881 helmet. Massive stamped design has approx. 86mm-wide wingspan. Silver-plated finish. Loop attachment to back. Avg. cond. $290

Helmet Frontplate, EG&A, USA, USMC, c1900. Sb. 3" x 3½" dimensions. Gilded eagle, globe and anchor. Suitable for helmet wear. Likely enlisted helmet 1900 era. Exc. cond. $177

Kepi Device, Army, Infantry, USA, Army, Civil war. Stamped brass Infantry horn device. 88mm wide. Lacks one of two wire loop attachments on back. Above avg. cond. $33

Kepi Device, Army, Infantry, USA, Army, Civil War. Gilt finished brass horn for kepi with two soldered loops for mounting. Shows some wear to the finish. Avg. cond. $37

Shako Device, Army, Cavalry, USA, Army, Civil War.

Army Civil War Shako Device

68mm wide. Stamped brass. Crossed saber design over "bursting" rays. Some corrosion. Avg. cond. $59

Shako Device, Army, Infantry, USA, Army, Civil War. Bugle brass. For Infantry shako, lug back and some wear evident. Avg. cond. $27

Shako Plate, Army, Infantry, USA, Army, c1815. Brass 3¼" x 2" plate with American eagle carrying banner "OLD RELIABLE" over montage of cannon, flags and gear. At bottom reads "FEDERAL GOVERNMENT" Pierced for sewing to cap. Avg. cond. $135

Helmet Frontplates—Germany

Eagle, Pith Helmet, Luftwaffe, Germany, Luftwaffe, WWII. Stamped brass with silver finish. Above avg. cond. $44

Frontplate, Spiked Helmet, Infantry, Officer, Bavarian, Imperial Germany, Army, WWI. Large size high gold gilt. Pierced crowns on lions, wappen. Pb. Exc. cond. $180

Frontplate, Spiked Helmet, Infantry, One-Year Volunteer, Bavarian, Imperial Germany, Army, WWI. Pierced central crown brass. Lug back. Mint cond. $66

Frontplate, Spiked Helmet, Leibgarde, Hessen, Imperial Germany, Army, WWI. Silver. Full oak and laurel leaves lion with silver "Gott Ehre Vaterland" star. Loop back. Near mint cond. $345

Shield, Pith Helmet, Army (pair), Germany, Army, WWII. Eagle and Tri-color. Stamped gray metal with painted details. Avg. cond. $20

Shield, Pith Helmet, Army (pair), Germany, Army, WWII. Eagle and Tri-color. Both stamped with painted details. Three prongs each. Avg. cond. $24

Helmet Frontplates—Other

Frontplate, Spiked Helmet, Life Guards, Austro-Hungary, Army, c1900. Pre-WWI. 75 x 40mm. Brass Hungarian shield with crown of St. Stephen above finely detailed. Prong back for attachment to helmet body. Exc. cond. $166

Frontplate, Royal Military College Canada, Canada, Army, c1930s. Pierced brass planchet with Victorian, inscribed "Royal Military College Canada," Pb. Above avg. cond. $55

Shako Plate, Army, Officer, France, Army, c1830. Gilt brass plate pierced with regimental numeral for the First Imperial Regiment. Exc. cond. $460

Shako Plate, Army, Officer, France, Army, c1810. Diamond-shaped brass plate bearing the Imperial eagle. Above avg. cond. $748

French Officer's Shako Plate

ID Badges—U.S.

Dog Tag, USA, Navy, WWI. Oval shaped. Man's name, 1917 dated and USN marked on front with thumb print on reverse side. Above avg. cond. $28

Dog Tags & Chain, USA, Army, WWII. Pair of tags with name, address and with t-43 date. Avg. cond. $24

Dog Tags and Chain, USA, Army, WWII. Have name, address and 1941 date. Avg. cond. $20

US Army WWII ID Tags (Dog Tags)

German WWII Era ID Tag

ID Badges—Germany

ID Tag, Germany, Army, WWII. Alum oval. Perforated at center. With name, unit, serial number and blood type of soldier. No cord. Avg. cond. $35

ID Tag, Imperial Germany, Army, WWI. Gray zinc with two hanger holes and stamped "I.E.B.J.R.81. 2.K. 1830 Wilh.Bernhardt." Above avg. cond. $44

ID Tag, M1915, Imperial Germany, Army, WWI. Gray zinc oval with two hanger holes and stamped "Georg Anielsperger Bring. 15.3.80.Abt.bay.7.Fd.Autl.K.Nr.4 etc." Avg. cond. $37

Identification Badge, Army, Bavarian, Imperial Germany, Army, WWI. 36mm. Domed. Hallmarked. Pb. White and blue field with red cross. Gilt inscription, "Bayr. Rotes Kreuz Sanitatskolonne." Issued by German Red Cross. Above avg. cond. $90

Wings—U.S.

Para Wing, Airborne, On Para Oval, USA, Army, WWII, Gaunt, London. English made. Sterling wing is Gaunt/London hmkd with open-catch pb and two combat stars and one arrowhead device. On rare 507th British-made para oval with silk embr border on black felt base. Above avg. cond. $142

Wing, Aerial Gunner, USA, AAF, WWII. 3". One piece. Cb. Sterling hmkd. Exc. cond. $25

WWII AAF Air Gunner Wing

Wing, Aerial Gunner, USA, AAF, WWII, Moody Bros. Moody Bros/sterling hmkd. 3". Multi-piece. Pb. Above avg. cond. $139

Wing, Aerial Gunner, USA, AAF, WWII, Amico. 2". Pb. Multi-piece design. Amico/sterling hmkd. Above avg. cond. $23

Wing, Aerial Gunner, USA, AAF, WWII, Meyer. 2". Multi-piece. Pb. Sterling/Meyer hmkd. Above avg. cond. $25

Wing, Aerial Gunner, USA, AAF, WWII, Sterling. 3". One piece. Cb. Sterling hmkd. Above avg. cond. . . . $24

Wing, Airborne Para, USA, Army, WWII. 1½". Sterling. With two bronze stars and brass arrowhead. Cb. Avg. cond. $31

Wing, Airborne Para, USA, Army, WWII. 1½" wide. Pb. Sterling hmkd. Avg. cond. $30

Wing, Airborne, Para Jump Wing, USA, Army, WWII. PB. Sterling 1½". Bronze arrowhead on shroud. Above avg. cond. $55

Wing, Aircrew, USA, AAF, WWII, Meyer. 2". One piece. Pb. Sterling/Meyer hmkd. Above avg. cond. $25

WWII AAF Aircrew Wing

Wing, Aircrew, USA, AAF, WWII, Gemsco. 3⅛". Multi-piece. Gemsco/sterling hmkd. Pb. Above avg. cond. $35

WWII AAF Aircrew Wing (Gemsco)

Wing, Aircrew, USA, AAF, WWII, LGB. 3". Pb. Hmkd "LGB/STERLING." Above avg. cond. $61

Wing, Aircrew, USA, AAF, WWII, Gemsco. 3⅛". Pb. Gemsco/sterling hmkd. Above avg. cond. $75

Wing, Aircrew, USA, AAF, WWII, Gemsco, NY. 3", Pb, Sterling with hmkd "Gemsco, NY." Die struck. Above avg. cond. $72

Wing, Aircrew, USA, AAF, WWII, N.S. Meyers, NY. 3", cb. "N. S. Meyers, NY" hmkd. Above avg. cond. ... $16

Wing, Aircrew, USA, AAF, WWII, Juarez Mexico. 3¼". Pb. Juarez Mexico/sterling marked. One piece. Above avg. cond. $100

Wing, Aircrew, USA, AAF, WWII, Amico. 3", frosted sterling, cb,"Amico" hmkd. Avg. cond. $20

Wing, Aircrew, USA, USAF, c1950s. 3". CB. Unmarked. Avg. cond. $20

Wing, Astronaut, USA, Navy, c1960s, Vanguard. 2¾". Gilt. Multi-piece. Cb. "1/20 10k GF/Vanguard/154" marked. Exc. cond. $55

Wing, Aviator Pilot, USA, Army, c1920s, B-B. Pb open catch, 68mm, S/S, hmkd B-B on back. 1921 pattern. Above avg. cond. $100

Wing, Bombardier, USA, AAF, WWII, A.E. Co. 3⅛". One piece. Pb. Sterling/A.E. Co. hmkd. Exc. cond. $145

Wing, Bombardier, USA, AAF, WWII, Amico. 2". Multi-piece. Pb. Amico/sterling hmkd. Above avg. cond. ... $36

WWII AAF Bombardier Wing In Case

Wing, Bombardier, USA, AAF, WWII, Meyer. 2". Multi-piece. Pb. Sterling/Meyer hmkd. Above avg. cond. . $32

Wing, Bombardier, USA, AAF, WWII, Gemsco. 3⅛". Multi-piece. Pb. Gemsco/sterling marked. Above avg. cond. $70

WWII AAF Bombardier Wing (Gemsco)

Wing, Bombardier, USA, AAF, WWII, C Luke, Melbourne, Australia. Australian made. Multi-piece design. Open-catch. "C Luke, Melbourne, Australia" hmkd. Above avg. cond. $325

WWII AAF Bombardier Wing

Wing, Bombardier, USA, AAF, WWII. 3". Sterling hmkd. Cb. Avg. cond. $28

WWII AAF Bombardier Wing (Meyer)

Wing, Bombardier, USA, AAF, WWII, Meyer. 3". Multi-piece. Pb. Meyer/sterling marked. Avg. cond. $82

Wing, Cloth, Aircrew, USA, AAF, WWII, England. English made. Bullion 3" design on uncut dark blue felt base. Avg. cond. $38

Wing, Cloth, Bombardier, USA, AAF, WWII. 3⅛"-wide heavy silver bullion design on uncut dark OD gabardine base. Exc. cond. $43

Wing, Cloth, Bombardier, USA, AAF, WWII, England. English made. 3½" x 1½" blue felt padded rectangular base with 3"-wide hand-embr design. Above avg. cond. $61

Wing, Cloth, Bombardier, USA, AAF, WWII. 3⅛" wide in heavy silver bullion. On uncut dark OD gabardine. Avg. cond. $21

Wing, Cloth, Gunner, USA, AAF, WWII. 3". Silver bullion on blue wool. Above avg. cond. $45

Wing, Cloth, Naval Aviator, USA, Navy, WWII. 2⅞"-wide heavy gold bullion design on uncut 3¼" x 1⅜" navy blue felt backing. Exc. cond. $31

Wing, Cloth, Naval, Aviator, USA, Navy, WWII. 2¾"-wide heavy gold bullion design on uncut tan gabardine. Near mint cond. $40

Wing, Cloth, Naval, Aviator, USA, Navy, WWII. 3" wide heavy gold bullion design on uncut 3½" x 1½" navy blue felt backing. Exc. cond. $34

Wing, Cloth, Naval, Aviator, USA, Navy, WWII. 2¾" wide heavy gold bullion design on uncut navy blue felt. Avg. cond. $22

Wing, Cloth, Observer, USA, AAF, WWII. 3" wide in heavy silver bullion on 4" x 1¾" blue felt base. Above avg. cond. $55

Wing, Cloth, Observer, USA, AAF, WWII. 3" wide in heavy silver bullion on uncut dark OD gabardine. Above avg. cond. $40

Wing, Cloth, Pilot, USA, AAF, WWII. 3¼". Bullion/glitter wire on dark blue wool field. Black thread for detail outlines. Above avg. cond. $65

Wing, Cloth, Pilot, USA, AAF, WWII. Dark green twill with embr edge and silk backing, multi-color bullion and theater made. Above avg. cond. $50

Wing, Cloth, Pilot, Naval, USA, Navy, WWII. Gold bullion on black wool. Exc. cond. $150

Wing, Cloth, Pilot, Naval, USA, Navy, WWI. 2¾" wide heavy bullion wing on navy blue felt backing. Avg. cond. $75

Wing, Cloth, Pilot, Naval, USA, Navy, WWII. 2⅜". Gold bullion on aviation green gabardine. Avg. cond. $29

Wing, Cloth, Technical Observer, USA, AAF, WWII. Silver bullion with black highlights on tan cloth. Avg. cond. $65

Wing, Combat Aircrew, USA, Navy, WWII. 2¾". Multi-piece. Pb. Sterling marked. Above avg. cond. $40

WWII AAF Command Pilot Wing

Wing, Command Pilot, USA, AAF, WWII, Jostens. 3". Cb. Marked "JOSTENS/STERLING." Exc. cond. . $135

Wing, Command Pilot, USA, AAF, WWII, Jostens. 3". Pb. Josten hmkd. Sterling. Exc. cond. $165

Wing, Command Pilot, USA, AAF, WWII, Meyer. 3". Pb. Meyer Hmkd. Sterling. Exc. cond. $145

WWII AAF Command Pilot Wing

Wing, Command Pilot, USA, AAF, WWII, NS Meyer. 2". Pb. Hmkd "N S MEYER." Avg. cond. $20

Wing, Command Pilot, USA, AAF, WWII, Amico. 3⅛". Pb. Amico/sterling hmkd. Avg. cond. $95

Wing, Command Pilot, USA, USAF, Korean War Era, Meyer. 3". Cb. Sterling and Meyer marked. Avg. cond. $35

Wing, Crewmember, USA, AAF, WWII, J.R. Gaunt/London. English made. 3⅛" wide. Silver finished brass. Multi-piece construction. Open-catch pb. "J.R. Gaunt/London" hmkd on reverse. Above avg. cond. $74

Wing, Flight Nurse, USA, AAF, WWII, Amico. 2". Pb. Sterling. "AMICO" hmkd. Above avg. cond. $170

WWII AAF Flight Nurse Wing

Wing, Flight Surgeon, USA, Navy, WWII, Vanguard, NY. 2¾". Pb with "fall-in" catch. Vanguard NY/sterling hmkd. Exc. cond. $100

Wing, Flight Surgeon, USA, Navy, WWII, Amico. 3". 2 piece. Pb. "Amico Sterling 10k gold filled" marked. Medical emblem fixed to observer disc in center. Exc. cond. $235

Wing, Glider Pilot, USA, AAF, WWII, J. Gaunt, London. 3". Pb. English made (J. Gaunt). Silver-plated wing with large "G" imposed on shield in center. Exc. cond. . $136

Wing, Glider Pilot, USA, AAF, WWII, Amcraft. 3". Pb. One piece. Amcraft/sterling hmkd. Above avg. cond. $177

Wing, Glider Troop, USA, Army, WWII. 1½". Sterling. Pb. Brass "M" in center and copper battle star on each side. Above avg. cond. $45

Wing, Glider Troop, USA, Army, WWII. 1½". Sterling. Pb. Small bronze star applied. Avg. cond. $32

Wing, Glider Troop, USA, Army, WWII. 1½". Sterling. Pb. Glider in center. Avg. cond. $21

Wing, Gunner, USA, AAF, WWII, Meyer. 3". Pb. Sterling and Meyer marked. Exc. cond. $65

Wing, Gunner, USA, AAF, WWII, Gemsco. 3". PB. Sterling. Unmarked. With Gemsco box. Exc. cond. $50

WWII AAF Gunner Wing (Gemsco) in Case

Wing, Gunner, USA, AAF, WWII. 3". Pb. Sterling. Unmarked. Avg. cond. $35

Wing, Instructor Pilot, USA, Army, WWI. For US

instructor at French airfields in WWI 1917–18. 88mm gilt wing S/B, with square nuts. Exc. cond. $250

Wing, Liaison Pilot, USA, AAF, WWII, Meyer. 3". Pb. Meyer marked. Exc. cond. $118

Wing, Naval Aviator, USA, Navy, WWII, Blackington. 2¾". Gold filled. CB. Blackington marked. Exc. cond. $93

Wing, Navigator, USA, AAF, WWII, A.E. Co. 3⅛". Pb. A.E. Co./sterling hmkd. Exc. cond. $122

WWII AAF Navigator Wing

Wing, Navigator, USA, AAF, WWII. 3". Pb. Unmarked sterling. Exc. cond. $45

Wing, Navigator, USA, AAF, WWII, Meyer. 3". PB. Meyer/sterling hmkd. Above avg. cond. $45

Wing, Navigator, USA, AAF, WWII, Amico. 3". Pb. Amico/sterling hmkd. Above avg. cond. $139

Wing, Navigator, USA, AAF, WWII. 2". Pb. Sterling hmkd. Avg. cond. $30

Wing, Navigator, USA, Navy, WWII, Amico. Pb. 10k gold on sterling. Two piece. "Amico" marked. Navigator emblem fixed to center over crossed anchors. Exc. cond. $145

Wing, Observer, USA, AAF, WWII, Luxembourg. 2". Sterling. Luxembourg. Pb. Pivot hinge and closed clasp. Exc. cond. $82

Wing, Observer, USA, AAF, WWII, Meyer. 2". One piece. Pb. Meyer/sterling hmkd. Above avg. cond. . . $35

WWII AAF Observer Wing

Wing, Observer, USA, AAF, WWII, Meyer. 2". One piece. Pb. Meyer/sterling hmkd. Above avg. cond. . . $40

Wing, Observer, USA, AAF, WWII. 35mm. Pb. Sterling hmkd. Above avg. cond. $20

Wing, Observer, USA, AAF, WWII, Gemsco. 3⅛". Pb. Gemsco/sterling hmkd. Avg. cond. $93

Wing, Observer, USA, AAF, WWII, Amico. 3". Pb. Sterling marked. Amico marked. Avg. cond. $80

Wing, Pilot, USA, AAF, WWII. 2¾". Pb. Unmarked sterling. Exc. cond. $95

Wing, Pilot, USA, AAF, WWII. 3" wide. Feather detail. Pb. Sterling hmkd. Exc. cond. $135

Wing, Pilot, USA, AAF, WWII, Gemsco. 3". Pb. Sterling. Gemsco hmkd. In maroon velour-lined box. Exc. cond. $135

WWII AAF Pilot Wing in Lined Box

Wing, Pilot, USA, AAF, WWII. 3¹⁄₁₆" wide. Cb. Sterling hmkd. Feather detail. Above avg. cond. $61

Wing, Pilot, USA, AAF, WWII, Amcraft. 3". Pb. Sterling. Amcraft hmkd. Above avg. cond. $50

Wing, Pilot, USA, AAF, WWII, Meyer. 3". Pb. Meyer/sterling hmkd. Above avg. cond. $45

WWII AAF Pilot Wing

Wing, Pilot, USA, AAF, c1930s. Pre-WWII, unmarked, Pb, 73mm with unusual curved and bowed wing. Above avg. cond. $145

Wing, Pilot, USA, AAF, WWII, Amico. 2". One piece. Pb with "fall-in" catch. Amico/sterling hmkd. Avg. cond. $25

Wing, Pilot, USA, AAF, WWII, Amico. 2". One piece. Pb. Amico/sterling hmkd. Avg. cond. $20

Wing, Pilot, USA, AAF, WWII. 3". Pb. Unmarked. Avg. cond. $35

Wing, Pilot, USA, Army, WWI. 1¼" gilt brass spread wing with enameled "US" on red, white and blue shield design. Open catch pb. Exc. cond. $100

Wing, Pilot, USA, Army, WWI. Unusual variant of 1918 pattern. Pb. Hmkd "Meyer rolled plate," silver 3" wing with interesting patina and detail. The US normally on shield is omitted. Exc. cond. $192

AAF Pilot Wing (Pre-WWII)

Wing, Pilot, USA, Navy, WWI. Bullion embr on black wool. Wing with shield over anchor. Exc. cond. ... $195

Wing, Pilot, USA, Navy, WWII, H-H. 2¾". Cb. H-H/sterling/307 hmkd. Above avg. cond. $31

Wing, Pilot, USA, Navy, WWII. 3". Pb. Sterling with gilt finish and marked "Balfour." Above avg. cond. $65

WWII AAF Pilot Wing

Wing, Pilot, USA, Navy, c1950s, Balfour Co./Attleboro, MA. 2¾". Pb. Hmkd "Balfour Co./Attleboro, Mass./B-21 1/20 10k G.F." Above avg. cond. $66

WWII Navy Pilot Wing (Balfour)

Wing, Pilot, USA, USAF, Korean War Era. 3". Cb. Sterling. Above avg. cond. $27

USAF Pilot

Wing, Pilot, 3rd Pattern, USA, AAF, WWII, Luxembourg. CB, 3" sterling Luxembourg 3rd pattern

wing with crisp features. Hmkd on back. Exc. cond. .
. . . . $175

Wing, Pilot, 3rd pattern, USA, AAF, WWII, A.E. Co. 3".
Cb. Luxembourg 3rd pattern in A.E. Co. style. Sterling.
Exc. cond. $125

Wing, Sr Astronaut, USA, USAF, c1960s. 3". Multi-
piece. Cb. Sterling/G-22 marked. Exc. cond. $30

Wing, Sr Pilot, USA, AAF, WWII, Luxembourg, NY. 2".
Pb. Hmkd "LUXEMBURG, NY." Sterling. Exc. cond. .
. . . . $195

Wing, Sr Pilot, USA, AAF, WWII, Jostens. 3". Cb.
Jostens/sterling marked. Above avg. cond. $125

WWII AAF Sr. Pilot Wing

Wing, Sr Pilot, USA, AAF, WWII, Amcraft. 3". Pb. Sterling, Amcraft hmkd. Above avg. cond. $177

Wing, Sr Pilot, USA, AAF, WWII, Amcraft, Attleboro
MA. 3". Pb. Hmkd "Amcraft Attleboro Mass." Sterling.
Above avg. cond. $118

WWII AAF Sr. Pilot Wing

Wing, Sr Pilot, USA, USAF, c1960s, Vanguard. 3". CB.
Sterling. Vanguard marked. Above avg. cond. $60

USAF Sr. Pilot Wing

Wing, Technical Observer, USA, AAF, WWII. One of
the rarest WWII AAF wings. 3". Solid back with pierced
"O" and superimposed "T." Pb. Sterling. Unmarked. Exc.
cond. $189

WWII AAF Technical Observer Wing

Wings, Combat Crewmember, USA, Navy, c1990s. 2",
pb, sterling, "22-M" marked. Currently used wing with
frosted silver finish and gilt disk at center with anchor, jas
"ribbon" at top with holes to accommodate three stars.
Near mint cond. $30

Wings, Senior Pilot, USA, Air Force, Korean War Era,
NS Meyer. Sterling, 3", cb, hmkd "NS Meyer" and 9-M
marked. Frosted finish to the silver with patina highlights.
Near mint cond. $35

Wings—Other

Wings, Para, England, Army, c1970s. Silver finish with
crown over parachute. Above avg. cond. $10

Medals, Ribbons, Badges, and Awards

Chapter Eleven covers the broad category of medals and awards for such things as recognition for special service, bravery or other marks of distinction. Medals and badges have been used since ancient times to honor individuals for their heroic deeds and accomplishments. It wasn't until the mid 1800s that what we now think of as medals came into wide use. Some of the first of these early medals included the US Medal of Honor, the English Victoria Cross, the French Legion of Honor with Croix de Guerre, and the German Iron Cross.

The English have a wide and distinctive variety of medals and badges, as well as metal insignias which are discussed in Chapter Ten. But even with their attractive appearance and distinctiveness, English medals are still not widely collected in the United States. American and German medals continue to be the most desirable and widely collected.

The Third Reich medals are some of the most highly

WWII and Post WWII Collection of US Medals

sought after, especially the Iron Cross (EK), First Class and Second Class, and the War Order of the German Cross or German Cross (DK). War badges and wound badges are also very popular collectibles. Over 40 varieties of war badges were authorized during the war. Wound badges came in three degrees: gold, silver and black.

Fakes and Frauds

Many reproduction medals and badges are on the market. Because of their popularity and the prices they command, Third Reich medals and badges are especially big targets for reproductions. Generally, the only distinguishing characteristic between originals and reproductions are the detail of the casting, ribbon detail and definitive signs of wear and age.

Collectors Clubs

Orders and Medals Society of America, Glassboro, NJ, Newsletter

Medals—U.S.

Medal, Achievement, USA, Air Force. Recent strike on mounted ribbon. Mint cond. $10

Medal, Achievement, USA, Army. Recent strike on mounted ribbon. Mint cond. $10

Medal, Achievement, USA, Navy. Recent strike on mounted ribbon. Mint cond. $10

Medal, Achievement, USA, Coast Guard. Recent strike on mounted ribbon. Mint cond. $14

Medal, Achievement, USA, Army Reserve. Recent strike on mounted ribbon. Mint cond. $8

Medal, Achievement, USA, Navy, 1990s. Recent strike on mounted ribbon. Mint cond. $10

Medal, Achievement, USA, Air Force. Recent strike on mounted ribbon. Mint cond. $10

Medal, Achievement, USA, Army. Recent strike on mounted ribbon. Mint cond. $8

Medal, Achievement, USA, Army. Cased with lapel pin and ribbon bar. Mint cond. $10

Medal, Achievement, USA, Army. Cased with lapel pin and ribbon bar. Mint cond. $10

Medal, Air Force Cross, USA, USAF, c1960s. Bronze satin finish multi-piece pendant with enamel detail on crimp brooch-mounted ribbon. Older strike. Above avg. cond. $40

US Air Force Cross

Medal, Air Force Cross, USA, USAF, c1960s. Award originally authorized 1960. Bronze satin finish multi-piece pendant with enamel detail on crimp brooch-mounted ribbon. Above avg. cond. $25

Medal, Air Medal, USA, AAF, WWII. Issue box dated July 24, 1943. Above avg. cond. $60

Medal, Air Medal, USA, AAF, WWII. Named. Bronze pendant on wrap brooch-mounted ribbon. In case with ribbon. Above avg. cond. $50

Medal, Air Medal, USA, AAF, WWII. Bronze-toned pendant. Pb brooch. Reverse privately machine engraved and reads "S/SGT/(name)/AC." With lapel pin and ribbon bar. Cased. Above avg. cond. $100

Medal, Air Medal, USA, AAF, WWII. Wrap brooch ribbon. With ribbon bar. In WWII leatherette case. Avg. cond. $30

Medal, Airman Medal, USA, USAF, 1990. Bronze satin finish pendant on crimp brooch-mounted ribbon. With ribbon bar and lapel pin. In "Arrow" presentation case and 1990 dated government issue carton. Above avg. cond. $20

Medal, Airman, USA, USAF. Cased, unissued, USAF contract strike bronze finish pendant on crimp brooch-mounted ribbon, full size "Arrow" style case with RB. $10

Medal, Airman, USA, USAF, 1990. Cased, unissued, USAF contract strike-bronze finish pendant on crimp brooch-mounted ribbon, full size "Arrow"-style case with ribbon bar and lapel pin, case comes in original cardboard carton with contract data and info, dated 1990. Mint cond. $10

Medal, American Defense, USA. Recent strike on mounted ribbon. Mint cond. $12

Medal, American Defense, USA, All, c1980s. Recent strike on mounted ribbon. Mint cond. $12

Medal, Antarctic Service, USA, Various. Recent strike on mounted ribbon. Mint cond. $18

Medal, Arctic Service, USA, USCG. Recent strike on mounted ribbon. Mint cond. $30

Medal, Armed Forces Expeditionary, USA. Recent strike on mounted ribbon. Mint cond. $10

Medal, Bronze Star, USA, Army, c1960s. Slot brooch-mounted ribbon. In full-size "Arrow" presentation case with ribbon and lapel pin. Exc. cond. $20

Medal, Bronze Star, USA, Army, WWII. Machine engraved. With case, ribbon and lapel pin. Avg. cond. . $34

Medal, Bronze Star, USA, Army, WWII. Cased, dark bronze pendant on crimp brooch-mounted ribbon, in hinged lid, "Arrow"-style case with ribbon bar and lapel device. Near mint cond. $20

Medal, Bronze Star, USA, WWII. Recent strike on mounted ribbon. Mint cond. $17

Medal, Civilian Humanitarian Service, USA, various,

1990s. Bronze pendant on crimp brooch-mounted ribbon, in blue carton. Mint cond. $15

Medal, Combat Readiness, USA. Recent strike on mounted ribbon. Mint cond. $10

Medal, Commendation, USA, Air Force. Recent strike on mounted ribbon. Mint cond. $10

Medal, Commendation, USA, Navy. Recent strike on mounted ribbon. Mint cond. $10

Medal, Defense Logistics Agency Distinguished Career, USA. Bronze pendant on crimp brooch-mounted ribbon. Mint cond. $22

Medal, Defense Logistics Agency Superior Civilian Service, USA. Bronze pendant on crimp brooch-mounted ribbon. Mint cond. $22

Medal, Distinguished Flying Cross, USA, AAF, Other. Deep bronze finish on Sb mofted ribbon. Rev privately machine engraved "1st Lt./(Name)/USAAC." With lapel pin and ribbon bar. Cased. Exc. cond. $150

Medal, Distinguished Flying Cross, USA, AAF, WWII. On slot brooch-mounted ribbon. In WWII-era leatherette presentation case. Above avg. cond. $27

Medal, Distinguished Flying Cross, USA. Recent strike on mounted ribbon. Mint cond. $20

Medal, Distinguished Service Cross, USA, Army, c1970s. Bronze satin finish cross on crimp brooch-mounted ribbon. Above avg. cond. $35

Medal, Distinguished Service Cross, USA, Army. On crimp brooch-mounted ribbon. Above avg. cond. . . . $24

Medal, Distinguished Service Cross, USA, Army, WWII. Numbered. Bronze pendant stamped. Above avg. cond. $65

Medal, Distinguished Service Cross, USA, Army, WWII. Bronze satin finish. Slot brooch. Good cond. $59

Medal, Distinguished Service Cross, USA, Army. Recent strike on mounted ribbon. Mint cond. $20

Medal, Distinguished Service, USA, Coast Guard. Recent strike on mounted ribbon. Mint cond. $35

Medal, Distinguished Service, USA, Army. Recent strike on mounted ribbon. Mint cond. $65

Medal, Expeditionary, USA, USMC. Unissued, mint frosted bronze finish pendant on crimp brooch-mounted ribbon, on original plastic sealed card. Near mint cond. $20

Medal, Expeditionary (in issue envelope), USA, Navy. Well marked on envelope, dated Nov. 1982, full-size

medal with bronze pendant on crimp brooch-mounted ribbon, pb, in sealed plastic bag. Mint cond. $14

Medal, Expert Pistol Shot Qualification, USA, Navy, 1989. On crimp brooch mounted ribbon. In 1989 dated issue envelope. Exc. cond. $10

Medal, Expert Pistol Shot, USA, Coast Guard, c1980s. On crimp brooch-mounted ribbon. Above avg. cond. $20

Medal, Good Conduct, USA, Army, WWII. Machine engraved name on reverse in block letters. On slot brooch mounted ribbon. Avg. cond. $20

Medal, Good Conduct, USA, Army, 1945. Slot brooch-mounted ribbon. In 1945 dated issue box with ribbon and lapel pin. Reverse of medal is machine engraved with name. Avg. cond. $11

Medal, Good Conduct, USA, Coast Guard. Pb brooch. Bar reads "US COAST GUARD." Above avg. cond. $36

Medal, Good Conduct, USA, Navy, 1940. Medal machine engraved in block letters with man's full name and 1940 dated. On slot brooch-mounted ribbon. Above avg. cond. $28

Medal, Good Conduct, USA, Navy, 1928. Ribbon sewn to brooch and holding three brass bars for 1933, 1937, 1940 awards. Reverse of pendant is machine engraved with name and 1928 date. Avg. cond. $164

Medal, Good Conduct, USA, USMC, c1920s. Pendant is machine engraved on reverse "No.15826/(name)/1st Enlistment/1918–1922." On short drape ribbon on rope trimmed "U.S.Marine Corps" pb brooch. Near mint cond. $68

Medal, Good Conduct, USA, Navy. Recent strike on mounted ribbon. Mint cond. $10

Medal, Good Conduct, USA, Army. Recent strike on mounted ribbon. Mint cond. $8

US Navy Good Conduct Medal

Medal, Good Conduct, USA, Air Force. Recent strike on mounted ribbon. Mint cond. $8

Medal, Humane Action, USA, c1950. For Berlin Airlift. Authorized July 1949. On slot brooch-mounted ribbon. With ribbon. In pressed blue paper box. Avg. cond. . $11

Medal, Humanitarian Service, USA. Recent strike on mounted ribbon. Mint cond. $8

Medal, Joint Service Achievement, USA. Recent strike on mounted ribbon. Mint cond. $15

Medal, Joint Service Commendation, USA. Recent strike on mounted ribbon. Mint cond. $20

Medal, Medal of Honor, USA, Army, c1960s. With full neck ribbon. Above avg. cond. $318

Medal, Medal of Honor, USA, Army. Light blue neck ribbon with snaps, throat knot with 13 stars and brass suspender in Army emblem likeness holding five-point star pendent with enameled green wreath. Above avg. cond. $150

Medal, Medal of Honor, USA, USAF. Light blue neck ribbon with snaps, throat knot with 13 stars and brass suspender with Valor bar and AF emblem holding five-point star pendent with enameled green wreath. Near mint cond. $263

Medal, Medal of Honor, USA, USAF. With full neck ribbon. Above avg. cond. $250

Medal, Meritorious Service, USA. Recent strike on mounted ribbon. Mint cond. $15

Medal, Mexican Service (1911–17), USA, Navy, c1920s. Pb brooch. Above avg. cond. $29

Medal, Multinational Force, USA. Recent strike on mounted ribbon. Mint cond. $20

Medal, National Defense, USA, All, c1960s. Bronze pendant on crimp brooch-mounted ribbon. With ribbon. In box. Above avg. cond. $28

Medal, National Defense, USA. Recent strike on mounted ribbon. Mint cond. $10

Medal, National Defense, USA, All, c1990s. Recent strike on mounted ribbon. Mint cond. $10

Medal, Navy and Marine Corps, USA, Navy and Marine Corps. Recent strike on mounted ribbon. Mint cond. $24

Medal, Navy Cross, USA, Navy, WWII. 63 x 120mm. Navy blue leatherette-covered "Coffin"-style case has white silk and blue velvet lined interior. Dark bronze Navy cross on dark bronze split brooch-mounted ribbon. With ribbon bar. Near mint cond. $710

Medal, Navy Cross, USA, Navy, Korean War Era. Wrap-mounted ribbon on pb brooch suspending pendant. Reverse with name engraved (unofficial). Above avg. cond. $343

Medal, Navy Cross, USA, Navy, WWII. Satin finished bronze cross pendant on crimp brooch-mounted ribbon. Above avg. cond. $55

Medal, Navy Expert Rifleman Shot Qualification, USA, Navy, 1988. On crimp brooch-mounted ribbon. In 1988 dated issue envelope. Exc. cond. $92

Medal, Occupation Service, USA, USMC. Recent strike on crimped brooch-mounted ribbon. Mint cond. . . . $18

Medal, Occupation Service, USA, USN, 1990s. Recent strike on mounted ribbon with Asia clasp. Mint cond. $17

Medal, Occupation Service, USA, USMC, 1990s. Recent strike on crimped brooch-mounted ribbon. Mint cond. $18

Medal, Organized Reserve, USA, Marine Corps. Recent strike on mounted ribbon. Mint cond. $16

Medal, Philippine Campaign (1899–1903), USA, USMC, c1900s. Thick pendant in bronze satin finish with ring suspender on wrap brooch-mounted ribbon. Above avg. cond. $51

Medal, POW, USA. Recent strike on mounted ribbon. Mint cond. $12

Medal, Purple Heart, USA, AAF, WWII. Gilt pendant with plastic insert. Named in block letters. With ribbon bar. Cased. Above avg. cond. $47

Navy Cross with Case and Ribbon Bar

Medal, Purple Heart, USA, Army, WWII. Machine-engraved pendant. With case. Includes documentation on individual covering unit and state of residence at death (KIA). Near mint cond. $175

Medal, Purple Heart, USA, Army, WWI. Enamel pendant with numbered rim is hand engraved with name on reverse. Split brooch-mounted ribbon. With original carton numbered to match medal. Includes brief research for man WIA with 59th Inf. Sept. 28, 1918. Exc. cond. $150

Medal, Purple Heart, USA, Army, WWII. Numbered. Mounted. On slot brooch. With ribbon bar and lapel pin. In leatherette presentation case. Above avg. cond. . . $38

Medal, Purple Heart, USA, Army, WWI. Wrap-mounted ribbon to split brooch and suspending pendant. Enameled heart behind Washington's profile. Serial numbered and named. With ribbon bar. Avg. cond. $83

Medal, Purple Heart, USA, Army, WWII. Numbered. Gilt and enamel. Mounted slot brooch. With lapel pin. In WWII-style presentation case. Avg. cond. $31

Medal, Purple Heart, USA. Unissued, recent strike. Mint cond. $30

Medal, Silver Star, USA, Army, 1942. Slot brooch. 1942 dated box, numbered. Avg. cond. $29

Medal, Silver Star, USA. Recent strike on mounted ribbon. Mint cond. $16

Medal, Soldiers, USA, Army. Recent strike on mounted ribbon. Mint cond. $25

Medal, Southwest Asia Service, USA. Recent strike on mounted ribbon. Mint cond. $10

Medal, UN Kuwait Service, c1992. 42mm-diam bronze pendant on pin brooch-mounted ribbon with star device affixed. Mint cond. $15

Medal, Victory, USA, Army, c1920. On wrap brooch-mounted ribbon with "France" clasp. Avg. cond. . . . $11

Medal, Volunteer Service, USA, Various, c1990s. New issue on crimp brooch-mounted ribbon. Mint cond. . $25

Medal, WWI Victory, USA, Army, WWI. On wrap brooch-mounted ribbon with Defensive Sector clasp. Avg. cond. $23

Medal, WWI Victory With Clasp, USA, Navy, WWI. Wrap brooch. Naval pattern "Patrol" clasp. Above avg. cond. $66

Medal, WWI Victory With Clasp, USA, Navy, WWI. Wrap brooch. Naval pattern "Atlantic Fleet" clasp. Above avg. cond. $40

Medal, WWI Victory With Clasp, USA, Navy, WWI. Pb brooch. "Naval Battery" clasp. Avg. cond. $30

Medal, WWI Victory With Clasp, USA, Navy, WWI. Bronze pendant on wrap brooch-mounted ribbon with "Transport" clasp affixed. Avg. cond. $25

Medal, WWI Victory With Clasp, USA, c1920. Ribbon sewn to pb brooch and holds brass "Siberia" bar. Above avg. cond. $106

Medal, WWI Victory With Clasp, USA, 1920. Clasp reads "France." On wrap brooch mounted ribbon. In 1920 issue box. Avg. cond. $20

Medal, WWI Victory With Five Clasps, USA, Army, USMC, WWI. On long drape ribbon mounted on wrap brooch. With Defensive Sector, Champagne-Marne, Aisne-Marne, St. Mihiel and Meuse-Argonne clasps. Avg. cond. $32

Medal, WWI Victory With Two Clasps, USA, Army, c1920. Pb brooch. With two bars — Meuse Argonne and Defensive Sector. Avg. cond. $27

Medal, WWII Victory, USA, Merchant Marine, WWII. Crimp brooch. Above avg. cond. $20

Metal, Bronze Star, USA, Army. Bronze star pendant on slot brooch-mounted ribbon with machine-engraved name to back in block capitals. Avg. cond. $27

Metal, Distinguished Flying Cross, USA, Army, WWII. On slot brooch-mounted ribbon. In WWII-style leatherette presentation case. Avg. cond. $30

Mounted Collection of German Medals and Ribbons

Medals—Germany

Black Eagle Order, Prussian, Imperial Germany, Army, WWI, Wagner. Silver gilt 1916 issue. With "W" for Wagner maker mark. Bright yellow ribbon sash. Near mint cond. $2597

Iron Cross 1870, 2nd Class, Imperial Germany, Army, c1870s. Silver frame. Exc. cond. $182

Iron Cross Oak Leaves, For 1870 EK, 2nd Class, Imperial Germany, Army, c1870s. 27mm wide, three dark silver oak leaves with "25" center, two flat prongs and 3½"-long ribbon. Exc. cond. $167

Lapel Chain, Six Place, Imperial Germany, Army, WWI. 4" double gold chain with stickpins to each side with 1914 EK, Friedrich August Konig von Sachsen medal, 1914 "FA" Cross, silver 20-Year Cross, Kriegsmarine 1914/18 Cross with swords and Schlesien eagle. Above avg. cond. $145

Medal Bar, Four Place, Germany, Army, WWII. Four medal bar with 1939 Iron Cross, 2nd class/1939 War Service Cross, 2nd class with swords/Russian Front medal/Four-Year Armed Services medal. Above avg. cond. $147

Medal Bar, Four Place, Germany, Navy, WWII. Medals are mounted on an angle and in reverse order for naval frock coats. Group consists of 1914 Iron Cross, 2nd class/Hindenburg Cross with swords/Kriegsmarine 25-Year Service Cross with miniature Spanish Victory medal in gilt, black as issued to Condor Legion members. Parade furled ribbons. Iron Cross is original old jeweler's piece with old solder repair to suspension ring. Above avg. cond. $167

Medal Bar, Four Place, Bavarian, Imperial Germany, Army, WWI. Group includes 1914 Iron Cross 2nd class. Bavarian Military Service Cross 4th class with swords. Hindenburg Cross with swords. Bavarian 9-Year Service medal. Pb. Above avg. cond. $133

Medal Bar, Four Place, Saxon, Imperial Germany, Army, WWI. Bar consists of 1914 Iron Cross 2nd class/General Saxon Honor Cross with swords for combatant/Friedrich August medal/Hindenburg Cross with swords. Above avg. cond. $129

Medal Bar, Six Place, Germany, Army, WWII. Double wrapped ribbons are padded. 1914 EK, Crowned Prussian gold WR medal, Hindenburg with swords, 18-Year Army Service Cross with eagle, Service Ribbon lacks medal and Turkish WWI Service medal. Black wool back with bevo maker "Grabow & Matthes Kiel" and brass pin. Above avg. cond. $200

Medal Bar, Three Place, Germany, Luftwaffe, WWII. Double wrapped ribbons show age with silver LW eagle device. 1939 EK, Four-Year Service and Czech Occupation. Red felt backing with brass pin. Above avg. cond. $143

Medal Bar, Three Place, Imperial Germany, Army, WWI. 1914 Iron Cross 2nd class with three-letter hallmark on ring/1871 Victory medal with inscribed rim (on improper Hesse ribbon)/Hindenburg Cross with swords. Large furled-style ribbons. Above avg. cond. $61

Medal Bar, Three Place, Imperial Germany, Army, WWI. Iron Cross 2nd class 1914/Ducal 1914 Service medal/Hindenburg Cross with swords. Above avg. cond. $145

Medal Bar, Three Place, Imperial Germany, Army, WWI. 1914 Iron Cross 2nd class/1914 Hamburg Service Cross/Hindenburg Cross with swords. Above avg. cond. $85

Medal Bar, Two Place, Germany, Luftwaffe, WWII. Double wrapped ribbons, Four-Year Service medal with Luftwaffe eagle device and 1938 Czech Occupation medal. Moth felt backing and brass pb. Avg. cond. $60

Medal, 15 Year Service Cross For Officer, Hessian, Imperial Germany, Army, c1890s. Silvered and gilt cross with old original ribbon. Above avg. cond. $70

Medal, 1814–15 Napoleonic War Medal For Combat, Hesse-kassel, Imperial Germany, Army, c1815. Dated brass pendant and engraved edge "In captured cannon." Above avg. cond. $102

Medal, 1848 War Service Cross, 2nd Class, Mecklenburg-schwerin, Imperial Germany, Army, c1850. With old original ribbon. Above avg. cond. $293

Medal, 1849 Military Merit Cross, Mecklenburg-schwerin, Imperial Germany, Army, WWI. Gilt-plated bronze 40mm Maltese Cross FF center, crown at top and date base on arms and wording on other side. Above avg. cond. $250

Medal, 1849 War Service Medal, Baden, Imperial Germany, Army, c1850. Antique bronze finish. Yellow and silver ribbon. Avg. cond. $32

Medal, 1864 War Medal, Prussia, Imperial Germany, Army, WWI. War against Schleswig-Holstein. Bright bronze finish. Proper black ribbon with yellow, white stripes. Avg. cond. $51

Medal, 1870 Campaign Medal, Oldenburg, Imperial Germany, Army, WWI. Silver finish with head of duke. Red, blue and yellow ribbon. Above avg. cond. . . . $293

Medal, 1870 Service Cross, 2nd Class, Mecklenburg-schwerin, Imperial Germany, Army, c1870s. Complete with original ribbon. Gilt finish. Avg. cond. $117

Medal, 1870–71 Victory Medal, Prussian, Imperial Germany, Army, WWI. With ribbon and inscribed rim. Avg. cond. $20

Medal, 1870/71 War Medal, Oldenburg, Imperial Germany, Army, c1870s. Made from melted down cannon bronze. With ribbon. Exc. cond. $260

Medal, 1871 Service Cross, 2nd Class, Mecklenburg-schwerin, Imperial Germany, Army, c1870s. Complete with ribbon. Gilt remains. Exc. cond. $527

Medal, 1871 War, Combatant, Prussian, Imperial Germany, Army, c1870s. Complete with ribbon. Avg. cond. $40

Medal, 1914 Bravery, Wurttemberg, Imperial Germany, Army, WWI. Silver. With black and yellow ribbon. Mint cond. $39

Medal, 1914 Service Cross, 2nd Class, Mecklenburg-schwerin, Imperial Germany, Army, WWI. With ribbon. Avg. cond. $47

Medal, 1914 War Merit Cross, 2nd Class, Brunswick, Imperial Germany, Army, WWI. With ribbon. Exc. cond. $35

Medal, 1914 War Service Cross, 1st Class, Oldenburg, Imperial Germany, Army, WWI. Black wartime finish. Pb. Exc. cond. $100

Medal, 1914 War Service Cross, 1st Class, Oldenburg, Imperial Germany, Army, WWI. Nice even dark wartime finish. Above avg. cond. $82

Medal, 1914 War Service Cross, 2nd Class, Lippe, Imperial Germany, Army, WWI. With half-size rib. High gilt gold finish. Exc. cond. $31

Medal, 1914 War Service Cross, 2nd Class, Mecklenburg-schwerin, Imperial Germany, Army, WWI. 1914 issue. Fine gold finish with excellent details. Yellow, blue and red ribbon. Exc. cond. $52

Medal, 1914 War, Schwarzburg, Imperial Germany, Army, WWI. Silvered finish. Large size with cipher, date and crown. Blue and yellow ribbon. Above avg. cond. $65

Medal, 1914/15 War Medal, Saxe-meinigen, Imperial Germany, Army, WWI. With beautiful dark bronze finish. Proper black, yellow, ribbed-style ribbon. Exc. cond. . $75

Medal, 1914/18 War Service, Saxe-coburg-gotha, Imperial Germany, Army, WWI. In wartime gray finish with ribbon and rare unattached bar with crossed swords, 1914/18 dates. Exc. cond. $49

Medal, 1916 Charlotten Cross, Wurttemberg, Imperial Germany, Army, WWI. In silver finish with black and yellow ribbon. Above avg. cond. $47

Medal, 1916 War Service Cross, Prussian, Imperial Germany, Army, WWI. Gray wartime finish. Avg. cond. $30

Medal, Armed Forces Service Cross, 12 Year, Germany,

Army, WWII. Gold medal with ring. Above avg. cond. $31

Medal, Armed Forces Service Cross, 18 Year, Germany, Army, WWII. Silver cross with National eagle affixed to blue ribbon. Avg. cond. $103

Medal, Armed Forces Service Cross, 25 Year, Germany, Army, WWII. Dark finish to magnetic body. Above avg. cond. $35

Medal, Army Service, Four Year, Germany, Army, WWII. Frosted silver finish and blue ribbon with eagle. Includes envelope with two-line title and maker. Exc. cond. $48

Medal, Army Service, Four Year, Germany, Army, WWII. Frosted silver finish and blue ribbon with eagle. Exc. cond. $48

Medal, Austrian Occupation With Case, Germany, Army, WWII. Red leatherette body with gold eagle, white satin lid lining and maroon velvet base. Darkening to silver medal with ribbon having pin. Above avg. cond. $69

Medal, Bravery, Bavarian, Imperial Germany, Army, WWI. Formal dress. 35mm size with fine details and bust. Proper black, white and blue ribbon. Exc. cond. . . . $97

Medal, Bravery, Wurttemberg, Imperial Germany, Army, WWI. With yellow and black ribbon. Bust of king. Above avg. cond. $30

Medal, Czech Occupation, Germany, Army, WWII. On medal bar mount. Dark bronze metal on padded double wrapped ribbon mount. Red wool backing and brass pin. Above avg. cond. $40

Medal, Czech Occupation With Case, Germany, Army, WWII. Maroon leatherette body with gold eagle, white satin lid lining and maroon velvet base. Bronze medal with ribbon and pin coming unsewn. Above avg. cond. $61

Medal, Eastern People, 1st Class Gold, With Swords, Germany, Army, WWII. Black leatherette case with faint award to lid, white satin and black velvet inside. Faded gray award with traces of silver wide pin. Exc. cond. . . . $130

Medal, Eastern People, 1st Class Gold, Without Swords, Germany, Army, WWII. Good finish on star with shield center, dished out back and wide pin. Exc. cond. $90

Medal, Eastern People, 1st Class Gold, Without Swords, Germany, Army, WWII. Black leatherette case with gold award to lid, white satin and black flock inside. Faded gray award with traces of gold and wide pin. Avg. cond. $133

Medal, Eastern People, 1st Class Silver, With Swords, Germany, Army, WWII. Black leatherette case with silver decoration at top. White satin and black flock base. Solid badge is fading gray and has wide pin. Above avg. cond. $145

Medal, Eastern People, 1st Class Silver, Without Swords, Germany, Army, WWII. Shield to starburst and pb. Age darkening. Avg. cond. $40

Medal, Eastern People, 2nd Class Bronze, With Swords, Germany, Army, WWII. Faded gray, green ribbon and pin. Avg. cond. $25

Medal, Eastern People, 2nd Class Bronze, Without Swords, Germany, Army, WWII. Graying to finish and green ribbon. Avg. cond. $30

Medal, Eastern People, 2nd Class Gold, Without Swords, Germany, Army, WWII. Graying to gold finish. Red stripes on green ribbon lacks pin. Above avg. cond. $50

Medal, Faithful Service Cross 25 Year, Germany, Army, WWII. Frosted cross, black enamel swastika and blue ribbon with pin. Avg. cond. $20

Medal, Faithful Service Cross 25 Year, Germany, Army, WWII. Frosted silver finish, black enamel swastika and soiled blue ribbon. Avg. cond. $20

Medal, Faithful Service Cross 40 Year, Germany, Army, WWII. Bright finish, black swastika and blue ribbon with pin. Avg. cond. $25

Medal, Faithful Service Cross 40 Year, Germany, Army, WWII. Dark finish, good enamel swastika and replacement ribbon ring. Avg. cond. $20

Medal, Frankfurt 1815 War, Germany, Army, c1815. Napoleonic period. Large silvered badge with crowned eagle design. White-red ribbon. Exc. cond. $300

Medal, German Cross in Gold (Cloth Pattern), Germany, Army, WWII. Still sealed in cellophane wrapper. Excellent embr details on gray wool with gold 1941/wreath. Exc. cond. $222

Medal, German Cross in Gold (Cloth Pattern), Germany, Army, WWII. Embr details on gray wool with gold 1941/wreath and paper backing. Exc. cond. $195

Medal, German Cross in Gold (Cloth Pattern), Germany, Army, WWII. Nice embr work to star on gray felt with dark brass/bronze 1941 wreath. Part of paper backing remains. Exc. cond. $210

Medal, German Cross in Gold (Cloth Pattern), Germany, Army, WWII. Colored embr work on gray felt star. Corrosion on alum details. Gold 1941 wreath. Paper backed. Above avg. cond. $181

Medal, German Cross in Gold (Cloth Pattern), Germany, Army, WWII, C.A. Westmann Dresden. Colored embr work on gray felt star. Corrosion on alum star details. Gold 1941 wreath. Paper backing has inked maker tag "C.A. Westmann Dresden." Above avg. cond. $145

Medal, German Cross in Gold (Cloth Pattern), Germany, Army, WWII. Colored embr work on gray felt star. Gold 1941 wreath. Black mesh cloth backing. Above avg. cond. $137

Medal, German Cross in Gold (Cloth Pattern), Germany, Army, WWII. Good embr work on blue felt backing with many moth holes. Dark 1941 gold wreath. Removed from tunic. Avg. cond. $139

Medal, German Cross in Silver, Germany, Army, WWII. Black enamel swastika shows scuffs, worn silver finish to brass 1941 wreath, red enamel background and two-part starburst backing has four hollow rivets. Pin stamped "20." Avg. cond. $1426

Medal, German Eagle Order Merit Bronze, With Swords, Germany, Army, WWII. Dark finish, Latin script, affixed swords, ring stamped "30" and pin on ribbon. Exc. cond. $650

Medal, German Eagle Order Merit, With Swords, Germany, Army, WWII. Good silver finish, Gothic script, affixed swords and ribbon with pin. "835 etc." on rim. Exc. cond. $600

Medal, Hindenburg Cross, With Swords, Germany, Army, WWII. Black two-piece cardboard box with black velvet fitted compartment for medal and area for the folded ribbon, included both, ribbon has age stains and also has small ribbon bar with crossed gilt swords. Avg. cond. $79

Medal, Hindenburg Cross, Without Swords, Germany, Army, WWII. Faded dark bronze cross with soiled ribbon

German Cross in Gold, Cloth Pattern (DK)

and 1¼"-wide ribbon bar with swords device. Pb. Avg. cond. $20

Medal, House Order Silver Service, Hohenzollern, Imperial Germany, Army, WWI. Last model. Finely struck with black, white ribbon bordered with gold border. Exc. cond. $227

Medal, Iron Cross 1813, 1st Class, Imperial Germany, Army, c1815. 41mm dark silver frame with magnetic center. Two silver loops to reverse of each arm. Above avg. cond. $748

Medal, Iron Cross 1870, 1st Class, Imperial Germany, Army, c1870s. 42mm dark silver frame and magnetic black center. Pin is stamped "2" at underside. Avg. cond. $654

Medal, Iron Cross 1870, 2nd Class, Germany, Army, c1870s. With ribbon. Avg. cond. $282

Medal, Iron Cross 1914, 1st Class, Imperial Germany, Army, WWI. Double screw back. Magnetic black center and very dark tarnished frame. Slightly vaulted. Below avg. cond. $63

Medal, Iron Cross 1914, 1st Class, Imperial Germany, Army, WWI. Screw back. Magnetic black center with frosted silver frame and slightly vaulted. Large stamped brass rayed disc with threaded post. Exc. cond. . . . $160

Iron Cross, 1914, First Class

Medal, Iron Cross 1914, 1st Class, Imperial Germany, Army, WWI. Screw back. Magnetic. Vaulted. Reverse with two threaded posts-one on upper arm and one on lower. Two large disc-shaped backing plates with four holes. Two hexagon-shaped nuts. Above avg. cond. $187

Medal, Iron Cross 1914, 1st Class, Imperial Germany, Army, WWI. Screw back. Magnetic. Vaulted. Threaded stud in center of back. With 38mm-diam backing plate and hexagon-shaped wing nut. Above avg. cond. $130

Medal, Iron Cross 1914, 1st Class, Imperial Germany, Army, WWI. Variation. Magnetic black center, dark silver frame with stamped "800," slightly vaulted and two threaded posts with nuts. 2" diam gray metal backing disc with 12 sew-on holes. Above avg. cond. $136

Medal, Iron Cross 1914, 1st Class, Imperial Germany, Army, WWI. Three-piece construction with iron center and two screw-back posts. "800" hmkd on back. Above avg. cond. $93

Medal, Iron Cross 1914, 1st Class, Imperial Germany, Army, WWI. Magnetic black center with darkening to silver frame that is vaulted. Wire pb. Above avg. cond. $124

Medal, Iron Cross 1914, 1st Class, Imperial Germany, Army, WWI. Non-magnetic. Appears entire slightly vaulted body is made from brass with black paint and silver frame highlights. Wide pin. Above avg. cond. $97

Medal, Iron Cross 1914, 1st Class, Imperial Germany, Army, WWI. Screw back. Magnetic black center to vaulted body. Two threaded posts on unmarked back. 48mm gray zinc disc. Above avg. cond. $180

Medal, Iron Cross 1914, 1st Class, Imperial Germany, Army, WWI. Screw back. Magnetic black center, slightly vaulted silver frame, threaded stud and nut and gray metal backing disc. Avg. cond. $250

Medal, Iron Cross 1914, 1st Class, Imperial Germany, Army, WWI. Screw back. Magnetic black center, vaulted dark silver frame, socket back, domed disc and threads on wheel. Avg. cond. $149

Medal, Iron Cross 1914, 1st Class, Imperial Germany, Army, WWI. Magnetic black center with darkening to silver frame that is vaulted. Wide pb. Avg. cond. $72

Medal, Iron Cross 1914, 1st Class, Imperial Germany, Army, WWI. Magnetic black center, silver frame, pb and maker mark. Avg. cond. $85

Medal, Iron Cross 1914, 1st Class, Imperial Germany, Army, WWI. Magnetic center. Silver frame and wide pin. Stamped by "KO." Avg. cond. $59

Medal, Iron Cross 1914, 1st Class, Imperial Germany, Army, WWI. Non-magnetic. Vaulted body has dark silver frame and black painted gray center. pb. Avg. cond. $72

Medal, Iron Cross 1914, 1st Class, With 1939 Spange, Germany, Army, WWII. Sb. Darkening on silver eagle with dated scroll. Threaded stud at back and rayed disc with socket. Above avg. cond. $164

Medal, Iron Cross 1914, 1st Class, With Case and Box, Imperial Germany, Army, WWI. Maroon leatherette case with paper 1914 EK affixed. White satin and purple velvet lining. Magnetic black center, tarnished frame, swollen pin and stamped "KO." Four-line title label to storage box. Above avg. cond. $200

Medal, Iron Cross 1914, 1st Class, With Case, Imperial Germany, Army, WWI. Black leatherette case with EK outline on lid, white satin and velvet lined. Magnetic black vaulted body, bright silver frame, wide pin and stamped "950" with double headed eagle trademark. Exc. cond. $306

Medal, Iron Cross 1914, 1st Class, With Case, Imperial Germany, Army, WWI. Paper EK affixed to black leatherette body with white satin and purple velvet lining. Magnetic black center on tarnished silver frame. Wide pin and stamped "WS." Above avg. cond. $149

Medal, Iron Cross 1914, 1st Class, With Case, Imperial Germany, Army, WWI. Leatherette body with silver EK outline, white satin lid lining and purple velvet base. Magnetic black center, dark silver frame is vaulted. Pb, and stamped "800." Avg. cond. $125

Medal, Iron Cross 1914, 2nd Class, Imperial Germany, Army, WWI. Magnetic black centers with dark silver frame. "P" on ring. Above avg. cond. $28

Medal, Iron Cross 1914, 2nd Class, Imperial Germany, Army, WWI. Magnetic black centers, dark frame, tri-fold ribbon and bronze crossed swords bar. Above avg. cond. $66

Medal, Iron Cross 1914, 2nd Class, Imperial Germany, Army, WWI. Magnetic black centers, dark silver frame and long ribbon. Above avg. cond. $40

Medal, Iron Cross 1914, 2nd Class, Imperial Germany, Army, WWI. Magnetic black centers, dark silver frame and ribbon. Above avg. cond. $28

Medal, Iron Cross 1914, 2nd Class, Imperial Germany, Army, WWI. Magnetic black centers, dark silver frame and ribbon. Above avg. cond. $30

Medal, Iron Cross 1914, 2nd Class, Imperial Germany, Army, WWI. Non-combatant. Magnetic black centers, dark silver frame, ring stamped "N" and white ribbon with black stripes. Above avg. cond. $49

Medal, Iron Cross 1914, 2nd Class, Imperial Germany, Army, WWI. Ribbon has patriotic national color bow mounted to it with celluloid picture of von Mackensen in hussar busby in center shield. Above avg. cond. . . . $65

Medal, Iron Cross 1914, 2nd Class, Imperial Germany, Army, WWI. Hmkd ring "WILM." With ribbon. Avg. cond. $29

Medal, Iron Cross 1914, 2nd Class, Imperial Germany, Army, WWI. Magnetic black center, dark silver frame and long ribbon. Avg. cond. $37

Medal, Iron Cross 1914, 2nd Class, Imperial Germany,

Army, WWI. Magnetic black centers, dark silver frame and short ribbon. Avg. cond. $30

Medal, Iron Cross 1914, 2nd Class, Imperial Germany, Army, WWI. Magnetic black centers with dark silver frame. Unmarked ring. Avg. cond. $20

Medal, Iron Cross 1914, 2nd Class, Imperial Germany, Army, WWI. Magnetic black centers, dark silver frame and ribbon. Avg. cond. $28

Iron Cross, 1914, Second Class

Medal, Iron Cross 1914, 2nd Class, Imperial Germany, Army, WWI. Magnetic black centers, dark silver frame and ring stamped "KO." Avg. cond. $20

Medal, Iron Cross 1914, 2nd Class, Imperial Germany, Army, WWI. Magnetic black centers, dark silver frame and ring stamped "Z." Good ribbon. Avg. cond. $27

Medal, Iron Cross 1914, 2nd Class, With 1939 Spange, Germany, Army, WWII. Medal very clean with high silver content frame. With spange. Ribbon. Exc. cond. . . . $79

Medal, Iron Cross 1914, 2nd Class, With Case, Imperial Germany, Army, WWI. Austrian issue. Gold title on maroon leatherette case with rounded end. White satin lid lining has gold maker "Rothe & Neffe Wien etc." With eagle trademark. White velvet fitted base. Magnetic EK, frosted silver frame and tri-fold ribbon. Near mint cond. $370

Medal, Iron Cross 1914, 2nd Class, With Case, Imperial Germany, Army, WWI. Blue pressed cardboard box with gold inscription "Eisernes Kreuz 2 Klasse" having gold border, brass hinges and stud release. White silken liner with form-fitted white flocking for medal and mounted. Tri-fold ribbon. Near mint cond. $360

Medal, Iron Cross 1914, 2nd Class, With Case, Imperial Germany, Army, WWI. Black leather body, paper maker tag to back "Max Pinnow Duisburg," white lid lining with elastic loops for ribbon and fitted white velvet base. Magnetic black center, bright silver frame and long ribbon. Exc. cond. $200

Medal, Iron Cross 1914, 2nd Class, With Case, Imperial Germany, Army, WWI. Gray leatherette body with paper EK on lid, purple satin and velvet fitted base. Magnetic black center. Exc. cond. $269

Medal, Iron Cross 1939, 1st Class, Germany, Army, WWII. Bright and frosted silver finish. Wire pb. Broken black leatherette case missing four sides. Near mint cond. $100

Medal, Iron Cross 1939, 1st Class, Germany, Army, WWII. Sb. Magnetic black center and dull silver frame. Socket on back and stamped rayed disc with threaded stud. Exc. cond. $144

Medal, Iron Cross 1939, 1st Class, Germany, Army, WWII. Sb. Magnetic black center, dark silver frame, threaded socket and prong at back. "800" stamped EK shaped backing plate and disc with threaded stud. Variation. Exc. cond. $212

Medal, Iron Cross 1939, 1st Class, Germany, Army, WWII. Magnetic black center is old repaint. Darkening to silver frame. Wide pin stamped "L/58." Early example. Above avg. cond. $69

Medal, Iron Cross 1939, 1st Class, Germany, Army, WWII. Magnetic black center, darkening to silver frame and wide pin stamped "65." Above avg. cond. $88

Medal, Iron Cross 1939, 1st Class, Germany, Army, WWII. Magnetic black center shows some rust and dull silver frame. Wide pin stamped "L15." Avg. cond. ... $85

Medal, Iron Cross 1939, 1st Class, Germany, Army, WWII. Magnetic black center and dull silver frame. Wide pin stamped "L15." Avg. cond. $75

Medal, Iron Cross 1939, 1st Class, Germany, Army, WWII. Non-magnetic black center, dark silver frame and wide pin. Avg. cond. $120

Medal, Iron Cross 1939, 1st Class, Germany, Army, WWII. Sb. Dull silver frame and magnetic black center with some rust. Socket and pin. Domed disc by "L/21." Avg. cond. $110

Medal, Iron Cross 1939, 1st Class, Germany, Army, WWII. Sb. Magnetic black center, dull silver frame, threaded socket and fluted disc with threaded stud. Avg. cond. $156

Medal, Iron Cross 1939, 1st Class, Germany, Army, WWII. Sb. Magnetic. Screw disc hmkd "L/21." Avg. cond. $122

Medal, Iron Cross 1939, 1st Class, Germany, Army, WWII. Sb. Tarnish on silver frame and magnetic black center showing wear. Avg. cond. $92

Medal, Iron Cross 1939, 1st Class, With Case, Germany, Army, WWII. Black leatherette body with silver EK outline, white satin and velvet interior. Magnetic black center, silver frame and wide pin stamped "L/15." Exc. cond. $186

Medal, Iron Cross 1939, 1st Class, With Case, Germany, Army, WWII. Black leatherette case with silver EK outline on lid with white satin lining. White velvet base. Magnetic black center shows use. Dark tarnish to silver frame with wide pin. Exc. cond. $244

Medal, Iron Cross 1939, 1st Class, With Case, Germany, Army, WWII. Clean black center is magnetic and dull nickel frame. Wide pin stamped "L15." Black leatherette case has silver EK outline. White satin lid lining and velvet base. Old tape repair on hinge. Case. Exc. cond. $160

Medal, Iron Cross 1939, 1st Class, With Case, Germany, Army, WWII. Black leatherette body with silver EK outline, white satin and velvet interior. Magnetic black center, silver frame and wide pin stamped "L/56." Above avg. cond. $165

Medal, Iron Cross 1939, 1st Class, With Case, Germany, Army, WWII. Black leatherette case is style without latch, white flock inside and black stenciled "LDO" logo to lid flock. Magnetic black center, bright silver frame, wide pin and stamped "L/11." Above avg. cond. $168

Medal, Iron Cross 1939, 1st Class, With Case, Germany, Army, WWII. Black leatherette case, with silver EK outline, white satin and velvet lined. Magnetic black center,

Iron Cross, 1939, First Class

tarnished frame and wide pin stamped "L15." Above avg. cond. $123

Medal, Iron Cross 1939, 1st Class, With Case, Germany, Army, WWII. Black leatherette with silver EK outline, white satin and flock lining. Magnetic black center has some peeling, bright silver frame and wide pin stamped "107." Storage age only. Above avg. cond. $110

Medal, Iron Cross 1939, 2nd Class, Germany, Army, WWII. Magnetic black centers, dull silver frame and long ribbon. Rust peeled back. Below avg. cond. $20

Medal, Iron Cross 1939, 2nd Class, Germany, Army, WWII. Magnetic, dark silver frame, ring stamped "75" and long ribbon. Early example. Above avg. cond. . $40

Medal, Iron Cross 1939, 2nd Class, Germany, Army, WWII. Magnetic centers, darkening to silver frame and long ribbon. Avg. cond. $37

Medal, Iron Cross 1939, 2nd Class, Germany, Army, WWII. Magnetic, bright frame, stamped "23" ring and clean ribbon. Avg. cond. $42

Medal, Iron Cross 1939, 2nd Class, Germany, Army, WWII. Darkening to silver finish, four flat prongs and "L/4." Avg. cond. $44

Medal, Iron Cross 1939, 2nd Class, Germany, Army, WWII. Magnetic black centers, dark tarnished frame and clean ribbon. Avg. cond. $40

Medal, Iron Cross 1939, 2nd Class, With Case, Germany, Army, WWII. Black leatherette body with tan bottom inked "EK.II. L/54." "LDO" to tan lid inside with fitted flock base. Magnetic black centers, frosted ridge, bright silver frame, ring stamped "65" and clean loose ribbon. Near mint cond. $195

Medal, Iron Cross 1939, 2nd Class, With Case, Germany, Army, WWII. Black leatherette body with inked "L/11" on back, yellow inside with printed "LDO" on lid with tape damage. Magnetic black center, silver frame and 4" ribbon. Exc. cond. $165

Medal, Iron Cross 1939, 2nd Class, With Envelope, Germany, Army, WWII. Magnetic black centers, frosted ridge, darkening to frame and clean ribbon. Three-line title on blue envelope with maker at back. Exc. cond. . . . $76

Medal, Iron Cross 1939, 2nd Class, With Envelope, Germany, Army, WWII. Magnetic. Darkening to frame. With ribbon. Large blue titled envelope. Hard to find with envelopes. Above avg. cond. $54

Medal, Iron Cross 1939, 2nd Class, With Envelope, Germany, Army, WWII. Unmounted folded ribbon, nickel

silver metal frame and some oxidation on black painted center. Envelope is blue with black printing. Above avg. cond. $52

Medal, Iron Cross 1939, 2nd Class, With Envelope, Germany, Army, WWII. Magnetic black centers, dull-silver frame, ring stamped "5" and 14"-long clean ribbon. Large light blue envelope with three-line title shows age. Avg. cond. $75

Medal, Knights Cross of the Iron Cross 1939, Germany, Army, WWII. Bright heavy silver frame is stamped "800" below ring. Magnetic centers have peeling to black paint. Silver loop has faint "65 800." 12½"-long ribbon. Above avg. cond. $2029

Medal, Knights Cross of the War Merit Cross In Silver Without Swords, Germany, Army, WWII. 53mm-cross with some age darkening. Stamped "900" on lower arm. Smooth ring mount and loop for 20"-long ribbon with mini KVK ribbon tie-strings. Only 137 awarded. Above avg. cond. $1700

Medal, Life Saving, Prussian, Imperial Germany, Army, WWI. Fine silver finish with yellow and white ribbon. Above avg. cond. $58

Medal, Long Service Cross 25 Year, Prussian, Imperial Germany, Army. Gilt with dark blue ribbon. Exc. cond. $25

Medal, Luftschutz Cross, 1st Class, Germany, Luftwaffe, WWII. Wartime gold-plated body has some worn highlights showing gray base metal. Style with small ring holding ribbon ring with long ribbon. Above avg. cond. $387

Medal, Luftschutz Cross, 2nd Class, With Case, Germany, Army, WWII. Clean gray leatherette body, three-line title and gray flock inside. Clean gray finished alum medal, ribbon and pin. Exc. cond. $145

Medal, Military Merit Cross 3rd Class, With Swords, Bavarian, Imperial Germany, Army, WWI. Blue leatherette case with silver title, blue satin and velvet fitted base. Copper finished cross with swords. Avg. cond. $50

Medal, Military Merit Cross, 3rd Class, With Swords, Bavarian, Imperial Germany, Army, WWI. In issue box. Avg. cond. $39

Medal, Mother Cross Gold, With Case, Germany, Army. Full-length neck ribbon with gold-plated rayed star center on blue and white enameled cross. Has correct inscription on back. Case is blue leatherette with gold-embossed cross on front, hinged and push-button catch. Exc. cond. $96

Medal, Naval 1914–18 War Service Cross, With Ribbon, Imperial Germany, Navy, WWI. Dark bronze finish. Avg. cond. $39

Medal, People's Army Reservist, East Germany, c1960s. Silver finish, 35mm, bust of soldier to obverse, national emblem to reverse, pb, enamel finish hanger with crest and "NVA." Above avg. cond. $20

Medal, Red Cross Medal, Prussian, Imperial Germany, Red Cross, WWI. Dark bronze disc pendant with cross engraved. Bow-style ribbon for presentation to Women. Ribbon shows light soiling. Avg. cond. $36

Medal, Red Eagle Order, Prussian, Imperial Germany, Army, WWI. Gilt-plated bronze 25mm round with Maltese Cross center and eagle, reverse is gothic letters, on unmounted white ribbon with golden yellow border stripes. Above avg. cond. $73

Medal, Russian Front, Germany, Army, WWII. Silver rim, ring stamped "19" and long ribbon. Above avg. cond. $40

Medal, Russian Front, Germany, Army, WWII. Wear to blued center and graying to rim. Good ribbon. Above avg. cond. $35

Medal, Russian Front, With Envelope, Germany, Army, WWII. Silver rim, gray center, long ribbon and small envelope with four-line title. Exc. cond. $45

Medal, Service Cross, Prussian, Imperial Germany, Army, 1912. 1912 issue. Fine gold finish to cross pattee with cipher. Yellow and blue ribbon. Exc. cond. $97

Medal, Service Cross, Saxon, Imperial Germany, Army. In gold gilt finish with proper green and white banded ribbon. Exc. cond. $75

Medal, SS Service, Eight Year, Germany, Army, WWII. Bronze strike with good details, tear-drop loop and water-pattern blue ribbon. Above avg. cond. $191

Medal, St. John Order, Luxury Grade, Prussian, Imperial Germany, Army. Heavy gilt gold body with full white enamel arm. Pb. Also known as the Malta Cross. Near mint cond. $270

Medal, Star of Brabant House Order Service, Hesse-darmstadt, Imperial Germany, Army, WWI. Silvered finish with polar star logo, crown and cipher. Yellow and black ribbon. Exc. cond. $204

Medal, War Merit 1939, Germany, Army, WWII. Early bronze with 11"-long ribbon. Exc. cond. $20

Medal, War Merit Cross 1939, 1st Class, With Swords, Germany, Army, WWII. Black leatherette with silver cross to lid, white satin and black velvet inside. Frosted silver

finish with bright highlights showing some darkening. Pb and stamped "L/12." Exc. cond. $125

Medal, War Merit Cross 1939, 1st Class, With Swords, Germany, Army, WWII. Early silver finish, pb and stamped "1." Above avg. cond. $60

Medal, War Merit Cross 1939, 1st Class, With Swords, Germany, Army, WWII. Graying to silver finish. Wide pin stamped "65." Late war example. Above avg. cond. . $40

Medal, War Merit Cross 1939, 1st Class, Without Swords, Germany, Army, WWII. Black leatherette with silver cross to lid, white satin and black velvet inside. Frosted silver finish with bright highlights showing some darkening. Wide pb stamped "56." Above avg. cond. $110

War Merit Cross (KVK1) First Class with Swords

Medal, War Merit Cross 1939, 2nd Class, With Swords, Germany, Army, WWII. Early bronze finish and long ribbon. Small tan envelope with four-line title and maker. Above avg. cond. $30

Medal, West Wall, With Envelope, Germany, Army, WWII. Faded gray, 6" ribbon and tan envelope with three-line title and maker. Avg. cond. $20

Pour Le Merite, Prussian, Imperial Germany, Air Corps, WWI. Also known as the "Blue Max." Silver gilt wartime piece, c1916. Full original old neck ribbon. Toned finish to gilt with enamel Malta Cross, gold lettering. Exc. cond. $1994

Red Eagle Order 4th Class, Prussian, Imperial Germany, Army, WWI. Silver rib-style border. White enamel center with red eagle design. Above avg. cond. $190

Ribbon Bar, Two Place, Germany, Army, WWII. Two ribbons. With devices for Bronze and Silver Long Service medals with devices. Pb. Above avg. cond. $28

Spange, Iron Cross 1939, 1st Class, Germany, Army, WWII. Nice frosted and bright silver finish. Pin stamped "L21." Exc. cond. $76

Spange, Iron Cross 1939, 1st Class, Germany, Army, WWII. Frosted finish and pin stamped "L/11." Exc. cond. . . $99

Spange, Iron Cross 1939, 1st Class, Germany, Army, WWII. Frosted silver finish. Shows age. Pb and stamped "L/56." Avg. cond. $114

Spange, Iron Cross 1939, 2nd Class, Germany, Army, WWII. 25mm. Good frosted and bright silver finish on eagle with four flat prongs through 4" ribbon. Near mint cond. $180

Medals—Other

Badge, Polish Two Armored Battalion, Poland. Red/black enamels, SB. Exc. cond. $120

Lapel Chain, Eight Place, Austrian, Army, WWI. Group consists of two Military Crosses of Merit (one with swords)/WWI Red Cross medal with war decoration/Military Medal of merit in silver/two Silver Crosses of Merit, one with crown and two Republic Orders of Merit. Above avg. cond. $187

Medal of the Great Patriotic War, Bulgaria, 1944–45. Silver finish with folded ribbon. Above avg. cond. . $30

Medal, 1914–18 Honor Legion Service, Austrian, Austrian, Army, WWI. Gilt Malta Cross with wreath. Pro Patria inscription verso with Honor Legion inscription. Unmounted black and yellow ribbon. Near mint cond. $80

Medal, 1914–18 War, France, Army, c1920. Bronze with ribbon. Above avg. cond. $35

Medal, 1914–19 War, England, Army, WWI. Gilt gold clasp on blue-white ribbon. Above avg. cond. $28

Medal, 1939–45 Star, England, Army, WWII. Bronze planchant with ribbon. Above avg. cond. $20

English, 1939–1945 Star

Medal, 60th Anniversary of the Red Army, Soviet Union, 1918–78. 33mm-diam gilt brass pendant on hard mounted, bi-fold ribbon. Mint cond. $10

Medal, Bravery, Austria, Army, WWI. Large silver planchet, without ribbon. Above avg. cond. $37

Austrian WWI Bravery Medal with Ribbon

Medal, Service Cross, Austria, Army, WWI. Bronze, dated 1912–13, with incorrect ribbon. Above avg. cond. $15

Medal, Signum Memoriae, Austria, Army, WWI. Bronze, with ribbon. Above avg. cond. $20

Medal, 1914–18 Honor Cross, Austria, Army, WWI. Bronze, with swords and tri-fold ribbon. Above avg. cond. $20

Medal, Military Cross of Merit, Austria, Army, WWI. Silver cross with red, white enamel, medallion has silver inscription. Above avg. cond. $64

Medal, Cross of Merit, Belgium, Army, 1920s. Silver planchet, with ribbon. Above avg. cond. $80

Medal, Military Medal For Acts of Bravery, Belgium, Army, WWI. Gilded planchet, white silk case and ribbon, both with black velvet interior and red exterior. Above avg. cond. $37

Medal, WWI Victory, Belgium, WWI. Bronze with ribbon. Above avg. cond. $50

Medal, WWII Military, Belgium, WWII. Gilded planchet, with ribbon. Exc. cond. $50

Medal, Long Service Cross, Belgium, Army, WWII. Gilded planchet with ribbon. Above avg. cond. $40

Medal, Order of Military Merit, Belgium, Army, WWII. Oversized planchet, white enamel, old repairs, with ribbon. Good cond. $85

Medal, Order of the Crown, Belgium, WWII. Silver, blue-white enamels, with ribbon. Above avg. cond. $125

Medal, WWII Resistance, Belgium, WWII. Bronze planchet, with ribbon. Above avg. cond. $20

Medal, Order of the Crown, Belgium. Silver planchet,

blue-white-green enamel highlights, ribbon with rosette. Above avg. cond. $120

Medal, British Defense, England, 1939–45. Silver planchet with ribbon. For military and civilian service. Above avg. cond. $25

Medal, Medal Bar, England, Army, WWII. Four awards; War Medal 1939–45/Defense Medal/Italy Star/1939–45Star/, awards named. Above avg. cond. $55

Medal, WWI Victory, England, Army, c1920. Bronze, with ribbon, rim named to member of Royal Engineers, with ribbon. Above avg. cond. $20

English WWI Victory Medal

Medal, WWI 1914–19, England, Army, c1920. Silver planchet, rim named to member of Artillery Rgt, ribbon missing. Above avg. cond. $30

Medal, Defense, England, WWII. With ribbon. Above avg. cond. $25

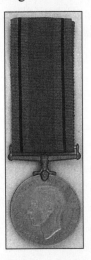

English WWII Defense Medal

Medal, WWI War, Bulgaria, WWI. Gilded bronze planchet with ribbon. Above avg. cond. $20

Medal, Distinguished Officer, Bulgaria, Army, WWII. Silver, depicting profile of helmeted soldier with oak leaf

border, Bulgarian cross and shield, red-green-white enamels, hmkd, Sb. Above avg. cond. $250

Medal, Croix de Guerre, France, Army, WWI. Bronze with ribbon. Above avg. cond. $36

Medal, Croix de Guerre, France, Army, WWI. Bronze with ribbon with laurel device. Above avg. cond. . . $30

French Croix de Guerre Medal (WWI)

Medal, Croix de Guerre, France, Army, WWII. Bronze with ribbon mounted by star device. Above avg. cond. $43

Medal, 1870–71 War, France, c1870s. Bronze, with ribbon. Above avg. cond. $25

Medal, General Service, India, Army, c1946. Antique silver finish with ribbon. Mint cond. $75

Medal, WWII Defense Forces, Ireland, WWII. Bronze planchet, obverse depicting Victory with sword and Irish wolfhound, with two bars inscribed "1939–1946," with ribbon. Above avg. cond. $20

Medal, Long Service Medal, Italy, Air Force, c1970s. Bronze with ribbon. Exc. cond. $50

Medal, Gulf War, Italy, Army, c1992. Recent strike with ribbon. Boxed. Mint cond. $28

Medal, Italian Navy Medal, Italy, Navy, WWII. Bronze planchet having "LEGA NAVALE ITALIANA" inscription, missing ribbon. Above avg. cond. $25

Medal, Cross of Military Formation, Italy, Army, WWI. Gilded brass planchet with white and red enamel, with ribbon. Above avg. cond. $125

Medal, Life Saving, Vietnam. U.S. strike in bright gilt on crimp brooch-mounted ribbon. Near mint cond. . . . $30

Medal, Merit Cross, Greece, Air Force, c1946. Silver finish cross with propeller and wreath, crown and ribbon above "1945" to reverse. Above avg. cond. $65

Medal, Military Service Cross, With Case, Austrian,

Austria, Army, WWI. Beautiful old red leatherette case with full inscription fancy gold Rothe Jeweler hallmark inside on upper silk lining black flocking. Full red, white enameled cross with wreath mounted. proper ribbon. Above avg. cond. $145

Medal, Military Valor, Italy, Army, WWI. Bronze with blue ribbon. Above avg. cond. $20

Medal, Order of the First Palestinian War, Iraq, 1948. Eight-pointed enamel star embossed to flat disc, depicts soldier with bayonet and mosque in Jerusalem, pb ribbon. Above avg. cond. $65

Medal, Philippine Liberation, Philippines, cWWII. Gilded planchet of red, white, blue enamels, with ribbon. Exc. cond. $20

Medal, 15 Year Military Service, Poland, Army. Silvered with ribbon. Good cond. $75

Medal, 1919 POW, Poland, Army, 1919. Silver eagle planchet, numbered, POW camps on reverse, with ribbon. Above avg. cond. $130

Medal, 1921 Soviet War Medal, Poland, Army, 1921. Bronze with ribbon. Above avg. cond. $65

Medal, 1928 Ten Year Military Service, Poland, Army, 1928. Bronze with ribbon. Above avg. cond. $50

Medal, 1938 Defense War, Poland, Army, 1938. Silvered with ribbon. Above avg. cond. $85

Medal, 1939 War of Defense, Poland, Army, 1939. Silvered with ribbon. Above avg. cond. $75

Medal, 1944 Field of Glory, Poland, 1944. Gilded with ribbon. Above avg. cond. $125

Medal, 1944 Virtuti Militari, Poland, Army, 1944. First class, gilded, with ribbon. Above avg. cond. $150

Medal, 1991 Republic National Defense Merit, Poland, 1991. Silvered with ribbon. Above avg. cond. $100

Medal, 20 Year Military Service, Poland, Army. Gilded with ribbon. Above avg. cond. $65

Medal, 20 Year Military Service, Poland, Army. Silvered, enameled, Sb. Above avg. cond. $100

Medal, 22 Argonsky Rifle Regiment, Poland, Army, WWII. Bronze with ribbon. Above avg. cond. $50

Medal, 240th Infantry Regiment, Poland, Army. Silvered, numbered, with ribbon. Above avg. cond. .. $150

Medal, Polish for Berlin, Poland. Silver planchet, with ribbon. Above avg. cond. $70

Medal, Manifest Lipcowy, Poland. Sterling with ribbon. Above avg. cond. $100

Medal, Medal of Merit, Poland, Army. Silver planchet, blue enamel. Above avg. cond. $95

Medal, National Defense, Poland, c1970s. gilded, with ribbon. Above avg. cond. $50

Medal, Red Cross, Poland, WWII. Bronze planchet, reverse with "PCK," with ribbon. Above avg. cond. . $44

Medal, Sept. 1939 War, Poland, Army, WWII. Silvered, with ribbon. Above avg. cond. $55

Medal, Soviet War, Poland, Army, WWII. Bronze with ribbon. Above avg. cond. $80

Medal, Polish WWI 1918 POW, Poland, 1918. silver, numbered, camp names on reverse, with ribbon. Above avg. cond. $140

Medal, Armed Forces in the West, Poland, Army, WWII. Silver with ribbon. Above avg. cond. $120

Medal, Army, Poland, Army, WWII. Bronze with ribbon. Good cond. $60

Medal, WWII Victory Over Germany, Soviet Union. 32mm-diam bronze pendant on hard mounted, bifold ribbon, pendant tarnished, ribbon lightly soiled. Avg. cond. ... $16

Medal, Technical Service, 1st Class, Vietnam. U.S. strike in bright gilt, crimp brooch-mounted ribbon. Near mint cond. $30

Medal, Technical Service, 2nd Class, Vietnam. U.S. strike in bright gilt, crimp brooch-mounted ribbon. Above avg. cond. $20

Medal, WWI Campaign, Austrian, Army, WWI. Dull silver finish mounted ribbon. Avg. cond. $25

Medals, Assorted, North Vietnam. Avg. 30mm with metal hanger and ribbon insert, various designs and sizes. Avg. cond. $15

Ribbons, Aiguillettes and Lanyards—Germany

Aiguillette, Germany, Army, WWII. Double plaited alum bodies with both cords and silver painted metal tips. Complete. Above avg. cond. $125

Aiguillette, Germany, Army, WWII. Two plaited alum bodies with two cords and silver painted metal tips. Above avg. cond. $124

Aiguillette, Germany, Army, WWII. Early alum bullion plaited body with cords and two dark silver tips. Above avg. cond. $117

Aiguillette, Germany, Army, WWII. Two plaited alum bodies with two cords and silver painted metal tips are worn gray. Both bodies have broken inside string that holds shape. Avg. cond. $115

Aiguillette, Germany, Army, WWII. Variation gray/silver bullion plaited body with loop cord. Faded dark gold finish to two metal tips. Avg. cond. $103

Aiguillette, Germany, Army, WWII. Two alum plaited bodies with silver painted metal end tips, two loops, buttonhole, braided slide and end loops. Avg. cond. $87

Aiguillette, Germany, Army, WWII. Heavy gold plaited body with two loops, braided slide, end loop and brass swivel fitting instead of buttonhole. Avg. cond. $76

Aiguillette, Germany, WWII. Two plaited alum bodies with two cords. Avg. cond. $85

Funeral Ribbon, Party, Germany, WWII. 27" red silk 2½" wide with two bevo white circles and swastika centers. Avg. cond. $20

Funeral Ribbon, SS, Germany, SS, WWII. 6½"-wide red satin ribbon has black printed border stripes to give armband look. 6½' long with dark silver fringe at ends. Printed black SS runes in circle on sewn white disc on each end. Avg. cond. $720

Funeral Sash Ribbon, Imperial Germany, Army, WWI. 32" long. Blue. 2" gilt bullion fringe on a beautiful water-pattern ribbon and 4" x 4" black with silver border iron cross at base. Above avg. cond. $25

Lanyard, Duty Service, Germany, Luftwaffe, WWII. 30"-long plaited body with loop ends and two short cords with silver painted gray metal tips. Only worn by NCO or officer of the day. Above avg. cond. $151

Lanyard, Marksmanship, Germany, Army, WWII. Alum plaited body and wool backing. Later pattern dark alum eagle/wreath with crossed swords on shield. Above avg. cond. $60

Lanyard, Marksmanship, Germany, Army, WWII. Alum plaited body with soiled gray satin backing. First pattern alum eagle/shield and gray wool back side with moth hole. Avg. cond. $61

Lanyard, Marksmanship, Germany, Army, WWII. Plaited alum body with early stamped alum eagle shield. Gray satin and wool backing. Avg. cond. $44

Lanyard, Marksmanship, Germany, Army, WWII. Alum plaited body, gray satin backing, early alum eagle/shield and no wool backing. Avg. cond. $60

Lanyard, Marksmanship, Germany, Luftwaffe, WWII. Blue-gray plaited body with alum zigzag design. Alum eagle-wreath with wool back side. Above avg. cond. $71

Lanyard, Marksmanship, Germany, Luftwaffe, WWII. Blue-gray plaited body with alum zigzags. Stamped gray eagle/wreath and gray felt backing. Above avg. cond. $65

Lanyard, Marksmanship, With Four Acorns, Germany, Army, WWII. Alum plaited body with gray satin backing. Four alum acorns. Later pattern alum eagle/wreath with crossed swords on shield. Gray wool backing. Avg. cond. $80

Lanyard, Marksmanship, With One Acorn, Germany, Army, WWII. Plaited alum body, gray satin backing, gray wool backing, one alum acorn and alum eagle shield. Exc. cond. $63

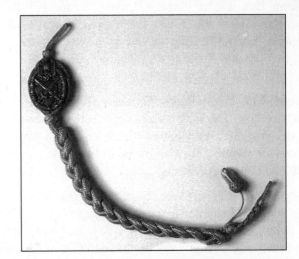

German Army Marksmanship Lanyard with Acorn (Later Pattern)

Lanyard, Marksmanship, With One Acorn, Germany, Navy, WWII. Blue wool plaited body lacks wreath/shield device. Has metal end clip with affixed silver metal acorn that unscrews. Frayed edge to body. Below avg. cond. $60

Lanyard, Marksmanship, With One Artillery Shell Device, Germany, Army. Alum plaited body, gray satin and felt backing. Gray-alum eagle/wreath with crossed swords on shield. Turned alum shell devices instead of acorns. Exc. cond. $68

Lanyard, Marksmanship, With Three Acorns, Germany, Army, WWII. Plaited alum body, gray satin backing, gray wool backing, three alum acorns and alum eagle/wreath with crossed swords. Exc. cond. $120

Lanyard, Marksmanship, With Three Acorns, Germany, Army, WWII. Plaited alum body has three acorns, gray satin backing, original pattern alum eagle/shield and gray wool backing. Shows age. Avg. cond. $65

Lanyard, Marksmanship, With Two Acorns, Germany, Army, WWII. Plaited alum body, gray satin backing, gray wool backing, two alum acorns and later pattern alum eagle/wreath with crossed swords. Above avg. cond. $59

Lanyard, Marksmanship, With Two Acorns, Germany, Army, WWII. Plaited alum body has frayed side and lacks section of gray satin backing. Two alum acorns. Original alum eagle/shield and gray wool backing. Above avg. cond. $61

Ribbon Bar, Eight Place, Germany, Army, WWII. About 5½" clean ribbons. 1914 EK with 1939 spange, KVK with swords, Russian Front, Spanish Communist, Spanish Survivor, Hindenburg with swords, two Long Service with eagles and Westwall. Gray wool backing and brass pin. Above avg. cond. $83

Ribbon Bar, Eight Place, Germany, Army, WWII. 5" long. Starts 1939 EK, KVK, faded red with white edges, Olympic, Luftwaffe long service with eagle device, two blue Service and Austrian Occupation with device. Black wool and brass pb. Avg. cond. $35

Ribbon Bar, Eight Place, Germany, WWII. Two WWI Iron Crosses, one with eagle, 1939, other swords and crown, War Service Cross with swords, War Cross of honor with swords, Austrian medal of valor, Tyrol Service medal and more. Above avg. cond. $40

Ribbon Bar, Eleven Place, Germany, Army, WWII. 6½" long with 1914 ribbon having 1939 spange device, KVK, red ribbon with white edges, Olympic medal, blue ribbon with two white edge stripes, Hindenburg cross with swords device having silver wound badge, NSDAP 10 Year Service with device, LW Service with eagle, Austrian and Czech Occupations with medal devices and Italian/German 1941 DAK medal. Gray wool backing with brass pin. Above avg. cond. $69

Ribbon Bar, Eleven Place, Germany, Army, WWII. Pb older bar with signs of wear. Ribbons include Iron Cross (WWII), War Service Cross and War Cross of Honor and more. Avg. cond. $30

Ribbon Bar, Five Place, Germany, Army, WWII. About 3" long and age soiled. 1914 EK, Hindenburg with swords, yellow and white, blue and Olympic with Army eagle device. Mothed wool and brass pin. Above avg. cond. $67

Ribbon Bar, Five Place, Germany, Army, WWII. 3" wide with double wrapped ribbons showing age soiling. 1914 EK, Hindenburg with swords, Customs Service with eagle/wreath, Faithful with cross and faded pink stripe on white with swords device. Pb. Avg. cond. $32

Ribbon Bar, Five Place, Germany, Army, WWII. War Merit Cross with swords, Czech Occupation, a purple ribbon with white bands on either side, Hungarian Occupation Combat with swords and Tyrol Annexation with swords. Avg. cond. $23

Ribbon Bar, Five Place, Germany, Army, WWII. 3" long. 1939 EK, two Long Service ribbons with eagles, Czech Occupation and Memel Occupation Service ribbon. Pb. Avg. cond. $30

Ribbon Bar, Four Place, Imperial Germany, Army, WWI. Pb. WWI Iron Cross. Hindenberg Cross with swords. WWI Hungarian War medal with swords. Tyrol War Service with swords. Avg. cond. $23

Ribbon Bar, Nine Place, Germany, Army, WWII. Ribbons include Iron Cross, 2nd class, War Service Cross, 2nd class with swords with device, Russian Front, Life Saving medal, 10 Year Party Faithful Service with device, SS Long Service with silvered S runes, Czech Anschluss, West Wall/DAK Italo-German ribbon. Proper gray backing with brass pin. Appears unissued. Ideal for tunic. Exc. cond. $55

Ribbon Bar, Seven Place, Germany, Army, WWII. Group includes 1914 EK, Bavarian Military Service with swords, Hindenburg and War Service with swords, Civil Faithful Service with device, NSDAP Political Medal with bronze device and unknown red-white ribbon. Above avg. cond. $40

Ribbon Bar, Seven Place, Imperial Germany, Army, WWI. Group includes two swords for Hindenburg Cross, Hungarian Service ribbon, ribbons for Iron Cross, Wurtemberg, War Service ribbons, etc. Parade furled. Pb. Above avg. cond. $37

Ribbon Bar, Seven Place, Imperial Germany, Army, WWI. Ribbons are 1914 EK, Hindenburg cross with swords, Austrian War Service medal with swords, Long Service, Prussian Life Saving, Hungarian War Service with swords, Bulgarian War Service. Brass pin. Above avg. cond. $36

Ribbon Bar, Six Place, Germany, Army, WWII. Group includes EK, Russian Front, Two Luftwaffe Long Service ribbons with devices plus Austrian and Czech Anschluss. Pb. Above avg. cond. $30

Ribbon Bar, Six Place, Germany, Army, WWII. 3½"-long bar. Starts 1939 EK, KVK with swords, Russian Front, Olympic, NSDAP 10 Year Service with device and Long Service with gold eagle. Gray wool and brass pin. Avg. cond. $30

Ribbon Bar, Six Place, Germany, Army, WWII. Half-size pattern. Group includes EK 1914, Hindenburg Cross, Wurtemberg WWI Bravery medal, two Army Nazi Long Service medals with devices and Civil Long Service device with blue ribbon. Pb. Avg. cond. $25

Ribbon Bar, Six Place, Germany, Army, WWII. Moisture stains on ribbons with six devices. 1914 EK with swords,

KVK, Hindenburg, Russian, Czech and Faithful 25 Year Service. Pb. Avg. cond. $32

Ribbon Bar, Six Place, Imperial Germany, Army, WWI. Group includes Hindenburg Cross, Prussian 1916 War Service Cross, Long Service ribbon, Kaiser Wilhelm Centennial and Nazi Civil Service badge with miniature gilt device. Pb. Avg. cond. $28

Ribbon Bar, Ten Place, Germany, Army, WWII. 6" long. 1914 EK with 1939 spange, EK with crown, EK with crowned crossed swords, yellow with black stripes and wreath, green with yellow stripes and oak leaves, tri-colored and Hindenburg with swords and two blue Service with runes and Czech Occupation. Gray wool backing and brass pin. Exc. cond. $177

Ribbon Bar, Three Place, Germany, Army, WWII. Includes Military Service with eagle, Entry into Sudetenland with castle bar and Spanish Campaign medal. Pb bar. Avg. cond. $25

Ribbon Bar, Three Place, Imperial Germany, Army, WWI. Iron Cross, 2nd Class/Hindenburg Cross with swords and Stahlhelm (round silver metal with profile of man and wreath). Avg. cond. $65

Ribbon Bar, Three Place, Imperial Germany, Army, WWI. Ribbons are 1914 EK, green, yellow and black striped, Hindenburg cross with swords. Pb. Gray wool backing. Avg. cond. $27

Ribbons, Aiguillettes and Lanyards—Other

Ribbon Bar, Five Place, Italy, Army, WWII. Five items; mounted on white cotton field. Good cond. $20

Badges—U.S.

Badge, "Sharpshooter," USA, Army, c1930s. Sterling bar and pendant. Avg. cond. $20

Badge, AAF Technician, USA, AAF, WWII. Pb. Sterling marked. Avg. cond. $25

Badge, Combat Crew Qualification, USA, USAF, 1970s, Meyer. Full size. Frosted silver with enamel detail. Cb. Meyer/sterling marked. Above avg. cond. $25

Badge, Combat Infantryman, USA, Army, WWII. Cast body with blue painted inset. Reverse has two small Sb fastening posts. Above avg. cond. $21

Badge, Combat Infantryman, USA, Army, WWII. Unmarked. Pb. Enameled face. Avg. cond. $30

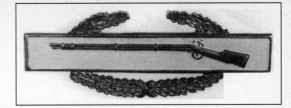

US Combat Infantryman's Badge (CIB)

Badge, Combat Infantryman, USA, Army, WWII. Cb. Sterling marked. Avg. cond. $11

Badge, Combat Infantryman, USA, Army, WWII. Cb. Sterling marked. Avg. cond. $12

Badge, Combat Infantryman, USA, Army, WWII, England. English made. 76mm. Pb. Enameled blue center. "J&J.B Ham." marked. Avg. cond. $50

Badge, Joint Chiefs of Staff, USA, Various, c1990. Silver, gilt and enamel, Cb. Mint cond. $39

Badge, Marksman, USA, Army, WWII. Gilt bar with "Marksman" in center and target symbols at each end. Pb. Avg. cond. $20

Badge, Marksman, USA, USMC, WWI. Large "Distinguished" brooch with "Sharpshooter" suspender and sharpshooter grade pendant. Pb. Above avg. cond. .. $45

Badge, Marksman, USA, USMC, WWII. Pb. Bronze finish. Marked "Expert Rifleman." Avg. cond. $20

Badge, Marksman, "New York State," USA, Army, Militia, c1900, Tiffany. 37mm bronze. Cross shaped with NY seal in wreath. Marked "18 USV 98" and "Ye 2 ar" suspenders with Pb "Marksman" brooch. Hmkd Tiffany. Above avg. cond. $45

Badge, Missileman, USA, USAF, c1970s. Cb. Gray alloy finish. Above avg. cond. $20

Badge, Navy Submarine Qualification, USA, Navy, c1960s. 3". Sterling. Pb. Above avg. cond. $60

US Navy Submarine Qualification Badge

Badge, PT Boat, USA, Navy, WWII. 64mm. Sterling marked. Pb. Above avg. cond. $75

Badge, Senior Missileman, USA, USAF, c1970s. 55mm. Frosted silver finish. Cb. Above avg. cond. $20

Badge, Senior Missileman, USA, USAF, c1970s, Vanguard. 77mm. Vanguard marked. Cb. Frosted silver finish. Avg. cond. $20

Badge, Technician, USA, AAF, WWII. Four-blade prop with Radio Mech and Radio Operator bars. Pb. Avg. cond. $20

Badge, Technician, USA, AAF, WWII. Sterling marked. Pb. Avg. cond. $20

Breast Badge, "IX Corps," USA, Army, Civil War. Bronze brooch with ribbon and bronze pendant. Crossed cannon and anchor on shield design. Exc. cond. . . $240

Breast Badge, Aid to President, USA, Various, c1940s. 50mm. Multi-piece. Cb. Near mint cond. $166

Breast Badge, Dept. of Defense, USA, Various, c1980s. Full size. Cb. Multi-piece. Near mint cond. $24

Breast Badge, Joint Chiefs of Staff, USA, Various, c1980s, Meyer. Full size. Multi-piece. Frosted-silver, gilt and enamel finish. Cb. Meyer marked. Above avg. cond. $24

Badges—Germany

Badge, Sleeve, Machine Gunner, Imperial Germany, Army, WWI, C.E. Juncker. Stamped steel oval with MG08 on sledge. Gold painted finish. Gray wool oval and gray backing plate stamped "C.E.Juncker etc." Avg. cond. $136

Badge, Anti-aircraft, Germany, Luftwaffe, WWII, C.E. Juncker. Early quality nickel-silver badge shows hard use with broken catch repaired with nail soldered through gun mount hole. By "C.E.Juncker etc." Below avg. cond. $182

Badge, Anti-aircraft, Germany, Luftwaffe, WWII. Heavy quality silver wreath, gun and affixed eagle. Pb and stamped "Brehmer etc." Exc. cond. $208

Badge, Anti-aircraft, Germany, Luftwaffe, WWII. Faded gray wreath/gun and attached eagle. Pb and "WH." Above avg. cond. $125

Badge, Anti-aircraft, Germany, Luftwaffe, WWII. Dark nickel-silver wreath, gun and attached eagle. Stamped "Brehmer etc." Wire pin and bent catch with crack. Avg. cond. $120

Badge, Anti-aircraft, Germany, Luftwaffe, WWII. Late war gray wreath, gun and attached fixed eagle. Some white corrosion. Pb and stamped "W" trademark. Avg. cond. $79

Badge, Anti-aircraft, Germany, Luftwaffe, WWII. Dark gray finished eagle/wreath and gun. Pb. Avg. cond. $175

Badge, Anti-partisan, Bronze, Germany, Army, WWII. "Junker" style construction with semi-hollow back. Good finish overall and cut-out snake heads. Wide pin. Above avg. cond. $475

Badge, Anti-partisan, Gold, Germany, Army, WWII. "Junker" style construction with semi-hollow back. Good finish overall and cut-out snake heads. Wire Pb. Above avg. cond. $906

Badge, Anti-partisan, Silver, Germany, Army, WWII. Heavy solid-style body with good details and silver-gray finish. Wide pin. Avg. cond. $600

Badge, Auxiliary Cruiser, Germany, Navy, WWII. Frosted gold eagle/wreath and Viking ship. Domed rivet on silver globe. Wide silver pin. Unmarked early example. Exc. cond. $450

Badge, Auxiliary Cruiser, Germany, Navy, WWII. Late war style. Gold finish on eagle/wreath and Viking ship. Wire pin. Above avg. cond. $135

Badge, Blockade Runner, Germany, Navy, WWII, Fec. Otto Placzek. Early heavy quality with gray ship and frosted silver eagle. Wide pin. By "Fec. Otto Placzek etc." Above avg. cond. $150

Badge, Blockade Runner, With Case, Germany, Navy, WWII, Fec. Otto Placzek, Berlin. 49mm diam. Weight 36 grams. Blue leatherette hinged case with satin lining and blue flocking. Frosted finish on eagle and chain wreath with excellent bright silver highlights. Hmkd "Fec.Otto Placzek Berlin etc." 26mm-diam stickpin with wear to gray and good frosted silver finish. Knurled pin. Exc. cond. $375

Badge, Coastal Artillery, Germany, Navy, WWII. Early heavy quality with gold finished eagle/wreath and silver/gray gun center. Wide pin. By "Schwerin Berlin." Exc. cond. $257

Badge, Coastal Artillery, Germany, Navy, WWII, Schwerin, Berlin. Heavy quality, gold eagle/wreath and silver-gray gun. Wide horizontal pin, hook at top and hmkd "Schwerin Berlin." Exc. cond. $328

Badge, Coastal Artillery, Germany, Navy, WWII. Early heavy quality with gold eagle/wreath and dark silver gun. Pb. Above avg. cond. $98

Badge, Coastal Artillery, Germany, Navy, WWII. Late war gray eagle/wreath and gun center. Wide pin. Avg. cond. $65

Badge, Destroyer, Germany, Navy, WWII. Gold finished eagle/wreath and gray ship center. Horizontal wire pin, top hook, hmkd "JFS." Above avg. cond. $131

Badge, Destroyer, Germany, Navy, WWII. Late war gray body with worn gold finish on eagle/wreath and silver center. Hmkd "R.S." Pb. Avg. cond. $135

Badge, Destroyer, Germany, Navy, WWII. Mid-war style by "S.H.u.Co." with horizontal pin and hook. Some graying on gold eagle/wreath and to silver ship/water center. Avg. cond. $200

Badge, E-boat, 1st Type, Germany, Navy, WWII. Medium weight with gold finished eagle/wreath showing gray metal base at highlights. Silver boat/water shows some graying. Dished-out back has wide pin stamped "20" and hook on top. Avg. cond. $270

Badge, E-boat, 2nd Type, Germany, Navy, WWII. Gold finished eagle/wreath, silver-gold-black finished boat/water and by "A.S." in triangle. Horizontal wire pin and hook at top. Light wear. Above avg. cond. $237

Badge, General Assault, Germany, Army, WWII. "JFS" maker marked badge. Frosted silver oak leaf wreath with gray number 50 panel attached. Four domed rivets on dark gray eagle with crossed bayonet and stick grenade. Wide pin. Exc. cond. $525

Badge, General Assault, Germany, Army, WWII. "JFS." Frosted silver wreath with affixed number 25 plate. Black eagle with crossed bayonet and stick grenade have worn silver highlights and four domed rivets. Wide pin. Exc. cond. $473

Badge, General Assault, Germany, Army, WWII. Good silver finish on wreath with attached gray number 50 panel. Dark gray eagle has fracture crack on left wing and is held by four domed rivets. Wide pin and "RK" marked. Above avg. cond. $399

Badge, General Assault, Germany, Army, WWII. Silver frosted wreath shows light graying, attached number 50 panel and four domed rivets on dark eagle with crossed grenade/bayonet. Wide pin and "RK." Above avg. cond. $420

Badge, General Assault, Germany, Army, WWII, G.H. Osang, Dresden. Solid heavy body has frosted silver finish with some darkening to highlights. Pb and stamped "G.H.Osang Dresden." Rare to find maker marked badge. Above avg. cond. $164

Badge, General Assault, Germany, Army, WWII. Solid with frosted silver finish dark at highlights. Pb. Above avg. cond. $45

Badge, General Assault, Germany, Army, WWII. Solid body with silver finish showing faint graying. Pb. Early example. Above avg. cond. $72

Badge, General Assault, Germany, Army, WWII. Solid

with silver finish showing bubbles. Pb. Avg. cond. . $25

Badge, General Assault, Germany, Army, WWII, Assmann. Solid gray body with indented back by "A" for Assmann. No pin on hinge and solder repair to catch. Fair cond. $20

Badge, Ground Assault, Germany, Luftwaffe, WWII. Mid-war style with riveted gray eagle on silver painted wreath and gray center. Single rivet. Pb. Above avg. cond. $60

Badge, Ground Assault, Germany, Luftwaffe, WWII, G.H. Osang, Dresden. Gray wreath with dark gray cloud and lightning bolt center. Single rivet to frosted silver eagle. Wide pin and stamped "G.H.Osang Dresden." Mid-war example. Above avg. cond. $132

Badge, Ground Assault, Germany, Luftwaffe, WWII, G.H. Osang, Dresden. Normal age graying to frosted silver wreath and center. Affixed frosted silver eagle with rivet. Stamped "G.H.Osang Dresden." Pb lacks catch. Avg. cond. $91

Badge, Gunner/Engineer, Germany, Luftwaffe, WWII. Frosted silver wreath with cut-out swastika arm, two domed rivets on black eagle stamped "W.Deumer etc." Pb. Early example. Exc. cond. $370

Badge, Gunner/Engineer, Germany, Luftwaffe, WWII. Gray swastika wreath and eagle with two rivets. By "W.Deumer etc." Pb. Late war solid swastika. Above avg. cond. $210

Badge, High Seas Fleet, Germany, Navy, WWII. Early one by "Fec. Adolf Bock etc." with wear on highlights of gold eagle/wreath and silver ship center. Wide pin. Above avg. cond. $250

Badge, High Seas Fleet, Germany, Navy, WWII. Late war gray body with about half of gold finish to eagle/wreath and faded gray ship. Hmkd "R.S." Pb. Avg. cond. $125

Badge, High Seas Fleet, Germany, Navy, WWII. Mid-war style with gold finished eagle/wreath and silver-gray ship center. Wire pin. By "R.S.&S." Avg. cond. $165

Badge, Infantry Assault, Bronze, Germany, Army, WWII. Stamped body with good details. Pb. Near mint cond. $62

Badge, Infantry Assault, Bronze, Germany, Army, WWII. Solid body with crack to wreath. Pb with fair finish. Above avg. cond. $70

Badge, Infantry Assault, Bronze, Germany, Army, WWII. Solid body with wear to finish. Pb. Above avg. cond. $70

Badge, Infantry Assault, Bronze, Germany, Army, WWII. Solid with faded gray details having traces of bronze finish. By "RSS." Lacks pin and hinge. Fair cond. $29

Badge, Infantry Assault, Bronze, With Envelope, Germany, Army, WWII. Solid with finish, Pb and by "JFS." Small envelope, three-line title, same maker and torn top corner. Above avg. cond. $80

Badge, Infantry Assault, Silver, Germany, Army, WWII. Solid gray body lacks finish, appears dug at back with corrosion and Pb. Maker trademarked "AS" in triangle. Below avg. cond. $72

Infantry Assault Badge in Silver

Badge, Infantry Assault, Silver, Germany, Army, WWII. Original tissue wrapped solid badge has nice silver finished front. Near mint cond. $135

Badge, Infantry Assault, Silver, Germany, Army, WWII. Solid body with good details. Pb. Exc. cond. $76

Badge, Infantry Assault, Silver, Germany, Army, WWII. Solid body with wear to finish. Pb. Above avg. cond. $72

Badge, Infantry Assault, Silver, Germany, Army, WWII. Solid body, finish fading gray and pb. Above avg. cond. $50

Badge, Infantry Assault, Silver, Germany, Army, WWII. Solid with faded gray body having good details. Pb and by "f.o." Avg. cond. $45

Badge, Infantry Assault, Silver, Germany, Army, WWII. Solid with faded gray body showing traces of silver. Pb. Avg. cond. $36

Badge, Infantry Assault, Silver, Germany, Army, WWII. Solid faded gray body. Riveted hinge and catch on Pb. Avg. cond. $34

Badge, Infantry Assault, Silver, Germany, Army, WWII. Solid with good finish. Pb. Avg. cond. $54

Badge, Infantry Assault, Silver, Germany, Army, WWII. Late war solid body with cast hinge/catch, finish fading gray and pb. Stamped "GWL." Avg. cond. $50

Badge, Member, Luftschutz, Germany, Luftschutz or RLB, WWII. Eagle with rayed star and swastika center. Pb. Hmkd. Avg. cond. $21

Badge, Member, Luftschutz, Germany, Luftschutz or RLB, WWII. 25mm silvered metal rayed star with blue enameled lettering over swastika. Pb. Hmkd. Avg. cond. $27

Badge, Member, Red Cross, Germany, Red Cross, WWII. 20mm winged black enameled eagle with swastika center and red cross at base. Pb. Hmkd. Above avg. cond. $32

Badge, Member, SA, Germany, SA, 1930s. 16mm steel framed round with black border and intertwined SA on off-white field insert. Avg. cond. $59

Badge, Member, SA Reserve, Germany, SA, WWII. 25mm winged black shield with white swastika center. Machined pin and hmkd. Above avg. cond. $20

Badge, Member, SS, Germany, SS, WWII. 13mm disc with darkening on silver runes, good black enamel, stamped maker and "213xx." Knurled pin comes with spring lock. Above avg. cond. $229

Badge, Minesweeper, Germany, Navy, WWII. Heavy quality with dark gold finish on eagle/wreath. Silver water. Wide pin. Hmkd "Fec.Otto Placzek Berlin Ausf.Schwerin Berlin." Exc. cond. $279

Badge, Minesweeper, Germany, Navy, WWII. Gold finished eagle/wreath shows some graying at highlights, gray water and wide pin. Above avg. cond. $75

Badge, Minesweeper, Germany, Navy, WWII. Early brass quality. Die struck 55mm x 42mm. 25 grams. Wide vertical pin. No maker. Avg. cond. $75

Badge, Naval Flight Observer, Imperial Germany, Navy, WWI. Hollow body with vent hole, Pb and stamped "800" double headed eagle trademark. Frosted gold finish. Exc. cond. $1440

Badge, Naval Pilot, Imperial Germany, Navy, WWI. Prinzen size. Antique gilt gold finish with flying eagle and sunburst. Vertical pin. Exc. cond. $162

Badge, Observer (Cloth), Germany, Luftwaffe, WWII. Same gray to eagle/wreath on blue-gray wool. Below avg. cond. $25

Badge, Observer (Cloth), Germany, Luftwaffe, WWII. Two-tone gray eagle, gray wreath, blue-gray wool backing and padded back side. Early version. Exc. cond. $79

Badge, Observer (Cloth), Germany, Luftwaffe, WWII. Padded blue-gray wool oval with subdued gray wreath and eagle with swastika cloth backed. Exc. cond. $75

Badge, Observer, Germany, Luftwaffe, WWII. Silver frosted wreath shows darkening. Gray eagle has two rivets and stamped "A" for Assmann. Pb. Above avg. cond. $375

Badge, Observer, Germany, Luftwaffe, WWII. 41 x 53mm frosted silver wreath. Two domed rivets on dark eagle 52mm wide. Pb. Eagle stamped "CEJ." Above avg. cond. $607

Badge, Observer, Prussian, Imperial Germany, Air Force, WWI, C.E. Juncker. Hollow silver body, vent hole, two prongs on enamel square center, pb, and stamped "C.E.Juncker Berlin 800" on rayed backing. Exc. cond. $750

Badge, Paratrooper (Cloth), Germany, Luftwaffe, WWII. Thick gold eagle, gray wreath and blue-gray wool oval. Exc. cond. $33

Badge, Paratrooper (Cloth), Germany, Luftwaffe, WWII. Padded blue-gray wool oval with gray embr wreath and golden yellow eagle in center. Removed from uniform. Avg. cond. $96

Badge, Paratrooper, Germany, Luftwaffe, WWII, Assmann. Gray wreath and faded gray eagle with traces of gold finish. Pb. Two rivets and marked "A L/64" for Assmann. Avg. cond. $177

Badge, Paratrooper, Germany, Luftwaffe, WWII, G.H. Osang, Dresden. Wartime faded gray wreath with two rivets holding gold finished eagle having worn gray highlights. Pb. Stamped "G.H.Osang Dresden." Avg. cond. $350

Badge, Paratrooper, Germany, Luftwaffe, WWII. Wartime gray wreath, wear to gold finished gray eagle, two rivets, stamped "B&N L." Pb. Avg. cond. $225

Badge, Pilot (Cloth), Germany, Luftwaffe, WWII. Gray eagle/wreath on blue-gray wool. Above avg. cond. . $72

Badge, Pilot (Cloth), Germany, Luftwaffe, WWII. Used by NCO pilots. Silver-gray machine embr on blue-gray wool. Removed from uniform. Above avg. cond. . . . $65

Badge, Pilot (Cloth), Germany, Luftwaffe, WWII. Blue-gray wool oval with white wreath and gray eagle with swastika cloth backed. Avg. cond. $75

Badge, Pilot (Cloth), Germany, Luftwaffe, WWII. Blue-gray wool oval with silver-white embr of wreath. Straight ahead flying eagle in two tones of gray and steel blue. Back with cloth and several minor moth nips. Avg. cond. . . . $45

Badge, Pilot, Germany, Luftwaffe, WWII, C.E.Juncker. 43x54mm silver wreath, 62mm gray eagle with two domed rivets and stamped "C.E.Juncker etc." Pb. Exc. cond. $300

Badge, Pilot, Germany, Luftwaffe, WWII. Nice age tarnish on silver eagle and wreath. 43x53mm and 64mm wingspan. Pb. Two domed rivets and eagle stamped "CEJ." Exc. cond. $492

Badge, Pilot, Germany, Luftwaffe, WWII. Frosted silver wreath, dark eagle with two domed rivets. Pb. Stamped "JMME." Above avg. cond. $350

Badge, Pilot, Germany, Luftwaffe, WWII. Mid war style. Frosted silver wreath, faded gray eagle with two rivets. Pb. Avg. cond. $275

Badge, Pilot, Germany, Luftwaffe, WWII, G.H. Osang, Dresden. Wartime example with eagle stamped "G.H.Osang Dresden." 43 x 54mm silver wreath. 64mm gray eagle with two rivets and fracture crack on wreath. Pb. Avg. cond. $265

Badge, Pilot, Bavarian, Imperial Germany, Air Force, WWI, Karl Pollath. Hollow constructed silver body with Bavarian crown on wreath and good details. Rayed reverse with vent hole shows. Stamped maker "Karl Pollath." Above avg. cond. $435

Badge, Pilot, Prussian, Imperial Germany, Air Force, WWI. Prinzen size. 30 x 47mm stamped silver badge with applied smooth back. Thin wire pin with wire loop catch. Above avg. cond. $225

Badge, Pilot, Prussian, Imperial Germany, Air Force, WWI. Stamped hollow construction, frosted silver finish and straight pin. 71 x 45mm size. Finely detailed with deluxe finish. Avg. cond. $395

Badge, Pilot/Observer (Cloth), Germany, Luftwaffe, WWII. Blue-gray felt body, gray eagle and gold wreath. Avg. cond. $57

Badge, Pilot/Observer, Germany, Luftwaffe, WWII, C.E. Juncker, Berlin. Heavy 43 x 53mm dark gold wreath. 65mm dark silver eagle with good details and two domed rivets. Pb. Maker stamped "C.E.Juncker Berlin S68." Near mint cond. $944

Badge, Pilot/Observer, Germany, Luftwaffe, WWII, C.E. Juncker. Eagle stamped "CE Juncker etc.," two domed rivets and faint gold wash to gray wreath. Traces of silver finish on eagle. Pb. Avg. cond. $339

Badge, Radio/Gunner (Aluminum), Germany, Luftwaffe, WWII, C.E. Junker. Four-rivet construction. Lightweight special hook is held by rivets. Near mint cond. $538

Badge, Sea Battle, Germany, Luftwaffe, WWII. 44 x 57mm gold painted oak leaf wreath with gray eagle attached by two rivets. Silver-gray finish on ship center with details at back giving stamped look. Pb. Late war quality. Above avg. cond. $1000

Badge, Sleeve, Artillery, Bavarian, Imperial Germany, Army, WWI. Dark green wool oval with brass crown over oak leaf wreath and crossed cannons center and 1904 date at bow. Stamped and five prongs attached to steel backing plate. Above avg. cond. $135

Badge, Tank Battle, Imperial Germany, Army, c1920. Die struck hollow with backplate open through the eyes of the skull to the backplate. 44 x 67mm in size. Weight 19.7 grams. These badges were made after WWI for a very small group of men, tank crews. Long vertical flat-sided pin. Exc. cond. $795

Badge, Tank Battle, Bronze, Germany, Army, WWII. Solid with good finish and maker "W." Pb lacks catch. Below avg. cond. $42

Badge, Tank Battle, Bronze, Germany, Army, WWII. Solid body has very dark finish, pb and by "L/5." Exc. cond. $135

Badge, Tank Battle, Bronze, Germany, Army, WWII. Solid, indented back side, finish fading, "L/53" and Pb. Above avg. cond. $50

Badge, Tank Battle, Bronze, Germany, Army, WWII. Stamped with some darkening to details. Pb. Above avg. cond. $63

Badge, Tank Battle, Bronze, Germany, Army, WWII. Solid with bronze finish fading gray. Pb. Avg. cond. $51

Badge, Tank Battle, Bronze, Germany, Army, WWII. Solid with dark finish worn at highlights showing copper shade. Pb. Avg. cond. $32

Badge, Tank Battle, Silver, Germany, Army, WWII. Silver-plated eagle/wreath has good details and attached number 25 plate. Two domed rivets on gray tank showing many corrosion pits to details. Wide pin and unmarked style. Below avg. cond. $334

Badge, Tank Battle, Silver, Germany, Army, WWII. Graying to silver eagle/wreath and attached number 50 plate. Two domed rivets on gray-black tank. Wide pin and marked "JFS." Above avg. cond. $300

Tank Assault Badge for 50 Engagements

Badge, Tank Battle, Silver, Germany, Army, WWII. Gray body with silver finish worn and indented back. By "RK." Pb. Above avg. cond. $87

Badge, Tank Battle, Silver, Germany, Army, WWII. Solid with finish showing light age. Pb. Above avg. cond. $61

Badge, Tank Battle, Silver, Germany, Army, WWII. Faded gray stamped eagle/wreath with indented back. Number 100 plate has rivet. Silver finished tank has two rivets that show through to front. Late war unmarked example. Avg. cond. $275

Badge, Tank Battle, Silver, Germany, Army, WWII. Graying to highlights, indented back by "A.S." Pb. Avg. cond. $59

Badge, Tank Battle, Silver, Germany, Army, WWII. Solid, indented backside finish fading gray. Pb. Avg. cond. $50

Badge, Tank Battle, Silver, With Box, Germany, Army, WWII, Aurich. Gray cardboard box has stapled corners and tissue wrap inside. Solid silver finished badge by "A" for Aurich. Pb. Near mint cond. $177

Badge, U-boat (Cloth), Germany, Navy, WWII. Age darkening to flat gold bevo badge on blue and uncut black. Avg. cond. $85

Badge, U-boat, Germany, Navy, WWII. Heavy early quality with gold finish having brighter highlights. Cut-out swastika and wide pin. Exc. cond. $300

Badge, U-boat, Germany, Navy, WWII. Heavy body with gold wash worn at highlights showing brass base. Wide pin and stamped "Schwerin Berlin 68." Exc. cond. $500

Badge, U-boat, Germany, Navy, WWII. Heavy brass body with gold finish. Cut-out swastika. Wide pin. Above avg. cond. $166

Badge, U-boat, Germany, Navy, WWII, Frank & Reif, Stuttgart. Darkening to early brass/bronze body. Wide pin. Stamped "Frank & Reif Stuttgart." Above avg. cond. $135

Badge, U-boat, Germany, Navy, WWII. Wartime gray badge with gilt wash worn from highlights. Wire horizontal pin and hmkd "f.o." Catch shows past repair. Avg. cond. $100

Badge, U-boat, Germany, Navy, WWII, Frank & Reif, Stuttgart. Early dark brass/bronze body with cut-out swastika. Faint gold finish traces. Wide pin. Hmkd "Frank & Reif Stuttgart." Avg. cond. $159

Badge, U-boat, Imperial Germany, Navy, WWI. Thin stamped bronze oval with crown over U-boat. Pb. Gilt finish. Exc. cond. $93

Badge, U-boat, Imperial Germany, Navy, WWI, Walter Schot. Solid brass body with horizontal pin. Stamped "Walter Schot fpc." Avg. cond. $247

Campaign Shield, Crimea, Germany, Army, WWII. Faded gray shield, gray wool backing and paper-covered backing plate. Removed from tunic. Avg. cond. $87

Campaign Shield, Demjansk, Germany, Army, WWII. Magnetic shield, soiled gray wool oval and paper backed. Above avg. cond. $218

Campaign Shield, Demjansk, Germany, Army, WWII. Magnetic silver finished shield shows wear, gray wool oval, paper backing, metal plate and four rim prongs. Avg. cond. $203

Campaign Shield, Krim, Germany, Army, WWII. Blue-gray wool. Convex steel plate with four prongs. Bronze finish. Above avg. cond. $85

Campaign Shield, Kuban, Germany, Army, WWII. Bronze shield with darkening, blue-gray wool, paper backing covers plate with four prongs. Above avg. cond. $164

Campaign Shield, Kuban, Germany, Army, WWII. Magnetic bronze finished shield shows wear, gray wool shield, paper backing on metal plate and four rim prongs. Removed from tunic. Avg. cond. $90

Campaign Shield, Narvik, Germany, Army, WWII. Gold non-magnetic shield with blue wool oval, wool oval backing, oval backing plate with cut corners and four flat prongs. Above avg. cond. $212

Campaign Shield, Narvik, Germany, Army, WWII. Gray non-magnetic shield on gray wool oval with paper backing over metal. Above avg. cond. $196

Clasp, Close Combat, Bronze, Germany, Army, WWII.

100mm bronze oak leaf bar with Nazi eagle over crossed bayonet and stick grenade, has anodized steel backing plate and hmkd "JFS & Peekhaus Berlin" on back. Large flat pin with stamped-in hinge and catch. Near mint cond. . $177

Clasp, Close Combat, Bronze, Germany, Army, WWII. Dark bronze body has gray corrosion area. Good details, blued panel, wide pin and by "JFS FEC WE etc." Avg. cond. $135

Clasp, Close Combat, Bronze, Germany, Army, WWII. Dark finish shows age and worn gray highlights. Wide pin, blued plate, raised "JFS" and stamped "Fec.W.E. etc." Avg. cond. $135

Clasp, Close Combat, Bronze, Germany, Army, WWII. Gray body shows remains of dark bronze finish. Blued panel, wide pin, stamped "Peekhaus etc." and raised "JFS." Avg. cond. $101

Clasp, Close Combat, Silver, Germany, Army, WWII. Gray body shows no traces of finish. Wide bronze fluted pin is usually silver on a silver clasp. Blued panel and unmarked late war example. Below avg. cond. . . . $165

Clasp, Close Combat, Silver, Germany, Army, WWII. Faded gray body with worn bright highlights. Metal panel. Wide pin, hinge and catch all have silver finish intact. Above avg. cond. $150

Clasp, Close Combat, Silver, Germany, Army, WWII. Good frosted finish. Wide pin. Lacks blued panel. Above avg. cond. $196

Combat Clasp, U-boat, Silver, Germany, Navy, WWII. Frosted silver finish shows some light darkening. Fluted, wide pin and "Schwerin" and "Peekhaus" marked. Above avg. cond. $545

Operational Flight Clasp, Bomber Squadron, Bronze, Germany, Luftwaffe, WWII. Dark body with rivet to silver winged bomb. Wide pin. Above avg. cond. $175

Operational Flight Clasp, Bomber Squadron, Silver, Germany, Luftwaffe, WWII. Traces of silver finish on gray oak and laurel leaves. Domed rivet on silver winged bomb. Wide pin. Shows use with fracture crack above swastika that holds bomb. Late war style. Above avg. cond. $175

Operational Flight Clasp, Day-fighter Squadron, Gold, Germany, Luftwaffe, WWII. Bright gold finish on oak and laurel leaves. Domed rivet on dark winged arrow. Wide pin. Near mint cond. $550

Wound Badge, 1914, Black, Imperial Germany, Army, WWI. Cutout. Stamped steel with good paint and pb. Exc. cond. $39

Wound Badge, 1914, Black, Imperial Germany, Army, WWI. Cutout. Stamped. Pb. Above avg. cond. $45

Wound Badge, 1914, Black, Imperial Germany, Army, WWI. Stamped brass with faint traces of black to recesses. Pb. Avg. cond. $45

Wound Badge, 1914, Black, Imperial Germany, Army, WWI. Stamped steel. Pb. Avg. cond. $20

Wound Badge, 1914, Gold, Imperial Germany, Army, WWI. Custom made of high quality material with beautiful toned gold finish for officer tunic. Exc. cond. . . $38

Wound Badge, 1914, Gold, Imperial Germany, Army, WWI. Stamped brass with gold finish. Pb. Exc. cond. $58

1914 Wound Badge in Gold

Wound Badge, 1914, Silver, Imperial Germany, Army, WWI. Private purchase style with fine silver finish. Delicate work. Exc. cond. $32

Wound Badge, 1914, Silver, Imperial Germany, Army, WWI. Stamped magnetic body has silver finish and two screw posts back side. Large backing disc and two nuts. Sb. Exc. cond. $140

Wound Badge, 1914, Silver, Imperial Germany, Army, WWI. Stamped brass body with silver finish worn at highlights. Threaded stud at back and rayed disc with socket. Sb. Above avg. cond. $135

Wound Badge, 1914, Silver, Imperial Germany, Army, WWI, R. Sedlatzeck, Berlin. Stamped steel, silver paint and maker marked "R.Sedlatzeck Berlin etc." Pb. Above avg. cond. $135

Wound Badge, 1914, Silver, Imperial Germany, Army, WWI. Cutout. Stamped brass with frosted silver finish. Pb. Avg. cond. $55

Wound Badge, 1914, Silver, Imperial Germany, Army, WWI. Stamped silver-gray magnetic body and "DRGM" stamped. Pb. Avg. cond. $62

Wound Badge, 1939, Black, Germany, Army, WWII. Stamped magnetic body with Pb and "81." Exc. cond. $24

Wound Badge, 1939, Black, Germany, Army, WWII. Stamped dark brass with worn paint. Pb. Early example. Above avg. cond. $20

Wound Badge, 1939, Black, Germany, Army, WWII. Stamped non-magnetic gray metal with worn paint. Pb. Marked "ESP." Above avg. cond. $20

1939 Wound Badge in Black

Wound Badge, 1939, Black, Germany, Army, WWII. Stamped steel with good paint. Pb. Above avg. cond. $27

Wound Badge, 1939, Black, Germany, Army, WWII. Stamped steel with good paint. By "88." Pb. Above avg. cond. $25

Wound Badge, 1939, Black, Germany, Army, WWII. Early stamped sheet brass version with worn paint. Pb. Avg. cond. $20

Wound Badge, 1939, Black, Germany, Army, WWII. Stamped brass body with worn paint. Pb and "L/52." Avg. cond. $20

Wound Badge, 1939, Black, Germany, Army, WWII. Stamped steel with fair paint. Pb. By "100." Avg. cond. $20

Wound Badge, 1939, Black, Germany, Army, WWII. Stamped steel with paint worn at highlights. Pb. Avg. cond. $20

Wound Badge, 1939, Black, Germany, Army, WWII. Stamped steel with black paint showing some rust. Pb. Avg. cond. $20

Wound Badge, 1939, Black, With Envelope, Germany, Army, WWII. For one or two wounds. Stamped steel with good paint and pb. Tan envelope with three-line title and maker. Avg. cond. $34

Wound Badge, 1939, Gold, Germany, Army, WWII. Solid with good finish. Wide pin and by "L/14." Above avg. cond. $80

Wound Badge, 1939, Gold, Germany, Army, WWII. Solid gray body with gold finish worn at swastika. Pb. Above avg. cond. $95

Wound Badge, 1939, Gold, Germany, Army, WWII. Solid, frosted gold finish. Pb. Marked "127." Above avg. cond. $95

Wound Badge, 1939, Gold, With Case, Germany, Army, WWII. Black leatherette, white satin and flock lined. Solid with bright gold finish. Pb and stamped "30." Early version. Exc. cond. $183

Wound Badge, 1939, Gold, With Case, Germany, Army, WWII. Black leatherette body with paper maker tag, damaged satin lining with hinged area intact and white flock base. Gold finished solid badge by "30." Pb. Avg. cond. $139

Wound Badge, 1939, Gold, With Case, Germany, Army, WWII. Blue leatherette-covered body "LDO" logo to inside of lid. Solid brass/bronze body is dark at highlights and traces of gold finish to recesses. Wide pin and by "L/63." Avg. cond. $97

Wound Badge, 1939, Silver, Germany, Army, WWII. Solid with silver finish fading gray. Pb. By "100." Above avg. cond. $30

1939 Wound Bandage in Silver

Wound Badge, 1939, Silver, Germany, Army, WWII. Solid body with graying. Pb. Avg. cond. $24

Wound Badge, 1939, Silver, Germany, Army, WWII. Late war solid gray body. Pb. By "30." Avg. cond. . . $24

Wound Badge, 1939, Silver, Germany, Army, WWII. Solid faded gray body. Frosted silver Pb. By "L/53." Late war. Avg. cond. $22

Wound Badge, 1939, Silver, Germany, Army, WWII.

Solid with finish faded mostly gray. Pb. By "107." Avg. cond. $23

Wound Badge, 1939, Silver, Germany, Army, WWII. Solid with finish fading gray. Pb. By "65." Late war example. Avg. cond. $25

Wound Badge, 1939, Silver, With Case, Germany, Army, WWII. Maroon leatherette body with maroon flock base. Frosted silver finish on solid body. By "100." Pb. Exc. cond. $75

Wound Badge, 1939, Silver, With Case, Germany, Army, WWII. Maroon leatherette body, red flock inside. Lid needs glue repair at corners. Solid body with frosted finish. Pb. By "65." Avg. cond. $100

Wound Badge, 1939, Silver, With Case, Germany, Army, WWII. Maroon leatherette case with gold "LDO" on maroon paper lid lining and flock base. Early solid badge by "30" with needle pin and dark age tarnish. Shows tunic use. Avg. cond. $113

Wound Badge, 1939, Silver, With Case, Germany, Army, WWII. Maroon leatherette body, faint "LDO" on paper lid lining and maroon velvet base. Early solid brass body with dark silver finish worn at highlights. Pb. Avg. cond. $85

Wound Badge, 1939, Silver, With Envelope, Germany, Army, WWII. Solid body with frosted silver finish. Pb. By "100." Green envelope with three-line title and maker. Above avg. cond. $70

Wound Badge, 1939, Silver, With Envelope, Germany, Army, WWII. Solid body with frosted silver finish and by "100." Pb. Small gray-green envelop with three-line title and maker. Avg. cond. $67

Wound Badge, 1939, Silver, With Envelope, Germany, Army, WWII. Solid with silver finish, fading gray and by "100." Pb. Green envelope. Three-line title and maker. Tear at back. Avg. cond. $50

Wound Badge, Naval, Black, Imperial Germany, Navy, WWI. Stamped steel with black paint on chain, wreath with crossed swords and anchor center. Pb. Above avg. cond. $42

Wound Badge, Naval, Black, Imperial Germany, Navy, WWI. Stamped magnetic oval with black painted front and rust patina back. Pb. Avg. cond. $72

Wound Badge, Naval, Silver, Imperial Germany, Navy, WWI. Stamped with frosted silver finish. Pb. Exc. cond. $160

Wound Badge, Naval, Silver, Imperial Germany, Navy, WWI. Stamped steel with silver paint. Pb. Avg. cond. $130

Badges—Other

Badge, Assault (Sturm) Troop, Austria, Army, WWI. 1¾" x 2" in size. Silver oval wreath with Austrian soldier throwing M1896 stick grenade with shrouded skeleton in cape embracing him. Hungarian inscription below. Pb. Above avg. cond. $48

Badge, Pilot Wings, Australia, Royal Australian Air Force, WWII. Embr with RAAF and blue wreath on dark blue wool background. Above avg. cond. $95

Royal Australian Air Force Pilot Wings (Cloth)

Badge, Pilot Wings, England, Royal Air Force, c1960. Brown wreath around white parachute and dark blue padded field. Above avg. cond. $20

Royal Air Force Pilot Wings, WWII (Cloth)

Badge, Military Families Nursing Service, England, WWII. Silvered metal badge. Queen Alexandra's Military Families Nursing Service. Above avg. cond. $45

Badge, Pilot Wings, England, Royal Air Force, WWII. Embr on padded cloth. Above avg. cond. $125

Badge, Military Academy, Czechoslovakia, Army, 1954. Silver planchet with red star having silver rampant lion motif. Dated. Sb. Above avg. cond. $200

Badge, WWII Partisan, Czechoslovakia, c1950s. Silver star planchet, Sb. Above avg. cond. $120

Badge, Infantry Search Light Unit, Austria, Army, WWI. 45mm gold finished heavy brass disc with crown over lightning bolts and oak leaf wreath border. Clip on back for right breast use. Exc. cond. $61

Badge, Pilot Wings, Japan, Army, WWII. Silver wings with yellow wreath, gold star and propeller on blue field. Above avg. cond. $20

Badge, Pilot Wings, Japan, Navy, WWII. Gold bullion

chain with silver bullion anchor and star. Above avg. cond. $18

Badge, Merit Cross, Greece, Air Force, 1945. Silver finish cross with propeller and wreath, crown and ribbon above, 1945 to reverse. Above avg. cond. $65

Badge, Military Parachutist, Argentina, Army, c1970s. 82mm antique silver finish wings with parachute in center, enamel ring with inscription "Paracaidista Militar." Above avg. cond. $25

Badge, Observer, Austria, Army, WWI. Green enameled oval gilt wreath with red gilt crown over riveted-on-brass eagle and white shield, brass, pb and hand numbered. Avg. cond. $276

Badge, Parachute, Saudi Arabia, Army, 1980s. Stamped 90mm wings, silver finish and pb. Above avg. cond. $20

Badge, Pilot, Austria, Air Force, WWI. 60 x 65mm dark green enameled bronze wreath with bronze spread-winged flying eagle. Creme-colored shield below with national colors and propeller. Two-piece construction with vertical pin. Above avg. cond. $79

Badge, Pilot, Hungary, Air Force, WWII. Gilt eagle with crown. 3½" wingspread. Pb. Above avg. cond. $35

Badge, Pilot, Mexico, Navy, c1970s. Silver finish Sb eagle with anchor, 75mm wingspread. Above avg. cond. $20

Badge, Pilot Wings, Japan, Army, WWII. Army Air Force with silver bullion wings, wreath and propeller star on blue wool field. Above avg. cond. $15

Badge, Pilot, Argentina, Navy, c1970s. 88mm gilt with enamel crest to center. Above avg. cond. $30

Badge, Pilot, Romania, Air Force, c1970s. Silver finish eagle with enamel crest on center. Above avg. cond. . $30

Badge, 1st Warsaw Infantry Div, Poland, Army, WWII. Silvered, enameled. Sb. Above avg. cond. $90

Badge, 10th Field Artillery Regt, Poland, Army, WWII. Silvered. Sb. Above avg. cond. $60

Badge, 19th Infantry Regt, Poland, Army, WWII. Silvered, three-piece construction. Sb. Above avg. cond. $60

Badge, 1st Western Infantry Corps, Poland, Army, 1919. Silvered. Sb. Above avg. cond. $50

Badge, Pilot Wings, Rhodesia, Rhodesian Royal Air Force, WWII. Embr, padded crown with Rhodesian national insignia on blue wool field. Above avg. cond. $225

Badges, Naval Military Academy Graduation, Soviet Union, Navy, c1975. Two enameled and gilded badges. Exc. cond. $22

Badge, Naval Radio Electronic School Graduation, Soviet Union, Navy, 1980s. Enameled and gilded badge. Exc. cond. $26

Badge, Naval Engineering Academy Graduation, Soviet Union, Navy, 1980s. Enameled, silver finish. Exc. cond. $20

Badge, Artillery Best Soldier, Soviet Union, Army, WWII. Enameled, gilded finish. Above avg. cond. . $26

Badge, Infantry Best Soldier, Soviet Union, Army, WWII. Enameled, gilded finish. Exc. cond. $26

Badge, Nationalist Aviation Armshield, Spain, Nationalist Aviation Unit, Spanish Civil War. Brass inscribed planchet, center-winged badge with crown and corners pierced for sewing on tunic sleeve. Above avg. cond. $43

Badge, Paratrooper Wings, Spain, Army, Paratrooper, WWII. Brass eagle with wings holding parachute and loop back. Good cond. $45

Badge, Paratrooper Wings, Portugal, Army, c1980s. 4th series pattern, gilded planchet with silvered parachute canopy. Pb. Above avg. cond. $20

Badge, Glider Pilot, England, Army, WWII. Brass glider facsimile with brass backing plate and loop back. Above avg. cond. $150

Medal, service, Kuwait. UN Kuwait Service Medal, 42mm-diam bronze pendant on pin brooch-mounted ribbon with star device affixed. Mint cond. $15

Badge, Guard Unit, Yugoslavia, Army, c1980s. Gilded planchet, red, white, and blue enamels, depicting Yugoslavian and Soviet flags. Exc. cond. $50

Awards——Germany

Award, Infantry Regt 131, Germany, Army, 1938. 18" x 14" mounted, shows fortress gate with unit history displayed on each side. Gate contains presentation from Infantry Regt. 131 in thanks to their comrade Lt-Colonel A.D. Von Ballujeck. Dated May 8,1938 and signed. Fancy litho design work of Imperial and Nazi party flags above gate. Near mint cond. $85

Awards——Other

Award, Long Aerial Navigation, Italy, Air Force, c1980s. Bronze planchet, 20 years service, with ribbon. Above avg. cond. $25

CHAPTER TWELVE

Military Images

Photographic collectibles appear mostly from the Civil War era through modern conflicts. Older images come in many formats including albumins, ambrotypes, cartes-de-visites, cabinet cards, daguerreotypes, salt prints, stereographs and tintypes. Modern collectible photographs are typically film and paper print formats.

Albumins were so named because albumins from eggs were used as a binder with the silver salts. This photographic process was used to make glass negatives and was popular in the 1870s. Ambrotypes are positive photographs on glass, backed by black color, making negative appear as positive. It was a popular process started in the mid 1850s, but lost popularity when paper print images were introduced in 1858. Specimens are rare and rank high on the advanced image collector's list.

Cartes-de-visites (French visiting cards) were inexpensive paper portraits popular during the 1850s through the 1860s. The CDV process took multiple exposures of a subject in one sitting with four lenses to make them look as if they were in a more natural and relaxed position and allowed for multiple duplications of the same pose. To help raise war funds during the Civil War, the government charged a small tax on all CDVs and stereocards. Specimens may be dated by their Federal Revenue stamp on the back dating from September 1, 1864 to August 1, 1866. Cabinet cards were introduced in 1867 primarily as mass-produced celebrity portraits. Although slightly larger, they are the most important of the cartes-de-visites images.

Daguerreotypes were popular during 1843 through 1855. An estimated 30 million were run off in assembly line fashion between 1840 and 1860 in the United States alone. "Dags" are shiny, precise images on silver coated copper plates. Even with their massive production, good specimens can command healthy prices in the market.

The double-pictured stereographs were popular through the 1870s and experienced a revival in 1887 through the turn of the century, and again in the 1930s. Depending upon the era, both illustrations (pre-paper print photography) and photographic images were used.

Popular well into the twentieth century, tintypes were created on iron plates, not copper, and a black japan varnish was applied. The quality was inferior to other methods, but the process was cheaper. Good specimens may be difficult to find because of the darkening of the image.

More modern photographic methods were introduced during the late 1800s, such as platinum and silver prints and were first used to create photos from earlier negative types, including Civil War depictions. The value and collectibility of modern photos, from World War One to Vietnam, lies in the events captured on film.

Fakes and Frauds

Many old photographs, such as Civil War photos, are actually copies or restored versions of the originals. Research types of images before deciding to buy. Close examination should be made for date, location and subject markings and natural wear.

Care and Display

If openly displaying your collection, avoid excessive handling, dust, humidity, pollutants, insects, and direct sunlight. Images may depreciate or worse, become irreparably damaged. If displaying, rotate artifacts in the display. Mount or store in boxes lined with acid-free paper. Cardboard releases gases and peroxides which can damage photos.

Cabinet Cards—U.S.

Cabinet Card, Cavalry Officer, USA, Army, c1870s. 6½" x 4¼". Studio pose of officer in 1872 regulation uniform with M1872 chasser-style kepi. Also wearing private purchase saber and GAR medal. Avg. cond. $44

Cabinet Photograph, c1870s, Cavalry Officer

Cabinet Card, Cavalry Soldier, USA, Army, c1898. 4" x 6" of full standing soldier with leather gloves, spats, slouch hat and side arm pistol. Made in Manila, 1890s. Some flaking to the edges but photo has clear detail. Avg. cond. $34

Cabinet Card, Infantry Soldier, USA, Army, c1870s. 6½" x 4¼". Studio pose of infantryman wearing five-button coat, M1872 belt plate and waistbelt, white gloves, kepi with 1876 hat device and sky blue trousers. Carrying Springfield rifle. Avg. cond. $48

Cabinet Cards—Other

Cabinet Photograph, Cavalry Officer, Austria, Army, 1912. 6¼" x 4", studio pose of cavalry officer in dress uniform with sword. Above avg. cond. $20

Cabinet Photograph, Colonial Soldier, England, Army, c1900. 6½" x 4¼", artilleryman in New Zealand in Model 1900 khaki uniform. Above avg. cond. $25

Cabinet Card Lot, Military Officers, Denmark, Army, c1870. Four CDV images, studio poses of officers and enlisted men in uniform. Above avg. cond. $20

Cabinet Photos, Military, Denmark, Army, c1870s. Three cabinet photos of Danish troops in studio pose. Above avg. cond. $30

Cartes-de-visites (CDV's)—U.S.

CDV's, Set of Three, Civil War Soldiers, USA, Army, Civil War. One is of a soldier seated with hands crossed wearing frock coat with shoulder insignias. The other two are busts of soldiers. Corners trimmed. Avg. cond. . $88

CDV, Civil War Naval Officers, Signed, USA, Navy, Civil War, F. Kindler, Newport, RI. Signed Civil War CDV of four naval officers in full uniform, posed in front of ship side and around cannon. Backstamped "F. Kindler, Newport, R.I." and signed "Compliments of Mid'm J. D. Adams." With orange 2-cent George Washington revenue stamp. Above avg. cond. $345

CDV, Civil War Naval Officer, USA, Navy, Nov. 1864, F. Kindler, Newport, RI. Civil War naval officer, J.D. Adams, posed in full uniform with sword and hand on cannon. Hand dated "Nov. 1864" on mount. Backstamped "F. Kindler, Newport, R.I." and signed "Compliments of Mid'm J. D. Adams." Above avg. cond. $259

CDV, Civil War EM, USA, Army, Civil War, C. Gullman, Poughkeepsie, NY. Full stand-up view of Union soldier in full uniform, not identified. By C. Gullman, Poughkeepsie, NY. Tax stamp on verso. Above avg. cond. $92

CDV, Confederate Soldier, USA, Army, Civil War. 70 x 100mm, chest-up shot of a man in light gray Northern Virginia depot jacket with stand-up collar and single button done. Above avg. cond. $125

CDV, CSA General Manfred Lovell, USA, Army, Civil War. 2½" x 4". Bust and head. New York studio maker marks on verso. Details on CSA general uniform with Lovell shown having full mustache. He was in command of the Confederate Forces at Mobile. Above avg. cond. $55

CDV, Enlisted Trooper, USA, Army, Civil War. Federal artillery man enlisted and holding cap in hand. Avg. cond. $25

CDV, Federal Camp at Baton Rouge, USA, 1863, McPherson and Oliver. Image of Federal Camp at Baton Rouge, LA. McPherson and Oliver backmark. Some soiling. Avg. cond. $270

CDV, Federal Signal Tower, USA, Army, Civil War. Outdoor view of Union signal tower. Image taken in the Petersburg or Bermuda Hundred area. No backmark. Minor spotting on background. Good cond. $161

CDV, Federal Warship, USA, Civil War, J.W. Black, Boston. Federal frigate USS Sautee. Close-up image of vessel at anchor close to shore. "J. W. Black, Boston" imprint on verso. Image has faded somewhat. Avg. cond. $178

CDV, Federal Warship, USA, Civil War, Black & Case, Boston. Federal frigates USS Sautee and USS Constitution. Close-up image of vessels at anchor in harbor. On ruled mount with "Black & Case, Boston" imprinted on recto and verso. Image has some minor spots. Avg. cond. $288

CDV, General Fitzhugh Lee, CSA, USA, c1866, C. R. Rees & Bro., Richmond, VA. CDV of General Fitzhugh

Lee, CSA and Charles Minnengrode. Waist-up seated view in civilian attire. Backmarked C.R. Rees & Bro., Richmond, VA. Mount trimmed (touches photo) and light soil. Taken shortly after war. Good cond. $345

CDV, General McClellan, USA, Army, Civil War. 2¼" x 4" with portrait head pose and autograph of General at bottom. Above avg. cond. $45

CDV, General McClellan, USA, Army, Civil War. 2¼" x 4" with engraving. Washington maker marked. Avg. cond. $27

CDV, General Phil Sheridan, Engraving, USA, Army, Civil War. 2½" x 4". General looking across right shoulder, shoulderboard with two stars very clear. Avg. cond. $30

CDV, Lincoln and Grant, USA, Civil War. 60 x 100mm with edges clipped for mounting. Both chest-up. Lincoln with engraving around photo of period events and patriotic style. Grant with scenes of the battle at base. Avg. cond. $35

CDV, Lincoln Mourning, USA, Civil War. 1865. 3½" x 4½" card art of Washington holding Lincoln and putting wreath on head of great leader. Has been professionally framed. Above avg. cond. $50

CDV, Lucuro B. Marsh, USA, Army, Civil War. 60 x 100mm with edges, full standing shot of man in long frock coat and kepi and officer sword in hand. Identified in pencil on back. Above avg. cond. $50

CDV, Marine, USA, USMC, c1900. 6" x 8" size, bust-up studio photo of marine in tunic. Good view of stripes and braided shoulder straps. Reverse caption. Above avg. cond. $118

CDV, Union EM, USA, Army, Civil War. 2½" x 3¾" full standing shot of two men in dark overcoats with light color tunics and kepis. Probably a state unit. Good clear detail. Above avg. cond. $93

CDV, Union EM, USA, Army, Civil War. 2½" x 3¾" full standing shot of seven men in dark overcoats with light color tunics and kepis. Probably a state unit. Good clear detail. Above avg. cond. $100

CDV, Union General Ben Butler, USA, Army, Civil War. 2½" x 4" partial right profile showing dress collar, epaulettes, and two rows of buttons on tunic. Above avg. cond. $72

CDV, Union General Weitzel, USA, Army, Civil War. 60 x 100mm with chest-up shot of the man with double breasted tunic and single star on shoulderboards. Identified in pencil on back. Revenue stamp. Avg. cond. $27

Cartes-de-visites (CDV's)——Germany

CDV, 9th Uhlan Officer, Imperial Germany, Army, WWI. Photo shows a Lieut standing with sword held in left hand, full dress ulanka with banjo boards and with number 9 high polished tschaka worn with large Prussian eagle. Excellent details of uniform and headgear. Above avg. cond. $27

CDV, Austrian Officer, Imperial Germany, Army, c1870s. Man shown with the Grand Cross of the Iron Cross, 1870 EK 1, 2, Mecklenburg Schwerin 2nd class 1864 medal, 1871 Victory medal, etc. Plus Malta Order. Very unusual as Austria fought Prussia in 1864 and largely remained neutral in the Franco-Prussian War of 1870. Above avg. cond. $20

CDV, Bavarian EM, Imperial Germany, Army, c1905. Hand tinted. Full-length posed studio shot with man dressed in pre-war blue tunic with red Brandenburg cuffs, piping number 16 shown on shoulder straps. Dress bayonet with white troddel blue and red visor cap. Studio marked. Avg. cond. $20

CDV, Bavarian EM, Imperial Germany, Army, WWI. Nice details to pillbox cap and concealed-button-style tunic with dark collar tabs. Studio marked. Avg. cond. $20

CDV, Garde EM, Imperial Germany, Army, WWI. Man shown in dress tunic of the unit with litzen, white breeches. White horsehair plumed helmet resting on table behind him. Avg. cond. $20

CDV, Garde EM, Imperial Germany, Army, c1905. Soldier shown in full dress tunic with garde litzen plumed helmet with horsehair top and trichter sitting on table beside him. Avg. cond. $20

CDV, Hussar NCO, Imperial Germany, Army, 1906. Man shown in attila and breeches with visor cap resting on chair. He clutches his sword with both hands and also carries gloves. Dated. NCO rank insignia on collar with lacing. Avg. cond. $20

CDV, Kurassier EM, Imperial Germany, Army, c1900. Man shown in standing position with tall boots, sword, full kurass and holding helmet against right thigh. Umhang or overcoat displayed across shoulders. Formal studio-style pose with good equipment details. Avg. cond $20

CDV, Kurassier EM, Imperial Germany, Army, c1900. Subject shown in koller and kurass with nice details to sword handle of a straight-bladed pallasch. White cartouche box strap across shoulders. Avg. cond. $20

CDV, Leib Garde Infantry EM, Bavarian, Imperial Germany, Army, c1900. Three-quarter-length, showing man in dress tunic with full collar litzen and cuff work visor cap, belt, etc. Crown ciphers on shoulderboards to indicate Leib Garde Inf Regt. Avg. cond. $23

CDV, Prussian One Year Volunteer Group, Imperial Germany, Army, WWI. 4¼" x 6½" photo of three young Prussian one year volunteers in dress uniforms and swords. Sepia tone. Avg. cond. $20

CDV, Prussian Soldier in March Rig, Imperial Germany, Army, WWI. Full-length view showing man with number 2 on field cover, full cartridge box, assault pack, leather leggings and GEW98 rifle with flower in barrel. Avg. cond. $20

CDV, Prussian Soldier With His Iron Cross, Imperial Germany, Army, WWI. Bust and head. Man dressed in M1915 tunic with crown buttons and EK mounted on 2nd button hole. Studio marked in gold lettering. Avg. cond. $20

CDV, Soldier, Imperial Germany, Army, 1915. Frame approx 5" x 9" with wooden half-moon design on side and hand-carved facing decorated with flowers and inscription. Dated. Soldier shown in studio picture in dress tunic without helmet or cap. Avg. cond. $20

CDV, Uhlan EM, Imperial Germany, Army, 1890s. 2" x 5" size. Formal studio picture of man in pillbox cap, ulanka with dress epaulettes with ciphers. Subject holds a sword and carries white gloves in free hand. Studio marked. Avg. cond. $20

CDV, Wurttemberg EM, Imperial Germany, Army, C1905. 2" X 4½" matted. Pre-war EM in dress tunic with visor cap. Shooting cord on chest. Indoor studio shot. Ulm photo logo. Avg. cond. $20

Daguerreotypes and Other Early Formats

Ambrotye, Army Officer, USA, Army, c1860. Pre-Civil War. 2½" x 3" gilt framed showing military officer with retouched collar, button cuffs and shoulderboards. Thermoplastic case with ornate covers and red velvet protective pad for picture. Above avg. cond. $111

Pre-Civil War Ambrotype in Frame

Image on Glass, Cadet, USA, Army, Civil War. 2" x 2½" full-length image of little boy wearing neat haircut and light colored military-style uniform with lacy black frogging on jacket and gold-tone buttons. Also a spindle wood chair in background. Image is still in thin brass "framette" with glass. Exc. cond. $76

Image on Glass, Union Soldier, USA, Army, Civil War. Cased. 50 x 60mm bust image of Union soldier in shell jacket. In brass framette with glass and in hinged gutta-percha-style case. Below avg. cond. $125

Civil War Image on Glass, Union Soldier

Image on Glass, Young Sailor, USA, Navy, 1862. 11" X 14". Photo of the man seated, in V-neck shirt with rolled-up shirt sleeves. Has ID on back and stated that sailor was killed at New Orleans. Some flaking on edges and one broken area at base. Avg. cond. $80

Albumin, Union Soldier, USA, Army, Civil War. Union soldier sitting with saber across his lap. Full view. Image has been hand tinted. Size: 6½" x 9" on 8½" x 10" heavy stock. Some staining. Good cond. $98

Ambrotype, Confederate Officer, USA, Army, Civil War. 1/6 plate ambrotype in case. Seated image of officer, tinted buttons, stars on collar, "CSA" on belt buckle. Case is missing cover. Above avg. cond. $1093

Ambrotype, Confederate Soldier, USA, Army, Civil War. 1/6 plate ambrotype in thermoplastic case. Seated image of Virginia CSA soldier. Hand-tinted brass coat buttons. Case has minor scratches and image is slightly solarized. Avg. cond. $489

Ambrotype, Federal Soldier, USA, Army, Civil War. 1/6 plate ambrotype. Waist-up image of soldier in jacket with epaulettes. Gold tint to epaulettes and buttons. In unhinged case. Light scratches and some minor tarnishing around perimeter. Avg. cond. $52

Photo Albums—U.S.

Photo Album, Army Air Force, USA, AAF, WWII. 11½" x 15" album. Photographs embossed in cover, string-bound with approx. 100 b&w photos. Many shots of planes, such as B-29, B-24 and B-17. Shots of docks, supplies, vehicles, and troops. Some captioned. Exc. cond. $90

Photo Album, WWI EM, USA, Army, WWI. 11½" x 15½" album with approx. 640 postcards of an excursion tour of Europe. Many in color. Tour included France, Germany, Mediterranean coastline, and England. Also includes approx. 100 personal snapshots. Album is string-bound but with many loose pages. Above avg. cond. $93

Photo Albums—Germany

Photo Album, Army Life, Germany, Army, c1936. 69 photos. Linen cover with steel helmet and silvered eagle and service time inscription. Album has mostly 1936 training pics, with infantry, cavalry; equipment shots, also rare brownie pic of Hitler in his Mercedes talking to massed troops. Good views of troops, personal equipment and army items. Early transitional period. Exc. cond. .. $152

Photo Album, Cruiser Emden, Germany, Navy, c1936. 18" x 14". 1936 period. Stiff cloth covers with metal binding. Hundreds of photos of a cruise around the world (goodwill type) showing excellent details of men, ship, work teams, visits to foreign ports to include Washington, DC and New York City (shots of men visiting Washington's grave, Lincoln memorial) plus some early photos of Erich Raeder while serving on the Emden. Early album with good historical background on pre-WWII Kriegsmarine. Avg. cond. $700

Photo Album, Early WWII, Germany, Army, c1940. 96 photos. 1940 era. 9" x 13" size with cloth-stock-covered body and onion skin dividers. Early part of album shows horse artillery men with stables, training horses and working with guns. Latter section shows war damage; bombed out buildings and sunken ships along the Channel ports in France or Belgium. Clear pictures with excellent uniform and equipment details. Above avg. cond. $137

Photo Album, French Campaign, Germany, Army, WWII. 8" x 10". 137 photos. Album kept by a private soldier and contains photos he took of the campaign in France, 1940, with shots of black French troops, white soldiers, stops along road, traditional Channel pictures, some leave, etc. Good shot of bicycle German troops and shots of officers. Above avg. cond. $85

Photo Album, Luftwaffe, Germany, Army, WWII. 9" X 12". Green stock covers. Photo of owner in front with steel helmet on and enlisted single-gull-style uniform. 70 photos. Shots of early Luftwaffe training, officers with many medals, athletic competition and of owner's girlfriend and family. Captures spirit of the early German Air Force. Above avg. cond. $164

Photo Album, Military Family, Imperial Germany, Army, Pre-WWI. Set of two large albums with 270+ photos. Albums are all from one family with men in the military and they record military events, maneuvers, gatherings from 1908 up into 1913 with nice shots of units on Kaiser maneuvers, soldiers at balls, on horseback, hussars, dragoons, etc. Many shots of young officers in pre-war uniforms, some photos going into 1930 period but mostly they stop around 1913. Avg. cond. $325

Photo Album, Naval, Germany, Navy, cWWI–c1930s. Some great pictures of Hindenburg's 80th Birthday in 1927. The launching of two new ships, the Sea Adler and the Falke. 7½" x 10" size. Pressed paper stiff covers. Onion skin dividers. Album contains 69 photos from 1917 into Nazi era. Early photos of destroyers and torpedo boats in WWI with crews, officers. Excellent details of life aboard ships, mid-album contains 1927 dated photos of battleships, naval reviews, latter portion shows Nazi naval and memorial activities. Above avg. cond. $165

Photo Album, Naval, Germany, Navy, c1932. Complete with 41 photos taken on board the Silesia - views of its fighting top, deck life, sailors, ships in formation, "Niobe," fjords, shore leaves, etc. Above avg. cond. $75

Photo Album, Sailor Cruise SMS Schleswig-Holstein, Imperial Germany, Navy, c1908. Pre-war Mediterranean cruise. Pseudo-brown crocodile skin covers with "Mit Linienschiff Schleswig-Holstein ins Mittlemeer." Album contains approx. 97 large-format b&w pictures of the ship, crew, officers, visits to Greece, Italy, Spain. Photos of jolly boats, fighting bridge, firing practice, etc. The Schleswig-Holstein later served as a training ship for the Nazis and bombarded Danzig at the beginning of WWII. Above avg. cond. $130

Photo Album, Sailor in China, Imperial Germany, Navy, c1905. 138 large captioned pictures showing sailor's voyage through Suez Canal through South Seas to China, 1905 period. Excellent pictures of natives, German sailors on SMS Fuerst Bismarck, other capital ships, soldier on leave in Japan. Album has large lacquered covers obviously made in China with delicate bird and foliage motifs. Above avg. cond. $301

Photo Album, WWI Army Life, Imperial Germany, Army, WWI. 5" x 8" gray leatherette cover with title and 22 photo postcards depicting military life in WWI. Each postcard is mounted in pre-cut slots and some have been used and canceled. Avg. cond. $30

Photo Album, WWI, Imperial Germany, Army, 1916. 9" x 11" black leatherette cover with gold "Album." Missing binding. Approx. 123 postcards. Starts with two Red Cross troopers wearing holstered pistols. 1916 captioned group shots, Ausweis "Sachs.San.-Komp.Nr.253." Combat, uniforms, natives, war damage, ruptured Arty gun, large mortar, dead tank and ends with post-war civilian dress shots. Above avg. cond. $167

Photo Album, WWI Naval, Imperial Germany, Navy, WWI. Contains 63 photos of ships, U-boats, crashed German airplane in sea, Zeppelin, mine damage to ship, downed British airplane, portrait shots of officers, and men, etc. Most photos captioned. 1914 Iron Cross on cover, red, white and black corded binding, 9" x 12" size. Above avg. cond. $93

Photo Album, WWI Sailor, Imperial Germany, Navy, WWI. Fully captioned. 26 photos. Covers 1913–17 period with early pictures of a squadron visit to the fjords of Norway. Latter pictures show minesweepers, submarines and battleships. Good pictures of officers and sailors in wartime uniforms. Captions all typed and easy to read. Avg. cond. $68

Photo Album, WWI Saxon Soldier, Imperial Germany, Army, WWI. 9" x 12" album with black covers. Onion skin dividers. Early pictures all have captions. Owner apparently served with a Pionier battalion and fought in Russia. Mixture of color cards of Eastern territories with postcard-sized photos of soldiers. Superb details of equipment in transition from 1915–17 with good shots of assault soldiers with grenade bags, specialized equipment, etc. Above avg. cond. $114

Photo Album, WWI Soldier, Imperial Germany, Army, WWI. 10" x 13" brown cover. Approx. 177 photos and 10 postcards. Various sizes with most 3" x 4". Uniforms, rest, war damage, trenches, map "Cambrai 13C," 1917 parade with officers "Falkenhausen." Most captioned. Above avg. cond. $150

Photo Album, WWI Soldier, Imperial Germany, Army, WWI. 107 photos. Mixture of pre-war family shots with people in traditional Bavarian peasant garb and group of war photos showing early spikes to later 1917 period uniforms. Full range of shots of barracks, field installations, etc. End of album has family, posed shots, etc. Above avg. cond. $90

Photo Album, WWI Soldier, Imperial Germany, Army, WWI. Covers period 1912–38. About 7" x 9½" plaid paper front on blue cover. Approx. 82 photos with most military shots postcard size. Captions on each page and starts with young man in 1912, 1915 in uniform, combat group shots with steel helmets, general, trenches, plane in flight, Arty bursts, 1925 motorcycle with side car, family 1930s, etc. Above avg. cond. $167

Photo Album, WWI Soldier, Imperial Germany, Army, WWII. 3x4" small format, with tiger spotted cover.

Includes twenty photos of soldiers on move, with horses, girls, houses and railroad tracks. Above avg. cond. . $27

Photo Album, WWI Soldier, Imperial Germany, Army, WWI. 5" x 7½" black cover with EK, title and tri-color affixed ribbon. Approx. 73 postcards. Starts with Bismarck, etc., Kaiser Wilhelm II, Hindenburg, field troops with Red Cross wagon, kitchen, Arty and some post-war color shots of monuments and gravestones. Above avg. cond. $300

Photo Album, WWI Soldier, Imperial Germany, Army, WWI. 5" x 8" black leatherette cover has silver stamped 1914-EK and gold "Erinnerungen an das Kriegsjahr 1914–15." Album shows use with pages for postcard. Approx 75 cards with many Prussian uniform shots. Some color illustrated troop cards and some scenic. Most used or captioned. Some interesting uniforms and equipment shots. Above avg. cond. $90

Photo Album, WWI Soldier, Imperial Germany, Army, WWI. 7" x 9½" black/red cover with 70 pictures. Photos cover soldiers in formation, in field exercises, artillery, family and friends. No captions. Above avg. cond. . $60

Photo Album, WWI Soldier, Imperial Germany, Army, WWI. Titled "In the 219th." 8" x 10" with 79 photos showing Eastern operation, trenches, buildings, Christmas party, officers, field kitchen, block houses, HQ's and cemetery. Great detail on field conditions. All pictures have caption giving names, dates, etc. Long interesting at end of album. Above avg. cond. $76

Photo Album, WWI Soldier, Imperial Germany, Army, WWI. Twenty-five pictures and postcards. Vast majority field taken by soldier with 482nd Telephone Bn as evidenced by feldpost stamps. All pics are of high quality and show men in the field with some rather unusual equipment, some armed with 88 Commission rifles with M71 bayonets, etc. Mix of frontline and reservist equipment typical of some reserve formations. Avg. cond. $75

Photo Album, WWI Soldier, Imperial Germany, Army, WWI. 98 photos. Pictures show prepared defensive positions, war damage, French POW's and German officers and men. Period appears to be 1917 with many photos of devastated landscapes, snowbound and barren. Paper covers. 8" x 12" with design of Iron Crosses on cover. Avg. cond. $145

Photo Album, WWI Veteran, Imperial Germany, Army, 1933. 9" x 12" size, cloth-covered album, string-bound with approx. 140 photos. This professionally done b&w photo album illustrates the WWI battle entrenched locations throughout Europe. This album was put together to commemorate a 1933 visit by former German soldiers to WWI battle sites. Avg. cond. $50

Photo Album, WWII Soldier, Germany, Army, c1940. Half-tracks, MG-34s, 88 cannons, tanks, generals remembrance photo. Standarts telegraph unit, etc. Metallic helmet on cover, "MEINE DIENSTZEIT." 166 photos of a man with the 73rd Field Artillery Unit in 1940. Many fine pics of prime movers, some 88s ready to fire, half-tracks, leave, soldiers on maneuvers and clowning around as Arabs pulling "cannon," etc. Above avg. cond. $250

Photo Albums—Other

Photo Album, Fascist Dictator Mussolini, Italy, 1926. 24 period images all 6½" x 4½" of subject in formal dress uniform on board ship *Esperia* during inspection. Above avg. cond. $675

Photos—U.S.

Photo, 449th FIS, USA, USAF, 1949. 10" x 59" b&w rolled photo of officers and enlisted men standing in front of hanger with P-82 aircraft in background. Taken at Ladd AFB, Alaska. Avg. cond. $30

Photo, Admiral Philip Andrews, Autographed, USA, Navy, 1920. 9½" x 5½" framed photo. Shows admiral on deck in dark blue uniform and visor cap. Autographed and dated July 21, 1920. Above avg. cond. $75

Photo, Admiral Philip Andrews

Photo, Battleship USS Wyoming, USA, Navy, WWI. Framed. 18" x 32"approx. size, in period wooden frame. Depicts a side view of the ship with good details of its guns. Above avg. cond. $160

Photo, Black Army Band in France, USA, Army, WWI. Official signal corps photo. 5" x 7". WWI black officer leading all-black army band in the street under the sign of Hotel Tunis. Near mint cond. $145

Photo, Black Unit, USA, Army, 1929. 8" x 20" b&w rolled photo. Shows soldiers wearing 1926-style uniform. No sleeve insignia. Could be a pioneer unit. Shows water stains. Above avg. cond. $129

Photo, British WWI, Framed. 17" x 8", walnut frame in form of aircraft propeller end section, central oval compartment containing image of pilots in outdoor formal seated pose, interior with standing arm and inscription "Pilot Cadets With Instructors Number 2, S. M. A. Oxford 1917." Good cond. $1200

Photo, Medal of Honor Winner, USA, USAF, c1970s. Two 5" x 7" photos of Captain Lance Sijan, first AF Academy graduate to win Medal of Honor. One in color in full position as drawing. Exc. cond. $40

Photo, Medal of Honor Winner, USA, USMC, WWII. 5" x 7" b&w press-released and signed photo of Joe Foss, 1943 USMCR VMF-121. Above avg. cond. $37

Photo, Medal of Honor Winner, USA, USN, WWII. 8" x 10" b&w autographed photo of medal winner David McCampbell. Good details of ribbons, medal and uniform. Above avg. cond. $45

Photo, Signed By Claire Chennault, USA, WWII. 8" x 10" size. Framed. A head and shoulders portrait of Chennault dressed in full military attire. He was an American aviator. Following the Japanese invasion of China, 1937, he became Chiang Kai-Shek's air adviser and formed a volunteer air corps, "The Flying Tigers," to aid China in the war against Japan. Near mint cond. $433

Photo, Union Soldier, USA, Army, Civil War. 12" x 17" size, sepia color print depicting young Union soldier, standing position in frock coat and cap. Above avg. cond. $93

Photos, Press Release of Battle Dead, USA, Army, WWII. 25 8" x 10" b&w photos of the most graphic, detailed and clear shots of dead men on battlefield and in morgue. Most photos are captioned and dated. Exc. cond. $44

Portrait, Four Cadets, USA, Army, Civil War. Framed. 2½" x 4" studio posed showing four cadets in a casual pose. Kepis, sleeve tabs and stripes on pants all show well. Could be NY cadets or West Point cadets. Above avg. cond. $72

Portrait of Four Civil War Cadets

Photos—Germany

Photo, One Year Volunteers in 74th Inf Rgt, Imperial Germany, Army, WWI. 7" x 12" matted studio posed picture with men reclining, standing, seated. Good details of cording on shoulder straps, pre-war uniforms with tunics, polished shoes, etc. Avg. cond. $20

Photo, Aerial Ace Pilot Lt. Voss, Imperial Germany, Air Force, WWI. Man shown seated by fireplace in dress tunic with Blue Max, EK1, pilot badge and House Order hung in 2nd buttonhole of tunic. Above avg. cond. $45

Photo, Captured US Soldiers, Germany, WWII. Rare image of captured US soldiers being marched through Rome. The Coliseum is visible in the background. Above avg. cond. $66

Photo, Captured US Soldiers

Photo, Crown Prince and His Wife, Imperial Germany, 1907. 4" x 6". The Prince is shown in infantry general dress uniform with many breast orders and medals, plumed helmet resting on chair beside him, his wife is dressed in princely skirt, etc. Avg. cond. $23

Photo, E-Boat, Germany, Navy, WWII. 8½" x 10½" silver painted wood frame with glass front. 5" x 7" photo mounted at center showing E-Boat at speed in water. Typed label to back "Zur Erinnerung & Anerkennung an Ihre Frontfahrzeit bei der 2. Schnellbootsflottille vom 4.4.1940 bis 25.3.1944" with signature of the "Oberlt.zur See & Kommandant." Hanger loop. Exc. cond. $165

Photo, Framed and Autographed Image of Hitler, Germany, WWII. 7" x 5" overall framed size. Studio-posed photograph of Hitler standing wearing political uniform, riding boots, and armband. Complete with period penned autograph. Period wooden frame retains 90% of original gilding. Above avg. cond. $1750

Photo, Guard Dragon Group, Imperial Germany, Army, WWI. 8" x 11" b&w photo of 15 Dragons, five in spiked

helmets with field covers all in uniform plus four horses. Has "Welt Krieg 1914" on front. Above avg. cond. . $40

Photo, Hamburg Bandsmen, Imperial Germany, Army, 1905. 8" x 6". Matted. Three soldiers shown seated around table with service tunics, swallows' nests on shoulders and Hamburg, Reichs rosettes in pillbox caps. Avg. cond. $20

Photo, Kaiser and Officers, Germany, WWI. 9" x 7" b&w of Kaiser and officers at the Kaiser maneuvers. All are mounted on horseback with Kaiser standart in picture. Above avg. cond. $45

Photo, Kaiser Wilhelm As Commander of the Garde Du Corps, Imperial Germany, Army, WWI. 2½" x 4". Detailed picture showing Kaiser on horseback wearing the cuirass and helmet of the unit with ornate shabraque trimmed with Garde du Corps star and all fittings. Large frosted silver eagle on top of helmet. Near mint cond. $32

Photo, Naval Ship SMS Danzig, Imperial Germany, Navy, WWI. Large 11" x 15" backed b&w photo of officers and EM's on the Danzig. All seamen are in either whites or blues with Donald Duck hats. One standing officer has naval dagger hanging on left side. Above avg. cond. $35

Photo, Naval Ship SMS Kaiser Barbarossa, Imperial Germany, Navy, 1902. Signed on the back by all of the

Framed Photo and Autographed Image of Hitler

officers. Is marked property of Captain Fr. Krause. In old period frame. Approx. 12" x 15". B&w sepia-toned photo showing ship making speed with smoke pouring from the stacks and bow wave. Excellent details to guns and superstructure. Dated. Ship's name on matte. Above avg. cond. $100

Photo, Naval Ship's Crew on Foredeck, Imperial Germany, Navy, WWI. 5" x 7" matted formal picture with captain seated, deck officers about him. EM lined up at back. Avg. cond. $25

Photo, Remembrance 1917 Pilot School, Imperial Germany, Army, WWI. 15" x 17½" brown finished wood frame with ornate details in plaster. Glass front, 7" x 9" photo showing partial biplanes and 40 uniformed men in various dress. Most wear visor caps, four officers, some leather coats and one crash helmet. Gray matte title marked in black reads "Herzog Carl Eduard-Schule Gotha, August 1917." Near mint cond. $234

Photo, Reserve Men in Leather Visor Caps, Imperial Germany, Army, WWI. Small group posing by barracks, men all wear light tunics with collar litzen and all have on black leather visor caps with large metal Reserve crosses. Good details to uniforms. One man carries a small regimental pipe in his hand. Feldpost stamped on reverse with short message. Avg. cond. $20

Photo, Saxon Infantry Officer and Wife, Imperial Germany, Army, WWI. Man dressed in walking-out tunic and breeches with white topped visor cap having both rosettes complete with sword in hand. Excellent detail. 4" x 6". Avg. cond. $20

Photo, Service Time 55th Field Arty Group, Imperial Germany, Army, WWI. 12" X 14". In original black wooden frame and glass. Picture shows recruits of the 55th Field Arty Regt in barracks posing at dining table with two men in dress uniforms and ball-top helmets standing at guard position with sabers. Avg. cond. $30

Photo, Soldier in Stable Gear, Imperial Germany, Army, WWI. Subject shown with pillbox cap, white tunic, gray woolen breeches and leggings, man carries a shovel in his right hand. Avg. cond. $20

Photo, Soldiers By Barracks, Imperial Germany, Army, c1905. Pre-war period. 9" x 12" matted photo shows a formation of men in dress tunics with pillbox hats assembled behind NCOs with shooting cords band with spiked helmets assembled to side. Many men staring out of open barracks windows. Avg. cond. $24

Photo, SS Riechsfuhrer Himmler, Germany, SS, WWII. 7" x 5" image of Himmler in SS uniform in conversation with another SS officer. SS entourage visible in background. Avg. cond. $160

Photo, Himmler

Photo, WWI Aerial Pilot, Imperial Germany, Army, WWI. 7" x 11". Man dressed in visor cap and greatcoat. 2nd Lieut straps with winged propeller clearly evident. Early wartime picture. Avg. cond. $20

Photo, WWI Arty NCO and Family, Imperial Germany, Army, WWI. 4" x 6½" b&w matted photo shows man in NCO dress tunic with single military medal on chest posing with his little girl and wife. Soldier has a shooting cord and carries his custom purchase dress Arty saber with cannons on larget. Avg. cond. $20

Photo, WWI Garde Officer in Dress Parade Attire, Imperial Germany, Army, WWI. Matted. Full dress uniform with white Sam Browne belt, overcoat, man has on white plumed Garde officer helmet and carries dress saber. 4" x 6". Avg. cond. $22

Photo, WWI Landsturm Soldier, Germany, Army, WWI. M15 tunic with metallic insignia on collar. Avg. cond. $20

Photo, WWI Landsturm Soldier, Imperial Germany, Army, WWI. M15 tunic with metallic insignia on collar, subject shown wearing a pillbox cap. Avg. cond. . . . $20

Photo, WWI Naval Officer, Imperial Germany, Navy, WWI. 14" x 10" portrait of naval officer. One-half view of seated officer in dress uniform. Avg. cond. $35

Photo, WWI German Naval Officer

Photo, WWI Officer, Imperial Germany, Army, WWI. 6" x 8". In modern matte frame. Man shown with officer Litewka having Iron Cross ribbon in buttonhole. No damage to picture. Avg. cond. $20

Photo, WWI Prussian NCO in Dress Uniform, Imperial Germany, Army, WWI. 3" x 6". Matted. Man dressed in walking-out uniform with visor cap holding sword and gloves. Prussian 1916 War Cross and other order on breast. Avg. cond. $20

Photo, WWI Prussian Officer, Imperial Germany, Army, WWI. 8" x 4". Subject shown in studio pose with spiked helmet and double breasted overcoat having Lieut shoulderboards. Brown leather belt with trench knife having ribbed grip clearly seen. Posed picture showing man wearing spurs though his helmet indicates infantry foot service. Above avg. cond. $25

Photo, WWI Soldiers Posing With Nurse Outside of Hospital, Imperial Germany, Army, WWI. Picture unusual as men are shown in a wide variety of different style uniforms ranging from those with numbered shoulder straps to tunics without straps. Large spectrum of button- and concealed-button tunics shown with equally wide range of field caps. Avg. cond. $20

Photos—Other

Photo, Soldier, Austria, Army, WWI. Color-retouched photo depicting portrait pose of Austrian soldier wearing medal and aiguillette. In period wood frame. Above avg. cond. $39

Photo, Austrian Officer, Austria, Army, Imperial Era. 25" x 17". Color-retouched portrait pose of Austrian officer. Above avg. cond. $34

Photos, Press Release, Canada, Army, 1942. 8" x 6". Canadian Armour Div training. Above avg. cond. . . $20

Postcards—U.S.

Postcard, Patriotic, USA, WWII. Comical, oversized, five different cards, unused. Avg. cond. $12

Postcard, Commemorative, Confederate General Joseph Johnston, USA, c1900. With three color flags of army above photo of man with birth and death dates and poem written for him. Unused. With gilt outline of flags. Above avg. cond. $25

Postcard, Union Soldier, USA, c1870s. Photo illustration of E.E. Ellsworth. Was reportedly the first soldier killed in the Civil War. Was Col of NY Fire Zouave Regiment. Above avg. cond. $25

Postcard, European Views, USA, WWII. 121 images

typical of era. Postcards of Paris, Verdun, Luxembourg. Above avg. cond. $35

Postcards—Germany

Postcard, Anti-fascist, Germany, WWII. Colored comical card depicting Third Reich leader with comical inscription. Above avg. cond. $20

Postcard, Anti-fascist, Germany, WWII. Depicting Goebbels figure with Hitler figure, comic inscription relating to subjects asking for work. Above avg. cond. $20

Postcard, "Deutsche Weihnacht" or German Christmas, Germany, WWII. By Hoffmann. VDA print depicting profile of Hitler and a lightened Christmas tree. Unused. Above avg. cond. $40

Postcard, "unsere Waffen SS" or Our Waffen SS, Germany, WWII. Waffen SS MG crew in urban fighting. MG 34 crew firing from rubble, from the EA Schwertfeger series, well marked, titled "Kampf um eine Ortschaft im Osten." Above avg. cond. $36

Postcard, Aerial Ace Hauptmann Buddecke, Imperial Germany, WWI. War Hero #433. Shown in uniform from knees up with EK, Pilot badge, Blue Max and visor cap. Avg. cond. $27

Postcard, Aerial Ace Lieut Anslinger, Imperial Germany, WWI. War Hero #565. Shown standing with Pilot badge, EK, two awards and visor cap. Avg. cond. . . $25

Postcard, Aerial Ace Lieut Bernert, Imperial Germany, WWI. With medals, Pilot badge, parade belt. Unused. Above avg. cond. $20

Postcard, Aerial Ace Lieut Bohme, Imperial Germany, WWI. Subject shown seated in dress tunic with EK1, Prussian Pilot badge. Four-ribbon bar on chest. Near mint cond. $36

Postcard, Aerial Ace Lieut Frank Seydler, Imperial Germany, WWI. Studio shot shows Seydler wearing a German-style tunic favored by the Turks with EK1, Pilot badge, two ribbons in buttonhole and Turkish medal above EK. He holds a dress sword in his left hand and wears a Turkish-style pile fur fez. Unusual also in that Seydler was not awarded the Blue Max at the time of the picture and therefore lacks that essential medal. Above avg. cond. . . . $36

Postcard, Aerial Ace Lieut Hohndorf, Imperial Germany, WWI. With Blue Max. Above avg. cond. $25

Postcard, Aerial Ace Lieut Leffers, Imperial Germany, WWI. Three-quarter standing studio pose showing Leffers in dress tunic with Blue Max, EK 1, Pilot badge and medal bar with three orders. Above avg. cond. $36

Postcard, Aerial Ace Lieut Mulzer, Imperial Germany, WWI. Waist to head profile showing dress tunic being worn with Blue Max plus EK1 and Pilot badge. Above avg. cond. $36

Postcard, Aerial Ace Lieut Pfeifer, Imperial Germany, WWI. War Hero #428. Shown in uniform from knees up with EK and visor cap. Avg. cond. $24

Postcard, Aerial Ace Lieut Schleich, Imperial Germany, WWI. Formal dress tunic with two-button front. Blue Max clearly seen as are the EK1 and Pilot badge (Bavaria). EK2 & Bav Mil Serv ribbons in 2nd buttonhole. Sword seen to lower right. Above avg. cond. $44

Postcard, Aerial Ace Lieut Wendelmuth, Imperial Germany, WWI. Photo shows him seated beside a table while holding cap in right hand. Two-medal bar with EK2 and unknown House Order. Man wears both Prussian and Turkish Pilot badges, has on an EK1 and also a 1915 Gallipoli Star. Above avg. cond. $36

Postcard, Aerial Ace Naval Lieut Christiansen, Imperial Germany, WWI. Nicely detailed with man in naval dress tunic wearing four-medal bar to include EK, Hohenzollern Order, Hamburg Service medal and EK1 on tunic with Naval Flying badge. Blue Max at neck. Above avg. cond.   . $36

Postcard, Aerial Ace Naval Oberflugmeister Fabeck, Imperial Germany, WWI. War Hero #635. Shown from waist up with Naval Pilot badge, EK, medal bar, leather belt with bayonet and visor cap. Avg. cond. $25

Postcard, Color Art Style, Boy With SMS Deutschland Cap, Imperial Germany, 1908. 1908 postcard is used. Good colors of young boy with striped coveralls and neckerchief. Above avg. cond. $40

Postcard, Color Art Style, Von Hindenburg, Imperial Germany, WWI. Color art drawing of Hindenburg. Unused. Above avg. cond. $21

Postcard, Hitler, Germany, 1943. Patriotic Hitler as leader and father of the nation. Has stamp and postmark 1943, Vienna. Above avg. cond. $40

Postcard, Hitler, Germany, 1938. Has b&w drawing of chest-up profile with overcoat and peaked hat. Unused. Above avg. cond. $28

Postcard, Naval Aerial Ace Oberlt. Christiansen, Imperial Germany, WWI. War Hero #608. Shown from waist up with Naval Pilot badge, EK, medal bar and Blue Max. Above avg. cond. $28

Postcard, WWI Bavarian Military Band, Imperial Germany, WWI. Men all wearing pillbox caps with M15 tunics having swallows nests and good detail of all band instruments. Above avg. cond. $20

Postcard, WWI Bavarian Musician in Field Tunic, Imperial Germany, WWI. Taken outdoors by barracks. Good details to visor cap, swallows nests, wrap leggings, breeches and shoes. Feldpost stamped to unit on back. Above avg. cond. $25

Postcard, WWI Bavarian NCO, Imperial Germany, WWI. Man shown wearing M15 concealed button tunic with NCO lace on collar and dress bayonet on left side with troddel. Soldier has visor cap on. Above avg. cond.   . $20

Postcard, WWI Bavarian NCO, Imperial Germany, WWI. Subject shown wearing M15 tunic with lower slash pockets and crown buttons. Subdued Garde litzen on collar with NCO lace. NCO-style visor cap shown with both rosettes. Above avg. cond. $20

Postcard, WWI Bavarian Soldiers, Imperial Germany, WWI. Two older men shown with beards. Figure on left wears a four-pocket-style tunic with concealed buttons, man on right dressed in M15 tunic with concealed buttons and lower slash pockets. Both shown wearing visor caps. Avg. cond. $20

Postcard, WWI Black African Colonial Soldier, Imperial Germany, WWI. Unused. Caption on back, has full standing black man in uniform with rifle and black with red flag. Above avg. cond. $24

Postcard, WWI German Officer, Imperial Germany, WWI. In field gray uniform. Above avg. cond. $20

Postcard, WWI German Sailor, Imperial Germany, WWI. Nice details to knot, bib and standard jumper with large chevron and flaming shell specialty patch with two small chevrons below it. Above avg. cond. $20

Postcard, WWI Landssturm Man With Wife and Daughter, Imperial Germany, WWI. Man shown wearing Bavarian pillbox cap with M15 tunic having "I. II. S" insignia in metal on turn-down collar. Above avg. cond. $20

Postcard, WWI NCO With Wife, Imperial Germany, WWI. Man shown wearing M15 tunic with crown devices on shoulderboards and stand-up collar and Brandenburg cuffs with NCO tressing. Soldier has what appears to be a Bavarian Military Service Cross ribbon in buttonhole. Dated. Above avg. cond. $20

Postcards—Other

Postcard Lot, Russian Art, Soviet Union, c1980s. Collection of modern colored photograph/postcards depicting arms, armor, jewels, etc. Exc. cond. $20

Postcard, Patriotic, Italy, WWII. Depicting Italian female victory figure with Italian soldiers advancing across battlefield. Above avg. cond. $20

Postcard, Patriotic, Japan, WWII. Colored card depicting artillery crew in jungle. Above avg. cond. $20

Postcard, Soviet Anti-German Art, Soviet Union, WWII. Color comic figure of French politician being on German chain. Above avg. cond. $47

Postcard Lot, British Military Art and Photographs, England. 200 cards, art cards, postcard/photographs of men in dress uniform, paintings of famous battles. Above avg. cond. $45

Postcard Lot, British Military Art, England, WWI. Five cards, painting of soldier leading blind comrade. Above avg. cond. $30

Postcard Lot, Russian Military Uniforms and Moscow Views, Imperial Russia, c1900. One set of Russian Military Uniforms from 1700–1800 and one set of everyday life scenes in Moscow around 1900. Above avg. cond. $20

Postcard, Patriotic, Dictator Mussolini, Italy, c1930s. Depicts portrait of subject wearing civilian clothes. Above avg. cond. $20

Postcard, Patriotic, Italy, WWII. Depicts Mussolini wearing top hat and civilian frock coat. Above avg. cond. $20

Postcard, WWI Austrian Soldiers, Austria, 1916. Chest up shot. Good detail of rank insignia and shoulder straps and two are wearing three medals each and one has a whistle lanyard. Dated on back. Above avg. cond. $30

Postcard Lot, British Military Art, England. 275 cards, from all eras, mixed lot. Above avg. cond. $64

Stereographs—U.S.

Stereograph, Viewing Card, St. Augustine, Florida, USA, c1865. Titled "St. Augustine Views" by George Pierron. Civil War-Era view of Fort De San Marcos showing the interior of the fort, Parrot Rifled Artillery Piece, and cannon balls. Avg. cond. $28

Stereograph, Viewing Cards, US Fleet, USA, c1900. 25 cards on the American Fleet. Color tinted with several on USS Maine and on the first US submarines. In original box. Avg. cond. $38

Stereograph, Viewing Cards, WWI Scenes, USA, WWI, Keystone View Co. Complete boxed set of WWI Keystone cards numbered 1–50. Come in the original "book" case. These are b&w photos of surpassingly grisly scenes in some instances - wounded, dead and the aftermath of battle. Avg. cond. $96

Stereograph, Viewing Cards, WWI Scenes, USA, WWI,

Keystone View Co. Series titled "World War Through the Stereoscope Vol 1 & 2." 105 cards. B&w photos. Box in shape of two books. Avg. cond. $240

Stereograph, Viewing Cards, WWI Scenes, USA, WWI, Keystone View Co. Boxed set of 88 cards. Come in their original box/case. Photos of all branches of the service, warfare, dead, wounded, trench conditions, men in field activity, equipment, etc. Covers all aspects of the war. Avg. cond. $176

Stereographs—Other

Stereograph, Viewer Card, Scottish Military Band, England, Army, 1900. Scottish military pipers in kilts standing near "The Great Forth Bridge." Good cond. $20

Tintypes

Tintype, Civil War Soldier, USA, Civil War Era. Small tintype of a soldier with a forage cap. In a scrimshaw bone frame. Clear image. Avg. cond. $137

Tintype, Civil War Soldier, USA, Civil War Era. In case. Civil War soldier in cavalry coat with beard. Clear image with some bends in tin. Case has some edge damage. Avg. cond. $138

Tintype, Civil War Soldier, USA, Civil War. Civil War soldier wearing a sack coat. In a case. Good image with three scratches on plate. Size: 2¾" x 3¼". Avg. cond. $110

Tintype, Federal Artilleryman, USA, Civil War Era. 1/6-plate tintype of full standing Federal artilleryman with sword. In half case. Tinted highlights. Good cond. . $201

Tintype, Indian War Era Soldiers, USA, Army, State Militia, c1870s. 3½" x 3" plate. Studio pose of two state militia EM wearing white M1872 helmets with spikes, dress uniforms and white leather belts. Both are holding muskets. Avg. cond. $115

Tintype, Indian War, Era Soldiers

Tintype, Jefferson Davis, USA, c1860, Abbot & Co., NY. A 1/9-plate tintype of Jefferson Davis. Bust view housed in brass preserver frame. Good image despite spotting. Avg. cond. $288

Tintype, c1870s, Enlisted Man

Tintype, Soldier or Cadet, USA, Army, Civil War. 1/6-plate. Studio portrait in gilt frame, part of folding frame (cover missing). Shows young man in dress uniform with kepi and four-button colored sleeve tabs. Tabs and collar buttons suggest he may be West Point cadet. Above avg. cond. $80

Tintype, Union Soldier, USA, Army, Civil War. Simulated gutta-percha-style case. Image of seated Union soldier in shell jacket. Holds musket across his chest, wearing belt with oval "US" plate, large ammo pouch and socket bayonet attached. Above avg. cond. $180

Tintype, Union Soldier, USA, Army, Civil War. Size 2½" x 2½". Seated pose of Union soldier in forage cap, civilian frock coat and vest with watch chain. Complete with case with maroon velvet lining and scrollwork decorated cover. Avg. cond. $110

Tintype, Union Soldier, USA, Army, Civil War. One-sixth plate size. Union EM posing in front of 13 star national flag wearing oversized four-button fatigue blouse, unbuttoned

to reveal gray wool issue shirt. Avg. cond. $300

Tintype, Union Soldier, USA, Civil War. Cased. 70x80mm waist up image of young man in dark shell jacket and lighter shade kepi. In brass framette with glass. In gutta percha style, hinged lid case. Above avg. cond. . . .
. . . . $125

Tintype, Union Soldier, USA, Civil War. Cased. 3" x 4" image of young, seated Union soldier. Photo backdrop of camp scene with waving US flag. In brass framette with glass. Avg. cond. $125

Tintype, Union Soldier, USA, Civil War. Shows young gentleman in Bummer cap and old sack coat. One-sixth of a plate size image. Oval framed in gilded metal 2¼" x 3" photo case with lid missing. Avg. cond. $58

Tintype, Union Soldier, USA, Civil War. Cased. 70 x 80mm full-length shot of Union soldier in frock coat and kepi. Oval "US" belt plate and Eagle cross strap plate have been gold toned. Avg. cond. $125

Civil War Tintype, Union Soldier

Tintypes, Pair, Civil War Soldiers, USA, Civil War. Uncased. One shows an officer holding a saber. Other is of a soldier in a forage cap. Sizes: 2½" x 3¼" and 2½" x 4". Avg. cond. $105

CHAPTER THIRTEEN

Military Paper

A nation at war requires massive amounts of paper to support it. Items such as books, manuals, documents, propaganda materials and other "ephemera" (ration books, personal letters, ID cards, postcards, special currency, newspapers, periodicals and so on) create a broad collecting base and appeal to different kinds of collectors. Regardless of their specialization, militaria collector often possess or need to acquire at least some form of printed material to support their collection. For example, the specialty collector may desire or need to obtain: service manuals for the restoration of equipment and vehicles; dress regulations for headgear and uniforms; drill guides and training manuals for firearms and edged weapons; or rank lists and official materials to research medals, badges, patches and insignias. Original service manuals, especially for weapons, vehicles or aircraft, often command high prices, because they represent the nearest many collectors get to owning the "real thing."

This chapter concentrates specifically on military related items. Published materials such as newspapers and periodicals are covered in Chapter Fifteen of this book. Some examples of other ephemeral objects can be found in Chapter Sixteen.

Collecting Tips

Books and documents relative to specific events and specific regiments are popular items, especially if they are related to well-known World War units. Books about Marine units tend to be more popular than Army and Naval information. Book and document prices are usually governed by the item's condition, rarity, and production quantity.

Fakes and Frauds

Manuals for service vehicles have become so popular for preservation work that companies are starting to reproduce facsimile editions. They are exactly the same in appearance or content, but have no collectible value. Research well and examine items carefully.

Care and Display

The biggest concern among collectors with regard to paper items, and the thing that typically creates the scarcity of certain paper items, is the paper's tendency to easily age and deteriorate. Because of the lack of resources during war time, often poor quality or re-circulated waste was used to produce paper items. Extra care and attention needs to be shown if the collectibles are to survive and maintain their value.

Original pieces should be carefully stored in plastic sheeting or metal boxes to impede any further deterioration. Avoid exposing items to temperature extremes, moisture and insects. Complete lamination or hermetic sealing of items may be necessary, if they are starting to break down severely. Have originals carefully copied and then preserved if you will be using the information regularly, such as you would with service or repair manuals for vehicle maintenance and restoration.

Books—U.S.

Book, "A Compendium of the War of the Rebellion," USA, 1959. Vol. I, II, III, in box. Hb, large format, dated. Vol. I contains number and organization of the Armies of the U.S. Vol. II Chronological record of the campaigns, battles, engagements, etc. 1861–1865. Vol. III regimental histories. Avg. cond. $69

Book, "A Guide to the American Battlefields in Europe," USA, 1927. American Battle Monuments Commission. 281 pages with lots of period photos of the war and fold-out maps and back cover sleeve with folded maps. Great WWI battle reference. Avg. cond. $23

Book, "Air Service Boys Flying For France," USA, 1919. By Charles Amory Beach. Story of the young heroes of the Lafayette Escadrille. Hb, medium format, 218 pages. Shows some age. Above avg. cond. $26

Book, "13th Airborne Division—Fort Bragg, North Carolina," USA, 1945. Hb, large format, 200+ pages. Dated. Editorial and pictorial history of Div, with roster. Padded leatherette cover with Div Insignia. Autograph, Lieut General Lesley J. McNair. Exc. cond. $132

Book, "82nd Airborne Division, Vietnam History," USA, Army, Vietnam War Era. 3rd Brigade, 82nd Airborne Div. Hb. Large format with illustrations. In original mailing sleeve. Avg. cond. $30

Book, "Annual Register, Or a View of the History, Politics, and Literature for the Year 1798, The," 1798. By T. Burton. British chronicle book, presents court cases, military action, promotions, etc. Avg. cond. $43

Book, "3rd Armor Division Spearhead in the West 1941–45," USA, Army, 1946. Hb. 260 pages with illustrations. Avg. cond. $65

Book, Spearhead of the West, 3rd Armored Division

Book, "Australian Army Insignia, 1903–1966," 1967. By A.N. Festberg. Reference book with illustrations. Above avg. cond. $30

Book, "12th Armored Division Hellcats," USA, 1947. Hb, large format, 90+ pages. Exc. cond. $49

Book, "1st Battalion, 406th Telegraph Battalion," USA, WWI. WWI. Hb, large format, 300+ pages of photos and roster in back, gold embossed cover of US line man and plane passes. Avg. cond. $22

Book, "73rd Bomb Wing in ATO," USA, 1945. Large format, 150 pages. Above avg. cond. $150

Book, "12th Bomber Group The Earthquakers in ETO," USA, AAF, 1948. Embossed cover, large format, 150 pages. With photos. Above avg. cond. $150

Book, The Earthquakers

Book, "487th Bomber Group, Sept. 1943–Nov. 45, in the ETO," USA, AAF, 1946. Large format, 150 pages with b&w photos. Avg. cond. $300

Book, "456th Bomber Group 1944–45 in Italy," USA, AAF, c1946. Large format, sb, 120 pages. Sqdn insignia on cover. Above avg. cond. $150

Book, "14th Bomber Wing 8th AAF in ETO," USA, 1945. Large format, 150 pages, b&w photos. Avg. cond. $244

Book, "Cadillac Motor Company History of WWI," USA, 1939. Hb, 78 pages with detailed history of the company with lots of photos of the production during the war and with roster and records of the employees that served. Avg. cond. $19

Book, "Carrier War: History of Task Force 58," USA, Navy, 1945. By Jensen. Medium format, hb, 173 pages. Avg. cond. $24

Book, "1st Cavalry Division," USA, 1947. Large format, sb, 2nd print 1947, 250 pages with photos. Avg. cond. $45

Book, "Combat Narrative 10th Infantry Regiment 1944–1945," USA, Army, 1946. Hb, medium format, 165 pgs. Avg. cond. $55

Book, "4th Division," USA, 1920. WWI. Hb, medium format, 368 pages with rosters and some photos. Has stain on bottom of pages and cover but still readable. Avg. cond. $20

Book, "32nd Division," USA, 1920. WWI. Hb, large format, 315 pages with lots of photos and roster in back. Avg. cond. $50

Book, "89th Division," USA, WWI. WWI. Hb, large, 500+ pages of photos and maps. Sound shape with flaking on binder cover. Avg. cond. $36

Book, "90th Division," USA, 1919. WWI. Hb, 259 pages with photos, fold-out maps and roster. Has one page loose in center. Avg. cond. $25

Book, "40th Division—1917/1919," USA, 1920. Hb, large format, 179 pages. Many photos, with personnel roster, and charts. Cover shows some age. Above avg. cond. $88

Book, "35th Division—Camp Robinson, Arkansas 1941," USA, Army, 1941. Medium format, sb, with large Div insignia on the cover. Photos of pre-war equipment in use, "General" Harry Truman in uniform, etc. Exc. cond. $59

Book, "28th Division Pennsylvania's Guard in WWI," USA, 1924. History of Keystone or Iron Div. Also Pennsylvania Guard and predecessor Pennsylvania Militia. Hb, large format, 558 pages, with roster and illustrations. 1924 dated. Cover shows wear and some water damage. Avg. cond. $69

Book, "88th Division in the WW of 1914–1918, The," USA, 1919. Hb, large format, 236 pages. With photos and roster. Above avg. cond. $48

Book, "Eight Stars to Victory—9th Infantry Division," USA, 1948. Hb, large format, 406 pages. Exc. cond. $59

Book, "Fifth Infantry Division in the ETO, The," USA, 1945. Hb, large format, 150+ pages. Exc. cond. ... $65

Book, "64th Fighter Wing 1942–45," USA, AAF, WWII. Hb, large format, 200 pages. With photos. Exc. cond. $111

Book, "Fighting the Flying Circus," USA, 1919. Signed copy "With every best wish to Wm Sears" signed by Captain Eddie Rickenbacker. Hb, medium format, 371 pages by commanding officer 94th Pursuit Sqdn US Air Service. Exc. cond. $150

Book, "Follow Me—2nd Marine Division in WWII," USA, USMC, 1946. Hb, large format, 293 pages. Above avg. cond. $61

Book, "Fourth Armored Division—From the Beach to

Bavaria, The," USA, 1946. Hb. By Captain Kenneth Koyen. 295 pages with line drawing illustrations and photo illustrations section. Above avg. cond. $118

Book, "History of the 77th Division," USA, 1919. Hb, large format, 225 pages. Many photos, roster and citation list. Also includes cartoons and battle songs. Color embossed design on cover. Above avg. cond. $35

Book, "History of the 77th Division, 1917–1918," USA, 1919. Hb, large format, with 228 pages of photos and rosters of the unit. Avg. cond. $33

Book, "History of the 87th Infantry Division," USA, 1946. Hb, large format, 500+ pages. Avg. cond. .. $229

Book, "History of WAC Detachment, 9th Air Force," USA, Army, WWII. Hb, 198 pages with narrative and photos. Cover has color 9th AF emblem. Personalized autograph on fly leaf. Exc. cond. $139

Book, "In Memoriam George S. Patton, Jr., General US Army," USA, 1946. Medium format, sb, 29 pages. Prepared at 3rd Army HQ Bad Tolz, Germany, March 1946, to commemorate the death of this great general. Booklet has pictorial and historical account of his great battles, other achievements. Exc. cond. $40

Book, "108th Infantry," USA, Army, 1918. WWI. Medium magazine format, sb, 150 pages of captioned photo roster of all soldiers. Tear on cover. Avg. cond. $22

Book, "45th Infantry Division," USA, 1946. Hb, large format, 200 pages. Avg. cond. $87

Book, "351st Infantry Division," USA, 1919. WWI. Hb, large format, 117 pages. Many photos. Color patch design embossed on cover. Exc. cond. $61

Book, "305th Infantry Division Second to None," USA, 1949. 1st edition. Hb, medium format, 243 pages with roster and photos. Avg. cond. $63

Book, "103rd Infantry, 43rd Infantry Division," USA, Army, 1942. Hb, large format, 107 pages. History and picture account of unit in WWII, plus roster of personnel in Camp Shelby 1942. Avg. cond. $30

Book, "304th Infantry Regiment, The," USA, Army, 1946. Hb, large format, 349 pages. Above avg. cond. $55

Book, "81st Infantry Wildcat Division in WWII, The," USA, 1948. Hb, large format, 305+ pages. Exc. cond. $111

Book, "345th Infantry Regiment—87th Infantry Division," USA, 1946. Hb, large format, 195 pages. Exc. cond. $74

Book, "4th Marine Division In WWII, The," USA, USMC, 1946. Hb, large format, 1946 dated, 225 pages. Exc. cond. $60

Book, 4th Marine
Division in WWII

Book, "Memoirs of France and the 88th Division," USA, 1920. WWI. Hb, large format, 172 pages. Many photos, charts and personnel roster. Shows some age. Above avg. cond. $30

Book, "Merrill's Marauders—Feb/May 1944," USA, Army, WWII. Medium format, sb, 117 pages. History and pictorial account of 5307th Composite Unit to reconquer Burma. Fold-out map. Annex lists casualties and decorations. American Forces in Action Series published by Historical Div of the War Dept. With "Marauders" patch, curved, yellow letters on red background, and gray edging. Approx. 3" long. Exc. cond. $315

Book, Merrill's Marauders

Book, "Michigan Volunteers of '98," USA, 1898. Hb, large format, dated, 50+ pages. A complete photographic record of Michigan's part in the Spanish-American War of 1898. Many photos and muster roll of volunteers. Patriotic design of American flag and soldier on cover. Exc. cond. $101

Book, "Military Improvisations During the Russian Campaign," USA, 1951, Department of the Army publi-

cation. Russian WWII historical reference work, standard tactical reference study. Good cond. $20

Book, "Military Science and Tactics," USA, 1890. Pocket size, sb, 665 pages, prepared for military students and profusely illustrated. Above avg. cond. $40

Book, "Mission Completed," USA, Army, 1945. 854th Aviation Engineers from Jan. 1, 1943 to Sept. 2, 1945. Dated 1945, hb, large format, 130 pages with numerous photos. Avg. cond. $59

Book, "New Testament," USA, Army, WWII. Distributed by the Pocket Testament League. Brown cover has WAAC imprint and PTL emblem. Shows slight age. Above avg. cond. $25

Book, "Pictorial Handbook of Military Transportation," USA, 1945. ETO Unit. Large format, sb, 80 pages of photos and captions. Avg. cond. $18

Book, "Pictorial History Of 27th Division, US Army, Ft. McClellan 1940–41," USA, 1941. Hb, large format, 400 pages with hundreds of photos and rosters of the pre-WWII history of unit. Avg. cond. $45

Program, "Army-Navy 25th Annual Football Game," USA, 1922. Nov. 25, 1922, Franklin Field, Philadelphia. Large format, sb, 96 pages. Many photos of football players, and advertisements. Exc. cond. $40

Book, "42nd Rainbow Infantry Division," USA, Army, WWII. Hb, annual size, 200 pages with photos. Avg. cond. $37

Book, "42nd Rainbow Infantry Division," USA, 1946. Hb, large format, 100 pages. Above avg. cond. $54

Book, 42nd Rainbow
Infantry Division

Book, "Red Army Uniforms and Insignia, 1944," 1968, Deep River Armory, publisher. Russian WWII uniform reference book, illustrated with line drawings and photographs. Good cond. $26

Book, "Russian Combat Methods of WWII," USA, Army, 1950. Russian WWII reference book, official American Army manual. Above avg. cond. $20

Book, "Saga of the USS Essex (CV-9)," USA, Navy, 1946. Hb, large format, 141+ pages. Picture history of war operations. Exc. cond. $133

Book, "Second Division American Expeditionary Forces—1917/1919, The," USA, 1919. Medium format, sb, 31 pages. Publication of General Orders, bulletins and newspaper articles will illustrate the great part the 2nd Div played in WWI. Avg. cond. $30

Book, "Sixth Infantry Division US Army," USA, Army, 1941. Hb, large format, 305 pages. Above avg. cond. $40

Book, "Soviet Partisan Movement, 1941–1944, The," Army, 1956. Russian WWII partisan history book, Department of the Army publication, illustrated with maps. By E.M. Howell. Good cond. $20

Book, "Sky Lancer 417th Bomb Group, The," USA, 1946. Hb, large format, 100+ pages. Exc. cond. . . $175

Book, "The Story Of The 91st Division," USA, 1919. Medium format, hb, 177 pages with b&w photos and maps. WWI history. Avg. cond. $48

Book, "Story of the War of 1898, The," USA, 1901. 1901. Hb, 11" x 17", 271 pages with lots of photos, war art, illustrations. Cover is loose and binder strings have broken, most page sections are intact but the 1st section pages are loose. Avg. cond. $24

Book, "Tarawa to Tokyo—1943–46," USA, Navy, 1946. Story of the USS Lexington (CV-16). Hb, large format. Above avg. cond. $85

Book, "Third Marine Division," USA, USMC, WWII. Hb, medium format, 335 pages. Avg. cond. $34

Book, "12th US Infantry 1798–1919," USA, 1919. Unit history. Hb, large format, 330 pages with some photos of the unit's history. Avg. cond. $20

Book, "USAAF Ninth Air Force," USA, c1947. Hb, large format, 20+ pages. Book consists of collection of color action paintings. All are captioned. Signed copy. Color printed patch design on cover. Avg. cond. $55

Book, "USS Boxer Far East Cruise 1956–1957," USA, 1957. Hb, large format, 260 pages. Above avg. cond. . $30

Book, "Vietnam 3rd Brigade, 82nd Airborne Division, Jan. to Dec. 1969," USA, 1970. Hb, large format, 140 pages. Above avg. cond. $38

Book, "War of the Rebellion," USA, 1899. Compilation of the official records of the Union and Confederate Armies. Series II, Vol. VIII. Washington Government Printing Office. Dated. Hb, medium format, 1059 pages. Above avg. cond. $27

Book, "West Point Furlong Book," USA, 1913. Suede leather cover embossed with logo, 111 pages with lots of photos and illustrations of the cadets, sport roster photos and other. Has some rodent damage to small area on the binder and to several of the last page edges but readable. Below avg. cond. $28

Book, "What Sammy's Doing," USA, 1917. Medium format, sb, 141 pages with hundreds of captioned photos of doughboy training in WWI. Avg. cond. $28

Book, "Rear Area Security in Russia," USA, Army, 1951. Department of the Army publication. Russian WWII historical reference work, historical study covering the Soviet second front behind the German lines. Good cond. $20

Books—Germany

Advertisement Catalog, Germany, WWII. "WKC" edged weapons. About 10" x 12½" light blue paper cover with silver and blue details. 15 pages with illustrated examples of various edged weapons. Above avg. cond. $75

Book, "Adolf Hitler," Germany, 1940. By Reichleiter Philipp Bouhlet. Hb, medium format, 93 pages. Few photos of Hitler throughout book. Blue binding shows minor separation and fading. Avg. cond. $25

Book, "Das Antlitz Des Fuhrers," Germany, 1939. By H. Hoffmann. Hb, medium format, 20 pages. Each page illustrated. with a portrait of Hitler with text starting in 1919 through 1939. Binding shows minor age separation. Avg. cond. $30

Book, "Das Marne Drama," Germany, 1926. Covers the battles from Sept. 5-8, 1914 of the Garde Corps on the right wing of the German Army. Excellent order of battle. 275 pages with 10 maps and illustrations. Above avg. cond. $20

Book, "Das War Der Krieg in Polen," Germany, 1939. Pictorial account of the Polish campaign. Hb, medium format, 111 pages, with text and 50-page photo section. 1939 dated personal note in front of book. Above avg. cond. $30

Book, "Defeat in the West," Germany, 1948. Hb, medium format, 336 pages, with a few photos. Account of campaigns on the Western Front as seen from German perspective written by the official Canadian Army historian, with great emphasis on D-Day to the surrender. Above avg. cond. $28

Book, "Der Rote Kampfflieger," Germany, 1933. The Red Baron. Medium format, hb with dust jacket, 261 pages. With rare photos of Richthofen and other WWI fighter pilots. Cover showing him in dress tunic with plane in background. Exc. cond. $40

Book, "Der Technische Krieg" 1938, Germany, 1938. Hb, medium format, by Karl Justrow, 128 pages. With text and 62 photos/illustrations of warfare. Avg. cond. . . $75

Book, "Deutsche Wehr Jahrgang 1929," Germany, 1929. Hb, large format, 1091 pages. A collection of newspapers for army and navy in book form. With photos and advertisement. Above avg. cond. $45

Book, "Deutsche Wehr Jahrgang 1931," Germany, 1931. Hb, large format, 1216 pages. Collection of newspapers loose in cover. With photos and ads. Issues 1–5 are missing. Avg. cond. $45

Book, "Deutsche Wehr Jahrgang 1932," Germany, 1932. Hb, large format, 888 pages. Collection of newspapers put in binder. Avg. cond. $45

Book, "Deutschlands Aussenpolitik 1933–1940," Germany, 1941. By Axel Freiherrn v. Freytagh. Medium format, sb, 266 pages. Publication for the army. Avg. cond. $20

Book, "Die Deutsche Armee Vor Dem Weltkriege," Germany, c1920. By Moritz Ruhl. Medium format, sb, with complete list of regiments and battalions of the Imperial Army. 12 fold-out color lithos of the uniforms of the Imperial Army from all parts of Germany. Exc. cond. . . $130

Book, "Die Deutsche Kriegsflotte," Germany, 1940. Small format, sb, 72 pages, and many photos and illustrations. Overview of German Navy. Exc. cond. $40

Book, "Die Kriegswaffen: Ein Handbuch der Waffenkunde," Imperial Germany, 1869. By August Demmin. Hb, medium format, 628 pages. With text, illustrations of pre-gunpowder weapons and armor. Ends with cannons, rifles and pistols up to 1869. Avg. cond. $250

Book, "Die Roten Teufel Find Die Holle!" Germany, 1941. Red Devils From Hell. By Starche, medium format, hb, 111 pages of German text with b&w photos. Excellent photos of the Belgian French campaign with rare shots of field police, ordnance, knocked-out French tanks and captured allied soldiers. With a heavy emphasis on the use of black colonial troops against Germans. Early war propaganda book. Above avg. cond. $26

Book, "Die Wehrmacht 1941," Germany, 1942. Hb. 319 pages with photos and stories of the different arms, navy, army and SS. Early war photo history. Avg. cond. . . $20

Book, "Die Wehrmacht Das Buch Des Krieges 1939/40," Germany, 1940. Published by the German Army. Hb, medium format, 1940, 318 pages. Filled with photos and German text. Avg. cond. $25

Book, "Division Sintzenich," Germany, 1941. Account of the French campaign 1940. Many photos and art sketches.

Signed copy by Generalmajor and Div Commandeur Sintzenich. Shows some age. Above avg. cond. $30

Book, "Grossdeutschland," Germany, 1939. Hb, large format, 357 pages and cardboard sleeve. By Hans Lerch. Covering pre-war Nazi Germany triumphs with photos of civil and military subjects. Exc. cond. $134

Book, "Hitler Abseits Vom Alltag," Germany, 1937. By Hoffmann. Hb, large format, 80+ pages, 100 picture documents of Hitler in everyday activities. Exc. cond. . $59

Book, "Hitler In Polen," Germany, 1941. By H. Hoffmann. Hb, medium format, 50 unnumbered pages of Hoffmann photographs with good details of Hitler's visit to Poland. Each photo is captioned. In front of book is a personal note dated 1941. Gray-white cloth cover. Above avg. cond. $44

Book, "Jahrbuch Der Deutschen Luftwaffe 1939," Germany, 1939. Hb, large format, 186 pages. Many photos of Goering and Hitler. Cloth cover is embossed with gold winged eagle and title. Shows some age. Avg. cond. . . .
. . . . $40

Book, "Klar Zum Gefecht!" Imperial Germany, WWI. Battle Stations! Covers the Imperial Navy in 1914/15. By Heinrich Liersemann. Medium format, 271 pages with color plates of naval battles. Covers the activities of the navy in the early days of WWI. Avg. cond. $20

Book, "Kommt Krieg In Europa?" Germany, 1934. Will War Come to Europe? Knickerbocker, medium format, 178 pages of German text. Also includes copied pages with a bio of the author. Book is hb with color dust jacket. Early book theorizing that if the plutocratic and corrupt democracies of England, France, Poland and Czechoslovakia. And Hitler, he will take by force what he should otherwise be given as rightful leader of the Germans. A tinge of the horror of the coming war emanates from this small and probably not widely read book that predicted the coming of WWII. Avg. cond. $20

Book, "Kriegslagge," Imperial Germany, 1900. (The War Flag) 1900. 160 pages. with 64 photos and illustrations of naval life in the Imperial Navy. Fine rare pictures of deckboard life, sailor uniforms and equipment. Fancy stiff cover with sailor hoisting the famous battle flag. Avg. cond. $27

Book, "Kriegstagebuch U202 Spiegel," Germany, 1916. War history of the U-Boat 202. Medium/small format, sb, 133 pages. German text. Above avg. cond. $36

Book, "Mein Kampf," Germany, 1934. By Hitler. Hb, small format, 781 pages. With Hitler's portrait in front. Blue cloth cover with golden party eagle embossed. Exc. cond. $100

Book, "Mein Kampf," Germany, 1935. By Hitler. Hb, medium format, 780 pages. With photo of Hitler in front. Above avg. cond. $40

Book, "Mein Kampf," Boxed Edition, Germany, 1937. Leather binder with gold embossed title, 780 pages, all German text and medium size. Box shows tearing and wear to ends. Avg. cond. $58

Book, "Rang-liste Der Koniglich Preussischen Armee," Imperial Germany, 1907. Hb, medium format, 1407 pgs. Rank list of the Imperial Prussian Army. Red cover with gold embossing. Pages have a multi-colored peacock design around edges. Above avg. cond. $187

Book, "Reichstagung In Nuernberg 1937," Germany, 1937. Hb, large format, 406 pages. With German text. By Hanns Kerrl. Many photos of Hitler, parades and other events at the rally. High quality edition. Blue cover shows slight wear. Above avg. cond. $237

Book, "Schiessvorschrift Fur Die Feartillerie," Imperial Germany, 1911. Field exercises of the field artillery. Berlin published. Stiff stock covers. 80 pages with fold-out maps, tables, etc. Avg. cond. $20

Book, "SS Kavallerie Im Osten," Germany, WWII. SS Cavalry in the East. Published only for the unit. This volume is serial number 6 Hb, large format, 191 pages with photos and history of the SS in Russian. Has large photo section with great uniform references and candid photos of the Waffen SS in action. Above avg. cond. $675

Book, "Vollgross!" Germany, 1939. Hearty Greetings. Medium format, hb, 235 pages with b&w photos of military activity, aerial photos, planes, hangers, etc. Subtitled "The Life of an Airman." Covers early training, romanticism of the Luftwaffe, spirit de corps, etc. Early propaganda book. Avg. cond. $20

Book, "Weyer's Taschenbuch Der Kriegsflotten 1911," Imperial Germany, 1911. Pocket book on the Military Navy. 536 pages with pics and data on military ships of Japan, Germany, USA, England, etc. Avg. cond. $20

Book, "Weyer's Taschenbuch Der Kriegsflotten 1941–42," Germany, 1941. Small format, hb, 486 pgs with b&w photos of various countries' ships and charts of specs for each type. Minor wear, many hand-written notes on various ships. Below avg. cond. $45

Book, 1900 Prussian-Wurttemberg Army Rank List For All Officers, Imperial Germany, 1900. Deluxe dark red stiff covers with gold embossed Iron Cross and Imperial eagle. Covers all active and reserve officers of both armies with service entry dates, awards, commands, etc. Exc. cond. $139

Book, German Army Rank List 1896, Imperial Germany, 1896. Medium format, hb cardboard, 1299 pages. Superb listing of all active and reserve officers and all corps and units of the Imperial German army at the turn of the century. Minor wear to spine. The standard work for looking up names of officers who appear on gift swords, presentation goblets, statues. Lists all medals, service patents and transfers. Avg. cond. $124

Book, "Lachen unterm Stahlhelm," Imperial Germany, 1915. Jokes and humorous stories designed for troops during off-duty hours. Good cond. $20

Booklet, "WWI Deutsche Armee Militar-album," Imperial Germany, WWI. By Moritz Ruhl. 16 fold-out color lithos of the field gray uniforms of the Imperial Army from all parts of Germany. Period reference. Avg. cond. $135

Booklet, Die Bundeswehr, West Germany, Army, 1970s. German army recruiting book, color photographic illustrations, complete with guide to flags and rank insignia. Good cond. $20

Catalog, "Assmann & Sohns" Insignia, Medals and Buckles, Germany, c1930s. Hb. Large format. 89 pages filled with b&w photos and illustrations of items produced. Much Nazi-related insignia as well as Weimar and some Imperial items. Excellent period reference. Above avg. cond. $40

Books—Other

Book, Formation Badges of World War II, England. By H. Cole. Illustrated British WWII insignia reference from British, Commonwealth, and Empire units, with color plates. Exc. cond. $23

Book, I Gia Di Capitani Italiani, Italy, 1930s, F. Grazioli. Italian WWII Fascist history. Illustrated. Good cond. $65

Book, Kaiser Huldigungs Festzug Wien-Juni 1908, Austria. Austrian Imperial-era patriotic booklet, discusses Kaiser's patriotic festival, with illustrations. Above avg. cond. $140

Book, Now It Can Be Told, England, 1920. By Sir Phillip Gibbs. WWI reminiscences. Above avg. cond. $25

Book, Officers Who Died in the Great War 1914–1919, England, 1979. Listing British officers who died in WWI. Above avg. cond. $35

Book, The Nations at War, England, 1917. British WWI history to 1916, illustrated, some color, lacking covers and ending pages. Good cond. $20

Documents—U.S.

Bond, $1000 Confederate States of America, USA, 1863. 14" x 14" bond dated 1863 with coupons on bottom attached for payment of interest at 8%. Bond is signed and recorded. One coupon has been removed. Above avg. cond. $50

Confederate Bond

Booklet, WWI Soldiers Individual Pay Record and Envelope, USA, WWI. Brown small envelope with typed name and number of HQ Co. 19th FA and small black booklet, dated from 1917 to 1919 with some entries. Avg. cond. $23

Broadside, Deserters, USA, 1863. Approx. 34½"x 18¾" size. Headed "List of Men Drafted in the 14th Congressional District of Pennsylvania, who have failed to report, and are Deserters." Printed in Harrisburg in Nov. 1863. Avg. cond. $690

Broadside, Military General Orders, USA, Army, c1861. Approx. 12" x 6½" size. Titled "General Order, No. 1. Head-Quarters, Camp Godard, June 1, 1861." Small broadside on green stock. Early Civil War period. Lists general rules of military discipline. Printed in Ohio c1861. Avg. cond. $258

Broadside, Recruiting, USA, Army, Civil War. Approx. 27" x 21½" size. Titled "23D P.V. 23D P.V. Bounty! Bounty! Regiment Penn'a Volunteers, late Burney's Zouaves." Recruiting broadside printed in Philadelphia in 1862. A few small holes. Mounted. Above avg. cond. $632

Document, Appointment For Soldier, USA, Army, 1863. 10" x 12" document. Soldier was appointed as third cor-

poral in Co. D 15th Rgt in Ohio Militia. Avg. cond. $60

Document, Artillery Service, USA, Army, Vietnam War Era. 9½" x 11½" color printed document for 77th Artillery, 1st Cavalry Div. In vinyl folder with 1st Cav logo on front. Above avg. cond. $45

Document, Award of Combat Infantryman Badge, USA, Army, WWII. 8" x 10" official document copy issued to a PFC in the 255th Inf. Dated 1945. Includes Combat Inf badge. 1" x 3" in size, with rifle on blue background with oak leaves. Avg. cond. $38

Document, Capture Certificate, USA, Army, WWII. Has been filled out for Luger pistol and cane sword. On official ETO form. Avg. cond. $19

Document, Honorable Discharge, USA, Army, 1865. 8¾" x 11" document discharges sergeant from 2nd Regt US. Document is handwritten with several signatures. Reverse side has an official stamp. Below avg. cond. $45

Document, Honorable Discharge, USA, Army, 1899. 9" x 11". After Spanish American War service. Honorable discharge document from 7th Regt of Cavalry in 1899. Has signature of a captain. Reverse side of document contains his military record. Avg. cond. $35

Document, NCO Commission, USA, Army, Civil War. Made out to soldier in First Wisconsin Cavalry, March 15, 1862 in Kenosha, WI. Signed by commanding officer and adjutant. Above avg. cond. $100

Document, NCO Commission, USA, Army, Civil War. For soldier in the 114th Regt Illinois Inf Vols promoting him to sergeant on Sept. 18, 1862 at Camp Butler. Signed by Col and adjutant. Folded. Avg. cond. $50

Document, Pay Voucher Record, USA, Army, Civil War. To Capt. C.J. Baily 17th Maine Inf. Dated Feb 6, 1864. Large fold-out with many signatures of people he mustered into service and ranks. Above avg. cond. $75

Document, Soldier Killed in Action, USA, Army, WWI. 16" x 20" with b&w graphics of Columbia knighting a doughboy and named to a Pvt in the 139th Inf Div. Avg. cond. $37

ID Card, Officer, USA, Army, WWII. Early tri-fold pattern issued by the War Department. Has ID "mug shot" photo in the center, fingerprints on side and data on the other. Serial number is also printed on the outside of the card. Issued to a 2nd Lieut in the Signal Corps, November 20, 1942. Has official embossed seal over lapping photo. Avg. cond. $20

Memoriam, Soldier, USA, Army, WWI. 10½" X 14½". WWI document with Pershing's signature and handwritten entries on deceased. Memorializes death of soldier in heroic terms on formal army document. Wood frame. Avg. cond. $135

Sheet Music, "Der Fuehrer's Face," USA, 1942. From Walt Disney's motion picture Donald Duck in Nutzi Land. Three pages. Large format. Above avg. cond. $25

Sheet Music, "Motor Transport Corps," USA, Army, WWI. Cover has graphic of army trucks in convoy. March for the piano. Avg. cond. $11

Documents—Germany

Broadside, Danger of Typhus in District Radom, Germany, 1942. 12" x 18" document prohibiting solicitations. All law breakers will be punished. For Occupied Poland. In German and Polish. With official stamp dated 1942. Exc. cond. $68

Broadside, SS From Occupied Poland, Germany, SS, 1942. 26" x 38". Light red poster with German and Polish text. Poster issued by order of the SS and Highest Police Fuhrer, Rosener at Chilli, Poland, 23 June 1942. Text announces the mass execution of Communist-Jewish partisans who are claimed to have murdered German and pro-German persons. Long list of dead ranging from accountants to insurance salesmen to day laborers, farmers. Also list of six women executed for murdering a German mother in front of her children. Old creases from storage but not detractive. In modern glassless frame for display. Above avg. cond. $538

Document Grouping, SS, Germany, SS, WWII. One-page orange SS Stammkarte with all the information and three SS units. 8" x 10" document with the same information Wehrpass with some water damage to photo pages and loose cover. Has the SS units listed and other Nazi ink stamps. Avg. cond. $171

Document Grouping, SS, Germany, Waffen SS, WWII. One-page orange SS Stammkarte with all the information. Sept. 1944 dated, Waffen SS ink stamped Wehrpass with some water damage to photo pages and loose cover. Has the SS mountain troops Unit number 6 listed and other SS vol unit. Avg. cond. $162

Document, Army Service, Germany, Army, 1936. 13" x 19" Dated 1936 and has standard photos of military service. Rolled and named to a man in an Inf reserve unit 1935–36. Filled in and Nazi eagle ink stamped. Surrounded by b&w photos of the army in all phrases of training. Has vehicles, dogs, artillery, etc. Avg. cond. $61

Document, Award, Hindenburg Cross For Combatant, Germany, Army, 1934. Issued in 1934 to soldier for WWI service. Complete with official rubber stamp seal plus 1918 document written in the field by an officer on his

taking part in offensive operations from 15 to 19 July 1918 of a especially heroic nature. Avg. cond. $27

Document, Iron Cross 1914 1st Class Award, Imperial Germany, Army, 1915. 5" x 8" document dated 13 June, 1915 with official Imperial stamp and signature. Folded. Avg. cond. $39

Document, Iron Cross 1914 2nd Class Award, Imperial Germany, Army, 1917. 6½" x 8" printed paper with typed "Musk. Weiss, Phil. 3. Kompagnie Infanterie- Regiment Nr. 87" and issued 28.5.1917. Folded. Above avg. cond. $61

Document, Iron Cross 1914 2nd Class Award, Imperial Germany, Army, 1915. 1915 dated. 10½" x 15½" b&w printed document with EK and kneeling soldier in bordered center and awarded by his Majestat to Unteroffizier in Inf Regt, Markgraf Karl (7.Brandenburg) Nr. 60 with inked signature and faint ink stamp. Avg. cond. $45

Document, Iron Cross 1914 2nd Class Award, Imperial Germany, Army, 1918. 6½" x 8¼" printed ornate paper with hand-inked name and dated 24.7.1918. Folded. Avg. cond. $95

Document, Leave Pass For a Leib Grenadier, Imperial Germany, Army, Grenadier, 1816. 7" x 9" document with emblem and hand-written info. Regiment Garde-Grenadier dated 12 January 1816 and signed by his captain. Valid to 17 Marz 1817. Gives age and description of the Grenadier for identification. Presumably for him to go home and tend the crops, family matters etc. Europe was still very unsettled and the battle of Waterloo occurred only seven months earlier in June 1815. Above avg. cond. $101

Document, Memorial, Zeppelin Death, Imperial Germany, Army, WWI. 14" x 11". Printed litho death memorial showing figure of Christ at sea holding out his hands above sinking cruiser. Bottom design shows furled Imperial battle flag with inscription, "Zum Gedachtnis des Signal-Maaten Julius Petitjean. Marine-Luftschiff R34. Er starb fur das Vaterland." With facsimile Wilhelm signature. Top of document shows about 1" trimmed off to fit in old period frame that comes with it. The R-34 went down with all hands during a bombing run against England. Above avg. cond. $150

Document, Russian Front Medal Award, Germany, Army, 1942. Named and dated 1942. Has official Army eagle ink stamp. Above avg. cond. $58

Document, Wound Badge 1914, Black, Imperial Germany, Army, 1918. To telegraph operator in 6. Infanterie-Division, Koeniglich Preussen. Nov. 1918 dated. Avg. cond. $35

Document, Russian Front Medal Award

ID Booklet, "Ausweiss," Germany, WWII. ID booklet issued to a Polish worker in 1939. It certifies owner to be admitted at a certain construction site. Photo ID on oil cloth. Avg. cond. $20

ID Booklet, "Deutsches Reich Reisepass," Germany, 1937. Issued to photo ID owner in 1937 for travel in Germany and abroad. With official stamps and signatures. Avg. cond. $30

ID Booklet, "Heer Wehrpass," Germany, Army, WWII. Owner was inducted into service in 1940 and served in Panzer Regt. Many entries reveal his training and assignments. Last entry shows he was killed in Russia in 1943. Has photo ID. Above avg. cond. $50

ID Booklet, "Heer Wehrpass," Germany, Army, WWII. Owner was born in 1874 and served in WWI and WWII. He had several promotions and became an officer in the army. His ID photos show a middle-aged man in civilian clothes. Avg. cond. $30

ID Booklet, "Luftwaffe Wehrpass," Germany, Luftwaffe, WWII. 2nd issue. 1944 issue shows youth in civilian dress. With 1936 volunteer service through 1944 listing various flak assignments and ends with 1945 "Luftkriegsschule 8." Weapons training included 2 cm and 3,7cm flak guns and awarded three medals including EK 2nd. Above avg. cond. $160

ID Booklet, "Militaer-pass," Imperial Germany, Army, c1865. 3½" x 5½" ID booklet to soldier with many entries, where he served and when. All done in handwriting very neatly. Attached in back is a permit for leave from 3rd Com des Koniglichen Landwehr Bataillons dated 1867. 8½" x 13" in size. With official stamp and signature. Avg. cond. $20

ID Booklet, "Soldbuch," Germany, Army, WWII. Cover shows most age, good photo of youth in "GD" uniform with large collar tabs. Lots of hospital marks and awarded black wound badge, Inf silver badge, EK 2nd and silver wound in 1943. Above avg. cond. $163

ID Booklet, "Soldbuch," Germany, Army, WWII. Issued 1940 to named soldier as a driver. Various entries up to 1944, hospitalized for grenade injuries and three awards,

Russian front medal, KVK 2nd with swords and Black Wound badge. Shows use and photo as army EM with rank changes. Above avg. cond. $121

ID Booklet, "Soldbuch," Germany, Army, WWII. Photo shows man in wrap-around Panzer tunic with skull collar tabs. Entries show he served with the 367th (mot.) Inf Regt and survived the war. Additional sheet added to front with signature attesting to fact that the owner read and agreed with all entries. Signed on 6 July 1945 and counterstamped with de-Nazified eagle stamp. Man won the 2nd class War Service medal with swords in 1944. Avg. cond. $159

ID Booklet, "Soldbuch," Germany, Army, WWII. Belonging to Obergefreiten in 2.Vet. Ers Abt 8. Records show clothing allowance, his weapons, his immunization. He was wounded on the Eastern Front and was in several field hospitals. Last hospital entry was Feb. 1945. Also many entries on his leaves during his many years of active duty. Shows some wear. Avg. cond. $65

ID Booklet, "SS Soldbuch," Germany, Waffen SS, WWII. Issued to soldier who served with the 4 (SS) Waffen Gren. Regt. of the SS 34 (Lettische 5) from 1943–44. Book notes he was awarded the War Service Cross with swords in 1944. Many stamps and notes on service career. Covers show wear from being used but pages intact. Avg. cond. $147

ID Booklet, "SS Wehrpass," Germany, Waffen SS, WWII. Issued with photo in civilian dress. Nine army units from 1940 through 1944 and ends with 1944 Unit 9.SS Totenkopf Wachbatallion Sachsenhausen. Many combat listings and received Russian Front medal. Above avg. cond. $131

ID Booklet, "SS Wehrpass," Germany, Waffen SS, WWII. 1939 issued with photo of soldier in civilian. 1944 inducted 18./SS-Flak A.u.e.Rgt. and ends with 1945 unit. Few entries. Avg. cond. $76

ID Booklet, "Wehrpass," Germany, Army, WWII. 1937 issue with photo of man in suit. Shows WWI service and EK 2nd class. 1939–1941 military desk service and discharged in 1941. Above avg. cond. $70

ID Booklet, "Wehrpass," Germany, Army, WWII. Man born 1913, inducted into service 1939. Served in 7. Erg. Batterie Artilleri Regiment 48 Gustrow I. M. Rank 1940 Gegreiter, 1941 Obergefreiter, 1944 Stabsgefreiter. Record of battles fought in 1941 on the way to Moscow. Received East medal 1944. 1944 record of battles in Italy. Very detailed records. Good cond. $40

ID Booklet, "Wehrpass," Germany, Army, WWII. Issued to man in 1936, with photo in civilian clothing. His induction record indicates that he was unfit for military service in 1936 and 1937. But in 1942 he was drafted. No further entries. Cover shows some age. Avg. cond. $30

Leaflet, Propaganda, Germany, WWII. Suggests postwar and post-victory over Germany will not get Americans sent home. Implies war will continue indefinitely in Pacific. Taken out of context from Stars and Stripes. Avg. cond. $26

Leaflet, Propaganda, Germany, WWII. Leaflet suggesting Americans are dying while draft dodgers are running everything their way in the states. Graphic. Avg. cond. ..
.... $36

Leaflet, Propaganda, Germany, 1944. "How Long Has It Been Since You Had a Good Night's Sleep?" 5" x 8" with red graphic of beautiful woman in a very sexy nightgown asleep. Other side is ten lines on how it would be not to sleep in the woods on pine needles, and other good things you could do in bed. Has been folded in center and a small hole on fold. Dropped on Allied troops fighting their way across France and Belgium in 1944. Avg. cond. $38

Map, "Grossdeutsches Reich," Imperial Germany, WWI. Color printed detail map of Germany showing all cities. Folded. Above avg. cond. $25

Map, Military Topography, Annaberg Area, Imperial Germany, Army, WWI. 19" x 19" gray fabric backed paper and folded, color graphics and very detailed. Avg. cond. .
.... $36

Map, Military Topography, Konigslein Area, Imperial Germany, Army, 1907. 14" x 15" gray fabric backed paper and folded, color graphics and very detailed. Has complete legend at base and dated with several embossed stamps at base. Avg. cond. $36

Personnel File, Army, Germany, Army, WWII. 6" x 8" file booklet filled in with information. Also with medical file booklet and 11 other added pieces of separate documents and papers on man, has civilian photo ID size, and lots of Nazi army ink stamps and entries. Avg. cond. $77

Personnel File, Luftwaffe Lieut, Germany, Luftwaffe, WWII. 16 pages on official forms with ink stamps and original signatures. 1943–45 dated. All studies of his character, military performance with recommendations for good service and promotions. Man won both the War Service Cross, 2nd class with swords and the EK, 2nd class. Served with the Tel.-Baukp. (motor) from Jan 1, 1942. Avg. cond. $45

Service Document, SS Death, Germany, Waffen SS, 1944. 8¼" x 11¾" with gold eagle embossed white stock with black "Getreu seinem etc." and hand inked "SS Sturmmann Eberhard Kling 9./SS-Pz.Gren.Rgt.7 etc."

Died 2.7.1944, ink signature and eagle stamp of "SS-Pol.Pz.Gren. Rgt.7 9.Kompanie." Avg. cond. $76

Service Document, SS Marriage, Germany, SS, WWII. 5¾" x 8¼"-size document granting permission to marry to SS officer. Large Nazi stamp and ink signature. Included is a postcard-size photo of a young woman seated by table reading a book. Exc. cond. $145

Sheet Music, Military, Imperial Germany, Army, 1900. 10" x 13". Color cover litho of red plumed bandsmen marching in Berlin with a bearded Kapelmeister at the fore. Four music selections inside for piano and violin. Avg. cond. $20

Sheet Music, SA March Music, Germany, Army, 1941. Dated May 1941. Complete musical score for wartime patriotic song. Cover reads "Die SA" and has sport badge illustration on it. Avg. cond. $40

SA March Sheet Music

Sign, Do Not Tamper With Air Defense Equipment, Germany, WWII. 10" x 15". Issued at Salzburg. Red border, tan field. Large black lettering reads "Air Defense Equipment. Do not tamper with or disturb. Any unauthorized activity will be treated as sabotage subject to severest penalties." No rips or tears. Above avg. cond. ... $40

Documents—Other

ID Booklet, Soviet Post-Graduate Identification, Soviet Union, 1946. Named to original owner, with subject's photograph and burgundy cover. Above avg. cond. $69

Broadside, Napoleonic Era, England, Army, 1803. 12" x 7" document. Broadside dated 1803 calling for volunteers to join the army to fight Napoleon or "an Usurper, a Corsican by birth" as he is referred to in the document. Has a few stains. Above avg. cond. $546

Broadside, Recruiting, France, Army, 1814. 21" x 17" size. Issued by Baron de Talleyrand on May 15, 1814. Issued in Orleans. Shows folds, stains and tears. Avg. cond. $345

Broadside, Recruiting, France, Army, 1811. 20½"x 16"

size. Issued by Count De Gavre and dated Nov. 29, 1811. Announces the formation of the "Regiment Des Flanqueurs De La Garde Imperiale." Show folds and light stains. Avg. cond. $547

Commission, Aide-De-Camp, France, Army, 1806. Size 15" x 10". Dated Sept. 20, 1806. Appoints M. Rebillot, "Chef d' Escardron" of the 8th Hussars, to the position of aide-de-camp on the staff of Marshal Kellermann. Signed by Dejean for the Ministry of War. With folds and minor stains. Above avg. cond. $317

Document, Austrian Award 1812, Austria, Army, c1815. 15½" x 21½" hand inked on parchment, with three signatures underneath and wax seal in wood disk, missing lid. Folded. Above avg. cond. $181

Document, Austrian Award 1853, With Imperial Seal, Austria, Army, 1853. 17" x 25" parchment with inked "MI Elnoeke, Dekana etc." named to soldier with much script writing and four signatures with 1853 dates. Wax seal attached. Exc. cond. $100

Document, Military Discharge, France, Army, 1798. Size 9½" x 12". Dated "10 Fructidor L'An 6" (Dec. 10, 1798). For the 13th Demi-Brigade, 12th Div of the "Armee de Angleterre" and issued in La Rochelle. Shows light stains. Above avg. cond. $345

French Army Discharge, December 10, 1798

French Military Dispatch,
October 24, 1802

Document, Military Dispatch, France, Army, 1802. Dated "24 Messidor An 10" (Oct. 24,1802). From Gen. Murat to the Minister of War. Written and signed by the general from Cisalpine (Gaul Region). Above avg. cond. . . $690

Pamphlet, British Victory, England, Army, 1809. 13" x 8" document. Announces Wellington's victory over the French at Talvera. Some minor stains and folds. Above avg. cond. $432

**British Victory Pamphlet,
Dated 1809**

Royal Proclamation, George III, England, 1803. 15" x 10" size. Four-page document detailing Napoleon's invasion of Malta and the recall of the English ambassador to France. Light stains and center fold. Avg. cond. . . . $173

Letters—U.S.

Letter, Civil War EM, USA, Army, Civil War. From soldier of 14th Regt, New Hampshire Volunteers. Dated Nov. 1862. Has letterhead and envelope named to unit. Four pages and tells father of returning from picket duty and finding tent burned to ground and loss of personal items including an armor vest which cost $8, and tells of his girlfriend. Avg. cond. $45

Letter, Civil War, USA, Army, Confederate, 1862. Approx. size 9" x 12" folded into four-page letter. From Lieut in Co. B, 3rd North Carolina Regt. Dated July 4, 1862. Describes fighting near Richmond and recent involvement of his regiment in those battles. Above avg. cond. $489

Letter, Civil War, USA, Army, 1864. 5" x 7"-size lined paper. Dated June 5, 1864. From soldier in 12th Regt, Massachusetts Volunteers, to his wife. Discusses ongoing fighting. Includes envelope addressed to wife in Natick, Massachusetts. Posted with 3-cent stamp. Avg. cond. $115

Letter, Civil War, USA, Army, 1865. Folded 8" x 9½" from the HQ of the 16th Ohio Battery at New Orleans. Dated March 23, 1865 giving veteran status to 2d Lieut.

All printed and has embossed building header of stationery with US eagle watermarked paper. Has a received ink stamp and two signatures. Avg. cond. $21

Letter, Civil War, USA, Army, 1864. Folded 8" x 12" from the HQ of the 16th Ohio Battery at New Orleans Aug. 3, 1864 to Washington with information about stores lost or destroyed in the field for the 3rd quarter of 1863. Signed by commanding captain and all hand written. Avg. cond. $21

Letters—Germany

Letter, German Soldier Regarding Iron Cross, Imperial Germany, Army, 1918. 6" x 8" lined notebook paper with typed message from the soldier's battalion commander. Addressed to a corporal where he was staying in Berlin and is dated 8 June 1918. Letter simply states that the sender has the honor of posting the Iron Cross 2nd class to him which he was awarded on 26 May 1918 and trusts that he will receive it soon. Writer notes that he is sending the EK and its award document under separate cover. Avg. cond. $20

Manuals—U.S.

Flight Manual Set, B-24D, USA, AAF, WWII. Set of seven hb Consolidated Vultee logoed manuals covering complete flight operations for aircraft. Standard size with text, photos and diagrams. Each volume covers different area of flight regime, e.g., power plants, fuel systems, hydraulics, radio maintenance, etc. Two related documents and a pilot flight training test are also included. In a company-provided pilot's briefcase in brown leather with double carry strap and brass latch. Exc. cond. $355

Manual, "Army Model UH-1D/H Helicopters," USA, Army, 1971. For Bell Huey Helicopters. Apparently covers D through H Models. TM 55-1520–210-20. issued by Dept of the Army, 1971, sb, medium format, 300+ pages. Above avg. cond. $32

Manual, "B-25C/D Flight Manual," USA, AAF, WWII. In original loose-leaf binder, 8" x 7". Produced by North American Aviation and distributed by AAF. 326 pages separated into flight operations sections. With b&w photos, diagrams and text. Above avg. cond. $161

Manual, "B-29 Gunner's Information File," USA, AAF, WWII. Small format, sb, red leatherette with two snaps for closure, spiral bound, 30 pages. Duties and responsibilities of B-29 Gunner. Above avg. cond. $35

Manual, "B-36 Gunnery," USA, USAF, 1950. Hb, 165 pages text, photos and diagrams. Strategic Air Command marked. Avg. cond. $45

Manual, B36 Gunnery

Manual, "Blue Book of Coastal Vessels South Vietnam," USA, Navy, 1967. Hb. Medium format. 556 pages with illus and data. Avg. cond. $87

Manual, "Engine Change Manual Boeing B-29," USA, AAF, 1944. By Boeing Aircraft. Heavy snap-shut vinyl cover, medium format, 326 pages and with b&w illus. Avg. cond. $35

Manual, "F-102A USAF Series Aircraft To 1f-102a-1," USA, Air Force, 1960. 1960 dated. In binder. For first model of Convair Delta Dagger jet fighter interceptor. Above avg. cond. $59

Manual, "Flight Manual B-24D Airplane," USA, AAF, 1942. By Consolidated Aircraft Corp. Hb, large format, dated 1942, 180+ pages. With photos, illus and charts. Exc. cond. $50

Manual, "Flight Manual Basic-USAF Series C-130b, C-130e, C-130h Aircraft," USA, USAF, 1986. Hb. Large format. Avg. cond. $34

Manual, "Flight Operating Instructions USAF F-89C Aircraft," USA, USAF, 1951. For Northrop F-89C Scorpion all-weather fighter. Large format, sb, for three-ring binder, 157 pages. Exc. cond. $90

Manual, "FM 21-150, Unarmed Defense For The American Soldier June 30, 1942," USA, Army, 1942. Small format, sb, 315 pages, by War Dept with illus. Avg. cond. $20

Manual, "French-English Military Technical Dictionary," USA, Army, 1917. US Government Printing Office. Hb, medium format, 581 pages with WWI supplement on the latest French terms. Avg. cond. $12

Manual, "German Infantry Weapons," USA, Army, 1943. US Army Intelligence. Medium format, sb, 190 pages with b&w illus and photos on the German Army small weapons. Good period reference. Avg. cond. $25

Manual, "Get Tough," USA, Various, 1942. How to win in hand-to-hand fighting as taught to the British commandos and US Armed Forces. Medium format, sb, dated 1942. 120 pages with illus. Avg. cond. $26

Manual, "Handbook For Combat Air Intelligence Officers," USA, AAF, 1944. By AAF Air Intelligence School, Harrisburg, PA. Dated Jan. 1944. Hb. Large format, 159 pages. Avg. cond. $93

Manual, "Maintenance Manual B-17 Bomber," USA, AAF, WWII. Large format, sb, For three-ring binder. 481 pages. Marked T.O. No. 01-20ef-2. Exc. cond. . . . $177

Manual, "Maintenance Manual B-29 Airplane," USA, AAF, WWII. Large format, sb, for three-ring binder, 600+ pages. T.O. No. 01-20EJ-2. Exc. cond. $196

Manual, "Military Intelligence ID of US Government Aircraft," USA, Various, 1942. 151 pages with hundreds of photos and profiles of all US planes at the start of the war, sb. Dated Feb. 21, 1942. Small format. Avg. cond. $12

Manual, "Recognition-Pictorial Manual," USA, AAF, Navy, WWII. Contains silhouettes and description of US Army, US Navy, British, German, Japanese, Italy, Soviet and other aircraft. String bound, sb, issued by War Dept and Navy. Above avg. cond. $55

Manual, "Revised US Army Regulations 1861," USA, Army, 1861. Hb, medium format, 558 pages with illus, charts and tables. Shows age. Avg. cond. $135

Manual, "The German Rifle Company For Study and Translation," USA, Army, 1942. 1942 US Army. Medium format, sb, 376 pages with exact reprint of the German Army manual including photos and illus. Has English aids in back for help in translation. Avg. cond. $34

Manual, "Thompson Submachine Gun, Cal .45 M1928a1," USA, Army, 1941. 80 pages, sb, with photos and illus. Avg. cond. $30

Manual, "United States Rifle Cal .30, Model of 1917," USA, Army, 1918. For US Model 1917 Enfield rifle. Medium format, sb, 78 pages with fold-outs and illus. Avg. cond. $21

Manual, "US Navy Uniform," USA, Navy, 1927. Hb, medium format, 1927, 60 pages. Photos and illus. Avg. cond. $53

Manual, Axis Submarines, USA, Navy, 1942. By US Naval Intelligence. Medium format, sb, dated 1942. With 50 pages of text, illus, profiles and photos. Excellent reference on German and Italian classes of submarines. Facts on weapons and diving specs. Above avg. cond. $37

Manual, Erection and Maintenance Instructions for

AT-6C/SNJ-4 Aircraft, USA, AAF, Navy, 1942. For Harvard basic training aircraft. Cover AAF and Navy versions. Loose-leaf manual for binder. Avg. cond. $52

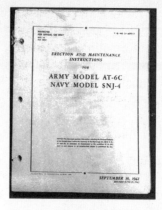

Manual, Erection and Maintenance Instructions

Manual, M1941.30 cal Johnson Light Machine Gun, USA, USMC, WWII. Medium format, sb, first horizontal feed model, 88 pages. With fold-out drawing of Johnson Light Machine Gun. Really an automatic rifle, it was originally adopted by the USMC to replace the BAR. Used on a limited basis, it was found to be easily damaged under combat conditions. Above avg. cond. $72

Manual, M50 and M55, .45 cal Reising Submachine Gun, USA, USMC, 1942. Small format, sb, 47 pages with illus and photos on assembly. This unsuccessful weapon was adopted by the USMC in 1940. Found to be prone to jamming and accidental firing, it saw little wartime service and production was stopped in 1942. Avg. cond. $27

Manual, Submarine Safety Respiration and Rescue Devices, USA, Navy, 1938. Issued by Navy Dept 1938, sb, 135 pages. Avg. cond. $32

Manuals—Germany

Manual, "Anhang Zum Exerzier-Reglement Fur Die Feldartillerie," Imperial Germany, 1913. Official Field Artillery manual. Small format, hb, 1913, 250 pages with b&w graphics of equipment and field-related articles. Interesting coverage of the topic immediately prior to the outbreak of war. Exc. cond. $45

Manual, "Ausbildungsvorschrift Fur Die Artillerie 1939," Germany, Army, 1939. Training manual for the artillery, 1939. Medium format, sb, 151 pages with photos and illus on small arms use. Avg. cond. $85

Manual, "Ausbildungsvorschrift Fur Die Infanterie," Germany, 1941. Training manual for the Inf. Small format, sb, dated 1941, 253 pages with photos and illus. Blue cover has small grease stain. Avg. cond. $28

Manual, "Ausbuldungsvorschrift Fur Die Infanterie 1942," Germany, Army, 1942. Training manual for the Inf,

1942. Medium format, sb, 255 pgs with photos and charts. Avg. cond. $28

Manual, "der Rekrut 1935," Germany, Army, 1935. The Recruit. Small format, sb, 162 pages. Has color plates showing uniforms and insignia. With b&w photos and drawings. Has army eagle on cover. Above avg. cond. $35

Manual, "die Schutzenkompanie," Germany, Army, 1939. By Ludwig Queckborner. Hb, medium format, dated 1939, 375 pages. Many photos and illus of the German rifle company for the Military Intelligence Service Information Bulletin No. 15. Marked for study and translation. Exc. cond. $40

Manual, "die Soldatenfibel," Germany, Army, 1920s. Medium format, sb, 115 pages of text with photos and illus covering Inf tactics in 1920s by Major A.D. Bodo Zimmermann. Slightly faded cover. Avg. cond. $75

Manual, "Electronic Equipment of the German Navy," Germany, Navy, 1945. Medium format, sb, printed April 1945. Over 400 pages and hundreds of photos and specs on the electronic equipment on all German ships and subs. Very rare hard-to-find reference manual. Avg. cond. $263

Manual, "Schiessvorschrift Fur Die Feldartillerie," Imperial Germany, Army, 1914. Artillery and Firing Drill. 170 pages. Hb. Avg. cond. $20

Manual, "Artillerieunterricht 10cm Feldhaubitze M.99," Imperial Germany, Army, 1909. Illustrated manual for 100mm Field Howitzer, Model 1899. Good cond. $20

Manual, "Schiezzanleitung Fur Feldkanonen," Imperial Germany, Army, 1908. Illustrated Field Artillery manual. Above avg. cond. $21

Manuals——Other

Manual, Lot, Military, Austria, Army, c1910. Two manuals, one considering Inf, the other considering general military aspects. Above avg. cond. $25

Manual, "The Manual and Platoon Exercises," England, Army, 1804. British military manual discussing all aspects of verbal military commands. Above avg. cond. $108

Manual, Messerschmitt Me109, Croatia, Air Force, 1940. Illustrated manual discussing the Messerschmitt Me109. Croatian text. Above avg. cond. $100

Manual, Model 1895 Styer-Mannlicher Rifle, Austria, Army, 1899. Full title "Instruction uber die Einrichtung und Verwendung des Repetier-Carabiners M.95." With fold-out schematic drawings. No front cover. Good cond. $21

Manual, 25mm Naval Cannon, Soviet Union, Navy, 1952. Soviet 25mm naval cannon manual. Hb, large format, 51 pages with illus and detail drawings. Marked secret and hand numbered. Avg. cond. $20

Manual, "Principles and Practice of Aerial Navigation," England, RAF, 1920, London. By Lieut J.E. Dumbleton. British aerial navigation manual, published in London, with illus. Above avg. cond. $20

Manual, 45mm Quad Naval Cannon Mount, Soviet Union, Navy, 1951. For Soviet 45mm quad naval cannon mount. Hb, large format, 52 pages with illus and detail drawings. Avg. cond. $20

CHAPTER FOURTEEN
Military Art

This chapter includes examples of fine art, posters, prints, and the unusual category of trench art. Most items in these collecting categories come from the twentieth century because of the lack of interest and market for military art before World War One.

Posters, such as recruitment and war bond posters, are popular collectibles. Even though thousands were produced during World War Two, their value comes primarily from the survival of those in good condition. Like most paper collectibles, posters and prints tend to age, fade, and deteriorate unless properly preserved.

Also included in military art are items made by soldiers out on the front lines or in the field to pass the time. These items are referred to as "trench art." The common availability of these types of items comes from the efforts of US servicemen made to bring home their World War Two "souvenirs from the front." Objects survived generations of attic storage before hitting the market as a collectible. Lamps, ashtrays, and statuary were constructed from the likes of spent ammunition shells, helmets, and foreign coins.

Fakes and Frauds

Even when well done, it is often impossible to perfectly match old paint with today's on pictures and prints because of composition and pigment variances. Because of its toll on a piece's value, cosmetic alterations should only be made by the collector if they feel the restoration enhances the art. Black light tests can easily detect retouches with new paint by the differences in colors exhibited by new versus old paints.

Only when items are going to be resold does the restoration issue come up, both from an ethical and value standpoint.

Care and Display

When not mounted for display, posters and prints should be stored flat in the dark or in wood or metal flat files for artwork. Posters and prints should not be exposed to environmental factors which may destroy paint, ink or paper. Avoid exposure to excessive heat, sunlight, moisture, and insects.

Fine Art——U.S.

Bust, Admiral Sampson, USA, c1900. Bronze. 4" disc with raised profile of Admiral Sampson's left side, titled and signed by artist in lower right. Above avg. cond. $76

Bust, General Pershing, USA, c1920s. 4½"-high desk-size cast-metal bust of Pershing in full dress with medals. Has bronze tone, fair features and name on base. Avg. cond. $30

Litho, Chance Vought F4U-1 Corsair, USA, Navy, WWII, Chance Vought. 11" x 15" size. Shows an unmarked Corsair attacking a Japanese ship. Avg. cond. $24

Statue, Aviator, USA, AAF, 1943. 9½"-tall white plaster statue with army aviator figure in flight helmet and goggles, coat with large collar, flight trousers and A-9-style boots. Has large aircraft tire design behind him. Overall copper finish. Felt-lined base. 1943 dated. Above avg. cond. $40

Statue, WWI Doughboy, USA, c1920s. 13½" tall. Bronze statue of WWI US doughboy in full battle dress with upraised arm holding grenade and rifle in opposite hand. Mounted on black-green variegated marble base having ornate bronze-footed corner mounting. Statue retains nearly 100% of original lacquer finish. Exc. cond. $608

Soldier Statue

Statuette, Bronzed Doughboy, USA, WWI. 11"-high portrayal of officer leading forces. Holding grenade in hand and in full equipment, presents the classic "follow me" pose. Details of pack, ammo belt, chest pack and helmet show well. Shown moving through barbed wire field. Loose on base and left hand missing. Below avg. cond. $95

Statuette, Doughboy, USA, WWI. 9"-tall cast metal with copper-tone finish showing doughboy standing resolutely with rifle. Much of uniform and equipment is well detailed from his leg wraps to the pouches on his cartridge belt. Avg. cond. $56

Statuette, French Sailor, USA, c1900. Bronze. Portrays French sailor/marine of 1870 era in tasseled beret and uniform with medal. Equipped with cartridge belt, pouches and bayonet. Rifle is attached in bag and can be remounted. Superior detail. Below avg. cond. $45

Statuette, Iwo Jima Flag Raising, USA, c1948. Cast metal with bronze finish showing replica of famed photo. Shows six Marines raising flag on Suribachi. Avg. cond. $58

Fine Art——Germany

Color Portrait, German Officer, Imperial Germany, 1850. 6" x 8" current black frame with ornate floral design. Glass, red, matte and hanger to back. 4" x 5" image is shown from waist up with details. Artist signed "B. Raimond de Bauer Berlin 1850." Light age. Exc. cond. $100

Desk Weight, Flaming Bomb, Imperial Germany, WWI. Cast brass. 5" x 5" device of winged, flaming bomb (AA unit). Posts on back for mounting to marble base. Above avg. cond. $60

Desk Weight, Hussar Officer, Imperial Germany, WWI. Green and black veined carian marble base approx. 4" x 5½" in size. Full red-blue enameled miniature sabretasche on body with FWR and crown device. Exc. cond. . . $91

Oil Painting, Imperial German General, Imperial Germany, 1936. Approx. 20" x 26" on original stretchers. Painting is full face with good details of tunic. Subject wears 1910 service tunic with general officer boards and collar tabs, on the neck are suspended the Red Eagle and Royal Crown Orders 2nd class with swords left breast, has an Iron Cross 1914 and the commander's breast badge of the Order of Malta, St. John of Jerusalem. Painting signed and dated 1936. Avg. cond. $492

Oil Painting, Kaiser, Wilhelm II, Imperial Germany, c1905. 20" x 14" gold leaf frame. Beautiful portrait shows Kaiser standing in army field marshal dress dark blue tunic with aiguillettes and neck order. Right hand clasps a GdC helmet by its spike. The left, withered arm is held behind a sword. Dark red background. Exc. cond. $175

Oil Painting, Landsturm NCO, Imperial Germany, 1916. 21" x 26" old frame with linen cloth field having superb painting of man in dress uniform with unit and NCO insignia on collar, three gold chevrons on left sleeve and 1914 Iron Cross ribbon in buttonhole. Artist signed and dated "Lille, 1916," showing it was done in occupied France. Exc. cond. $349

Oil Painting, Saxon Garde Reiter, Imperial Germany, 1907. Approx. 18" x 24". Three-quarter body painting of a young Garde Reiter in full Saxon helmet with lion top. Painting depicts subject in blue and white kurassier koller with white belt, brass buckle and brass epaulettes. Good details to helmet and lion with full Saxon crest. Dated 1907 and artist signed. Painting is mounted on wooden stretchers. Above avg. cond. $292

Oil Painting, Uhlans and Kurassiers on Reconnaissance, Imperial Germany, WWI. In modern frame measuring 19½" x 14". Painting shows two Prussian Uhlans in foreground with one man pointing at a small town with a tower while two mounted kurassiers in armor move off to examine it. Linen body. Exc. cond. $591

Oil Painting, Wehrmacht NCO, Germany, 1943. 18" x 22" painting of oil on canvas. Chest and head of an NCO in the Army with a ribbon bar having War Service Cross 2nd class with swords and Russian Front ribbon. Good details of face and good depth of field, old original heavy wooden frame. Painting dated July 13, 1943 with artist's initials at lower right. Exc. cond. $289

Porcelain Figure, SS Allach, Brown-Colored Resting Dog, Germany, c1930s. 7½" long, 4½" tall. No chips. Beautiful details to muzzle with brown eyes, claws and haunches. Colored Allach is rarer than the white work. Signed Prof. Th. Karner 13 with green SS logo and Allach. Exc. cond. $2260

Porcelain Figure, SS Allach, Standing Bavarian Peasant Man, Germany, c1930s. Part of a grouping of "Oberyabrisches Bauenpaar" (Upper Bavarian Farmer Pair) made by Prof. Richard Forster. This particular figure is artist-signed "R. Forster" and is numbered 48. White ceramic figure has slightly yellow-colored feather in Tirol cap. Small chip to lower leather tab on left side of breeches. Exc. cond. $375

Statues, Wilhelm II and Hindenburg, Germany, c1915. White plaster. Each studio marked to a Munich art company. Each offers full shoulder and bust with superb detail to neck orders, medal bars, general officer collar insignia and facial expressions. Plinth of Wilhelm statue has spread-winged eagle, base of Hindenburg statue shows man battling with dragon. Both date to c1915. Avg. cond. $675

Studio Portrait, Soldier, Imperial Germany, 1918. 11" x 15" photo shows uniformed trooper outside with early bayonet, knot and pillbox cap. Overall 18½" x 24½" gray matte with gold embossed crowned eagle and 1914 EK. Script name and date to back. "Jos.Ott Singen etc." pho-

tographer. Above avg. cond. $62

Tapestry, General Hindenburg, Imperial Germany, c1920s. 17½" x 24½" color shoulders-up portrait of Hindenburg in uniform with neck order. Recent gold and black wooden frame has antique look, 23½" x 30½" size with wire. Exc. cond. $280

Fine Art——Other

Bust, Franz Josef, Austria, c1900. Approx. 10". In silver finished metal. Tall with black wooden cylindrical base bearing 1848–98 dates on Imperial crest with crown above, crossed scepter with orb and sword. Bust shows emperor in open coat displaying hussar-style tunic with many orders and decorations. Double shields below bust with arms of Austria and Hungary. Fine toned silver finish. Exc. cond. $450

Bust, Mussolini, Italy, WWII. 11"-high bust of the Italian dictator. Bronze portrait bust of the Italian dictator in civilian dress coat with necktie, cravat and fascist insignia on lapel. Comes with matching bronze capstan plinth. Reverse signed by "Rossi." Shows age patina. Above avg. cond. $510

Bust of Mussolini

Charcoal Drawing, Army Volunteer Officer, Prussia, 1866. 18" x 22" with convex glass and original plaster green semi-oval frame with floral decor. Superb drawing of Lieut. John Moss (self-portrait), done by himself in 1866 when he was an officer in the German 6th (King William Guard) Grenadier Regt. To the lower right of the picture Moss has hand-written in English that this is a self-portrait, that he was born in 1839 and that his father's name is Wm. L. Roda. He has also noted that he served in the war against Austria. The charcoal portrait is very finely executed with good facial and uniform competency and he is shown wearing two German decorations. Exc. cond. $110

Painting, Naval Scene, Greece, c1910. 16½" x 10½" size.

Oil painting on tin. Depicts Early 20th-century Greek torpedo boat steaming at sea with crew on deck and Greek flag flying on aft mast. In period plaster and wood frame. Above avg. cond. $500

Oil Painting, Russian Czar Alexander I, Imperial Russia, 1825. 29½" x 14" framed dimension, oil on linen portrait pose of the Czar wearing period general's uniform. Signed by Mikhail Ivanovich Terebenyev. Above avg. cond. $4900

Watercolor, Aviation, France, 1916. 17½" x 12½" overall framed dimensions. Watercolor by French artist Rene Prejelan, depicts British biplanes, bombing Allied coastline at Tharos, artillery firing at German planes, English soldiers looking on. In period wooden frame. Dated. Above avg. cond. $447

Watercolor, Aviation, France, WWI. 17½" x 12½" size. Watercolor by French artist Rene Prejelan. Depicts a French biplane in climbing flight pattern with gunner at machine gun. In period wooden frame. Above avg. cond. $447

Posters and Prints—U.S.

Chromolithograph, Battle of Gettysburg, USA, Late 19th Century, Kurz & Allison. Titled "The Battle of Gettysburg." Bright colors with minor margin tears and stains. Size 22" x 28". Avg. cond. $220

Lithograph, Currier and Ives, USA, Late 19th Century. Size 12" x 16". Titled "Battle of New Bern, NC. Mar. 14th 1862." Bright colors with margin stains and pinholes from binding. Avg. cond. $193

Lithograph, Currier and Ives, USA, Late 19th Century. Handcolored. Titled "Battle of Chancellorsville, Va." Good colors. Minor margin tear and some stains. Size 12" x 16". Avg. cond. $138

Lithograph, Currier and Ives, USA, Late 19th Century. Hand colored. Titled "Battle of Corinth, Miss. Oct. 4th 1862." Minor margin stains and pinholes from binding. 1" margin tear. Size 12" x 16". Avg. cond. $165

Lithos, Mexican War Scenes, USA, c1850s. Set of four Mexican War scenes. First is a view of Chapultepec castle under attack. Size 19½" x 12½". Second is another view of Chapultepec and of Molino Del Ray. Size 17½" x 13". Third is a view of Churubusco. Size 17½" x 13". Fourth is a view of Mexico Guerrilleros in 1848. Size 19½" x 14". All have some minor staining. Above avg. cond. . $1725

Poster, "3rd War Loan Back the Attack," USA, 1943. 10" x 14", never folded, color graphics of paratroopers coming down in background while a GI with tommy gun is on the ground. Exc. cond. $45

Poster, "Buy US Defense Bonds," USA, WWII. 15½" x 17" approx. size color poster showing worker "I'm Buying Bonds Are You?" Published by Bethlehem Steel Co. Rolled. Above avg. cond. $36

Poster, "Duty Calls," USA, 1917. 16" x 20" color graphics of doughboys marching off to war and young soldier and sweetheart stand at the front gate, dog at his feet. Below avg. cond. $27

Poster, "Gen. John Pershing," USA, 1918. 16" X 20". Never folded and with bright colors and with flag background. Near mint cond. $86

Poster, "Gentlemen Prefer Blondes," USA, 1945. Small, 6" x 8" color printed poster reading "Gentlemen Prefer Blondes" and on reverse side "But Blondes Don't Like Cripples" depicting soldier on crutches without one leg. Above avg. cond. $22

Poster, "Halt the Hun," USA, WWI. 20" x 29" approx size. Color printed poster "Halt the Hun—Buy US Government Bonds, Third Liberty Loan." Depicts group of soldiers, red flaming battlefront. Rolled. Exc. cond. $40

Poster, "Hun or Home?" USA, WWI. Approx. 20" x 30" in size. Color printed illust of German soldier with his spike helmet in pursuit of a woman and child. Big letters on top read "Hun or Home? Buy More Liberty Bonds." Above avg. cond. $66

Poster, "Know Your Enemy," USA, Army, 1967. 16" x 25" size. MACV Command color poster of four different soldiers of the North Vietnamese armies; Viet Cong officer and soldier, NVA soldier and medic and with the flags of each, captioned. Avg. cond. $223

Poster, "Victorious Allies," USA, 1918. 16" x 20" size. Color graphics of a battle scene with the three flags of the Allies with tanks and planes, shows US and French troops fighting together as a long line of German POW's are led through trenches. Above avg. cond. $49

Mexican War Scene, Litho

Poster, "Victory and Peace," USA, WWI. 16" x 20". Color graphics of a peaceful countryside scene over three flags of the Allies draping over two-color art of a Army soldier and another of a sailor telling the tales of the great war deeds. Avg. cond. $40

Poster, Patriotic, USA, WWII. 18" x 24", "Confidence" over picture of FDR. Avg. cond. $9

Poster, Recruiting, USA, Army, WWII. Framed poster is 20" x 32". Color photo of army nurse in full uniform, "You are Needed Now Join the Army Nurse Corps." Avg. cond. $97

Poster, Recruiting, USA, Navy, WWI. 10" x 14" size. Color print "Gee I Wish I Were a Man, I'd Join the Navy." Shows pretty girl in Navy uniform. Above avg. cond. $55

Poster, Recruiting, USA, USMC, 1961. 8" x 10½" heavy card stock with design of young Marine in dress blues with background scene of helicopters and attacking Marines. Reads "Teamwork Join the Marines." Avg. cond. $30

Poster, Red Cross, USA, 1918. 29" x 39" approx. size. Color printed poster of Red Cross nurse depicting "I summon you to comradeship in the Red Cross," 1918 dated. Rolled. Exc. cond. $72

Poster, Red Cross, USA, WWI. 20" x 30"-size color printed Red Cross Roll Call poster. Rolled. Above avg. cond. $55

Poster, Sullivan Brothers, USA, Navy, 1943. 30" x 42" color printed poster. Has red background with five US Navy sailors in black and five blue stars on top. Reads "The five Sullivan brothers missing in action off the Solomons. They did their part." Exc. cond. $82

Poster, US Treasury, USA, 1943. 10" x 14" color print sketch depicting fighting man ready to throw a hand grenade. "Let 'em Have It" printed on top. "Buy Extra Bonds 4th War Loan" printed across bottom. Dated 1943. Exc. cond. $38

Poster, US Treasury, USA, 1944. 10" x 14" color print sketch depicting face of fighting man with camo helmet, "Next" in center. Island of Japan in background, "6th War Loan" printed in lower right-hand corner. Published by US Government Printing Office, 1944. Exc. cond. $45

Poster, War Saving Stamp "Your War Saving Pledge," USA, WWI. 21" x 32" color graphics of doughboy/Uncle Sam/civilian, "Our Boys Make Good Their Pledge, Are You Keeping Yours?" Avg. cond. $28

Poster, Recruiting, USA, USMC, 1980s. Gold and black reads "A Few Good Men." Above avg. cond. $12

Poster, Recruiting, USA, USMC, 1980s. Color reads "Semper Fi." Above avg. cond. $12

Poster, Recruiting, USA, USAF, 1980s. Color poster reads "Aim High." Above avg. cond. $12

Vue d' Optique, Revolutionary War, USA, c1800. Size 18½" x 16½". Hand-colored engraving depicts the sea battle between the Bon Homme Richard and Serapis in which John Paul Jones uttered his "I have not yet begun to fight." One tear into image, otherwise intact. Above avg. cond. $518

Revolutionary War Vue de Optique

Posters and Prints—Germany

Lithograph, Stukas in Battle, Germany, WWII. 11" x 15" b&w Ju 87 Stukas and Ju 88 bombers attacking English ships. Printed litho on art paper and framed with paperboard. Shows Stuka Ju 87 and Ju 88 bombing the gun deck of a ship and an aircraft carrier. Excellent detail and well done. Captioned at base. Facsimile artist signature. Exc. cond. $40

Poster, "Ewig Das Reich," Germany, WWII. 9" x 13", folded. Poster is etching of Henry the Fowler, on tan paper with black etching and cinnamon lettering. "The Reich Forever." Avg. cond. $27

Poster, "Mein Kampf," Germany, WWII. 12" x 19" size. Folded. Printed advertising poster showing Hitler, title and "Lerne Hitler durch sein buch kennen" print. Small tear at top. Avg. cond. $30

Poster, Anti-British, Germany, 1940. "Heuchelei, Terror und Meuchelmord." 32" x 48" color printed poster as published by NSDAP in 1940. Poster illustrates in large black print anti-British propaganda statements. With larger print in bottom section of poster. Photo of Chamberlain is illustrated in left part of poster. Minor separation. Above avg. cond. $145

Poster, Patriotic, Imperial Germany, WWI. 38" x 48" approx. size. Red gold crowned Imperial eagle depicted with outspread wings on mountain top. Strong and powerful. Full lower lettering advertises the exploits of the Tylolian heroes in the Galizien campaign. Avg. cond. $135

Poster, SS Belgium/Flanders Recruiting, Germany, SS, WWII. 14½" x 21½" size white paper with black, red and yellow print. Offers special placement as engineer, music or other trades. Report to "Ersatzkommando Flandern der Waffen-SS Antwerpen etc." Original that has storage-rolled age only. Exc. cond. $285

Poster, SS Nachrictentruppe, Germany, SS, WWII. 20" x 28" size. Orange body with seven troops in action photos with captions for various communication styles. Title center with wording about communication use. Storage-folded brittle yellowed paper. Above avg. cond. $360

Poster, SS Recruiting "Dich Ruft Die Waffen-SS," Germany, WWII. 21½" x 30" illustrated camo SS-NCO trooper pointing finger over title. Done by "Anton" and lists "SS-Hauptamt etc.Prag IV." Shows folds and mounting age. Exc. cond. $1268

Poster, SS Recruitment, Germany, Waffen SS, WWII. 21½" x 33" illustrated camo SS trooper and HJ trooper by "Anton" with title on upper corner and 12 combat photos of various trades of the Waffen SS in action with captions. Style by "SS-Hauptamt etc. Prag IV." Folded from storage. Exc. cond. $1125

Print, German Troops Cheering Wilhelm I, Imperial Germany, 1870s. In old brown period frame with glass print matted and done by well-known artist Franz Anling. Approx. 30" x 20". Sepia, black and white drawing shows 9th Laurenberg Jaeger troops cheering Wilhelm I as his carriage passes by destroyed French field artillery unit. Above avg. cond. $150

Print, Light Cruiser, Imperial Germany, c1900. 18" x 14" print in modern gold frame with full glass. Matted. Color 1900 print showing SMS Hela, a light cruiser at sea. Superb details with ram bow, full stack, fighting rig, etc. Ship completed in 1896 was torpedoed and sunk by British submarine in 1914. Gold name of ship appears on matte below. Above avg. cond. $30

Print, Navy Cruiser, Imperial Germany, Navy, c1905. 14" x 18" print in modern gold frame with glass. Cruiser is SMS Vineta, a protected cruiser completed in 1899. Ship has a pronounced ram-style bow beautifully detailed with black matte having gold lettering "S.M.S. Grossere Kreuzer "Vineta." Exc. cond. $30

Posters and Prints——Other

Print, Crimean War Political Satire, Imperial Russia, Crimean War Era. 27" x 23" size. Political satire of the major nations engaged in the Crimea, depicting French, British, and Turkish figures devouring bodies, boat loads of troops arriving, winged devils fly overhead, in mottled brown frame. Russian Cyrillic language inscription on border. Above avg. cond. $181

Print, Patriotic, Austria, WWI. 17" x 12½", color litho depicting portrait vignettes of Austrian Emperor Franz Joseph, German Kaiser Wilhelm and Italian King Humberto, with heraldic crests from each country, oak leaf motif and crossed flags. Good cond. $100

Poster Set, Army Rank and Specialist Insignia, England, Army, WWII. Three 30" x 20" posters depicting British Army ranks and cloth specialist insignia. Above avg. cond. $30

Poster, Revolutionary Propaganda, China, 1968. 30" x 21" poster depicting Asian, African, and South American revolutionary freedom fighters. Chinese language inscription. Above avg. cond. $53

Poster, War Loan, Austria, 1917. About 27½" x 41" rolled body. Illustrated helmeted soldier about to throw stick grenade and signed by "W. Kuhn 1917." Color crowned double headed eagle shield below with "K.K. Priv. Allgemeine Verkehrsbank, Wien Zeichnet Die Siebente Osterr. Kriegsanleihe etc." By "Wagnersche K.K. Universitats Buchdruckerie, R.Kiesel, Innsbruck." Exc. cond. $213

Print, Anti-Kaiser "The Him of Hate," England, 1917. 11½" x 15½" gold-painted wood frame with glass. 9½" x 13½" color print from newspaper of mean looking Kaiser head with spiked helmet. Title below, done by "David Robinson" and "Copyright Leslie's 1917." Exc. cond. $55

Trench Art——U.S.

Airplane Model, USA, WWI. From scrap brass, a bullet and coins. Fuselage is safed rifle round and wings and tail are from scrap. Coins make wheels moveable prop. Upper wing missing. Below avg. cond. $26

Ashtray, USA, Navy, 1959. Nickel plated with mounted .50-cal round converted to lighter and DI-style flags on each side of alum plaque for USS Roosevelt (CVA-42) Mediterranean cruise. Dated 1959. Avg. cond. $45

Ashtray, USA, WWII. British 3" Mark II shell cut down with two half pennies bent and soldered in as holders. Basic. Avg. cond. $12

Ashtray, From Japanese Artillery Shell, USA, WWII. Center (detonator area inside) has metal engraved with Japanese emblems. Base has ordnance marks in Japanese. Avg. cond. $23

Candlesticks From Helmet Plume Socket, USA, c1900. Brass plume socket from Army dress parade helmet (1870–90) with brass leaf base added and attached to walnut base. Brass candle holder attached to top. Handsome candlestick and documentation on bottom. Avg. cond. $66

Chromed Projectile on Display Base, USA, WWI. Special 105mm ID's as "SCAIFE" on display stand. Middle third slightly smaller diam than rest of projectile. Fused warhead with safing pin. Wood base with two metal struts on support projectile. Chromed plates for ID. Exc. cond. $165

Cobra Chopper Model in Brass, USA, Vietnam War Era. Solid brass with moving rotor and tail rotor. Even shows bulge of chin turret. Other features average. Avg. cond. $100

Display, 75mm Round, USA, WWI. Wooden base with felt-padded supports holding immaculate 75mm round. Perforated casing is lacquered and base has detonator removed. Projectile has open tip and grooved compression band. Black finish shows minor spotting. Exc. cond. $150

Display, From 57mm Shell, USA, WWI. Two-tiered wood base with nickel-plated cartridges on each corner and silver-plated eagle on rifle round with "US CARTRIDGE CO" on it. Center is plated 57mm artillery shell with miniature hat and Army shield. Three looped candlestick bulb holders with simulated candle extensions. Sides of main piece are attached by screws, tall torches with three wreaths. Avg. cond. $150

Display, Small Arms and Artillery Shells, USA, WWII. Arrangement of seven artillery shells cut down and stacked in decreasing size to form tower. Nickel-plated 20mm shells with gilded .50-cal rounds surround the base. .30-cal rifle and carbine rounds form a ring around the 37mm round that crowns the piece. Crossed cannons and a DI of an artillery unit are on the side. Above avg. cond. $120

Lamp Base, USA, WWII. Metal three-tiered base with mounted Japanese 75mm shell and projectile. Polished brass base with chromed plaque with Japanese characters at top and "JAPANESE 75MM SHELL /FIRED AT AMERICAN TROOPS/GUADALCANAL 1942" at bottom. Nickel-plated projectile with harp and socket mount at tip. Channeled for wiring. Exc. cond. $175

Lamp From Artillery Round, USA, WWII. Brass base with four feet. Foreign 25mm artillery round drilled safed and wired for socket assembly at top. Cord included. Avg. cond. $20

Lamp, USA, WWI. Round four-footed metal base has plain 57mm artillery shell projectile in center surrounded by several smaller rounds of various sizes. Conical-shaped shade. Complete with on and off pull-chain and wire with wall plug. Avg. cond. $80

Trench Art Lamp

Letter Opener, USA, WWI. 5" bolo-style brass blade with ornate guard and rifle round for grip. Austrian Hungarian empire uniform button on grip. Avg. cond. $21

Napkin Ring, 1st Aero Squadron, USA, WWI. Made from brass shell and etched with "1ST AERO SQ/SEPT 12–14, 1918." Brass St. Mihiel coat of arms on side. Avg. cond. $45

Pair of Lamps, USA, WWII. 81mm mortar shells inverted and attached to nickel-plated metal bases, drilled for wiring and sockets installed in motor exhaust outlet. Shells and fins are nickel plated. Wiring and sockets should be replaced for safety. Avg. cond. $70

Salt and Pepper Shakers, USA, WWII. Teak base with nickel-plated carrier hook and two salt/pepper holders from 20mm projectiles. Nickel plated with lead tops. Avg. cond. $20

Salt and Pepper Shakers, USA, WWII. From turned alum, with threaded tops for filling and holes for using. Names are engraved on each. This set looks like a pair of 60mm mortar rounds in miniature. Avg. cond. $55

Ship's Cannon Model, USA, WWI. 6"-long solid brass cannon on wheeled alum metal stand similar to 18th-century naval six or eight pounders. Number seven on base, well made with steel wheels. Avg. cond. $26

Trench Art, Decorated Shell, USA, WWI. 75mm shell cut down to 10" height and decorated with raised profile of General Pershing with name below and crossed American and French flags with dates 1914 to 1918 above and below cross. Star pattern textured background. Above avg. cond. $115

Trench Art, Decorated Shell, USA, WWII. 1941 dated 37mm shell. 8½" tall with decor from top to bottom in tropic theme. No writing or dates on sides. Avg. cond. $22

Trench Art, Decorated Shell, Verdun Memorial, USA, WWI. British brass shell dated 1918. Polished and given fluted top. On side is added banner with "VERDUN" under "Le Coc D" on bas relief. Avg. cond. $34

Trench Art, Lamp From Shell, USA, WWI. 22½" tall with base from large-cal shell and column from 40mm round drilled for wire. Three .50-cal rounds mounted about half way up column. Assembly for two lights and harp for shade at top. Shade is WWI helmet with original hand-painted unit designator for 21st Engineers, 1st Army and a likely anti-aircraft emblem. Will need rewiring. Avg. cond. $69

Trench Art, V For Victory, USA, WWII. Constructed from 2" aerial gunner's pb sterling wings with two halves of a .50-cal MG bullet mounted to form a "V" for victory below. Shows light tarnish. Avg. cond. $53

Urn, From 105mm Shell, USA, Vietnam Era. Beautiful brass urn from 1943 dated 105mm shell. Polished brass with fluted top and inscribed for named soldier from Da Nang Vietnam/Nov 66/Nov 67. Needs good cleaning. Avg. cond. $30

Vase, USA, WWII. 13" tall with wooden plug at base and artwork with owl and butterfly on peened background. Needs some polish. Above avg. cond. $70

Vase, USA, WWI. 9" cut down 75mm shell decorated with flowers and diagonal Verdun band, stippled background. Bronze tone on exterior. Avg. cond. $36

Vase, From 75mm Shell, USA, WWI. Brass shell 14" tall with elaborate peened decoration showing "VERDUN" and oak branches. Nice polished finish. Above avg. cond. $72

Vase, From 75mm Shell, USA, WWI. Foreign-shell American art. Unusual copper color brass, fluted bottom third. Arrowhead design with "CHATEAU THIERRY" on rim, unit shield in center and "Souvenir" over shield with "1918" below. Lip is dented slightly. Avg. cond. . . . $55

Vase, Verdun Memorial, USA, WWI. US 75mm shell with flutes near base, etched flowers and "VERDUN" and "1919" engraved on side. 13½" tall. Avg. cond. $34

Vases, USA, WWI. Designed to carry a message on both vases. Each 14" tall, fully decorated with oak leaves and branches. Both have "WORLD WAR" on upper part of vase, one has "MEUSE" and the other has "ARGONNE" at the bottom. Well polished. Above avg. cond. . . . $143

Vases, From 75mm, USA, WWI. Brass shells with fluted bases and decorated upper sections. Shows flower pattern with one reading "ARGONNE/1918," the other "VERDUN/1918" in raised relief. Decorative pattern in background. These have been polished and lacquered. Above avg. cond. $129

Vases, Pair, USA, WWI. From 75mm shells of American issue. Lower third fluted, decor art at top and "Argonne Meuse" on one, "St Mihiel" on the other. Well polished. Above avg. cond. $141

Vases, Pair, USA, WWI. Two 13½", 75mm shells fluted and engraved in flower pattern with roses and star pattern background. Avg. cond. $85

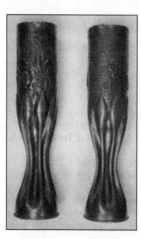

Trench Art Vases

Vases, Set of Three, USA, WWI. From 75mm shells of American issue. Two with lower third fluted, religious decor at top with crucifix and acorn and oak leaves. One dated 1919. The third vase is not fluted and is decorated with a shield and flag design marked RF (Republic of France) and a "fleur-de-lis." Above avg. cond. $120

Wind Chimes, USA, WWI. From brass shells, hanger is base of 75mm and chimes are cut-down 20mm shells with length selected for sound. Avg. cond. $35

Zeppelin, USA, WWI. 6"-long solid brass with finned tail, props on side and cabin structure with windows underneath. Light tarnish. Above avg. cond. $80

**Set of Three
Trench Art Vases**

Trench Art—Germany

Ashtray, Imperial Germany, WWI. Made from wooden aircraft propeller. 6" x 7½" crosscut section is 3" tall with hammered brass inset tray. Above avg. cond. $100

Ashtray, Imperial Germany, WWI. Made from artillery shell. 3" tall 3½" diam, fuse-shaped metal body has four rifle slugs for feet and full rifle bullet affixed across top, head stamped "DM 8 15 S67." Avg. cond. $55

Lamp, Imperial Germany, WWI. Made from 1916 brass artillery shell. 19½"-tall brass body has about 4½" diam on brass lamp fitting that is 5½" tall. Head stamped "Karth 851 Dez.1916 etc." Avg. cond. $24

Letter Opener, Imperial Germany, WWI. Copper. Made from pounded-out driving band of shell warhead. Approx. 10" long with handle and double edged dagger-shaped blade. Above avg. cond. $22

Letter Opener, Imperial Germany, WWI. Rough shrapnel style handle with polished diamond formed steel cutting blade. 5¾" long with art work. Above avg. cond. . . . $25

Letter Opener, Imperial Germany, WWI. Made from artillery shell driving band. 7½"-long copper band with 4" blade. Hand engraved "VERDUN 1914–17." Avg. cond. .
. . . . $50

Paperweight, Imperial Germany, WWI. 3" tall, brass fuse was fired and has scale up to number 12. On brass base. 4" x 5". Avg. cond. $20

Photo Frame With Photo, Imperial Germany, WWI. 4" x 8" size. Three bullets on either side of a b&w photo of officer and wife. With brass crown and small frame at top. Has wire stand on back. Avg. cond. $75

Tea Pot, Imperial Germany, WWI. Made from artillery shell. About 12½" tall and 3½" diam, nickel body with copper base, band and brass handle with copper heart, spout with cork stopper on chain and removable brass fuse lid with scale. Bottom stamped "01077." Above avg. cond. . .
. . . . $135

Trench Art, "Battle of St. Mihiel 1918," Imperial Germany, WWI. Brass. About 8½" long with French Lebel rifle bullet for handle, slug holes, scimitar-style blade with engraved title, oak leaves and affixed 1898 5-pfennig coin. Avg. cond. $30

Trench Art, Decorated Shell, Imperial Germany, WWI. 75mm shell. 13½" tall, dark body with fluted lower end, female figure, leaves, date and "Jcnomeh." Head stamp "A RS L481." Above avg. cond. $50

Trench Crucifix, Imperial Germany, Army, WWI. 6"-tall nickel-plated body, dark wood inlay, affixed title scroll, metal Jesus and skull/crossbones. Stamped "Germany" and hanger ring. Avg. cond. $35

Trench Crucifix, Imperial Germany, WWI. 55 x 110mm heavy cast nickel-silver cross with 3D Christ over skull and letters on each arm and hanging loop. Above avg. cond. $213

Trench Art—Other

Ashtray, Canada, Army, 1915. Brass artillery shell base, in form of visor hat with 104 Canadian Infantry Regt front insignia, copper chinstrap, side buttons lacking. Above avg. cond. $83

Letter Opener, England, Army, WWI. Brass, curved scimitar-type blade,.303 bullet grip with crown decoration, inscribed "Sir De France," crossed Allied flags motif on blade. Above avg. cond. $40

CHAPTER FIFTEEN

Homefront Collectibles

Collecting of homefront objects is one of the biggest changes to World War Two collecting in the past 15 years. However, these items still are secondary when compared with true military collectibles, even though collectors are beginning to pay more attention to this collecting category. Homefront collectibles are items that represented the battle fought "at home" to help support the war effort and include, but are not limited to civil defense items, jewelry, newspapers and periodicals, patriotic items, and sweetheart items. A number of items were specifically made to be sold to troops as souvenirs.

Most homefront collectibles are not very expensive and represent a reasonable market in which the new collector can participate. Collections can be as broad as paper items to more specialized collections, such as Nazi rings.

Civil defense was practiced in every nation represented in World War Two; however items distributed in the United States are more readily available because of their lack of use, since German bombing raids presented little threat to U. S. cities. Raids were practiced for morale and citizen unification efforts. British civil defense items, such as blackout kits, were readily consumed because of genuine threats and blackout practices.

Many newspapers and periodicals did not survive their respective eras because they were considered disposable items and were deliberately recycled to support the war effort. Those that did are plagued by deterioration because of the poor quality of papers used. The highest prices for newspapers and periodicals come from those items that cover significant events or conflicts. Collectible specimens should be complete and in good condition.

Many of the collectors in the homefront collectibles market are buying for sentimental purposes, because of their own or a family member's participation in World War Two. Only after the wave of nostalgia passes will the market for these items be truly tested.

Collecting Tips
Because the categories are so broad, it may be best to begin by specializing in one type of collectible, such as Civil Defense leaflets, and expand later.

Fakes and Frauds
Nazi political collectibles tend to be one of the most frequently reproduced items in this category. Examine items carefully.

Civil Defense Items—U.S.

Armband Lot, Civil Defense, USA, WWII. Two armbands; first is for a first-aid volunteer and second is for a coffee volunteer. Avg. cond. $28

Civil Defense Lot, USA, WWII. Mixed lot of 45 items including armbands, shoulder insignias, booklets, vehicle pennant with fender pole, CD identification card, license plate, gilded brass buttons and window decal. Avg. cond. $110

Marker Flag, New Jersey Civil Defense, USA, WWII. Triangular pennant on 20" pole with red triangular CD emblem in center. Some wear and staining. Avg. cond. $41

Civil Defense Badge, "Aux Police Erie County NY," USA, WWII. Pb. Blue "CD" emblem in center. Avg. cond. $20

Civil Defense Badge, "Aux. Police Erie County, New York Patrolman," USA, WWII. 54 x 83mm nickel body with enameled CD appliqué in center. Patent marked. Pb. Above avg. cond. $24

Helmet, Civil Defense, USA, WWII. WWI M1917 helmet with white sand finish and CD emblem painted on front. Interior has leather chinstrap and headband with pads of WWI converted helmet. Avg. cond. $23

Visor Cap, Civil Defense Officer, USA, c1950s. Dark green gabardine top with wire stiffener, ventilated woven black band, black visor and black finish smooth side buttons. Has Sb numbered CD badge on front of crown. $1 Sears price tag still attached. Size 7. No chinstrap. Above avg. cond. $40

Civil Defense Police Badge, "Wilmington, Delaware," USA, WWII. Pb. Avg. cond. $25

Gas Mask, Child, USA, WWII. Rubber face-mask marked Small Child's. One-piece curved lens above respirator valve. Attached canister/ filter and elastic headband. Avg. cond. $25

ID Silhouettes, Allied Aircraft, USA, WWII. 7" x 12" size. Cardboard planes used for identification purposes and ready for assembly. All in brown envelopes. Models included are Scout Bomber, US Navy SB2U-3 Vindicator, British Chesapeake Fighter, US Navy F2A-3 Buffalo, British Buffalo Fighter, AAF P-39D, British Airacobra Fighter, AAF A-31, British Vengeance. Exc. cond. $83

Sign, Civil Defense Headquarters, USA, WWII. Size 13" x 14". Double sided depicting Civil Defense red-white striped triangle on blue field, inscribed "HDQTS POST AIR RAID WARDEN." Finish worn. Below avg. cond. $65

Civil Defense Sign,
Air Raid Warden

Civil Defense Items—Germany

Gas Mask, Civilian, Germany, WWII. Green rubber mask with straps. Flat alum filter. Inked Waffenamt stamp on filter. Avg. cond. $20

Gas Mask, Civilian With Box, Germany, WWII. Gray cardboard box holds green mask with straps, alum filter and four-page instruction sheet showing "VM40" use. Avg. cond. $20

Gas Mask, Civilian With Box, Germany, WWII. Cardboard box. Owner-named printed RLB label on underside of lid with 1939 date up to 1944 for use. Full green rubber mask with alum filter and instruction leaflet on use. Avg. cond. $26

Gas Mask, Civilian, M1930, Germany, Air Raid, WWII. Includes gray painted fluted canister with shoulder strap and pivot lid latch. Stamped 1936 and maker marked on inside lid with inked "WaA" and extra lens packet. M1930 mask with straps and "S-filter Luftschutz etc." filter. Exc. cond. $93

Gas Mask, Civilian, M1930, Germany, Air Raid, WWII. M1930 mask with straps and "Auer" filter with paper Luftschutz label. Dated and eagle proofed fluted canister with gray paint. Extra lens packet. Above avg. cond. $74

Gas Mask, Civilian, M1930, Germany, Air Raid, WWII. M1930 mask with straps and "FE41" marked filter with plug. "Auer" stamped name on lid "Luftschutzgesetz etc." Gray paint and thin shoulder strap with hook strap. Avg. cond. $61

Civil Defense Items—Other

Gas Mask, Civilian Gas Mask Ensemble, England, 1942. Black rubber mask, clear glass eyepieces, forward-mounted filter with black enamel finish and black rubber butterfly valve with black cloth headstraps. With carrier of khaki canvas with white cotton straps. Good cond.   . $32

Helmet, Air Raid Warden, England, WWII. Of spun alum with 90% olive green finish remaining. Obverse pierced for badge, adjustable interior lining of khaki canvas and worn black leather chinstrap. Above avg. cond. $0

Jewelry—U.S.

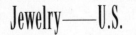

Bracelet, USA, AAF, WWII. Likely English made, nickel- or chrome-plated metal with AAF emblem in center and ETO/1945 on each side, England and USAAF on each arm. Nicely engraved "With Love" on back. Avg. cond. $34

Bracelet, 8th Air Force, USA, AAF, WWII. Bright nickel-plated brass band with incised, short wing 8th Air Force patch design in center, "England-ETO-1945-USAAF" on band. Generic inscription inside "With Love." Avg. cond. $48

Bracelet, Allied Powers/Victory, USA, WWII. Comprised of four rectangular links that have enameled designs of USSR, US, Great Britain and Chinese flags. Larger center piece has appliqué design of aviation wing with "V" in center. Engraved with woman's name. All links are sterling hmkd. Above avg. cond. $40

Bracelet, CBI, USA, WWII. Chain link with clasp and large oval metal disk in center. Sunburst around CBI emblem with "MARY" at top, dates (1942, 43, 44) on sides and Burma, India, China and CBI at bottom. Back reads "ALL MY LOVE FROM/FLORIN INDIA." Above avg. cond. $114

Compact, USA, WWII. 3½" brass with snap lid and still containing powder puff, powder and mirror. Top is blue enamel with raised Army brass emblem in center of lid. Some tarnish on brass. Above avg. cond. $55

Compact, Patriotic, USA, WWI. Enameled picture on face showing flag "God Bless America" and winged foot of Mercury. Inside has mirror and powder chamber. Above avg. cond. $48

Earrings, USA, WWII. Pair Sb earrings with AAF emblem on face. S/S. Avg. cond. $20

Finger Ring, USA, USCG, WWII. Sterling hmkd. Silver color. Has official seal design at top and patriotic eagle designs on each side. Medium finger size. Avg. cond. $17

Finger Ring, USA, WWI. Gold-plated ring with "tiger eyes" stone with raised relief shoulders-up design of

doughboy in WWI helmet. Hmkd. Large finger size. Avg. cond. $82

Finger Ring, 84th Div, USA, Army, WWII. Silver colored body has enameled 84th Div patch design at top and patriotic eagle/shield design on each side. Maker/sterling hmkd. Medium finger size. Avg. cond. $35

Gold Watch, NCO Retirement, USA, Army, 1938. Mounted to heavy woven fob. Hmkd "Waltham Premier" and still works. Engraved on back "PRESENTED TO/1ST SERGT H H WILBUR/BY OFFICERS AND MEN OF/A CO. 66TH INFANTRY LT/30 YEARS SERVICE/SEPT 24TH 1938." A proud piece for a proud moment. Exc. cond. $209

ID Bracelet, USA, AAF, WWII. S/S with AAF winged prop raised on crest name and rank of owner on back. Some tarnish. Avg. cond. $52

ID Bracelet, USA, AAF, WWII. S/S with ID bar and name, serial number of soldier and second bar with AAF winged prop logo. Light tarnish. Avg. cond. $55

ID Bracelet, USA, Navy, WWII. Has gilt Navy pilot wing in center, reinforced links and signs of wear on pilot wing. Above avg. cond. $44

ID Bracelet, USA, Navy, WWII. Sterling silver with fouled anchor and "USN" in center and hand-engraved name and serial number on back. Avg. cond. $37

ID Bracelet, USA, USMC, WWII. 2" oval with worn emblem with name and home town. Chain with clasp. Avg. cond. $36

ID Bracelet, USA, WWII. Classic heavy link bracelet with bombardier's wing on bar and name and serial number on back. Some wear on wing. Sterling. Above avg. cond. $49

ID Bracelet, USA, WWII. Sterling. Regular links and clasp, ID bar is curved CIB with enamel removed and chemically darkened. Avg. cond. $33

Id Bracelet, Officer, USA, Navy, WWII. 36" x 33" oval-shaped flat body (appears sterling) engraved to officer (full name), "169341/LT.USNR/T 7/42 O." Body only, no wrist chain. Below avg. cond. $25

ID Locket, USA, USMC, WWII. Engraved with name and USMC. Heavy link chain shows some tarnish. Avg. cond. $30

Lapel Pin, Aircraft Contractor, USA, WWII. Metal wings on shield. Shield has blue enamel field with "1" in center. Across top of wing is "CHANCE VOUGHT." Pb displayed in plastic box with clear top. Avg. cond. ... $11

Lapel Pin, Martin Aircraft Co., USA, WWII. 10kt gold

filled with pb and Martin on blue diagonal. "20 yrs" at top and green jewel between words. Above avg. cond. . . $59

Lapel Pin, Remember Pearl Harbor, USA, WWII. 63mm-wide pierced cast "Remember Pearl" body with appliqué simulated pearl. Pb. Avg. cond. $21

Lapel Pin, UCV, USA, 1914. Sb enameled Union of Confederate Veterans pin for dues paid at 1914 convention. Good job on flag. Above avg. cond. $118

Pendant and Earring Set, USA, AAF, WWII. Set displayed in blue velvet-lined box. Screw post-style earrings featuring winged prop AAF emblem in sterling silver. Matching chain with pendant. Shows frosted crystal in S/S frame with AAF wings attached to crystal. Avg. cond. $47

Pin, Curtis Wright, USA, WWII. Sb winged disk with company name in center and production/soldier around rim and 100% in tab below. Avg. cond. $20

Pin, Naval Academy Graduation, USA, Navy, 1948. Gold with naval emblems, wings, sabers, ships, seahorses and 1948 graduation year. Above avg. cond. $54

Pin, Son in Service, USA, WWII. Gilt and enamel pb brooch with Great National Seal design attached by small lined chain. In maker carton with sliding lid. Avg. cond. $20

Ring, USA, AAF, WWII. Sterling with AAF emblem on crest. Some wear. Avg. cond. $56

Ring, POW, USA, WWII. Sterling signet ring for German POW's at Camp Robinson, SD. Has buffalo on one side and Indian head on other and camp gate on crest. Above avg. cond. $110

Seabee Bracelet, USA, USN, WWII. Enameled Seabee emblem on brass disc fixed to dark stone. Gilt links for bracelet. Above avg. cond. $65

Signet Ring, USA, AAF, WWII. S/S with eagles on sides and AAF emblem (winged prop) for crest. Plus, crest swings away to expose a picture pocket like a locket. Above avg. cond. $91

Signet Ring, USA, AAF, WWII. 10kt gold filled with AAF emblems (winged props) on both sides and forms the crest. Reads around crest "UNITED STATES AIR CORPS." Some wear. Above avg. cond. $117

Signet Ring, Airborne, USA, ARMY, WWII. Sterling. Red stone in face with airborne images on sides and "AIRBORNE U.S. ARMY" around stone. Miniature jump wings fixed on stone. Some light patina. Avg. cond. $46

Signet Ring, Airborne, USA, Army, WWII. S/S with air-

borne eagles on each side and blue stone in crest. "AIRBORNE/ US ARMY" around stone. Avg. cond. . . . $48

Signet Ring, Airborne, USA, Army, WWII. Has chute on signet with copper inserts on each side spelling "82," chute has Airborne on the canopy. Avg. cond. $40

Signet Ring, Signal Corp Memorial, USA, Army, WWI. Signal Corps memorial ring for WWI. Sterling silver with Signal Corps crest and war dates on rim. Military emblems on each side. Some wear on raised features. Above avg. cond. $77

Souvenir Bracelet, German Occupation, USA, 1946. Shop-made slip-on alum bracelet engraved 1946 souvenir of Bremerhaven, Germany. Avg. cond. $25

Sword Pin, West Point Graduate, USA, Army, 1935. 50mm likeness of West Point cadet's sword in sterling. Pb with early style safety catch. Has West Point eagle on shield crest affixed to blade with "1935" on shield. Above avg. cond. $42

Watch Fob, 44th Division, USA, Army, WWI. Brass. Reads "Co/A/114 INF/ 44dth Div" in raised letters and cowhide strap with hair still on. Avg. cond. $28

Watch Fob, Mexican Border Service, USA, Army, 1916. Bronze heart-shaped metal with dates of raid on other side. Avg. cond. $21

Watch Fob, Navy, USA, Navy, c1900. 36 x 46mm brass with attached motif of a sailor with crossed flags behind him, flags still have 95% of original red-white-blue paint. Never used. Avg. cond. $37

Jewelry—Germany

Finger Ring, Swastika, Germany, WWII. Size 8½ silver band is broken, 14mm panel and black enamel swastika on silver disc with chipped red borders. Shows its age. Avg. cond. $145

Wrist Watch, Luftwaffe, Germany, Luftwaffe, WWII. Model Helvetia Fl.23883. 40mm silver case shows use with stamped Fl.# on back. Luminous hands and numbers on black face with second hand face and propeller on title maker. Still winds up and works! Replacement brown leather band. Above avg. cond. $702

Bracelet, Western Front, Germany, WWII. Double link with nine round bronze panels, each being 16mm in size. Catch present. Each panel depicts flying planes, tanks, motorcycles, pill boxes, etc. Central disc inscribed "Gruss von der West Front" (Greetings From the Western Front). Very attractive. No damage. Above avg. cond. $112

Bracelet, With Six Miniature Medals, Imperial Germany, WWI. Ladies. Includes Hindenburg cross with swords, silver wound badge, Prussian long service, German WWI combat, and more. Exc. cond. $85

Cigarette Case, DAK, Germany, Army, WWII. Native made. Alum. About ¾" x 3½" x 4½" body made from downed airplane. Ornate cut-out design affixed to each side with red leatherette background, Africa continent side has engraved palm tree and set stones for major coastal cities. Nice Arabic domed building scene with set colored stones. Hinged with more engraved designs inside. Highest quality for a native-made item. Above avg. cond. $114

Cuff Links, NSDAP, Germany, WWII. Black leather case has gold border outline. Maker name on white satin lid lining and black velvet base. 16mm diam on red enamel border with black swastika on white center. Curved and pivoting fitting to backs. Above avg. cond. $174

Finger Ring, 1939/1940 Helmet, Germany, WWII. Size 10½ brass body is worn thin. 16mm-tall brass panel riveted to front with engraved date and affixed helmet. Avg. cond. $63

Finger Ring, DAK, Germany, Army, WWII. 8½ size. 19mm-tall oval with raised camel, palm tree and pyramid. Silver finish is worn and shows brass base. Owner added swastika engraved to back side of oval. Avg. cond. $61

Finger Ring, Luftwaffe Eagle, Germany, Luftwaffe, WWII, L.G. Nitz, Hannover. Brown box with faint maker name on lid "L.G.Nitz Hannover etc." Size 9½. 12mm-tall panel with raised eagle details. Above avg. cond. $342

Finger Ring, Luftwaffe Paratrooper, Germany, Luftwaffe, WWII. Size 12½. 18mm-tall rectangular front with raised badge details. Oak leaves and acorns on sides. Stamped "800." Highlights show use. Above avg. cond. $328

Finger Ring, SS, Germany, SS, WWII. Hmkd "800" silver. Black enameled rectangular front panel with silver SS-style totenkopf skull over "SS" runes. Small size. Rare. Above avg. cond. $548

Watch Fob, Geb. Jager Regt 100, Germany, Army, WWII. 37mm brass body with raised title and edelweiss. Reverse has seven raised battle areas. "Cassino, Abruzzen etc." Avg. cond. $79

Watch Fob, Panzer, Germany, Army, WWII. In the form of a miniature shoulder strap with silver finished projectile suspended from bottom. Strap of dark green wool with pink piping and pink hand-embr "S 3." Suspension clip at top. Some damage to strap. Avg. cond. $25

Jewelry——Other

Finger Ring, Austria, 1914. 1914 Austrian. Nickel with bust of Franz Josef. Medium size. Avg. cond. $21

Newspapers and Periodicals——U.S.

Magazine, "Leatherneck," USA, USMC, 1950. 1950 issue on the 175th Anniversary of the Marine Corps. Avg. cond. $30

Magazine, "Rendezvous With Destiny," USA, Army, 1971. 101st Airborne Division Magazine. Magazine format, sb, 40 pages. Summer/Fall 1971 issue. Avg. cond. . . . $20

Magazine, "Rendezvous With Destiny," USA, Army, 1970s. Publication of the 101st Airborne Division. Large format, sb, 1970s, 29+ pages. Avg. cond. $40

Magazine, "The Indian," USA, Army, WWII. Eight issues. Titled "The Indian." Published by the 2nd Division occupation forces. Size 11½" x 9". Some color. Under 20 pages. Each copy sealed in plastic and cover assorted volumes and issues. Above avg. cond. $60

Magazine, TPE Indian

Magazines, "Yank The Army Weekly," USA, Army, 1945. Jan.–July 1945 issues. European Edition. With headlines such as "How Germans Killed American Prisoners of War," "Normandy Invasion Beach, One Year After," "7th Division Veterans Compare Three Campaigns," etc. Avg. cond. $30

Magazines, "Yank The Army Weekly," USA, Army, 1945. May-Dec. 1945 issues. Reporting on Freedom and Food, Washington Faces the Peace, etc. Avg. cond. $21

Newspaper, "Nation Weekly," USA, c1941. Aug. 4, 1941 issue with headlines "US Takes Lead For War Against Japan." July 28, 1941 reports "English People Turn Against War Directors." July 21, 1941 front news "Britain Wants US Expeditionary Force." Avg. cond. $48

Newspaper, "Negroes and the War," USA, WWII. Published by the OWI during the war. With pictures and illus. Above avg. cond. $72

Newspaper, Negroes
and the War

Newspaper, "The World" With the Headline on the Sinking Lusitania, USA, 1915. NY paper dated May 9, 1915. Has partial list of the famous Americans killed in the torpedoing of the ocean liner. Folded and a complete paper. Avg. cond. $38

Newspaper, "US Orders Kaiser to Explain Deaths Of 136 Americans," USA, 1915. NY paper dated May 8, 1915. "The Evening Telegram" extra edition with total killed in the torpedoing of the ocean liner. Folded and complete paper with no tears. Above avg. cond. . . . $32

Periodical, "Japan Times Weekly," USA, Army, WWII. Nov. 1942, with reports from war with Japan. Avg. cond. $20

Periodical, "Outpost Report," USA, WWII. OWI publication. Medium format magazine, sb, 32 pages with photos and articles on the war. Avg. cond. $20

Periodical, "Prisoners of War Bulletin," USA, Red Cross, WWII. Three issues dated 1944 and 1945. Published by the American National Red Cross. Reports on Japanese and German camps. Avg. cond. $55

Periodical, "The Forward Observer," USA, Army, WWII. Publication of the 492nd Armored Field Artillery Battalion at Camp Cooke, CA. One dated 5 August, 1944 and another 29 July, 1944. Avg. cond. $12

Newspapers and Periodicals—Germany

Periodical, "Der SA-Mann," Germany, 1935. In orange and black print, with party eagle in corner. 21 September 1935 issue shows soldiers in parade in stadium and Hitler. Headline "Das programm wird durchgefuhrt Parteitag-Kongress" Folded. Above avg. cond. $40

Periodical, "Der SA-Mann," Germany, 1935. 28 September, 1935. Headlines "Bindet den Helm fester" (fasten your helmets) with photos of Hitler saluting the new flag, in orange and black bold print, with party eagle in corner. With news reports of Reichsparteitag. Folded and shows some age. Avg. cond. $40

Periodical, "Der Weltkrieg," Germany, 1915. Small format, sb, 24 pages with all German text with history of the war and photos of the weapons, combat and leaders. A weekly magazine for 1st week Aug. 1915. Avg. cond. $20

Periodical, "SS Leithheft," Germany, 1944. Year 10, 1944, Vol. 8. Medium format, sb, 46 pages with photos and illus, has women, historical finds and Waffen SS soldiers getting decorated and others. All German text. Avg. cond. $50

Newspapers and Periodicals—Other

Newspaper, Spanish Blue Division Regimental, Spain, 1942. Published in Russia for Spanish volunteers, dated Feb. 16, 1942. Above avg. cond. $95

Newspaper, Spanish Civil War, Spain, 1937. Spanish fascist headline dated April 2, 1937. Good cond. . . . $20

Patriotic Items—U.S.

Badge, Liberty Loan, USA, WWI. For fourth liberty loan drive. 31 x 43mm oval body with Statue of Liberty design. Numbered. Pb. Avg. cond. $20

Badge, Navy, Civilian Employee, USA, Navy, 1930s. Stamped white metal with black enameled lettering "C and R Inspector USN 407." Pb. Maker marked. 2½" x 1¾". Above avg. cond. $26

Badge, San Francisco Naval Shipyard, USA, Navy, WWII. 75mm-wide seven-point star design with great national eagle design clutching anchor in center. Pb. Avg. cond. $100

Banner, Relative in Service, USA, WWII. 11" x 15" with black wood post and gold cord. Red with white field and blue star center. Some fading. Avg. cond. $28

Banner, Relative in Service, USA, WWI. Brown felt with embr "SIGNAL CORPS" at top and embr relative serving

"Relative in the Service" Pennant

banner in center and Signal Corps embr emblem at bottom. One edge discolored. Avg. cond. $25

Banner, Relative Serving in the US Marines, USA, WWII. On wooden pole with gold cord. Narrow red border with bottom gold fringe. White center with USMC emblem in middle and "SERVING IN THE" above and "US/MARINES" at bottom. Two small stains. Avg. cond. $15

Banner, Sixth War Loan, USA, WWII. Hand painted. White cotton with red and yellow fringe and blue and red images for the Sixth War Loan/Buy Bonds campaign. Above avg. cond. $339

Figurine, Anti-Hitler Plaster Skunk, USA, WWII. 5" long and 5" tall painted b/w skunk body with Hitler head. Solid plaster construction. Exc. cond. $160

ID Wheel, By Wonder Bread, USA, WWII. 4" x 5" paperboard wheel with b&w graphics of the rank and insignia of the US military during WWII. Avg. cond. $20

Pendant, Gold Star Mother, USA, WWI. 1½" round bronze with gold star insert over a liner and statue of Liberty and Eiffel tower. Given by the US Lines. Numbered on the rim. Loop for hanging. Avg. cond. $26

Pin Cushion, Anti-Hitler, USA, WWII. 6½" tall painted bent-over Hitler figure with cushion affixed at rump. Base marked "Stick a Pin in the Axis" with maker "Mason Co." Above avg. cond. $145

Pin, Liberty Loan Pin, USA, WWI. Official representative liberty loan ID pin. Gray metal with US above eagle. Avg. cond. $20

Remembrance Pillow Case, 11th Evac Hospital - Pusan Korea, USA, Korean War Era. 17" x 17" red cotton body with large color machine-embr 8th Army patch design in center. Yellow machine-embr "11th Evac Hospital Pusan Korea." Avg. cond. $30

Patriotic Items——Germany

Advertisement Calendar, WKC, Germany, WWII. About 1" x 9½" x 14" size with wood frame backing having two hanger loops. Two dial adjustment knobs at each side, day/month. Blue and silver "WKC" center with knight head, two color swords and bayonet "Blanke Waffen Aller Art" with address below. Above avg. cond. $240

Advertisement Sign, WKC, Germany, WWII. Self-framing. Metal. 12½" x 19" size. Still wrapped in original brown paper. Colorful. Has likeness of two swords and bayonet with knight trademark. Near mint cond. . . $150

Ashtray, Imperial Germany, WWI. Oval white porcelain. 7" x 3¾" in size. White field. Cigarette retainers on ends trimmed in national colors. Center field has oak and laurel wreath bound with ribbons of Germany and Austria. Center has litho b&w portraits of Kaiser and Franz Josef. Avg. cond. $27

Ashtray, Hitler Profile, Germany, WWII. White ceramic ashtray with picture of Hitler in brown with clear overglaze. Has gilt decorative stripe to upper edge, shows some wear from use. Maker marked on bottom, "CKW Buringia." Three-sided design. Exc. cond. $145

Ashtray, With Bust Of Bismarck in Center, Imperial Germany, WWI. 7" x 5" oval. White metal. Scrolled edges with Imperial crown and eagle design, radiant sun above bust of Bismarck in center with "Unser Bismarck" lettering. Hmkd. Avg. cond. $72

Beer Stein, Imperial Germany, WWI. 6" tall overall with domed pewter lid having lyre design, wreath, edelweiss thumblift and rim engraved "Ludwig Holzapfel." White china body with handle, size "1/2L," color front with "Gen.-Feldmarschall von Hindenburg," Hindenburg profile, 1914 EK, wreath with crossed equipment and tricolor flags. Tri-color lower edge. Avg. cond. $176

Box With Iron Cross, Imperial Germany, WWI. 1¼" x 3" x 4½" black and gray cloth-covered box with stamped metal full-size EK affixed to lid with small ribbon above. Deluxe inside is lined with blue velvet. Above avg. cond. $114

Cigarette Case, Imperial Germany, 1915. 1915 dated. Silver finished. Approx. 3" x 4". Flip-open pattern. Scrolled silver field with blue enameled house order on lid with gilt crown and FR device. Miniature EK 1st class. Verso with silver oak leaf sprig with "Gorlice 2v 1915" lettering. Exc. cond. $280

Decanter, Naval Sailor, Imperial Germany, WWI. Porcelain. 10" tall. Decanter is in shape of Imperial signal man sailor in dress blues with rate on left sleeve, signal flags in hand, sailor carries M09 binoculars in left hand, white sailor cap removable with original cork stopper. Hand painted and fired. Above avg. cond. $75

Feldpost Box, Imperial Germany, WWI. 7" x 12". Pseudo black pebbled leather body with "Feldpost Grusse" (Field Post Greetings). Flip open with white metal ornate hasp. Lettering is done in raised work with miniature design of EK 1914. Avg. cond. $28

Feldpost Letter Box, Imperial Germany, WWI. 11" x 8½" x 2½" hinged box with metal clasp lock. Gray cloth body with black border. EK 1914 2nd class on lid with ribbon. National colored ribbon for hinge opener. Inside has two lid compartments for letters and card. White and gray paperwork design liner. Above avg. cond. $100

Flower Stand, With Iron Cross, Imperial Germany, WWI. Pressed glass. 8" tall, 2¼" wide with gold work rim. Beautiful incised floral work with large gold trimmed oval in center having clear field and black Iron Cross 1914, 1st class with good detail. Squared-style base. Above avg. cond. $151

Goblet, From Oldenburg, Imperial Germany, c1900. 6½"-tall body has relief views of Imperial monuments featuring Bismarck and Wilhelm I, gray pewter color. Lip inscribed in German "Greetings from Oldenburg from your brother Dietrich." Above avg. cond. $84

Ink Well Desk Set, Imperial Germany, WWI. 5" x 12" oak base has a 2" rounded groove, with two cover compartments for ink bottles. Flying eagle attached to oak base. Above avg. cond. $75

Ink Well in Form of Spiked Helmet, Imperial Germany, WWI. 2½"-long nickel body is 1½" tall with removable 1" brass spike lid. Brass eagle frontplate shows past repair to head and brass bayonet placed through helmet behind eagle. Black leatherette chinstrap. Avg. cond. $105

Letter Box, With Iron Cross, Imperial Germany, WWI. Pressed paper with black pebbled finish. Silver impressed facsimile of 1914 Iron Cross and national colors band on lid, brass worked key entry lug with silver metal key. Functional lock. 6" x 4" x 2" in size. Avg. cond. ... $69

Match Safe, Imperial Germany, WWI. Three-sided brass with affixed "Gott Mit Uns" roundel. Back stamped "Reuben Burch Dayton Ill" using dog tag letters/dies. Avg. cond. $20

Member Badge, NSDAP, Germany, WWII. 18mm size, tri-color with small chip on red. Pb and "Ges.Gesch." Avg. cond. $34

Member Badge, NSDAP, Germany, WWII. 23mm with enamel and silver lettering. Pb and "RZM M1/155." Avg. cond. $35

Member Badge, NSDAP, Golden Honor, Germany, WWII. 25mm. Gold finished wreath is worn on copper base. Tri-color enamel work shows use with scratches and small chips overall. Bent pb with faint maker. No vent hole and stamped "63628." Shows its age. Below avg. cond. .. $275

Member Badge, NSDAP, Golden Honor, Germany, WWII. 25mm. Dark gold wreath, enamel shows wear, vent hole in back, stamped "28672" and pb. Early civilian dress badge. Above avg. cond. $538

Member Badge, Stahlhelm, Germany, 1924. Good black enamel, silver oak leaves/date and loose helmet from rivet shows past glue-repair attempts. Pb and engraved "VI.Ns.1396 1.5.24." Avg. cond. $100

Member Badge, Stahlhelm, Germany, 1930. Good black enamel, silver oak leaves/date and helmet. Pb, engraved "Wm.2687 26.10.30" and maker "sth 935 ges.gesch." Avg. cond. $108

Memorial to the Garde Infantry, Imperial Germany, WWI. Black turned wooden column with fluted general officer spike on top. Approx. 13" tall with round 4½" base tapering to fine finial top. Original large officer Garde star with full enamel mounted on side in silver starburst backing. Near mint cond. $643

Memorial, to a Bavarian Infantry Officer, Imperial Germany, WWI. Hand made. Desk-style wooden stand on base approx. 13" x 2" in black wood. Tall 9" fan in red and gold wood and paint. Large Bavarian Reservist officer frontplate mounted on body with "Ludwig Konig von Bayern" lettering. Exc. cond. $217

Mortar and Pestle, Imperial Germany, WWI. Mortar has high polish with raised band having dates and design in relief of heavy Skoda mortar. Matching iron pestle. Exc. cond. $124

Mother's Cross Medal, Miniature, Bronze, Germany, WWII. 21mm tall with good enamel and faded bow tie ribbon with pin. Avg. cond. $28

Mother's Cross, Gold, Germany, WWII. Mint enamel and finish. Ribbon still tied and wrapped with tissue. Gold plated for eight or more children. Near mint cond. $82

Mother's Cross, Silver, Germany, WWII. Darkening to silver finish, good enamel and full ribbon. Avg. cond. $32

Mother's Cross, Silver, Germany, WWII. Darkening to silver finish with soiling to enamel and 13" ribbon. For mother of six or seven children. Avg. cond. $30

Pen Case, Imperial Germany, WWI. 8" x 2" x 1" with hinged lid. Black lacquered case opens to reveal three compartments for pen, nibs, accessories. Domed lid has beautiful color design of helmeted soldiers drawing a large field gun into position while companions man a cannon on the line and officers radio in position. Flying early "Taube" aircraft shown doing aerial reconnaissance to upper left. Above avg. cond. $87

Plaque, Admiral Scheer, Germany, WWII. 18" x 14" black wooden frame with silver metal high-relief view of the ship at speed with good detail of weapons and superstructure. Lower front has silver metal plaque inscribed "Gr. 4/1.9.41–30.9.41." Reverse has large hand-written paper pasted to frame with 14 signatures of men who took the cruise in 1941. Above avg. cond. $195

Plaque, Luftwaffe Flak Regt 804, Germany, WWII. Probably came from regimental headquarters and is one of a kind. Bronze shield of oak base. 5" x 7". Bronze plaque with 804 at upper left top, 88mm gun in firing position above scrolled unit crest shield. Hook back. Above avg. cond. $124

Plate, Party Eagle, Germany, WWII. 9½" x 13" dark copper plate has 12"-wide party eagle at center. Above avg. cond. $185

Plate, Wood, Germany, WWII. Plate is 8¾" diam, wood-burned design around edges and color painted emblem of Munich in center with crest of five different cities/regions around edge. The Munich insignia is crested with the Nazi flag. Wall decoration. Avg. cond. $25

Remembrance Pillow, Naval Painted Scene, Imperial Germany, Navy, WWI. 14" x 19½" black velvet front with purple cloth backing and open seam on lower edge with no stuffing. Shows burning ship with sailor on floating wreckage holding small kriegs flag over head. Above avg. cond. $28

Reservist Stein, "4.garde Feld=art.regt., potsdam 1910/1912," Imperial Germany, Army, WWI. 8½" tall off-white crockery body with color details to raised designs around base, three painted artillery scenes to body with crowned display at center. Named to "Reservist Blohm" at rim, small roster at back near handle with crowned eagle thumblift, metal Garde star hanging from beak and view-glass has named "Podsdam etc." image. Domed pewter lid has fuse details, artillery crew and mounted trooper finial. Exc. cond. $906

Reservist Stein, 8th Rheinish Foot Artillery Regt, Imperial Germany, Army, c1906. 12" high. Half-liter. Named to Reservist Heis of the 6th Company, Metz, 1904–06. Roster. Field howitzer finial with two ball topped helmeted soldiers, crowned spread-winged eagle thumblift. Bright colors. Man, woman departing in field litho. Front panel shows field gun being ready for firing with officer in background with telescope. Two side panels depict artillery in firing position. No damage. Cannon barrel moves on pewter lid. Exc. cond. $460

Reservist Stein, Bavarian 4th Infantry Regt, Infantry Germany, Army, c1905. 10½" tall overall, 6½" white china body with color details, roster at back, named to "Res. Zapf" and "8. Cp. Konigl. Bayr. 4. Inftr. Regt. (Koenig Wlh. v. Wurttemberg) Metz 1901–1903." Domed pewter lid with military motif and soldier finial. Lion shield thumblift. King lithopane. Avg. cond. $300

Smoking Pipe Bowl, Imperial Germany, WWI. 3½" ceramic pipe bowl. Hand-painted details to two WWI medics with armbands, side packs and cloth service caps working on a wounded and bleeding soldier who has a severe chest wound. Background shows other medics with stretcher. Back of pipe is inscribed in German "Badly Wounded." Avg. cond. $50

Stein, Imperial Germany, WWI. Cobalt blue potbelly. This stein is about 5½" tall. The lid is a domed style with pebbled edges having feather-style thumblift. Front panel shows a lyre motif with floral design and raised motto "Gruss Gott mit hellem Klang. Heil Deutschen Wort und Sang" (Greet God With Bright Music. Hail German Words and Song). Above avg. cond. $180

Stein, Bavarian Artillery Regt, Imperial Germany, Army, WWI. Tall, half-liter crockery body. Named to soldier who served 1910–12. Obverse with image of Prince Regent Ludwig surrounded by Bavarian crests. Other scenes of military life and roster. With pewter lid with floral motifs, inscriptions, field cannon finial and lion motif. Exc. cond. $600

Stein, Bavarian
Artillery Regiment

Stein, Bavarian Infantry Regt, Imperial Germany, WWI. Half-liter tall body of white porcelain. Named to soldier who served from 1912–14. Various colorful scenes of Bavarian royalty, soldiers in pre-war uniforms, blue wreath banding, unit roster and image of soldier and his girlfriend. Cast-pewter lid with inscriptions, garlands, and scrollwork. Finial in form of standing soldier and lion and thumblift in form of lion. Exc. cond. $855

Stein, Bavarian Infantry

Stein, Hamburg 18th-Century City Outline, Imperial Germany, WWI. 7" tall. Silvered flat-pattern lid with ball thumblift. Glazed in dark brown with sepia transfer of the old city. Modified cylinder pattern. Avg. cond. $36

Stein, Reservist Holstein Field Arty Regt 24, Imperial Germany, Army, WWI. 11" tall. Beautiful bright colors. Named to Gefreiter Wigger of the 5th Battery Holstein Field Artillery Regt 24, stationed at Gustrow, 1906–08. Gray domed lid with two artillery soldiers standing by field cannon, crowned Prussian eagle thumblift. Lithopane of man and woman departing from one another. Double-column roster. Center panel shows cannon and caisson pulled by horses, lower device depicts shoulder strap, shells, crown, flags and swords. Two side panels show firing practice and placement of weapons. Exc. cond. $538

Stein, With Iron Cross, Imperial Germany, WWI. 4½" fat body with half-liter capacity. Blue and gray glazed work design of helmeted soldiers with field packs on charge flanked by two panels with 1914 Iron Crosses. Incised motto, "Mit Gott fur Konig und Vaterland." White metal domed lid with raised-work Iron Cross and ball thumblift. Minor 1mm separation at joint of lid and thumblift. Above avg. cond. $284

Tile, 1914 Iron Cross, Imperial Germany, WWI. 6"-diam white body with black EK center and green oak leaves wreath with acorns. Back marked "1914." Above avg. cond. $75

Veteran Badge, Long Service 25 Year, Imperial Germany, WWI. 40mm black-white-red shield bronze with "K.S.M. iron cross D.K.V. 25 jahre Mitglied & Glauchau." Pb. Avg. cond. $25

Wall Calendar, Imperial Germany, WWI. 18" x 23". Stiff cardboard with four-color picture of all the crests of all the states of Imperial Germany in full color. Center shows Teutonia holding her crown aloft. Beside the date holder appear soldiers of the Napoleonic and 1913 period in full color uniforms. Holder on lower front center for dates. Company advertised military provisions from old Hannover. Original hanging cord with Prussian crowned eagle in center. Avg. cond. $175

Wall Plaque, Imperial Germany, WWI. 17" x 12½" size. Carved wooden plaque. Depicts Bismarck standing carrying sword and scrolled document. With Prussian eagles and crown. Base inscribed "IN TRINITATE ROBAR." Small repair to base. Above avg. cond. $250

Patriotic Wooden Wall Plaque, Bismarck

Watch Carrier, Bavarian Officer, Imperial Germany, WWI. Custom made. Silver metal finish snap open with raised Iron Cross, "In Treue Fest" motto on front reverse, has clear celluloid viewer for watch face. Type carried in trench war to protect watch from shocks and impacts. Above avg. cond. $95

Wax Seal Stamp, "Waffen SS," Germany, WWII. Brass head with wooden handle. Waffenamt stamped, serial numbered. Large eagle with Waffen SS and circular inscription. Approx. 5" tall. Exc. cond. $328

Wooden Cigar Box With Steel Plate Litho Designs, Imperial Germany, WWI. 5" x 7" x 2". Hinged lid with brass stud pull. Yellow paper covering with scenes of seven different historical homes and peasants. Inner liner has rubberized support for cigars. Lid has view of the Albrecht Hall in Landeck. Avg. cond. $25

Patriotic Items—Other

Souvenir Handkerchief, French Navy, France, Navy, WWI. 9" x 9" white silk handkerchief having sepia-toned picture of French cruiser Duquesne, with identification inscription. Above avg. cond. $75

Sweetheart Items—U.S.

Ankle Bracelet, Sweetheart, USA, WWII. S/S bracelet with small oval disc and AAF winged prop emblem. Fine chain with spring catch. Avg. cond. $25

Bracelet, Bombardier Wing, USA, AAF, WWII. 3" size stamped sterling "Amcraft"-style bombardier wing with bomb design applied over observer center. Curve formed (pin has been removed) wing tips drilled for wrist chain. Includes chain with safety catch. Above avg. cond. $45

Bracelet, Sweetheart, USA, WWII. Woman's bracelet with brass and enamel Army emblem in center. Remainder appears silver plated. Scissors latch. Avg. cond. $35

Bracelet, Sweetheart, Airborne, USA, WWII. Features Airborne wings on crest and "love, Joe" on back. Link chain and chute worn smooth. Avg. cond. $28

Hankie, Sweetheart, USA, WWII. Pink-red with pink side-embr Sweetheart over AAF emblem. Avg. cond. $21

Heart-shaped Locket, Sweetheart, USA, USMC, WWII. Gold-finished heart locket has EGA device on the front. Has loop for wear on chain. Avg. cond. $20

Lapel Badge, Sweetheart, USA, USMC. With blank pendant for name. USMC lettered. Avg. cond. $20

Pin, Sweetheart, Airborne, USA, Army, WWII. 14 x 14mm 82nd A/B Div patch design. Pin with "82nd Division/U.S.A." lettering and crest design pin with motto "Honor and Country" attached to each other by small linked chain. Both are pb with "fall-in" catch. Sterling/maker hmkd. Above avg. cond. $49

Pin, Sweetheart, USA, WWII. Pb, CPO hat device with relative in service banner below USN. One anchor hook tarnished. Avg. cond. $25

Pin, Sweetheart, USA, AAF, WWII. Pb stamped polished metal looks like fighter with AAF stars on wings. Avg. cond. $20

Pin, Sweetheart, USA, AAF, WWII. Small gilt and enamel ferry command patch chain linked to small USA pin. Avg. cond. $20

Pin, Sweetheart, USA, Navy, WWII. Sterling pb shield

with enameled "NAVY" at top and Navy wings below and "V-5" at bottom. Avg. cond. $24

Pin, Sweetheart, USA, WWII. Brass pb pin with enameled relative in service banner in center. Brass frame has images of branches of Army. Mint on sales card. Near mint cond. $30

Pin, Sweetheart, USA, WWII. 13mm. 2nd lieut bar design attached to "U.S." design by small linked chain. Both pieces are 10k, hmkd and Pb with "fall-in" catch. Exc. cond. $45

Pin, Sweetheart, USA, WWII. Pb, 1" heart from layered red-white-blue plastic with sterling graphic "Mother" and dangling star with red jewel. Exc. cond. $90

Pin, Sweetheart, USA, WWII. Constructed from CW belt buckle, disc removed from remainder and pb added. Above avg. cond. $55

Pin, Sweetheart, USA, WWII. Pb. S/S. Qm pin with "US" fixed at bottom. Good detail. Avg. cond. $20

Pin, Sweetheart, USA, WWII. Hand painted eagle with "IN SERVICE" on chest and open. Sweetheart banner in talons. Avg. cond. $20

Pin, Sweetheart, Air Cadet, USA, AAF, WWII. 2½" pb sterling cadet wing with prop in center. Marked on back. Good detail and finish. Avg. cond. $28

Pin, Sweetheart, Keesler Field, USA, AAF, WWII. 1½" S/S, pb, pilot wing with good details and has tip to tip bow across top with KEESLER FIELD in blue enamel on bow. Avg. cond. $59

Pins, Sweetheart, USA, AAF, WWII. Both gold-filled S/S, pb with winged prop and rank dangle. One is 1st Lieut, the other Captain Rank shows wear. Avg. cond. $25

Ring, Sweetheart, USA, WWII. Sterling from Lieut Col's leaf. Above avg. cond. $32

Ring, Sweetheart, USA, WWII. Copper ring with Air Cadet Wings on crest and other symbols on sides. Above avg. cond. $34

Pin, Boy in Service, USA, WWII. 17mm wide, gilted sterling and enamel. Good cond. $9

Wing, Sweetheart Aircrew, USA, AAF, WWII. 72mm, pb, S/S, unmarked with 17 stones set in wing, six on each pelican beak inner wing and five in the center disc. Simulated diamonds. Avg. cond. $82

Wing, Sweetheart, USA, AAF, WWII. 1½", pb, S/S pilot wing with enameled stars, bars in center and bow across tip to tip with "CRIDER FIELD." Avg. cond. $70

Wing, Sweetheart, USA, AAF, WWII. Pilot-style wing, pb with gilded center disc and Army emblem surrounded by jewel chips. Avg. cond. $22

Wing, Sweetheart, Pilot, USA, AAF, WWII. Sterling 1/20th 10k marked. Pb with safety catch. 1¼" size. Hmkd. Avg. cond. $20

Sweetheart Items—Germany

Rouge Case, Sweetheart, Imperial Germany, WWI. 3¼" diam, 1¼" tall. Silver metal. Brass Garde star on top. Flip-up silvered lid. Above avg. cond. $65

Sweetheart Items—Other

Brooch, Sweetheart, England, WWII. 42 mm diam, gold, upswept wings with small pearls at wing top arches, surmounted by green enamel wreath, red and gold enamel crown, pierced planchet with blue enamel script "R.A.F." center, reverse inscribed "14Kt.," pb. Above avg. cond. $125

Bracelet, Sweetheart, England, WWI. Two officer's rank pips, gilded with red and green enameled highlights, two gilded crowns on silvered chain bracelet with spring-clip closure. Above avg. cond. $20

Brooch, Sweetheart, England, WWII. 42mm diam, gilded brass, outstretched wings surmounted by blue enamel field, "RAF" center, red enamel crown, reverse inscribed "Official Bundles For Britain By Monet." Above avg. cond. $25

Brooch, Sweetheart, England, WWII. Silver with light blue and dark blue enamel, enameled suspension and marked "Silver." Has original sales card. Exc. cond. $20

Brooch, Sweetheart, England, WWI. Silver, suspension with clear glass crystal, Peruvian blue butterfly wing decoration, surmounted by full-color Royal Army Artillery insignia, marked "Sterling Silver." With original sales card. Good cond. $20

CHAPTER SIXTEEN

Miscellaneous Militaria

A vast array of items fall under miscellaneous collecting categories. They often include practical and personal items used by both servicemen and civilians. In this chapter examples of flags, banners, glassware, kitchenware, china, lighters, plaques and trophies, tin soldiers, toys and games will be presented. Values within the category vary greatly. Many common items are plentiful and priced reasonably for collectors. Other special or rare pieces can command higher market prices.

Serviceman often brought home souvenirs of their travels and campaigns. These sentimental collectibles have survived as they have been passed down through the generations and have entered the collectible markets. Some items, such as china with patriotic pictures or sayings, were given as gift premiums or propaganda souvenirs.

Flags commonly fell during conflicts and were prized World War souvenirs for servicemen. Both unit flags and personal flags, such as those carried by Japanese soldiers, are popular items. Nazi flags are especially desirable.

"Ephemera" is a broad collectible category that includes a wide array of military and civilian items. These items include ration books, ID cards, occupational currencies, postcards, recruiting items, servicemen's personal papers and letters, and much more. Some ephemeral print items were discussed in Chapters Fourteen and Fifteen.

Collecting Tips
Personal items are generally more identifiable and collectible when engraved with a person's name, unit, and/or date, such as cigarette cases or lighters.

Fakes and Frauds
Nazi collectibles tend to be one of the most frequently reproduced items in this category. Examine items carefully.

Flags—U.S.

Flag, 3 Star General, USA, USAF, c1960s. Yellow fringe around blue nylon field. Stars are sewn on and two sided. Size 3' x 4'. Exc. cond. $50

Flag, Rear Admiral, USA, Navy, WWII. Dark blue wool blend with two white vertical stars sewn on. Two sided with bunting and grommets. Some wear with holes and some repairs. Avg. cond. $45

Flag, USMC, USA, USMC, c1930s. 4' x 5' flag that was used in the China service of 1930s and retained by Marine NCO when he retired. Wool blend with dark blue panel and colored USMC emblem. Two sided with reinforced bunting. Some minor cracking of paint and slight soiling. Documentation included. Above avg. cond. $641

Guidon, Swallowtail, Artillery, USA, Army, WWII. Scarlet field with yellow crossed cannons. Swallowtail design 29" x 18". Two-sided sewn construction. Exc. cond. $20

Guidon, Swallowtail, Qm Corps, USA, Army, 1961. 29½" x 20" buff-colored cotton body with appliqué design. 1961 dated Qm label. Some mothing but no soiling. Above avg. cond. $30

Signal Flags Signal, USA, Army, WWI. Nine flags with 42" wood rods. Avg. cond. $20

Flags—Germany

Flag, Imperial Battle, Imperial Germany, Army, WWI. 4' x 6½' wool printed body with good details. Bunting has rope and loop end. Exc. cond. $450

Flag, Imperial Battle, Imperial Germany, Army, WWI. 2½' x 4' printed cotton body with good details. Roped bunting with loop. Avg. cond. $278

Flag, Kriegs, Germany, Army, WWII. 3' x 5' printed wool body. Red cotton bunting has rope with loop ends. Above avg. cond. $177

Flag, Kriegs, Germany, Army, WWII. 6' x 8' printed wool body. Variation cloth bunting with end loops. Avg. cond. $125

Flag, Kriegs, Naval, Germany, Navy, WWII. 5' x 8' printed wool body. Rope on bunting and loop. Inked Eagle-M "Reichskriegsfl. 150 x 250 etc." Above avg. cond. . $160

Flag, Kriegs, Naval, Germany, Navy. 5' x 8' printed body has old white sheet sewn to back side as reinforcement. Body shows some frayed areas. Bunting lacks rope. Inked Eagle-M and "Reichskriegsflg 150 x 250 etc." Avg. cond. $87

Flag, Kriegs, Prussian, Imperial Germany, Army, WWI. 2' x 3' printed wool body. Rope on bunting with loop end. Good printed details. Fair cond. $180

Flag, Party, Germany, WWII. 15" x 22" red cotton body, composite swastikas on sewn white centers and pole sleeve with bevo "Stetter etc." Exc. cond. $150

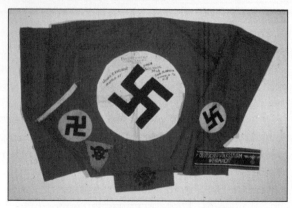

Nazi Party Flag and Pennants Group

Flag, Party, Germany, WWII. 2½' x 5' red cotton body with printed swastikas on sewn white centers. Small rope on bunting with looped ends. Avg. cond. $40

Flag, SS, Germany, SS, WWII. 5' x 8' black cotton body with white composite runes to each side, 32" tall. Rope on bunting with steel swivel clip. Exc. cond. $551

Standard, Kriegerbund, Naval, Germany, Navy, WWII. 4' x 4' printed red body with black swastika, anchor and EK center. Avg. cond. $370

Flags—Other

Flag, Pipe Major Banner of the Scots Guards, England. 28" x 21". Double sided with red silk field with hand-embr gold bullion crown, shield with red rampant lion, and sphinx with laurel wreath, complete with gold bullion border fringe, red field and museum quality. Above avg. cond. $2500

Flag, Denmark, WWII. 140" x 54", wool bunting, German manufacture. Above avg. cond. $49

Flag, SS Trumpet Banner, Holland, SS, WWII. 15" x 15", double sided with red wolf hook insignia outlined in gray, black cotton twill field with gray border fringe with ties. Above avg. cond. $2500

Flag, War Flag, Greece, Army, WWII. 48" x 34", embr gold crown on white cotton cross with royal blue cotton field, complete with hanging rope. Hmkd. Above avg. cond. $350

Flag, Naval, Italy, Navy, 1988. 52" x 35" printed wool flag. Exc. cond. $43

Flag, Italy, WWII. 37" x 24½", Italian tri-color with Savoy shield and crown. Avg. cond. $20

Flag, Lot, Japan, WWII. 28" x 28", red ball with white field and Japanese character inscriptions, with corner gold foil hanging reinforcements, lot also includes white silk 12" x 12" banner. Good cond. $125

Flag, Japan, WWII. 40" x 27", silk, national pattern having two corners with grained paper grommet reinforcements. Above avg. cond. $55

Flag, Japan, WWII. 34¼" x 28¼", red ball on white cotton field, two corners with cloth reinforcements, black printed Japanese character inscription. Above avg. cond. . . . $75

Japanese Flag

Flag, Vice Admiral Flag, Japan, Navy, WWII. 102" x 62", sewn composition, red and white cotton, rising sun motif with top red horizontal field. With hanging rope. Good cond. $535

Banner, Patriotic, Japan, WWII. 44" x 20", white silk with green silk edges, golden fringe bottom, depicts crossed national and rising sun war flags with star in center, zigzag pattern in blue with Japanese characters. Above avg. cond. $150

Flag, War, Japan, Army, WWII. 6' x 4', red and white rising sun style. With wooden stick. Above avg. cond. $23

Flag, Japan, WWII. 88" x 68", printed linen with hanging ties. Above avg. cond. $87

Flag, South Korea, Korean War Era. 25" x 14", white printed silk. Above avg. cond. $26

Flag, Recognition, Italy, Navy, WWII. 18" x 14", sewn composite wool construction with red-white Savoy cross with dark blue field and hanging rope. Above avg. cond. $39

Flag, Air Force, Soviet Union, Air Force, 1954. 35" x 27" printed wool flag. Good cond. $34

Flag, War Banner, Soviet Union, Army, WWII. 15" x 8" banner with blue embr inscription over gray, red, and green hammer and sickle and wreath finials, and orange suspension cord. Above avg. cond. $20

Flag, Falangist Banner, Spain, c1937. 28" x 22" single-sided banner with embr "Yoke and Arrows" insignia with unit inscription, with blue floral brocade field and bullion trimmed fringe. Above avg. cond. $235

Flag, Turkey, WWII. 64" x 35" sewn composite construction, white star and crescent on red linen field with hanging loops. Above avg. cond. $125

Flag, Viet Cong, Vietnam, Vietnam War Era. 82"x40" silk flag with gold star on sky blue and red field. Above avg. cond. $127

Glassware, Kitchenware and China——U.S.

Beer Mug, USA, Army, c1946. German made. Tan ceramic 5" beer mug style with "BATTERY C, 440TH AAA AW BN/YANKEE CLUB/ON THE RHEIN IN 1945." Above avg. cond. $90

China, Medical Service, USA, Army, WWII. Large creamer and two small bowls, saucers and salad plates. All have logo, dishes have maroon band also. Above avg. cond. $28

Coffee Cup, Medical Service, USA, Army, WWII. Single coffee cup with maroon US Army Medical Service emblem on side. Above avg. cond. $11

Coffee Mug, 22nd Troop Carrier Sqdn, USA, USAF, c1950s. China. Full-color Sqdn emblem on one side featuring burro with pack and neat portrayal of C-124 Globemaster on the other. Some light crazing on finish. Above avg. cond. $93

Gravy Boat, Medical Dept, USA, Army, WWII. White china gravy boat with maroon Army Medical Dept emblem on one side. Above avg. cond. $16

Saucer, West Point Cadet Mess, USA, c1960s. Expressly made for the cadet mess and so marked on bottom. White china with blue border and West Point emblem on side. Avg. cond. $21

Glassware, Kitchenware and China——Germany

Bread Bowl, With Portrait of U-Boat Ace Otto Weddigen, Imperial Germany, WWI. China. Approx 8" x 12" with integral gold-trimmed handles, pierced side walls. Bottom has large green oak wreath with national colored ribbon. Center shows star with portrait of Kapt.-Lt. Weddigen of the Navy in white summer dress uniform. Weddigen became an early ace after sinking three British cruisers in one day within the space of an hour. All sank with tremendous loss of life, occasioning a scandal in the admiralty offices. Exc. cond. $215

Bread Dish, With Iron Cross, Imperial Germany, WWI. Porcelainized. 2"-tall formed metal oval body has open design around sides. 9" wide and 12" long. Tri-color rim and color wreath center with crowned 1914/15 EK. Above avg. cond. $180

Butter Dish, With Iron Cross, Imperial Germany, WWI. White porcelain 3¼"-diam small personal butter pat dish. Ceramic dish with design of Iron Cross on bottom and motto. Black, white and red border to rim. With wire stand. Exc. cond. $70

Chocolate Mugs, Imperial Germany, WWI. Set of six. 3½" tall and 3½" wide at top with gold rim. Colored panels around base. Wreath with Iron Cross and b&w ribbon. Near mint cond. $152

Creamer, Naval Motif, Imperial Germany, WWI. 5½". White china. National color rim with gold trim on pourer and handle. White field with oval green wreath enclosing fouled blue anchor with crossed national and battle flags above lettering "Kriegsjahr 1914." Exc. cond. $65

Cup and Saucer, With Hitler Portrait, Germany, c1932. Pedestal cup of white porcelain with portrait of Hitler in early political uniform surrounded by wide oak leaf frieze in two-tone gold leaf highlight. Underside inscribed "HEIL HITLER! 24 APRIL 1932." Underside further presents KPM cobalt blue hallmark and painter's signature. Matching saucer has oversized red swastika, similar trim and matching hallmark and signature. Exc. cond. $1750

**Cup and Saucer
with Hitler Portrait**

Cup, Iron Cross, Imperial Germany, WWI. 3" tall white china with 2½" diam and handle. Black EK on center of colored wreath with ribbon. Avg. cond. $20

Cup, With Iron Cross, Imperial Germany, WWI. White china. 2½" wide, 2½" tall with white field. National color design on lip. Center panel has green wreath with 1914 Iron Cross in black work. Gold-trimmed handle. Near mint cond. $41

Demitasse Set, Imperial Germany, WWI. China cup and saucer. 4" saucer, 2" tall cup. Matching set. Cup lip trimmed in national colors design of two eagles on

cup–German and Austrian with black, gold details. Saucer and cup trimmed also in gold. Above avg. cond. . . . $61

Drinking Boot, Imperial Germany, WWI. Glass boot has Iron Cross at top dated 1914. Gold bands below cross and gold straps for spur. Engraved "Mit Gott Fur Konig v Vaterland." Near mint cond. $100

Egg Cup, With Iron Cross, Imperial Germany, WWI. 2½" tall, white china with national color band around lip. Body has black-work Iron Cross 1st class with motto "Mit Gott fur Konig u. Vaterland." Avg. cond. $35

Glass, Germany, WWII. Crystal. Czech made for higher-ups in the Nazi party, design of pre-1939 Czech rampant lion with crown engraved and frosted on ochre-colored oval to one side. Has rounded fluted base with walls of glass rising at an angle upward and outward. The base is also flashed in the ochre color with cut concave discs encircling it. The rim has another flashed ochre stripe and has an engraved patriotic slogan in sutterlin-style script. Dated on this stripe 1938. Flat-cut and polished bottom and rim. Has original maker sticker affixed. 4½" high. Near mint cond. $85

Glass, Lead Crystal, Germany, WWII. Golden yellow tinted, engraved, ground and polished. Known by Glass Collectors as Czechoslovakian Art Glass. Made for higher-ups in the Nazi party, design of pre-1939 Czech rampant lion with crown engraved and frosted in golden yellow oval. Has rounded fluted base with walls of glass rising upward and outward. The base is also flashed in the same color with cut concave discs encircling it. The rim has another flashed stripe and has an engraved patriotic slogan in sutterlin-style script. Dated on this stripe 1938. Flat-cut and polished bottom and rim. 4¼" high. Still has original maker's paper label. Near mint cond. $160

Goblet, "1914 Kriegsjahr," Imperial Germany, WWI. Etched bubble glass. 7½" tall clear body with wheel-cut title to crowned wreath with crossed swords. Nine small bubble design to stem with 3"-diam base. Near mint cond. $225

Goblet, Iron Cross, Imperial Germany, WWI. 5"-tall heavy clear glass body has 3½"-diam ground rim. Ruby red finish on body with large base having ground clear design and ruby outlines. Frosted/etched 1914 EK on side with excellent oak leaf wreath details having acorns and wrap-around branches on body. Exc. cond. $223

Pitcher and Tumbler Set, Imperial Germany, WWI. Six clear glass tumblers, each with ornate national color bowed ribbon and wreath in green, gold rimmed. 5¾" tall, 2¾" wide at mouth. Pitcher is fancy art deco clared style with handle, gold work and Imperial tri-color flag, pole and oak leaves in bright green decor. Approx. 10" tall. Near mint cond. $125

Plate, Imperial Germany, WWI. China. 11" with integral handles to each side. Black-white-red border on lip center has black uncrowned Hohenzollern eagle with national and battle flags to left and right. Bavaria maker marked. Near mint cond. $75

Plate, "Mit Gott Fur Konig Und Vaterland 1914," Imperial Germany, WWI. 9½"-diam white porcelain with blue title to rim and charging lancer in center. Green "Von Professor Anton Hoffmann Munchen" and "Rosenthale Kunst-Abteilung Selb-Bavaria." Exc. cond. $176

Plate, Bavarian "Ludwig III Konig Von Bayern Gekront 10.Nov.1913," Imperial Germany, 1913. 8½"-diam white porcelain with blue title on rim having two monument scenes. Blue crowned shield held by lions at center. Ludwig III takes the throne. Green maker "Rosenthal etc." Near mint cond. $203

Plate, Bavarian, "In Treue Fest 1914," Imperial Germany, WWI. 9½"-diam white porcelain with blue title to rim and spiked helmeted trooper on horse at center in blue. Green "Von Professor Anton Hoffmann Munchen" and "Rosenthal etc." Near mint cond. $176

Plate, Christmas 1914, Imperial Germany, WWI. 10"-diam china plate with blue Christmas scene showing five German soldiers in trench celebrating around small candlelit Christmas tree. Center soldier playing concertina while others enjoy gifts or letters. One soldier on watch. Dated 1914 on rim. Marked on back with blue crossed swords. Bottom rim pierced for hanging. Near mint cond. $339

Plate, Commemorative 12th Jager BN, Imperial Germany, 1910. Meissen. 10" diam. White field with blue worked oak and laurel wreath at sides, 1810–1910 commemorative centennial dates at top. Center has large Royal crown with JB 12 below. Near mint cond. $375

Plate, Heroes of the World War, Imperial Germany, WWI. 10" white glazed porcelain plate with scalloped edges and alternating national color shields. Center has b&w litho of Wilhelm and Franz Josef in wreath with national eagles, national color ribbons. Top and bottom has b&w portraits of U-Boat Ace Weddigen and Hindenburg. "In grosser Zeit. Weltkrieg 1914–15" lettering in gold. Above avg. cond. $135

Plate, Hindenburg Portrait, Germany, WWII. Beautiful gold worked porcelain plate with pierced edges having gold rim and side panel trim. Center of plate has fine color portrait of Hindenburg in his field marshal uniform with

Grand Cross of the Iron Cross and Red Eagle, Orders bar from Franco-Prussian War and gold aiguillettes. Avg. cond. $75

Plate, Saxon 6th Inf Regt, Imperial Germany. 10" diam. White china body in glazed finish with cobalt blue toned view of a cathedral, medieval town in center, blue cobalt style lettering on rim of plate–"Kgl. Sachs. 6. Infanterie Rgt. No. 105. Konig Wilhelm II. v. Wurttemberg" with Imperial eagle and 1701 founding date. Each side of plate has crest of Wurttemberg and Saxony. Crossed sword maker mark on reverse, bright colors. Near mint cond. $252

Plate, With Iron Cross, Imperial Germany, WWI. Gold and silvered china. Maker is "C.T. Altwasser Silesia" with a green Eagle and serial numbered. 160mm square with a perfect 1914 Iron Cross in the center. Exc. cond. . . $220

Presentation Goblet, Royal Prussian, Imperial Germany, 1913. To Prince Oscar of Prussia. Enameled crystal on a pewter base. Delicate 6½" flared lip crystal goblet with gold-filled rim body has Prussian eagle shield showing "Kaiserhaus Goslar" above in wreath, base is flared pewter with banded arbor design above raised inscription "21 July 1908. His Highness, the Crown Prince of the German Nation/18, 19, 20 July 1913 His Royal Highness, Oscar Prince of Prussia." Exc. cond. $538

Serving Tray, Shnapps, With Iron Cross, Imperial Germany. White metal. 11½" x 9" with rigid surface and rim having struck raised Iron Cross in center. Steel-style finish. Near mint cond. $185

Sugar Bowl, Imperial Germany, WWI. White china. 5" tall, 4½" wide with double handles. Complete with lid. Lid and upper bowl trimmed in national colors. Oval green wreath on pot with blue fouled anchor and crossed national and Imperial battle flags above "Kriegsjahr 1914" lettering. Exc. cond. $65

Sugar Bowl With Gold-Topped Lid, Imperial Germany, WWI. 5" x 3". Two handles. White glazed porcelain with double design of crowned Prussian-style eagle in half green wreath of laurel. National color design on top. Near mint cond. $60

Vase, With Iron Cross, Imperial Germany, WWI. Meissen. White glazed china body with flared rim. Approx. 9" tall with 5½" flared lip. Blue cobalt design of laurel on front encloses a radiant EK 1914 1st class, reverse has oak leaf sprig with 1914–16 dates. Near mint cond. $245

Wine Decanter, 49th Field Artillery, Imperial Germany, 1902. 1902 dated with presentation inscription on flat silver lid with spout cover scrolled cipher with #49 below on center of lid, edge dated 27 January 1902, having two men's names. Ball-top lifter, upper 2" of glass body sheathed in silver metal finish, decanter is 10½" tall with clear crystal glass body in gentle flare configuration. Exc. cond. $225

Lighters

Lighter, SAC "Peace Is Our Profession," USA, Universal. Boxed, brushed chrome lighter with SAC shield on front, lettering on lid. Above avg. cond. $23

Lighter, 5th Air Force, USA, USAF, Korean War Era, Prince. Brushed silver finish case with flip top. One side brass and enameled 5th Air Force patch design DI and engraved "Officers Open Mess." Other side engraved "K. 55" and with likeness of Korea and locations. Exc. cond. $41

Lighter, Service, USA, Army, WWII, Dunhill. Dark brownish red painted metal body with hinged cover for wick. Well marked. In pressed paper maker's carton. Exc. cond. $40

Lighter, Navy Ship, USA, 1970, Zippo. Color enhanced etching of ship and title "USS WREN/DD568." Back side shows small bird clutching sub in talons and airplane in beak. Above avg. cond. $67

Lighter, USMC, USA, USMC, 1953, Zippo. Brushed silver finish case with flip top. Has small EG&A appliqué with "Bronx Platoon/November 10, 1953" engraved on one side and initials engraved on other. Above avg. cond. $177

Lighter, USN Aviator, USA, Navy, Zippo. USN aviator lighter, standard size, brushed silver finish flip-top case with small gold-tone USN aviator wing applied to one side, in folding stand-up black plastic Zippo carton. Above avg. cond. $14

Lighter, USN, USA, Navy, Zippo. Black finish, stand size, flip-top case has small gold-tone USN anchor motif applied to one side, in folding black plastic stand-up case. Above avg. cond. $16

Lighter, Navy Ship, USA, c1952, Zippo. Early 1950s. For escort destroyer, etched on side is picture of ship and title "USS DE LONG/DD 884." Initials scratched on back. Avg. cond. $90

Lighter, Service, USA, Army, WWII, Park Sherman. Od finish, needs repair to hinge, well made and shows wear to finish. Avg. cond. $28

Lighter, Trench, USA, Army, WWI, Dunhill. S/S in orig box with wick. Some tarnish. Glo-type wick. Avg. cond. $30

Lighter, Army, USA, 1969, Zippo. 1969 dated, with "SAIGON VIETNAM/69-70" on lid and map of in country below. Back has "Going to Hell" verse. Avg. cond. $35

Lighter, Army, USA, 1968, Zippo. 1968 dated and showing nearly all finish removed from brass base. Lid reads "KHE SANH/ 67-68." MACV Emblem below and verse on back side. Avg. cond. $55

Lighter, Japanese Occupation, USA, USAF, 1959, Zippo. Penguin Zippo-style flip top. From Yokota Japan with 5th AF DI-style emblem on lid and 6102nd Air Base Wing emblem on body. Marked "SAYONARA/1958–9 // OFFICERS OPEN MESS/ YOKOTA AIR BASE/JAPAN." Much wear on edges and back. Avg. cond. $30

Plaques and Trophies——U.S.

Commemorative Plate, Ordnance, USA, Army, 1945. 10½". The Army Ordnance Assoc. Membership banquet March 2, 1945. Top has picture of General Joseph Stillwell, sides has committee heads and program chairmen. Center shows map of CBI theater and the Stillwell road. Avg. cond. $20

Commemorative Plate, Signal Corps, USA, Army, WWI. Pewter-style alloy plate 12" in diam commemorating the Signal Corps, US Army with images on center and rim displaying activities in many wars. Commissioned by the Ft. Ritchie, MD OWC. Exc. cond. $20

Commemorative Plate, USS Enterprise, USA, Navy, 1961. Issued at the formal christening of the USS Enterprise, it shows new carrier in center and other enterprises of history around rim. 11" diam and in original issue box. Avg. cond. $20

Lincoln Medallion, USA, 1898. GAR National Encampment, Cincinnati, OH, 1898. 36mm with Lincoln profile and encampment data on back. Avg. cond. $72

Medal, Encampment, USA. For 1900 GAR Chicago Encampment. Orante multi-piece pendant with pierced design with message on back from C-I-C of GAR that this medal was made from captured cannon. On dark bronze pb brooch. Marked. Above avg. cond. $91

Medal, GAR, USA, GAR, c1900. Black ribbon on pb mount. Brass patee cross with white enamel and brass center with national emblem. Avg. cond. $40

Medal, Liberty Loan Essay, USA, 1918. Bronze pendant showing child giving money to seated Liberty and reverse showing Liberty Bell with engraved winners name and May 21, 1918 date. Brown leather cord attached. Above avg. cond. $65

Medal, SAW Veteran Convention, USA. Bronze eagle with national shield inside wreath with American flag ribbon. Crossed sword, rifle, cannon and anchor serve as hanger for pendant. Bronzed Spanish War veterans emblem centered on cross. Avg. cond. $20

Medallion, UCV Convention, USA, Union of Confederate Veterans, c1900. 1¾" domed disc with Confederate battle jack in center and UCV initials on three sides. Celluloid covered and metal trimmed. "Pettebone Co. of Cincinnati" marked. Above avg. cond. $125

Plaque, USA, Navy, 1967. Wood plaque 8" x 7" with enameled 5" metal disc showing Viking-like profile, banner reads "VMA9AW0 225." Brass plate reads "TO/THE MAD RUSSIAN/BIG BIG THANKS/VIETNAM 1966–1967." Above avg. cond. $34

Plaque, 1st Marine Division, USA, USMC, Vietnam War Era. 8" x 12" painted wood plaque with raised wood 1st Marine Div logo and Vietnam banner. Brass plaque at bottom is generalized presentation by General Wheeler, USMC Commandant. Avg. cond. $28

Plaque, 5th Air Force, USA, USAF, Korean War Era. Oak. Hand-painted emblem in center with "5th AIR FORCE" above and "KOREA" below. Above avg. cond. $53

Plaque, Aviation, USA, Navy, c1950s. Ceramic. Mounted on wooden base, ceramic shows clouds and sea with "AIR FORCE" at top and gold Navy wings against black with "PACIFIC FLEET/NAMED INDIV" below. Avg. cond. $20

Plaque, Remembrance, USA, Korean War Era. 15" x 13" rectangle with 13" x 11" metal presentation display for named corporal. Framed in Army branch and Div emblems and image of forces landing. Presentation gives soldier's name, enlistment date (1/16/1951), assigned units and service number. Saw combat in Korea and display includes CIB and ribbon bar. Avg. cond. $30

Plaque, Tactical Fighter Squadron, USA, USAF, c1960s. 8" x 6" wood shield with 3" painted disc of angry bee in boxing gloves and banner "22ND TACTICAL FIGHTER SQUADRON." Avg. cond. $20

Plaque, Union General, USA, Civil War Era. Cast iron with black paint finish showing bust profile of general in dress blouse. 12" oval presentation. Avg. cond. $28

Plaque, USS Helena (CA-75) Proud and Fearless, USA, Navy, c1950s. 10½" x 12" thick wood shield-shaped body is varnished. Has cast 7½"-wide appliqué with painted details. Hanger device on back. Above avg. cond. $80

Plaque, WWI Victory, USA, WWI. "A TRIBUTE TO ONE WHO SERVED 1917–18." Above avg. cond. . $28

Remembrance Plaque, USA, WWII. Shield 8" x 7" with "World War II" at top, outline map of Southern Italy and North Africa, painted unit emblems for 2nd corps, 5th Army, 442RCT, 34th Div, 3rd Div (mislabeled "Marines") 1st Armored, etc. Interesting. Above avg. cond. $38

Remembrance Tray, 9th Air Force, USA, AAF, 1946. Artist quality. Hand carved. Done in 1946, 10½" circular tray with "GOPPINGEN GERMANY/9TH AIR FORCE" on rim and masterful presentation of 9th AF emblem in center, centered on five-point star. Background stained dark so light wood is highlighted. Signed and dated on back. Above avg. cond. $48

Reunion Medal, "Union Veteran Legion," USA, 1903. From UVL, Dayton, OH, 18th National Encampment, Oct. 1903. 36mm-diam bronze finish pendant with ring suspender with striped ribbon on bronze finish. Pb brooch. Above avg. cond. $59

Souvenir Medal, Admiral Dewey Hero's Welcome, USA, c1899. 36mm-diam bronze wreath-design pendant with gilt inlay with bust design of Dewey and reads "New York Welcomes the Hero 1899." Reverse has Battleship Olympia design. Marked. On ring suspender with striped ribbon on bronze "souvenir" brooch. Above avg. cond. $41

Trophy Mug, USA, USAF, Vietnam War Era. Silver plated. Named mug with etched candlestick over individual name and "IN APPRECIATION FOR FLYING/OVER 160 NIGHT COMBAT MISSIONS/OVER THE TRAIL WITH THE/CANDLESTICKS." Light tarnish patina and dark spotting. Above avg. cond. $61

Plaques and Trophies—Germany

Honor Goblet, Air War, Germany, Luftwaffe, WWI. About 8" tall, hammered steel body with stamped eagle in battle, "Dem Sieger im Luftkampfe" base and four ball mounts. Base stamped "Chef des Feldflugwesens" with Imperial eagle. Exc. cond. $3500

Medallion, Battle of Mulhausen 10 Aug. 1914, Imperial Germany, WWI. 35mm. Bronze finish. Obverse has bust of bare-headed Kaiser in uniform, verso has wreath with commemorative inscription. Avg. cond. $20

Plaque, "U-boat Honor Memorial," Germany, WWII. 8½" x 10½" black wood backing. 5" x 7" cast plaque with good raised details to eagle monument with view of bay/harbor. Title along lower edge. Lacks two nails in front and has hanger loop. Minor age toning, good patina. Above avg. cond. $130

Plaque, Heroic Soldier Profile, Germany, WWII. Silver painted profile of army soldier with helmet on. Mounted on black painted oak 10" x 13" rectangular base. Full profile of soldier in dress tunic with Nazi eagle on steel helmet, antique-toned silver finish, nice heavy wood backing. Original hook remains. Avg. cond. $125

Plaque, Hindenburg Head Profile, Germany. Artist signed K. Kuhl. Very fine likeness. Approx. 16½"-inch diam. Circular raised edge center has raised head and shoulders of Hindenburg subject wears field marshal uniform with Pour le Merite medal on neck. Has bracket for mounting on back. Near mint cond. $195

Plaque, Hitler Profile, Germany, 1933. 8½" tall x 6½" wide, fine antique glazed bronze finished terra cotta. Nice profile of Hitler facing to his right. Hmkd on the back "MEISSEN." Made in 1933 when Hitler came to power. Near mint cond. $217

Wall Plaque, General Officer Memorial, Imperial Germany, WWI. 11" with oak leaf border. Plaque has head of general with open collar-type tunic, very heroic style. Back of plaque has massive lugs for mounting. Above avg. cond. $265

Wall Plaque, Kaiser Wilhelm II, Imperial Germany, WWII. Silvered on copper. Approx. 5" x 7¾" in size. Raised profile relief of Kaiser from chest to head with all medals, decorations, laurel leaf trim with PAX (Peace) motto beautifully hand engraved. Artist signed and dated at Cassel, 1899. Avg. cond. $85

Wall Plaque, Pilot Badge, Imperial Germany, WWI. All worked metal is hand cut and hand detailed. 7" x 11½" size. Dark oak backing with hand-made copper, white metal front having raised relief of 1913-style pilot badge with early Taube in flight above field, rising sun, green velvet backing. Near mint cond. $300

Wall Plaque, Serpent and Torch, Imperial Germany, WWI. Bronze. 14" long with single serpent intertwined on stylized torch with bulbous head. Back of torch has two posts for mounting. From military hospital. Avg. cond. $79

Plaques and Trophies——Other

Table Medallion, France, WWI. 66mm diam, bronze, obverse depicting profile of French hero Marshal Petain, rim inscribed "Philippe Petain Marechal De France 1918," reverse with kneeling French soldier extending French Marshall's baton over soldiers' graves. Exc. cond. . . $80

Table Medallion, War Ministry, Italy, WWII. 55mm diam, silver planchet, obverse depicting classical warrior in chariot pulled by lions, superimposed on royal crest, reverse with Italian eagle, inscribed "Ministero Della Guerra." Above avg. cond. $127

Plaques, Military Building, Italy, WWII. 125mm diam, bronze, star and fascio motif on pebbled ground, inscribed "Ro Eto," with cogged-wheel border, reverse has two screw posts, with retainer and bolts. Above avg. cond. $71

Plaques, Patriotic Wall, Poland, WWII. 5" x 5", brass crowned Polish eagle on red fabric field and contemporary frame. Above avg. cond. $75

Wall Plaque, Spanish Paratrooper Brigade, Spain, 1970s. 9" x 5½", gilded metal central medallion depicting eagle with crown and parachute motif, bottom of presentation plaque finished in colored laurel leaf highlights, inscribed "Trunifar O Morir," wooden base, reverse with mounting loop. Above avg. cond. $22

Tin Soldiers——Germany

Duro Soldier-Charging Officer, Germany, c1930s. 70mm figure in helmet with upraised sword. Figure is crack free and has normal paint wear. Above avg. cond. $37

Duro Soldier-Marching With Rifle at Shoulder, Germany, c1930s. Full combat gear and excellent facial detail. Avg. cond. $20

Duro, Soldier-Rifleman, Germany, c1930s. Kneeling and firing rifle. Full combat dress and full backpack. Good detail. No visible cracks. Above avg. cond. $20

Elastolin, Army Artillery Loader, Germany, WWII. Soldier kneeling next to wicker box that was used to move artillery shells. Figure is in red piped tunic and has on helmet. Figure is free of cracks and has very good paint. Above avg. cond. $91

Elastolin, Army Medic With Red Cross Dog, Germany, WWII. Walking with dog. Cracks and chip to dog foot. Avg. cond. $50

Elastolin, Army Officer On Horseback, Germany, ELAS, c1930s. Rectangular green base marked "Elastolin." Nicely detailed work to roan horse with map case, blanket, rolled blanket and reins, bridle. Officer shown in black boots, light green breeches, OD tunic with helmet. Officer carries an upright sword in his right hand. Finely detailed. Exc. cond. $85

Elastolin, Artillery Gun, Germany, c1930s. Sheet metal. Cap firing. 10"-long camo-painted body in tan, brown and green. Black rubber "Hausser" tires. Cap device shows use but still works. Hinged arms to back show one missing spade from end. Avg. cond. $215

Elastolin, Artillery Soldier With Shell, Germany, WWII. 3" standing figure shown holding large artillery shell in green finish. Soldier in brown tunic, pants with black jack boots. Red artillery piping on tunic and shoulder straps. Avg. cond. $23

Elastolin, BMW Motorcycle With Soldier, Germany, c1930s. Two-seater model, with rolling wheels. 4" in size. Painted details show some wear. Above avg. cond. $275

Elastolin, British Officer, Germany, c1930s. 70mm figure of officer in British-style helmet with raised arm holding pistol while running. Above avg. cond. $37

Elastolin, Cavalry Musician With Horn on Horseback, Germany, c1930s. Helmeted soldier with large horn wrapped around back and brown horse. Marked rectangular base. Above avg. cond. $155

Elastolin, Horse-drawn Artillery Rig With Box, Germany, c1930m. 4½" x 4½" x 12" red cardboard box with Elastolin knight, color label to bottom and contents label to lid. Two brown horse teams on wood platforms with wheels, mounted driver with whip and helmet, chains for hitch and camo-painted sheet-metal cart and Artillery cannon. Above avg. cond. $425

Elastolin, Hussar on Horseback, Germany, c1930s. 5½" tall with black uniformed soldier with busby seated on brown horse. Age cracks to both and show use. Avg. cond. $205

Elastolin, Machine Gunner, Germany, WWII. 70mm prone German soldier in helmet behind machine on sled mount. Figure has cracks around both knees but paint is good. Below avg. cond. $38

Elastolin, Marching Drummer, Germany, c1930s. 70mm figure in helmet with red piping to uniform and playing snare drum. Figure has small crack to right elbow and good paint. Avg. cond. $23

Elastolin, Personality Figure, Dr. Josef Goebbels, Germany, c1930s. Oval base marked "Elastolin." Figure approx. 3" tall and complete with moving right arm that allows a Heil Hitler salute to be made. Very detailed with Goebbels in brown party uniform with armband, crossbelt and black breeches. Goebbels holds his party leader visor cap with his left hand. Avg. cond. $203

Elastolin, Personality Figure, Naval Admiral Doenitz, Germany, WWII. Doenitz is shown in blue frock coat, sword, Fore-Aft hat and saluting. Oval base marked "Elastolin Germany." Avg. cond. $85

Elastolin, Prussian Rifleman, Germany, c1930s. 4" tall with blue and red tunic, white pants and rifle on left shoulder. Oval base with title. Avg. cond. $45

Elastolin, Radio Operators, Germany, c1930s. Two soldier with headsets on, around a field radio. One is writing on a white chart. Base has metal plate with complete Morse code table on it. This plate folds under the base for storage. Antenna is missing from silver holder in right front. Avg. cond. $145

Elastolin, SA Leader, Germany, WWII. Shown marching in brown tunic, visor cap and armband. Oval base marked "Elastolin Germany." Avg. cond. $40

Elastolin, SA Parade Trooper, Germany, c1930. Shown in brown shirt with kepi. Oval base with "Elastolin Germany." Above avg. cond. $37

Elastolin, Soldier in Fighting Position, Germany, WWII. 70mm-figure of soldier with rifle raised in clubbing position. Figure has helmet, pack and red piped tunic. Figure has good paint with crack around left knee. Below avg. cond. $25

Elastolin, Soldier Playing Accordion, Germany, WWII. Shown seated playing instrument. Some paint wear. Avg. cond. $43

Elastolin, Soldier With Flamethrower, Germany, WWII. 70mm-figure in helmet with tank on back and gun in hands shooting flame. Figure has cracks to flame that is common and some to normal body area. Avg. cond. $55

Elastolin, Soldier With Megaphone, Germany, c1930s. 70mm soldier with helmet and has megaphone to mouth. This is a hard to get figure and free of cracks with good paint. Avg. cond. $59

Elastolin, SS Officer, Germany, WWII. Entire black uniform and visor cap. Parade marcher. Exc. cond. . . . $93

Elastolin, SS Trooper, Germany, WWII. 3"-tall black painted parade marcher with rifle on left shoulder. Wears helmet and full pack. Marked base with glue repair to boot and no right hand. Below avg. cond. $144

Elastolin, Winter Sentry, Germany, WWII. Standing figure with greatcoat collar turned up, helmet and rifle cradled in right arm. Oval base marked "Elastolin." Some paint wear. Avg. cond. $50

Leyla, Luftwaffe Pilot, Germany, WWII. Shown in gray flight suit, parachute harness, flight helmet and goggles. Fracture cracks. Title marked rectangular base. Avg. cond. $38

Lineol, 88mm Flak Gun, Germany, WWII. Three-color camo body with black rubber trailer tires, maker marked. Lacks gear adjustment to rear trailer. Avg. cond.   . $1100

Lineol, Army MG08 Gunner Firing, Germany, WWII.

Cracks to legs and bent wire stand to MG08. Avg. cond.
. . . . $45

Lineol, Army MG08 Loader, Germany, c1930s. Prone soldier feeding broken ammo belt to the gunner. Avg. cond. $32

Lineol, Artilleryman With Rabbit-ear Optics, Germany, WWII. Standing with three wires on optics for tripod stand. Avg. cond. $50

Lineol, Camo Flak Gun With Carrier, 88mm Flak 36, Germany, WWII. 15"-long sheet-metal construction with three-color camo painted finish. Four black rubber tires title marked. Near mint cond. $750

Lineol, Charging Officer, Germany, WWII. 70mm figure of officer charging with raised sword. Figure has small crack on left arm but good paint. Avg. cond. $40

Lineol, Command Car With Figures, Germany, WWII. 10" in length. Tinplate body with camo painted finish. Cloth top with same design. Black rubber tires. Has two spare tires. Battery operated electric lights. Figures with painted details. Includes two rifles. Has Luftwaffe fender pendent. Exc. cond. $1600

Lineol, Marching Officer, Germany, WWII. 70mm figure in helmet with sword on shoulder. Avg. cond. . . $24

Lineol, Personality Figure, Goring in SA Uniform, Germany, c1930s. 3" tall, tan tunic with awards and silver neck cross. Right arm salute over head. Age cracks to back and square base title marked. Avg. cond. $180

Lineol, SA Torchlight Parade Trooper, Germany, c1930s. 3" tall with brown shirt, kepi and flaming torch in left hand. Title marked rectangular base. Exc. cond. .
. . . . $135

Lineol, Soldier Throwing Stick Grenade, Germany, WWII. Crawling on ground with grenade bags, rifle at back and grenade in hand. Crack on leg and no toes on boot. Avg. cond. $51

Lineol, Soldier With Searchlight Holder, Germany, c1930s. Helmeted trooper holding searchlight and pack on back. Above avg. cond. $45

Heyde, Mixed Lot, Germany, Early 1900s, Heyde. Twenty-two soldiers. Various armies. Includes mounted figures and horse-drawn wagons. Below avg. cond. $173

Umarked, SS Trooper Motorcycle Rider, Germany, WWII. Unmarked motorcycle with fracture crack on front wheel, brown shirted rider with SS party armband and black kepi. Avg. cond. $165

Unmarked, Fighting Soldier, Germany, WWII. 70mm figure of soldier with rifle raised in clubbing position. Sol-

dier has on helmet and red piped tunic. Comes on square unmarked base, and is free of cracks with good paint. Avg. cond. $24

Tin Soldiers—Other

Britains, #32 Royal Scots Greys (Second Dragoons), England, Pre-WW II, Britains. Five mounted figures. Missing three horse hooves. Original box has edge wear and tape repairs. Avg. cond. $92

Britains, #44 2nd Dragoon Guards, England, Pre-WWII, Britains. Original box. Five mounted figures. Two horses missing one leg. Box has edge wear, missing side flap and tape repairs. Good cond. $80

Britains, #69 Pipers of the Scots Guards, England, Pre-WWII, Britains. Original Whisstock box. Six figures. Box has edge wear. Good cond. $242

Britains, #114 Queens's Own Cameron Highlanders, England, Pre-WWII, Britains. Original Whisstock box. Eight figures with good finish. Box has edge wear and tape repairs to flaps. Above avg. cond. $144

Britains, #115 Egyptian Cavalry, England, Pre-WWII, Britains. Original Whisstock box. Five mounted figures. One horse missing a hoof. Box has edge wear and a torn flap. Avg. cond. $115

Britains, #182 11th Hussars, England, Pre-WWII, Britains. Original Whisstock box. Four dismounted figures. One figure missing a sword. Box has edge wear, tears and creases. Good cond. $144

Britains, Tin Soldiers, 11th Hussars in Box

Britains, #192 Infanterie de Ligne (French Infantry), England, Pre-WWII, Britains. Types of the French Army. Original Whisstock box. Six marching figures. Box in good condition. Above avg. cond. $115

Britains, #299 West Point Cadets (Summer Dress), England, Pre-WWII, Britains. Original Whisstock box. Eight marching figures. Box has edge wear. Good cond. . . .
. . . . $115

Britains, #400 Life Guards (Winter Dress), England, Pre-WWII, Britains. Original Whisstock box. Five mounted figures. One horse missing a leg. Box has edge wear. Good cond. $80

Britains, #1711 French Foreign Legion, England, Britains. Six marching troopers and one mounted officer. Two broken bayonets. Good cond. $58

Lineol and Brevetteo, Italian Soldiers, Italy, c1940, Lineol and Brevetteo. Composition soldiers. Includes two Mussolinis (one with missing arm), machine gun, two soldiers climbing telegraph poles, two flag bearers and other infantry figures. Avg. cond. $460

Toys and Games——U.S.

Game, "Coast Defense," USA, 1930s, Marx. Wind-up game with original box. Features circling tin litho plane and cannons. Box intact with graphics featuring Zeppelins and early planes. All parts are functional. One end flap detached but it is included. Size: 8½" diam. Above avg. cond. . . $75

Puzzle, Yank, USA, WWII. 4" x 6" printed cardboard design which allows player to reconstruct scene to enable objective to be obtained. In original folder. Copyright 1942. Near mint cond. $13

Truck, Anti-Aircraft, USA, c1950s. Air defense truck. Friction vehicle with battery operated pom-pom guns positioned on truckbed. Battery powered features not working. Size: 14". Avg. cond. $200

Truck, Army Artillery, USA, Late 1920s, Dayton Toy and Specialty Co. Pressed steel with OD finish. One original Firestone slip-on rubber tire. Cannon inoperative. Finish has some surface rust. Avg. cond. $402

Dump Truck, Army, USA, c1930s, Kelmet. White Big Boy Army dump truck. Black body with red chassis. Original canvas cover included but needs repair. Size: 25½" x 8" x 10½". Good cond. $200

Transport Truck, Army, USA, 1931, Marx. Army transport friction truck. Mack front end styling. Original canvas top. Size: 5". Above avg. cond. $140

Truck, Army, USA, c1928, Sturditoy. Sturditoy #20, Army truck. Pressed steel, khaki color with original canvas color. Steering wheel missing. Some paint flaking. Avg. cond. $920

Military Vehicles, USA, c1950s, Dale Model Co., Chicago, IL. Five die-cast Army combat vehicles. Army green. Size: 5" to 7". Good cond. $25

Truck, Missile Launcher, USA, 1950s, Structo. Flatbed with missile launcher at rear. AG color. Size: 13" x 6½" x 5¼". Avg. cond. $55

Puzzle, Tank, USA, WWII. 4" x 6" printed cardboard design can be assembled in manner that allows US tank to go through German lines. In original envelope. Copyright 1942. Near mint cond. $13

Puzzle, Tokyo, USA, WWII. 4" x 6" printed cardboard puzzle can be assembled in manner that allows US planes to bomb Tokyo. In original folder. Copyright 1942. Near mint cond. $13

Toys and Games——Germany

Artillery Gun, Germany, WWII, Marklin. Sheet metal. Cap firing. 6"-long body with green painted carriage and wheels. Blued metal barrel works with cap firing device and elevation wheel that all work. Stamped oak leaf wreath to maker marked barrel "GM&Cie." Highest quality. Exc. cond. $90

Board Game, "Spiele," Germany, WWII. 1½" x 6½" x 12" cardboard box has color printed top showing four Army soldiers around game table. Instructions on underside of lid for three fold-open game boards. Many wood and plastic game pieces and some wood dies. Exc. cond. $90

Boxed Aero Game, "Luftverteidigungs Spiel," Germany, WWII. (Air Defense Game). Published by Adler in stiff cardboard box, approx. 9" x 12". Color litho cover shows 88mm crew blasting British Blenheim bomber out of sky. Game board, counters appear based on dice roll to determine if Allies take your city by air. Some wear to box. Some counters appear to be missing. Avg. cond. . . . $38

Checkers Game, Germany, WWII. In original box with cartoon soldiers playing checkers on it. No counters. "Ein Gruss aus der Heimat" lettering indicates it was equivalent of a German Red Cross gift for front soldiers. Complete fold-out board inside. Above avg. cond. $25

Chess Game, "Schach-dame and Muhle," Germany, WWII. ½" x 5" x 9½" blue cardboard box with printed title label having scene of two Army soldiers playing chess. Folded cardboard game board is double sided and one panel is loose. Sixteen green cardboard pieces and 13 maroon. Avg. cond. $45

Chess Set, Party Eagle Marked, Germany, WWII. In 2½" x 4½" x 7" wooden box with slideout lid and two inked eagle stamps of "Luftgaupostamt Nurnberg etc." Complete with 16 white turned pieces and 16 black. Exc. cond. $66

Gama Tank, Mark-I, Germany, c1930s. Sheet metal. Pre-WWII toy. White rubber tracks. Gray and green camo paint, with black and silver details. Wind-up motor inoperable-it is missing the spring. Has the shovel and wrench on the fenders. Avg. cond. $282

Toys and Games——Other

Playing Cards, Russian Playing Cards Lot, Russia, 1990. Two decks in original packages, one having zodiac symbols and other being regular deck. Exc. cond.   . . $20

Armored Car, Soviet Union, c1960s. Die-cast 1/43-scale metal armor car in box, 2" x 5" dark green with four plastic wheels and moving turret, number and Soviet guard star decals on either side. Box graphics in Russian. Near mint cond. $18

Tank, Soviet Union, c1960s. 1/43 die-cast T-34 tank, 3" x 8" OD painted all-metal body with working rubber tracks and plastic wheels, Soviet guard flag and number decals, hmkd on base and all Russian graphics on box. Near mint cond. $13

Glossary

Aiguillette: A decorative cord (usually gold color) worn over the shoulder by designated aides to senior-level officers.

Alpaca: The wool of llama-like mammal (an Alpaca) that was widely used as the lining for cold weather and flight clothing during the WWII period.

Blood Chit: A note or message carried by aircrews (usually) to be used in the event of a crash or bailout over hostile territory. It usually identified the nationality of the crewman and had messages of assistance in the local languages. Often a monetary reward was offered for the safe return of the crewman.

Brassard: A cloth armband usually worn for identification purposes.

Breeches: A style of pants worn by military personnel that were characterized by a baggy or loose fit around the thighs and a tight fit below the knees.

Briquet: Type of short bladed sword (22"–27"), with a single-edged, slightly curved blade and a cast brass hilt. Most commonly of French origin.

Browning Automatic Rifle (BAR): A light machine gun first developed in 1917 and used widely in U.S. service from WWI into the 1960s.

BuAero: U.S. Navy Bureau of Aeronautics. Responsible for design and testing of aviation-related equipment and vessels.

Bullion: Gold or silver lace, thread, or braid used as decoration on military uniforms.

Collar Tabs: Small embroidered cloth insignia worn on the collar. Usually designated a soldier's rank, branch of service, or unit affiliation.

Crossguard: Part of a knife or bayonet that separates the blade from the handle and protects the hand of the person holding the weapon.

Cuirass: A piece of armor covering from the neck to the waist. Similar to a breastplate.

Epaulettes: Ornamental, fringed shoulder pads worn as part of a uniform.

ERDL Camouflage: A four-color, random pattern camouflage designed in 1948 by the Army Engineer Research and Development Laboratory and widely used in Vietnam.

Frog: A loop or other device used to attach a knife scabbard or sheath to a belt.

Fuller: A groove or indentation found on the blade of many types of edged weapons.

Garand M1: A semi-automatic .30 caliber rifle adopted by the U.S. Army in 1936. It was the standard American infantryman's weapon in WWII and Korea.

Gorget: A collar or ring of armor worn to protect the throat and neck. Later (Nazi Germany) a metallic badge or shield worn around the neck on a chain. Usually designated a soldier's specialty or branch of service.

Grand Army of the Republic (GAR): An organization of Union veterans of the Civil War.

Greatcoat: A long, heavy coat worn as part of a uniform or over a uniform. Widely used by European armies from WWI into early WWII.

Guidon: A small flag or pennant carried by military organizations to identify individual units.

Hallmarked (Hmkd): A mark or method of identification used to indicate the source or manufacturer of an item.

Herringbone Twill (HBT): A special weaving pattern used with various fabrics known for its strength and durability. Widely used in uniforms in the WWII era.

Katana: A Japanese long sword.

Kepi: A style of military hat identified by a round flat top which slopes toward the front visor.

Krag: Officially the Krag Jorgensen M1896 .30 caliber rifle. Widely used by U.S. forces in the Spanish American War. Other versions used by several nations.

Kevlar: Special fiber developed by Du Pont in 1965. Widely used for bulletproof vests and other types of protective clothing.

LAW: Tube-launched light antitank weapon widely used by the U.S. Army in Vietnam and later.

Leggings: Cloth or leather covering worn as part of military uniforms. It usually covers the top of the shoes to the bottom of the knee. Worn widely through WWII.

Luger: Generic name applied to a family of German self-loading pistols. Adopted by the Imperial German Army in 1904, it was widely used in WWI. Usually found in 9mm caliber, although others were produced. Also manufactured in Switzerland and England.

Morion: A type of armored helmet characterized by a high skull cap and a high, peaked front and back brim.

Nomex: A special fire-resistant polyamide fiber developed by Du Pont. Widely used in aviation-related clothing.

Pommel: The knob found on the hilt of a sword or on the end of the handle or grip of a knife or bayonet.

Puttees: Similar to leggings (see above).

Quatrefoil: An elaborate decoration found on uniforms, which is in the form of a flower with four petals or set of four leaves.

Quartermaster Corps: The branch of the U.S. Army that has responsibility for the design, testing, procurement, and supply of clothing, food, and other items needed by the Army for its soldiers.

Quillion: An extended crossguard (see above) found on many types of swords. Often straight or S-shaped, it is used to protect the hand of the person holding the weapon or to entangle an opponent's blade.

Ricasso: The area of the blade of an edged weapon that is below the crossguard or quillions.

Shako: A style of military hat identified by a high crown and stiff construction, and often decorated with a plume.

Smatchet: A multipurpose edged weapon that combined the characteristics of a fighting knife and machete into one.

Springfield M1903: The standard infantry rifle used by American troops in WWI. It was a .30 caliber design that was adopted for use prior to WWI and remained in limited service until 1945 as a sniper weapon.

Targe: A small light shield.

Tinnie: Generic name used to describe a wide variety of small metallic badges issued during the Nazi German era for civilian, political, and sporting awards.

Bibliography

There are many books in and out of print that can be very helpful references for historians, re-enactors and general and specialized collectors of militaria. The following list is by no means comprehensive, but includes many recent titles that should be of great use to those with an interest in militaria.

Ball, Robert W. D. and Paul Peters. *Military Medals, Decorations, & Orders of the United States & Europe: A Photographic Study to the Beginnings of WW II.* Atglen, PA: Schiffer Publishing Ltd., 1994.

Berndt, Thomas. *Standard Catalog of U.S. Military Vehicles 1940–1965.* Iola, WI: Krause Publications, 1993.

Britton, Jack and George Washington, Jr. *Military Shoulder Patches of the United States Armed Forces.* Tulsa, OK: M.C.N. Press, 1985.

Bull, Stephen. *An Historical Guide to Arms & Armor.* New York: Facts on File, Inc., 1991.

Clarke, J. *Gallantry Medals and Awards of the World.* Osceola, WI: Motorbooks International Publishers and Wholesalers, 1994.

Coe, Michael D., Peter Connolly, Anthony Harding, et al. *Swords and Hilt Weapons.* New York: Barnes & Noble Books, 1993.

Cohen, Stanley. *To Win the War: Homefront Memorabilia of World War II.* Missoula, MT: Pictorial Histories Publishing Company, Inc., 1995.

Davis, Brian Leigh. *Badges & Insignia of the Third Reich 1933–1945.* London: Arms and Armour Press, 1992.

———. *German Army Uniforms & Insignia 1933–1945.* London: Arms and Armour Press, 1992.

———. *Uniforms & Insignia of the Luftwaffe Volume 1 & 2, 1933–1945.* London: Arms and Armour Press, 1995.

Fisch, Robert. *Field Equipment of the Infantry 1914–1945.* Sykesville, MD: Greenberg Publishing Co., Inc., 1989.

Flayderman, Norm. *Flayderman's Guide to Antique American Firearms . . . and Their Values,* sixth edition. Northbrook, IL: DBI Books, Inc., 1994.

Fosten, D. S. V., R. J. Marion, and G. A. Embleton. *The British Army 1914–18.* London: Osprey Military Books, 1996.

———. *The German Army 1914–18.* London: Osprey Military Books, 1996.

Foster, Frank and Lawrence Borts. *U.S. Military Medals 1939–Present.* Fountain Inn, SC: Medals of America Press, 1995.

Fowler, E. W. W. *Nazi Regalia.* Edison, NJ: Chartwell Books, Inc., 1996.

Friz, Richard. *Official Price Guide to Civil War Collectibles.* New York: House of Collectibles, 1995.

Gotz, Hans Dieter. *German Military Rifles and Machine Pistols 1871–1945.* Atglen, PA: Schiffer Publishing Ltd., 1994.

Green, Michael. *Illustrated Tank & AFV Buyer's Guide.* Osceola, WI: Motorbooks International Publishers and Wholesalers, 1993.

Howard, Gary. *America's Finest: U.S. Airborne Uniforms, Equipment, and Insignia of World War II (ETO).* London: Greenhill Books, 1994.

Hogg, Ian V. and John Weeks. *The Illustrated Encyclopedia of Military Vehicles.* Englewood Cliffs, NJ: Prentice-Hall, Inc., 1980.

Katcher, Philip and Jeffrey Burn. *The U.S. Army 1890–1920.* London: Osprey Publishing Ltd., 1990.

Katcher, Philip and Bryan Fosten. *U.S. Infantry Equipments 1775–1910.* London: Osprey Publishing Ltd., 1989.

Katcher, Philip and Michael Youens. *Army of the Potomac.* London: Osprey Publishing Ltd., 1991.

Kirsner, Gary. *German Military Steins 1914–1945,* second edition. Coral Springs, FL: Glentiques Ltd., Inc., 1996.

Lumsden, Robin. *A Collector's Guide to Third Reich Militaria.* New York: Hippocrene Books, Inc., 1994.

———. *A Collector's Guide to Third Reich Militaria: Detecting the Fakes.* New York: Hippocrene Books, Inc., 1994.

Maguire, Jon A. *Gear Up! Flight Clothing & Equipment of USAAF Airmen in WWII.* Atglen, PA: Schiffer Publishing Ltd., 1995.

———. *Silver Wings, Pinks, & Greens: Uniforms, Wings, & Insignia of USAAF Airmen in WWII*. Atglen, PA: Schiffer Publishing Ltd., 1994.

Matthews, Jack. *Toys Go to War: World War II Military Toys, Games, Puzzles, & Books*. Missoula, MT: Pictorial Histories Publishing Company, Inc., 1994.

Mirouze, Laurent. *World War I Infantry in Colour Photographs*. London: Windrow & Greene Ltd., 1995.

———. *World War II Infantry in Colour Photographs*. London: Windrow & Greene Ltd., 1995.

Rottman, Gordon and Francis Chin. *U.S. Army Air Force, vol. 1*. London: Osprey Publishing Ltd., 1993.

Rottman, Gordon and Ron Volstad. *U.S. Army Combat Equipments 1910–1988*. London: Osprey Publishing Ltd., 1992.

Schwing, Ned. *Standard Catalog of Firearms,* seventh edition. Iola, WI: Krause Publications, 1997.

Snider, Nicholas D. *Antique Sweetheart Jewelry*. Atglen, PA: Schiffer Publishing Ltd., 1996.

———. *Sweetheart Jewelry and Collectibles*. Atglen, PA: Schiffer Publishing Ltd., 1995.

Stanton, Shelby. *U.S. Army Uniforms of the Korean War*. Harrisburg, PA: Stackpole Books, 1992.

———. *U.S. Army Uniforms of the Vietnam War*. Harrisburg, PA: Stackpole Books, 1989.

———. *U.S. Army Uniforms of World War II*. Harrisburg, PA: Stackpole Books, 1991.

Sweeting, C. G. *Combat Flying Equipment: U.S. Army Aviator's Personal Equipment, 1917–1945*. Washington, DC: Smithsonian Institution Press, 1989.

Walter, John. *The Luger Book*. London: Arms and Armour Press, 1988.

Wilkinson, Frederick. *Handguns: A Collector's Guide to Pistols and Revolvers from 1850 to the Present*. Secaucus, NJ: Chartwell Books, Inc., 1993.

Zaloga, Steven J. and Ron Volstad. *The Red Army in the Great Patriotic War 1941–45*. London: Osprey Publishing Ltd., 1996.

Index

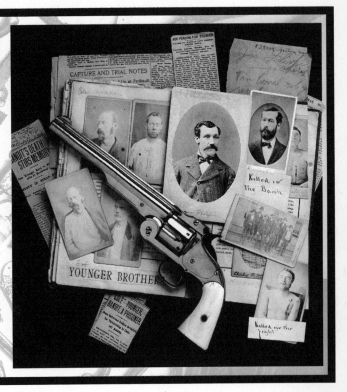